Lecture Notes in Computer Science 1783

Edited by G. Goos, J. Hartmanis and J. van Leeuwen

Springer

Berlin
Heidelberg
New York
Barcelona
Hong Kong
London
Milan
Paris
Singapore
Tokyo

Tom Maibaum (Ed.)

Fundamental Approaches to Software Engineering

Third International Conference, FASE 2000
Held as Part of the Joint European Conferences
on Theory and Practice of Software, ETAPS 2000
Berlin, Germany, March 25 – April 2, 2000
Proceedings

Springer

Series Editors

Gerhard Goos, Karlsruhe University, Germany
Juris Hartmanis, Cornell University, NY, USA
Jan van Leeuwen, Utrecht University, The Netherlands

Volume Editor

Tom Maibaum
King's College London
Department of Computer Science
Strand, London WC2R 2LS, UK
E-mail:tom@maibaum.org

Cataloging-in-Publication Data applied for

Die Deutsche Bibliothek - CIP-Einheitsaufnahme

Fundamental approaches to software engineering : third international
conference ; proceedings / FASE 2000, held as part of the Joint
European Conferences on Theory and Practice of Software, ETAPS 2000,
Berlin, Germany, March 25 - April 2, 2000. Tom Maibaum (ed.). - Berlin ;
Heidelberg ; New York ; Barcelona ; Hong Kong ; London ; Milan ;
Paris ; Singapore ; Tokyo : Springer, 2000
    (Lecture notes in computer science ; Vol. 1783)
    ISBN 3-540-67261-3

CR Subject Classification (1991): D.2, D.3, F.3

ISSN 0302-9743
ISBN 3-540-67261-3 Springer-Verlag Berlin Heidelberg New York

Springer-Verlag is a company in the BertelsmannSpringer publishing group.
© Springer-Verlag Berlin Heidelberg 2000
Printed in Germany

Typesetting: Camera-ready by author, data conversion by Boller Mediendesign
Printed on acid-free paper   SPIN 10719952   06/3142   5 4 3 2 1 0

Foreword

ETAPS 2000 was the third instance of the European Joint Conferences on Theory and Practice of Software. ETAPS is an annual federated conference that was established in 1998 by combining a number of existing and new conferences. This year it comprised five conferences (FOSSACS, FASE, ESOP, CC, TACAS), five satellite workshops (CBS, CMCS, CoFI, GRATRA, INT), seven invited lectures, a panel discussion, and ten tutorials.

The events that comprise ETAPS address various aspects of the system development process, including specification, design, implementation, analysis, and improvement. The languages, methodologies, and tools which support these activities are all well within its scope. Different blends of theory and practice are represented, with an inclination towards theory with a practical motivation on one hand and soundly-based practice on the other. Many of the issues involved in software design apply to systems in general, including hardware systems, and the emphasis on software is not intended to be exclusive.

ETAPS is a loose confederation in which each event retains its own identity, with a separate program committee and independent proceedings. Its format is open-ended, allowing it to grow and evolve as time goes by. Contributed talks and system demonstrations are in synchronized parallel sessions, with invited lectures in plenary sessions. Two of the invited lectures are reserved for "unifying" talks on topics of interest to the whole range of ETAPS attendees. The aim of cramming all this activity into a single one-week meeting is to create a strong magnet for academic and industrial researchers working on topics within its scope, giving them the opportunity to learn about research in related areas, and thereby to foster new and existing links between work in areas that were formerly addressed in separate meetings. The program of ETAPS 2000 included a public business meeting where participants had the opportunity to learn about the present and future organization of ETAPS and to express their opinions about what is bad, what is good, and what might be improved.

ETAPS 2000 was hosted by the Technical University of Berlin and was efficiently organized by the following team:

Bernd Mahr (General Chair)
Hartmut Ehrig (Program Coordination)
Peter Pepper (Organization)
Stefan Jähnichen (Finances)
Radu Popescu-Zeletin (Industrial Relations)

with the assistance of BWO Marketing Service GmbH. The publicity was superbly handled by Doris Fähndrich of the TU Berlin with assistance from the ETAPS publicity chair, Andreas Podelski. Overall planning for ETAPS conferences is the responsibility of the ETAPS steering committee, whose current membership is:

Egidio Astesiano (Genova), Jan Bergstra (Amsterdam), Pierpaolo Degano (Pisa), Hartmut Ehrig (Berlin), José Fiadeiro (Lisbon), Marie-Claude Gaudel (Paris), Susanne Graf (Grenoble), Furio Honsell (Udine), Heinrich Hußmann (Dresden), Stefan Jähnichen (Berlin), Paul Klint (Amsterdam), Tom Maibaum (London), Tiziana Margaria (Dortmund), Ugo Montanari (Pisa), Hanne Riis Nielson (Aarhus), Fernando Orejas (Barcelona), Andreas Podelski (Saarbrücken), David Sands (Göteborg), Don Sannella (Edinburgh), Gert Smolka (Saarbrücken), Bernhard Steffen (Dortmund), Wolfgang Thomas (Aachen), Jerzy Tiuryn (Warsaw), David Watt (Glasgow), Reinhard Wilhelm (Saarbrücken)

ETAPS 2000 received generous sponsorship from:

the Institute for Communication and Software Technology of TU Berlin
the European Association for Programming Languages and Systems
the European Association for Theoretical Computer Science
the European Association for Software Science and Technology
the "High-Level Scientific Conferences" component of the European
    Commission's Fifth Framework Programme

I would like to express my sincere gratitude to all of these people and organizations, the program committee members of the ETAPS conferences, the organizers of the satellite events, the speakers themselves, and finally Springer-Verlag for agreeing to publish the ETAPS proceedings.

January 2000   Donald Sannella
                                        ETAPS Steering Committee chairman

Preface

The conference on Fundamental Approaches to Software Engineering (FASE) is one of the confederated conferences within ETAPS. It aims at providing a forum where rigorous methods (in the sense used by scientists and engineers) for the software production process may be discussed. FASE is related to the correspondingly 'acronymed', but differently named conference that was traditionally part of the late TAPSOFT series. There is thus a tradition to uphold, but also a shift in emphasis: we wish to address issues in software engineering rigorously, but not necessarily simply mathematically. Engineers in the classical disciplines use a mixture of formal and heuristic methods in a design process, which has been legitimized by being well founded with respect to scientific and mathematical foundations, and by repeated and repeatable successes in delivering artefacts that are 'fit for purpose'.

The call for papers stated this view as follows:

To achieve the status of a proper engineering discipline, software engineering requires engineering design and analysis METHODS which are firmly grounded on scientifically sound concepts as well as well-founded software tools and analyses based on sound engineering principles. Fundamental approaches are sought, integrating formal approaches with principled methods, providing the bridge between theory and practice and aimed at producing engineering methods and tools for the various phases of software development. FASE is intended to provide a forum where fundamental approaches to software engineering are presented, compared and discussed. Contributions should focus on the problems and methods of software engineering; papers are especially welcome on the following topics:

- Methods for the design of high quality software, relying on formal approaches to specification, refinement, testing, and validation
- The use of program derivation and transformation methods to support software production
- Integration of formal notations and methods with engineering notations and methods
- Combining programming in the small and programming in the large software architectures
- Principled approaches to reverse engineering, legacy software, reuse and evolution
- Case studies of the application of principled software engineering methods
- Reports evaluating industrial experience of the use of software engineering methods
- Rigorous experimental studies of the effectiveness and applicability of principled methods

The program committee consisted of:

Gul Agha, University of Illinois Urbana
David Basin, Albert-Ludwigs-Universität Freiburg
Dan Craigen, ORA Canada
Peter Dybjer, Chalmers University of Technology
José Luiz Fiadeiro, University of Lisbon
Jean-Pierre Finance, University of Nancy
Hans-Dieter Ehrich, Technical University of Braunschweig
Heinrich Hußmann, Technical University of Dresden
Michael Lowry, NASA Ames Research Center
Jeff Magee, Imperial College
Tom Maibaum (chair), King's College London
Dino Mandrioli, Politecnico di Milano
Narciso Martí-Oliet, Universidad Complutense Madrid
Peter Mosses, University of Aarhus
Andrzej Tarlecki, University of Warsaw

We received almost 60 papers and used an electronic method of review. We did not actually meet physically. This has been tried before and worked well. I believe that this was again the case. This was in no small measure due to the PC and to the referees that agreed to help them. The names of these referees are listed immediately after the preface and I would like to take this opportunity to heartily thank them all! I would also like to thank Anna Maros for her administrative help and particularly Kelly Androutsopoulos for her hard extensive efforts in making the electronic system work!

The result of all this effort is on display in this volume. I hope that you will find the 21 papers useful and inspirational. Three short papers related to tools demonstrations relevant to FASE further supplement the volume. The demonstrations were chosen using a different, global mechanism and then assigned to relevant conferences. Also, we have the contributions of 3 invited speakers assigned to this volume. The FASE invited speaker, Wlad Turski, has contributed an intriguing assessment of software engineering at the turn of the century. He looks back to the original conference 'establishing' the discipline, its focus over the last few decades, and the need to refocus our efforts in different directions so as to better support the present needs of software engineering. He ends on a somewhat pessimistic note.... I look forward to the discussions which I am certain will be generated at the conference.

The two 'global' invited speakers, David Harel and Richard Mark Soley, have made short contributions related to their invited talks. Harel focuses on the need to do further research on bahaviour and how to represent it, a topic also taken up extensively by Turski. Soley focuses on the need to develop the capability of dynamically linking information on the Web so as to enhance our ability to find and use information.

I want to thank Don Sannella, chair of the ETAPS steering committee for his many great efforts on behalf of the ETAPS community. The organizers in Berlin should also be thanked for their work in making the conference a great success. Finally, I would also like to thank Matt Bishop for his hard work in putting together the proceedings.

January 2000   Tom Maibaum

Referees

Agha, Gul
Alexandre, Francis
Ambroszkiewicz, Stanislaw
Andrade, L.
Andreu, I. Pita
Ayari, Abdelwaheb
Baresi, Luciano
Basin, David
Baumeister, Hubert
Bednarczyk, Marek
Bidoit, Michel
Blanc, B.
Boyd, Mark
Brat, Guillaume
Craigen, Dan
Cugola, Giampaolo
Danvy, Olivier
de Frutos-Escrig, David
de Groote, Philippe
Demuth, Birgit
Duran, Francisco
Dybjer, Peter
Eckstein, Silke
Ehrich, Hans-Dieter
Festor, Olivier
Fiadeiro, José Luis
Finance, Jean-Pierre
Fischer, Bernd
Fischer, Mike
Fitzgerald, J. S.
Friedric, Stefan
Fuenfstueck, Falk
Galan Corroto, L. Antonio
Godart, Claude
Grau, Antonio
Grudzinski, Grzegorz
Havelund, Klaus
Hussmann, Heinrich
Jabłonowski, Janusz
Jacquot, J. P.
Jamali, Nadeem
Jaray, Jacques
Kubica, Marcin
Kuester Filipe, Juliana

Kumichel, Frank-Ulrich
Laprie, Jean-Claude
Lasota, Sławomir
Llana-Diaz, Luis F.
Lopes, A.
Lowry, Michael
Lukaszewicz, Witold
Magee, Jeff
Maibaum, Tom
Mandrioli, Dino
Marroquin Alonso, Olga
Martí-Oliet, Narciso
Monga, Mattia
Mosses, Peter D.
Méry, Dominique
Neumann, Karl
Nipkow, Tobias
Nunes, I.
Orso, Alex
Park, Seungjoon
Pecheur, Charles
Penczek, W.
Penix, John
Pinger, Ralf
Pressburger, Thomas
Roegel, Denis
Rossi, Matteo
Schumann, Johan
Segura, Clara
Sernadas, Cristina
Souquières, Jeanine
Tarlecki, Andrzej
Thati, Prasannaa
Thiemann, Peter
Varela, Carlos
Verdejo, Alberto
Vigano, Luca
Visser, Willem
Wermelinger, M.
Whittle, Jonathan
Winkowski, J.
Wolff, Burkhart
Ziaei, Reza

Table of Contents

Invited Papers

Real-Time Systems

Formally Engineering Systems

Software Engineering

Object Orientation

Formally Engineering Systems

Theory and Applications

Case Studies

Demonstrations

Essay on Software Engineering at the Turn of Century

Władysław M. Turski

Institute of Informatics, Warsaw University
Banacha 2, 02-097 Warsaw, Poland
wmt@mimuw.edu.pl

Abstract. Presents a personal view of the development of software engineering and its theoretical foundations, assesses the current state, lists (some) unresolved problems and identifies (some) directions of fruitful research. The Y2K problem is ignored.

0 Disclaimer

When asked to prepare this presentation, I was given a broad description of its desired content: about software engineering, something appropriate for the year 2000, a look backward and few hints on future development, perhaps a little about important research topics.

It could have been a very boring presentation, full of references and technical jargon. Even if I decided to go this way, I am sure I would have missed some references and some technical terms very dear to some of my esteemed audience and/or readers. I do not need more enemies than absolutely necessary, therefore I decided not to include *any* references and limit the use of technical jargon to bare essentials. There is one exception: in several places I quote from the proceedings of the 1968 Garmisch Conference on Software Engineering[1]; it is there that it all began.

There is no widely accepted hierarchy of topics in software engineering, or if it exists, I am left out of the common knowledge. I decided to follow my own preferences (and if you wish to call them predilections, or even prejudices, I will not argue).

There is always the perplexing matter of style. I believe that even without references I could have produced a very learned-looking document, but I decided to follow another pattern. I have chosen the form of an essay: at least at first glance it seems easy to read.

I realise that writing this essay in the autumn of 1999 to be presented in the spring of 2000 I am facing the difficulty of guessing the computer events of the 99/00 changeover and their consequences for our systems/economies/lives.

---

[1] Software Engineering. Report on a conference sponsored by the NATO Science Committee. Garmisch, Germany, 7th to 11th October 1968. Editors: Peter Naur and Brian Randell. January 1969.

T. Maibaum (Ed.): FASE 2000, LNCS 1783, pp. 1–20, 2000.

I am no seer, I cannot tell the future, but I am sure that in the *long run* the whole Y2K affair shall have beneficial effects for software engineering practice because some very bad systems will have been discontinued (or destroyed), some bad systems will have been mended a little and — most of all — a few more practicing software engineers and their bosses would have realised that proper discipline in programming and documentation is not just for academic birds: it pays, handsomely.

Finally, all opinions expressed in this essay are mine and I accept the whole, undivided responsibility for them.

1   Background

The ancient Greeks were excellent mathematicians. Despite a relatively high level of mathematical education, (at least some) Greek engineering projects clearly exceeded cost and — one presumes — time limits.

To celebrate their victory over the Macedonian king Antigonus I in 306 B.C., proud citizens of the island of Rhodes decided to erect at the entrance to their main harbour a bronze statue of Apollo. The design and project management were entrusted to the famous sculptor and architect, Chares. When he submitted the cost estimates, the Rhodians asked what would it cost to build the statue twice as high. The answer "twice as much" accepted and corresponding budget allocated, Chares started the construction. According to Sextus Empiricus, when funds ran out *long before* the statue was completed, Chares committed suicide. Colossus, one of the Wonders of the Ancient World, was eventually completed (70 cubits high) by others. It was severely damaged by an earthquake in 224 B.C., never restored, and finally (in A.D. 672) sold for scrap to a merchant of Edessa, who carried it off piecemeal on 900 camels. One wonders if the drastic change of project management was responsible for structural heterogeneity of the monument: one part was destroyed barely 80 years after construction (albeit by an earthquake), another stood for nearly a millennium. This question can be answered only by speculation; the glaring error in estimation of the cost of change in specifications is a historic fact.

The Roman legionnaire, who in 212 B.C. killed Archimedes while the latter was engrossed in solving a mathematical problem, gained a dubious kind of immortality being the *only* ancient Roman ever mentioned in the history of mathematics. A very comprehensive textbook on the subject may add that an inscription prohibiting dogs and mathematicians adorned the doors of many a Roman tavern. Mathematics was not among the subjects dear to a Roman mind, yet Romans were excellent engineers.

And so it continued throughout the centuries. The contemporary structural analysis of medieval cathedrals bristles with mathematics which certainly was neither available nor even accessible to the inspired master masons who built them. Yet, very few cathedrals collapsed on their own. The relationship between mathematical and engineering excellence (and, indeed, proficiency) is not as simple and straightforward as the popular view would have it.

Software, or should I say "the software engineering product", is by no means unique in that it is less than completely satisfactory, reliable, trouble-free. In fact, no engineering product ever is. Yes, there were a few actual disasters caused by software, some — regretfully — cost human life. It is pointless and distasteful to run a scoreboard of tragedies, but software engineering surely is not a clear leader. A brief analysis of two catastrophes may throw some light on issues we are to discuss later on.

Owners of the White Star Line raising toasts in April 1912 as their new liner set course for New York were a little precipitate. Getting the Titanic launched and selling the tickets were not really the issue. In retrospect, knowing all we know today, what was the single most important "error"? I claim it was an incomplete specification in which hardly any attention was paid to life-saving features under conditions of the total failure of disaster-prevention features. Apart from considerations of cruising speed, cost-effectiveness and passengers' (somewhat graduated) comfort, designers worked to the best of their ability to make the ship seaworthy and unsinkable. It did not enter their heads that all precautions could fail under the impact of a North Atlantic iceberg, or, few years later, if a U-boot would score a hit. The Titanic's lifeboats did not have sufficient capacity.

The Chernobyl disaster is often quoted as an example of nightmares that the technology could unleash. To be sure, the reactor design in the Chernobyl power station was not the safest known. But what is conveniently overlooked in most analyses and — especially — in dramatic writings intended for popular consumption is that the actual catastrophe was due entirely to a *human operator error*, with control software intentionally switched off. There is absolutely no reason to suspect that had the software operated as usual on that fateful day in April 1986 there would have been an explosion. This realisation opens a very difficult problem, one that may be truly insoluble, to wit: in safety-critical situations, where computer-based *i.e.* software control is installed, should it be possible for a human operator to override it? (Switching off being a rather special instance of overriding.) The Chernobyl disaster points towards a negative answer; most car manufacturers seem to go in the same direction, some aircraft crashes perhaps could have been avoided if the pilot's reactions were not overridden. But the problem is deeper than this; the classical answer "it depends" is more than a little disturbing.

Finally, let us note that at least some disasters clearly emanating from faulty computer calculations can hardly be attributed to *software errors*. Stupidity, for example, needs no software to show its ugly face, even though software is by no means immune to it, as follows from a fairly recent piece of news:

The United States space agency Nasa admitted that the disastrous loss of its $130m Mars Climate Orbiter last month was due to faulty flight calculations based on the simple failure to convert imperial measurements into their metric equivalents. (The Guardian Weekly, October 7 - 13, 1999.)

2 A Bit of History

There is a tendency to consider the evolution of the software field as a kind of more or less systematic progression from individual machine code programs written in binary (or, indeed, wired by cables plugged into a switchboard) to contemporary mammoth systems and networks, heterogeneous in every respect: written in dozens of high (and very high) level languages, interconnected at several levels by message passing mechanisms, produced by a variety of tools, relying on vast depositories of non-uniformly structured information. This view is correct only insofar as the term "software" is used in the loosest possible sense of "all that makes computers run". For any analytical use such an interpretation of the term is inadequate because it blurs the essential distinction between programs which prescribe *computations* and those that prescribe *behaviours*.

Historically, computers were first used for computations or — in a slightly more abstract phraseology — for effecting well-defined state transformations, from a *given* to a *result*. Computations have been a part and parcel of human civilisation for several millennia; for most of that period they were performed by people. Algorithms were invented to formalise the process of human computations and thus to facilitate them, *i.e.* to make them performable by less qualified persons. The sequentiality of computation (and its particularly important variant: iteration), born from the human propensity to do one thing after another, has become a part of our cultural heritage. It was *not a consequence* of the von Neumann architecture, quite the opposite: *it dictated its principles*.

The essence of computation is captured by the familiar $\{P\}p\{Q\}$ triple; the fundamental problems of computation software are easily expressible in terms of this paradigm: termination and correctness nicely merged into notions of partial and total correctness. It took about 20 years of programming practice and its analysis by the more mathematically inclined to find this succinct representation; in another 10 years or so there emerged a fully-fledged discipline based on this paradigm. Originally concerned (almost) exclusively with proofs of program correctness, the discipline developed a number of logics (more or less) well-suited for this task. Subsequently, with the $\{P\}p\{Q\}$ triples embedded in predicate calculus (as predicate transformers), the discipline embraced algebra-like calculi of program derivation.

For software engineering, the most interesting aspects of the discipline were those in which $\{P\}p\{Q\}$ was considered as an equation in p, *i.e.* methods (or at least hints) for constructing an unknown program p for a given characterisation of the initial and final states. The big white hope was *automatic program construction i.e.* in fact an algorithmic solution for the program construction problem, a goal very hard to achieve in restricted circumstances and most probably impossible to reach in general. A number of limited-application solutions resulted in experimental systems implemented in academic and industrial research environments; none have passed into general use. A relaxation of the notion of algorithmicity, for example by admitting a heuristic trial and error approach or by exploiting interaction with a human operator, resulted in several more systems, some actually used, albeit primarily for educational purposes.

Insofar as programming remains essentially a human activity, the greatest impact of the $\{P\}p\{Q\}$ paradigm on software engineering comes through its influence on and absorption by programmers. As is usual with intellectual advances, the time needed for an innovation to reach its social fruition is measured in academic generations: first it is absorbed by peers, then it enters curricula, finally those educated with the innovation firmly established as an integral part of the "craft" (or "science", or "technology") they were taught apply it in their daily work. Assigning roughly five years for each generation, we arrive at the mid-80s as the epoch when the calculational view of program correctness and derivation (and, therefore, program manipulation) should have become a more or less established norm amongst educated programmers. Unfortunately, by that time the demand for programming bodies far outstripped the supply of programming graduates. The balance was made up by persons trained in program writing at various "intensive courses" and by self-taught amateurs, who attained a rudimentary ability to put down program texts with a reasonably small number of syntactic errors. (Easily available tools quickly convert such texts into syntactically perfect programs.) It is only in those establishments where the concentration of educated programmers is high enough that the impact of the calculational approach is felt. Such establishments tend to be found in the better part of academia and in the highly specialised industries. A very large part of the software industry has yet to discover the only tool (so far) for dealing with the *semantic problems of computations, i.e.* to reap the benefits of using the $\{P\}p\{Q\}$ paradigm in a calculational fashion.

The mentality that came up with and eagerly embraced the $\{P\}p\{Q\}$ paradigm was shaped by the computations culture, predominantly in science or in some other previously mathematicised fields. This mentality was also formed by the *scientific work ethic* in which criteria of success (although not the success itself!) were impersonal and Occam's razor was ever present. Thus there was little currency for "almost correct" programs, the value attached to "user satisfaction" (other than a perfect outcome of computations) was nil, and frugal use of computer resources was not only a necessity dictated by severe hardware limitations, but also a sign of one's maturity and professionalism. To be quite honest, this mentality could not really conceive of a million or more people running a particular program. Hence, for instance, a very cautious attitude towards program testing was taken: a pretty complex program *could not possibly* be thoroughly tested within a reasonable time by a programmer and his/her several friends/colleagues. In the realm of software for mass use, guided by market forces and paltry user expectations, firmly established by the end of the 80s, the fundaments of that world-view became decidedly outmoded.

For example, wide distribution of the so-called beta versions of popular packages increases the number of testers by several orders of magnitude. From the producer's point of view the beta version testing certainly is practically free, although collecting and processing the test results is not. An additional advantage of beta version testing by a large subpopulation of the intended users comes from an ample representation of the variety of use modes. Indeed, it is very probable that the several hundred thousand testers using the beta version for several months will find nearly all bugs in a fairly large software product. That the product finally brought to the market still contains a number of errors is to be expected, but these should relate to "exotic" modes of use, or to rare configurations of interactions. Unfortunately, the challenges of managing the tidal wave of bug reports pouring in after the beta version release, and the time pressure to deliver the market version within a reasonable period after the beta version, cause a large proportion of information generated by the beta release to be wasted and/or misinterpreted, which — combined with the poor workmanship inevitable in a hasty patching-up — results in a market product much inferior to what could have been expected after such massive testing. The residual unreliability bears witness to the unmastered complexity and unresolved contradictions characteristic of the software process.

Apart from a few and, frankly, well isolated special cases, software is no longer expected to be *mathematically* correct. With this change, the whole edifice of mathematically-founded software technology appears irrelevant, a folly.

As early as the Garmisch Conference, the incipient change was noted: *If the users are convinced that if catastrophes occur the system will come up again shortly, and if the responses of the system are quick enough to allow them to recover from random errors quickly, then they are fairly comfortable with what is essentially an unreliable system.* (J. W. Smith)

Since the time of the Garmisch Conference the scope of the notion of software has vastly changed. The change is not only of size, even though the volume of software written and used is several orders of magnitude larger today, it is not only of kind, even though numeric computations and sequential file processing then dominant now constitute a barely discernible fraction of computer use, it is not even just the change of mode, even though interactive programs swept from a mere curiosity very prominently into the forefront. The most important change has occurred in the public perception of software.

Two equally powerful and interrelated factors contributed to the change of attitude: emergence of the mass market and an essential shift in the mode of computer use. To the great majority of users constituting the mass market any notion of scientific work ethic is quite alien: they are guided by (and expect) much more relaxed criteria, often "not too bad" taken literally (*i.e.* not as an understatement) means "good enough". Computers are not any longer used primarily as machines to execute computations, instead they are employed to perform a variety of functions defined in terms of contexts taken from everyday life. Windows is a bad idea whose time has come.

It is a serious educational fault that the software consumer population earnestly expects miracles. A vast majority of current PC users are "first-time" users. With no prior first-hand experience of pain and misery, they take an advertising copy for the gospel truth. For example, we talk of software maintenance, when in fact we mean software change. Nobody expects house maintenance to encompass addition of an extra floor or of an Olympic-size swimming pool in the attic. Accomplishments of this calibre are routinely expected of software maintenance. Regrettably, in the realm of software, consumer education is just as neglected as are consumer rights.

Computer today is typically used as a multimedia communication device or as a glorified switchboard enabling multidirectional flow, transformation, storage and retrieval of discrete signals. There is a growing tendency to eliminate any visible barrier (such as, *e.g.* typing) between the computer and its environment. Some applications still do heavily depend on large volume of repetitive computations (for instance, many medical applications rely on extensive FFT computations), but even then the user is hardly aware of it. In many applications, the individual computations invoked in the course of performing a visible function are trivial (*e.g.* in word processing); the usefulness of an application obtains not from any particular computation, but from the available set of "applications" and the simplicity of their invocation[2]. This situation has profound consequences for the present state of software engineering.

Individual programs of the $\{P\}p\{Q\}$ paradigm are visible neither in the mass market, nor in the field of special applications. Computer systems and instruments with embedded computers are bought and sold for the visible functions they perform, these functions defined in terms of the environment in which the systems and instruments are to be used. Definitions of such functions are seldom mathematical or even simply precise. Correspondingly, the criteria of performance are often diffused. There is no clear relationship between the qualities of the software, as expressed in the framework of the $\{P\}p\{Q\}$ paradigm, and the users' assessment of the quality of the system or instrument. Moreover, the observable deficiencies may just as likely be due to the software buried in its bowels as to other components of the system or instrument. For instance, a poor quality image on the screen of a medical instrument may be due to a defective sensor, bad software, a glitch in the screen electronics or an imperfection in its coating, just to name a few causes with *identical* visible results; naturally, all these causes may be independently present, can interfere with each other, and (don't we all love it?) could be transient. Strict adherence to the $\{P\}p\{Q\}$ school dicta would make software engineering quite insensitive to demands posed by the marketplace; unfortunately even the best software will not sell an erratically behaving instrument, and no programmer can claim that the excellence of software implies an overall good quality of the system.

As resources that used to be scarce got cheaper and cheaper, the economic reasons for many good programming practices started to evaporate, soon to be replaced by their near opposites. As storage units grew in capacity to previously unimaginable sizes, and processing units grew very fast indeed, the premises for the programmer's frugality assumed the flavour of a sectarian ethic. Combined with the growing cost of waste disposal, this has led to an abominable practice of not removing obsolete parts of system software, just shunting them off in new releases. The percentage of dead wood in current releases of popular systems is quite large. So, of course, is the risk that the bypasses put in shall not always

---

[2] At the Garmisch Conference, A. Perlis prophetically observed: *Almost all users require much less from a large operating system than is provided.*

stay firm. But as long as the havoc resulting from an occasional activation of a shunted off program can be cured by hitting the famous combination CTRL ALT DEL, even with a loss of a file or two, the catastrophe is fully acceptable to most users, immunised by occasional failures of other appliances.

Thus even in that part of software engineering which is concerned with programming for computations, the frame of reference has changed dramatically since the epoch dominated by programs written by scientists for scientists. It is tempting to say that in $\{P\}p\{Q\}$ the emphasis has shifted from p to the two predicates, *i.e.* to specification. If this is indeed the case — and I believe it is — we ought to note a remarkable success of the research carried out under the banners of the $\{P\}p\{Q\}$ paradigm: its original and initially considered the most important goal, to wit: the development of technology for construction of correct programs satisfying specifications given by firm initial and final conditions on computational processes, has been reached.

3   A Linguistic Aside

In English, there is a bit of confusion about the meaning of the noun "model": it can denote either something that sets a pattern to be followed (*model for*, as in "model citizen"), or something that mirrors some other (real) entity (*model of*, as in "models of World War II aircraft"). Sometimes the noun is employed with both meanings simultaneously, which greatly adds to the confusion. Unfortunately, such is the case when speaking of software specifications one uses expressions like "model of real-world (relationships)".

4   A Short Treatise on Model Theory with Applications

The confusion of the natural language usage of "model" is avoided in mathematics, where two terms are assigned to its two roles: *theory* and *model*. Pure mathematics deals with abstract entities which possess only such properties as by accepted rules of reasoning follow from their definition; *e.g.* it is meaningless to ask about the colour of the number π. Some entities are known as *domains*, usually they have a structure: elements, relations, functions etc. A *fact* is a property "observed" in the domain, perhaps involving its structure. Thus in the domain of natural number arithmetic it is a fact that all even numbers divisible by 3 are divisible by 6.

Theories are sets of sentences generated by application of listed rules of inference to a listed set of axioms. It is said that theory T *is satisfied* in domain D, $\text{sat}(D, T)$, or that D *is a model* of T, $\text{mdl}(T, D)$, iff there is an interpretation of sentences by means of facts, such that to each true sentence there corresponds an observable fact. It is important to note that even if $\text{sat}(D, T)$ there very well may be facts in D which under the chosen interpretation correspond to no sentences in T. Indeed this is what Gödel's famous theorem on incompleteness is all about. In this sense a *model is richer than its theory*. For example, the domain of natural number arithmetic is richer than Peano's axiomatisation (a theory expressly designed to succinctly capture the arithmetic of natural numbers). It follows that a given theory T can have different models, *i.e.* domains which in addition to "core" facts (all corresponding to true sentences of the theory, albeit perhaps under different interpretations, specific for each domain) exhibit their own "additional" facts not necessarily convertible from one domain to another. Thus two perfectly valid models of the same theory need not be very similar (isomorphic). Peano's axiomatisation, for instance, has two well-known models: arithmetic of natural numbers and arithmetic of transfinite numbers. If a theory is consistent (*i.e.* not self-contradictory) it is guaranteed to have a model, and *vice versa*, a theory that has a model is consistent; the latter is often used to prove consistency.

In exact sciences it is usually the case that a theory has two important models: the physical world, W, and a suitable mathematical model M. The theory and its mathematical model being both artefacts, it is (at least in principle) possible to *prove* the $\mathrm{sat}(M, T)$ relation. On the other hand no proof of $\mathrm{sat}(W, T)$ is ever possible; the scientist use *experiments* to check if (important) statements of T correspond to facts in W. Long series of confirmatory experiments increase the likelihood that the theory is OK, a single irrefutable failure is enough to shoot it down. A time-honoured scientific practice is to select for experimental verification the most implausible statements of T.

So far we considered an idealised static picture. In practice, a theory is often the last-to-arise element of the trio. The physical world precedes all man-made artefacts, but in scientific analysis it is usually presented by means of a class of observations which filter out most aspects of the reality. Thus in theory formation and subsequently in verification, if $\mathrm{sat}(W, T)$ holds, W is seldom the whole wide world but instead a specific view of it chosen by the scientist. It is also possible first to construct an elegant mathematical structure, then to invent a theory for which it would serve as a model, and only then look for an aspect of the physical world that could be considered as the physical model; it is rumoured that some Nobel Prize winners in physics have worked exactly in this manner.

5   Specifications

In software engineering, it is the specification that acts as the theory, the corresponding software as one model, the application domain as another. As in science, two elements of the trio are artefacts (specification and software), one is (an aspect of) the real world. Thanks to the discipline of the $\{P\}p\{Q\}$ paradigm, the relations between (properly presented) specifications and programs (software) are calculable, at least in principle. This means we can prove that a program satisfies its specification (if it indeed does so), or — which is much better — given a non-contradictory specification, we can construct a program that provably ("by virtue of construction") satisfies it.

The relationship between the specification and the application domain is much harder to deal with. The chief problem with software for non-formal application domains is that no matter how well-educated and conscientious are the specification builders, the informality of the domain precludes any strict verification of the abstraction process that leads from the application model to the specification. This plain fact is sometimes masked by the nature of specification-making tools which are increasingly more sophisticated and whose use yields specifications that are formal entities with desirable pragmatic properties. Thus, as far as formal criteria are concerned, we are getting excellent specifications from which it is increasingly easy to design correct programs, indeed, to obtain them automatically. Nevertheless, from the application (*i.e.* ultimate user's) point of view, the quality of the program is determined by how well the informal abstraction process semantically captures the intended application model. (Let us stress that we assume all subsequent steps in program construction and implementation to be faultless, hence the program given to a user is correct wrt informally derived, but itself formally structured and impeccably formal, specification.)

Thus, even in the simplest cases (just as in exact sciences) there is no finite calculational procedure to establish the satisfaction; rapid prototyping and on-site tests — which in this context play the role of experiments — are not conclusive when positive. When negative, following the pattern of exact sciences, the first failure should *invalidate the specification*, but in many application domains the specifications are so rickety that such a clean cut decision is seldom taken. A negative result may simply be dismissed ("it was not really that important"), the specification could be mended in an *ad hoc* fashion ("it really should have been the other way"), or the view of the domain could be changed in a way that invalidates the test ("don't worry, in practice it never happens"). There could (and often is) a powerful incentive for such a cavalier attitude, notably when large sums of money and a considerable effort have been expended on construction of the other model, *i.e.* on software: a slight mismatch between the specification and reality is not reason enough to throw that effort away[3], especially when the specification is a bit woolly and the view of reality a bit foggy. Needless to say, the tenuous link between the software and the application does not get any firmer by employing such practices.

In addition, in many instances software is written for application domains which do not have the intransigence of the physical world . Often, especially in the world of business applications, but also in a plethora of services and entertainment applications, the time span needed to produce software satisfying a given specification exceeds the life-span of the particular world view that served as the specification's other model. This gives rise to the phenomenon of *evolving specifications*: theories that evolve to reflect an ever changing world-model.

A closer analysis of the situation in exact sciences shows that the phenomenon is not entirely absent there. As the views of the physical world evolved, so did their theories and the computation programs that were their models. Today we compute planets' positions according to algorithms quite different from 2000

---

[3] This is not to say that I advocate the other extreme, vividly described at the Garmisch Conference by R. M. Graham: *We build systems like the Wright brothers built airplanes - build the whole thing, push it off the cliff, let it crash, and start over again.*

years ago; indeed, to compute positions of some planets and most comets we use programs modelling (mildly) relativistic dynamics, while for most other planets and asteroids the plain Newtonian dynamics will do very nicely. The point is that in exact sciences the theories tend to stay fixed for periods much longer than the software life-cycle.

Note, however, that *in mathematics* the phenomenon of evolving specifications is practically unknown. There, a theory once formulated stays unchanged forever, because the wholly artificial world of mathematical structures knows no internal evolution whatsoever. (Its expansion is an altogether different thing.) A circle for Archimedes was the same as for Gauss, even though to compute its circumference to diameter ratio (*i.e.* the number π) they would have used quite different algorithms. The assumption of immutability of theories permeates mathematical culture. The mathematically minded founders of the $\{P\}p\{Q\}$ discipline established a didactic paradigm in which the specifications are considered as given once and for all; they are so firmly fixed that any question of the kind "what would happen if the specification changed?" is easily dismissed as totally irrelevant. Much too easily!

Programming methods cultivated in the $\{P\}p\{Q\}$ discipline — and they are the best there is! — are often spurned on the grounds of frivolity of the examples used to convey the methods. (From the *Problem of Dutch National Flag* to the *Problem of Welfare Crook*, they all are "toy" examples, are they not?) The issue is not in the examples being too simple, because they are not *that* simple and no sane teacher would use much more challenging ones, but in the tacit yet very convincing acceptance of the sacro-sanctity of the specifications (problem statement). Students reared on the exclusive diet of such examples, particularly, the bright students, are likely to consider the problems entailed by evolving specifications as a can of worms carried around by simpletons unaware that good programming practice requires unambiguous and (of course!) fixed specifications. Therein lies one of the reasons for the *mutual* mistrust between software specialists and programmers brought up in the $\{P\}p\{Q\}$ discipline. It is deep and divisive, its background is cultural, and therefore it will not be easy to remove.

It would be untrue to say that the theoreticians have totally disregarded the problem of changing specifications or, to use a more elevated terminology, the problem of theory manipulation. The research under this heading took two main directions: logic-based and functional-programming-based. Despite significant internal achievements, none of them has yet had an appreciable impact on software making. Because of the novelty of approaches developed in this research, it is only to be expected that their social acceptance would take a few more years (*cf.* the academic generations phenomenon discussed earlier). I am afraid, however, that this is only a part of the explanation. The other part is related to some inherent features of the research, features that in the context of a desired wide acceptability appear to be weaknesses.

The logic-based theory manipulation has two such weaknesses. In logic itself the theory manipulation is quite awkward and computationally expensive. Perhaps yet more importantly, the required model manipulations following from theory manipulation are seldom straightforward, indeed often are non-algorithmic. As a matter of fact, the only known instances of simple model manipulations restoring the satisfaction relation (after theory manipulation) correspond to rather uninteresting kinds of theory manipulation (such as renaming or definition unfolding). In addition, the logic-based approach has a strange relationship with mundane programming practice: its programming vehicle of choice, programming in logic, has obviously missed its chance of becoming the working tool of programming community (very active special interest groups notwithstanding), while the direct use of logic for specification of imperative programs leads to difficulties that the $\{P\}p\{Q\}$ community avoided by using algebraic-like specifications.

The use of algebraic specifications has also been the choice of the functional-programming school. With this choice, a very rich source of mathematical inspirations has been tapped and a lot of energy spent on establishing mathematical credibility of the school. While this activity generated a large number of elegant papers and created a legion of Ph.D. students and graduates, it did nothing for the working programmer and her boss[4]. If anything, the use of forbiddingly mathematical jargon (a PR fault assiduously avoided by the logic-based research community) alienated the functional-programming school from the software industry. Recently there are signs that functional-programming-based specification manipulation is making some inroads into industrial programming practice, where the object-oriented programming mania created a receptive ground.

Time will show how deep the fertile layer for cross-breeding is. The imperative programming habits of a working programmer seem as firmly established as ever, even as the quality of the programming languages in common use is rapidly deteriorating. On the other hand there is a growing tendency to use "fourth generation" and similar "very high level" languages even for professional work in software firms, despite their gargantuan appetite for computer resources. (Is it plausible that in the near future the professional programming languages will degenerate into two classes: one being machine language with object syntax, another — a catalogue of pictographically invoked "intelligent" components?)

Yet, if we accept that software is produced for applications, and applications are increasingly frequent in poorly formalised (or quite informal) domains, there is no escaping the problem of evolving specifications, not least because the (views of) application domains change as a result of implementation of computer systems. Paradoxically, the more successful — in terms of an application — is an

---

[4] For the vast majority of software engineers, the perennial question of whether ($undefined = undefined'$) ≡ **true** or ($undefined = undefined'$) ≡ **false** is of precious little significance and even less consequence. There, what matters is that $undefined$ should never be encountered and — if it happens — should raise all sorts of alarms. The same, of course, goes for similar concerns with other errors of design: while they could be viewed as a fertile ground for subtle considerations, in the bread–earning community the need to *avoid* them is dominant, and the guarantee that errors, if made, will not remain undetected is a prime concern.

implementation, the more profoundly it changes the application domain, and, therefore, the less valid becomes the original specification.

The only proper way to proceed in case of a changed application model and an existing program is to modify the specification and then see how to modify the program so that it remains a model of the changed specification-theory. The specification's "resistance" to change (expressed in the effort needed to do so properly) is not an *obstacle*, but a *warning* about the real magnitude of effort required to accommodate a change in the application domain. Attempts to make it easier remind me of the policy of taking ever increasing doses of painkillers in order to avoid visiting a dentist when a tooth aches. Follow this policy, if you wish, but then do not complain that your teeth are unreliable and fail the simple test of taking a bite of a nice, hard, juicy apple.

In the realm of software for humdrum applications, the major research challenge is to develop a usable specification calculus equipped with corresponding algorithmic transformations of software models. In short, for a class of specifications Σ we need the following:

1. a set of meaningful and useful monadic operations $U : \Sigma \to \Sigma$
2. a set of meaningful and useful diadic operations $B : \Sigma \times \Sigma \to \Sigma$
3. an indexed set of algorithms $\{\alpha\}_{i \in U \cup B}$

such that given specifications $s_1, s_2 \in \Sigma$ and their software models p_1, p_2, $\mathrm{mdl}(s_1, p_1)$, $\mathrm{mdl}(s_2, p_2)$, we would have $\mathrm{mdl}(u(s_1), \alpha_u(p))$ for any $u \in U$ and $\mathrm{mdl}(b(s_1, s_2), \alpha_b(p_1, p_2))$ for any $b \in B$.

It is a very tall order indeed, one that certainly cannot be fulfilled in its full generality, because it is not true that *any* meaningful and useful operation on a satisfiable specification yields another satisfiable specification. On the other hand, restricting the sets U and B to such operations that are guaranteed to preserve satisfiability for *all* operands would be self-defeating as such sets would consist of very few and mostly uninteresting operations. Yet, I believe this challenge to be most important for software research well into the next century.

6   Production of Software

The idealised view of software being produced by a programmer who was given precise and complete specifications is very far from the prevailing reality. We have already analysed one aspect, *viz.* specification evolution. There are two more that are best considered jointly:

- software very seldom is written "from scratch"
- software is most often produced in large organisations

The existence of large software systems and — in many instances — continuing dependence of users on their performance mean that a very large proportion of software is produced as enhancements (updates, extensions, new releases etc.)

of systems already in use. This entails additional constraints on writing software: not only must it satisfy whatever specifications are provided but it must also allow "seamless integration" of the fresh code with the existing body of the system code. The exact meaning of "seamless integration" varies somewhat from case to case, but in most instances it means that it should be possible to insert the fresh code without seriously interfering with the productive use of the existing system, and it always means that the writer(s) of the fresh code must take into consideration all kinds of interactions between the old and new parts of the system; needless to say, such interactions fall into two categories: expected (well documented, desirable etc.) and unexpected. It is the latter that cause royal headaches. Not infrequently "seamless integration" also implies that the actual users' procedures and habits evolved during their work with the old system should be respected, *i.e.* preserved as much as possible.

Of course all this is nothing new if software engineering is considered as a provider of utilities. Most other kinds of engineering are thoroughly familiar with such requirements: neither a new bridge, nor an additional water reservoir bring about major disruption to services provided (although the construction of a new bridge may occasionally create local havoc!). But implications for software engineering are far reaching. A very substantial part of the effort involved in a successful design and implementation of a piece of software needs to go not into the conversion of specifications into working code, but into all sort of peripheral activities that ensure the "seamless integration". Some of this extra activity is of a programming kind, some is closely related to programming; some, however, belongs to entirely different fields (such as, *e.g.*, public relations or ergonomics).

This alone would indicate that to provide software one needs an organisation which, in addition to programmers, employs other kinds of specialists. (Remember, we are not selling programs any more, we provide software services!). Add to it the sheer volume of contemporary software systems, bloated by prevalent practices, but also necessitated by the scope of activity covered, and the need for large teams becomes pretty obvious.

It is important to note that quite a few of existing large systems were not conceived as large systems, they just grew by repeated extensions, by adding features and functions, each, perhaps, of a moderate size, and by a permissive attitude to waste disposal. Thus, it is not necessarily the case that S. Gill's Garmisch warning: *It is of utmost importance that all those responsible for large projects involving computers should take care to avoid making demands on software that go far beyond the present state of technology, unless the very considerable risks involved can be tolerated* went unheeded.

One way or another, large and very large software systems exist[5], are being updated, extended, modified etc. Other large systems are manufactured, often from large components, much less often - from scratch. Work on a large software system requires a large organisation, a large organisation requires a managerial structure and a defined *modus operandi*. The question, whether the management

---

[5] *It is large systems that are encountering great difficulties. We should not expect the production of such systems to be easy.* — K. Kolence at the Garmisch Conference

of a software-making organisation is essentially different from that of any other complex-product making concern or not, has not been conclusively resolved[6].

Superficially, the differences seem dominant. The distribution of costs between design and actual production seems very peculiar in software-making: no matter how expensive an architect, his fee is minuscule as compared to the cost of steel, concrete, pipes, cables and other supplies that go into construction of a largish building; even the cost of construction labour is often larger than the architect's fee. In software construction the supplies and raw materials cost next to nothing and cost of labour is mostly subsumed in costs of design, particularly so if modern tools are used for churning out the actual lines of code. Many large software systems are unique (for application on a single site), hence the famous economies of scale hardly matter. And so on.

A closer look, however, casts some doubts on the simple conclusion. In any large organisation a fair share of costs is consumed by the infrastructure, both physical (offices, energy, various services etc.) and managerial (personnel, meetings, reporting etc.); these costs are a function of organisation size and structure regardless of what it does. Economy of scale *does* matter for software making, although in a somewhat different sense: a company supplying its tenth banking system spends less effort per line of code than it did for the first one, even if all ten systems are truly different, because it gained experience[7] in making systems for banks. And so on.

A very substantial volume of national expenditure on software in nearly all developed countries has been a powerful incentive for seeking managerial solutions to the high cost of software construction and its odious companions: budget and deadline overruns. A number of modelling techniques have been proposed for representing the software-making process in a variety of metrics. Not surprisingly, the predictive capability of these techniques is not very impressive: insofar as software-making remains chiefly a creative process, modelling based on statistics is bound to produce results applicable — at best — to collections, and quite inadequate for individual instances. Thus, even if we can predict that *on the average* projects of a certain kind are likely to cost X dollars and last for T months, any particular project of this very kind may cost $2X$ or $0.5X$ dollars and last $0.5T$ or $2T$. To get better predictions we should make the software process more homogeneous, less dependent on human idiosyncrasies; but this is not going to be an easy task. Actually, I am not sure it is possible at all, because as soon as technical means (tools) are introduced to automate (*i.e.* algorithmise) an aspect of the software process, the process itself is extended on "the other end"

---

[6] *cf.* K. Samelson at the Garmisch Conference:*By far the majority of problems raised here are quite unspecific to software engineering, but are simply management problems. ... Perhaps programmers should learn management before undertaking large scale jobs.*

[7] In a hard to describe way it is indeed the organisation, as distinct from individuals it employs, that gains the relevant experience. Of course, the employees, each in her/his special way, also gain experience from the completed tasks, but there seems to be a clear synergy effect, making the *combined* gain larger than the sum of individual ones.

by inclusion of tasks previously considered outside the software process proper, for example, by processing preliminary requirements.

Another direction taken in an attempt to improve the management of the software process in order to make it (*i.e.* the process) more predictable, consists in developing organisational patterns which supposedly impose best structure on the process and its managerial infrastructure. The success of this approach is the greatest in the most chaotic organisations, where imposition of *any* order, rules, procedures and standards cannot fail to improve co-ordination and internal communication, which in turn is bound to improve productivity and work discipline. Thus, as a means of combating chaos, such patterns are very good; whether they can produce improvements in a disciplined environment is open to some doubt. Needless to say, in this approach there is very little truly specific to software; it is a sad reflection on the state of many software companies that such simple "law and order" prescriptions yield appreciably positive results. What makes it even sadder is the realisation that the essence of the proper approach was clear at the time of Garmisch Conference: *The ability to estimate time and cost of production comes only with product maturity and stability, with the directly applicable experience of the people involved and with business-like approach to project control* (R. McClure) Why this simple message did not reach all concerned during more than 30 years and why substantial organizations can prosper doing very little other then embellishing this message with irrelevant charts and tables remains a psychological puzzle.

Because managerial remedies often do bring positive results in terms of better productivity and more realistic scheduling, and because these effects are eagerly sought after, and because — being managerial in nature and packaged as any other "product" on the managerial market — they look appealingly familiar to managers, such remedies sell very well to the top management of software companies. No wonder then that there is a fierce competition between various schools and institutions offering managerial remedies. The evidence for an objective assessment of individual competitors is (at best) scant, it would be foolish to attempt any ranking; the more so because it is very probable that any one of them is just as good as any other: very helpful to a chaotic organisation, and of little value where a stable and workable *modus operandi* has been established. If the latter hypothesis is correct, we should observe an industry-wide conversion to regimented production units structured on conveyer-belt-like principles, accompanied by a painful demise of traditional loose co-operatives of artist-programmers, followed by a rather rapid loss of interest in all-encompassing "managerial solutions".

7   Programming for Behaviour

As mentioned earlier in this essay, the interest in computer applications is shifting from calculations to behaviours. To be sure, computers still perform calculations and shall continue doing so, if only because they cannot do anything else. The shift occurs in the *external perception* of computing activity: it is perceived less and less as a purposeful combination of calculations, and more and more as an unordered collection of *reactions to external stimuli*. A computer is no longer expected to be turned on to achieve a (calculational) result and then be switched off, instead it is expected to be on all the time and, while being on, to behave in conformance with its (independently and often unpredictably) changing environment.

What does this shift spell for software? There is a level at which the simple answer is: nothing new. Each individual reaction needs to be programmed just as any old fashioned procedure, except for one significant difference: The execution of any routine takes time, during this interval the environment, which now is assumed to be quite independent from the computation, can change in a way which makes the reaction being computed obsolete, inappropriate, unwanted or even plainly harmful. This is not an entirely new problem, we have faced it ever since programming concurrently running processes started. However, there is an important *novum*: we are not in control of all processes. Even if there could arise a harmful interference, we are not allowed the luxury of mutual exclusion of critical sections, the environment will not patiently wait suspended at a semaphore nor languish inactive in a monitor until our routine completes its critical section and releases the catch.

In other words, we have two problems

- a theoretical one: how to deal with continuous concurrency?
- a practical one: how to implement the theoretical solution on discrete (digital) computers?

There are other problems which programming for behaviours brings to the surface:

- how to express (specify) and program (implement) modalities: **do** *something* **as long as** R , where predicate R does not depend on *something*, indeed, may be totally outside our control, and: **do** *something else* **before** S, where *something else* does not influence S ?
- how to cope with situations in which several behaviours are indicated in the same state of the environment and there is no reason to expect that choosing one (or, for that matter, any subset) could be justified? Note that the collection of behaviours required in a state need not to recur in any other state and that its components may belong to other collections indicated in other states.

All these problems share one essential property: absence of a granularity of "time" common to all participating computational processes. This vitiates most (if not all) classical approaches to concurrence. Indeed, the principle of a common discrete time-like dimension permeates the temporal logic approach and its variants. Sometimes the common time is replaced by a common synchronisation principle, where the pattern of interactions (no matter whether synchronous or not) weaves a braid of time-like progression. Even in seemingly time-less mutual exclusion co-ordination there is an implicit pattern of sequencing which corresponds to a time-like dimension[8]. There are two reasons why the granular time-like dimension (whether explicit or implicit) was chosen as the framework for (nearly) all research on concurrent programming and — by extension — for (nearly) all work on software systems: (i) it is a simple discrete version of "smooth" time which was and remains a basis of Western religions, philosophies and science, (ii) it allows us to play down the role of the interrupt, a phenomenon all too common in hardware and singularly difficult to deal with in theories based on logic, mathematics or computations.

A simple example should convince us about how eager we are to invent time-based solutions to problems in which time plays no role at all. Consider the problem of boiling a breakfast egg. To solve it means to bring the yolk and the white to specific conditions, *e.g.*, the white set, and the yolk semi-liquid. Assuming we start with a reasonably fresh egg, the solution will be achieved by heating the egg until the desired condition is reached. Simple, isn't it? But in deference to our scientific tradition (and also because measuring the consistence of white and yolk without breaking the shell is a little difficult), we invent the notion of a "three minute" egg and proclaim that under average conditions most eggs immersed for three minutes in boiling water *are* proper breakfast eggs. And so we cook breakfast eggs not to reach a satisfactory condition, but for three minutes. Indeed, most people consider this a proper (scientific?) solution to the original problem. In many instances, programming for behaviour is just restoring the original sense to problems falsified by simplifications.

It seems that there are two major avenues of approach to behavioural programming. In one of them, we decide to design perennially watchful programs, *i.e.* programs which after each atomic action would evaluate the state of the environment and progress according to the outcome of the evaluation. In the other approach we may decide to advance individual computations in larger chunks, but be prepared to roll them back if they progress beyond the limits of validity determined by the environment. Both solutions appear quite expensive in terms of control and/or restorative computations; the second approach is not unlike some techniques used in fault-tolerance and distributed database updating. A common aspect of both approaches is an attempt to simulate an event-driven behaviour within the framework of traditional computations. It may thus appear that these approaches are implementation oriented, or even implementation motivated. Indeed, with the prevalent computer architectures there is hardly any other way to implement behavioural computations.

An entirely different approach would result from taking an event-driven structure of computations as the basic paradigm, and all actions triggered by an observed event as atomic. The latter assumption implies that an action produces no externally observable events while it is being carried out (any possible visible effects occur only when the action terminates) and cannot be influenced by external events occurring while it is being executed. In recognition of the fact that the execution of any atomic action takes some time, we should equip an

---

[8] I am using the expression "time-like" in order to avoid any suspicion that what is implied is the well-behaved, uniform time of classical physics and theology.

action with two guards: one, call it the preguard, describing the state of the environment in which the action is fired, another, call it the postguard, describing the state of the environment in which the effects of the executed action are acceptable. Operationally speaking: As soon as the environment enters (creates) the state in which action is to be fired, its execution is initiated (on a *private copy of the universe*). As soon as the execution terminates, the state of the environment is tested by (evaluating) the postguard; if the postguard is satisfied, the action effects (if any) instantaneously update the environment, otherwise the action's execution and possible effects are completely ignored. This model can be completed by an assumption on the number of agents able to execute any action, for example, by stating that there are sufficiently many agents, or that their number is infinite[9].

The simplicity of behavioural specifications obtained in this fashion is very enticing. For instance, the specification for a fork-picking action in the *Dining Philosophers Problem* may look as follows

(has left fork and right fork on table, right fork on table)→ pick right fork,

where the two guards are separated by the comma. This specification corresponds to verbal behavioural instruction: "if you have the left fork and the right fork is available for taking, take it, provided you can pick the right fork before anybody else grabs it". In the same problem, the deadlock is prevented by a pair of specifications for each philosopher:

(has left fork and right fork on table, right fork not on table) → release left fork,

(has right fork and left fork on table, left fork not on table) → release right fork

Note that the deadlock-breaking actions are purely local to each philosopher.

Unfortunately, even this unorthodox approach cannot cope with the limitations unavoidably introduced by the discrete nature of digital computing. In specification $(P, P) \to \alpha$ there is no way to distinguish between the environment *unchanged* during α's execution and one changed but *restored* to a state satisfying P just in time for α's termination. A very careful formulation of guards may include terms that would reflect some "tracing" information, in which case the two guards above will not be identical, but the generality of this solution remains doubtful. Indeed, if the "observer" has a time constant $\tau > 0$ such that two consecutive observations must be separated by at least τ, then any cycle (*change, restore*) in the environment with period much less than τ is likely to be missed or miscounted by the "observer".

The problem of providing software for behaviour-oriented systems has been recognised long ago. So far, however, nearly all attempts to solve it have been based on extensions of the sequential calculational paradigm. Some extensions were brilliant, others — less so. A number of very interesting disciplines have been created, among them various schools of parallel programming, especially for

---

[9] On closer scrutiny, the apparently insurmountable implementational difficulties of this approach turn out much less forbidding.

numeric calculations, where the power of specially designed parallel processors obviously needed a corresponding development on the programming side. None of these addressed the main issues of behavioural programming. A pessimistic conclusion appears inevitable: the possibilities of extending the calculational paradigm towards a behavioural one have been exhausted without ever getting near the goal.

Thus the challenge is there, clearly visible to any impartial observer. It seems possible that in order to meet this challenge, we shall have to make an entirely fresh start, perhaps discarding not only much of what we learned about programming (and accepted as "natural"), but also largish parts of logic (in particular, some classical rules of reasoning, such as *modus ponens* and *tertium non datur*). It will be interesting to see if the programming/software community can take the dare. Modern physics took a similar step in the first quarter of this century; ever since then, the common sense and science remain at odds on many issues. In the next century, shall *we* take the plunge?

8   Conclusions

The basic elementary step in software construction, the derivation of a program correct wrt its fixed and consistent specification, has been fully intellectually mastered and can now be performed orders of magnitude faster and safer than 50 years ago. The mathematical clarity of these developments enabled the construction of tools which greatly facilitate the mechanics of programming. The process of making larger software constructs from smaller ones can be carried out safely in limited, highly constrained circumstances. The problem of adopting existing software to evolving specifications remains largely unsolved, perhaps is algorithmically insoluble in full generality. Development of a realistic specification calculus is badly needed and does not seem impossible. Managerial aspects of large-scale software production are important insofar as many software companies are still managed in an amateurish way, which certainly leaves a lot of room for improvement. Whether good management practices for large-scale software production differ in an essential way from those for any other large-scale team effort or not remains an open question. Prevailing criteria of commercial success in the software market are shifting away from strict notions of correctness towards much vaguer notions of user satisfaction; this tends to de-emphasise the role of hard science in programming. Computers are increasingly perceived not as calculating machines, but instead as elements of larger systems whose purpose is to react, or enable other system elements to react, to stimuli provided by the environment. This creates a need for a new programming paradigm, oriented towards behaviour rather than towards calculations. It is likely that such a new paradigm shall be radically different from what we consider as familiar.

I am not sure there exists a software engineering at all.

Memex Is Not Enough

Richard Mark Soley

Object Management Group, Inc.
Needham, Massachusetts

Turning his thinking finally from the application of science to military needs, in 1946 the great scientist and research organizer Dr. Vannevar Bush of the United States' wartime Office of Scientific Research and Development wrote a seminal paper entitled *As We May Think*. In it, he challenged us to discover ways to encode, link and in general make more accessible the huge store of human knowledge developed to that date.

In the last decade, the emergence of the World Wide Web has been held up as the embodiment of that half-century-old vision. While this is a reasonable claim, even if true it is simply not enough. Human beings, and more importantly our silicon-based information processors, do not simply encode, store and index static data; they create new data every nanosecond. Links between static data, stale the moment they are created, are simply not enough; the real challenge is to link the information processing power we have directly.

At the core of this effort must be sufficient consensus for interfaces not only to store and link data, but to forward and link computational power. This effort has informally been underway for decades, with thousands of "stovepiped" system thrown together without any planning. We must renew our efforts to agree standards for linking information assets, for mundane (but economically critical) "business to consumer" as well as "business to business" supply/service-chain integration, and for more interesting problems as well.

Typically such standardization efforts have centered on the lowest levels of the interoperability protocol stack, including the physical cable or the byte-transfer level. Even newer approaches based on document type extensions (e.g., XML) have focussed only on data movement. Unfortunately, it is the much more difficult piece of the puzzle that is required for true processing power synchronization: transactional, persistent, secure application interfaces (at the lower level) and market-specific interface definitions (at the higher level) are absolutely critical.

Memex—the availability of linked, indexed data—is a great starting point for integrating the sum total of human knowledge, as Bush saw a half century ago. By simply implementing this vision we abandon it; instead we should focus on providing true application-level integration across worldwide networks so that knowledge may be shared the moment it is discovered.

T. Maibaum (Ed.): FASE 2000, LNCS 1783, pp. 21–21, 2000.
© Springer-Verlag Berlin Heidelberg 2000

From Play-In Scenarios to Code:
An Achievable Dream
(Preliminary Version, January 2000)

David Harel

The Weizmann Institute of Science, Rehovot, Israel.
`harel@wisdom.weizmann.ac.il`

Abstract. We discuss the possibility of a complete system development scheme, supported by semantically rigorous automated tools, within which one can go from an extremely high-level, user-friendly requirement capture method, which we call *play-in scenarios*, to a final implementation. A cyclic process consisting of verification against requirements and synthesis from requirements plays an important part in the scheme, which is not quite as imaginary as it may sound.

Over the years, the main approaches to high-level system modeling have been structured-analysis and structured design (SA/SD), and object-oriented analysis and design (OOAD). The two are about a decade apart in initial conception and evolution. SA/SD started out in the late 1970's by DeMarco, Yourdon and others, and is based on 'lifting' classical procedural programming concepts up to the modeling level and using diagrams for visualization [3, 6]. The result calls for modeling system structure by functional decomposition and the flow of information, depicted by hierarchical data-flow diagrams. As to system behavior, the mid 1980's saw several methodology teams (such as Ward and Mellor [35], Hatley and Pirbhai [17] and our Statemate team [14]) enriching the basic SA/SD model with means for modeling behavior, using state diagrams or the richer language of statecharts [9]. A state diagram or statechart is associated with each function or activity, describing its behavior.[1]

Many nontrivial issues had to be worked out in order to properly connect structure with behavior, enabling the modeler to construct a comprehensive and semantically rigorous model of the system (see Fig. 1); it is not enough to simply decide on a behavioral language and then associate each function or activity with a behavioral description.[2] The above teams struggled with this issue, and their decisions on how to link structure with behavior ended up being very similar.

---

[1] Of course, there are many other possible choices for a language to specify behavior, including such visual languages as Petri nets [29] or SDL diagrams [33], and more algebraic ones like CCS [24] and CSP [19].

[2] This would be like saying that when you build a car all you need are the structural things — body, chassis, wheels, etc. — and an engine, and you then merely stick the engine under the hood and you are done...

T. Maibaum (Ed.): FASE 2000, LNCS 1783, pp. 22–34, 2000.

Detailed descriptions of the way this is done in the SA/SD framework appear in [35, 17, 16].

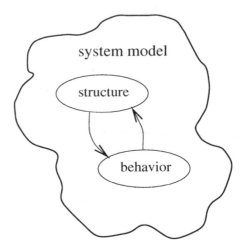

Fig. 1. A system model

Careful behavioral modeling and its close linking with system structure are especially crucial for embedded, reactive systems [15, 26], which constitute the kinds of systems this paper is most concerned with, and of which real-time systems are a special case. The availability of a rigorous semantical basis for the model — notably for the behavioral parts — is what leads to the possibility of executing models and running actual code generated from them. The first commercial tool to enable model execution and code generation from high-level models was Statemate from I-Logix in 1987 (see [14, 20]). We shall have more to say about executability and code generation later on. Here, code need not necessarily be of the kind that results in software; it could be code in a hardware description language, resulting ultimately in real hardware.

Turning to object-orientation, following developments in OO programming, proposals for object-oriented modeling (analysis and design; that is, OOAD) started to show up in the late 1980's. Here too, the basic idea for system structure was to 'lift' concepts from the programming level up to the modeling level, and to use diagrams, or what has been termed *visual formalisms* in [10]. For example, the basic structural model for objects in Booch's method [1], in the OMT method of Rumbaugh and his colleagues [31], in the ROOM method [34], and in many others (e.g., [4]), features a graphical notation for such OO notions as classes and instances, relationships and roles, and aggregation and inheritance. Visuality is achieved by basing this model on an enriched form of entity-relationship diagrams. As to system behavior, most object-oriented modeling approaches, including those just listed, adopted the statecharts language [9] for this (or a variant thereof). A statechart is associated with each class, and its role is to describe the behavior of the instance objects.

The issue of connecting structure and behavior in the OOAD world is more subtle and a lot more complicated than in the SA/SD one. Classes represent dynamically changing collections of concrete objects, and behavioral modeling must address issues related to their creation and destruction, the delegation of messages, the modification and maintenance of relationships, aggregation, inheritance, etc. The test of whether these have been dealt with properly is, of course, whether the inter-links of Fig. 1 are defined sufficiently well to allow model execution and code generation. This has been achieved only in a couple of cases. One is the ObjecTime tool, which is based on the ROOM method of [34], and the other is the Rhapsody tool (see [20]), which is based on the executable object modeling work of [12]. Executable object modeling is a carefully worked out language set based on the class/object diagrams of [1, 31], driven by statecharts for behavior, and addressing the issues above in a rigorous way.

The pair of languages described in [12] also serve as the heart of the recent UML language set [36, 30], which was adopted in 1997 as a standard by the Object Management Group. In fact, we shall refer to this part of the UML, namely the class/object diagrams and the statecharts, as described in [12] or in the UML documents [36, 30], by the term *Base-UML*. Thus, Base-UML is that part of the UML that is used to specify unambiguous, executable, and therefore implementable, models. Perhaps it should be called *Executable-UML*, or simply *XUML* or *X-UML*. In any event, we shall stick to 'Base-UML' here.[3]

Indeed, if we have the ability to generate full code, we would eventually want that code to serve as the basis for the final implementation. Current tools are in fact capable of producing quality code, good enough for the implementation of many kinds of systems. And there is no doubt that the techniques for this kind of 'super-compilation' from high-level visual formalisms will improve in time. Providing higher levels of abstraction with automated downward transformations has always been the way to go, as long as the abstractions are ones with which the engineers who do the actual work are happy. The broad arrow on the right-hand side of Fig. 2 is now relevant: with the convention that solid broad arrows denote automated processes, it shows the system model giving rise to automatic generation of the full runnable code.

∗   ∗   ∗

Let us now discuss model execution.[4] Why would we want to execute models? Clearly, in order to test and debug them. Against what should we be carrying out the testing? Clearly, against requirements. What kinds of requirements are

---

[3] The UML has several means for specifying more elaborate aspects of the structure and architecture of the system under development (for example, packages and components), but we shall not get into these here. Our emphasis is on classical object-oriented structure and full behavior.

[4] See also [11] for a more detailed discussion of various kinds of model execution that one might desire.

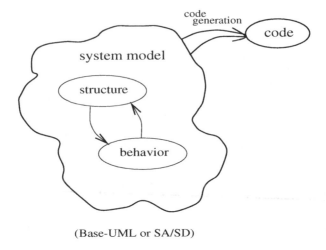

(Base-UML or SA/SD)

Fig. 2. System modeling with full code generation

relevant to high-level system modeling with visual formalisms? Well, requirements are, by their very nature, the constraints, desires and hopes we entertain
concerning the system under development. We want to make sure, both during
development and when we feel development is over, that the system does, or will
do, what we intend or hope for it to do.

Since in this paper we concentrate on processes that can be automated, we
shall not discuss informal requirements, written in natural language or pseudo
code. Instead, we concentrate on rigorous, precisely defined requirements. Ever
since the early days of high level programming, computer science researchers
have grappled with the question of how to best state what we want of a complex
program or system. Notable efforts are those embodied in the early work of Floyd
and Hoare on invariant assertions and termination statements [8, 18], and in the
many variants of temporal logic [26, 22, 23]. These make it possible to express
the two main kinds of requirements of interest: safety properties (a bad thing
can't happen; e.g., this program will never terminate with the wrong answer, or
this elevator door will never open between floors), and liveness properties (good
things must happen; e.g., this program will eventually terminate, or this elevator
will open its door on the desired floor within the allotted time limit).

A more recent way to specify requirements, which is popular in the realm of
object-oriented systems, is to use *message sequence charts* (*MSCs*). This graphical language was adopted long ago as a standard by the CCITT telecommunication organization, currently the ITU (see [25]), and in the UML it manifests
itself — in a slightly weaker way – as the language of *sequence diagrams*. MSCs,
or UML's sequence diagrams, are used to specify scenarios as sequences of message interactions between object instances. This approach meshes very nicely
with Jacobson's methodological notion of *use-cases* [21]: In the early stages of
system development, engineers typically come up with use-cases, and then pro-

ceed to specify the scenarios that instantiate them. This captures the desired inter-relationships between the processes, tasks, or object instances (and between them and the environment) in a linear or quasi-linear fashion, in terms of temporal progress.[5] In other words, we are specifying the scenarios, or the 'stories', that the final system should, and hopefully will, satisfy and support. See Fig. 3.

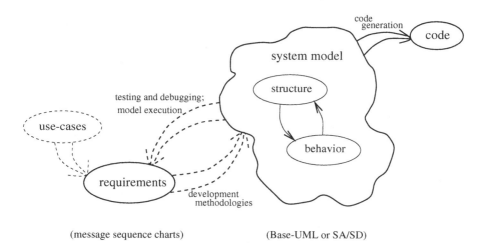

Fig. 3. System modeling with 'soft' links to requirements

However, it is important to realize that these scenarios are not part of the system. They are part of the requirements *from* the system. They are constructed (often based on the less detailed and more abstract use-cases) in order to capture the scenarios that we hope, desire, and want our system to satisfy, when implemented. Of course, one can ask why these scenarios cannot be part of the implementable system model. We shall return to this question soon, but we should first contrast this inter-object 'one-story-for-all-objects' approach with the dual intra-object 'all-stories-for-one-object' approach manifest in the Base-UML modeling of objects using statecharts. In contrast to scenarios, modeling with statecharts is typically carried out at a later stage, and results in a full behavioral specification for each of the (tasks or processes or) object instances, providing details of its behavior under all possible conditions and in all possible 'stories'. This intra-object specification is what we need as an output from the design stage, since it is directly implementable (ultimately, the final software will consist of code specified for each object). It is at the heart of the system model of Figs. 1 and 2, which must support, or satisfy, the scenarios as specified in

---

[5] We mention tasks and processes here, since although we couch much of our discussion in the terminology of object-orientation and the UML, there is nothing special to objects in what we are discussing.

the MSCs. The MSCs themselves cannot be implemented; only the model can.[6] MSCs and sequence diagrams are thus the requirements, whereas Base-UML provides the implementable model.

*   *   *

Let us now turn to the broad dashed arrows in Fig. 3, those between the requirements and the system model. Going from the requirements to the model is another long-studied issue, and many system development methodologies provide guidelines, heuristics, and sometimes carefully worked-out step-by-step processes for this. The reason this left-to-right arrow is dashed is obvious: however good and useful, such processes are 'soft' methodological recommendations as to how to proceed, and are not rigorous and automated.

The arrow going from the system model to the requirements depicts the testing and debugging of the model against the requirements, using, e.g., model execution. Here is one of the neat ways this can be done, as supported by the Rhapsody tool. The user specifies the requirements as a set of sequence diagrams (perhaps instantiating previously prepared use-cases), and then puts them aside for the moment. Suppose this results in a diagram called A. Later, when the system model has been specified, it can be executed[7] and Rhapsody can be instructed to automatically construct, on the fly, animated sequence diagrams that show the dynamics of object interaction as they actually happen during execution. Suppose this results in diagram B. Upon completion of the execution, Rhapsody can be asked to compare diagrams A and B, and it will highlight any inconsistencies, thus helping debug the behavior of the system against the requirements. While this is a powerful and extremely useful way of working, we must remember that it is really limited to those executions of the model that we actually carry out, and is thus akin to classical testing and debugging. Since in general there will be infinitely many inputs or runs of the system, there could always be some out there that were not checked, and which could violate the requirements by being inconsistent with, e.g., the sequence chart A. As Dijkstra famously put it years ago, "testing and debugging cannot be used to demonstrate the absence of errors, only their presence" [7]. This 'softness' of the debugging process is the reason this arrow is dashed too. So much for Fig. 3.

Two points must now be made regarding MSCs and sequence diagrams. The first is one of exposition: by and large, the true role of these is not made clear in the literature. Again and again, one comes across articles and books in which the very same phrases are used to introduce sequence diagrams and statecharts. At one point such a publication might say something like "sequence diagrams can be used to specify behavior", and later it might say that "statecharts can be used to

---

[6] You can't simply prepare a collection of 1000 scenarios and call that your system. How would it operate? What would it do under general dynamic circumstances? How are these scenarios related? What happens if things occur that simply do not fall under any of the scenarios? And on and on.

[7] Rhapsody actually executes its Base-UML models by generating code from them and running the code in a way that is linked to the visual model.

specify behavior". Sadly, the reader isn't told anything about the fundamental difference between the two — their different roles and indeed the very different ways they are to be used. This obscurity is one of the reasons many naive readers come away confused and puzzled by the multitude of diagram types in the UML and the incoherent recommendations as to what it means to 'specify' a system.

The second point is more substantial. As a requirements language, all known versions of MSCs, including the ITU standard [25] and the sequence diagrams adopted in the UML [36, 30], are extremely weak in expressive power. Their semantics is little more than a set of simple constraints on the partial order of possible events in some possible system execution. Virtually nothing can be said in MSCs about what the system will actually do when run! These diagrams can state what *may possibly* occur, not what *must* occur. Thus, amazingly, if one wants to be puristic, then under most definitions of the semantics of MSCs, an empty system (i.e., one that doesn't do anything in response to anything) satisfies any such chart. So just sitting back and doing nothing will make your requirements happy....[8] Another troublesome drawback of MSCs is their inability to specify 'no-go' scenarios (or, as we may call them, *anti-scenarios*), which are crucial in setting up safety requirements. These are scenarios whose occurrence we want to forbid; they are to be explicitly *dis*allowed. In short, there is a serious need for a more powerful language for sequences.

In a recent paper with Damm [5], this need has been addressed, by proposing an extension of MSCs, called *live sequence charts* (or *LSCs*). One of the main extensions deals with specifying liveness, i.e., things that must occur. This is done by allowing the distinction between possible and necessary behavior both globally, on the level of an entire chart, and locally, when specifying events, conditions and progress over time within a chart. The live elements, the *hot* ones, as we call them in [5], make it possible to specify anti-scenarios too. LSCs also support subcharts, synchronization, branching and iteration. It is not clear yet whether this language is exactly what is needed, and a lot more work on it is definitely required. Experience using it must be gained and an implementation is badly needed. But the proposal is there, and LSCs are a preliminary candidate for a far more powerful way of visually specifying behavioral requirements of a system model, and thus of the system's final implementation.

*   *   *

Since their expressive power is far greater than MSCs (it is essentially that of Base-UML itself), LSCs also make it possible to start looking more seriously at this 'grand dichotomy' of reactive behavior, namely, the relationship between the aforementioned dual views of behavioral description — the inter-object requirements view captured by LSCs and the intra-object implementable view captured by statecharts in Base-UML. Let us try to do so, by referring to Fig. 4.

---

[8] Usually, however, there is a minimal, often implicit, requirement that there should be at least one run of the system that winds its way correctly through any specified sequence chart.

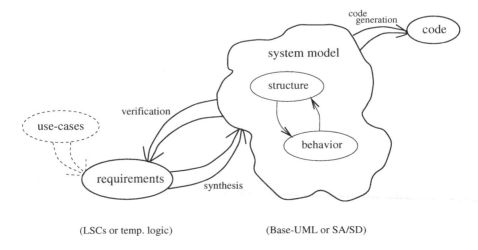

Fig. 4. System modeling with 'hard' links to requirements

The difference between Figs. 3 and 4 is in the two arrows between the requirements and the model, which have been 'un-dashed'. We are now talking about the possibility of having at our disposal 'hard', formal and rigorous, and mainly fully automatable, links between the system model (e.g., Base-UML) and the requirements (e.g., LSCs).[9]

Going from right to left, instead of testing and debugging by executing models, we are now interested in checking the system model against the requirements using true *verification*. This is not what CASE-tool people in the 1980s often called "validation and verification", which did not amount to much more than consistency checking of the model's syntax. What we have in mind is a mathematically rigorous and precise proof that the model satisfies the requirements. And we want this to be done automatically by a computerized verifier. Since we are using LSCs (or the analogous temporal logics or timing diagrams) this means far, far more than merely executing the system model and making sure that the sequence diagrams you get from the run are consistent with the ones you prepared in advance. It means making sure, for example, that the things an LSC specifies as *not* allowed to happen, will indeed never happen, and things it specifies as *having* to happen (and/or having to happen within certain time constraints), will indeed happen — facts not verifiable in general by any amount of execution. And it means a lot more too. This paper is not a treatise on verification, so we shall say no more about this here, except to note that although verification in general constitutes a non-computable algorithmic problem, ever since the early work of Floyd and Hoare [8, 18], and through the work on temporal logic [23] and model checking verification [2], rigorously verifying programs

---

[9] Requirements could equally well have been specified using some powerful form of temporal logic with path quantifiers; see, e.g., [22, 23] or certain kinds of timing diagrams [32].

and systems — hardware and software — has matured, and has become more and more viable. These days we can safely say that it *can* be carried out in many, many cases, especially in the finite-state ones that arise in the realm of reactive, real-time systems. Work is in progress these days on enriching the Statemate tool [14, 16, 20] with true verification capabilities. Doing the same for an OOAD tool like Rhapsody or Rose-RT is just a matter of time. Before long, I believe, we will be routinely using such tools to verify models agains requirements.

In the opposite direction, from the requirements to the model, instead of guiding system developers in informal ways to try to build models according to their dreams and hopes, we would very much like our tools to be able to carry out true *synthesis* directly from those dreams and hopes, if they are indeed implementable. We want to be able to automatically generate a system model (say, statecharts) from the requirements (say, LSCs). This is a whole lot harder than synthesizing code from a system model, which is really but a high-level kind of compilation. The duality between the scenario style and the statechart style in saying what a system does over time renders the synthesis of an implementable system model from sequence-based requirements a truly formidable task. It is not too hard to do this for the weak MSCs, which can't say much about what we really want from the system. It is a lot more difficult for far more realistic requirements languages, such as LSCs.

How can we synthesize a good first approximation of the statecharts from the LSCs? Several researchers have addressed this issue in the past, including work on certain kinds of synthesis from temporal logic [27, 28] and timing diagrams [32]. More recently, in [13], we have been able to present a first-cut attempt at algorithms for synthesizing state-machines and statecharts from LSCs (albeit, in a slightly restricted setup, and resulting in models that could become too large to work with). This is done by first determining whether the requirements are consistent (i.e., whether there is *any* system model satisfying them), and then using the proof of consistency to synthesize a model. There is still a lot of rather deep research to be done here, and work is in progress as we write. I believe this problem will eventually end up like verification — hard in principle, but not beyond a practical and useful solution.

What does all this mean? Well, it is tempting to say that if we have the picture set up as in Fig. 4, we don't even need verification or testing: just go directly from left to right. State your requirements, have one part of your tool synthesize the system model and another part generate code, and you are all set. Again, this in not a treatise on incremental development of systems (although the more ambitious parts of this paper implicitly suggest that the classical life cycle models might eventually have to be modified somewhat), but obviously one would want to go through a cycle of development phases, producing continuously refined and extended versions of the system. This cycle, we suggest, would repeatedly and incrementally follow some combination of the dashed arrows of Fig. 3 — development methodologies and testing and debugging — and the solid ones of Fig. 4 — synthesis and verification — in both horizontal growth of the system under development and in its vertical refinement. This will have to be done based not on quick-and dirty methods written up hastily in shallow methodology books, but on the deep and profound wisdom that will have to be accumulated over years of experience using these techniques. It will not happen overnight, even if all the required tools were just around the corner.

*   *   *

To complete the dream this paper has tried to sketch, albeit superficially, I would like to introduce one additional idea, that of *play-in scenarios*. When you execute a model, you play-*out* a scenario. This becomes apparent when you use the tool's ability to execute models interactively, and it becomes especially transparent and impressive (useful too) when you work with a soft panel mock-up of the system's final interface or even a hard version of the system's actual hardware, as is possible in Statemate and Rhapsody. You can play-out a scenario by standing in, so to speak, for the system's environment, introducing events and changes in values, etc., and observing the results as they unfold (see [11]). What is proposed here is to play-*in* scenarios in order to set up the requirements, perhaps driven by use-cases. This will be done by working directly opposite such a mock-up of the system's interface (think of a cell-phone, for example), using a highly user-friendly method of 'teaching' your tool about the desired and undesired scenarios. The interactive process will also include means for refining the system's structure as you progress, e.g., forming composite objects and their aggregates and setting up inheriting objects, all reflected in a modified mock-up interface. As the process of playing in the scenario-based requirements continues, the underlying tool will automatically and incrementally generate LSCs (not merely MSCs) that are consistent with these 'teachings'. Thus we are automating the construction of rigorous and comprehensive requirements from a friendly, intuitive and natural play-in capability, which could even be carried out by the customer.

Here too, there is much research still to be done. While there is a nontrivial mathematical/algorithmic side to this too, we must deal with the human aspect: we have to find powerful, yet natural and easy-to-use means for interacting with an essentially behavior-free 'system shell', in order to tell it what we want from it. We are currently at work on this rather exciting possibility, and hope to be able to report pretty soon on an initial proposal for play-in scenarios and a first-cut prototype implementation of such a capability.

Fig. 5 is a schematic attempt to summarize the story as a grand dream. In the figure, we have also included a second broad arrow in the right-hand upper part. It indicates the ability of the user to 'round-trip' back from the code to the model: making changes in the former reflects automatically back as changes in the visual formalisms of the latter. A modest (but very useful) form of this model-code association is already available in the Rhapsody tool. There is reason to believe that this ability too will become commonplace in the future, and that the techniques enabling it will become more powerful and far broader in applicability.

*   *   *

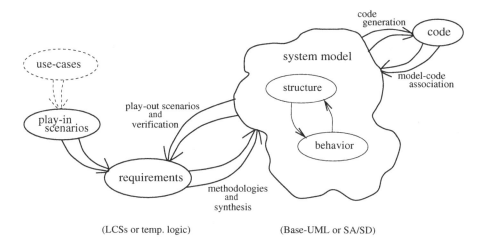

Fig. 5. The dream in full

In summary, it is probably no great exaggeration to say that there is a lot more that we *don't* know and *can't* achieve yet in this business than what we do know and can achieve. The efforts of scores of researchers, methodologists and language designers have resulted in a lot more than we could have hoped for ten or twenty years ago, and for this we should be thankful and humble. Still, I maintain that there is a dream in the offing. It is a dream of many parts — several of which are not even close to being fully available to us yet — but one that is not unattainable. If and when it comes true, it could have a significant effect on the way complex systems are developed.

References

[1]   Booch, G., *Object-Oriented Analysis and Design, with Applications* (2nd edn.), Benjamin/Cummings, 1994.

[2]   Clarke, E.M., O. Grumberg and D. Peled, *Model Checking*, Mit Press, 1999.

[3]   Constantine, L. L., and E. Yourdon, *Structured Design*, Prentice-Hall, Englewood Cliffs, 1979.

[4]   Cook, S. and J. Daniels, *Designing Object Systems: Object-Oriented Modelling with Syntropy*, Prentice Hall, New York, 1994.

[5]   Damm, W., and D. Harel, "LSCs: Breathing Life into Message Sequence Charts", *Proc. 3rd IFIP Int. Conf. on Formal Methods for Open Object-based Distributed Systems (FMOODS'99)*, (P. Ciancarini, A. Fantechi and R. Gorrieri, eds.), Kluwer Academic Publishers, 1999, pp. 293–312.

[6]   DeMarco, T., *Structured Analysis and System Specification*, Yourdon Press, New York, 1978.

[7]   Dijkstra, E.W., "Notes on Structured Programming", in *Structured Programming*, Academic Press, New York, 1972.

[8]   Floyd, R.W., "Assigning Meanings to Programs", *Proc. Symp. on Applied Math.*, (Vol. 19: "Mathematical Aspects of Computer Science"), American Math. Soc., Providence, RI, pp. 19–32, 1967.

[9]   Harel, D., "Statecharts: A Visual Formalism for Complex Systems", *Sci. Comput. Prog.* **8** (1987), 231–274. (Preliminary version appeared as Tech. Report CS84-05, The Weizmann Institute of Science, Rehovot, Israel, Feb. 1984.)

[10]   Harel,D., "On Visual Formalisms", *Comm. Assoc. Comput. Mach.* **31**:5 (1988), 514–530.

[11]   Harel, D., "Biting the Silver Bullet: Toward a Brighter Future for System Development", *Computer* (Jan. 1992), 8–20.

[12]   Harel, D., and E. Gery, "Executable Object Modeling with Statecharts", *Computer* (July 1997), 31–42.

[13]   Harel, D., and H. Kugler, "Synthesizing Object Systems from Live Sequence Charts", submitted for publication, 1999.

[14]   Harel, D., H. Lachover, A. Naamad, A. Pnueli, M. Politi, R. Sherman, A. Shtull-Trauring, and M. Trakhtenbrot, "STATEMATE: A Working Environment for the Development of Complex Reactive Systems", *IEEE Trans. Soft. Eng.* **16** (1990), 403–414. (Preliminary version in *Proc. 10th Int. Conf. Soft. Eng.*, IEEE Press, New York, 1988, pp. 396–406.)

[15]   Harel, D., and A. Pnueli, "On the Development of Reactive Systems", in *Logics and Models of Concurrent Systems*, (K. R. Apt, ed.), NATO ASI Series, Vol. F-13, Springer-Verlag, New York, 1985, pp. 477-498.

[16]   Harel, D., and M. Politi, *Modeling Reactive Systems with Statecharts: The STATEMATE Approach*, McGraw-Hill, 1998.

[17]   Hatley, D., and I. Pirbhai, *Strategies for Real-Time System Specification*, Dorset House, New York, 1987.

[18]   Hoare, C.A.R., "An Axiomatic Basis for Computer Programming", *Comm. Assoc. Comput. Mach.* **12** (1969), 576–583.

[19]   Hoare, C.A.R., "Communicating Sequential Processes", *Comm. Assoc. Comput. Mach.* **21** (1978), 666–677.

[20]   I-Logix, Inc., products web page, http://www.ilogix.com/fs_prod.htm.

[21]   Jacobson, I., *Object-Oriented Software Engineering: A Use Case Driven Approach*, ACM Press/Addison-Wesley, 1992.

[22]   Manna, Z., and A. Pnueli, *The Temporal Logic of Reactive and Concurrent Systems: Specification*, Springer-Verlag, New York, 1992.

[23]   Manna, Z., and A. Pnueli, *Temporal Verification of Reactive Systems: Safety*, Springer-Verlag, New York, 1995.

[24]   Milner, R., *A Calculus of Communicating Systems*, Lecture Notes in Computer Science, Vo. 92, Springer-Verlag, Berlin, 1980.

[25]   MSC: ITU-T Recommendation Z.120: Message Sequence Chart (MSC), ITU-T, Geneva, 1996.

[26]   Pnueli, A., "Applications of Temporal Logic to the Specification and Verification of Reactive Systems: A Survey of Current Trends", *Current Trends in Concurrency* (de Bakker et al., eds.), Lecture Notes in Computer Science, Vol. 224, Springer-Verlag, Berlin, 1986, pp. 510–584.

[27]   Pnueli, A., and R. Rosner, "On the Synthesis of a Reactive Module", *Proc. 16th ACM Symp. on Principles of Programming Languages*, Austin, TX, January 1989.

[28]   Pnueli, A., and R. Rosner, "On the Synthesis of an Asynchronous Reactive Module", *Proc. 16th Int. Colloquium on Automata, Languages and Program-*

ming, Lecture Notes in Computer Science, vol. 372, Springer-Verlag, Berlin, 1989, pp. 652–671.

[29]   Reisig, W., *Petri Nets: An Introduction*, Springer-Verlag, Berlin, 1985.

[30]   Rumbaugh, J., I. Jacobson and G. Booch, *The Unified Modeling Language Reference Manual*, Addison-Wesley, 1999.

[31]   Rumbaugh, J., M. Blaha, W. Premerlani, F. Eddy and W. Lorensen, *Object-Oriented Modeling and Design*, Prentice Hall, 1991.

[32]   Schlor, R. and W. Damm, "Specification and verification of system-level hardware designs using timing diagrams", *Proc. European Conference on Design Automation*, Paris, France, IEEE Computer Society Press, pp. 518 – 524, 1993.

[33]   SDL: ITU-T Recommendation Z.100, Languages for telecommunications applications: Specification and description language, Geneva, 1999.

[34]   Selic, B., G. Gullekson and P. T. Ward, *Real-Time Object-Oriented Modeling*, John Wiley & Sons, New York, 1994.

[35]   Ward, P., and S. Mellor, *Structured Development for Real-Time Systems* (Vols. 1, 2, 3), Yourdon Press, New York, 1985.

[36]   Documentation of the Unified Modeling Language (UML), available from the Object Management Group (OMG), http://www.omg.org.

Parallel Refinement Mechanisms for Real-Time Systems

Paul Z. Kolano[1], Richard A. Kemmerer[2], and Dino Mandrioli[3]

[1] Trusted Systems Laboratory, Lockheed Martin M & DS – Western Region
3200 Zanker Road, San Jose, CA 95134 U.S.A.
paul.z.kolano@lmco.com
[2] Reliable Software Group, Computer Science Department,
University of California, Santa Barbara, CA 93106 U.S.A.
kemm@cs.ucsb.edu
[3] Dipartimento di Elettronica e Informazione,
Politecnico di Milano, Milano 20133, Italy
dino.mandrioli@polimi.it

Abstract. This paper discusses highly general mechanisms for specifying the refinement of a real-time system as a collection of lower level parallel components that preserve the timing and functional requirements of the upper level specification. These mechanisms are discussed in the context of ASTRAL, which is a formal specification language for real-time systems. Refinement is accomplished by mapping all of the elements of an upper level specification into lower level elements that may be split among several parallel components. In addition, actions that can occur in the upper level are mapped to actions of components operating at the lower level. This allows several types of implementation strategies to be specified in a fairly natural way, while the price for generality (in terms of complexity) is paid only when necessary. The refinement mechanisms are illustrated using a simple digital circuit and a much more complex example is sketched.

1 Introduction

Refinement is a fundamental design technique that has often challenged the „formal methods" community. In most cases, mathematical elegance and proof manageability have exhibited a deep trade-off with the flexibility and freedom that are often needed in practice to deal with unexpected or critical situations. A typical example is provided by algebraic approaches that exploit some notion of homomorphism between algebraic structures. When applied to parallel systems, such approaches led to the notion of observational equivalence of processes [8] (i.e. the ability of the lower level process to exhibit all and only the observable behaviors of the upper level one). Observational equivalence, however, has been proved too restrictive to deal with general cases and more flexible notions of inter-level relations have been advocated [5].

The issue of refinement becomes even more critical when dealing with real-time systems where time analysis is a crucial factor. In this case, the literature exhibits only a few, fairly limited proposals. [3] is the origin of the present proposal. [6] addresses the issue within the context of timed Petri nets and the TRIO language. In this approach, a system is modeled as a timed Petri net and its properties are described as TRIO formulas. Then, mechanisms are given that refine the original net into a more detailed one that preserves the original properties. The approach is limited, however,

T. Maibaum (Ed.): FASE 2000, LNCS 1783, pp. 35–50, 2000.
© Springer-Verlag Berlin Heidelberg 2000

by the expressive power of pure Petri nets, which do not allow one to deal with functional data dependencies. In [11], a system is modeled by an extension of finite state machines and its properties are expressed in a real-time logic language. Refinement follows a fairly typical algebraic approach by mapping upper level entities into lower level ones and pursuing observational equivalence between the two layers. In this case, observable variables (i.e. variables that are in the process interface), must be identical in the two levels. This leads to a lack of flexibility, as pointed out above, that is even more evident in time dependent systems where refined layers must also guarantee consistency between the occurrence times of the events.

In this paper, we propose highly general refinement mechanisms that allow several types of implementation strategies to be specified in a fairly natural way. In particular, processes can be implemented both sequentially, by refining a single complex transition as a sequence or selection of more elementary transitions, and in a parallel way, by mapping one process into several concurrent ones. This allows one to increase the amount of parallelism through refinement whenever needed or wished.

Also, *asynchronous implementation policies* are allowed in which lower level actions can have durations unrelated to upper level ones, provided that their effects are made visible in the lower level exactly at the times specified by the upper level. For instance, in a phone system, many calls must be served simultaneously, possibly by exploiting concurrent service by many processors. Such services, however, are asynchronous since calls occur in an unpredictable fashion at any instant. Therefore, it is not easy to describe a call service that manages a set of calls within a given time interval in an abstract way that can be naturally refined as a collection of many independent and individual services of single calls, possibly even allowing a dynamic allocation of servers to the phones issuing the calls. In Section 8, we outline how this goal can be achieved by applying the mechanisms described in this paper.

Not surprisingly, generality has a price in terms of complexity. In our approach, however, this price is paid only when necessary. Simple implementation policies yield simple specifications, whereas complex specifications are needed only for sophisticated implementation policies. The same holds for the proof system, which is built hand-in-hand with the implementation mechanisms.

Furthermore, the proof system is amenable both for traditional hand-proofs, based on human ingenuity and only partially formalized, and for fully formalized, tool-supported proofs. Finally, although experience with the application of the proposed mechanisms is still limited, it is not difficult to extract from meaningful examples suitable guidelines for their systematic application to many real cases.

This work is presented in the context of ASTRAL, which is a formal specification language for real-time systems with the following distinguishing features:

- It is rooted in both ASLAN [1], which is an untimed state machine formalism, and TRIO [7], which is a real-time temporal logic, yielding a new, logic-based, process-oriented specification language.
- It has composable modularization mechanisms that allow a complex system to be built as a collection of interacting processes. It also has refinement mechanisms to construct a process as a sequence of layers, where each layer is the implementation of the layer above.
- It has a proof obligation system that allows one to formally prove properties of interest as consequences of process specifications. This proof system is incremental since complex proofs of complex systems can be built by composing small proofs that can be carried out, for the most part, independently of each other. ASTRAL's proofs are of two types. Intra-level proofs guarantee system properties on the basis of local properties that only refer to a single process type.

Inter-level proofs guarantee that layer i+1 is a correct implementation of layer i without the need to redo intra-level proofs from scratch.

In this paper, we resume the issue of ASTRAL layering mechanisms and the inter-level proofs, which were addressed in a preliminary and fairly restrictive way in [3].

This paper is structured as follows. Section 2 provides the necessary background on the ASTRAL language. Section 3 summarizes previous purely sequential refinement mechanisms. Section 4 motivates the need for their extensions through a simple running example and illustrates the essentials of the generalized and parallel refinement mechanisms. Section 5 shows their application to the running example. Section 6 presents the proof obligations needed to guarantee implementation correctness and section 7 applies them to the running example. Section 8 briefly summarizes a more complex example. Finally, section 9 provides some concluding remarks. For the sake of conciseness in this paper, we concentrate only on the essentials. Complete technical details can be found in [9].

2 ASTRAL Overview

An ASTRAL system specification is comprised of a single global specification and a collection of state machine specifications. Each state machine specification represents a process type of which there may be multiple, statically generated, instances. The *global specification* contains declarations for the process types that comprise the system, types and constants that are shared among more than one process type, and assumptions about the global environment and critical requirements for the whole system.

An ASTRAL *process specification* consists of a sequence of *levels*. Each level is an abstract data type view of the process being specified. The first („top level") view is a very abstract model of what constitutes the process (types, constants, variables), what the process does (state transitions), and the critical requirements the process must meet (invariants and schedules). Lower levels are increasingly more detailed with the lowest level corresponding closely to high level code.

The process being specified is thought of as being in various *states*, where one state is differentiated from another by the values of the *state variables*, which can be changed only by means of *state transitions*. Transitions are specified in terms of entry and exit assertions, where *entry assertions* describe the constraints that state variables must satisfy in order for the transition to fire, and *exit assertions* describe the constraints that are fulfilled by state variables after the transition has fired. An explicit non-null duration is associated with each transition. Transitions are executed as soon as they are enabled if no other transition is executing in that process.

Every process can export both state variables and transitions. Exported variables are readable by other processes while exported transitions are callable from the external environment. Inter-process communication is accomplished by inquiring about the values of exported variables and the start and end times of exported transitions.

In addition to specifying system state (through process variables and constants) and system evolution (through transitions), an ASTRAL specification also defines system critical requirements and assumptions about the behavior of the environment that interacts with the system. Assumptions about the behavior of the environment are expressed by means of *environment clauses* that describe the pattern of calls to external transitions, which are the stimuli to which the system reacts. Critical requirements are expressed by means of *invariants* and *schedules*. Invariants represent requirements that must hold in every state reachable from the initial state, no matter what the behavior of the external environment is, while schedules represent additional properties that must be satisfied provided that the external environment behaves as assumed.

Invariants and schedules are proved over all possible executions of a system. A system execution is a set of process executions that contains one process execution for each process instance in the system. A process execution for a given process instance is a history of events on that instance. The value of an expression E at a time t1 in the history can be obtained using the *past* operator, past(E, t1). There are four types of events in ASTRAL. A *call event*, Call(tr1, t1), occurs for an exported transition tr1 at a time t1 iff tr1 was called from the external environment at t1. A *start event*, Start(tr1, t1), occurs for a transition tr1 at a time t1 iff tr1 fires at t1. Similarly, an *end event*, End(tr1, t1), occurs if tr1 ends at t1. Finally, a *change event*, Change(v1, t1), occurs for a variable v1 at a time t1 iff v1 changes value at t1. Note that change events can only occur when an end event occurs for some transition. An introduction and complete overview of the ASTRAL language can be found in [2].

The example system used throughout the remainder of the paper is shown in figure 1. This system is a circuit that computes the value of a * b + c * d, given inputs a, b, c, and d. The ASTRAL specification for the circuit is shown below.

```
PROCESS Mult_Add                 AXIOM      TRUE
EXPORT    compute, output        INVARIANT
    CONSTANT   dur1:pos_real         FORALL t1:time, a, b, c, d:integer
    VARIABLE     output:integer       (Start(compute(a, b, c, d), t1)
TRANSITION compute(a, b, c, d:integer)  → FORALL t2:time
    ENTRY     [TIME:dur1]                  (t1 + dur1 ≤ t2 & t2 ≤ now
      TRUE                                 →past(output, t2) = a * b + c * d))
    EXIT   output= a * b + c * d
```

3 Sequential Refinement Mechanism

A refinement mechanism for ASTRAL was defined in [3]. In this definition, an ASTRAL process specification consists of a sequence of levels where the behavior of each level is implemented by the next lower level in the sequence. Given two ASTRAL process level specifications P_U and P_L, where P_L is a refinement of P_U, the implementation statement, hereafter referred to as the IMPL mapping, defines a mapping from all the types, constants, variables, and transitions of P_U into their corresponding terms in P_L, which are referred to as *mapped* types, constants, variables, or transitions. P_L can also introduce types, constants and/or variables that are not mapped, which are referred to as the *new* types, constants, or variables of P_L. Note that P_L cannot introduce any new transitions (i.e. each transition of P_L must be a mapped transition). A transition of P_U can be mapped into a sequence of transitions, a selection of transitions, or any combinations thereof.

A selection mapping of the form $T_U == A_1$ & $T_{L.1}$ | A_2 & $T_{L.2}$ | ... | A_n & $T_{L.n}$, is defined such that when the upper level transition T_U fires, one and only one lower level transition $T_{L.j}$ fires, where $T_{L.j}$ can only fire when both its entry assertion and its associated „guard" A_j are true.

A sequence mapping of the form $T_U ==$ WHEN $Entry_L$ DO $T_{L.1}$ BEFORE $T_{L.2}$ BEFORE ... BEFORE $T_{L.n}$ OD, defines a mapping such that the sequence of transitions $T_{L.1}; ...; T_{L.n}$ is enabled (i.e. can start) whenever $Entry_L$ evaluates to true. Once the sequence has started, it cannot be interrupted until all of its transitions have been executed in order. The starting time of the upper level transition T_U corresponds to the starting time of the sequence (which is not necessarily equal to the starting time of $T_{L.1}$ because of a possible delay between the time when the sequence starts and the time when $T_{L.1}$ becomes enabled), while the ending time of T_U corresponds to the ending time of the last transition in the sequence, $T_{L.n}$. Note that the only transition that can modify the value of a mapped variable is the last transition in the sequence. This further constraint is a consequence of the ASTRAL communication model. That is, in the upper level, the new values of the variables affected by T_U are broadcast when T_U terminates. Thus, mapped variables of P_L can be modified only when the sequence implementing T_U ends.

The inter-level proofs consist of showing that each upper level transition is correctly implemented by the corresponding sequence, selection, or combination thereof in the next lower level. For selections, it must be shown that whenever the upper level transition T_U fires, one of the lower level transitions $T_{L.j}$ fires, that the effect (i.e. changes to variables) of each $T_{L.j}$ is equivalent to the effect of T_U, and that the duration of each $T_{L.j}$ is equal to the duration of T_U. For sequences, it must be shown that the sequence is enabled iff T_U is enabled, that the effect of the sequence is equivalent to the effect of T_U, and that the duration of the sequence (including any initial delay after $Entry_L$ is true) is equal to the duration of T_U.

4 Parallel Refinement Mechanism

In the sequential mechanism, refinement occurs at the transition level, where the behavior of each upper level transition can be specified in greater detail at the lower level. We now extend the ASTRAL refinement mechanism to include process level refinement, which allows a process to be refined as a collection of components that operate in parallel. For example, a reasonable refinement of the Mult_Add circuit is shown in figure 2. Here, the refinement of the system consists of two multipliers that compute a * b and c * d in parallel and an adder that adds the products together and produces the sum. This refinement cannot be expressed in the sequential mechanism due to the parallelism between the two multipliers. The new parallel mechanism introduced below, however, easily expresses this refinement.

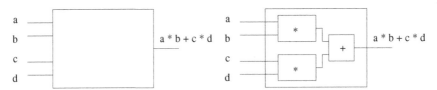

Fig. 1. Mult_Add circuit   **Fig. 2.** Refined Mult_Add circuit

In parallel refinement, an upper level transition may be implemented by a dynamic set of lower level transitions. To guarantee that an upper level transition is correctly implemented by the lower level, it is necessary to define the events that occur in the lower level when the transition is executed in the upper level. It must then be shown that these events will only occur when the upper level transition ends and that the effect will be equivalent. Like the sequential refinement mechanism of [3], an IMPL mapping is used, which describes how items in an upper level are implemented by items in the next lower level. The items of the upper level include variables, constants, types, and transitions. In addition, the implementation mapping must describe how upper level expressions are transformed into lower level expressions.

The following sections only discuss the transition mappings. A complete description of the IMPL mapping is given in [9].

4.1 Parallel Sequences and Selections

A natural but limited approach to defining parallel transition mappings is to extend the sequential sequence and selection mappings into parallel sequence and selection mappings. Thus, a „‖" operator could be allowed in transition mappings, such that „P_1.tr1 ‖ P_2.tr2" indicates that tr1 and tr2 occur in parallel on processes P_1 and P_2, respectively. With this addition, the compute transition of the Mult_Add circuit could be expressed as the following.

```
IMPL(compute(a,b,c,d)) == WHEN TRUE DO
    (M1 multiply(a,b) ‖ M2 multiply(c,d))
        BEFORE A1 add(M1 product, M2 product) OD,
```

where M1 and M2 are the multipliers and A1 is the adder.

Although parallel sequences and selections work well for the example, they do not allow enough flexibility to express many reasonable refinements. For example, consider a production cell that executes a produce transition every time unit to indicate the production of an item. In a refinement of this system, the designer may wish to implement produce by defining two „staggered" production cells that each produce an item every two time units, thus effectively producing an item every time unit. The upper level production cell P_U and the lower level production cells P_{L1} and P_{L2} are shown in figure 3. Note that the first transition executed on P_U is init, which represents the „warm-up" time of the production cell in which no output is produced.

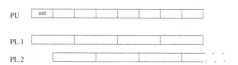

Fig. 3. Production cell refinement

This refinement cannot be expressed using parallel sequences and selections because there is no sequence of parallel transitions in the lower level that corresponds directly to produce in the upper level. When produce starts in the upper level, one of the lower level produce's will start and when produce ends in the upper level, one of the lower level produce's will end and achieve the effect of upper level produce, but the produce that starts is not necessarily the produce that achieves the effect of the corresponding end.

4.2 Parallel Start, End, and Call Mappings

The desired degree of flexibility is obtained by using transition mappings that are based on the start, end, and call of each transition. For each upper level transition T_U, a start mapping „IMPL(Start(T_U, now)) == $Start_L$" and an end mapping „IMPL(End(T_U, now)) == End_L" must be defined. If T_U is exported, a call mapping „IMPL(Call(T_U, now)) == $Call_L$" must also be defined. These mappings are defined at time now, which is a special global variable that holds the current time in the system; thus, the mappings are defined for all possible times.

Here, $Start_L$, End_L, and $Call_L$ are well-formed formulas using lower level transitions and variables. For the most part, the end and call mappings will correspond to the end or call of some transition in the lower level, whereas the start mapping may correspond to the start of some transition or some combination of changes to variables, the current time, etc. Call mappings are restricted such that for every lower level exported transition T_L, $Call(T_L)$ must be referenced in some upper level exported transition call mapping $IMPL(Call(T_U), now))$. This restriction expresses the fact that the interface of the process to the external environment cannot be changed. For parameterized transitions, only the call mapping may reference the parameters given to the transition. Any parameter referenced in a call mapping must be mapped to a call parameter of some lower level transition and the corresponding start mapping must contain the same transitions as the call mapping. Thus, the start and end parameters are taken from the associated set of unserviced call parameters.

With these mappings, the initialize and produce transitions can be mapped as follows. Note that the parallelism between P_{L1} and P_{L2} is implied by the overlapping start and end times of produce on each process and not by a built-in parallel operator.

```
IMPL(Start(initialize,now)) ==
    now = 0 & P_{L1}.Start(produce,now)
IMPL(Start(produce,now)) ==
    IF now mod 2 = 0
        THEN P_{L1}.Start(produce,now)
        ELSE P_{L2}.Start(produce,now)
    FI
```

```
IMPL(End(initialize,now)) ==
    now = 1
IMPL(End(produce,now)) ==
    IF now mod 2 = 0
        THEN P_{L1}.End(produce,now)
        ELSE P_{L2}.End(produce,now)
    FI
```

5 The Mult_Add Circuit

The specification of the refinement of the Mult_Add circuit in figure 2 is shown below using the new parallel refinement mechanism. Each multiplier has a single exported transition multiply, which computes the product of two inputs. The adder has a single transition add, which computes the sum of the two multiplier outputs.

```
PROCESS Multiplier
EXPORT
    multiply, product
VARIABLE
    product: integer
TRANSITION multiply(a,b:integer)
    ENTRY    [TIME:2]
        EXISTS t:time
            (End(multiply, t))
        → now -End(multiply) ≥ 1
    EXIT
        product= a * b
```

```
PROCESS Adder
IMPORT
    M1,M1.product,M1.multiply,
    M2,M2.product,M2.multiply
EXPORT      sum
VARIABLE    sum : integer
TRANSITION add
    ENTRY    [TIME:1]
        M1.End(multiply,now)
    &   M2.End(multiply,now)
    EXIT
        sum = M1.product+ M2.product
```

The lower level consists of two instances of the Multiplier process type, M1 and M2, and one instance of the Adder process type, A1. The output variable of the upper level process is mapped to the sum variable of the adder (IMPL(output) == A1.sum). The duration of the compute transition is the sum of the multiply transition and the add transition in the lower level (IMPL(dur1) == 3). When compute starts in the upper level, multiply starts on both M1 and M2. When compute ends in the upper level, add ends on A1. When compute is called in the upper level with inputs a, b, c, and d, multiply is called on M1 with inputs a and b and multiply is called on M2 with inputs c and d.

```
  IMPL(Start(compute, now)) ==        IMPL(End(compute, now)) == A1.End(add, now)
  M1.Start(multiply, now)             IMPL(Call(compute(a, b, c, d), now)) ==
& M2.Start(multiply, now)               M1.Call(multiply(a, b), now)
                                      & M2.Call(multiply(c, d), now)
```

6 Proof Obligations for Parallel Refinement Mechanism

The goal of the refinement proof obligations is to show that any properties that hold in the upper level hold in the lower level without actually reproving the upper level properties in the lower level. In order to show this, it must be shown that the lower level correctly implements the upper level. ASTRAL properties are interpreted over execution histories, which are described by the values of state variables and the start, end, and call times of transitions at all times in the past back to the initialization of the system. A lower level correctly implements an upper level if the implementation of the execution history of the upper level is equivalent to the execution history of the lower level. This corresponds to proving the following four statements.

(V)   Any time a variable has one of a set S of possible values in the upper level, the implementation of the variable has one of a subset of the implementation of S in the lower level.

(C)   Any time the implementation of a variable changes in the lower level, a transition ends in the upper level.

(S)   Any time a transition starts in the upper level, the implementation of the transition starts in the lower level and vice-versa.

(E)   Any time a transition ends in the upper level, the implementation of the transition ends in the lower level and vice-versa.

If these four items can be shown, then any property that holds in the upper level is preserved in the lower level because the structures over which the properties are interpreted is identical over the implementation mapping.

6.1 Proof Obligations

Instead of proving directly that the mappings hold at all times, it can be shown that the mappings hold indirectly by proving that they preserve the axiomatization of the ASTRAL abstract machine, thus they preserve any reasoning performed in the upper level. This can be accomplished by proving the implementation of each abstract machine axiom. The proof obligations are shown in figure 4 and are written in the specification language of PVS [4], which will be used to assist the proofs in the future.

To perform the proofs, the following assumption must be made about calls to transitions in each lower level process.

```
impl_call: ASSUMPTION
  (FORALL (tr_ll: transition_ll, t1: time):
     Exported(tr_ll) AND Call(tr_ll, t1)(t1) IMPLIES
        (EXISTS (tr_ul: transition_ul): (FORALL (t2: time):
           IMPL(Call(tr_ul, t2)(t2)) IMPLIES Call(tr_ll, t2)(t2)) AND
           IMPL(Call(tr_ul, t1)(t1))))
```

This assumption states that any time a lower level exported transition is called, there is some call mapping that references a call to the transition that holds at the same time. This means that if one transition of a „conjunctive" mapping is called, then all transitions of the mapping are called. That is, it is not possible for a lower level transition to be called such that the call mapping for some upper level transition does not hold. For example, consider the mapping for the compute transition of the Mult_Add circuit „IMPL(Call(compute(a, b, c, d), now)) == M1.Call(multiply(a, b), now) & M2.Call(multiply(c, d), now)". In this case, impl_call states that any time multiply is called on M1, multiply is called on M2 at the same time and vice-versa.

An assumption is also needed to assure that whenever the parameters of an upper level exported transition are distributed among multiple transitions at the lower level, the collection of parameters for which the lower level transitions execute come from a single set of call parameters. For example, in the Mult_Add circuit, the upper level compute transition may be called with two sets of parameters {1, 2, 3, 4} and {5, 6, 7, 8} at the same instant. In the lower level implementation, the multiply transition of each multiplier takes two of the parameters from each upper level call. Thus, in the example, multiply is enabled on M1 for {1, 2} and {5, 6} and on M2 for {3, 4} and {7, 8}. Without an appropriate assumption, M1 may choose {1, 2} and M2 may choose {7, 8}, thus computing the product for {1, 2, 7, 8}, which was not requested at the upper level. The *impl_call_fire_parms* assumption given in [9] prevents this.

```
impl_end1:OBLIGATION
  (FORALL (tr1:transition, t1:time):
    IMPL(End(tr1,t1)(t1)) IMPLIES
    t1 ≥ IMPL(Duration(tr1)))
impl_end2:OBLIGATION
  (FORALL (tr1: transition, t1: time, t2:
time):
    t1 = t2 - IMPL(Duration(tr1)) IMPLIES
    (IMPL(Start(tr1,t1)(t1)) IFF
    IMPL(End(tr1,t2)(t2))))
impl_trans_mutex:OBLIGATION
  (FORALL (tr1:transition, t1:time):
    IMPL(Start(tr1,t1)(t1)) IMPLIES
    (FORALL (tr2:transition):
      tr2 ≠ tr1 IMPLIES
        NOT IMPL(Start(tr2, t1)(t1)))
AND
    (FORALL (tr2:transition, t2:time):
      t1 < t2 AND
      t2 < t1 + IMPL(Duration(tr1))
IMPLIES
        NOT IMPL(Start(tr2,t2)(t2))))
impl_trans_entry:OBLIGATION
  (FORALL (tr1:transition, t1:time):
    IMPL(Start(tr1,t1)(t1)) IMPLIES
    IMPL(Entry(tr1,t1)))
impl_trans_exit:OBLIGATION
  (FORALL (tr1:transition, t1:time):
    IMPL(End(tr1,t1)(t1)) IMPLIES
    IMPL(Exit(tr1,t1)))
```

```
impl_trans_called:OBLIGATION
  (FORALL (tr1:transition, t1:time):
    IMPL(Start(tr1,t1)(t1)) AND
    Exported(tr1) IMPLIES
      IMPL(Issued_Call(tr1,t1)))
impl_trans_fire:OBLIGATION
  (FORALL (t1:time):
    (EXISTS (tr1:transition):
      IMPL(Enabled(tr1,t1))) AND
    (FORALL (tr2:transition, t2:time):
      t1 - IMPL(Duration(t2)) < t2 AND
      t2 < t1 IMPLIES
        NOT IMPL(Start(t2, t2)(t2)))
IMPLIES
    (EXISTS (tr1:transition):
      IMPL(Start(tr1,t1)(t1))))
impl_vars_no_change:OBLIGATION
  (FORALL (t1:time,t3:time):
    t1 ≤ t3 AND
    (FORALL (t2:transition,t2:time):
      t1 < t2 AND t2 ≤ t3 IMPLIES
        NOT IMPL(End(t2, t2)(t2))
IMPLIES
      (FORALL (t2:time):
        t1 ≤ t2 AND t2 ≤ t3 IMPLIES
          IMPL(Vars_No_Change(t1,
t2))))
impl_initial_state:OBLIGATION
  IMPL(Initial(0))
impl_local_axiom:OBLIGATION
  (FORALL(t1):IMPL(Axiom(t1))
```

Fig. 4. Parallel refinement proof obligations

In the axiomatization of the ASTRAL abstract machine [9], the predicate „Fired(tr1, t1)" is used to denote that the transition tr1 fired at time t1. If Fired(tr1, t1) holds, then it is derivable that a start of tr1 occurred at t1 and an end of tr1 occurred at t1 + Duration(tr1).   Additionally, since an end of tr1 can only occur at t1 when Fired(tr1, t1 - Duration(tr1)) holds and the time parameter of Fired is restricted to be nonnegative, it is known that an end can only occur at times greater than or equal to the duration of the transition. In the parallel refinement mechanism, the start and end of upper level transitions are mapped by the user, so it is unknown whether these properties of end still hold. Since the axioms rely on these properties, they must be proved explicitly as proof obligations. The *impl_end1* obligation ensures that the mapped end of a transition can only occur after the mapped duration of the transition has elapsed. The *impl_end2* obligation ensures that for every mapped start of a transition, there is a corresponding mapped end of the transition, that for every mapped end, there is a corresponding mapped start, and that mapped starts and mapped ends are separated by the mapped duration of the transition.

The other obligations are the mappings of the ASTRAL abstract machine axioms. The *impl_trans_mutex* obligation ensures that any time the mapped start of a transition occurs, no other mapped start of a transition can occur until the mapped duration of the transition has elapsed. The *impl_trans_entry* obligation ensures that any time the mapped start of a transition occurs, the mapped entry assertion of the transition holds. The *impl_trans_exit* obligation ensures that any time the mapped end of a transition occurs, the mapped exit assertion of the transition holds. The *impl_trans_called* obligation ensures that any time the mapped start of an exported transition occurs, a mapped call has been issued to the transition but not yet serviced.   The *impl_trans_fire* obligation ensures that any time the mapped entry assertion of a transition holds, a mapped call has been issued to the transition but not yet serviced if the transition is exported, and no mapped start of a transition has occurred within its mapped duration of the given time, a mapped start will occur.   The *impl_vars_no_change* obligation ensures that mapped variables only change value when the mapped end of a transition occurs. The *impl_initial_state* obligation ensures that the mapped initial clause holds at time zero.

Besides the abstract machine axioms, the local proofs of ASTRAL process specifications can also reference the local axiom clause of the process (which is empty (i.e. TRUE) in the Mult_Add circuit). Since this clause can be used in proofs and the constants referenced in the clause can be implemented at the lower level, the mapping of the local axiom clause of the upper level must be proved as a proof obligation. The *impl_local_axiom* obligation ensures that the mapped axiom clause holds at all times. In order to prove this obligation, it may be necessary to specify local axioms in the lower level processes that satisfy the implementation of the upper level axiom clause.

To prove the refinement proof obligations, the abstract machine axioms can be used in each lower level process.   For example, to prove the impl_initial_state obligation, the initial_state axiom of each lower level process can be asserted.

6.2 Correctness of Proof Obligations

The proof obligations for the parallel refinement mechanism given in figure 4 are sufficient to show that for any invariant I that holds in the upper level, IMPL(I) holds in the lower level. Consider the correctness criteria (V), (C), (S), and (E) above. (V) is satisfied because by impl_initial_state, the values of the implementation of the variables in the lower level must be consistent with the values in the upper level. Variables in the upper level only change when a transition ends and at these times, the implementation of the variables in the lower level change consistently by impl_trans_exit. (C) is satisfied because the implementation of the variables in the lower level can only change value when the implementation of a transition ends by impl_vars_no_change. The forward direction of (S) is satisfied because whenever an upper level transition fires, a lower level transition will fire by impl_trans_fire. The reverse direction of (S) is satisfied because whenever the implementation of a transition fires in the lower level, its entry assertion holds by impl_trans_entry, it has been called by impl_trans_called, and no other transition is in the middle of execution by impl_trans_mutex. (E) is satisfied because (S) is satisfied and by impl_end1 and impl_end2, any time a start occurs, a corresponding end occurs and vice-versa.

More formally, any time an invariant I can be derived in the upper level, it is derived by a sequence of transformations from I to TRUE, $I \vdash_{f1/a1} I_1 \vdash_{f2/a2} \cdots \vdash_{fn/an}$ TRUE, where each transformation f_i/a_i corresponds to the application of a series f_i of first-order logic axioms and a single abstract machine axiom a_i. Since the implementation of each axiom of the ASTRAL abstract machine is preserved by the parallel refinement proof obligations, a corresponding proof at the lower level $IMPL(I) \vdash_{f1'/impl\_a1} IMPL(I_1) \vdash_{f2'/impl\_a2} \cdots \vdash_{fn'/impl\_an}$ TRUE can be constructed by replacing the application of each abstract machine axiom a_i by $impl\_a_i$. Additionally, each series f_i of first-order logic axioms is replaced by a series f_i' that takes any changes to the types of variables and constants into consideration.

7 Proof of Mult_Add Circuit Refinement

This section shows the most notable cases of the parallel refinement proof obligations for the Mult_Add circuit. The full proofs can be found in [9]. The obligations below were obtained from the corresponding obligations in figure 4 by expanding the IMPL mapping appropriately, replacing quantification over transitions with the actual transitions of the Mult_Add circuit, rewriting the Curried PVS form (e.g. Start(tr1, t1)(t2)) to its ASTRAL equivalent (e.g. past(Start(tr1, t1), t2)), and performing some minor simplifications. For the impl_end2 obligation, the following must be proved.

```
FORALL t1 : time
    (   past(M1.Start(multiply, t1 - 3), t1 - 3)
     &  past(M2.Start(multiply, t1 - 3), t1 - 3)
 ↔      past(A1.End(add, t1), t1))
```

For the forward direction, it must be shown that add ends on A1 at t1, thus starts at t1 - 1. From the antecedent, multiply ends on both M1 and M2 at t1 - 1 so the entry assertion of add holds on A1 at time t1 - 1. A1 must be idle or else from the entry of add, multiply ended in the interval (t1 - 2, t1 - 1), which is not possible since multiply was still executing on M1 and M2 in that interval. Therefore, add starts at t1 - 1 on A1, thus ends at t1. The reverse direction is similar.

For the impl_trans_exit obligation, the formula below must be proved.

```
FORALL t1 : time
    (   past(A1.End(add, t1), t1)
 →      FORALL a, b, c, d : integer
            (   past(M1.Start(multiply(a, b), t1 - 3), t1 - 3)
             &  past(M2.Start(multiply(c, d), t1 - 3), t1 - 3)
         →      past(A1.sum, t1) = a * b + c * d))
```

By the exit assertion of add, past(A1.sum, t1) = past(M1.product, t1 - 1) + past(M2.product, t1 - 1). From the entry of add, multiply ends on both M1 and M2 at t1 - 1. Since multiply ends on M1 and M2 at t1 - 1, it starts on M1 and M2 at t1 - 3 for two pairs of parameters (a, b) and (c, d), respectively, which were provided by the external environment. By the exit assertion of multiply, past(M1.product, t1 - 1) = a * b and past(M2.product, t1 - 1) = c * d, so past(A1.sum, t1) = a * b + c * d. Thus, impl_trans_exit holds.

The impl_trans_fire obligation is given below.

```
FORALL t1:time
    (  EXISTS t2:time
          (  t2 ≤ t1
          &  past(M1.Call(multiply,t2),t1)
          &  past(M2.Call(multiply,t2),t1)
          &  FORALL t3:time
                (  t2 ≤ t3 & t3 < t1
                → ~ (  past(M1.Start(multiply,t3),t3)
                    &  past(M2.Start(multiply,t3),t3))))
       &  FORALL t2:time
              (  t1 - 3 < t2 & t2 < t1
           →  ~ (  past(M1.Start(multiply,t2),t2)
               &   past(M2.Start(multiply,t2),t2)))
    →      past(M1.Start(multiply,t1),t1)
    &      past(M2.Start(multiply,t1),t1))
```

To prove this obligation, it is first necessary to prove that M1.Start(multiply) and M2.Start(multiply) always occur at the same time. This can be proved inductively. At time zero, both M1 and M2 are idle. By impl_call, if multiply is called on either M1 or M2, multiply is called on both M1 and M2. At time zero, multiply cannot have ended, thus the entry assertion of multiply is true, so if both are called, both fire. If neither is called, then neither can fire. For the inductive case, assume M1.Start(multiply) and M2.Start(multiply) have occurred at the same time up until some time T0. Suppose multiply occurs on M1 (the M2 case is similar), then M1 was idle, multiply has been called since the last start, and it has been at least one time unit since multiply ended on M1. M2 cannot be executing multiply at T0 or else M1 must also be executing multiply by the inductive hypothesis, thus M2 must be idle. Similarly, it must have been at least one time unit since multiply ended on M2. By impl_call, multiply must have been called on M2 since it was called on M1. Thus, multiply is enabled on M2, so must fire. Therefore, M1.Start(multiply) and M2.Start(multiply) always occur at the same time. Based on this fact, the following two expressions are equivalent.

```
FORALL t3:time                       FORALL t3:time
  ( t2 ≤ t3 & t3 < t1                  ( t2 ≤ t3 & t3 < t1
→ ~ ( past(M1.Start(multiply,t3),t3)  → ~past(M1.Start(multiply,t3),t3)
    & past(M2.Start(multiply,t3),t3)))  & ~past(M2.Start(multiply,t3),t3))
```

Since nothing has started in the interval (t1 - 3, t1), nothing can end in the interval (t1 - 1, t1 + 2), thus the entry assertion of multiply on M1 is satisfied at t1. Since the entry of multiply holds, multiply has been called but not yet serviced, and M1 is idle, multiply starts on M1 at t1. Since multiply always starts on both M1 and M2 at the same time as shown above, impl_trans_fire holds.

The remaining proof obligations were all proved in a straightforward manner. Therefore, the lower level is a correct refinement of the upper level and the implementation of the upper level invariant, shown below, holds in the lower level.

FORALL t1:time,a,b,c,d:integer
  (M1.Start(multiply(a,b), t1 -3)
  & M2.Start(multiply(c,d), t1 -3)
→   FORALL t2:time
      (t1 + dur1 ≤ t2 & t2 ≤ now
   →   past(A1.sum , t2) = a *b + c *d))

8 Parallel Phone System

The previous example has shown that the parallel refinement mechanism can express the parallel implementation of a simple system in a simple and straightforward manner. Furthermore, the proof obligations for a simple implementation were themselves simple. In this section we briefly outline how our mechanisms can be applied to the specification and refinement of a much more complex case such as the control of a phone system.

The system considered here is a slightly modified version of the phone system defined in [2]. It consists of a set of phones that need various services (e.g. getting a dial tone, processing digits entered into the phone, making a connection to the requested phone, etc.) as well as a set of central controls that perform the services. Due to space limitations, this example cannot be described in full detail. Thus, we limit ourselves to an informal description of the main steps of the refinement process and refer the interested reader to [9] for the complete description and proof.

The specification of the central control, which is the core of the whole system, is articulated into three layers. The goal of the top level is to provide an abstract and global view of the supplied services in such a way that the user can have complete and precise knowledge of the external behavior, both in terms of functions performed and in terms of service times, of the central control but the designer still has total freedom on implementation policies. In fact, as a result, the description provided in [2] is just an alternative implementation of the top level description given here, which differs from this version in that services are granted sequentially rather than in parallel.

To achieve our goal (i.e. to allow the implementation of services both asynchronously in parallel and strictly sequentially, as suggested by figures 5 and 6), the top level is specified such that a *set* of services can start and a set of services can end at every time unit in the system (for simplicity we assume discrete time). In these figures, Ti_si.Pk denotes providing service si to phone k.

The service of a phone is split into the beginning of servicing and the completion of servicing through two transitions: Begin_Serve and Complete_Serve. In other words, instead of assigning ASTRAL transitions to single services or groups thereof, we only make the beginning and the end of services visible at the top level. In this way, we do not commit too early to a fixed duration of the implementation of the service, stating only when a service will begin and when it will be completed. Thus, the durations of Begin_Serve and Complete_Serve are set to „serve_dur", where 2*serve_dur is chosen to be a divisor of the duration of every service.

A parameterized variable „serving(P)„ records when each phone P began being serviced so that it can complete being serviced at the appropriate time. When serving(P) changes to true for a phone P at time t, P began being served at t - serve_dur. Thus, when the duration of the function that was serving the phone elapses from this time, Complete_Serve carries out the effect of the function on the phone's state and resets serving for that phone to false.

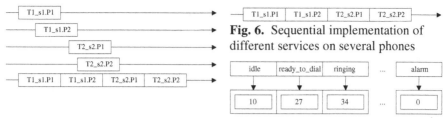

Fig. 5. Parallel implementation of different services on several phones

Fig. 6. Sequential implementation of different services on several phones

Fig. 7. Implementation of the phone state

To allow both a sequential and a parallel implementation, it is necessary for the top level specification to allow the possibility of multiple actions occurring at the same time without actually requiring multiple actions to occur. This is achieved by limiting the number of phones that can be serviced at any given time to be less than a constant „K_max". In the sequential refinement, K_max is mapped to one, indicating that only one phone at a time can be serviced. In the parallel refinement, K_max is mapped to the sum of the capacities of the individual servers, indicating that as many phones as it is possible for the servers to serve can be serviced in parallel.

Let us now look at the parallel implementation of the top level central control. As mentioned earlier, this is achieved through two refined layers. In the first refinement, the central control is split into several parallel processes, each of which is devoted to a single service of the top level central control. Thus, there is a process devoted to giving dial tone, a process devoted to processing entered digits, and so on. Each one of these processes executes two transitions that correspond to Begin_Serve and Complete_Serve at the top level.

The main issue in this step is the mapping of the global state of the central control into disjoint *components* to be assigned to the different lower level parallel processes. That is, the „Phone_State(P)" variable in the top level, which holds the state of each phone P (Phone_State can take the values idle, ready_to_dial, ringing, ...), needs to be split among all the servers in the lower level.

In the ASTRAL model, however, only a single process can change the value of a variable, thus it is not possible to let all of the lower level servers change the same variable directly. A solution to this problem is to split Phone_State into a set of „timestamp" variables, with one timestamp for each possible state of a phone. Each server is then allocated the timestamp variables associated with the phone state(s) it is responsible for. The state of a phone is the state associated with the timestamp that has last changed among all the servers. Figure 7 illustrates such a state variable mapping. In this figure, each component is managed by a different process and the current state of the phone is „ringing" because the corresponding timestamp component holds the maximum value.

Finally, in the third layer of the central control, each second level server is refined by a parallel array of „microservers", where each microserver is devoted to processing the calls of a single phone. Each microserver picks a phone from the set of phones waiting for the service according to some, possibly nondeterministic, policy and inserts its identifier into a set of served phones through a sequence of two transitions. The union of the elements of these sets over all the microservers implements the set of phones that are being served on the upper level server.

This example demonstrates that the parallel refinement mechanism can be used to express very complex parallel implementations. Not surprisingly, such generality is obtained at the cost of complicating the proofs of the proof obligations as shown in the major proofs of the phone system refinement, which were completed in [9]. We are confident that the approach adopted in this and other examples can be applied in a fairly similar way to a collection of real-life cases. As a result, we should obtain a general and systematic *method* for driving the specification and refinement of parallel and asynchronous systems.

9 Conclusions, Future Work, and Acknowledgments

ASTRAL aims to provide a disciplined and well-structured way of developing real-time systems. To achieve this goal it stresses modularization and incremental development through several refinement levels. In this paper, we presented an approach to accomplish these refinement steps in a flexible, general, and yet rigorous and provably correct way. A key feature of the proposed mechanism is the exploitation of parallelism so that global actions at a high level of abstraction may be described as individual transitions that can be refined at a lower level as several concurrent and cooperating activities. Our approach allows more generality and flexibility than the few independent ones available in the literature, which are more algebraic in nature (for an up-to-date survey of formal refinement methods see [5]).

Although our experience in the application of the mechanisms to problems of practical interest is still limited, we have already developed a number of case studies that show that the approach naturally scales up. Besides those summarized in this paper, we also mention the management of a hydroelectric reservoir system based on a real-life project. Early methods guiding the user throughout the development of real-life cases have already been extracted from these experiences [9].

As usual, when moving towards complex applications, the support of suitable tools is fundamental. ASTRAL is already equipped with several prototype tools [10] that allow the user to edit and manage complex specifications as well as providing support for their analysis. In particular, proof obligations can be automatically produced from specifications, and proofs are supported by both model checking and deductive facilities. The model checker can check the critical requirements of a particular instance of a specification over a finite time interval. ASTRAL has been encoded into the language of the PVS theorem prover to support deductive reasoning.

The ASTRAL toolset currently supports the sequential refinement mechanism of [3], but does not yet support the parallel refinement mechanism of this paper. To support the new mechanism, the design portion needs to incorporate a slightly different specification structure, an algorithm is needed to transform upper level expressions to lower level expressions using the implementation mapping, and the proof obligations must be incorporated into the current ASTRAL-PVS library for use with the theorem prover. It may be possible to use the PVS rewriting mechanism directly to transform upper level items to lower level items. This work is currently under way. In addition to tool support, more parallel refinements will be developed to test the expressiveness and applicability of the new parallel mechanism.

The authors would like to thank Klaus-Peter Loehr for his participation in the development of the parallel mechanism and Giovanna Di Marzo for her valuable comments. This research was partially supported by NSF Grant No. CCR-9204249 and by the Programma di scambi internazionale of the CNR.

References

1. Auernheimer, B. and R.A. Kemmerer. ASLAN User's Manual. Technical Report TRCS84-10, Department of Computer Science, University of California, Santa Barbara, Mar. 1985.
2. Coen-Porisini, A., C. Ghezzi, and R.A. Kemmerer. „Specification of Realtime Systems Using ASTRAL". *IEEE Transactions on Software Engineering*, Sept. 1997, vol. 23, (no. 9): 572-98.
3. Coen-Porisini, A., R.A. Kemmerer, and D. Mandrioli. „A Formal Framework for ASTRAL Inter-level Proof Obligations". *Proc. of the 5th European Software Engineering Conf.*, Sitges, Spain, Sept. 1995.
4. Crow, J., S. Owre, J. Rushby, N. Shankar, and M. Srivas. „A Tutorial Introduction to PVS". *Workshop on Industrial-Strength Formal Specification Techniques*, Boca Raton, Florida, Apr. 1995.
5. Di Marzo Serugendo, G. „Stepwise Refinement of Formal Specifications Based on Logical Formulae: From CO-OPN/2 Specifications to Java Programs". Ph.D. Thesis no. 1931, EPFL, Lausanne, 1999.
6. Felder M., A. Gargantini, and A. Morzenti. „A Theory of Implementation and Refinement in Timed Petri Nets". *Theoretical Computer Science*, July 1998, vol. 202, (no. 1-2): 127-61.
7. Ghezzi, C., D. Mandrioli, and A. Morzenti. „TRIO: a Logic Language for Executable Specifications of Real-time Systems". *Jour. of Systems and Software*, May 1990, vol. 12, (no. 2): 107-23.
8. Hennessy, A. and R. Milner. „Algebraic Laws for Nondeterminism and Concurrency". *Jour. of the ACM*, Jan. 1985, vol. 32, (no. 1): 137-61.
9. Kolano, P.Z. „Tools and Techniques for the Design and Systematic Analysis of Real-Time Systems". Ph.D. Thesis, University of California, Santa Barbara, Dec. 1999.
10. Kolano, P.Z., Z. Dang, and R.A. Kemmerer. „The Design and Analysis of Real-time Systems Using the ASTRAL Software Development Environment". *Annals of Software Engineering*, vol. 7, 1999.
11. Ostroff, J.S. „Composition and Refinement of Discrete Real-Time Systems". *ACM Transactions on Software Engineering and Methodology*, Jan. 1999, vol. 8, (no. 1): 1-48.

Applying RT-Z to Develop Safety-Critical Systems

Carsten Sühl

GMD FIRST, Kekuléstraße 7, 12489 Berlin, Germany
suehl@first.gmd.de

Abstract. We present the application of the formal specification language RT-Z, an integration of the model-based specification language Z and the real-time process algebra timed CSP, in the area of safety-critical systems. The characteristics underlying the development of safety-critical systems are identified, and criteria for specification languages to be used in this area are derived. It is demonstrated by means of a case study that RT-Z satisfies these criteria.

1 Introduction

The benefit of using formal methods in the area of safety-critical systems has already been discussed in detail, consult e.g. [2, 7, 13]. Craigen et al. [2, 7] surveyed the use of formal methods in the industrial context, where the majority of the considered projects concerned safety-critical systems. The conclusions drawn were by no means enthusiastic, but revealed the existing deficiencies of formal methods and provided recommendations to overcome the present situation. In [8, 9] we have presented a combination of the formal languages Z and timed CSP including a methodological framework for its application to safety-critical systems. The motivation to use a combined language was that a formalism intended to model safety-critical systems must take into account both the dynamic and the static behaviour of a system. Z [16] is a very successful formal language for specifying data and algorithmic aspects. However, it is not designed to model aspects of control and concurrency. The real-time process algebra timed CSP [3], on the other hand, is a powerful language to specify the dynamic control behaviour, including real-time aspects. However, it does not provide any constructs to model data-oriented aspects. Both formalisms can hence be considered as complementary, covering disjoint aspects of safety-critical systems. Further, their underlying concepts are well suited to each other.

In [15], we presented a successor of the initial approach of combining both languages, called RT-Z. The most relevant improvements of RT-Z concern the following aspects. Most importantly, RT-Z is able to structure a large and complex system specification into a collection of specification units, which interact with each other via well-defined interfaces. Further, it provides abstract and concrete language constructs to adequately express both abstract requirements and concrete designs, and, last but not least, RT-Z is based on a clearer and more

T. Maibaum (Ed.): FASE 2000, LNCS 1783, pp. 51–65, 2000.

strictly defined model of integrating both base languages than its predecessor. A unified denotational semantics serves to map each specification to a unique meaning.

RT-Z is designed to formally specify real-time embedded systems in general; the aim of this paper is to demonstrate the appropriateness of RT-Z in the area of safety-critical systems and to illustrate the merits of RT-Z with respect to its predecessor, especially in the context of safety-critical systems. To facilitate the comparison between both versions, we use a similar case study to discuss RT-Z as was used in [9], namely the specification of a railway network.

The paper is organised as follows. We first give a short overview of the specification language RT-Z in Section 2, which should be sufficient to understand the following case study. In Section 3, we discuss the characteristics of the development of safety-critical systems and the resulting criteria to specification languages used in this area. The railway network case study in Section 4 constitutes the main part of the paper. We then contrast RT-Z with another specification language and compare our case study with a similar one. We complete the paper by drawing conclusions in Section 6.

2   Overview of RT-Z

The aim of this paper is not to introduce RT-Z; a comprehensive description of the integrated formalism RT-Z including an outline of its unified denotational semantics can be found in [15]. Readers not familiar with the base languages Z and timed CSP are referred to [16] and [3], respectively. In this section, we shall only give a short overview of the main principles of RT-Z.

A system specification in RT-Z is composed of a hierarchy of so-called *specification units*. Each specification unit defines the structure and behaviour of a corresponding system component; therefore, a hierarchy of specification units corresponds to a hierarchy of system components constituting the considered system. Specification units interact with each other via well-defined interfaces.

Each specification unit consists of a Z part and a (timed) CSP part. The Z part defines aspects of the overall component behaviour like its data state, transitions thereon, or properties of data values communicated with interactions occurring at the component interface. The CSP part defines aspects of the component behaviour like the structure of its interface and the temporal order of interactions occurring at this interface and their real-time constraints. More precisely, each specification unit consists of several *sections*, where each section serves to define a specific, more restricted fragment of the overall component behaviour and belongs to exactly one part.

Each specification unit may *aggregate* any number of other specification units. Aggregated specification units may be arbitrarily arranged by the aggregating unit by means of CSP operators (e.g., parallel composition). The relationship between aggregating and aggregated specification units induces the mentioned hierarchy.

We distinguish two kinds of specification units: abstract and concrete ones. The former ones are used to abstractly specify properties of a system (software) component in the requirements phases, whereas the latter ones are used to express architectural and implementation aspects in the design phases.

Further details of the formalism are provided when discussing the case study.

3   Developing Safety-Critical Systems

In this section, we discuss the specific characteristics that—from our point of view—underlie the development of safety-critical systems, and we derive criteria for a formalism to be applied in this area. Following Leveson [12, Chapter 9], *safety* is the property of a system to be free from accidents, where *accidents* in turn are defined to be undesired and unplanned events that result in a specified level of loss. These two notions give no indication how to guarantee safety when developing a system that may potentially contribute to accidents; the notion hazard bridges this gap. A *hazard* is defined to be a state of a system that, together with conditions in the environment of this system, will lead inevitably to an accident.

One immediate consequence of these definitions is that software per se cannot be safe or unsafe, because (as an abstraction) it is not able to cause accidents. However, in the context of a system into which it is embedded software may contribute to accidents. Thus, one can only consider the safety of a software component in the context of the specific system within which it is embedded. Moreover, from the perspective of the system design, hazards are the only concept that can be influenced, because accidents (and consequently safety) result from an interaction of conditions inside *and* outside the considered system, where the latter ones cannot be influenced by the system design. As a consequence of these considerations, when we intend to develop "safe software" we have ultimately to aim at *system* safety by designing measures that prevent the whole system from reaching a hazardous state, i.e., one that may contribute to an accident. The identification and unambiguous formulation of these hazardous states should be the starting point of the development of any safety-critical system.

Which are the implications for a formal specification language that is intended to be employed in the development of software embedded in safety-critical systems? Firstly, because safety is intrinsically a system property, the formalism must be able to cope with whole systems rather than only with isolated (software) components. Therefore, the formalism must provide means to structure large and complex artifacts, namely systems. Secondly, it has to be expressive enough to be applied to software components and to general system components, including so different kinds of artifacts like mechanical, electrical, and electronic devices, human operators, etc. Finally, it must be capable of covering a wide range of abstraction layers in order to be applicable in various phases of a system development process, starting at the system requirements acquisition, where the hazardous states are identified and specified, and ending at the software de-

sign, where the identified software components are designed to meet their fixed
requirements.

4 Case Study: Railway Network

To demonstrate the applicability of RT-Z to safety-critical systems, we have
chosen the formal specification of a railway network for the following reasons.
First, it is undoubtedly safety-critical. Second, we had chosen the railroad crossing problem to discuss the predecessor of RT-Z, so that a comparison between
both is facilitated. Last but not least, the railway network has the appropriate
level of complexity. On the one hand, it is complex enough to demonstrate the
decomposition concepts of RT-Z, on the other hand it allows us to find an appropriate abstraction level that is not overwhelming. Our case study is based
on the 'Generalized Railroad Crossing' problem presented in [10] and [11]; it is,
however, lifted to the specification of a whole railway network in order to be able
to better motivate the use of Z.

We first outline how we will proceed in the phases of the development process
of the railway network that are supported by the use of RT-Z. The starting point
is the system requirements specification, in which the identified system hazards
are specified. A crucial task of this phase is to fix the system boundaries. In our
case study, the considered system, in terms of which the safety constraints[1] will
be formulated, is a railway network located in a certain area, which includes the
railway lines running through this area and the railway crossings at the intersec-
tions of the railway lines and the traffic lines in this area, see Figure 1. Certainly,
there are various hazards that can be identified for such a railway network. For
the sake of brevity, we consider one of them as an example: *the state in which a
train is in a railway crossing and its gates are not closed,* a state that can lead to
a collision between the train and a vehicle crossing the railway line. The purpose
of the subsequent system design is to work out an architecture of the considered
system that is able to realize the specified requirements and constraints. Such
an architecture provides the decomposition into a set of system components and
the definition of the channels via which these components interact. The general
aim of the following software requirements phase is to abstractly specify the
behaviour of the software components identified during the system design, i.e.,
to formulate requirements to their behaviour at their external interface without
restricting their internal realization. It is important to emphasise that in our
case study the component to be finally developed is only a part of the system
that is considered in toto: the component to be developed is the controller of
the railway network, but to express and analyse the conditions of its "safe" operation, we have to take into account the whole railway network within which
it is embedded. Finally, in the software design, an architecture of each software
component identified in the system design is worked out and fixed, so that the
constraints and requirements defined in the software requirements specification

---

[1] We consider safety constraints to be formalisations of system hazards in a negated
form.

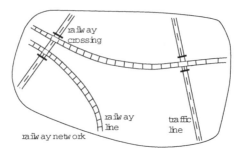

Fig. 1. System under development.

are met. It is one of the essential merits of RT-Z with respect to its predecessor to provide all necessary notational means to express such a software architecture.

4.1   System Requirements

The abstract specification unit *RailwayNetwork*, which fixes the results of the system requirements phase, formally expresses the selected safety constraint on the operation of the railway network. We first encapsulate general definitions within the specification unit *TechnicalPars*.

SPEC. UNIT   *TechnicalPars*

We make use of the powerful notation of the base language Z to formally express the technical parameters of operating the railway network, which include relatively complex data-oriented relationships.

TYPES & CONSTANTS

The constituting elements of the railway network are trains (*TRAIN*), railway lines (*RAIL*), and railway crossings (*CROSS*).

$[TRAIN, RAIL, CROSS]$

Each railway line can run through any number of railway crossings in the considered area and vice versa, see Figure 1.

$$runs\_through : RAIL \leftrightarrow CROSS$$
$$\mathrm{dom}\ runs\_through = RAIL \wedge \mathrm{ran}\ runs\_through = CROSS$$

When a train passes through the railway network, we consider four different kinds of events: the train's entry into and exit out of the network and the train's entry into and exit out of the various railway crossings.

The functions ϵ_1 and ϵ_2 model the durations that the fastest and slowest trains need to reach a particular railway crossing after having entered the railway network on a particular railway line. Further, the functions γ_{down} and γ_{up} represent the maximal time needed to completely lower and raise the gates at a particular crossing, respectively.

$$\epsilon_1, \epsilon_2 : RAIL \rightarrow (CROSS \nrightarrow \mathbb{T}^+)$$
$$\gamma_{down}, \gamma_{up} : CROSS \rightarrow \mathbb{T}^+$$

$$(\forall r : RAIL \bullet \mathsf{dom}(\epsilon_1\ r) = \mathsf{dom}(\epsilon_2\ r) = runs\_through(\!|\{r\}|\!) \land$$
$$(\forall c : runs\_through(\!|\{r\}|\!) \bullet (\epsilon_1\ r\ c) \leqslant_\mathbb{R} (\epsilon_2\ r\ c) \land (\epsilon_1\ r\ c) >_\mathbb{R} (\gamma_{down}\ c)))$$

The maximal time needed to lower a gate must be less than the time that the fastest train needs to reach the corresponding railway crossing after having entered the railway network.

END UNIT

SPEC. UNIT *RailwayNetwork*   **EXTENDS** *TechnicalPars*

The above **EXTENDS** clause causes the import of all definitions made in the previous specification unit.

Because of the chosen system boundaries[2], all relevant events occurring in the railway network are internal. The internal channels of the railway network, on which these internal events occur, are introduced and associated with a type in the **LOCAL** section.

LOCAL

> **channel** *enterN*, *exitN* **of type** *TRAIN* × *RAIL*;
> **channel** *enterC*, *exitC* **of type** *TRAIN* × *RAIL* × *CROSS*;
> **channel** *lowering*, *raising*, *down*, *up* **of type** *CROSS*

Events occurring on the channels *enterN* and *exitN* represent the entry into and the exit out of the railway network on a particular railway line, whereas events on the channels *enterC* and *exitC* represent the entry into and exit out of a railway crossing, respectively. Moreover, events occurring on the channels *down*, *up*, *lowering* and *raising* model that the gates of a particular crossing change into the state of being completely closed, being completely open, going down and going up, respectively.

BEHAVIORAL PROPERTIES

As claimed in Section 3, the most important task of the system requirements phase of the development of safety-critical systems is to identify the relevant system hazards and to formally express them in the form of safety constraints. In RT-Z, this can be achieved in the **BEHAVIORAL PROPERTIES** section, which serves, in general, to abstractly specify the requirements and the constraints on the dynamic and static behaviour. The notational means of this section is the predicate language of the timed failures model of timed CSP [3]. In our integration RT-Z, this predicate language is extended by allowing references to Z schemas in order to enable the compact formulation of properties of both the dynamic and the static behaviour within a single, coherent language.

---

[2] Trains and railway crossings (including gates) are part of the considered system. Certainly, the railway network is not a closed system from a physical point of view, because trains are entering and leaving the network's area; nevertheless, the corresponding events are internal, since a train is considered to be part of the railway network even in time intervals when it is outside the network's area.

The schema *SafeRailwayCrossing* specifies, for a particular railway crossing *cross* of the railway line *rail*, the required relationship between the last time instants a train has entered and left the railway crossing and the last time instants the corresponding gates have been completely closed and opened, respectively: the gates have to be closed whenever a train has entered but not already left the crossing.

SafeRailwayCrossing

$rail : RAIL;\ cross : CROSS$
$last\_enterC, last\_exitC, last\_down, last\_up, last\_raising : \mathbb{T}$

$(last\_enterC >_\mathbb{R} last\_exitC \wedge cross \in runs\_through(\!|\{rail\}|\!))$
$\Rightarrow last\_down >_\mathbb{R} max_\mathbb{R}\{last\_up, last\_raising\}$

The defined schema is used in order to specify the selected safety constraint, which is expressed by a predicate on timed traces s and timed refusals X, which, according to the timed failures model of timed CSP, constitute the timed observations of the system under consideration. This predicate basically defines how the values with which the Z schema is evaluated are extracted from the timed trace component s. The operators of the predicate language, e.g., $\lceil$, $\downarrow$ and $\lfloor$, are discussed in [15].

$Behavior(s, X)$ **sat** $\forall t : \mathbb{T};\ r : RAIL;\ tr : TRAIN;\ c : CROSS \bullet$
  $SafeRailwayCrossing(rail == r, cross == c,$
    $last\_enterC == \text{end}(s \lceil t \downarrow enterC \lfloor \{(tr, r, c)\}),$
    $last\_exitC == \text{end}(s \lceil t \downarrow exitC \lfloor \{(tr, r, c)\}),$
    $last\_down == \text{end}(s \lceil t \downarrow down \lfloor \{c\}), \ldots)$
  $\wedge \ldots$

Certainly, the railway network has to guarantee further constraints, e.g., utility constraints ensuring that the gates of railway crossings are not closed when not necessary. For reasons of space, we omit them.

END UNIT

The specification of the system requirements has illustrated that RT-Z is able to cope with system concepts (in addition to software concepts) and to abstractly specify properties that are related to both the dynamic and the static behaviour.

4.2   System Design

To guarantee the safety constraint expressed in the system requirements phase, the railway network is decomposed into three system components. The *train* component and the *gate* component model the assumptions on the behaviour of the trains and gates within the considered network. The task of the third component, *controller*, is to supervise all gates in the network according to the information about the current position of the trains, obtained by sensor reports via the channels $enterN$, $exitN$ and $exitC$. The gates of the network area are instructed by the controller via the channels $lower$ and $raise$.

The following concrete specification unit fixes the results of the system design.

SPEC. UNIT *RailwayNetworkDesign*   **EXTENDS** *TechnicalPars*

LOCAL

    channel $enterN, exitN$ **of type** $TRAIN \times RAIL$;
    channel $enterC, exitC$ **of type** $TRAIN \times RAIL \times CROSS$;
    channel $lower, raise, lowering, raising, down, up$ **of type** $CROSS$

SUBUNITS

The identified system components are associated with specification units defining their structure and behaviour.

    $train(TRAIN)$ **spec. unit** *Train*;
    $gate(CROSS)$ **spec. unit** *Gate*;
    $controller$ **spec. unit** *Controller*

BEHAVIOR

The *physical* structure of the system components and their physical interaction via channels is specified by the timed CSP process *Behavior*.

$$Behavior \,\widehat{=}\, \left(\left|\left|\right|_{id \in TRAIN} train(id).Behavior \right)$$
$$|[\, \{\!|\ enterN\ |\!\} \cup \{\!|\ exitN\ |\!\} \cup \{\!|\ exitC\ |\!\} \,]|$$
$$controller.Behavior$$
$$|[\, \{\!|\ lower\ |\!\} \cup \{\!|\ raise\ |\!\} \,]|$$
$$\left(\left|\left|\right|_{id \in CROSS} gate(id).Behavior \right)$$

END UNIT

The above specification unit demonstrates the ability of RT-Z to formally define architectural aspects fixed in the system design.

As already mentioned, the system component to be finally developed is the controller of the railway network. This means that the trains and gates constitute the environment of the component under development. The following specification unit documents the assumptions that underlie the development of the controller with respect to the behaviour of trains.

SPEC. UNIT   *Train*

INTERFACE

    channel $enterN, exitN$ **of type** $RAIL$;
    channel $enterC, exitC$ **of type** $RAIL \times CROSS$

BEHAVIOR

The behaviour of a train, as defined by the process term *Behavior*, is as follows: it enters the railway network on an arbitrary railway line at an arbitrary time instant, which is expressed by the combination of the internal choice operator ($\sqcap$) and the *Wait* operator parameterised with the interval $\mathbb{T}^+$. It then enters and leaves the different railway crossings of the current railway line, which is modelled by the interleaving operator ($\vert\vert\vert$) indexed with the set of crossings of the current railway line. The time distance between the entry into the network and the entry into a particular railway crossing c is restricted to the interval $[\epsilon_1\ r\ c, \epsilon_2\ r\ c]$.

$$Behavior \mathrel{\widehat{=}} \mu X \bullet \bigsqcap_{r \in RAIL} Wait\ \mathbb{T}^+;\ enterN!r \rightarrow$$
$$(\underset{c \in runs\_through(\!|\{r\}|\!)}{\vert\vert\vert} Wait[\epsilon_1\ r\ c, \epsilon_2\ r\ c];\ enterC!(r, c) \rightarrow$$
$$Wait\ \mathbb{T}^+;\ exitC!(r, c) \rightarrow Skip);\ Wait\ \mathbb{T}^+;\ exitN!r \rightarrow X$$

END UNIT

By treating the trains as components of the considered system, we have succinctly documented all assumptions that the controller can make about their behaviour. Since the specification of the gates' behaviour is analogous, we omit it.

4.3   Software Specification

The aim of the software requirements specification is to abstractly define the constraints on the operation of the railway network controller to be implemented by software.

We first define the interface of the software controller separately.

SPEC. UNIT   *SCInterface*

INTERFACE

The interface of the software controller does not contain all channels that we have chosen to express the system requirements and the system design. This is because we have performed the transition from the system into the software phases. The events occurring on the channel *enterC*, for instance, mark relevant points of a system observation, namely the entry of a train into a railway crossing. From the software controller's point of view, however, these events are not visible, because in the system design it has been decided that the entry of trains into the railway crossings is not observed by a sensor.[3] Similar remarks apply to the events on the channels *up*, *down*, *lowering* and *raising*, which label state transitions of the gates that the controller need not know.

> **channel** $enterN, exitN$ **of type** $TRAIN \times RAIL$;
> **channel** $exitC$ **of type** $TRAIN \times RAIL \times CROSS$;
> **channel** $lower, raise$ **of type** $CROSS$

END UNIT

---

[3] This is the case, because the controller need not know when a train really enters a crossing. It must simply guarantee that the gates are closed when a train could potentially reach the crossing.

SPEC. UNIT *Controller*   **EXTENDS** *TechnicalPars, SCInterface*

BEHAVIORAL PROPERTIES

The constraint on the behaviour of the software controller is, like the safety constraint on the behaviour of the whole railway network, expressed by a predicate of the timed failures model. The main difference between both formulations is the set of channels they refer to. Since the interface of the software controller is only a subset of the channels used in the system requirements specification, the occurrence of events outside the controller interface, e.g., the entry of a train into a railway crossing, must be appropriately traced back to the occurrence of events of the controller interface.

The schema *TrainInCrossing* specifies, for a particular railway crossing *crs* of a railway line *rail*, the situation that a train has entered but not already left the crossing.

$$
\begin{array}{l}
\rule{0pt}{0pt} \\
\hline
\textit{TrainInCrossing} \\
\hline
rail : RAIL; \ crs : CROSS \\
last\_enterN, last\_exitC : \mathbb{T} \\
\hline
crs \in runs\_through(|\{rail\}|) \wedge last\_enterN +_\mathbb{R} (\epsilon_1 \ rail \ crs) >_\mathbb{R} last\_exitC \\
\hline
\end{array}
$$

This schema is used to define the constraint on the behaviour of the software controller.

$$
\begin{aligned}
Behavior&(s, X) \ \textbf{sat} \ \forall \, t : \mathbb{T}; \ r : RAIL; \ tr : TRAIN; \ c : CROSS \bullet \\
&\exists_1 \ t1 : \mathbb{T} \mid t1 = \text{end}(s \upharpoonright t \downarrow enterN \downarrow \{(tr, r)\}) \bullet \\
&TrainInCrossing(rail == r, crs == c, last\_enterN == t1, \\
&\qquad\qquad last\_exitC == \text{end}(s \upharpoonright t \downarrow exitC \downarrow \{(tr, r, c)\})) \\
&\Rightarrow (((lower, c) \ \text{live from} \ (t1 +_\mathbb{R} (\epsilon_1 \ r \ c) -_\mathbb{R} (\gamma_{down} \ c)) \\
&\qquad \vee \ \text{last}(s \upharpoonright (t1 +_\mathbb{R} (\epsilon_1 \ r \ c) -_\mathbb{R} (\gamma_{down} \ c)) \downarrow \{(lower, c), (raise, c)\}) = \\
&\qquad\qquad (lower, c)) \\
&\qquad \wedge s \downarrow \{(raise, c)\} \upharpoonright [t1 +_\mathbb{R} (\epsilon_1 \ r \ c) -_\mathbb{R} (\gamma_{down} \ c), t] = \langle\rangle)
\end{aligned}
$$

If a train *tr* enters the network at *t1* on the railway line *r*, then the gates at the railway crossing *c* of *r* have to be closed at $(t1 +_\mathbb{R} (\epsilon_1 \ r \ c))$, which is the earliest time instant at which the train can reach the crossing. Because the maximal time needed to completely close the gates is $(\gamma_{down} \ c)$, the command to lower the gates must be given at $(t1 +_\mathbb{R} (\epsilon_1 \ r \ c) -_\mathbb{R} (\gamma_{down} \ c))$ at the latest unless the gates are already closed. Further, the gates have to remain closed until the corresponding sensor reports that the train has left railway crossing *c*.

END UNIT

4.4   Software Design

In this section, we shall discuss how to employ the language constructs offered by RT-Z to specify a safety-oriented software architecture. The software controller is decided to be composed of two components: a general control and a safety component. The redundant arrangement of the components *gen_control* and *safety*, both responsible for ensuring the specified (safety-related) constraint, is a means to enhance the fault-tolerance of the railway network controller. The only task of the safety component is to enforce satisfaction of the (safety-related) constraint; it is therefore essentially simpler than the general control component, which is additionally cluttered with functional requirements.

SPEC. UNIT *ControllerDesign*   **EXTENDS** *TechnicalPars, SCInterface*

SUBUNITS

> *safety* **spec. unit** *SafetyComp*;
> *gen_control* **spec. unit** *ControlComp*

BEHAVIOR

The parallel composition operator ($\lVert [\,] \rVert$) with the chosen synchronisation set is adequate to arrange the general control and safety components. Since the *raise* channel is a member of the synchronisation set, a command to a gate is sent if and only if both components agree on this command simultaneously. The safety component can hence prevent the general control component from issuing a raise command violating the (safety-related) constraint. Further, because the *lower* channel is not part of the synchronisation set, both components are able to send the lower command independently, so that the safety component cannot be prevented by the general control component from lowering gates.

> *Behavior* $\widehat{=}$ *safety.Behavior*
> $\lVert \{\!\mid raise \mid\!\} \cup \{\!\mid enterN \mid\!\} \cup \{\!\mid exitN \mid\!\} \cup \{\!\mid exitC \mid\!\} \rVert$
> *gen_control.Behavior*

END UNIT

Finally, we outline the specification of the safety component, where we concentrate on the discussion of the concrete language constructs of RT-Z for specifying implementation aspects. In the software design, we interpret the software component under consideration as encapsulating a data state and transitions thereon (operations), where both aspects are specified by the Z notation. The definition of the external stimulus-response and the internal control behaviour, i.e., how the software component reacts to external stimuli in terms of causing the execution of operations and sending responses into the environment, is specified by the process term language of timed CSP.

SPEC. UNIT *SafetyComp*   **EXTENDS** *TechnicalPars, SCInterface*

TYPES & CONSTANTS

Because we are faced with implementation aspects in the software design, we cannot abstract from the time needed to execute operations: accordingly, the constant Δ_{op} represents the duration of executing one of the operations.

$$TrainStatus ::= In \mid Out$$
$$GateStatus ::= Down \mid Up$$

$$phase, \Delta_{op} : \mathbb{T}^+$$
$$\overline{\Delta_{op} <_{\mathbb{R}} phase}$$

STATE

To meet its (safety-related) constraint, the safety component has to record some information for each train and gate. For each train in the network, it has to record the current railway line ($train\_in\_rail$) and the minimal time needed to reach a particular railway crossing ($sched\_time$). In this context, the (safety-related) constraint can be formulated as a state invariant: for each train in the network, the minimal time needed to reach a currently open gate must be greater than the maximal time needed to lower this gate.

State ─────

$train\_status : TRAIN \rightarrow TrainStatus$
$train\_in\_rail : TRAIN \nrightarrow RAIL$
$sched\_time : TRAIN \nrightarrow CROSS \nrightarrow \mathbb{T}$
$gate\_status : CROSS \rightarrow GateStatus$

$\mathsf{dom}\ sched\_time = \mathsf{dom}\ train\_in\_rail = \{tr : TRAIN \mid train\_status\ tr = In\}$
$(\forall\, cr : CROSS \mid gate\_status\ cr = Up \bullet$
$(\forall\, tr : TRAIN \mid tr \in \mathsf{dom}\ train\_in\_rail \wedge cr \in runs\_through(\!|\{train\_in\_rail\ tr\}|\!) \bullet$
$\quad (sched\_time\ tr\ cr) \geqslant_{\mathbb{R}} (\gamma_{down}\ cr)))$

OPERATIONS

We explain only one of the safety component's operations as an example.

The operation $enterN$ defines the reaction of the safety component to receiving the sensor report that a train has entered the railway network on a particular railway line.

---
enterN ─────

$\Delta State$
$id? : TRAIN \times RAIL$

$train\_status(first\ id?) = Out$

$train\_status' = train\_status \oplus \{first\ id? \mapsto In\}$
$train\_in\_rail' = train\_in\_rail \oplus \{id?\}$
$sched\_time' = sched\_time \oplus \{first\ id? \mapsto \epsilon_1(second\ id?)\}$
$gate\_status' = gate\_status$

BEHAVIOR

The process term *Behavior* defines the stimulus-response and the internal control behaviour of the safety component. As a result of the software design, it is decided that the safety component has to pass cyclically through two phases: in *Phase*1 it is ready to receive sensor reports about entering and leaving trains and records this information by executing the corresponding operations. After *phase* time units, it changes to *Phase*2 where it computes the commands to be sent to the gates according to the received sensor reports. For reasons of space, we show only a fragment of the behaviour definition.

$$Behavior \cong \mu\, Cycle \bullet (Phase1 \diagdown \{phase\}\ Phase2);\ Cycle$$

$$Phase1 \cong \ldots TrainCtrl \ldots$$

The process $TrainCtrl$ specifies the reaction of the safety component to receiving a sensor report, e.g., that a train has entered the network on a particular railway line. In this case, the execution of the operation $enterN$ is caused after a delay of Δ_{op} time units, which is modelled by the communication on the channel $enterN_X$; for a more detailed explanation of the interplay between the Z and timed CSP definitions see [15].

$$\begin{aligned}
TrainCtrl \cong\ &\mu\, X \bullet \\
&enterN?(id : TRAIN \times RAIL) \rightarrow Wait\, \Delta_{op}; \\
&\quad enterN_X?(par : enterN_{InMap}(id)) \rightarrow X \\
&\square \ldots
\end{aligned}$$

$\ldots$

END UNIT

The design specification of the safety component has demonstrated the ability of RT-Z to specify implementation aspects of a software component, including real-time aspects.

5   Related Work

Recently, combining formalisms has become a research field of growing interest. The conference on 'Integrated Formal Methods' [1] has been dedicated to this topic, where different combinations/integrations of behavioural and model-based formalisms and their varying underlying principles and concepts have been discussed. In this article, we have discussed the application of one of these integrations, RT-Z, in the area of safety-critical systems.

An overview of the general principles of combining model-based and behavioural formalisms can be found in [6]. Fischer [5] has provided a succinct survey of the more restricted field of combining Z with process algebras. Two formalisms closely related to RT-Z are TCOZ [14] and CSP-OZ [4], which integrate Object-Z with timed CSP and (plain) CSP, respectively.

In [11], the 'Generalized Railroad Crossing' (GRC) has been proposed as a benchmark problem for specifying and verifying real-time systems, to which different formal languages have been applied. As mentioned, we have based our case study on this benchmark problem but have extended the problem definition in order to be able to better motivate the use of Z in our integration RT-Z.

The GRC case study presented in [10] has demonstrated one merit of the timed automaton formalism, namely its means to verify that a design meets its requirements with the help of a more or less detailed (mathematical) argumentation. In our case study, in contrast, we have not addressed these verification tasks. It is part of further work to develop more powerful verification techniques for RT-Z than currently available, see also Section 6. The drawback of the timed automaton formalism, however, are its rather rudimentary constructs for specifying the data-oriented aspects of a system. The system state is constituted by a plain set of variables without any facility to structure the state by higher-level components, to specify invariant properties these variables have to satisfy, or to introduce new data types with an associated domain theory. In contrast, RT-Z is based on the Z notation, which supports these aspects in a very powerful way. Moreover, the concepts provided by the timed automaton formalism to express designs in terms of state-transition systems are less convenient than RT-Z's notation to define architectures. This is due to the fact that the concepts provided by timed automata only allow one to specify flat structures and that parallel composition is the only means to decompose systems into system components. From our point of view, these are obstacles to cope with complex systems.

6   Conclusion

The main contribution of this paper is the presentation of a formalism, RT-Z, which is able to support the development of software embedded within safety-critical systems in various phases of the development process. The demonstration of the appropriateness of RT-Z in this area has been achieved by means of a case study involving a safety-critical system.

The discussion of the notions related to safety in Section 3 has resulted in the criteria that a formalism must meet in order to be reasonably used to develop "safety-critical software". The presentation of the case study in Section 4 has demonstrated that RT-Z satisfies all these criteria:

- different phases of the development process have been successfully treated, starting with the system requirements specification and ending with the software design specification,
- RT-Z has been applied to an entire system as well as to software components, and
- RT-Z has accomplished to specify abstract requirements as well as concrete designs.

By treating a similar case study as has been used for RT-Z's predecessor in [9], we have demonstrated the merits of RT-Z with respect to this predecessor, which has not been able to cope with large and complex systems, to formally express architectures, and to specify abstract properties in an equally integrated way like RT-Z.

Planned further work includes to provide methodological support for the application of RT-Z to safety-critical systems as presented in [9] for its predecessor. As has already been pointed out in Section 5, a major point of further work concerns the development of an integrated proof system for RT-Z that enables us, e.g., to formally prove an RT-Z design specification correct with respect to an RT-Z requirements specification, i.e., to prove a refinement relationship between both.

Acknowledgement

Many thanks to Kirsten Winter and the anonymous referees for helpful comments and constructive criticism.

References

[1] K. Araki, A. Galloway, and K. Taguchi, editors. *Proceedings of the 1st International Conference on Integrated Formal Methods.* Springer, 1999.

[2] D. Craigen, S. L. Gerhart, and T. J. Ralston. Formal methods reality check: Industrial usage. In J. C. P. Woodcock and P. G. Larsen, editors, *FME'93: Industrial-Strength Formal Methods*, volume 670 of *LNCS*, pages 250–267. Springer, 1993.

[3] J. Davies and S. Schneider. Real-time CSP. In T. Rus and C. Rattray, editors, *Theories and Experiences for Real-Time System Development.* World Scientific Publishing Company, Inc., Feb. 1995.

[4] C. Fischer. CSP-OZ: A combination of Object-Z and CSP. In H. Bowman and J. Derrick, editors, *Formal Methods for Open Object-Based Distributed Systems (FMOODS '97)*, volume 2, pages 423–438. Chapman & Hall, 1997.

[5] C. Fischer. How to combine Z with a process algebra. In J. P. Bowen, A. Fett, and M. G. Hinchey, editors, *ZUM '98: The Z Formal Specification Notation*, number 1493 in LNCS, pages 5–23. Springer, 1998.

[6] A. Galloway and B. Stoddart. Integrated formal methods. In *Proceedings of INFORSID '97*, 1997.

[7] S. Gerhart, D. Craigen, and T. Ralston. Experience with formal methods in critical systems. *IEEE Software*, 11(1):21–28, Jan. 1994.

[8] M. Heisel and C. Sühl. Combining Z and Real-Time CSP for the development of safety-critical systems. In *Proceedings 15th International Conference on Computer Safety, Reliability and Security.* Springer, 1996.

[9] M. Heisel and C. Sühl. Methodological support for formally specifying safety-critical software. In *Proceedings 16th International Conference on Computer Safety, Reliability and Security.* Springer, 1997.

[10] C. Heitmeyer and N. Lynch. The generalized railroad crossing: A case study in formal verification of real-time system. Technical Memo MIT/LCS/TM-511, Laboratory for Computer Science, Massachusetts Institute of Technology, 1994.

[11] C. Heitmeyer and D. Mandrioli. *Formal Methods for Real-Time Computing.* Number 5 in Trends in Software. John Wiley & Sons, 1996.

[12] N. G. Leveson. *Safeware: System Safety and Computers.* Addison-Wesley, 1995.

[13] N. G. Leveson, M. P. E. Heimdahl, H. Hildreth, and J. D. Reese. Requirements specification for process-control systems. *IEEE Transactions on Software Engineering*, 20(9):684–707, Sept. 1994.

[14] B. Mahony and J. S. Dong. Blending Object-Z and Timed CSP: An introduction to TCOZ. In *Proceedings of the 20th International Conference on Software Engineering*, pages 95–104. IEEE Computer Society Press, 1998.

[15] C. Sühl. RT-Z: An integration of Z and timed CSP. In K. Araki, A. Galloway, and K. Taguchi, editors, *Proceedings of the 1st International Conference on Integrated Formal Methods.* Springer, 1999.

[16] J. C. P. Woodcock and J. Davies. *Using Z: Specification, Refinement, and Proof.* Prentice Hall, 1996.

A Process Algebra for Real-Time Programs*

Henning Dierks

University of Oldenburg, Department of Computer Science,
P.O.Box 2503, 26111 Oldenburg, Germany,
dierks@informatik.uni-oldenburg.de

Abstract. We introduce a generalised notion of a real-time specification language ("GPLC-Automata") that can be translated directly into real-time programs. In order to describe the behaviour of several GPLC-Automata implemented on one machine we introduce composition operators which form a process algebra. We give several algebraic laws and prove that each system is equivalent to a system in a certain normal form. Moreover, we demonstrate how a real-time specification in terms of GPLC-Automata can be decomposed into an untimed part and a timed part.

1 Introduction

In this paper we generalise PLC-Automata, a language to specify real-time systems that was motivated by the experiences we made in the UniForM-project [11] with an industrial partner. This notion has been successfully applied to specify a series of academic and industrial case studies [5].

The name stems from the fact that PLC-Automata are compilable into executable code for "Programmable Logic Controllers" (PLC), the hardware target of the project. For formal reasoning we presented in [4] (resp. [7]) a semantics in terms of Duration Calculus [20, 9], an interval based temporal logic, and in terms of Timed Automata [2].

These PLCs are very often used in practice to implement real-time systems. The reason is that they provide both convenient methods to deal with time and an automatic polling mechanism. Nevertheless, every computer system can be used to implement the proposed language if a comparable handling of time and an explicit polling is added.

The process algebra we introduce in this paper allows us to compose generalised PLC-Automata ("GPLC-Automata") which are intended to be implemented on the same PLC. In this case the automata are synchronised in a certain way by the PLC and the process algebra gives us means to exploit this synchronisation for transformations that preserve the semantics. Main benefits are a normal form and a decomposition of a system into its timed and untimed parts. Note that the generalisation of PLC-Automata to GPLC-Automata is necessary because PLC-Automata are not closed under the composition operator we need.

---

* This research was partially supported by the Leibniz Programme of the German Research Council (DFG) under grant Ol 98/1-1.

T. Maibaum (Ed.): FASE 2000, LNCS 1783, pp. 66–81, 2000.

The main difference between the algebra proposed in this paper and existing real-time process algebras like Timed CSP [3, 17] is that our algebra models real-time *programs* including the reaction time of the executing hardware in contrast to assumptions that synchronisation and communication may take place in 0 time units.

2 Programmable Logic Controllers

One goal of the UniForM-project [11] was to verify source code for Programmable Logic Controllers (PLCs). This hardware is often used in industrial practice to control real-time systems like production cells and it can be viewed as a simple computer with a special real-time operating system. PLCs have features for making the design of time- and safety-critical systems easier:

- PLCs have external input and output busses where sensors and actuators can be plugged in.
- PLCs behave in a cyclic manner. Each cycle consists of the following three phases:
  Polling: In this phase the external input bus of the PLC is read and the result is stored in special registers of the PLC. This phase is under the control of the PLC's operating system.
  Computing: After this, the operating system of the PLC executes the user's program once. At this point, the program can make arbitrary computations on the memory including the special registers for the input read. Furthermore, it can change the values in special registers for the output busses of the PLC.

  Moreover, the program can use "timers" which are under the control of the operating system. The program is allowed to set these timers with time values and to check whether this time has elapsed or not. To this end dedicated commands are part of all programming languages for PLCs.
  Updating: In this final phase the special registers for the output busses are read by the operating system. The read values become visible on the output busses.

  The repeated execution of this cycle is managed by the operating system. The only part the programmer has to adapt is the computing phase.
- Depending on the program and on the number of inputs and outputs there is an upper time bound for a cycle that can be used to calculate an upper time bound for the reaction time.
- Convenient standardised libraries are given for the programming languages to simplify the handling of time.

The time consumption of each cycle depends on the duration of actions of the operating system for the polling and updating phases and the duration of the execution of the user's program. The duration of the operating system's actions depends on the number of input and output busses whereas the duration of the program execution can consume an arbitrary amount of time.

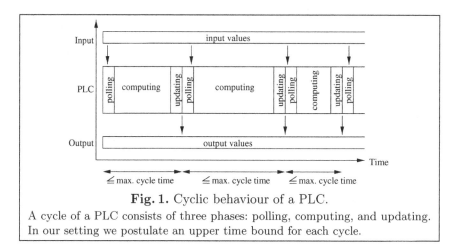

Fig. 1. Cyclic behaviour of a PLC.
A cycle of a PLC consists of three phases: polling, computing, and updating. In our setting we postulate an upper time bound for each cycle.

3   The Definition of GPLC-Automata

In this section we introduce an abstract notion of programs for PLCs. It is a generalisation of PLC-Automata [4] which have been proposed in the UniForM project [11] in order to serve as a common basis for computer scientists and engineers. The idea is that we use extended state-transition diagrams to describe the real-time behaviour of a PLC program. An example of these generalised PLC-Automata is given in Fig. 2

The purpose of this controller is to determine the behaviour of the gas burner. It starts in a state called "idle"; the output "out" is set to the value "id" initially. This state holds as long as the polling yields that a Boolean input "hr" (standing for heat request) is false. If the polling of the inputs produces "$hr=$ true ", then the system has to switch to the state "purge". When "purge" is entered a timer called "t1" is set to the value of 30 seconds. This means that the Boolean variable "t1" is true for the first 30 seconds after starting and false afterwards. Therefore the system will stay in state "purge" for at least 30 seconds. A timer is equipped with a set of states where it is activated ("activation region"). That means if the system switches into the activation region, then the timer is started. Within the activation region it is allowed to read the value of the timer variable.

The purpose of the "purge" state is to introduce a mandatory delay between attempts of ignition. If such a delay is not present it could happen that several failed attempts of ignition produce a dangerous concentration of gas. When the "purge" state is left, the output is changed to "ig". The state "ignite" holds for at least one second due to timer "t2" and the definition of the transitions. If state "burn" is entered the output is changed to "bn" and this state holds as long as the polling of input yields that there is still a request for heat ("hr") and the Boolean input "fl" (standing for "flame") indicates that a flame is present.

Figure 2 contains the equality $\varepsilon = 0.2$ s. This restricts the upper bound of the cycle of the executing hardware. That means the machine has to execute a cycle

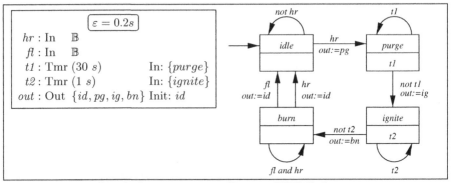

Fig. 2. A gas burner controller as GPLC-Automaton.

within the 0.2 seconds. In the following we will formalise the notion presented in Fig. 2 after some preliminaries.

Let Var be the set of all *variables* and assume that each $v \in Var$ has a finite *type* t_v associated with. With $BVar \subseteq Var$ we denote the set of all variables with *Boolean* type.

Let $V, W \subseteq Var$. We call a function val that assigns to each $v \in V$ a value of type t_v a *valuation* of V. We use $\mathcal{V}(V)$ to denote the set of *all valuations* of V. If $V \cap W = \emptyset$, $val \in \mathcal{V}(V)$, and $val' \in \mathcal{V}(W)$ we define the *composed valuation* $val \oplus val' \in \mathcal{V}(V \cup W)$ as follows:

$$(val \oplus val')(v) \stackrel{\mathrm{df}}{=} \begin{cases} val(v), & \text{if } v \in V \\ val'(v), & \text{if } v \in W \end{cases}$$

A generalised PLC-Automaton is in principle an automaton with a finite number of states and several typed variables which are either input, local, or output. Moreover, timer variables (of type Boolean) are allowed. To each timer we assign a running time and a set of states where the timer is active. An upper bound for the cycle time is also included.

Definition 1 (GPLC-Automaton). *A generalised PLC-Automaton (GPLC-Automaton) is a structure* $\mathcal{G} = (Q, \Sigma, L, T, \Omega, \longrightarrow, g_0, \varepsilon, \Xi, \Theta)$ *where*

- Q *is a nonempty, finite set of* states.
- $\Sigma \subseteq Var$ *is a finite set of* input variables.
- $L \subseteq Var$ *is a finite set of* local variables.
- $T \subseteq BVar$ *is a finite set of* timer variables.
- $\Omega \subseteq Var$ *is a finite set of* output variables.
- $\longrightarrow$ *is a function of type* $Q \times \mathcal{V}(L \cup \Omega) \times \mathcal{V}(\Sigma) \times \mathcal{V}(T) \longrightarrow 2^{Q \times \mathcal{V}(L \cup \Omega)} \setminus \{\emptyset\}$ *that describes the* transition relation.
- $\emptyset \neq g_0 \subseteq Q \times \mathcal{V}(L \cup \Omega)$ *is the* initial condition, *which restricts the initial state and the initial values of the local variables and output variables.*
- $\varepsilon > 0$ *is the* upper time bound *for a cycle.*
- Ξ *is a function of type* $T \longrightarrow 2^Q$ *assigning to each timer variable a set of states, where this timer is activated (*activation function*), and*

– Θ is a function of type $T \longrightarrow \mathbb{R}_{>0}$ assigning to each timer variable a running time.

Furthermore Σ, L, T, and Ω are disjoint and the well-formedness condition

$$\forall q \in Q, v \in \mathcal{V}(L \cup \Omega), \varphi \in \mathcal{V}(\Sigma), \tau_1, \tau_2 \in \mathcal{V}(T) : \qquad\qquad (1)$$
$$\tau_1|_{\{t \in T | q \in \Xi(t)\}} = \tau_2|_{\{t \in T | q \in \Xi(t)\}} \Longrightarrow \longrightarrow (q, v, \varphi, \tau_1) = \longrightarrow (q, v, \varphi, \tau_2)$$

has to hold which says that timer which are not active cannot influence the behaviour of the system.

We will use the notation $(q, v) \xrightarrow{\varphi, \tau}_{\mathcal{G}} (q', v')$ for $q, q' \in Q$, $v, v' \in \mathcal{V}(L \cup \Omega)$, $\varphi \in \mathcal{V}(\Sigma)$, and $\tau \in \mathcal{V}(T)$ if $(q', v') \in \longrightarrow_{\mathcal{G}} (q, v, \varphi, \tau)$.

Note that we allow a *set* of initial states and do not need a notion of final states since the polling systems are intended to run infinitely. The definition of the transition relation postulates that there is at least one allowed reaction but there may be several choices. In case that the transition relation allows more than one transition the system may choose a transition nondeterministically.

The Boolean timer variables T can be used to measure the time. If $tmr \in T$ is a timer variable with *activation region* $\Xi(tmr) \subseteq Q$, then it carries the value true if the systems stayed less than $\Theta(tmr)$ seconds in the activation region. It carries the value false if $\Theta(tmr)$ seconds have elapsed in the activation region.

Note that in Fig. 2 a syntax for both guards and actions annotated to transitions is given. Here we omit the formal definition of syntax and semantics of both since they are straightforward.

The operational behaviour of a GPLC-Automaton as in the definition above is as follows: in each cycle the system stores the polled input values in the variables of Σ. If there are more than one possible transition for the current state, the current valuation of the input variable, timer variables, local variables, and output variables, then the system chooses nondeterministically one of these transitions. Finally, the cycle is finished and the values of the output variables become visible from the outside.

In [5] it is shown how to generate systematically executable source code from GPLC-Automata for PLCs. The semantics that will be presented in the following section describes the behaviour of the PLC executing the source code within the given upper bound for the cycle time. The analysis whether a given PLC is able to execute the source code generated is not difficult since no loops or jumps are necessary for the implementation.

4   The Timed Automaton Semantics of GPLC-Automata

In this section we present an operational semantics of GPLC-Automata in terms of Timed Automata. For the definition of Timed Automata the reader is referred to App. A. We first present the components of the Timed Automaton $\mathcal{T}(\mathcal{G})$ that is associated to a given GPLC-Automaton $\mathcal{G}$, and then give some intuition.

Each location[1] of $T(\mathcal{G})$ is a 6-tuple $(i, \varphi, \phi, q, \pi, \tau)$, where

$i \in \{0, 1, 2\}$ describes the current status of the PLC ("program counter"),
$\varphi \in \mathcal{V}(\Sigma)$ contains the current input valuation,
$\phi \in \mathcal{V}(\Sigma)$ contains the last input valuation that has been polled,
$q \in Q$ is the current state of the GPLC-Automaton,
$\pi \in \mathcal{V}(L \cup \Omega)$ is the current valuation of local and output variables, and
$\tau \in \mathcal{V}(T)$ is the last timer valuation that has been tested.

There are three kinds of clocks in use:

x measures the time for which the current latest input valuation is stable,
y_t measures the time that has elapsed since the latest start of timer t, and
z measures the time elapsed in the current cycle of the PLC.

The idea of the program counter for GPLC-Automata is to model the internal status of the polling device. If the program counter is 0, then the polling has not happened in the current cycle. The change from 0 to 1 ((GTA-2) in Table 1) represents the polling of the system and hence we copy the second component of the location to the third. This is not allowed if the current input valuation has changed at the same point of time. Therefore we have to test whether the x-clock is greater than 0. This clock is reset whenever the environment changes the input valuation (GTA-1).

If the program counter is 1, then the polling has happened and the computation takes place. However, the *result* of the computation will not be visible before the cycle ends (cf. Fig. 1). For the semantics it is important which valuation of the timer variables was valid when the computing phase took place. Therefore, we will record this valuation in the sixth component in the location of the Timed Automaton (GTA-3). If the program counter has value 2, then the computation is finished and the updating phase takes place. When this phase is left and the counter is set to 0 again, the cycle ends and we change the state, local variables, and output variables accordingly (GTA-4).

Definition 2 (Timed Automata semantics of GPLC-Automata). *Let* $\mathcal{G} = (Q, \Sigma, L, T, \Omega, \longrightarrow, g_0, \varepsilon, \Xi, \Theta)$ *be a GPLC-Automaton. We define* $T(\mathcal{G})$ *to be the Timed Automaton* $(\mathcal{S}, \mathcal{X}, \mathcal{L}, \mathcal{E}, \mathcal{IV}, \mathcal{P}, \mu, S_0)$ *with*

- $\mathcal{S} \stackrel{df}{=} \{0, 1, 2\} \times \mathcal{V}(\Sigma) \times \mathcal{V}(\Sigma) \times Q \times \mathcal{V}(L \cup \Omega) \times \mathcal{V}(T)$ *as locations*,
- $\mathcal{X} \stackrel{df}{=} \{x, z\} \cup \{y_t | t \in T\}$ *as clocks*,
- $\mathcal{L} \stackrel{df}{=} \mathcal{V}(\Sigma) \cup \{poll, test, tick\}$ *as labels*,
- *the set of edges* $\mathcal{E}$ *is given in Table 1*,
- $\mathcal{IV}(s) \stackrel{df}{=} z \leq \varepsilon$ *as invariant for each location* $s \in \mathcal{S}$,
- $\mathcal{P} \stackrel{df}{=} \{obs = v | obs \in \Sigma \cup L \cup \Omega\}, v \in t_{obs}\}$ *as the set of propositions*,

---

[1] Note that the notion "locations" refers to the Timed Automaton and the notion "states" to the GPLC-Automaton.

$$(i, \varphi, \phi, q, \pi, \tau) \xrightarrow{\varphi', \text{true}, \{x\}} (i, \varphi', \phi, q, \pi, \tau) \qquad \text{(GTA-1)}$$

$$(0, \varphi, \phi, q, \pi, \tau) \xrightarrow{poll, 0 < x \wedge 0 < z, \varnothing} (1, \varphi, \varphi, q, \pi, \tau) \qquad \text{(GTA-2)}$$

$$(1, \varphi, \phi, q, \pi, \tau) \xrightarrow{test, \mathcal{C}(q, \tau'), \varnothing} (2, \varphi, \phi, q, \pi, \tau') \qquad \text{(GTA-3)}$$

$$(2, \varphi, \phi, q, \pi, \tau) \xrightarrow{tick, \text{true}, \mathcal{RS}(q, q') \cup \{z\}} (0, \varphi, \phi, q', \pi', \tau) \qquad \text{(GTA-4)}$$

$$\text{with } (q, \pi) \xrightarrow{\phi, \tau}_{\mathcal{G}} (q', \pi')$$

Table 1. Transitions of the Timed Automaton $\mathcal{T}(\mathcal{G})$.

with $i \in \{0, 1, 2\}$, $\varphi, \varphi', \phi \in \mathcal{V}(\Sigma)$, $q, q' \in Q$, $\pi, \pi' \in \mathcal{V}(L \cup \Omega)$, $\tau, \tau' \in \mathcal{V}(T)$,

$$\mathcal{C}(q, \tau) \stackrel{\text{df}}{=} \bigwedge_{\substack{q \in \Xi(t) \\ \tau(t)}} y_t < \Theta(t) \wedge \bigwedge_{\substack{q \in \Xi(t) \\ \neg\tau(t)}} y_t \geq \Theta(t), \text{ and}$$

$$\mathcal{RS}(q, q') \stackrel{\text{df}}{=} \{y_t | t \in T, q' \in \Xi(t), q \notin \Xi(t)\}$$

- $\mu(i, \varphi, \phi, q, \pi, \tau) \stackrel{\text{df}}{=} \{\sigma = \varphi(\sigma) | \sigma \in \Sigma\} \cup \{obs = \pi(obs) | obs \in L \cup \Omega\}$ as the propositions for each location $(i, \varphi, \phi, q, \pi, \tau) \in \mathcal{S}$,
- $S_0 \stackrel{\text{df}}{=} \{(0, \varphi, \phi, q, \pi, \tau) \in \mathcal{S} | (q, \pi) \in g_0\}$ as set of initial locations.

In [5] an alternative semantics in terms of the interval based temporal logic Duration Calculus [20, 9] was presented. In contrast to the Timed Automaton semantics above which is of operational kind, the Duration Calculus semantics for GPLC-Automata is of denotational kind. It was shown that both semantics are equivalent in an appropriate sense. The advantage of the Timed Automaton semantics is that it is easier to understand and that Model-Checkers for Timed Automata are applicable to GPLC-Automata. The advantage of the Duration Calculus semantics is that logical reasoning is easier. In [6] a synthesis procedure for GPLC-Automata was presented and proved to be correct with the help of the logical semantics.

5 A Process Algebra for GPLC-Automata

In this section we present operators to compose GPLC-Automata which are implemented *on the same PLC*. The most important operator is the sequential composition ("$\mathcal{G}_1; \mathcal{G}_2$"). The name stems from the fact that the computation of the composition is done by the computation of $\mathcal{G}_1$ first and second the computation of $\mathcal{G}_2$ in the same cycle of the implementing PLC (cf. Fig. 3). Note that we assume that the cycle time of a composition is at least as fast as the cycle times of the composed component. The reason is that in this case we get the property that an automaton $\mathcal{G}$ in sequential composition with an arbitrary automaton is still a refinement of the $\mathcal{G}$.

When we define the sequential composition we have to consider that inputs of one automaton which are triggered by outputs of the other automaton have to be handled in a different way than usual inputs. The reason is that polling is

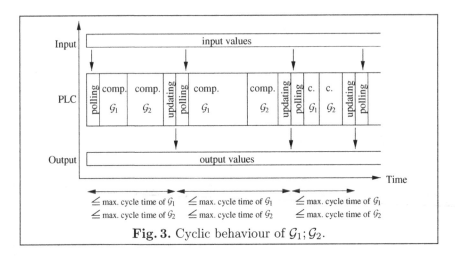

Fig. 3. Cyclic behaviour of $\mathcal{G}_1;\mathcal{G}_2$.

not necessary because the information is always present in the PLC. Therefore, we have three cases of inputs for the sequential composition $\mathcal{G}_1;\mathcal{G}_2$:

- the input is not an output of the other automaton. In this case the input values are determined by the polling phase.
- the input of $\mathcal{G}_1$ is triggered by an output of $\mathcal{G}_2$. Here the input value is determined by the corresponding output value of $\mathcal{G}_2$ in the *previous* cycle.
- the input of $\mathcal{G}_2$ is triggered by an output of $\mathcal{G}_1$. In this case the input value is determined by the corresponding output value of $\mathcal{G}_1$ in the *current* cycle.

Definition 3 (Sequential composition). *Let $\mathcal{G}_i$ be GPLC-Automata with $\mathcal{G}_i = (Q_i, \Sigma_i, L_i, T_i, \Omega_i, \longrightarrow_i, g_{0,i}, \varepsilon_i, \Xi_i, \Theta_i)$ for $i = 1, 2$ and disjoint variable sets $L_1, L_2, T_1, T_2, \Omega_1, \Omega_2$ and $\Sigma_i \cap (L_{3-i} \cup T_{3-i}) = \varnothing$ for $i = 1, 2$. We call the GPLC-Automaton*

$$\mathcal{G}_1;\mathcal{G}_2 = (Q_1 \times Q_2, \Sigma, L_1 \cup L_2, T_1 \cup T_2, \Omega_1 \cup \Omega_2, \longrightarrow, g_0, \varepsilon, \Xi, \Theta)$$

the sequential composition of $\mathcal{G}_1$ and $\mathcal{G}_2$ iff

$$\Sigma = (\Sigma_1 \cup \Sigma_2) \setminus (\Omega_1 \cup \Omega_2)$$
$$\longrightarrow ((q_1, q_2), v, \varphi, \tau) = \{((q_1', q_2'), v') \in Q \times \mathcal{V}(L \cup \Omega)|$$
$$(q_1, v|_{L_1 \cup \Omega_1}) \xrightarrow{(\varphi \oplus v)|_{\Sigma_1}, \tau|_{T_1}}_1 (q_1', v'|_{L_1 \cup \Omega_1}) \wedge$$
$$(q_2, v|_{L_2 \cup \Omega_2}) \xrightarrow{(\varphi \oplus v')|_{\Sigma_2}, \tau|_{T_2}}_2 (q_2', v'|_{L_2 \cup \Omega_2})$$
$$g_0 = \{((q_1, q_2), v) \in Q \times \mathcal{V}(L \cup \Omega)|\forall i : (q_i, v|_{L_i \cup \Omega_i}) \in g_{0,i}\}$$
$$\varepsilon = \min\{\varepsilon_i|i = 1, 2\}$$
$$\Xi(tmr) = \begin{cases} \Xi_1(tmr) \times Q_2, & \text{if } tmr \in T_1 \\ Q_1 \times \Xi_2(tmr), & \text{if } tmr \in T_2 \end{cases}$$
$$\Theta = \Theta_1 \oplus \Theta_2$$

This definition of sequential composition assumes that the interface between the automata is given by the sets $\Sigma_1 \cap \Omega_2$ (inputs of $\mathcal{G}_1$ connected with outputs of $\mathcal{G}_2$) and $\Sigma_2 \cap \Omega_1$ (inputs of $\mathcal{G}_2$ connected with outputs of $\mathcal{G}_1$). This concept of an interface definition by equality of names may be too weak. Moreover, we cannot express that we want to connect an input with an output of the same automaton or that we want to hide an output and conceive it as local.

Hence, we define ways to change the interface, i.e., the set of inputs and the set of outputs. First, we introduce renaming of inputs where it is possible to replace the current names of the inputs by other names. It is even possible to choose locals and outputs as new name for inputs. In this case the input is removed from the external interface.

Definition 4 (Renaming of inputs). *Consider a GPLC-Automaton $\mathcal{G} = (Q, \Sigma, L, T, \Omega, \longrightarrow, g_0, \varepsilon, \Xi, \Theta)$ and a function f with domain Σ which is type consistent $(\forall \sigma \in \Sigma : t_\sigma = t_{f(\sigma)})$ and which does not map into the timers $(f(\Sigma) \cap T = \varnothing)$. Then we call the automaton*

$$f : \mathcal{G} \stackrel{df}{=} (Q, f(\Sigma) \setminus (L \cup \Omega), L, T, \Omega, \longrightarrow_f, g_0, \varepsilon, \Xi, \Theta)$$

the automaton $\mathcal{G}$ renamed by f *where*

$$(q, v) \xrightarrow{\varphi, \tau}_f (q', v') \quad \textit{iff} \quad (q, v) \xrightarrow{(\varphi \oplus v) \circ f, \tau} (q', v')$$

With the next definition we allow to remove outputs from the interface. This transformation is called "hiding". The hidden outputs are shifted into the set of locals:

Definition 5 (Hiding of outputs).
Let $\mathcal{G} = (Q, \Sigma, L, T, \Omega, \longrightarrow, g_0, \varepsilon, \Xi, \Theta)$ be a GPLC-Automaton and $H \subseteq \Omega$. We call the automaton

$$\mathcal{G} \setminus H \stackrel{df}{=} (Q, \Sigma, L \cup H, T, \Omega \setminus H, \longrightarrow, g_0, \varepsilon, \Xi, \Theta)$$

the automaton $\mathcal{G}$ with hidden outputs H.

In the following we examine some properties of the operations defined above. To this end we define a notion of refinement and equivalence in usual manner. This definition employs a notion of simulation for Timed Automata that is defined in App. A.

Definition 6 (Refinement and equivalence). *Let $\mathcal{G}_1, \mathcal{G}_2$ be GPLC-Automata with $\Sigma_1 \cup L_1 \cup \Omega_1 \supseteq \Sigma_2 \cup L_2 \cup \Omega_2$ and $L_1 \cup \Omega_1 \supseteq L_2 \cup \Omega_2$. We say that $\mathcal{G}_1$ is a refinement of $\mathcal{G}_2$ (in symbols: $\mathcal{G}_1 \Longrightarrow \mathcal{G}_2$) iff*

$$T(\mathcal{G}_1) \precsim_\beta T(\mathcal{G}_2)$$

with

$$\beta(\{ obs = val(obs) \mid obs \in \Sigma_1 \cup L_1 \cup \Omega_1 \})$$
$$= \{ obs = val(obs) \mid obs \in \Sigma_2 \cup L_2 \cup \Omega_2 \}$$

for each valuation $val \in \mathcal{V}(\Sigma_1 \cup L_1 \cup \Omega_1)$.

If $\mathcal{G}_1 \Longrightarrow \mathcal{G}_2$ and $\mathcal{G}_2 \Longrightarrow \mathcal{G}_1$ hold we say that $\mathcal{G}_1$ and $\mathcal{G}_2$ are equivalent. In symbols: $\mathcal{G}_1 \equiv \mathcal{G}_2$. It is clear how to lift $\Longrightarrow$ and $\equiv$ to composed systems.

Note that equivalence of $\mathcal{G}_1$ and $\mathcal{G}_2$ implies $\Sigma_1 = \Sigma_2$.

Lemma 1 (Algebraic rules). *Let $\mathcal{G}, \mathcal{G}_1, \mathcal{G}_2, \mathcal{G}_3$ be GPLC-Automata. It holds:*

Associativity of sequential composition:
$$\mathcal{G}_1; (\mathcal{G}_2; \mathcal{G}_3) \equiv (\mathcal{G}_1; \mathcal{G}_2); \mathcal{G}_3 \tag{2}$$
Monotonicity: $(\Sigma_{\mathcal{G}_1} = \Sigma_{\mathcal{G}_2},\ L_{\mathcal{G}_1} = L_{\mathcal{G}_2},\ T_{\mathcal{G}_1} = T_{\mathcal{G}_2},\ \Omega_{\mathcal{G}_1} = \Omega_{\mathcal{G}_2})$
$$\mathcal{G}_1 \equiv \mathcal{G}_2 \Longrightarrow \mathcal{G}_1 \setminus H \equiv \mathcal{G}_2 \setminus H \quad \text{provided that } \mathcal{G}_1 \setminus H \text{ is legal} \tag{3}$$
$$\Longrightarrow f : \mathcal{G}_1 \equiv f : \mathcal{G}_2 \quad \text{provided that } f : \mathcal{G}_1 \text{ is legal} \tag{4}$$
$$\Longrightarrow \mathcal{G}_1; \mathcal{G} \equiv \mathcal{G}_2; \mathcal{G} \quad \text{provided that } \mathcal{G}_1; \mathcal{G} \text{ is legal} \tag{5}$$
$$\Longrightarrow \mathcal{G}; \mathcal{G}_1 \equiv \mathcal{G}; \mathcal{G}_2 \quad \text{provided that } \mathcal{G}; \mathcal{G}_1 \text{ is legal} \tag{6}$$
Commutativity of sequential composition:
$$\mathcal{G}_1; \mathcal{G}_2 \equiv \mathcal{G}_2; \mathcal{G}_1 \text{ if } \Sigma_{\mathcal{G}_1} \cap \Omega_{\mathcal{G}_2} = \Sigma_{\mathcal{G}_2} \cap \Omega_{\mathcal{G}_1} = \varnothing \tag{7}$$
Refinement by sequential composition:
$$\mathcal{G}_1; \mathcal{G}_2 \Longrightarrow \mathcal{G}_1 \tag{8}$$
$$\mathcal{G}_1; \mathcal{G}_2 \Longrightarrow \mathcal{G}_2 \tag{9}$$
Concatenation of renamings: $(\mathrm{dom}(f) = \Sigma_{\mathcal{G}},\ \mathrm{dom}(f') = \Sigma_{f\mathcal{G}})$
$$f' : (f : \mathcal{G}) \equiv f'' : \mathcal{G} \text{ with } f''(\sigma) = \begin{cases} f'(f(\sigma)), & \text{if } f(\sigma) \in \mathrm{dom}(f') \\ f(\sigma), & \text{if } f(\sigma) \notin \mathrm{dom}(f') \end{cases} \tag{10}$$
Concatenation of hidings: $(H \subseteq \Omega_{\mathcal{G}},\ H' \subseteq \Omega_{\mathcal{G}} \setminus H)$
$$(\mathcal{G} \setminus H) \setminus H' \equiv \mathcal{G} \setminus (H \cup H') \tag{11}$$
Hiding and sequential composition: $(H_i \subseteq \Omega_{\mathcal{G}_i},\ H \subseteq \Omega_{\mathcal{G}_1} \cup \Omega_{\mathcal{G}_2})$
$$(\mathcal{G}_1 \setminus H_1); \mathcal{G}_2 \equiv (\mathcal{G}_1; \mathcal{G}_2) \setminus H_1 \text{ where } H_1 \cap \Sigma_{\mathcal{G}_2} = \varnothing \tag{12}$$
$$\mathcal{G}_1; (\mathcal{G}_2 \setminus H_2) \equiv (\mathcal{G}_1; \mathcal{G}_2) \setminus H_2 \text{ where } H_2 \cap \Sigma_{\mathcal{G}_1} = \varnothing \tag{13}$$
$$(\mathcal{G}_1; \mathcal{G}_2) \setminus H \equiv ((\mathcal{G}_1 \setminus (H \setminus \Sigma_{\mathcal{G}_2})); (\mathcal{G}_2 \setminus (H \setminus \Sigma_{\mathcal{G}_1}))) \setminus (H \cap (\Sigma_{\mathcal{G}_1} \cup \Sigma_{\mathcal{G}_2})) \tag{14}$$
Hiding and renaming: $(\mathrm{dom}(f) = \Sigma_{\mathcal{G}},\ H \subseteq \Omega_{\mathcal{G}})$
$$f : (\mathcal{G} \setminus H) \equiv (f : \mathcal{G}) \setminus H \tag{15}$$
Renaming and sequential composition: $(\mathrm{dom}(f) = \Sigma_{\mathcal{G}_1; \mathcal{G}_2},\ \mathrm{dom}(f_i) = \Sigma_{\mathcal{G}_i})$
$$f : (\mathcal{G}_1; \mathcal{G}_2) \equiv ((\mathrm{id}_{\Sigma_{\mathcal{G}_1} \cap \Omega_{\mathcal{G}_2}} \oplus f|_{\Sigma_{\mathcal{G}_1} \setminus \Omega_{\mathcal{G}_2}}) : \mathcal{G}_1); \tag{16}$$
$$((\mathrm{id}_{\Sigma_{\mathcal{G}_2} \cap \Omega_{\mathcal{G}_1}} \oplus f|_{\Sigma_{\mathcal{G}_2} \setminus \Omega_{\mathcal{G}_1}}) : \mathcal{G}_2)$$
$$(f_1 : \mathcal{G}_1); \mathcal{G}_2 \equiv (f_1|_{\Sigma_{\mathcal{G}_1} \setminus f_1^{-1}(\Omega_{\mathcal{G}_2})} \oplus \mathrm{id}_{\Sigma_{\mathcal{G}_2} \setminus \Omega_{\mathcal{G}_1}}) : \tag{17}$$
$$(((f_1|_{f_1^{-1}(\Omega_{\mathcal{G}_2})} \oplus \mathrm{id}_{\Sigma_{\mathcal{G}_1} \setminus f_1^{-1}(\Omega_{\mathcal{G}_2})}) : \mathcal{G}_1); \mathcal{G}_2)$$
$$\mathcal{G}_1; (f_2 : \mathcal{G}_2) \equiv (f_2|_{\Sigma_{\mathcal{G}_2} \setminus f_2^{-1}(\Omega_{\mathcal{G}_1})} \oplus \mathrm{id}_{\Sigma_{\mathcal{G}_1} \setminus \Omega_{\mathcal{G}_2}}) : \tag{18}$$
$$(\mathcal{G}_1; ((f_2|_{f_2^{-1}(\Omega_{\mathcal{G}_1})} \oplus \mathrm{id}_{\Sigma_{\mathcal{G}_2} \setminus f_2^{-1}(\Omega_{\mathcal{G}_1})}) : \mathcal{G}_2))$$

Proof. of (8): It is clear from the definition of sequential composition that

$$\Sigma_{\mathcal{G}_1;\mathcal{G}_2} \cup L_{\mathcal{G}_1;\mathcal{G}_2} \cup \Omega_{\mathcal{G}_1;\mathcal{G}_2} = (\Sigma_1 \cup \Sigma_2) \setminus (\Omega_1 \cup \Omega_2) \cup L_1 \cup L_2 \cup \Omega_1 \cup \Omega_2$$
$$\supseteq \Sigma_1 \cup L_1 \cup \Omega_1$$

Also clear is $L_{\mathcal{G}_1;\mathcal{G}_2} \cup \Omega_{\mathcal{G}_1;\mathcal{G}_2} \supseteq L_1 \cup \Omega_1$. Hence, the requirements of Def. 6 are fulfilled. We have to construct for each run of $\mathcal{T}(\mathcal{G}_1;\mathcal{G}_2)$ a run of $\mathcal{T}(\mathcal{G}_1)$ with the same time stamps and the same propositions. Let $((s_j, v_j, t_j)_{j\in\mathbb{N}_0}) \in \mathcal{R}(\mathcal{T}(\mathcal{G}_1;\mathcal{G}_2))$. Due to the definition of the sequential composition we know that the clock valuations v_j are functions with domain $\{x, z\} \cup \{y_t | t \in T_1 \cup T_2\}$. Let $v'_j = v_j|_{\{x,z\}\cup\{y_t|t\in T_1\}}$ the restriction of v_j to the clocks of $\mathcal{T}(\mathcal{G}_1)$. Due to the definitions we can conclude that $s_j = (i_j, \varphi_j, \phi_j, q_j, \pi_j, \tau_j)$ with $i_j \in \{0, 1, 2\}$, $\varphi_j, \phi_j \in \mathcal{V}(\Sigma_{\mathcal{G}_1;\mathcal{G}_2})$, $q_j \in Q_1 \times Q_2$, $\pi_j \in \mathcal{V}(L_1 \cup L_2 \cup \Omega_1 \cup \Omega_2)$, and $\tau_j \in \mathcal{V}(T_1 \cup T_2)$. We construct the states s'_j as follows:

$$s'_j = (i_j, (\varphi_j \oplus \pi_j)|_{\Sigma_1}, (\phi_j \oplus \pi'(j))|_{\Sigma_1}, p_1(q_j), \pi_j|_{L_1\cup\Omega_1}, \tau_j|_{T_1})$$
with $\pi'(j) = \pi_{\max\{k\in\mathbb{N}_0|k\leq j, i_k=1\}}$

It is simple to verify that $((s'_j, v'_j, t_j)_{j\in\mathbb{N}_0})$ is a run of $\mathcal{T}(\mathcal{G}_1)$ with the property

$$\beta(\mu_{\mathcal{T}(\mathcal{G}_1;\mathcal{G}_2)}(s_j)) = \beta(\{obs = val(obs) \mid obs \in \Sigma_{\mathcal{G}_1;\mathcal{G}_2} \cup L_{\mathcal{G}_1;\mathcal{G}_2} \cup \Omega_{\mathcal{G}_1;\mathcal{G}_2}\})$$
$$= \{obs = val(obs) \mid obs \in \Sigma_{\mathcal{G}_1} \cup L_{\mathcal{G}_1} \cup \Omega_{\mathcal{G}_1}\}$$
$$= \mu_{\mathcal{T}(\mathcal{G}_1)}(s'_j)$$

Theorem 1 (Normal form). *Each system that is composed by sequential composition, renaming, and hiding is equivalent to a system of the form*

$$((f_1:\mathcal{G}_1); \ldots; (f_n:\mathcal{G}_n)) \setminus H$$

with appropriate GPLC-Automata $\mathcal{G}_1, \ldots, \mathcal{G}_n$, renaming functions $f_1, \ldots, f_n$ and H.

Proof. First note that (10), (11), (12), (13), (15), and (16), are all of the form $\mathcal{G}_{left} \equiv \mathcal{G}_{right}$ with $\Sigma_{left} = \Sigma_{right}$, $L_{left} = L_{right}$, $T_{left} = T_{right}$, and $\Omega_{left} = \Omega_{right}$. Therefore, the requirements of the monotonicity laws (3)–(6) are fulfilled. Hence, the above formulas are applicable to arbitrary subsystems of a composed system. To reach the normal form we first shift all hidings to the outermost position. To achieve this we can apply (12), (13), and (15) as long as possible. Then apply (11) to summarise all hidings in one operation. Then use (16) to shift the renamings to the innermost positions. Equivalence (10) can be applied to reach the normal form we desire.

Theorem 2 (Decomposition of timers). *Let $\mathcal{G}$ be a GPLC-Automaton with $\mathcal{G} = (Q, \Sigma, L, T, \Omega, \longrightarrow, g_0, \varepsilon, \Xi, \Theta)$ and $t \in T$. Then holds $\mathcal{G} \equiv$*

$(Timer_t^{\varepsilon\mathcal{G}}; \mathcal{G}_{-t}) \setminus \{act, runs\}$ *where act and runs are fresh variables of Boolean type. The GPLC-Automaton $\mathcal{G}_{-t}$ is defined as follows:*

$$\mathcal{G}_{-t} \overset{df}{=} (Q, \Sigma \cup \{runs\}, L, T \setminus \{t\}, \Omega \cup \{act\}, \longrightarrow', g_0', \varepsilon, \Xi|_{T\setminus\{t\}}, \Theta|_{T\setminus\{t\}})$$

with

$$g_0' \overset{df}{=} \{(q, \pi)|(q, \pi|_{L\cup\Omega}) \in g_0, \pi(act) \iff q \in \Xi(t)\}$$

$$\longrightarrow'(q, \pi, \sigma, \tau) \overset{df}{=} \{(q', \pi')|\pi'(act) \iff q' \in \Xi(t),$$

$$(q, \pi|_{L\cup\Omega}) \xrightarrow{\sigma|_\Sigma, (\tau\oplus(t\mapsto\sigma(t))))} (q', \pi'|_{L\cup\Omega}).$$

The automaton $Timer_t^{\varepsilon\mathcal{G}}$ is given in Fig. 4.

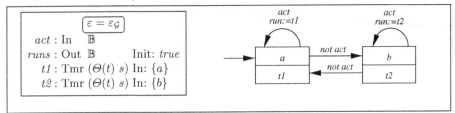

Fig. 4. Automaton $Timer_t^{\varepsilon\mathcal{G}}$.

The idea of this decomposition is to replace a timer t of an automaton $\mathcal{G}$ by a Boolean input (*runs*) that is triggered by another automaton ($Timer_t^{\varepsilon\mathcal{G}}$). The latter gets the information whether the reduced $\mathcal{G}$ is in the activation region of t by the Boolean channel *act*. Since $Timer_t^{\varepsilon\mathcal{G}}$ is executed before the reduced automaton $\mathcal{G}_{-t}$ is executed, $Timer_t^{\varepsilon\mathcal{G}}$ has to anticipate that $\mathcal{G}_{-t}$ changes into the activation region the in current cycle. Hence, $Timer_t^{\varepsilon\mathcal{G}}$ starts in each cycle a timer with the same time as t as long as $\mathcal{G}_{-t}$ is not in the activation region of t.

6   Application Example

In this section we apply the process algebra to the gas burner GPLC-Automaton GB given in Fig. 2. In order to control the gas valve we assume that another automaton ("*gas*") computes the signal for the valve depending on the output of GB. This automaton is given in Fig. 5. Analogously we assume that a controller ("*ign*") is given to control the ignition of the flame (cf. Fig. 5).

If we consider an alternative implementation where the variables *ignition* and *gas* are manipulated directly like the way as given in Fig. 6, the question arises whether both ways are equivalent. The answer is positive, ie. in symbols:

$$(GB; ign; gas) \setminus \{out\} \equiv GB' \equiv (GB; gas; ign) \setminus \{out\}.$$

By the decomposition theorem it is also possible to extract a controller which does not use timers:

$$GB' \equiv \underbrace{(Timer_{t1}^{0.2}; Timer_{t2}^{0.2};}_{\text{timed}} \underbrace{(GB'_{-t1})_{-t2})}_{\text{untimed}} \setminus \{act_{t1}, act_{t2}, runs_{t1}, runs_{t2}\}$$

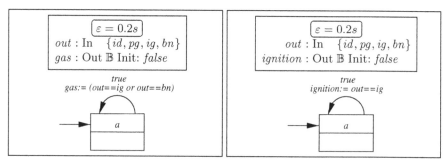

Fig. 5. Controller *gas* (LHS) and *ign* (RHS).

7   Conclusion

We introduced several composition operators for GPLC-Automata which are implemented on the same PLC. These definitions were motivated by the observable behaviour of the real machine executing the source code produced from the GPLC-Automata. Due to the equivalences that are proved in this paper we are allowed to transform a system into a normal form and/or into timed and untimed parts.

In the future we plan to exploit these results to improve the model-checking of PLC-Automata. In Moby/PLC [8, 18], a tool suite for PLC-Automata, it is possible to translate a system of PLC-Automata into its Timed Automaton semantics in the syntax of the model-checkers Uppaal [12] and Kronos [19]. With the help of the process algebra given in this paper we expect to improve this translation such that the system become smaller and hence faster to check. The reason is that the current translation of GPLC-Automata systems does not exploit the information whether two automata are in sequential composition. Hence, it introduces for each automaton the clocks x and z. If it would exploit the information it could save two clocks per sequential composition.

Acknowledgements: The author thanks E.-R. Olderog, J. Hoenicke, and other members of the "semantics group" in Oldenburg for detailed comments and various discussions on the subject of this paper. Furthermore, he likes to thank the anonymous referees for the valuable hints to improve the paper.

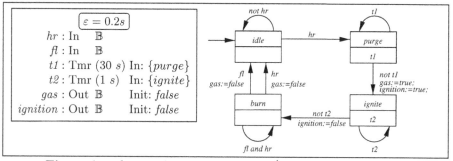

Fig. 6. An alternative controller GB' for the gas burner.

References

[1] R. Alur, C. Courcoubetis, and D. Dill. Model-Checking for Real-Time Systems. In *Fifth Annual IEEE Symp. on Logic in Computer Science*, pages 414–425. IEEE Press, 1990.

[2] R. Alur and D.L. Dill. A theory of timed automata. *TCS*, 126:183–235, 1994.

[3] J.W. Davies and S.A. Schneider. A Brief History of Timed CSP. *TCS*, 138, 1995.

[4] H. Dierks. PLC-Automata: A New Class of Implementable Real-Time Automata. In M. Bertran and T. Rus, editors, *ARTS'97*, volume 1231 of *LNCS*, pages 111–125, Mallorca, Spain, May 1997. Springer.

[5] H. Dierks. *Specification and Verification of Polling Real-Time Systems*. PhD thesis, University of Oldenburg, July 1999.

[6] H. Dierks. Synthesizing Controllers from Real-Time Specifications. *IEEE Transactions on Computer-Aided Design of Integrated Circuits and Systems*, 18(1):33–43, 1999.

[7] H. Dierks, A. Fehnker, A. Mader, and F.W. Vaandrager. Operational and Logical Semantics for Polling Real-Time Systems. In Ravn and Rischel [16], pages 29–40.

[8] H. Dierks and J. Tapken. Tool-Supported Hierarchical Design of Distributed Real-Time Systems. In *Proceedings of the 10th EuroMicro Workshop on Real Time Systems*, pages 222–229. IEEE Computer Society, June 1998.

[9] M.R. Hansen and Zhou Chaochen. Duration Calculus: Logical Foundations. *Formal Aspects of Computing*, 9:283–330, 1997.

[10] T. Henzinger, X. Nicollin, J. Sifakis, and S. Yovine. Symbolic Model Checking for Real-Time Systems. *Information and Computation*, 111:193–244, 1994.

[11] B. Krieg-Brückner, J. Peleska, E.-R. Olderog, D. Balzer, and A. Baer. UniForM — Universal Formal Methods Workbench. In U. Grote and G. Wolf, editors, *Statusseminar des BMBF Softwaretechnologie*, pages 357–378. BMBF, Berlin, March 1996.

[12] K.G. Larsen, P. Petterson, and Wang Yi. Uppaal in a nutshell. *Software Tools for Technology Transfer*, 1(1+2):134–152, December 1997.

[13] O. Maler and A. Pnueli. Timing Analysis of Asynchronous Circuits using Timed Automata. In *Proc. CHARME'95*, volume 987 of *LNCS*, pages 189–205. Springer, 1995.

[14] O. Maler and S. Yovine. Hardware Timing Verification using Kronos. In *Proc. 7th Conf. on Computer-based Systems and Software Engineering*. IEEE Press, 1996.

[15] X. Nicollin, J. Sifakis, and S. Yovine. Compiling Real-Time Specifications into Extended Automata. *IEEE Transactions on Software Engineering*, 18(9):794–804, September 1992.

[16] A.P. Ravn and H. Rischel, editors. *Formal Techniques in Real-Time and Fault-Tolerant Systems*, volume 1486 of *LNCS*, Lyngby, Denmark, September 1998. Springer.

[17] S.A. Schneider. An Operational Semantics for Timed CSP. *Information and Computation*, 116:193–213, 1995.

[18] J. Tapken and H. Dierks. MOBY/PLC – Graphical Development of PLC-Automata. In Ravn and Rischel [16], pages 311–314.

[19] S. Yovine. Kronos: a verification tool for real-time systems. *Software Tools for Technology Transfer*, 1(1+2):123–133, December 1997.

[20] Zhou Chaochen, C.A.R. Hoare, and A.P. Ravn. A Calculus of Durations. *IPL*, 40/5:269–276, 1991.

A   Timed Automata

Timed automata are an automaton-based mathematical model for real-time systems. Although the basic concepts are very similar, various definitions of syntax and semantics can be found in the literature [1, 15, 2, 10, 13, 14]. Here we use a variant of timed automata that is defined in [14]:

Definition 7 (Timed Automaton). *A* timed automaton $\mathcal{T}$ *is a structure* $(\mathcal{S}, \mathcal{X}, \mathcal{L}, \mathcal{E}, \mathcal{IV}, \mathcal{P}, \mu, S_0)$ *where:*

- *$\mathcal{S}$ is a finite set of* locations,
- *$\mathcal{X}$ is a finite set of real-valued variables called* clocks *whose values increase uniformly with time,*
- *$\mathcal{L}$ is a finite set of* labels.
- *$\mathcal{E}$ is a finite set of* edges *of the form* $e = (s, L, \phi, \rho, s')$, *or alternatively written as* $s \xrightarrow{L, \phi, \rho} s'$, *where* $s, s' \in \mathcal{S}$, $L \in \mathcal{L}$, ϕ *is a* clock constraint, *generated by the grammar* $\phi ::= x + c \leq d \mid c \leq x + d \mid x + c \leq y + d \mid \neg\phi \mid \phi_1 \wedge \phi_2$ *with* $x, y \in \mathcal{X}$ *and* $c, d \in \mathbb{R}$, *and* $\rho \subseteq \mathcal{X}$ *is the set of clocks which are to be reset to 0 by the transition,*
- *$\mathcal{IV}$ assigns to each location a clock constraint that serves as an* invariant *within the location,*
- *$\mathcal{P}$ is a finite set of atomic propositions,*
- *μ is a labelling of the locations with a set of atomic propositions over $\mathcal{P}$,*
- *$S_0 \subseteq \mathcal{S}$ is the set of* initial locations.

Usually only natural numbers are allowed as constants in the clock constraints, but in order to associate a timed automaton to each PLC-Automaton our definition allows for real-valued constants. The price we have to pay is that we cannot model-check this kind of timed automata. However, as long as the PLC-Automaton uses only discrete delays and a discrete cycle time, the corresponding timed automaton semantics uses only discrete time constants, too.

Definition 8 (Run of a timed automaton). *A* run *of $\mathcal{T}$ is an infinite sequence* $r = ((s_i, v_i, t_i))_{i \in \mathbb{N}_0}$ *where, for each* $i \in \mathbb{N}_0$, $s_i \in \mathcal{S}$ *is a location,* $v_i \in \mathcal{X} \longrightarrow \mathbb{R}_{\geq 0}$ *is a valuation of the clocks,* $t_i \in \mathbb{R}_{\geq 0}$ *is a time stamp, and* r *satisfies the following properties:*

- *the initial location is contained in S_0: $s_0 \in S_0$, initially all the clocks have value 0: $\forall x \in \mathcal{X} : v_0(x) = 0$, time starts at 0: $t_0 = 0$,*
- *the sequence of time stamps is monotonic and diverging: $t_i \leq t_{i+1}$, for all $i \in \mathbb{N}_0$, and $\lim_{i \longrightarrow \infty} t_i = \infty$,*
- *for all $i \in \mathbb{N}_0$ the invariant $\mathcal{IV}(s_i)$ is fulfilled during $[t_i, t_{i+1}]$: $\forall 0 \leq t \leq t_{i+1} - t_i : \mathcal{IV}(s_i)(v_i + t)$ with $(v_i + t)(x) \overset{df}{=} v_i(x) + t$ for all $x \in \mathcal{X}$ and $\mathcal{IV}(s)(v)$ denoting the evaluation of the constraint $\mathcal{IV}(s)$ at valuation v,*
- *for all $i \in \mathbb{N}_0$ there is an edge $e = (s_i, L, \phi, \rho, s_{i+1})$ such that*
  - *clock constraint ϕ holds at time t_{i+1}: $\phi(v_i + t_{i+1} - t_i)$, and*
  - *valuation v_{i+1} is updated according to ρ: $\forall x \in \mathcal{X} : v_{i+1}(x) = 0$ if $x \in \rho$ and $v_i(x) + t_{i+1} - t_i$ if $x \notin \rho$*

By $\mathcal{R}(\mathcal{T})$ we denote the set of runs of a timed automaton $\mathcal{T}$.

Definition 9 (Simulation, bisimulation). *Let $\mathcal{T}_i$ be Timed Automata with $\mathcal{T}_i = (\mathcal{S}_i, \mathcal{X}_i, \mathcal{L}, \mathcal{E}_i, \mathcal{IV}_i, \mathcal{P}_i, \mu_i, S_{0,i})$ for $i = 1, 2$ and let β be a function of type $\mu_1(\mathcal{S}_1) \longrightarrow \mu_2(\mathcal{S}_2)$. We say that $\mathcal{T}_2$ is a* simulation *of $\mathcal{T}_1$ with respect to β (in symbols: $\mathcal{T}_1 \lesssim_\beta \mathcal{T}_2$) iff holds:*

$$\forall((s^1_j, v^1_j, t_j)_{j \in \mathbb{N}_0}) \in \mathcal{R}(\mathcal{T}_1) :$$
$$\exists((s^2_j, v^2_j, t_j)_{j \in \mathbb{N}_0}) \in \mathcal{R}(\mathcal{T}_2) : \forall j \in \mathbb{N}_0 : \beta(\mu_1(s^1_j)) = \mu_2(s^2_j)$$

We say that $\mathcal{T}_1$ is a bisimulation *of $\mathcal{T}_2$ with respect to β (in symbols: $\mathcal{T}_1 \approx_\beta \mathcal{T}_2$) iff β is a bijection, $\mathcal{T}_1 \lesssim_\beta \mathcal{T}_2$ and $\mathcal{T}_2 \lesssim_{\beta^{-1}} \mathcal{T}_1$.*

System Fault Tolerance Specification: Proposal of a Method Combining Semi-formal and Formal Approaches

Giovanna Dondossola (contact author), Oliver Botti

ENEL R&D Department
Via Volta 1, Cologno Monzese 20093 Milan, Italy

E-mail: dondossola@pea.enel.it
Phone: +39 2 72245478
Fax. +39 2 72245465

Abstract. The topic of the present work is the specification of system Fault Tolerance (FT). FT is considered a valid technique for increasing the dependability of critical automation systems by adding them the ability to operate in presence of faults. Two basic considerations stimulated the development of the present work. Firstly although a considerable amount of concepts and theory have been published around FT, a full-organized method supporting their application to the FT needs of a specific system is still missing. Furthermore, the availability of a methodology oriented to the specification of system FT is especially useful in view of integrating available FT software layers according to specific system needs. Goal of the present work is therefore to develop a methodology for the FT specification, to be used as a tool supporting the configuration of the tailorable FT software layer, which is currently under development within the TIRAN Project[1]. The presented approach to the FT specification is based on a combined use of two general-purpose specification methods: the UML (Unified Modeling Language) graphical method and the TRIO (Tempo Reale ImplicitO) temporal logic. The main novelty of the proposed method consists in the identification and organization of a sequence of specification steps, which drive the industrial user in collecting and analyzing system dependability requirements and then in designing FT solutions, possibly tailoring already existing and configurable FT mechanisms.

1. Introduction

Purpose of this work is the construction of a methodological scheme in support to the development of *dependable systems*. Deterministic aspects of dependability properties, which concern how the system faces the possibility of faults independently by their occurrence probabilities, are specifically addressed. With respect to high-

---

[1] The TIRAN (TaIlorable fault toleRANce frameworks for embedded applications) Esprit Project is partially funded by the IT Programme of the Commission of the European Communities as project n° 28620. The partners of the TIRAN Project are ENEL-R&D (Italy), SIEMENS (Germany), TXT Informatica (Italy), EONIC Systems (Belgium), Katholic University of Leuven (Belgium) and University of Turin (Italy).

T. Maibaum (Ed.): FASE 2000, LNCS 1783, pp. 82-96, 2000.

level dependability means like fault prevention, fault removal, fault forecasting and fault tolerance the scheme focuses on *fault tolerance (FT) techniques* which increase system reliability, availability and integrity by preventing system faults from producing system failures [Lapr95].

Each system stating a set of FT requirements has to be realised by adopting a specific FT solution. More or less explicitly high level FT requirements express constraints on the FT strategy to be adopted and/or about suitable configurations/compositions of FT steps and their related mechanisms.

As an example, let us consider the following high level FT requirement:

"When a hardware fault occurs and remains unrepaired for at least δ time units, the system must be able to find the damaged part and put it off-line."

The above requirement expresses a FT strategy addressing hardware faults composed by FT steps such as error detection (*"When a hardware fault occurs..."*), fault diagnosis (*"...the system must be able to find the damaged part..."*) and system reconfiguration (*"...and put it off-line."*). The triggering of the FT strategy is due to output from the error detection step and conditioned by the duration of fault permanence in the unrepaired state (*"...and remains unrepaired for at least δ time units..."*), therefore requiring some time-out mechanism.

The proposed methodological scheme concentrates on the first steps in the development of a FT solution, which concern *high level FT requirement specification and how they constrain the FT solution*. It supports the collection and organization of FT requirements into a semi-formal model and their formal specification and analysis. The work is part of the TIRAN Esprit Project whose main objective is the development of a tailorable software framework providing a set of FT mechanisms amenable for real-time and distributed automation systems [Bott99]. In the context of the TIRAN project, the main goal of this work is the definition of a methodological support addressed to both

- *application designers,* in capturing system-specific high level FT requirements
- *users of the TIRAN framework,* in tailoring its use to the FT needs of the particular system.

The methodological scheme is based on a systematic organization of well-known dependability concepts (due to Laprie [Lapr95], [Lapr98] and recent R&D experiences [EFTOS97] about FT flexible solutions. The novelty of the approach consists of the definition of a methodology organized into a sequence of steps, which drive the user in first collecting and analyzing his/her FT requirements and then composing his/her FT solutions.

The whole scheme, overviewed in section 2, is composed by four distinct specification supports which make use of informal, semi-formal and formal techniques at the aim of producing, for a given system, a certifiable specification of its FT requirements. The present paper summarizes the first three steps of the scheme fully presented in [TIRAN99]:

1. in the first step, described in section 3, the FT specification is based on the UML [UML97a] [UML97b] semi-formal approach, as supported by the tool Rational Rose [Rose98]
2. the second step, described in section 4, exploits the TRIO formal language [Ciap97a] to express the requirements related to FT specification in a formal way
3. the third step exploits the formal techniques made available by TRIO to perform formal analyses on the FT requirements.

The scheme has been applied to model the FT requirements of an ENEL system, the Primary Substation Automation System (PSAS) which consists of different modules managing an electric substation[2]. The proposed application combines protection, command and control, monitoring and supervision capabilities and is a good representative for most of the dependability requirements of the energy field, in terms of integrity, security, availability and EMI immunity. It also demands for distributed and heterogeneous platforms with High Performance Computing capabilities. However, due to space reasons, only one example of the application of the formal part of the FT scheme to the PSAS system has been reported in sections 4 and 5.

2.   Scheme Overview

In order to allow its wide exploitation, the scheme has been developed by separating the use of semi-formal techniques for specifying FT requirements from the use of fully formal methods for performing formal V&V activities on FT requirements.

To non-formal specifiers the scheme proposes a model for the specification of FT requirements based on the Unified Modeling Language or UML [UML97a] [UML97b], in its version supported by the tool Rational Rose [Rose98]. As UML is

- *an object-oriented graphical language* $\Rightarrow$ therefore highly expressive
- *an OMG standard* $\Rightarrow$ a pre-requisite to its industrial spreading
- *supported by visual modeling tools* $\Rightarrow$ therefore an "easy to learn" technology
- *strongly emerging* in the market of semi-formal methods for system design

it showed to be an adequate mean for communicating the basics of the generic scheme for the specification of FT requirements, as well as for applying the scheme on specific FT systems.

The UML-based support to FT specification represents an entry-level use of the scheme, which requires a very low overhead, paid back by significant improvements in the specification inter-operability. It is centered on

- *System composition*, introducing system components/functions and their attributes
- *Fault/Error/Failure* (FEF) classes characterized by hierarchical relationships, attributes and associations with system components/functions
- *FT step* classes characterized by hierarchical relationships, attributes and associations with fault classes.

As a second step the scheme proposes to formalize the specification of FT requirements, thus endowing FT requirements with all the specification and V&V benefits recognized to formal methods [Rush95] [NASA95] [MOD91]. A specific formal method called TRIO is used to specify FT requirements. TRIO (Tempo Reale Implicito) [Ciap97a] is a product of ENEL research conceived for the specification of real time systems, also experimented by industries like Ansaldo, Volvo and Sextant.

---

[2] A joint project with the ENEL Distribution Division is ongoing to renew the existing PSAS. One of the goals of this joint project is to improve the efficiency and quality of service, by increasing the system dependability and by reducing its costs. Target plants are about 2000 existing and new Primary Substations (PS).

The TRIO formalization is finalized to produce a fully formal version of the FT requirement specification expressed in TRIO forms[3].

The third step of the scheme makes use of TRIO formal techniques to perform V&V activities on the FT requirement specification. Specifically two levels of support to V&V are provided:

- Level A: static analysis dealing with the V&V of the fault tolerance strategic plan
- Level B: dynamic analysis dealing with the V&V of system behaviors.

The fourth, final step of the scheme establishes generic links between system-specific FT requirements and their related FT solutions. A central issue towards FT design is the identification of appropriate FT mechanisms. There are several mechanisms supporting fault tolerance. Each mechanism may be used to realize several types of FT steps and may contribute fulfilling several system-specific FT requirements. FT mechanisms may be explicitly referred in the FT requirements of a specific system, but it may also be the case that the requirements do not refer to them. Some FT mechanisms could have alternative configurations, which need to be set in the FT design specification. The following design activities have to be considered by the fourth step of the methodology:

- choice of FT mechanisms: a set of FT mechanisms fulfilling the requirements has to be identified depending on the specified FT steps and design constraints
- choice of the target platform
- verification of design constraints: time/space/redundancy constraints stated in the requirements have to be satisfied by the correspondent bounds associated with the selected FT mechanisms and platform.

The instantiation of this step of the scheme on a specific application represents a support to a system-specific tailoring of the TIRAN framework driven by FT requirements. However, as this step has not been developed in detail yet, it will not be further described in the rest of the paper.

3.   UML-Based Support to FT Specification

The first step of the methodological scheme is expressed in the UML notation. This means that UML models, to be intended as meta-models to be instantiated by each application of the methodology to a specific FT system, capture methodological guidelines. The UML methodological step consists in a set of class hierarchies distributed into a structure of **Packages**[4]. Each Package encapsulates a set of inner packages/classes and their relationships, visualized by means of **Package/Class Diagrams**.[5]

---

[3] The possibility of supporting the non-formal specification of FT requirements by adopting the TRIO graphical editing capabilities [Bert97] has been investigated, this choice allowing the automatic integration of the semi-formal and formal steps of the scheme. However, in order to favor a wide usability of the first, semi-formal step of the methodology in industrial contexts, the adoption of the UML standard notation has been preferred.

[4] All the words referring to the UML terminology are written in **bold** face.

[5] Due to space constraints, this section visualizes only a simple example of the UML diagrams built by using the tool Rose but visualizes just one UML diagram. The application of the

The top-level **Package** is named *Methodology*[6] and includes three **Packages**, namely
1. *System Model* addressing system requirements relevant to FT specification
2. *FEF (Fault Error Failure) Model* supporting the description of fault/error/failure classes and modeling the *FEF chain*
3. *FT Strategy Model* concerning the identification of FT steps.

According to the object-oriented approach, using the UML scheme for specifying FT requirements of a given system means
- to select sub-parts of the scheme models which are relevant for the specific system
- to assign values to class attributes from the scheme models
- to refine/specialize sub-parts of models from the scheme.

3.1   System Model

The Package *System Model* includes four inner Packages supporting
- the definition of the conceptual structure of an FT system, i.e. the identification of (classes of) its components (Package *Composition*)
- the association of functions to system components (Package *Functions*)
- the association of real time requirements to system components and/or functions (Package *Time Requirements*)
- the association of dependability attributes to system components and/or functions (Package *Dependability*).

The model of a specific system is obtained specializing classes provided in the *System Model* and representing system-specific components, functions, time constraints, attributes and associations.

The Package *Composition* concerns system structure. The definition of system composition supports system partitioning in fault confinement area, which establish independence among faults at the aim of avoiding fault propagation. As the system structure is typically system-specific, it will be mainly defined at application level. The methodological level may provide generic structures for categories of systems. By addressing in particular the category of automation systems, the very basic meta-structure in Fig.1 is made available defining
- the decomposition of the class *Automated System* into *Automation System* and *Plant* (the field) as a UML aggregation relationship
- the decomposition of the classes *Automation System* and *Plant* in *Automation Component* and *Plant Component*, respectively
- the interface between *Automation Component* and *Plant Component* as a UML association called *commands*
- the class *Automation Operator* (which may be *local* or *remote*) associated with an *Automation Component* by the association *interfaces*.

As far as system functions are concerned, the methodology provides a very simple meta-model, which associates system functions to system components and operators.[7] Communication functions are characterised by the following attributes:

UML scheme to the PSAS system has been omitted here and the interested reader may refer to Chapter 7 of [TIRAN99] where a step by step instantiation of the scheme is reported.
[6] All the words referring to element identifiers of the UML model are written in *italic* face.

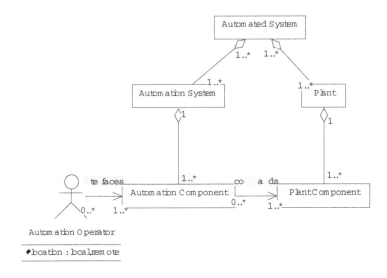

Fig. 1.: the Main Class Diagram in the Package Composition.

- *Transmission*: the mode in which data are transmitted
- *Channel*: the type of physical support to communication
- *Bandwidth*: the information quantum supported by the channel in the time unit
- *Location* that distinguishes communications internal to a component from communications towards the plant, remote systems/operators, local components/operators.

The Package *Time Requirements* identifies two attributes, which are considered particularly relevant for the FT specification of real time systems:

- the **attribute** *cycle time* (Tc) refers to the interaction between the system/component and its external environment (the plant)
- the **attribute** *execution time* (Texec[f_i]) which is the (maximum) response time required by a function f_i
- cycle and execution times are related by Tc < Min (Texec[f_i]).

In the case of automation systems the values of these attributes are tightly coupled with the real time constraints stated by the plant process on the automation system and their definition greatly influences the instantiation of the appropriate FT strategy with its associated mechanisms.

The methodology considers dependability attributes whose quantitative or qualitative estimates may be provided. Both repairable and non-repairable dependable systems are characterized by the following attributes:

- *criticality*: a qualitative estimate of the risk consequent to a failure of a given function/component/system. Its type is an enumerative that identifies criticality levels. A three-level criticality scale may be adequate for most critical domains

---

[7] A more detailed model for the Package *Functions* could be provided by identifying a set of generic classes of automation functions such as monitoring, command and control.

- *complexity*: a qualitative estimate of the complexity degree of the system. Its type is an enumerative, which identifies complexity levels. Complexity levels have to be determined on a strictly system-specific base
- *MTTF (MeanTimeToFailure):* the expectation of the mean time to failure.

In repairable systems/components three other dependability attributes may be added:

- *MTTR (MeanTimeToRepair)*: the expectation of the time to restoration
- *MTBF (MeanTimeBetweenFailures):* the expectation of the time between two failures
- *Availability:* the probability that the system is ready for specified usage.

Dependability attributes may be defined at system/component/function level.

3.2   Fault Error Failure Model

The FaultErrorFailure (FEF) model captures general concepts on the fault theory partially expressed in the literature and partially derived from previous experience. Three different Packages (*Fault Model, Error Model, Failure Model*) compose the FEF model, each package characterizing a different view of a fault evolution, from its appearance to its recovery and/or repair.

Faults are error causes that usually affect a system component but then may propagate to other components through their interactions.

The Package Fault Model contains a class diagram representing the fault classification due to Laprie [Laprie98][8] as a fault hierarchy. The root class *Fault* of the inheritance tree describes a generic fault in terms of the following attributes:

- *fault rate:* frequency of a fault occurrence
- *location:* faults may affect three logical parts of a system component, namely memories (MEM), elaboration units (ELAB) and communication units (COM)
- *latency:* the length of time between the occurrence of a fault and the appearance of the corresponding error.

The first level of the inheritance tree distinguishes *Physical Fault* from *Design Fault*.

Physical faults may be either *Permanent Fault* or *Temporaneous Fault*.

Permanent physical faults are specialised by the following sub-classes:

- *DevPerm Fault:* internal, permanent faults due to the development phase
- *OpInt Fault:* internal, operational faults that have their origin within hardware components and are constantly active
- *OpEx Fault:* external, operational faults induced on the system by the physical environment

Temporaneous physical faults are specialised by the following sub-classes:

- *DevTemp Fault:* internal, temporary faults due to the development phase
- *Intermittent Fault:* internal physical defects that become active depending on a particular pointwise condition
- *Transient Fault:* faults induced by environmental phenomena

---

[8] Only those classes that are relevant with respect to the FT scope have been included.

Design faults are specialised into

- *Systematic Fault:* accidental, permanent faults (flawed algorithms) that systematically turn into the same errors in the presence of the same input conditions and initial states
- *Intentional Fault:* intentional, though not malicious, faults (basically compromises introduced at design time).

Faults are related to system components by a multiple association named *location.*

Errors are deviations from the correct state of the system. They are caused by faults affecting system components and are related to some functions of the faulty component. The model assumes that errors affect locally the functions of the faulty component before propagating to another interacting component.

The Package Error Model contains a class diagram representing an error hierarchy that is especially useful for the associations between FT mechanisms and the kind of errors they are able to manage.

The root class *Error* introduces the following basic error attributes:

- *latency:* the length of time between the occurrence of an error and the eventual appearance of the corresponding failure
- *PE:* an estimate of the Probability of the Error.

The first level of the error hierarchy identifies three error sub-classes, namely *Processing Error, Communication Error* and *Memory Error.* A Processing Error may be sub-classified by one of [*Runtime Error, Late Processing Error, Memory Violation Error, Corrupted Processing Error*]. A Communication Error may be sub-classified as one of [*Late Communication Error, Corrupted Communication Error, Disordered communication Error*]. Additional attributes are introduced locally to error sub-classes. In particular a *BER* (Bit Error Rate) attribute is associated to the class *Corrupted Communication Error.*

Errors are related to system functions by a multiple association named *location.*

Failures are deviations of the service delivered by the system from fulfilling its intended function. The root class *Failure* of the inheritance tree in the Package Failure Model is characterized by the following basic attributes:

- *PF:* an estimate of the Probability of the Failure
- *criticality:* consequences on the environment or failure criticality level. The failure criticality level of a specific class of failure influences the specification of its related failure mode assumption.

The different failure mode assumptions generate the following failure classes [Cri91][9]:

- *Omission Failure:* it occurs when an agreed reply to a well-defined request is missing. The request appears to be ignored
- *Timing Failure:* it occurs when the service is supplied, though outside the real-time interval agreed upon in the specification. Sub-classes are *Early Timing Failure* and *Late Timing (or Performance) Failure*
- *Response Failure:* it occurs when the system provides a wrong response. Sub-classes are *Value Failure* (when the system supplies an incorrect output) and *State-transition Failure* (when the system executes an incorrect state transition)
- *Crash Failure:* it occurs when the system continuously exhibits omission failures. Sub-classes are *Pause-crash Failure* (the system restarts in the state it had before

---

[9] The failure classification is an updated version of that reported in [TIRAN99].

its crash), *Halting-crash Failure* (the system never restart), *Amnesia-crash Failure* (a restarted system re-initializes itself wiping out the state it had before its crash) and *Partial Amnesia-crash Failure* (some part of a system's state is re-initialized while the rest is restored to its value before the crash).

The cause-effect relationships in the chain fault ✐ error ✐ failure ✐ fault are captured by a UML class diagram named *FEF Chain*. The cause-effect association between a fault type and its provoked error type considers the value of the attribute *location* in the causing fault. Thus, for example, a fault localized on the memory of a system component may propagate as a memory error on some function of that component. An error may propagate into a failure and a failure may propagate into a fault located anywhere on a component related to the original faulty component.

3.3   FT Strategy Model

The UML model of the fault tolerance strategy proposed by the methodology includes the classification of FT steps due to Laprie [Laprie95]. Some extensions to that classification have been introduced in order to distinguish some FT steps concerning faults from steps belonging to the error processing family.

Any number of FT steps classified as *fault processing*, *error processing* and *fault treatment* may carry out fault tolerance.

Fault Processing aims at avoiding systematically the propagation of fault effects and includes two specialized sub-steps, namely

- *Fault Masking*: masks the fault using the available redundancy to enable the delivery of an error-free service. It does not assume error detection
- *Fault Containment*: prevents propagation of fault effects by means of either spatial (*Permanent Containment*) or temporal redundancy (*Temporary Containment*). Spatial redundancy may be on information (*Local Containment*), hardware or software (*Global Containment*) units

Error processing aims at removing errors from the computational state (if possible, before failure occurrence) and includes the following FT steps:

- *Error detection*: identifies states as being erroneous
- *Error diagnosis*: assesses the damages caused by error propagation before detection
- *Error isolation*: isolates the erroneous component from the other part of the system to prevent error propagation
- *Error recovery*: performs recovery after detection and includes
  - *Compensation*: recovery is performed using the present (erroneous, internal) state that contains enough redundancy to enable the delivery of an error-free service. Requires error detection
  - *Forward recovery*: recovers to a future state
  - *Backward recovery*: recovers to a past state

Fault treatment aims at assuring that the system fails according to the stated failure modes and at preventing faults from being re-activated and includes the following:

- *Failure handling*: performs a set of actions required to fulfil a given failure mode
- *Fault compensation*: after fault containment, it allows the system to provide a response to compensate for output of the faulty subsystem

- *Fault repair*: performs repairing actions
- *Fault diagnosis*: identifies the cause(s) of error(s)
- *Fault passivation*: removes faulty components and includes *Reconfiguration*, i.e. modifies the structure of the system such that non-failed components fulfil the system function, possibly at a degraded level.

FT steps are related to fault/error classes by a multiple association named *addresses*.

4.   TRIO-Based Support to FT Specification

The structure of a system FT specification in the TRIO language may be obtained by translating in TRIO the system-specific Rose-UML diagrams. However the FT formalization includes some parts which have not a correspondence with the semi-formal FT specification but whose introduction V&V purposes have motivated. Formal methods are typically endowed with automatic analysis capabilities requiring that the formalization be adequately instrumented for performing that type of analysis[10].

TRIO is a temporal logic language that supports a linear notion of time: the *Time Domain* is a numeric set equipped with a total order relation and the usual arithmetic relations and operators (it can be the set of integer, rational, or real numbers, or any interval thereof). TRIO formulae are constructed in the classical inductive way, starting from terms and atomic formulas. Besides the usual prepositional operators (& for *and*, | for *or*, ~ for *not*) and quantifiers (*all, ex*), TRIO formulae may be composed by using a single basic modal operator called *Dist* that relates the *current time* (which is left implicit in the formula) to another time instant. Thus the formula *Dist (F, t)*, where F is a formula and t a term indicating a time distance, specifies that F holds at a time instant at t time units from the current instant. For convenience, TRIO items (*variables, predicates,* and *functions*) are distinguished into time-independent (TI) ones, i.e., whose value does not change during system evolution and time-dependent (TD) ones, i.e., those whose value may change during system evolution. Several *derived temporal operators* (ex. *Alw(F), Som(F), Becomes(F), Futr(F,t), NextTime(F,t)*) can be defined from the basic *Dist* operator through prepositional composition and first order quantification on variables representing a time distance.

TRIO provides object-oriented concepts and constructs, which support writing modular reusable specifications of complex systems. Among the most important o-o features are the ability to partition the universe of objects into classes, to introduce inheritance relations among classes, and to exploit mechanisms such as genericity to support the reuse of specification modules and their incremental development.

Classes denote collections of objects that satisfy a set of axioms. They can be either *simple* or *structured* –the latter term denoting classes obtained by composing simpler ones. A simple class is defined through a set of axioms premised by a declaration of all items that are referred therein. Some of such items (declared *visible*) are in the

---

[10] The fact that some specification parts are missed in the correspondent semi-formal specification does not mean in general that the semi-formal language is unable to express the concepts but that that kind of information is relevant for analysis purposes not considered during the semi-formal specification.

interface of the class, i.e. they may be referenced from outside it in the context of a complex class that includes a module that belongs to that class.

As an example let us consider the following two textual FT requirements of the ENEL PSAS system, labeled FR2 and FR19[11]:

FR2: "Corruption on input/output, elaboration, memory and internal communications, caused by any first fault (transient, intermittent or permanent) must be tolerated

a) allowing to preserve a working state acceptable and coherent with the history of the system

b) avoiding or handling any loss of control

c) avoiding to transmit wrong output to the plant, the operator, the remote systems."

FR19: "Proper evolution according to the system history needs to be guaranteed:

a) the evolution must be guaranteed between acceptable states

b) leaving an acceptable state must be allowed only towards an other acceptable state
   - e.g. by using mechanisms which maintain the current state (judged correct) till a confirmation of correctness of the next state (e.g. by using a Stable Memory technique [Deco98])

c) the transitions between two subsequent acceptable states must be non interruptible and without uncertainties - e.g. by an atomic action

d) evolution must be coherent among the different system components - e.g. by synchronizing the state transition of all the components within a single atomic action."

The combination of FR2a with FR19 demands for a fault masking technique applied to the PSAS state. In the TRIO formalization reported below such requirements have been fulfilled by a fault masking mechanism called Stable Memory, which integrates temporal and spatial (triple modular) redundancy to stabilize the PSAS state.

For the purpose of providing an initial PSAS formal specification, the Rose-UML diagrams have been manually translated in the TRIO language. However, such translation could be made automatic by completely defining the translation rules mapping Rose-UML → TRIO[12]. The construction and refinement of the PSAS initial TRIO specification for V&V purposes has been supported by the TRIO Editor.

The above PSAS FT requirements have been formalized by two TRIO classes, namely *PSAS* and *PSAS_Stable_Memory*. The class PSAS is characterized by the TI value *cycle_time*, the TD values *stable_state* and *new_state* and by the TD propositions *begin_cycle, end_cycle* and *confirm_state*. The PSAS cycle time is assigned to 3 time units by the axiom *set_cycle_time*. The PSAS FT behavior is abstractly defined by the last five axioms allowing to cyclically producing a new state (axioms *cyclic_behavior, produce_new_state* and *maintain_new_state*) which is considered stable under confirmation (axioms *maintain_stable_state* and *change_stable_state*). The confirmation of the new state, provided by the *PSAS_Stable_Memory*, is conditioned by its triple repetition, as expressed by the axiom *stable_state*.

---

[11] PSAS textual requirements, extracted from documentation produced by ENEL technicians for a call for tender, have been grouped into 4 categories labeled SR (System Requirements), DR (Dependability Requirements), FR (FT Requirements) and TR (Time Requirements).

[12] The VDM (Vienna Development Method) formal method has already adopted such approach by providing a new tool from IFAD called Rose-VDM⁺⁺ Link. It supports round trip engineering between UML and VDM⁺⁺ through an automatic bi-directional coupling of Rational Rose and the IFAD VDM Tools (see the IFAD WWW Page at http://www.ifad.dk).

```
class PSAS
    visible      end_cycle, new_state, confirm_state;
    temporal domain    integer;
    types        state_values = {state0,state1,state2,state3,state4,state5,none};
                 cycle_values = 1 .. 15;
    TI Items
      values     cycle_time : cycle_values;
    TD Items
      values     new-state : state_values;
                 stable_state : state_values;
      propositions      begin_cycle; end_cycle; confirm_state;
    vars       s1, s2 : state_values;
               tc : cycle_values;

    axioms
    set_cycle_time:        cycle_time = 3;
    initialisation:        stable_state = state0 & new_state = none & begin-cycle;
    cyclic_behaviour:    Alw(all tc (cycle-time = tc →
               (begin-cycle ↔ Dist(end_cycle & Dist(begin_cycle,1),tc))));
    produce_new_state: Alw(all s1 (end_cycle & stable_state = s1 →
                                ex s2 (s2 <> s1 & Becomes(new_state = s2))));
    maintain_new_state: Alw(new_state = none ↔ ~end_cycle);
    maintain_stable_state:            Alw(all s1 (~confirm_state & stable_state = s1 ↔
                                Dist(stable_state = s1, -1)));
    change_stable_state: Alw(all s1 (confirm_state & new_state = s1 ↔
                                Becomes(stable_state = s1)));
end   PSAS
```

```
class PSAS_Stable_Memory
    visible      end_cycle, new_state, confirm_state;
    temporal domain    integer;
    types        state_values = {state0,state1,state2,state3,state4,state5,none};
    TD Items
    values       new-state : state_values;
    propositions        end_cycle; confirm_state;
      vars       s1, s2, s3: state_values;
                 d1, d2: integer;

      axioms
      stable_state:            Alw(confirm_state ↔ all s1, s2, s3, dist1, dist2
                                (Becomes(new_state = s1) &
                                NextTime(Becomes(new_state = s2) &
                                NextTime(Becomes(new_state = s3),d2),d1) &
                                s1 = s2 & s2 = s3))
end   PSAS_Stable_Memory
```

5.   TRIO-Based Support to FT V&V

Formal specifications may be analyzed by different Verification and Validation (V&V) techniques. Several formal V&V techniques have been developed characterized by different degrees of formality [Dond00]. By applying formal V&V techniques for analysing FT properties of dependable systems we may distinguish two main levels of formal support, namely *static analysis* (level A) and *dynamic analysis* (level B).

The static analysis of a FT specification allows the extraction of distinct views of the FT static model captured by the FT formalization. Static analysis may be referred either to the whole system or to specific functions/components. The following ones are some examples of static analysis:

- analysis of relevant fault/error classes
- analysis of FEF chains
- analysis of the defined FT strategy, e.g. fault/error classes (not) addressed, masked fault classes, contained fault classes, detected error classes, isolated error classes, recovered error classes, handled failure classes.

The dynamic analysis of a FT specification implies a detailed analysis of FT behaviours, sometimes requiring the formal specification to be refined and enriched with related functional requirements. Examples of dynamic types of analysis are:

- FT consistency analysis (satisfiability proofs), e.g. generation of system behaviors and check of the absence of contradictions in the FT specification
- FT adequacy analysis (truth/false proofs) checking specific FT conditions
- proof of system FT properties
- automatic generation of fault injection cases for the conformance testing of the final system.

By considering the PSAS system the following analysis could be addressed:

A1 Which fault classes are associated to which system components?

A2 Which system functions are affected by corrupted-communication errors?

A3 Which are the FT steps addressing PSAS permanent faults?

B1 Find PSAS histories stabilizing a new state.

B2 Find PSAS histories which revoke a new unstable state.

The TRIO method is endowed with tools supporting three basic V&V techniques, i.e. model generation, property poof and test case generation[13], which are suitable for performing both levels of FT analysis. In order to perform V&V activities, the following proof settings must be provided to the TRIO tool:

a) load of the formal specification

b) selection of the axiom set to be considered

c) selection of the V&V technique to be applied

d) selection of the Temporal Domain and the Evaluation Instant.

Let us consider the case B1 and assume that the following values are given to the required settings above:

a) TRIO classes PSAS and PSAS_Stable_Memory reported in section 4

b)   all axioms

c) model generation

d)   Temporal Domain = 1 .. 12; Evaluation Time = 1.

The TRIO tool builds all possible histories satisfying the chosen set of axioms, i.e. sequences of time dependent literals (positive and negative items) located on the time

---

[13] In particular such techniques are supported by a new version of TRIO, which will be available at the end of the FAST Esprit project No. 25581, integrating the TRIO model generation within the NP-tools, by Prover Technology.

axis. The output of the model generation process is a graph representing for each relevant item its truth-value on the temporal domain. A tabular version of the B1 results are visualized below, where at each time instant only positive items are given.

Time Domain	$\models$ Model
1	begin_cycle, stable_state = *state0*, new_state = *none*
2	stable_state = *state0*, new_state = *none*
3	stable_state = *state0*, new_state = *none*
4	end_cycle, new_state = *state1*, stable_state = *state0*
5	begin_cycle, stable_state = *state0*, new_state = *none*
6	stable_state = *state0*, new_state = *none*
7	stable_state = *state0*, new_state = *none*
8	end_cycle, new_state = *state1*, stable_state = *state0*
9	begin_cycle, stable_state = *state0*, new_state = *none*
10	stable_state = *state0*, new_state = *none*
11	stable_state = *state0*, new_state = *none*
12	end_cycle, new_state = *state1*, stable_state = *state1*

6.   Conclusions and Future Usage

The paper has presented a methodological approach to the specification and analysis of high level fault tolerance requirements, which makes use of two general purpose methods, namely UML and TRIO.
A main global result of the methodology is the systematization of FT concepts and their relations aimed at defining articulated FT strategies, eventually focussed on specific system components and/or functions. On one side, the UML-based support represents an easy way to collect and organize FT requirements. On the other side the TRIO-based support provides formal techniques to validate the specification of such requirements.
The experimentation of the methodological approach to the ENEL PSAS system has allowed assessing the original textual requirements, which are now traceable on both (UML and TRIO) model items.

The methodological scheme will be experienced by ENEL within the TIRAN project itself over the PSAS pilot application. An evaluation of this experience will be provided, together with the methodology itself, to the future users of the TIRAN framework. It will represent a guided support for the specification and analysis of FT requirements as well as for framework configuration and verification.

References

[Bott99] O. Botti, V. De Florio, G. Deconinck, F. Cassinari, S. Donatelli, A. Bobbio, A. Klein, H. Kufner, R. Lauwereins, E. Thurner, E. Verhulst, *TIRAN: flexible and portable fault tolerance solutions for cost effective dependable applications*, in: Proc. of 5ᵗʰ Int. Conf. Europar'99 - Parallel Processing, Toulouse, F, Aug. 1999, LNCS, No.1685, Springer-Verlag.

[Ciap97a] E. Ciapessoni, A. Coen-Porosini, E. Crivelli, D. Mandrioli, P. Mirandola, A. Morzenti, *From formal models to formally-based methods: an industrial experience*, submitted to Transaction on Software Engineering and Methodologies, 1997.

[Cri91] F. Cristian, *Understanding fault-tolerant distributed systems*, in Communications of the ACM, 34(2): 56-78, February 1991.

[EFTOS97] G. Deconinck, T. Varvarigou, O. Botti, V. De Florio, A. Kontizas, M. Truyens, W. Rosseel, R. Lauwereins, F. Cassinari, S. Graeber, and U. Knaak. (Reusable software solutions for more fault-tolerant) Industrial embedded HPC applications. *Supercomputer*, XIII(69):23-44, 1997.

[Deco98] G. Deconinck, O. Botti, F. Cassinari, V. De Florio, R. Lauwereins, *Stable Memory in Substation Automation: a Case Study*, in: IEEE Digest of Papers of the 28th Annual Int. Symp. on Fault-Tolerant Computing (FTCS-28), Munich, Germany, Jun. 1998.

[Dond00] G. Dondossola, *A Scheme for Formal Methods Assessment in the context of developing Certifiable Control Systems,* paper to be published.

[Lapr95] J.-C. Laprie, "Dependability — Its Attributes, Impairments and Means", Section II.A from B. Randell, J.-C. Laprie, H. Kopetz, B. Littlewood (Eds.), "ESPRIT Basic Research Series: Predictably Dependable Computing Systems" Springer-Verlag, Berlin Heidelberg New York, 1995, pp. 3-18.

[Lapr98] J.-C. Laprie, "Dependability of computer systems: from concepts to limits", in Proc. of IFIP International Workshop on Dependable Computing and Its Applications (DCIA98), Johannesburg (South Africa), Jan. 12-14 1998.

[MOD91] UK Ministry of Defence: *Interim Defence Standard 00-55: The procurement of safety critical software in defence equipment*, Part 1, Issue 1: Requirements; Part 2, Issue 1: Guidance, April 1991.

[NASA95] Formal Methods Specification and Verification Guidebook for Software and Computer Systems, Volume I: Planning and Technology Insertion, NASA-GB-002-95.

[Rose98] "Rational Rose 98i Using Rose", Rev. 6.0, December 1998, (Software Release 98i).

[Rush95] J. Rushby, *Formal Methods and their Role in the Certification of Critical Systems*, SRI Technical Report CSL-95-1, March 1995 (300 pages). This is a shorter (50 pages) and less technical treatment of the material in [Rushby 93]. It will become a chapter in the FAA Digital Systems Validation Handbook (a guide to assist FAA Certification Specialists with advanced technology issues).

[TIRAN99] *D1-1: Requirements specification – Version V2*, TIRAN Project deliverable, Oct. 1999, (confidential).

[UML97a] "UML Notation Guide", version 1.1 September 1997.

[UML97b] "UML Semantics", version 1.1 September 1997.

Structuring and Design of Reactive Systems Using RSDS and B

K. Lano[1], K. Androutsopoulos[1], and D. Clark[2]

[1] Department of Computer Science,
King's College London, Strand,
London WC2R 2LS
[2] Department of Computing,
Imperial College, London SW7 2BZ

Abstract. With the advent of comprehensive safety standards for software intensive safety related systems, such as IEC 61508 and its specialisations for particular industry sectors (medical, machinery, process, etc), there is a need to establish combinations of techniques which can be used by industry to demonstrate conformance to these standards for particular developments. In this paper we describe one such combination of techniques, involving statecharts and B, which is aimed at reactive control system development.

We define strategies for controller decomposition which allow safety invariants to be distributed into subcontroller requirements, and define techniques for the automatic synthesis of controllers from invariants. A case study of a train control system is used to illustrate the ideas.

1 Introduction

A control algorithm for a discrete event system describes the reactions (control signals to actuators) issued in response to each input event (from sensors) which may be sent to the controller. Typically this algorithm is represented as a finite state machine (FSM) or as a statechart. In current practice, control algorithms are usually developed by hand, thus introducing possibilities for perhaps very expensive or life-threatening design faults.

We aim to improve this practice by providing techniques for the systematic derivation of executable controllers from requirements statements. These techniques integrate control engineering techniques such as *procedural controller synthesis* [12] and the B formal method and toolset [1].

Section 2 summarises the method used and the structuring approaches. Section 3 identifies the semantic problems of existing statechart based notations and defines our restricted version, Structured Reactive System Notation (SRS), of statecharts designed to eliminate these problems. Section 4 describes the synthesis process for controllers from invariants, and how controllers represented in our restricted statechart notation are translated into B modules in a structured fashion. Section 5 illustrates the process on the case study.

T. Maibaum (Ed.): FASE 2000, LNCS 1783, pp. 97–111, 2000.

2   Development Method

We represent a reactive control system using standard DCFD notation, except that input event flows are indicated by dashed lines and output command flows by solid lines (see for example, Figure 1). This corresponds to the convention used on finite state machines. There may be a set of invariants (such as safety and operational behavior properties) associated with each process (representing a controller). Usually the behaviour of sensors, controllers and actuators will be

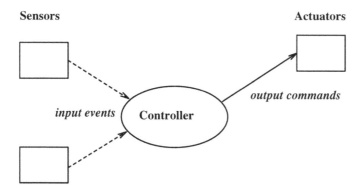

Fig. 1. Structure of Reactive Control Systems

specified by SRS modules in the statechart notation of Section 3. B specifications or implementations may be used interchangeably with SRS modules in these descriptions.

Except for the most trivial systems, it is necessary to modularise the specification of the control algorithm, in order to obtain analysable descriptions. There are several ways in which such a decomposition can be achieved:

1. *Hierarchical* composition of controllers: events e are dealt with first by an overseer controller S which handles certain interactions between components, and e (or derived events) are then sent to subordinate controllers responsible for managing the individual behaviour of subcomponents.

   This design is appropriate if some control aspects can be managed at an aggregate level separately from control aspects which can be managed at an individual component level. It can also be used to separate responsibility for dealing with certain subsidiary aspects of a control problem (such as fault detection) from the calculation of control responses.

   Subordinate controllers S_1 and S_2 should control disjoint sets of actuators, or be independent on shared actuators in the sense that for any two command sequences a_1 and a_2 issued by S_1 and S_2 respectively to a shared actuator A, any permutation of $a_1 \frown a_2$ has the same state-transformation effect on A as $a_1 \frown a_2$. The timing of the responses of S_1 and S_2 relative to each other must also not be critical.

2. *Horizontal* composition of controllers: events are copied to two separate control algorithms S_1 and S_2, which compute their reactions independently. As with hierarchical composition, S_1 and S_2 should control disjoint sets of actuators, or be independent on shared actuators.
3. *Decomposition by control mode:* a separate controller is specified for the control reactions to be carried out in each *mode* or *phase* of the system [5].
4. *Annealing:* creating a separate subcontroller to encapsulate repeated control sequences as single operations (eg: opening a number of valves and pumps to open one flow path between vessels in a chemical plant).
5. *Composition of standard controllers:* recognising common control patterns (priority, and-combination, etc) and chaining together suitable versions of these standard controllers to achieve a more complex control function.

The first two are based on the *physical* decomposition of the actual system, whilst the third is based on *temporal decomposition*.

Various strategies may be used in selection of a suitable decomposition approach, as described in Section 5. The decomposition is usually performed on the DCFD and statechart descriptions of the system, instead of on the B representation. Invariants of controllers are decomposed into invariants of subcontrollers when the controller is structurally decomposed. A control algorithm is then synthesised for each of the controllers, based on their invariants. This is usually done as part of a translation to B machines and implementations, as described in Section 4.

The B notation supports further verification techniques, such as internal consistency and refinement checks, and animation. If the statechart descriptions were translated directly to executable code, these additional verification steps could not be directly supported (a static analysis tool would need to be applied).

3   Restricted Statecharts

3.1   Problems with Statechart Semantics

The semantics of statecharts has proved to be fraught with problems and complications. The original operational semantics given by Harel and others in [3] was changed by Pnueli and Shalev in [11] since the semantics given in the first paper was highly operational and lacked global consistency.

Pnueli and Shalev's paper explored the extent to which the operational semantics, amended to provide global consistency, could be viewed as a declarative semantics – that is, a non-compositional functional semantics expressed in terms of fixed points. Correspondence with a declarative semantics proves to be fairly fragile as it can be destroyed by allowing disjunctions of events (and their absences, i.e. disjunctions of literals) as triggers for transitions. Nevertheless their paper set some sort of standard for elegance in the treatment of the semantics of statecharts.

The semantics in [11] was in turn criticised by Leveson and others in [10] as being counter-intuitive. Because generated events are considered in the same step as that in which they are generated and because transitions to add to the step are chosen one at a time, non-deterministically, it is possible to choose a transition triggered by a generated event rather than a conflicting transition triggered by an input event.

To overcome this problem [10] introduces an ordering in the way in which events are considered. In constructing a step as a series of micro steps they did not consider generated events in the micro step in which they were generated but only in the following one – once all the input events had been exhausted as triggers. This produced a more intuitive semantics but had the side effect of introducing potential cycles and hence steps whose calculation did not terminate.

Leveson and her colleagues have recently decided on eliminating generated events entirely from the syntax of RSML [9]. This not only removes the possibility of non-termination and makes the semantics of statecharts more intuitive but also simplifies the semantics considerably, albeit at the price of loss of expressiveness.

3.2   Structured Reactive System (SRS) Statechart Notation

To eliminate the above semantic problems of statecharts, we restrict statechart notation in the following ways:

1. Negations of events are not allowed as triggers to events, nor are logical combinations of events allowed.
2. Generated events are detected in subsequent steps to that in which they are generated, not in the same step.
3. A strict hierarchy of event generation and reception is enforced, so preventing cycles of sending and receiving.

Thus a transition in our restricted version has the form $t : e[G]/e_1 \frown \ldots \frown e_n$ where t is an (optional) transition label, e the name of the event triggering t (or e is a timeout specification $[min, max]$), G is a logical *guard condition*, and the e_i are the events generated by t. G is optional and defaults to *true*. The e_i are also optional. None of the e_i can lead directly or indirectly to a generation of e.

3.3   Modules and Subsystems

In restricted statecharts all systems are described in terms of *modules*: an OR state containing only basic and OR states. A system description S is given by the AND composition $M_1 \mid \ldots \mid M_m$ of all the modules contained in it, $modules(S) = \{M_1, \ldots, M_m\}$.

Each module M in a system description S has a set $receivers_S(M)$ of modules in S, which are the only modules of S to which it can send events:

$$generations_M(t) \in seq(Events_{R_1} \cup \ldots \cup Events_{R_k})$$

for all $t : Trans_M$, where $receivers_S(M) = \{R_1, \ldots, R_k\}$, and

$$\alpha \in \text{ran}(generations_M(t)) \ \wedge$$
$$\alpha \in Events_{M'} \ \Rightarrow \ M' \in receivers_S(M)$$

for any $M' \in modules(S)$.

   $receivers_S$ is acyclic – $M \notin receivers_S^*(M)$ where $receivers_S^*$ denotes the transitive closure of $receivers_S$ (considered as a relation). For each module, M, the set $receivers_S^*[\{M\}]$ is termed the *subsystem* S' defined by M. M is then the *outer module* of S'.

   Typically modules in a reactive system description represent sensors, controllers, subcontrollers, and actuators.

   Figure 2 shows the typical arrangement of subsystem modules for a reactive system, and the associated hierarchy of modules under the *receivers* relation. *Subcontroller* 1 and *Subcontroller* 2 are the receivers of *Controller*, etc, *Actuator* 3 has transitions for $g1$ and $g2$. Each module is a separate OR state within an overall AND state representing the complete subsystem.

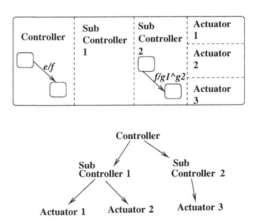

Fig. 2. Typical subsystem structure

4   Synthesis of Control Algorithms

The invariants for controller behaviour, both operational and safety, can be used to synthesise the required control algorithm, ie, the reaction to individual events.

   We assume that a typical operational invariant has the form:

$$sstate = s1 \wedge G \ \Rightarrow \ astate = on$$

where *sstate* is some sensor state, G a guard involving other sensor or actuator states, and *astate* is an actuator state. This represents an obligation that the actuator must be on if an associated switch or trigger sensor is in state $s1$ and the guard is satisfied. (The consequent may also be a disjunction of such equalities, more generally).

Then the reaction to any event that sets $sstate$ to $s1$ while G is true must set $astate$ to be on. Also, any event which results in G becoming true whilst $sstate = s1$ must also have a reaction which sets $astate = on$.

In detail, the algorithm for synthesising an abstract B specification from the invariants is as follows:

- For each event e (that affects the state of a particular sensor, for example setting $sstate$ to $s1$):
  1. Identify all invariants which may be invalidated by this state change – ie, invariants of the form

$$sstate = s1 \wedge G1 \;\Rightarrow\; astate = a1$$
$$sstate = s1 \wedge G2 \;\Rightarrow\; astate = a2$$

     or any other invariants involving $sstate$.
  2. Identify actuator changes needed to maintain these invariants – gather together in a single conditional clause all cases of changes to a particular actuator:
     ```
     IF G1
     THEN astate := a1
     ELSE
         IF G2
         THEN astate := a2
         . . .
     ```
     All possible cases should be defined in the invariants – for missing cases additional invariants will have to be provided by the developer. A simple completeness check is that for each sensor S, and reachable state x of S, there is some invariant containing $sstate = x$ in its antecedent.

     These then give rise to a hierarchically organised set of conditional clauses, with the most general conditions in the outer conditional tests and more specific subcases in the inner tests.

     Optionally, assignments to actuator states can be replaced by invocations of corresponding operations of a machine which encapsulates the actuator state. The controller then *INCLUDES* all machines representing actuators which it controls.
  3. Compose changes to different actuators by ∥.
  4. Restructure the operation definition if necessary to move all occurrences of ∥ inside conditional branches, so that no ∥ combinator occurs outside an *IF* statement.

Controller specifications expressed in an SRS module with invariants therefore produce B machines whose set of operations correspond to the events which the controller responds to, defined by the above synthesis procedure. The invariants translate directly to invariants of the B machine. The B machine needs to declare a variable $sstate$ to record the current state of each sensor whose events are detected by the controller. The operation e above then needs the additional assignment $sstate := s1$. Alternatively sensor states can be encapsulated in separate machines, making it easier to share read access to these sensors in a number of controllers.

If actuators are defined in separate machines, these machines need to be included in the controller.

In implementations, a fixed order of control actions is determined, and expressed in B by the use of the ; construct in place of $\|$ in controller operation definitions.

5   Case Study: Train Control System

The aim of this system is to safely control a train to ensure that the train only moves when the doors are locked. Its sensors are:

- Door: $dstate \in \{locked, closed, opening, closing, open\}$
- Motion sensor: $motstate \in \{stationary, moving\}$
- Switch (to start train): $swstate \in \{on, off\}$
- Door button (to open/close doors): $dbstate \in \{on, off\}$

Its actuators are:

- Motor: $mstate \in \{on, off\}$
- Brake: $bstate \in \{on, off\}$
- Door.

The safety invariants are:

1. $motstate = moving \Rightarrow dstate \in \{closing, closed, locked\}$
2. $dstate \neq locked \Rightarrow mstate = off \wedge bstate = on$
3. $bstate = off \equiv mstate = on$ (the motor is on iff the brake is off).

The operational invariants are:

1. $swstate = on \wedge dstate = locked \Rightarrow mstate = on$
2. $dbstate = off \Rightarrow dstate \in \{closing, closed, locked\}$
3. $swstate = off \Rightarrow mstate = off$
4. $dbstate = on \wedge swstate = off \wedge motstate = stationary \Rightarrow dstate \in \{open, opening\}$
5. $swstate = on \Rightarrow dstate \in \{closing, closed, locked\}$ (the train switch has priority over the door button).

Figure 3 shows the overall context diagram of this control system.

5.1   Structuring Alternatives

We can decompose control requirements in a number of ways: temporal mode or phase decomposition, hierarchical decomposition, annealing, or by recognition of standard controllers. In the following sections we detail how these are applied in practice and illustrate them using the train control system.

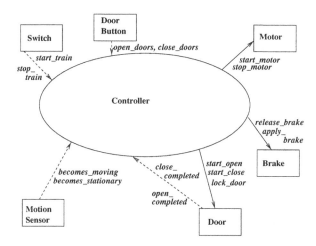

Fig. 3. DCFD of Train Control System

Temporal Mode/Phase Decomposition In order to decompose on the basis of temporal mode, we select a variable (or variables) representing sensor states, whose set of possible values are to be taken as the set of modes. In making this selection, it is useful to choose the variables which occur most frequently on the LHS of the safety and operational invariants: such variables will be involved in more control rules than others, and hence by fixing their values in particular modes, more control rules will be simplified than if less frequently occurring variables were chosen.

In the train control system, the variable $swstate$ occurs most frequently on the LHS of axioms (4 occurrences), and is therefore the prime candidate for constructing modes. The two possible states on and off of this variable give rise to two modes $SwOn$, $SwOff$. The control axioms for these modes are derived from those for the overall controller by substituting in the fixed values of $swstate$ in these two modes and simplifying. For $SwOn$ the axioms therefore become:

- Safety:
    1. $dstate \neq locked \ \Rightarrow \ mstate = off \wedge bstate = on$
    2. $bstate = off \ \equiv \ mstate = on$
  Operational invariants:
    1. $dstate = locked \ \Rightarrow \ mstate = on$
    2. $dstate \in \{closing, closed, locked\}$

Notice that only a record of $dstate$ needs to be kept in the controller for $SwOn$ (in order to express these invariants), other sensor states need not be recorded and hence $SwOn$ does not need operations for any of their events. Similarly for $SwOff$.

Operational axioms 1 and 5 of the train system define the actions the coordinator controller should take in switching from the $SwOff$ to the $SwOn$ phase controllers, and operational axioms 3 and 4 the actions to be taken in switching from *SwOn* to *SwOff*.

The structural decomposition resulting from this choice is shown in Figure 4. The controllers for *SwOn*, *SwOff* and the coordinator controller can now be derived from their respective sets of axioms. Because there are many shared

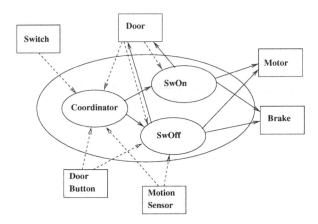

Fig. 4. Phase Decomposition of Train Controller

sensors and actuators between the two phase controllers, this decomposition is probably a bad choice for the train control system. In other systems, such as the milk plant of [7], where substantially different sets of equipment are used in the different phases of operation (eg: filling with milk, emptying, cleaning, etc), such a decomposition would be more effective.

A more sophisticated approach for phase decomposition is to identify an invariant of the form $P_1 \vee \ldots \vee P_n$ of the system, where each P_i involves at least one sensor variable, the P_i are logically disjoint: $P_i \Rightarrow \neg P_j$ for $i \neq j$, and the phases of the system are taken as those sets of states corresponding to the truth of each particular P_i.

Hierarchical Decomposition The second structural decomposition approach is to introduce hierarchical composition by selecting subsets of the actuators of the system and isolating the control rules which apply only to those actuators. The aim is to identify disjoint groups $A_1, \ldots, A_n$ of actuators such that there are relatively few axioms in the original requirements relating the states of actuators in A_i to those in A_j for $i \neq j$. If there are *no* such axioms, then horizontal structuring can be used, otherwise a coordinator controller will be needed which invokes the controllers for A_i and A_j in such a way that the invariants which link their states are maintained.

In the case of the train control system, a suitable grouping of actuators is $A_1 = \{Motor, Brake\}$ and $A_2 = \{Door\}$. This is because only one safety

invariant (number 2) and one operational invariant (number 1) link the states
of these two groups.

As with temporal mode decomposition, we generate new sets of axioms which
the subcontrollers for A_1 and A_2 must satisfy. These are obtained by selecting
the axioms which refer only to the actuators in each subgroup. Axioms which
refer to actuators in both A_1 and A_2 are not included in the subcontrollers but
remain as obligations on an overseer controller.

The structure of this decomposition of the system is shown on the LHS of
Figure 5, and the corresponding state machine module structure on the RHS.

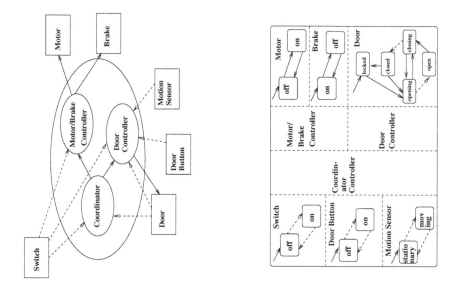

Fig. 5. DCFD and Module Structure of Hierarchical Decomposition

Annealing In this decomposition approach, we identify repeated groups of actuator commands issued by the controller, and package these groups of commands
into a single module, so that the controller needs to only issue single commands
to this module instead of sets of specific commands to particular actuators. This
decomposition assists in making the controller more maintainable (eg., if the
precise set of actuators changes in different versions or upgrades of the system).

In the train controller the natural candidates for such subsequences are

$$\rho_1 = start\_motor \frown release\_brake$$
$$\rho_2 = apply\_brake \frown stop\_motor$$

as generations of a monolithic controller for the system. These can be 'annealed'
into the generations of a module M' with a single state s and transitions for
events $start$ and $stop$ with the labels

$start/\rho_1$
$stop/\rho_2$

Since M' has no invariants, and no invariants are removed from the main controller, this step does not improve verifiability, unlike the phase and hierarchical decompositions. For this system hierarchical decomposition already achieves all the modularity provided by annealing, so is the preferable approach.

Recognition of Standard Controllers Certain simple control mechanisms occur quite frequently, so it is appropriate to keep a list of ready-built controllers for these cases, which can then be adapted to particular sensors and actuators by renaming, and chained together to define more elaborate control functions. In [8] we describe two common patterns, an 'And' controller which takes inputs from two switches, produces a *goon* command only if both switches have been set *on*, and produces a *gooff* command when either one or the other is set *off* (when the other is *on*). A similar controller is the *priority* controller, which switches on actuator A whenever switch A is on, and switches it off whenever switch A is off, and similarly for actuator B and switch B. However actuator B cannot be on if switch A is on, so A has priority over B.

By chaining together copies of these controllers, it is possible to achieve complex control functions. To select appropriate standard controllers for a new control problem, the invariant of this problem should be examined for patterns similar to those of (for example) the And and Priority controllers.

In the case of the train control system, the priority controller pattern can be recognised in the interaction between the *swstate* (playing the role of *sastate*) and *dbstate* (playing the role of *sbstate*), where an indication *mstate'* that the motor should be on/off plays the role of *aastate*, and an indication *dstate'* that the door should open/close plays the role of *abstate*. The following axioms result from this adaption of *PriorityController*:

1. $swstate = off \Rightarrow mstate' = off$ (cf. operational axiom 3)
2. $dbstate = off \Rightarrow dstate' = off$ (cf. operational axiom 2)
3. $swstate = on \Rightarrow mstate' = on$ (cf. operational axiom 1)
4. $dbstate = on \wedge swstate = off \Rightarrow dstate' = on$ (cf. operational axiom 4)
5. $swstate = on \Rightarrow dstate' = off$ (cf. operational axiom 5)

Further patterns can be applied until the axioms of the train control system are recovered. For example, the motor can only be on if $mstate' = on$ and $dstate = locked$.

5.2   Translation to B

Phase Decomposition The translation of control actions to B operations follows Section 4, with the addition that several phase controllers may include the same sensor or actuator components. For example, both *SwOn* and *SwOff* include *Motor*. Such a structure is not allowed in B, because invariants of the subordinate machines may be violated without any of their operations being executed: if machines B and C both include D, then C may change the state of D in such a way that B's invariant is violated despite the fact that all operations of B maintain the invariant. In an object-oriented language such as VDM^{++}, no such problem would arise, as the controller C would be dynamically swapped in for the controller B, and only C's invariant would contribute to the system invariant while the phase that it represents is in progress.

A way to 'trick' the B Toolkit into accepting such a structure is described in [6], however this naturally limits the benefits of the formal method in providing verification checks on the controllers.

Here the coordinator has the specification:

MACHINE *Coordinator*
SEES *TrainTypes*
INCLUDES *SwOn, SwOff*
VARIABLES *swstate*
INVARIANT *swstate* $\in$ *State* $\wedge$
    (*swstate* $=$ *on* $\wedge$ *dstate* $=$ *locked* $\Rightarrow$ *mstate* $=$ *on*) $\wedge$
    (*swstate* $=$ *off* $\Rightarrow$ *mstate* $=$ *off*) $\wedge$
    (*dbstate* $=$ *on* $\wedge$ *swstate* $=$ *off* $\wedge$ *motstate* $=$ *stationary* $\Rightarrow$
                                    dstate $\in$ { *open, opening* }) $\wedge$
    (*swstate* $=$ *on* $\Rightarrow$ *dstate* $\in$ { *closing, closed, locked* })
INITIALISATION *swstate* $:=$ *off*
OPERATIONS
    start_train $=$
        PRE *swstate* $=$ *off*
        THEN
            swstate $:=$ *on* $\|$
            init_swon
        END;

    close_completed $=$
        PRE *dstate* $=$ *closing*
        THEN
            IF *swstate* $=$ *on*
            THEN *swon_close_completed*
            ELSE *swoff_close_completed*
            END
        END;

   ⋮

END

Each operation e of *Coordinator* that corresponds to an event e of sensor S must forward e in renamed form P_e to any of the currently active phase controllers P which refer to the state of S (ie., to any P which is a target of an arrow from S in the DCFD of the system).

Hierarchical Decomposition The translation of control actions to B operations in this case follows Section 4, with the addition that there may be duplicate records of the same sensor state in different B machines representing controllers. For example, in the train control system, both *MBController* and the coordinator controller require a record of *swstate* in order to express their invariants. Such duplication is handled by renaming the variables in the subordinate controllers, and then asserting the equality of the different sensor state representations in the coordinator. Each subcontroller which needs read-only access to a sensor or actuator state to determine the validity of an action, must *SEE* the machine which encapsulates that state.

In this case the coordinator is:

MACHINE *Coordinator*
SEES *TrainTypes*, *Bool_TYPE*
INCLUDES *MBController*, *DoorController*
VARIABLES *swstate*
INVARIANT *swstate* ∈ *State* ∧
    swstate = *mb_swstate* ∧ *swstate* = *d_swstate* ∧
    (*dstate* ≠ *locked*   ⇒   *mstate* = *off* ∧ *bstate* = *on*) ∧
    (*swstate* = *on* ∧ *dstate* = *locked*   ⇒   *mstate* = *on*)
INITIALISATION
    swstate := *off*
OPERATIONS
    start_train =
        PRE *swstate* = *off*
        THEN
            swstate := *on* ||
            mb_start_train ||
            d_start_train
        END;

    stop_train =
        PRE *swstate* = *on*
        THEN
            swstate := *off* ||
            mb_stop_train ||
            d_stop_train
        END;

    open_door =
        PRE *dbstate* = *off*
        THEN
            d_open_door ||
            mb_open_door
        END;

        ⋮

END

Events are forwarded by this controller to all subcontrollers which need to respond to it, ie, those subcontrollers which refer to the state of the sensor which produced the event.

Annealing An extra machine is defined to act as the intermediary between the source of the annealed command sequences and the actuators it controls, otherwise the translation to B is as in Section 4.

Chaining of Standard Controllers In the translation to B, each copy of a standard controller produces a B machine (for example, a renamed version of the Priority controller of Section 5.1). In the hierarchical control structure there may be controllers which take inputs from sensors directly, rather than from hierarchically superior controllers. Whenever this is the case, we must promote such operations from the lower to the higher controller, in order to maintain the strict tree structure which B requires.

6   Tool Support

A suite of tools (collectively known as the RSDS tool [2]) have been developed in Visual C++ to support the specification of reactive systems using DCFD and statecharts and their translation into B specifications and implementations.

The RSDS tool currently provides the following features: (i) Supporting the visualisation of a correct DCFD for the entire reactive system and recording the operational, safety and liveness properties for its controllers. (ii) Checking on the existence or correctness of abstraction mappings between two statecharts, including construction of such mappings where they exist. (iii) Transformations (flattening) of statecharts with nesting, conditions, event generation and AND composition into state machines. (iv) Translating a statechart into B source for the purpose of invariant checking and animation/testing and code generation.

Extensions to the RSDS tool are under development allowing for: (i) Visual decomposition of the main controller in the DCFD using a suitable decomposition strategy. (ii) Checking the validity of the operational, safety and liveness properties of the statecharts.

The tool is also being ported to Java.

References

1. J-R Abrial. *The B Book: Assigning Programs to Meanings.* Cambridge University Press, 1996.
2. K. Androutsopoulos. *The Reactive System Design Tool,* ROOS Project report, Department of Computing, Imperial College, 1999.
3. D. Harel, A. Pnueli, J. Schmidt, and R. Sherman. On the formal semantics of statecharts. In *Proceedings of the first IEEE Symposium on Logic in Computer Science,* pages 54-64, 1986.

4. International Electrotechnical Commission, *IEC 61508: Functional Safety of Electrical/Electronic/Programmable Electronic Safety-Related Systems*, 1999.
5. International Society for Measurement and Control. *Batch Control Models and Terminology*, ISA-S88.01-1995, 1995.
6. P. Kan, K. Lano, *Reactive System Development in B*, 1st YUFORIC Workshop, Brisbane, Australia, 1998.
7. K. Lano, D. Clark. *Demonstrating Preservation of Safety Properties in Reactive Control System Development*, 4th Australian Workshop on Industrial Experience with Safety Critical Systems and Software, Canberra, ACT, November 1999.
8. K. Lano, J. Bicarregui, A. Sanchez, *Invariant-based Synthesis and Composition of Control Algorithms using B*, B User Group Meeting, Formal Methods '99.
9. N. G. Leveson. Designing a Requirements Specification Language for Reactive Systems. Invited talk, Z User Meeting, 1998, Springer Verlag 1998.
10. N. G. Leveson, Mats P.E. Heimdahl, Holly Hildreeth, and Jon D. Reese. Requirements specification for process-control systems. In *IEEE Transactions on Software Engineering*, volume 20, no. 9, pp. 684-707. 1995.
11. A. Pnueli and M. Shalev. What is in a step: On the semantics of statecharts. In *Proceedings of the Symposium on Theoretical Aspects of Computing Software*, Lecture Notes in Computer Science, Volume 526, Springer-Verlag, Berlin, 1991, pp. 244-264.
12. A. Sanchez. *Formal Specification and Synthesis of Procedural Controllers for Process Systems*. Springer-Verlag. Lecture Notes in Control and Information Sciences, vol. 212. 1996.

Using Domain-Specific Languages for the Realization of Component Composition

Matthias Anlauff[1], Philipp W. Kutter[2], Alfonso Pierantonio[3], and
Asuman Sünbül[4]

[1] GMD FIRST, Rudower Chaussee 5
D-12489 Berlin, Germany
ma@first.gmd.de
[2] Swiss Federal Institute of Technology
Gloriastr. 35, CH-8092 Zürich, Switzerland
kutter@tik.ee.ethz.ch
[3] Dipartimento di Matematica, Pura ed Applicata
Università di L'Aquila, I-67100 L'Aquila, Italy
alfonso@univaq.it
[4] Computer Science Department, Technical University Berlin
Einsteinufer 17, Sekr. EN-7, D-10587 Berlin, Germany
asu@cs.tu-berlin.de

Abstract. In recent years, component-based development has evolved
to one of the key technologies in software engineering, because it provides
a promising way to deal with large scale software developments. Due to
this, the realization of component interactions has become an important
task while implementing a system being assembled from (existing) components. Scripting languages, like Perl, Tcl, Unix-Shell, are often used
for implementing this so-called *glue code*, because they provide a flexible way to process string-based input, the most common data structures
used for component interactions. However, often it turns out that the
algorithms of the component interactions are too sophisticated to be adequately expressed in this kind of languages. In this paper, we propose
the use of language technology for that purpose: the strings passed between the components are treated as sentences in specialized component
interaction languages (CIL). The syntax of such a language defines the
input format of the components to be interconnected, and the semantics
represents the functionality of the glue code. The appropriateness of this
approach depends on the methodology and support functionality available for designing these languages. We report on the positive experiences
using *Montages* as methodology. We will also describe the support functionality of the Gem-Mex tool containing its graphical animation and
debugging facilities, which can be used as vehicle for the comprehension
of the interplay between the components of the overall system.

1 Introduction

The need for designing new programming languages is generally restricted to
those cases, where special applications require non-standard language constructs.

T. Maibaum (Ed.): FASE 2000, LNCS 1783, pp. 112–126, 2000.

These so-called Domain-Specific Languages (DSL) are usually designed for being used by domain experts who need languages consisting of terms and notions they are familiar with. Often, a DSL also diminishes the amount of source code, because domain-specific knowledge is already contained in the semantics of the language constructs. However, the design overhead is often the reason, why the definition of a DSL is chosen as the last alternative for solving a given problem. This fact also prohibits specialized programming languages being exhaustively used in other situations than the processing of human-written source code. In this paper, we will present a "language design environment" which – as we think – decreases the threshold of defining DSLs for solving given problems. Especially, if the transformation from source to target is a non-trivial task, the use of DSLs often leads to much better and less ad-hoc solutions.

In other words, the proposal of using syntax and semantics descriptions of DSLs for implementing algorithms can be seen as a novel style of programming: *Programming On Syntax Trees (PoST)*. That means that the input data defines the locations of computation by the nodes of the parse tree, each of these nodes is connected with a set of actions representing the computation, and the program is given as the union of all these actions occurring in a parse tree.

The method, we are using for supporting this new paradigm is *Montages* [17,3]. Unlike other methods for describing formally the syntax and semantics of programming languages, Montages is based strictly on techniques well known by programmers: EBNF, finite state machines, imperative code. We will show, how the Gem-Mex system automatically generates interpreters based on language definitions given as Montages specifications. Montages has a formal semantics based on Abstract State Machines [12,15], which makes it also interesting when security aspects of the target system must be considered.

In this paper, we will use the application domain of component-based software development in order to show that designing new specialized languages in our framework can compete with the technologies usually chosen in this domain.

This paper is organized as follows: We will first briefly describe some aspects of the composition of software components and will thereby categorize our approach in the work already done in this field. Section 3 explains the running example of the paper. We will then introduce the Montages method and briefly describe the Gem-Mex system. Section 7 concludes the paper and provides an outlook on future work.

2   Composition of Software Components

A lot of work has been done regarding the composition of software components. This fact is expressed by the large number of publications related to this issue. We will try to position ourselves wrt. the state of the art in component composition technology using a very recent publication by Schneider and Nierstrasz [21] where they distinguish between five techniques that are used for the realization of software component composition, namely[1]

---

[1] citation from the mentioned paper

- *component frameworks* provide software components that encapsulate useful functionality;
- *architectural description languages* explicitly specify architectural styles in terms of interfaces, contracts, and composition rules that components must adhere in order to be composable;
- *glue* abstractions adapt components that need to bridge compositional mismatches;
- *scripting languages* are used to specify compactly and declaratively how software components are plugged together to achieve some desired result [19]; and
- *coordination models* provide the coordination media and abstractions that allow distributed components to cooperate [6,9].

In this paper, we propose the use of domain-specific languages as a substitute for *scripting languages* for those cases, where it would be clumsy to use this kind of languages. We do *not* want to use DSLs for coordinating the architectural design of the composed software system, as proposed in [10]; we will focus on the use of DSLs for non-trivial component composition tasks on the implementation level. A more detailed discussion on aspects regarding the design of software systems that are assembled from components can also be found in [5] and [22].

2.1   Component Interaction Technologies

Important requirements for the technology that shall be used for realizing component interaction are *flexibility* and *adaptability* (see [11]). Flexibility in this context means the ability to process and generate any format of data occurring in a heterogeneous environment. Adaptability describes the possibility of the technology to adapt it for certain application domains. Therefore, scripting languages, like Unix-Shell-Script, Tcl/Tk, Python, Perl, are often used for the implementation of component interactions, because they meet these requirements. In [20], the importance of scripting language for the component interaction culminates in the statement: "The main purpose of a scripting language is to wire components in other languages".

In trying to analyze this elusive role of scripting languages for component interaction technology and knowing the drawbacks of this kind of languages concerning concepts of high-level programming languages, one might come to the conclusion, that the uncomplicated way of dealing with input and output data is the key factor for this rating. Most scripting languages provide very easy to use input/output primitives on a higher abstraction level than usually programming languages do. The data types that can be handled by scripting languages are restricted to one or two basic types (e.g. strings and integers); for the purpose of implementing component interaction this is usually sufficient.

2.2   The Implementation of Component Interaction Using DSLs

At the risk of oversimplifying somewhat, the functionality of the code implementing the component interaction can be characterized by two basic tasks:

processing data coming from and sending data back to components. The prereq-uisite for applying the "PoST" style of programming is therefore given for this kind of application: the execution of the code is mainly controlled by the struc-ture of the input data. The format of this data defines the syntax of a *Component Interaction Language* (CIL), and the functionality is expressed by the language semantics given by the actions attached to the nodes of the resulting parse trees. Thus, the component interaction code can be regarded as an interpreter for the CIL. Figure 1 illustrates this approach: The components $C_{i_1} \ldots C_{i_n}$ send strings

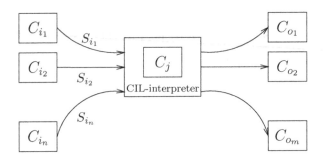

Fig. 1. Composition using a component interaction language

$S_{i_1} \ldots S_{i_n}$ to the component C_j, each of these strings is a sentence of the compo-nent interaction language CIL. The interpretation of these sentences in the CIL interpreter results in the output of data that is send back to the components.

The components on the left-hand-side and on the right-hand-side both rep-resent subsets of the set of components occurring in the system.[2]

2.3   Domain-Specific vs. Scripting Languages

The situations in which we propose to use DSLs as a substitute for scripting languages are those where non-trivial or at least non-linear transformations of the data exchanged between the components must be performed. On the one hand, we do not propose to get rid of scripting languages at all; this would be a big mistake because scripting languages have been proven to be a very good vehicle for a high percentage of component interaction problems. But on the other hand, often the expressive power of scripting languages does not suffice to provide an appropriate solution for a given composition problem. In these cases we propose to use domain-specific languages as an alternative component composition implementation techniques. Our running example introduced below will show a typical situation were we think that the overhead of designing an own language solely for the task of component interaction is justified. We will also show how this overhead can can diminished by using the Montages method,

---

[2] C_{i_j} may represent the same component as C_{o_k}, and both may coincide with C_j

a semi-visual framework for specifying syntax and semantics of programming languages, and its tool environment Gem-Mex.

3   Running Example: Transformation of Object Repository Decription Formats

As a running example for explaining our proposal we use the interaction of a object-based tool (e. g. a graphical editor) and a data repository. We assume that the tool wants to store its objects in the repository in order to make use of the configuration management functionality provided by the repository system. As it is common in practice, the meta-models of both components do not match so that the objects of the tool can not be stored in the repository as they are. In our special case, the tool has a notion of sub-classing while the repository system has not. In order to correctly reflect the interrelations of objects and their attributes, the inheritance relation should also be represented in the repository.

For illustration purposes, we assume, that the classes occurring in the object-based tool can consist of a list of attributes each of which has one of the basic types "int", "float", "string", or "bool". Furthermore, we assume, that a class has at most one super-class. For making things more concrete, we will further assume that the grammar for describing the object format of the object-based tool is given as follows:

Program	::= { ClassDefinition ";" }
ClassDefinition	= BasicClassDefinition | SubclassDefinition
BasicClassDefinition	::= "class" Ident "{" { Attribute ";" } "}"
SubclassDefinition	::= "subclass" Ident "of" Ident "{" { Attribute ";" } "}"
Attribute	::= Ident ":" AttrType
AttrType	= "Int" |"Float" |"String" |"Bool"

The repository component is only able to declare classes and attributes, no sub-classing is defined in the repository. The task of the DSL is to read the object definitions from the tool and generate for each object the corresponding entry in the repository. The attributes of an object's super-class must also be inserted for each object. Thus, the DSL must "flatten" the inheritance relationship introduced by the object-based tool, so that the corresponding objects in the repository contain the correct list of attributes.[3]

In the following, we will use this example to introduce the Montages approach, and demonstrate the functionality of the Gem-Mex system.

---

[3] This example is inspired by a problem that arose in the context of the "KobrA"-project which currently runs with industrial partners at GMD FIRST. The approach described in this paper is used to extend the repository system developed by one of the industrial partners to deal with sub-classing.

4   Visual Formal Semantics Descriptions: Montages

Montages [17,2] constitute a specification formalism for describing all aspects of programming languages. Syntax, static analysis and semantics, and dynamic semantics are given in an unambiguous and coherent way by means of semi–visual descriptions. The static aspects of Montages resemble control and data flow graphs, and the overall specifications are similar in structure, length, and complexity to those found in common language manuals.

In the same way Montages is used to describe the syntax and semantics of programming languages, it can be used to formulate application functionality based on the structure of input data. The difference lies on the conceptual level: While in the first case the *language* and its semantical description lies in the center of interest, in latter case one focuses on the *application* that processes data of a given format. Thus, the term "language" does not necessarily refer to a programming language, but may also refer to the description of the format of the input data of an application.

The mathematical semantics of Montages is given with Abstract State Machines (formally called Evolving Algebras) [13,15]. In short, ASMs are a state-based formalism in which a state is updated in discrete time steps. Unlike most state based systems, the state is given by an algebra, that is, a collection of functions and universes. The state transitions are given by rules that update functions point-wise and extend universes with new elements.

ASMs have already been used to model the dynamic semantics of a number of programming languages, such as C [14], Occam [7], C++ [23], Oberon [16], and Java [8] to mention a few. At the risk of oversimplifying somewhat, one defines the *initial state* of the functions and specifies how they evolve by means of *transition rules*. The *initial state* is assumed to include the results of a static analysis. After this analysis the program's control and data flow is represented in the form of functions between parts of the program text. As usual the control flow functions specify the order in which statements are executed, and the data flow functions specify how values flow via variables through operations. The corresponding *transition rules* update the system state and let the control evolve through the control flow.

The existing case studies showed that it is possible to model with ASMs the dynamic semantics of realistic programming languages, but they have the disadvantage that they do not formalize the static aspects. Montages engineered the ASMs approach to programming language semantics showing how to model consistently not only the dynamic semantics, but the static analysis and semantics as well. In particular, Montages describe how to define intensionally the control and data flow, starting from the concrete syntax.

In terms of the "PoST"-programming style this means that during the first phase – the static analysis – the locations of the computation – associated with a subset of the nodes of the syntax tree – are linked with each other using control flow arrows. Data access to other parts of the syntax tree is defined by data arrows. In the second phase – the dynamic execution – these locations are visited depending on firing condition on the flow arrows. In contrast to traditional programming languages, where the control flow graph is fixed by the source program, in our approach this graph is first constructed depending on the structure of the input data and then processed according to the rules and actions given for each node of that graph.

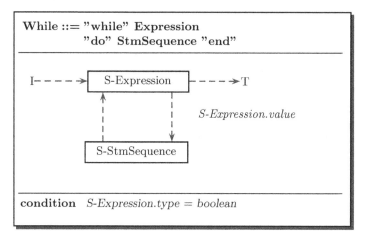

Fig. 2. The While Montage

In order to get an idea on how the the syntax and semantics is described for a typical language construct in an imperative language, Figure 2 contains the Montages specification of a "While" statement. The topmost part in the working area is the production rule defining the context–free syntax. Below is the local flow, i.e. the graphical definition of the mapping between syntax tree and flow graph. In the While-Montage the tree with the expression and the statement sequence descendants (denoted by the selectors S-Expression and S-StmSequence) is mapped to a control cycle. The dotted control flow arrows may be labeled by means of firing conditions, i.e. predicates which determine through which edges the control must flow. If the firing condition S-Expression.value evaluates to true, control cycles, otherwise it leaves the construct through the exit point denoted by the T node (terminal). The entry point for the control is the I node (initial).

Unlike the While construct, most other Montages contain additional points of computation. Such points, or *actions nodes* are visualized as labeled ovals. The action to perform is given in the fourth part (not contained in Figure 2) of a Montage, by using the label as reference. We will see examples of this in the following section.

5   Implementing Component Interaction Using Montages

In this section, we will illustrate how Montages and its support environment Gem-Mex can be used to implement the interaction of components using the examples introduced in Section 3. According to the grammar specified there we have specified a Montage for each language construct of the DSL implementing the component interaction between the object-based tool and the object repository.

In Figure 3 the Montage for the attribute definition is given. The action performed when an attribute node is reached is given by the lower part of the window: The name and the type of the attribute is written to stdout in a format that is accepted by the repository system.

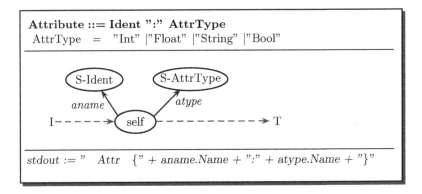

Fig. 3. The "Attribute"-Montage

In Figure 4, the Montage for a basic class definition is given. When the control flow reaches a basic class definition the return point is set to the "self" node. This is done, because the return point serves as register for storing the "next" class definition occurring in the input stream. The class definition header as it is expected by the repository system is printed to stdout. After the list of attributes has been processed, the control reaches the return point that has been set in the first action of this construct. This Montage represents the base case, only the local attributes are written to stdout.

The Montage in Figure 5 represents the most interesting part of this example, namely the case in which local and inherited attributes must be transfered to the repository system. The Montage is nearly identical to the "BasicClassDefinition"-Montage only that the control flow – after the local attributes has been processed – does not enter the return point immediately; instead the control flow is set to the "self" node of the super class. This node has been stored during the static analysis in the global table "ClassDef". From here, the inherited attributes are also reached and transfered to the repository component. The use of the "Return-Point" variable becomes clearer now: after processing the basic class definition

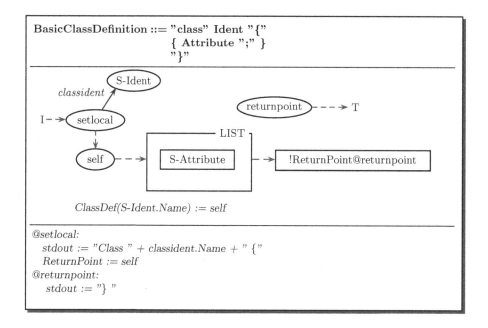

Fig. 4. The "BasicClassDefinition"-Montage

representing the root class for the current subclass, the control returns to the current class definition.

Example

In order to illustrate the functioning of the DSL described above, we have generated a language interpreter from the Montages described above using the Gem-Mex tool. Figure 6 contains an example input and the generated output. As one can see there, the attributes of the classes are flattened so that no information is lost in the repository.

6   Gem-Mex: The Development Environment for Montages

The development environment for Montages is given by the Gem-Mex tool [2,4]. The intended use of the tool Gem-Mex is, on one hand to allow the designer to 'debug' her/his semantics descriptions by empirical testing of whether the intended decisions have been properly formalized; on the other hand, to automatically generate a correct (prototype) implementation of programming languages from the description, including visualization and debugging facilities.

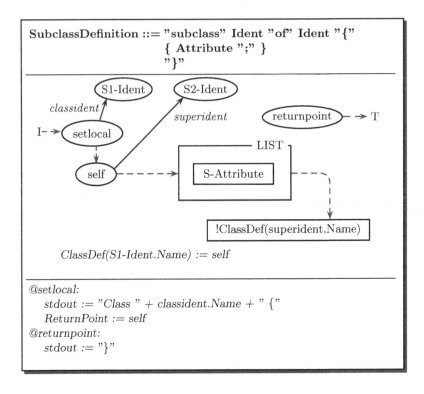

Fig. 5. The "SubclassDefinition"-Montage

Gem-Mex consists of a number of interconnected tools:

- a specialized graphical editor allows to enter and manipulate Montages in a convenient way;
- frames for the documentation of the specified languages are generated automatically;
- the Montages executable generator (Mex) generates a correct and efficient interpreter of the language;
- the generic animation and debugger tool visualizes the static and dynamic behavior of the specified language at a symbolic level; source programs written in the specified language and user-defined data structures can be animated and inspected in a visual environment; a snapshot of the debugging process is shown in Fig.7.

6.1   Generation of Language Interpreters

Using nothing but the formal semantics description given by the set of Montages, the Gem-Mex system generates an interpreter for the specified language. The core of the Gem-Mex system is *Aslan*, which stands for *A*bstract *S*tate Machine

```
                                        Class Rectangle {
                                           Attr  {x0:Int}
                                           Attr  {y0:Int}
                                           Attr  {x1:Int}
                                           Attr  {y1:Int}
  class Rectangle {                       }
    x0:Int; y0:Int; x1:Int; y1:Int;      Class Square {
  };                                         Attr  {length:Int}
                                           Attr  {x0:Int}
                                           Attr  {y0:Int}
  subclass Square of Rectangle {          Attr  {x1:Int}
    length:Int;                           Attr  {y1:Int}
  };                                      }
                                        Class Trapezium {
  subclass Trapezium of Rectangle {       Attr  {angle:Float}
    angle:Float;                          Attr  {x0:Int}
  };                                      Attr  {y0:Int}
                                           Attr  {x1:Int}
                                           Attr  {y1:Int}
                                        }
```

Fig. 6. Input (left) and output (right) of the DSL connector

*Lan*guage and provides a fully-fledged implementation of the ASM approach. Aslan can also be used as a stand-alone, general purpose ASM implementation. The process of generating an executable interpreter consists of two phases:

- The Montages containing the language definition are transformed to an intermediate format and then translated to an ASM formalization according to the rules presented in the previous sections.
- The resulting ASM formalization is processed by the Aslan compiler generating an executable version of the formalization, which represents an interpreter implementing the formal semantics description of the specified language.

Using Aslan as the core of the Gem-Mex system provides the user the possibility to exploit the full power of the ASM framework to enrich the graphical ASM macros provided by Montages with additional formalization code.

6.2 Generation of Visual Programming Environments

Besides pure language interpreters, the Gem-Mex system is able to generate visual programming environments for the generated ASM formalization of the programming language semantics[4]. This is done by providing a generic debugging and animation component which can be accessed by the generated executable.

---

[4] This feature is again available to all kind of ASM formalizations implemented in Aslan not only to those generated from a Montages language specification

During the translation process of the Montages/ASM code special instructions are inserted that provide the information being necessary to visualize the execution of the formalization. In particular, the visual environment can be used to debug the specification, animate the execution of it, and generate documents representing snapshots of the visualization of data structures during the execution. The debugging features include stepwise execution, textual representation of ASM data structures, definition of break points, interactive term evaluation, and re-play of executions.

Figure 7 shows an example of the graphical animation facility of the Gem-Mex system. On the right-hand-side of the window the source code program written in the specified programming language is displayed using position information generated during the compilation process of the Montages. This position information is used, for example, to highlight certain parts of the source code that correspond to values of data structures contained in the language formalization. In Figure 7, for example, the change of the value of the "current-task" function CT is animated by drawing an arrow from its old value to the new one. Similarly, after the rules of the static semantics are processed, the correspondence of the use occurrence of an identifier an its declaration position is visualized by drawing an arrow between the two positions in the "view source" window. Experiences show that especially this kind of animation is useful to explain and document the formal semantics as specified in the Montages.

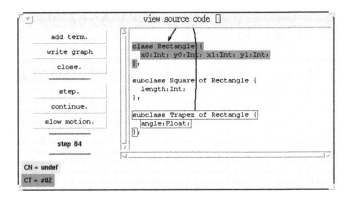

Fig. 7. Graphical animation in the Gem-Mex system

6.3   Generation of Documentation Frames

The Gem-Mex system also generates files that can be used as frames for the documentation of the language specification. Both, paper and online presentation of the language specification are automatically generated:

- LATEX documents illustrate the Montages and the grammar; such documents are easily customizable for the non-specialist user; all Montages in this paper are generated by Gem-Mex;
- HTML versions of the language specification allows to browse the specification and retrieve pieces of specification.

7   Conclusion

The implementation of component interaction mainly consists of processing input data coming from other components, analyzing this data, starting internal computation and sending output data back. Because of their flexibility and adaptability, scripting languages are often used for this task. They usually provide regular expressions for analyzing incoming data streams. This technique is very powerful, if the transformations that must be applied to the data aren't too complex. Using scripting languages in these cases often leads to nearly unmaintainable code. In this paper, we propose an alternative for the implementation of component interaction for these cases. Our approach is based an experiences in the field of the formal description of programming languages semantics using the Montages method.

We explicitly do not want to get rid of scripting languages at all, because they have been proven to be very useful for most cases of component interaction problems. Nevertheless, we think that DSLs are appropriate for implementing component interactions requiring non-trivial or at least non-linear transformations of data that is exchanged by the components to be interconnected. This assumption only holds, if an environment like Montages/Gem-Mex is used diminishing the overhead of designing DSLs and generating interpreters for them.

Originally Montages are used to give syntax and semantics of programming languages: syntax defines the possible programs and semantics defines the static and dynamic properties of programs. If used to implement component interaction, syntax defines the input format of components, while semantics is used to "code" the glue algorithms. We named this form of algorithm structuring the PoST programming style.

We have furthermore sketched, how the generated graphical tool environment, originally designed for debugging an animating the semantics of described programming languages, now serves as a tool for visualizing the component interactions.

In earlier work we designed two DSLs, which fall partly in the category of CIL. The Cubix DSL [18] is an interesting example for the proposed methodology. Cubix itself is used to initialize driver components. These components use as input CIL a query language for multi-dimensional data bases and generate as output corresponding SQL queries. The SQL-sentences are fed to a relational data base management system (DBMS). Hysdel [1] is designed in order to specify hybrid systems in a convenient way. Hysdel has two semantics: one is the direct simulation of the system for validation purposes. The second is the generation of the corresponding Matlab code. Hysdel together with the first semantics is used as a CIL for a simulation component, while the same language together with the second semantics is used as a CIL for a Matlab component.

As already mentioned in Section 3, we are applying our approach in the context of an research project with industrial partners. In this project, a commercial repository system should be connected with other components using an object definition language. First experiments with this industrial case study have shown, that our approach provides an efficient and elegant way to describe and implement component interaction, and that it represents a promising alternative to techniques traditionally used for the realization of component interaction.

References

1. M. Anlauff, A. Bemporad, S. Chakraborty, P. Kutter, D. Mignone, M. Morari, A. Pierantonio, and L. Thiele. From ease in programming to easy maintenance: Extending DSL usability with Montages, 1999. submitted for publication.

2. M. Anlauff, P. Kutter, and A. Pierantonio. Formal Aspects of and Development Environments for Montages. In M. Sellink, editor, *2nd International Workshop on the Theory and Practice of Algebraic Specifications*, Workshops in Computing, Amsterdam, 1997. Springer.

3. M. Anlauff, P. Kutter, and A. Pierantonio. Enhanced control flow graphs in Montages. In A. D.Bjoerner, M.Broy, editor, *Perspective of System Informatics*, LNCS, 1999. to appear.

4. M. Anlauff, P. W. Kutter, and A. Pierantonio. The Gem-Mex tool homepage. http://www.first.gmd.de/~ma/gem/, 1997.

5. M. Anlauff and A. Sünbül. Software architecture based composition of components. In *GI-Workshop Sicherheit und Zuverlässigkeit software-basierter Systeme*, 1999.

6. J. A. Bergstra and P. Klint. The ToolBus coordination architecture. In Ciancarini and Hankin [9], pages 75–88.

7. E. Börger, I. Durdanović, and D. Rosenzweig. Occam: Specification and Compiler Correctness. Part I: Simple Mathematical Interpreters. In U. Montanari and E. R. Olderog, editors, *Proc. PROCOMET'94 (IFIP Working Conference on Programming Concepts, Methods and Calculi)*, pages 489–508. North-Holland, 1994.

8. E. Börger and W. Schulte. Programmer Friendly Modular Definition of the Semantics of Java. In J. Alves-Foss, editor, *Formal Syntax and Semantics of Java*, LNCS. Springer, 1998.

9. P. Ciancarini and C. Hankin, editors. *Coordination and models, Proceedings of the first international conference, Cesena, Italy*, number 1061 in LNCS. Springer Verlag, 1996.

10. C. Consel and R. Marlet. Architecturing software using a methodology for language development. In C. Palamidessi, H. Glaser, and K. Meinke, editors, *Proceedings of the 10th International Symposium on Programming Language Implementation and Logic Programming*, number 1490 in LNCS, pages 170–194, Pisa, Italy, Sept. 1998.

11. F. Griffel. *Componentware*. dpunkt.verlag, 1998.

12. Y. Gurevich. Logic and the challenge of computer science. In E. Börger, editor, *Theory and Practice of Software Engineering*, pages 1–57. CS Press, 1988.

13. Y. Gurevich. Evolving Algebras 1993: Lipari Guide. In E. Börger, editor, *Specification and Validation Methods*, pages 9–36. Oxford University Press, 1995.

14. Y. Gurevich and J. Huggins. The Semantics of the C Programming Language. In E. Börger, H. Kleine Büning, G. Jäger, S. Martini, and M. M. Richter, editors, *Computer Science Logic*, volume 702 of *LNCS*, pages 274–309. Springer, 1993.

15. J. Huggins. Abstract State Machines Web Page   .
    http://www.eecs.umich.edu/gasm.

16. P. Kutter. Dynamic semantics of the programming language oberon. Technical report, ETH Zürich, 1997.

17. P. Kutter and A. Pierantonio. Montages specifications of realistic programming languages. *Journal of Universal Computer Science*, 3(5), 1997.

18. P. W. Kutter, D. Schweizer, and L. Thiele. Integrating formal domain-specific language design in the software life cycle. In *Current Trends in Applied Formal Methods*, LNCS. Springer, October 1998.

19. J. K. Ousterhout. Scripting: Higher level programming for the 21st century. *IEEE Computer*, 31(3):23–30, Mar. 1998.

20. J.-G. Schneider and O. Nierstrasz. Scripting: Higher-level programming for component-based systems. In *OOPSLA 1998*, 1998. Tutorial.

21. J.-G. Schneider and O. Nierstrasz. Components, scripts and glue. In L. Barroca, J. Hall, and P. Hall, editors, *Software Architectures – Advances and Applications*, pages 13–25. Springer, 1999.

22. A. Sünbül. Abstract state machines for the composition of architectural styles. In *Perspectives on System Informatics, PSI99*, 1999. to appear.

23. C. Wallace. The Semantics of the C++ Programming Language. In E. Börger, editor, *Specification and Validation Methods*, pages 131–164. Oxford University Press, 1995.

Analysing UML Active Classes and Associated State Machines - A Lightweight Formal Approach[*]

G. Reggio[1], E. Astesiano[1], C. Choppy[2], and H. Hussmann[3]

[1] DISI, Università di Genova - Italy
[2] LIPN, Institut Galilée - Université Paris XIII, France
[3] Department of Computer Science, Dresden University of Technology - Germany

Abstract. We propose a precise definition of UML active classes through associated labelled transition systems using the algebraic specification language CASL. We are convinced that the first step to make UML precise is to find an underlying formal model for the systems modelled by UML, and we argue that labelled transition systems are a sensible choice. This modelization will help understanding the UML constructs and will improve their use in practice. One of our aims is, in the future, to use the powerful animation and verification tools available for algebraic specifications with UML specifications. We simplify the problem of the applicability of our semantics by restricting the state machine constructs considered. This restriction does not, however, narrow the UML subset in study because the restricted constructs can be replaced by equivalent combinations of other constructs. Because of some ambiguities in the UML official semantics, we discuss the several options at hand and choose, for each ambiguous case, the semantics that either makes more sense or that allows to simplify the problem the most.

1 Introduction

The Unified Modeling Language (UML) [13] is an industry standard language for specifying software systems. This language is unique and important for several reasons:

- UML is an amalgamation of several, in the past competing, notations for object-oriented modelling. For a scientific approach, it is an ideal vehicle to discuss fundamental issues in the context of a language used in industry.
- Compared to other pragmatic modelling notations in Software Engineering, UML is very precisely defined and contains large portions which are similar to a formal specification language, as the OCL language used for the constraints.

---

[*] Work supported by CoFI (ESPRIT Working Group 29432) and MURST – Sistemi Formali per la Specifica, l'Analisi, la Verifica, la Sintesi e la Trasformazione di Sistemi Software.

T. Maibaum (Ed.): FASE 2000, LNCS 1783, pp. 127–146, 2000.

It is an important issue in Software Engineering to finally close the gap between pragmatic and formal notations and to apply methods and results from formal specification to the more formal parts of UML. This paper presents an approach contributing to this goal and has been carried out within the European "Common Framework Initiative" (CoFI) for the algebraic specification of software and systems, partially supported by the EU ESPRIT program. Within the CoFI initiative [8], which brings together research institutions from all over Europe, a specification language called "Common Algebraic Specification Language" (CASL) was developed which intends to set a standard unifying the various approaches to algebraic specification and specification of abstract data types. It is a goal of the CoFI group to closely integrate its work into the world of practical engineering. As far as specification languages are concerned, this means an integration with UML, which may form the basis for extensions or experimental alternatives to the use of OCL. This would allow for instance to specify user-defined data types that just have values but do not behave like objects, and/or to use algebraic axioms as constraints. These new constraints may cover also behavioural aspects, because there exist extensions of algebraic languages that are able to cope with them [4], whereas OCL does not seem to have any support for such aspects. The long-term perspective of this work is to build a bridge between UML specifications and the powerful animation and verification tools that are available for algebraic specifications.

To this end we need to precisely understand (and formally define) the most relevant UML features. In this paper we present the results of such formalization work for active objects with associated state machine [1], which was guided by the following ideas.

Real UML Our concern is the "real" UML (i.e., all, or better almost all, its features without simplifications and idealizations) as presented in the official OMG documentation [14] (shortly UML 1.3 from now on).

Based on an underlying model We are convinced that the first step to make UML precise is to find an underlying formal model for the systems modelled by UML, in the following called *UML-systems*.

Our conviction also comes from a similar experience the two first authors had, many years ago, when tackling the problem of the full formal definition of Ada, within the official EU project (see [1]). There too an underlying model was absolutely needed to clarify the many ambiguities and unanswered questions in the ANSI Manual.

We argue that labelled transition systems could be a sensible model choice; indeed, they were used quite successfully to model concurrent languages as Ada [1], but also a large part of Java [3].

Integrated with the formalization of the other fragments of UML The ultimate goal of this work is to have an approach by which it is easily possible to integrate semantically the most relevant diagram types. The underlying model

---

[1] Following UML terminology *state machine* is the abstract name of the construct, whereas *state chart* is the name of the corresponding diagram; here we always use the former.

plays a relevant role in that, because the UML diagrams of the various kinds either describe a part of such model or express some properties about it.

Lightweight formalization By "lightweight" we mean that we use the simplest formal tools and techniques: precisely labelled transition systems algebraically specified using a small subset of the specification language CASL (conditional specification with initial semantics). However, to further simplify the formalization CASL could be replaced by a simpler mathematical notation plus inductive definitions.

The formalization of active classes and state machines lead to perform a thorough analysis uncovering many problematic points. Indeed, the official informal semantics of UML, reported in UML 1.3, is in some points either incomplete, or ambiguous, or inconsistent or dangerous (i.e., the semantics of a part is clearly formulated but its allowed usage seem problematic from a methodological point of view). To stress this aspect and to help the reader we have used the mark pattern $\boxed{\textbf{PROBLEM} ....}$ to highlight them.

Some of these cases are "semantic variation points", i.e., points where intentionally the semantics allows for multiple interpretations. In such cases we have formalized the most general choice, in the sense that any behaviour in our semantics is a behaviour of an admissible semantic variation and a behavior of an admissible semantic variation is a behaviour in our semantics.

The use of an algebraic specification language allows for abstract, modular and easily modifiable definitions, and that could make easy to modify our semantics in some point to take into account instead a particular variation.

In Sect. 2 we shortly introduce the UML part that we consider. Then in the following sections we introduce the used formal techniques (labelled transition systems and algebraic specifications), and present step after step how we built the labelled transition system modelling the objects of an active class with an associated state machine. Due to lack of room part of the definition and the complete formal model (rather short and simple) are in [11].

2   Introducing UML: Active Classes and State Machines

The UML defines a visual language consisting of several diagram types. These diagrams are strongly interrelated by a common abstract syntax and are also related in their semantics. The semantics of the diagrams is currently defined by informal text only.

The most important diagram types for the direct description of object-oriented software systems are the following:

- Class diagrams, defining the static structure of the software system, i.e., essentially the used classes, their attributes and operations, possible associations (relationships) between them, and the inheritance structure among them. Classes can be passive, in which case the objects are just data containers. For this paper, we are interested in active classes, where each object has its own thread(s) of control.

- Statechart diagrams (state machines), defining the dynamic behaviour of an individual object of a class over its lifetime. This diagram type is very similar to traditional Statecharts. However, UML has modified syntax and semantics according to its overall concepts.
- Interaction diagrams, illustrating the interaction among several objects when carrying out jointly some use case. Interaction diagrams can be drawn either as sequence diagrams or as collaboration diagrams, with almost identical semantics but different graphical representation.

A UML *state machine* is very similar to a classical finite state machine. It depicts states, drawn as rounded boxes carrying a name, and transitions between the states. A transition is decorated by the name of an event, possibly followed by a specification of some action (after a slash symbol). The starting point for the state machine is indicated by a solid black circle, an end point by a solid circle with a surrounding line.

The complexity of UML state machines compared to traditional finite state machines comes from several origins:

- The states are interpreted in the context of an object state, so it is possible to make reference, e.g., in action expressions, to object attributes.
- There are constructs for structuring state machines in hierarchies and even concurrently executed regions.
- There are many specialized constructs like entry actions, which are fired whenever a state is entered, or state history indicators.

In order to simplify the semantical consideration in this paper, we assume the following restrictions of different kinds. Please note that none of these assumptions restricts the basic applicability of our semantics to full UML state machines!

We do not consider the following UML state machine constructs, because they can be replaced by equivalent combinations of other constructs.

Submachines We can eliminate submachines by replacing each stub state with the corresponding submachine as UML 1.3 p. 2.137 states "It is a shorthand that implies a macro-like expansion by another state machine and is semantically equivalent to a composite state".

Entry and exit actions Entry and exit actions associated with a state are a kind of shortcut with methodological implication, see, e.g., [13] p. 266, but semantically they are not relevant; indeed we can eliminate them by adding such actions to all transitions entering/leaving such state.

Internal transitions An internal transition differs from a transition whose source and target state coincide only for what concerns entry/exit actions. Because we have dropped entry/exit actions, we can drop also internal transitions. The following picture shows, on an example, how to eliminate entry actions and internal transitions.

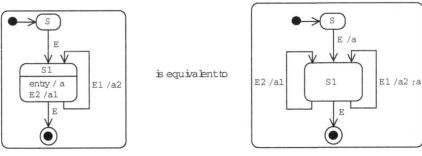

Different transitions leaving the same state having the same event trigger We can replace these transitions with compound transitions using junction states. The latter presentation seems better from a methodological point of view, because it groups together all transitions leaving a state with the same event trigger. The picture below shows on an example of this simplification.

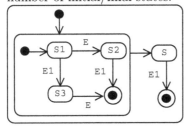
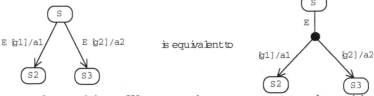
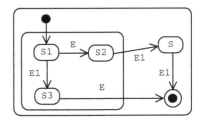

Compound transitions We assume there are no compound transitions except the complex ones and compound transitions of length two (e.g., as those needed in the above case). Indeed compound transitions are used only for presentation reasons and can be replaced by sets of simpler transitions.

Multiple initial/final states We assume that there is always a unique initial state that is placed at the top level (determine the initial situation of the class objects) and a unique final state that is placed at the top level too (when it is active the object will perform a self destruction). The remaining initial/final states can be replaced by using complex transitions. The picture below shows an example of equivalent state machines, differing only in the number of initial/final states.

Terminate action in the state machine Indeed it can be equivalently replaced by a destroy action addressed to the self.

We do not consider the following features just to save space; indeed we think that they present at the semantic level problems posed by other considered constructs.

- Operations with return type and return actions
- Synch and history states
- Generalization on the signals (type hierarchy on signals)
- Activities in states (do-activities).

3 Modelling Active Objects with Labelled Transition Systems

3.1 Labelled Transition Systems

A *labeled transition system* (shortly *lts*) is a triple $(ST, LAB, \rightarrow)$, where ST and LAB are two sets, and $\rightarrow \subseteq ST \times LAB \times ST$ is the *transition relation*. A triple $(s, l, s') \in \rightarrow$ is said to be a *transition* and is usually written $s \xrightarrow{l} s'$.

Given an lts we can associate with each $s_0 \in ST$ the tree (*transition tree*) whose root is s_0, where the order of the branches is not considered, two identically decorated subtrees with the same root are considered as a unique subtree, and if it has a node n decorated with s and $s \xrightarrow{l} s'$, then it has a node n' decorated with s' and an arc decorated with l from n to n'.

We model a process P with a transition tree determined by an lts $(ST, LAB, \rightarrow)$ and an initial state $s_0 \in ST$; the nodes in the tree represent the intermediate (interesting) situations of the life of P, and the arcs of the tree the possibilities of P of passing from one situation to another. It is important to note here that an arc (a transition) $s \xrightarrow{l} s'$ has the following meaning: P in the situation s has the *capability* of passing into the situation s' by performing a transition, where the label l represents the interaction with the environment during such a move; thus l contains information on the conditions on the environment for the capability to become effective, and on the transformation of such environment induced by the execution of the transition.

Notice that here by process we do not mean only "sequential process", but also concurrent processes that have cooperating components (that are in turn other processes – concurrent or not), and that can be modelled through particular lts, named *structured lts*. A structured lts is obtained from from another lts describing such components, say *clts*; its states are built by the states of *clts*, and its transitions starting from a state S are determined by those of *clts* starting from the subcomponents of S.

An lts may be formally specified by using the algebraic specification language CASL (see [10]) with a specification of the following form:

spec LTS =
    STATE **and** LABEL **then**
free {   **pred** $\_ \xrightarrow{\quad} \_ : State \mid Label \mid State$
      axioms ......
} **end**

whose axioms have the form $\alpha_1 \wedge \ldots \wedge \alpha_n \Rightarrow \alpha_{n+1}$, where for $i = 1, \ldots, n+1$, α_i is a positive atom (i.e., either a predicate application or an equation). The CASL construct **free** requires that the specification has an initial semantics [10]; if we forget about the algebraic apparatus, then this amount to use the conditional axioms as defining a set of inductive rules; hence the initial semantics corresponds to the inductively defined lts.

Assume we have an active class ACL with an associated state machine SM belonging to the subset of UML introduced in Sect. 2, and assume that ACL and SM are statically correct, as stated in UML 1.3. Here we present how we built the lts L modelling the objects of the class ACL, following the steps below, which will be detailed in the rest of the paper. It will be clear that our technique implies the possibility of defining a computable function associating with textual presentations of state machines the CASL specifications of the corresponding lts's.

1. determine whether L is simple or structured
2. determine the grain of the L-transitions
3. if L is structured, determine its components and the lts modelling them
4. determine the labels of L
5. determine the states of L
6. determine the transitions of L by means of conditional rules (in this case, because we are using CASL, by conditional axioms).

The constraints attached either to ACL or to SM are treated apart in Sect. 3.7, because they do not define a part of L, but just properties on it.

To avoid confusion between the states and the transitions of the state machine SM with those of the lts L, we will write from now on *L-states* and *L-transitions* when referring to those of L.

3.2   Is L Simple or Structured?

The first question is to decide whether L is simple or structured; in terms of UML semantics this means to answer the following question:

PROBLEM Does an active object correspond to a single thread of control (running concurrently with those corresponding to the other objects), or to several ones?

Unfortunately, UML 1.3 is rather ambiguous/inconsistent for what concerns this point. Indeed, somewhere it seems to suggest that there is exactly one thread, as in UML 1.3 p. 2-23, p. 2-149, p. 2-150:

> *It is possible to define state machine semantics by allowing the run-to-completion steps to be applied concurrently to the orthogonal regions of a composite state, rather than to the whole state machine. This would allow the event serialization constraint to be relaxed. However, such semantics are quite subtle and difficult to implement. Therefore, the dynamic semantics defined in this document are based on the premise that a single run-to-completion step applies to the entire state machine and includes the concurrent steps taken by concurrent regions in the active state configuration.*

Otherwise, UML 1.3 seems to assume that there are many threads, as in p. 2-133, p. 2-144, p. 3-141:

> *A concurrent transition may have multiple source states and target states. It represents a synchronization and/or a splitting of control into concurrent threads without concurrent substates.*

and in p. 2-150:

> *An event instance can arrive at a state machine that is blocked in the middle of a run-to-completion step from some other object within the same thread, in a circular fashion. This event instance can be treated by orthogonal components of the state machine that are not frozen along transitions at that time.*

However, this seems to be what is called in UML a "semantic variation point", thus we consider the most general case, by assuming that an active object may correspond to whatever number of threads, and that such threads execute their activities in an interleaving way. Thus L may be a simple lts. Perhaps, a better way to fix this point is to introduce two stereotypes: *one-thread* and *many-threads*, to allow the user to decide the amount of parallelism inside an active object.

3.3   Determining the Granularity of the L-Transitions

Using lts means that we model the behaviour of processes by splitting it into "atomic" pieces (the L-transitions); so, to define L, we must first determine the granularity of this splitting.

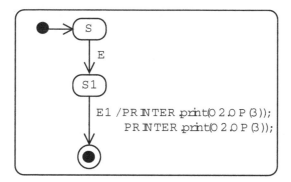

Fig. 1. A simple State Machine

PROBLEM By looking at UML 1.3 we see that there are two possibilities corresponding to different semantics.

1. each *L*-transition corresponds to performing all transitions of the state machine SM triggered by the occurrence of the same event starting from a set of active concurrent states. Because *L*-transitions are mutually exclusive, this choice corresponds to a semantics where *L*-transitions, and thus such group of transitions of SM, is implicitly understood as critical regions.
2. each *L*-transition corresponds to performing a part of a state machine transition; then the atomicity of the transitions of SM (run-to-completion condition) required by UML 1.3 will be guaranteed by the fact that, while executing the various parts of a transition triggered by an event, the involved threads cannot dispatch other events. In this case, also the parts of state machine transitions triggered by different events may be executed concurrently.

The example in Fig. 1, where we assume that there is another object O2 with an operation OP resulting in a printable value, shows an instance of this problem. Choice 1 corresponds to say that in any case pairs of identical values will be printed, whereas choice 2 allows for pairs of possibly different values (because the value returned by OP can be different in the two occasions due to the activity of O2.

Choice 2 seems to be what was intended by UML designers and so here we model it; however we could similarly also model choice 1.

3.4   Determining the *L*-Labels

The *L*-labels (labels of the lts *L*) describe the possible interactions/interchanges between the objects of the active class ACL and their external environment (the other objects comprised in the model). As a result of a careful scrutiny of UML 1.3 we can deduce that the basic ways the objects of an active class interact with the other objects are the following, and we distinguish them in "input" and "output":

input:
   – to receive a signal from another object
   – to receive an operation call from another object
   – to read an attribute of another object (+)
   – to have an attribute updated by another object (+)
   – to be destroyed by another object (+)
   – to receive from some clock the actual time (see [13] p. 475)

output:
   – to send a signal to another object
   – to call an operation of another object
   – to update an attribute of another object (+)
   – to have an attribute read by another object (+)
   – to create/destroy another object

However, UML 1.3 does not consider explicitly the interactions marked by (+), which do not correspond to send or to receive events, and does not say anything about when they can be performed (e.g., they are not considered by the state machines).

PROBLEM When may an object be destroyed?

A way to settle this point is to make "to be destroyed" an event, which may be dispatched when the machine is not in a run-to-completion-step and may appear on the transitions the state machine.

PROBLEM   The interactions corresponding to have an attribute read/ updated by other objects are problematic.
May an object have its attributes updated by some other object?
If the answer is yes, then when such update may take place? For example, is it allowed during a run-to-completion-step?
Are there any "mutual exclusion" properties on such updates? or may it happen that an object O1 updates an attribute A of O while O is updating it in a different way, or that O1 and O2 updates simultaneously A in two different ways?
May an active object have a behaviour not described by the associated state machine (see UML 1.3 p. 2-136), because another object updates its attributes? In the following example, another object may perform O.X = O.X + 1000, changing completely the behaviour specified by this state machine.

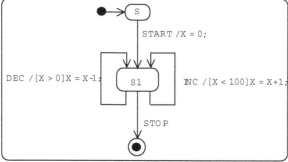

Notice also that reading/updating attributes of the other active objects is an implicit communication mechanism, thus yielding a dependency between their behaviours that is not explicitly stated in UML 1.3.

A way to overcome this point may be to fully encapsulate the attributes within the operations, i.e., an attribute of a class may be read and updated only by the class operations. As a consequence, the expressions and the actions appearing in the associated state machine may use only the object attributes, and not those of other objects. Here we take this choice, because we think that any reasonable software engineering methodology will assume it.

Then an *L*-label, which formalizes the interactions happening during an *L*-transition, will be a triple consisting of a set of input interactions, the received time, and a set of output interactions.

3.5   Determining the *L*-States

The *L*-states (states of the lts *L*) describe the intermediate relevant situations in the life of the objects of class ACL.

On the basis of UML 1.3 we found that to decide what an object has to do in a given situation we surely need to know:

- the object identity;
- the set of the states (of the state machine SM) that are active in such situation;
- whether the threads of the object are in some run-to-completion steps, and in such case which are the states that will become active at the end of such step, each one accompanied by the actions to be performed to reach it;
- the values of object attributes;
- the status of the event queue.

Thus the *L*-states must contain such information; successively, when defining the transitions we discovered that, to handle change and time events, we need also to know

- some information, named *history* in the following, on the past behaviour of the object, precisely the previous values of the attributes and the times when the various states became active.

The *L*-states are thus specified by the following CASL specification

spec L-STATE =
    IDENT **and** CONFIGURATION **and** ATTRIBUTES **and** EVENT_QUEUE **and** HISTORY
    then free types
        State ::= *Ident* : ⟨*Configuration*, *Attributes*, *History*, *Event_Queue*⟩ |
            Ident : *terminated*
    ......

where *Ident* : *terminated* are special elements representing terminated objects.

A configuration contains the set of the states that are active in a situation and of those states that will become active at the end of the current run-to-completion step (if any), the latter are accompanied by the actions to be performed to reach such states.

spec EVENT_QUEUE =
    SET[EVENT] **then**
    sort *Event_Queue*
    preds   *no_dispatchable_event* : *Event_Queue*
    %% checks whether there is no dispatchable event
        _ ∈ _ : *Event* × *Event_Queue*
    %% checks whether a given event in the queue may be selected for dispatching
    ops *put* : *Bag*[*Event*] | *Event_Queue* → *Event_Queue*
    %% adds some events to the queue
        remove : *Event* | *Event_Queue* → *Event_Queue*
    %% removes an event from the queue
    ......

> **PROBLEM** UML 1.3 explicitly calls the above structure a queue, but it also clearly states that no order must be put on the queued events (UML 1.3 p. 2-144) and so the real structure should be a multiset. This choice of terminology is problematic, because it can induce a user to assume that some order on the received events will be preserved.
> The fact that the event queue is just a bag causes other problems: an event may remain forever in the queue; time and change events may be dispatched disregarding the order in which happened (e.g., "after 10" dispatched before "after 5"); a change event is dispatched when its condition is false again; two signal or call events generated by the same state machine in some order are dispatched in the reverse order.

To fix this point, we can either change the name of the event queue in the UML documentation in something recalling its true semantics, or define a policy for deciding which event to dispatch first.

In a UML model we cannot assume anything on the order some events are received by an object (as the signal and operation calls); we conjecture that this was the motivation for avoiding to order the events in the queue. However, we think that it is better to have a mechanism ensuring that when two events are received in some order they will be dispatched in the same order, even if in many cases we do not know such order. Here, we make the most general choice, thus the event queue is just a multiset (bag) of events.

The specifications of the other components of the L-states are reported in [11].

3.6   Determining the L-Transitions

An L-transition, i.e., a transition of the lts L, corresponds to

1. either to dispatch an event,
2. or to execute an action,
3. or to receive some events; such events are either received from outside (signals and operation calls) or generated locally (self sent signals and operation calls, change and time events),
4. or to be destroyed by dispatching a special event.

Moreover, (3) may be also performed simultaneously with (1) and (2), because we cannot delay the reception of events.

It is important to notice that the L-transitions and the transitions of the state machine SM are different in nature and are not in a bijective correspondence. To clarify such relationship we report in Fig. 2 a fragment of the transition tree (see Sect. 3.1) associated with the simple state machine of Fig. 1 showing only the relevant parts of the states, where it is possible to see that one state machine transition corresponds to many L-transitions.

The L-transitions are formally defined by the axioms of an algebraic specification of the following form

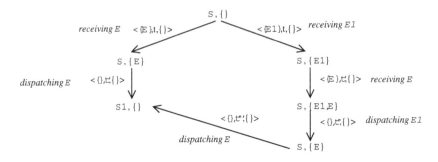

Fig. 2. A fragment of a transition tree

spec L-SPEC =
    L-LABEL **and** L-STATE **then**
free { **pred** _ $\xrightarrow{\ \ }$ _ : *State* × *Label* × *State*
    axioms   . . . . . . *cond* $\Rightarrow$ $s \xrightarrow{\ l\ } s'$ . . . . . .

In the following subsections we give the axioms corresponding to the four cases above To master complexity and to improve readability we use several auxiliary operations in such axioms, whose name is written in sans serif font. Some relevant problems come to light when defining some of such operations, and thus we consider them explicitly in Sect. 4. The others are reported in [11].

Dispatching an Event If the active object is not fully frozen executing some run-to-completion steps (checked by *not_frozen*), an event *ev* is in the event queue ready to be dispatched (checked by *dispatchable*), then there is an *L*-transition, with the label made by the events received from outside *in_evs*, and the time *t*, where the history was extended, and all received events was put in the event queue, as described by Receive_Events.

Recall that Dispatch(*ev*, *conf*, *e_queue*) = *conf₁*, *e_queue₁* means that dispatching event *ev* in the configuration *conf* changes it to *conf₁* and changes *e_queue* to *e_queue₁*.

$not\_frozen(conf) \land dispatchable(ev, e\_queue) \land$
$\mathsf{Dispatch}(ev, conf, e\_queue) = conf_1, e\_queue_1 \Rightarrow$
$id : \langle conf, attrs, history, e\_queue \rangle \xrightarrow{\langle in\_evs, t, \emptyset \rangle} id : \langle attrs, conf_1, history_1, e\_queue_2 \rangle$
where
    $e\_queue_2 = \mathsf{Receive\_Events}(e\_queue_1, in\_evs, attrs, history, t)$
    $history_1 = \langle active\_states(conf), attrs, \rangle, t \rangle \& history$

Executing an Action If the active object is executing at least a run-to-completion step, (checked by *frozen*), then there is an *L*-transition, with the label resulting from the events received from outside *in_evs*, the time *t*, and the set of events generated in the action to be propagated outside *out_evs*, where the attributes are updated due to executed action, the history was extended, and all received events was put in the event queue, as described by Receive_Events.

Exec($id, attrs, conf$) = $conf_1, attrs_1, out\_evs, loc\_evs$ means that the object id with configuration $conf$ executes an action changing its configuration to $conf_1$, updating its attributes to $attrs_1$ and producing the set of output events out_evs and the set of local events loc_evs.

$$frozen(conf) \land \text{Exec}(id, attrs, conf) = conf_1, attrs_1, out\_evs, loc\_evs \Rightarrow$$

$$id : \langle conf, attrs, history, e\_queue \rangle \xrightarrow{\langle in\_evs, t, out\_evs \rangle} id : \langle attrs_1, conf_1, history_1, e\_queue_1 \rangle$$

where

$e\_queue_1 = \text{Receive\_Events}(e\_queue, in\_evs \cup loc\_evs, attrs, history, t)$

$history_1 = \langle active\_states(conf), attrs, \rangle, t \rangle \,\&\, history$

Receiving Some Events If the active object is not executing any run-to-completion step (checked by $\neg\ frozen$), the event queue is empty (checked by $no\_dispatchable\_event$), then there is an L-transition, with the label resulting from the set of events received from outside in_evs and the time t, where the history was extended, and all received events was put in the event queue, as described by Receive_Events.

$$\neg\ frozen(conf) \land no\_dispatchable\_event(e\_queue) \Rightarrow$$

$$id : \langle conf, attrs, history, e\_queue \rangle \xrightarrow{\langle in\_evs, t, \emptyset \rangle} id : \langle attrs, conf, history_1, e\_queue_1 \rangle$$

where

$e\_queue_1 = \text{Receive\_Events}(e\_queue, in\_evs, attrs, history, t)$

$history_1 = \langle active\_states(conf), attrs, \rangle, t \rangle \,\&\, history$

Being Destroyed We consider a destruction request as an event and assume that an active object cannot be destroyed while it is fully frozen executing run-to-completion steps (checked by not_frozen).

$$not\_frozen(conf) \land dispatchable(destroy, e\_queue) \Rightarrow$$

$$id : \langle conf, attrs, history, e\_queue \rangle \xrightarrow{\langle in\_evs, t, \emptyset \rangle} id : terminated$$

3.7   Constraints

Constraints may be attached to any element of a UML model. For what concerns the fragment of UML considered in this paper we have constraints in the class diagram, attached to the class icon (e.g., invariants) and to the operations (e.g., pre-post conditions), and in the state machine (e.g., invariants). The language for expressing the constraints is not fixed in UML (though OCL is the most used), however the semantics of the constraints is precisely settled; indeed UML 1.3 p. 2-29,2-30 states:

A constraint is a semantic condition or restriction expressed in text. In the metamodel, a Constraint is a BooleanExpression on an associated ModelElement(s) which must be true for the model to be well formed. ... Note that a Constraint is an assertion, not an executable mechanism. It indicates a restriction that must be enforced by correct design of a system.

Such an idea of constraint may be easily formalized in our setting: the semantics of a constraint attached either to ACL or to SM is a property on L.

The CASL formulae allow to express a rich set of relevant properties (recall that the underlying logic of CASL is many sorted partial first-order logic), and CASL extensions with temporal logic combinators, based on [4] are under development. Moreover the constraints expressed using OCL may be translated into CASL without too many problems.

Assume we have the constraints $C_1, \ldots, C_n$ attached either to ACL or to SM, then the UML model containing ACL and SM is well formed iff for $i = 1, \ldots, n$, $L \models \Phi_i$, where Φ_i is the CASL formula corresponding to C_i. Techniques and tools developed for algebraic specification languages may help to verify the well-formedness of UML models.

PROBLEM The use of constraints without a proper discipline may be problematic, as in the following case, where the constraint attached to the icon of class C is an invariant that must hold always, and so must be respected also by the transitions triggered by the calls to OP and OP1. These inconsistencies may be hard to detect, because the problematic constraints are in the class diagram, while the state machine violating them is given elsewhere.

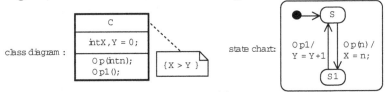

In UML there are also other constraint-like constructs raising similar problems; as the query qualification for operations (requiring that an operation does not modify the state of the object), or the "specifications" for signal receptions (expressing properties on the effects of receiving such signal). Also in these cases the behaviour described by the state machine may be in contrast with them.

We think that a way to settle those problems is to develop a clear methodology for using these constraints, making precise their role and their use them in the development process.

4   Auxiliary Functions

Receive_Events : *Event_Queue* × *Set[Event]* × *Attributes* × *History* × *Time* → *Event_Queue*

Receive_Events(e_queue, evs, $attrs$, $history$, t) = e_queue_1 means that e_queue_1 is e_queue updated by putting in it all received events: the signal and operation call events are given by a function parameter (evs), the time events are detected using t and $history$ (by TimeOccur), and the change events are detected by using $attrs$ and $history$ (by ChangeOccur).

PROBLEM May operation calls to other objects appear within the expressions of change and time events? May such expressions have side effects ?
If the answer is yes, then we can have more hidden constraints on the mutual behaviour of objects (e.g., a synchronous operation call in the expression of a change event may block an object), and, due to the side effects, the behaviour of the whole system may be scarcely predictable. We assume no, and this is the reason for the above simple functionality of Receive_Events.

Receive_Events(e_queue, evs, $attrs$, $history$, t) =

put(TimeOccur(t, $history$) $\cup$ ChangeOccur($attrs$, $history$) $\cup$ evs, e_queue)

We report the definitions of TimeOccur and of ChangeOccur in [11].

Dispatch : *Event* $\times$ *Configuration* $\times$ *Event_Queue* $\rightarrow$ *Configuration* $\times$ *Event_Queue*

Dispatch(ev, $conf$, e_queue) = $conf_1$, e_queue_1 means that dispatching event ev in the configuration $conf$ changes it to $conf_1$ and changes e_queue to e_queue_1.

It is defined by cases, and here we report the most relevant ones, the others are reported in [11].

Some transitions triggered by an event Assume that in the state machine SM there are the following branched transitions triggered by E starting from the states belonging to *Sset*

If *Sset* $\cup$ *Sset'* is the set of the active states, and $cond_{q_i}^i$ holds for $i = 1, \ldots, h$ ($1 \le h \le r$), then the active object may start a run-to-completion step going to perform the actions $act_{q_i}^i$ ($i = 1, \ldots, h$) and to reach the states $S_{q_i}^i$ ($i = 1, \ldots, h$) (the actual parameters of the event are substituted for its formal parameters within the actions to be performed). Notice that we do not require that $cond_{q_i}^i$ does not hold for $i = h + 1, \ldots, r$, $q = k_1^i, \ldots, k_{r_i}^i$.

$active\_states(conf) = Sset \cup Sset' \wedge \bigwedge_{i=1}^{h} \mathsf{Eval}(cond_{q_i}^i[p_j/x_j], attrs) = True \Rightarrow$

Dispatch($E(p_1, \ldots, p_n)$, $conf$, e_queue) = $conf_1$, $remove(E(p_1, \ldots, p_n), e\_queue)$

where

$conf_1 = run(\ldots run(conf, S_i, act_{q_1}^1[p_j/x_j], S_{q_1}^1)\ldots, act_{q_h}^h[p_j/x_j], S_{q_h}^h)$

active_states and *run* are operations of the specification CONFIGURATION returning respectively the active states of the state machine and recording the start of a run-to-completion step, going from an active state into another one performing a given action.

PROBLEM What to do if the conditions appearing on the transitions may have side effects, for example because they include operation calls ? In such case the order of evaluating the conditions and how many attempts have been done before to find those that hold are semantically relevant, and also in this case the behaviour of the whole system may become scarcely predictable.

Here we assume that the conditions on the transitions have no side effects.

PROBLEM What to do when the dispatched event is an operation call for whom also a method has been defined in the class ACL?

The solution in this case is just to prohibit to have a method for the operation appearing in some transition, and it is supported, e.g., by [13] p. 369 and other UML sources ([12]).

PROBLEM A similar problem is posed by the case below: what will happen when someone calls method Op, whose body is described by the note attached to its name in the class diagram? On one hand, assuming that such call is never answered, may lead to produce wrong UML models, because the other classes assume that Op is an available service, since it appears in the class icon. On the other hand, answering it (perhaps only when the machine is not in a run-to-completion-step) seems in contrast with the role of the state machine (UML 1.3 p. 2-136).

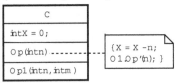

In general operations with an associated method seem to be problematic for the active classes, and so it could be sensible to drop them.

No transitions triggered by a deferred event Assume that in the state machine SM there are no transitions starting from states belonging to *Sset* triggered by E and that E is deferred in some elements of *Sset*.

PROBLEM UML 1.3 does not say what to do when dispatching E in such case. The possible choices are:
− remove it from the event queue
− put it back in the event queue
− put it back in the event queue, but only for the states in which it was deferred. Here we assume that it is deferred, and that after it will be available for any state; however, notice, that we could formally handle also the first cases, whereas to consider the last we need to assume that there are many threads in an object with the relative event queues (one for each active state).

If the active states are *Sset*, then the event $E(p_1, \ldots, p_n)$ is left in the event queue for future use.

$$active\_states(conf) = Sset \Rightarrow$$
$$\mathsf{Dispatch}(E(p_1, \ldots, p_n), conf, e\_queue) = conf, e\_queue$$

5   Conclusions and Related Work

The task of formalizing UML has been addressed using various available formal techniques, as we will discuss below. Most of these attempts are complementary, because they approach the task from different viewpoints and aims.

In this respect our work has several distinguishing features. First of all we are using a very elementary and well-known machinery, namely lts (which are at the basis of formalisms like CCS), and conditional algebraic specifications. As for Ada, [1], this simple model provides a powerful setting for revealing ambiguities, incompleteness and perhaps questionable features, both from the purely techni- cal and the methodological point of view. For example, we have discussed several naturally arising questions concerning UML, such as "what is the behaviour of an object with several active subthreads?", and "does the run to completion ex- ecution of a state machine transition imply that a transition is a kind of critical region?"

Furthermore we have used a modular framework where the various possible interpretations of the aspects of UML (and of its many variants) may be made precise and the various problems exemplified and discussed also with users lack- ing a formal background (a lightweight formal method approach).

Within the "Precise UML" group and also outside, several proposals for formalizing UML or parts of them have been presented; we briefly report on some paradigmatic directions.

Some papers are addressing specific questions; for example [5] shows how to use graph rewriting techniques to transform UML state machines into another simplified machine (a kind of normal form); but, e.g., the execution of actions is not considered. That paper could be seen as providing a method for precisely handling the constructs not considered here, because can be derived from others.

Some other papers try to formalize UML by using a particular specifica- tion language. For example, as in [6], using Real-Time Action Logic, a form of real-time temporal logic. With respect to these approaches we put less emphasis on the specification language and more on the underlying model, because we think that in this setting it is easier to explain UML features (also the possi- ble problems) and to derive a revised informal presentation. [7] also presents a formalization of the UML state machines using PROMELA, the specification language for the model checker SPIN.

The relevance of the underlying model for making precise UML has been considered in [2], where a different model, a kind of stream processing function, is used. But the main aim there is methodological: how a software engineering method can benefit from an integrative mathematical foundation. While one of the main results of our work could be a basis for a revised reference manual for UML.

Finally, we have not considered the large number of papers on the semantics of classical state machines (as those supported by the Statemate tool), because the semantics of the UML state machines is rather different; e.g., in the former the events are dispatched as soon as they are received, whereas they are enqueued (also forever) before being dispatched following some policy in UML (see [13] page 440).

We plan to go on analysing UML, to give a sound basis for our work in the CoFI project, trying to give an underlying formal (lightweight) model to the other constituents of a UML-system, i.e., to instances of passive classes and the system itself, and to consider the other kinds of diagrams, as class, sequence and collaboration.

The modular structure of our formalization of UML and the use of the algebraic specification CASL, allows us to easily modify the formalization of UML presented here to accommodate and to analyse particular choices for the variation points, and also the changes surely introduced by future versions.

This work could be also the basis for developing a "clean" profile for UML (see [9]), i.e., a variant of UML defined by extending it, using the various UML mechanisms as stereotypes, and by specializing its semantics, by means of natural language, without any of the problems presented here.

References

[1] E. Astesiano, A. Giovini, F. Mazzanti, G. Reggio, and E. Zucca. The Ada Challenge for New Formal Semantic Techniques. In *Ada: Managing the Transition, Proc. of the Ada-Europe Conference, Edimburgh, 1986*, pages 239–248. University Press, Cambridge, 1986.

[2] R. Breu, R. Grosu, F. Huber, B. Rumpe, and W. Schwerin. Systems, Views and Models of UML. In M. Schader and A. Korthaus, editors, *The Unified Modeling Language, Technical Aspects and Applications*. Physica Verlag, Heidelberg, 1998.

[3] E. Coscia and G. Reggio. A Proposal for a Semantics of a Subset of Multi-Threaded Good Java Programs. Technical report, Imperial College - London, 1998.

[4] G. Costa and G. Reggio. Specification of Abstract Dynamic Data Types: A Temporal Logic Approach. *T.C.S.*, 173(2):513–554, 1997.

[5] M. Gogolla and F. Parisi-Presicce. State Diagrams in UML- A Formal Semantics using Graph Transformation. In M. Broy, D. Coleman, T. Maibaum, and B. Rumpe, editors, *Proc. ICSE'98 Workshop on Precise Semantics of Modeling Techniques(PSMT'98)*, Technical Report TUM-I9803, 1998.

[6] K. Lano and J. Bicarregui. Formalising the UML in Structured Temporal Theories. In B. Rumpe H. Kilov, editor, *Proc. of Second ECOOP Workshop on Precise Behavioral Semantics, ECOOP'98*, Munich, Germany, 1998.

[7] J. Lillius and I Paltor. Formalising UML State Machines for Model Checking. In R France and B. Rumpe, editors, *Proc. UML'99*, LNCS. Springer Verlag, Berlin, 1999.

[8] P.D. Mosses. CoFI: The Common Framework Initiative for Algebraic Specification and Development. In M. Bidoit and M. Dauchet, editors, *Proc. TAPSOFT '97*, number 1214 in LNCS, pages 115–137, Berlin, 1997. Springer Verlag.

[9] OMG.   White   paper   on   the   Profile   Mechanism   – Version   1.0. http://uml.shl.com/u2wg/default.htm, 1999.

[10] The   CoFI   Task   Group   on   Language   Design.   CASL   Summary.   Version   1.0.   Technical   report,   1998.   Available   on http://www.brics.dk/Projects/CoFI/Documents//Summary/.

[11] G. Reggio, E. Astesiano, C. Choppy, and H. Hussmann. A CASL Formal Definition of UML Active Classes and Associated State Machines. Technical Report DISI-TR-99-16, DISI – Università di Genova, Italy, 1999.

[12] J. Rumbaugh. Some questions relating to actions and their parameter, and relating to signals. Private communication, 1999.

[13] J. Rumbaugh, I. Jacobson, and G. Booch. *The Unified Modeling Language Reference Manual*. Object Technology Series. Addison-Wesley, 1999.

[14] UML Revision Task Force. *OMG UML Specification*, 1999. Available at http://uml.shl.com.

Software as Learning:
Quality Factors and Life-Cycle Revised[*]

José Hernández-Orallo and Mª José Ramírez-Quintana

Universitat Politècnica de València. Dep. de Sistemes Informàtics i Computació
Camí de Vera s/n, E-46071, València, Spain
E-mail: {jorallo, mramirez}@dsic.upv.es

Abstract. In this paper Software Development (SD) is understood explicitly as a learning process, which relies much more on induction than deduction, with the main goal of being predictive to requirements evolution. Concretely, classical processes from philosophy of science and machine learning such as hypothesis generation, refinement, confirmation and revision have their counterpart in requirement engineering, program construction, validation and modification in SD, respectively. Consequently, we have investigated the appropriateness for software modelling of the most important paradigms of modelling selection in machine learning. Under the notion of incremental learning, we introduce a new factor, predictiveness, as the ability to foresee future changes in the specification, thereby reducing the number of revisions. As a result, other quality factors are revised. Finally, a predictive software life cycle is outlined as an incremental learning session, which may or may not be automated.

1 Introduction

Software engineering was considered a pure science just two or three decades ago. Theoretical and formal methods were prevalent. Nowadays, we have a much more realistic conception of software engineering as an experimental science [6]. Empirical studies of real problems are encouraged and their conclusions are usually much more successful in practice than theoretical results. Moreover, many times theoretical studies are not applicable because in the end they do not model the software construction process.

In our opinion, the formal methods in software engineering cannot be fully exploited due to still frequent conceptions of software as being "from specification to final product". This does not take maintenance nor the generation of that specification into account.

Fortunately, there is an increasing interest in requirements elicitation and evolution as the most important topics in software engineering. *Requirements Engineering* has made some important things patently clear: the need to take the *context* of a computer

---

[*] This work has been partially supported by CICYT under grant TIC 98-0445-C03-C1.

T. Maibaum (Ed.): FASE 2000, LNCS 1783, pp. 147-162, 2000.

system into consideration, i.e., *"the real-world environment in which the system operates, including the social structure and the people therein"* and the fact *"that requirements are always incomplete; each stage involves identifying new requirements based on experiences from previous stages... and requirements and design affect each other"* [8].

The other two fundamental (and more classical) areas of research for improving the economics of software have been reusability and modifiability, the latter being more relevant when a particular system is already implemented. The maintenance cost is greatly reduced by improving the modifiability and/or extensibility software quality factors. Another neglected but fundamental question is whether we are able to reduce the modification probability. The idea is to 'predict' requirement evolution as much as possible, in order to minimise the remaking of software as a trace of this evolution. In order to gain greater benefits, this "predictive model of requirements" should be made upon previous models by *reusing* parts of other specifications and taking context into account.

It should be explicitly stated that this predictive character of the model must be preserved during the remainder of the life-cycle: the design must be conceived to maintain the generality of the model, validation must be made according to this general model, and, more importantly, future modifications must consist of coherent revisions, not extensional 'patches' to the model.

With the appearance of new approaches, such as adaptive software [28] or intelligent software [30], which include techniques and languages for further generalisation, an empirical and theoretical study of when a generalisation of the model is useful and how it should be done seems necessary. The flippancy here would be to start from scratch or to reinvent the wheel. As we will see in the following sections, predictive modelling in particular and philosophy of science in general historically been able to provide us very useful terminology and tools to select the most likely or the most informative model.

This paper tries to emphasise the benefits of adapting the paradigm of theory construction to software, and to recognise and situate the role of induction in software engineering. In fact, recent popular subjects in the field such as adaptive software or intelligent software are in essence inductive. However, none of them use inductive tools and techniques in an explicit way.

Induction, as we use throughout this paper, is the process of theory abstraction from facts. Karl Popper proposed [36] the concept of *verisimilitude* as the level of agreement with the facts. Since there are an infinite number of theories which cover a finite number of examples, the question of verisimilitude must be contrasted with all the possible future examples that may appear in a given context. The quandary of whether there is any way to know, a priori, if a given hypothesis will be followed by future experiences in that context is obvious. If we know the initial distribution of hypotheses in that context, the plausibility of the hypothesis can be obtained in a Bayesian way. Since this initial distribution is generally unknown, many different measures of the quality of theories have been proposed in philosophy of science and Machine Learning (ML), generally in an informal way. From these, there are two main trends ([39]): *descriptional induction* ([5]), which is usually related to the simplicity criterion (or Occam's Razor) and the view of learning as compression; and *explanatory induction* ([39]), which is more closely related to coherence, cohesion or 'consilience' criteria ([41]).

In 1978, Rissanen formalised Occam's Razor under the Minimum Description Length (MDL) principle, quickly spreading over the theory and practice of ML and predictive modelling. In his later formulation ([5]), the MDL principle advocates that the best description of a given data is the shortest one. Apart from all the methodological advantages of simplicity, the major reason for using the MDL principle is that it usually avoids over-specialisation (underfitting) and over-generalisation (overfitting). From here it is usually argued that *"the shorter the hypothesis the more predictable it is"*. On the contrary, 'consilience' or coherence refer to the idea that the data must be covered by the same general rule. Thagard ([41]) postulated that *"explanatory coherence"* is more important for durability than prediction and confirmation: *"a hypothesis exhibits explanatory coherence with another if it is explained by the other, explains the other, is used with the other in explaining other propositions, or if both participate in analogous explanations"*. Another related notion is that of intensionality ([19]), which is based on the avoidance of extensional patches to the theory.

The convenience of both these trends will be studied for the case of software, in order to obtain predictive and coherent models for the requirements which will improve software quality factors. In the ML literature [31], there is a classical paradigm that is necessary for problems of medium or large complexity: incremental learning. The evidence is obtained incrementally and new evidence can appear which may force the revision of the model. Revision is then the most important process in incremental learning and is motivated by two kinds of errors: anomalies (cases which are not explained by the current theory) and novelties (new cases which are not covered). The incremental paradigm is the most appropriate one for software.

The paper is organised as follows. In Section 2 we introduce an analogy between software development and theory induction, which we contrast with previous (and very debated) analogies between software development and deduction and mathematics.

Section 3 reviews many software quality factors under the inductive paradigm. A new quality factor, 'predictiveness', is defined and is related to other software quality factors such as functionality, validation, reusability, modifiability, ...

Section 4 introduces a new life-cycle as an incremental learning session which attempts to reduce prediction errors. The automation is discussed, as applied to declarative programming (logic programming), because the techniques and stages required for the new life-cycle (ILP, evaluation, transformation, revision, etc.) are much more mature than in any other paradigm.

Finally, Section 5 concludes the paper with a discussion of the practical relevance of this work and future directions.

2   Programs as Scientific Theories

The statement "programs are scientific theories" or, alternatively, "software is a learning process" summarises the main idea developed in this section. Before presenting this analogy, we will review the most well-known analogies in order to understand software development. In our opinion, these analogies have failed to capture the essence of software, although partial mappings have been useful.

2.1 Existing Analogies

The use of analogies with pure mathematics to formalise the processes of computer programming was greatly influenced and promoted by the seminal paper from Hoare [24]. This first analogy, known as "Verifiers' Analogy", established that proofs are to theorems as verifications are to programs:

Verifiers' Analogy

Mathematics		Programming
theorem	↔	program
proof	↔	verification

After the first successes of some simple programs of algorithmic nature, the debate began precisely from the side of mathematics, exemplarised by the influential paper by De Millo, Lipton and Perlis [13]. The preceding analogy was criticised and replaced by the following one, which is based on the idea that programs are formal whereas the requirements for a program are informal:

De Millo-Lipton-Perlis Analogy

Mathematics		Programming
theorem	↔	specification
proof	↔	program
imaginary formal demonstration	↔	verification

The new trends in automated programming, popularised by the logic programming community, were very difficult to conciliate with an analogy with mathematics as a social science. Thus, the analogy was revised once again [38]:

Automated Programming Analogy

Mathematics		Programming
problem	↔	specification
theorem	↔	program
proof	↔	program derivation

However, Colburn [11] affirms that "for unless there is some sort of independent guarantee that the program specifications, no matter how formally rendered, actually specify a program which solves the problem, one must run the program to determine whether the solution design embodied by the specification is correct". In this way, he postulates that software is the final test for validating the specification.

Finally, Fetzer reopened the debate and introduced an analogy between computer programs and scientific theories [17]:

Fetzer's Analogy

	Mathematical Proofs	Scientific Theories	Computer Programs
Syntactic Entities:	Yes	Yes	Yes
Semantic Significance:	No	Yes	Yes
Causal Capability:	No	No	Yes

In our opinion, the difference between scientific theories and programs in *causal capability* disappears if we consider software to be a learning process (which shares the same paradigm with philosophy of science but *has* causal capability), where the learned theory (the program) can be used to interact with the environment.

2.2 Scientific Theories and Programs

The assumption that there is an "independent guarantee" that the specification is correct for a given problem is rather optimistic in the context of modern software development, where requirements and, consequently, applications are very complex. It is impossible to completely and definitely establish the intended behaviour that the system should show.

Current methodologies end up accepting the dynamic character of requirements, and include loops back to each of the stages, including a loop to requirement elicitation. Then it is finally recognised that requirements are never completely stated, that they evolve and that they are related to the environment, the context of specifications, the 'reality'.

The same idea is implicitly suggested by the maxim that "*testing can be used to show the presence of bugs, but never to show their absence*" [15], although applied to a restricted view of software. The extended maxim "requirements cannot be fully validated, just invalidated" conforms perfectly with Popper's conception of scientific methodology [36] where scientific hypotheses can possibly be shown to be false but can never be shown to be true.

This impels us to looking for more realistic conceptions of programming. We propose a new analogy between scientific methodology and programming methodology which shows the numerous links that can be established:

Programs as Scientific Theories Analogy

Science		Programming
reality	↔	requirements context
problem	↔	problem
experimentation data	↔	cases / interviews / scenarios
construed evidence	↔	requirements
evaluation	↔	analysis
best hypothesis	↔	specification
refinement	↔	transformation
theory	↔	program
verisimilitude	↔	correctness
anomalies	↔	exceptions

confirmatory experiments	↔	testing
confirmation	↔	validation
revision	↔	modification
background knowledge	↔	SW. repositories
technical books	↔	technical/programmer's doc.
science text books	↔	user documentation

The difference between best hypothesis and theory in Science is less than the difference between specification and program in software engineering. In both cases, however, a hypothesis-specification is not usually predictive/operational and it must be refined/transformed into a more manageable and applicable form, by the use of mathematisation/formalisation and a proper engagement with the background knowledge / repositories. As we have stated, the analogy should be well understood by regarding programs not only as simple scientific theories which predict the outputs for given inputs but also as systems that interact with an environment or reality according to the ontology and hypotheses that have been learned, i.e., interactive learning systems. This 'new' analogy offers many equivalences to work on and many of the results in one field can be applied to the other. Therefore, following this comparison, Figure 1 shows how deduction and induction are more or less used depending on the stage of the development of a scientific theory or a software system.

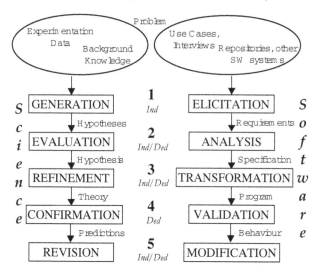

Fig. 1. Main stages in scientific theories and software systems development.

It is remarkable that, in some way, the philosophy of science and software engineering are complementary in experience and techniques because they have focused primarily on different stages.

For instance, the third and fourth stages (of a more engineering character) have been thoroughly addressed on the software side, especially the stage that is called 'transformation', which includes design and codification. In *automated programming*, this transformation stage is the most important one, because it is not convenient to *directly* execute the specification, and it is necessary to transform it by using program transformation techniques and further analyses [35]. The final program *evolves* from the specification to better performance characteristics, while still preserving semantics.

On the contrary, the first and second stages have been traditionally addressed by philosophy of science. Only recently these stages have been taken into consideration and they are included in the software construction paradigm under the banner of "requirement engineering". However, it is not usually recognised in the literature that the techniques should be mainly inductive. The information transmitted from the user to the developer is incomplete and inexact. The developer must complete and explain it by inductive methods. This inference process has recently given name to a different approach to software engineering: inductive programming [33]. According to Partridge: "*The science of creating software is based on deductive methods. But induction, deduction's ignored sibling, could have a profound effect on the future development of computer science theory and practice*". In our opinion, this effect will come true if both inferences can be effectively combined.

Finally, our concern is not to present software engineering as an experimental science but to show that each program can be seen as a scientific theory and that each software problem can be seen as a learning problem. We will work under this analogy for the rest of the paper, mostly investigating the implications from theory formation and revision to program generation and modification.

From theory formation we will translate the debate between descriptive and explanatory approaches to theory construction in science (see [39] for some contrasted positions in this debate). From theory revision (and abduction) we will try to identify which kind of software modifications are preferable: minimal extensional modifications or deeper coherent ones.

3   A Revision of Software Quality Factors

As we stated above, the role of the specification as a tentative hypothesis forces a revision of many software quality factors. The factors that are more directly related to the compliance with the specification are functionality, completeness, correctness, reliability and robustness. Other factors which are indirectly related such as testability, traceability, adaptability, flexibility, reusability, generality, maintainability /modifiability, practical modularity/granularity, ideal modularity or module independence, coupling, cohesion, efficiency/performance, comprehensibility and intelligibility will be discussed later[1].

The main factors are classically defined in terms of "the specification" or "requirements" ([26], [27]):

- *Functionality*: the degree to which a system "satisfies stated or implied needs".

---

[1] For the factors that are not explicitly defined here, we refer to [26] and [27].

- *Completeness*: usually assumed in functionality, it is the degree to which a system or component implements all required capabilities.
- *Correctness*: is the fundamental part of functionality (jointly with completeness): the degree to which software, documentation, or other items *meet specified requirements* (classical view) or *meet user needs and expectations*, whether specified or not (modern view).
- *Reliability*: "the ability of a component to perform its required functions under stated conditions for a specified period of time".
- *Robustness*: "the degree to which a system or component can function correctly in the presence of invalid inputs or stressful environmental conditions".

Most of them deal with "stated or implied needs", "required capabilities", "specified requirements", "expectations, whether specified or not" and "required functions". However, the question arises of what software feature measures the correctness of this specification or specified requirement wrt. the "stated or implied needs".

In our opinion, a new factor is required to measure the goodness of the requirement elicitation stage and the whole process of specification (hypothesis) revision during the overall life-cycle:

Definition 3.1. Software Predictiveness

Predictiveness is the degree to which the software system predicts present and future requirements in the context where the requirements are originated.

The key issue is that the behaviour of a program is seen as a prediction given from the hypothetical specification. The analogy from incremental learning is now as follows: software construction is an *incremental* process. The new goal is not necessarily to achieve the highest accuracy at the end of a first prototype or version (or even with the 'last' version), but to maximise the cumulative benefits (prediction hits) obtained *throughout* the entire life of the software.

Consequently, some concepts must be redefined. If we regard functionality equivalent to predictive accuracy, we must reconsider the components of functionality.

Functionality or *predictiveness* includes:

- *correctness* (prediction for normal situations),
- *robustness* (prediction for environment or abnormal situations),
- *reliability* (minimisation of anomalies), and
- *completeness* (minimisation of novelties).

Since a *modification* is required when there is a lack of *functionality*, modifiability (which includes extensibility) should cover both prediction errors (anomalies) and failure to predict (novelties). The former are motivated by a lack of correctness or reliability and the latter by a failure of robustness or completeness.

Finally, maintainability is redefined as considering both the predictiveness and modifiability factors. That is to say, it weights the frequency and scope of modifications. For instance, a software system can be non predictive at all and highly modifiable, resulting in a maintainable software. Conversely, a software system can be not modifiable at all but, if it has been predictive for changing requirements, then the resulting cost of maintenance could still be low.

Next we deal with how the learning/science analogy for software helps to redefined many of these and other quality factors in a more detailed way.

3.1 Functionality and Validation

In the reorganisation made after the introduction of predictiveness, one may still question why we have included reliability inside functionality. The reason that has been argued is that, since the requirements are never definite, reliability depends more on the accuracy of the requirements elicitation than on the rest of the design and implementation phases. However, the relationship between these later phases and reliability is, at first glance, not related to the predictiveness factor. We will see that this is not the case, and even the later phases of the software life-cycle can be better understood using the analogy with a learning session.

For example, it is widely accepted that redundancy compromises reliability because inconsistencies can easily arise, and checking them is *sparse* and consequently more difficult. An initial reflection would suggest that the removal of redundancies is the key to reliability. In [42], Gerard Wolff establishes the correlation between software and information compression in a direct way, arguing that "*the process of designing well structured software may be seen as a process of information compression*". Although the parallel between automated programming and pattern recognition was recognised by Banerji in the eighties [4], Wolff reminds us that patterns such as iteration, function, procedure or sub-routine, and the idea of recursion are all forms of information compression. The same applies to object-oriented abstraction through the use of inheritance.

The paradox arises when conditional statements (*if.. then.. else* and cases) are well justified by this approach. However, it has been recognised that the number of "cases" or "exceptions" in software increases the possibility of errors (and makes modifiability difficult). Moreover, there is a maintainability measure, known as *cyclomatic complexity* [25], which measures exactly this, the number of conditions in the source.

In this way, an intensional model (with few exceptions) seems much easier to check. In particular, apart from reusability, object-oriented methodologies (and especially the polymorphism technique) improve reliability because they generally eliminate long cases and exceptions with a considerable increase in code length.

As the software becomes more complex and requirements evolve during software validation, validation is finally applied to a whole which can be influenced by requirements elicitation errors, design errors or implementation errors. However, the idea of intensional and coherent models and structures applies to all the stages and must be preserved from specification to final code.

3.2 Reusability

The coherence and simplicity criteria are have long been known to improve reusability (keep in mind the claims *keep methods coherent* and *keep methods small* [37]). However, intensionality is more important for reusability than simplicity. For instance, we can make a very simple program work for a given specification or data, but if we have no foresight, the software will be not useful to slight changes in the specification. In this case, the problem resides in selecting the 'easy' or 'extensional' solutions, the most specific ones instead of the most general ones.

This avoidance of application specific procedures, methods, modules, etc, is directed by the following classical guidelines [37]:

- *provide uniform coverage*: if input conditions can occur in various combinations, write methods for all combinations, not just the ones that you currently need.
- *broaden the method as much as possible*: try to generalise argument types, preconditions and constraints, assumptions about how the method works, and the context in which the method operates. Take meaningful actions on empty values, extreme values, and out-of-bound values (anomalies). Often a method can be made more general with a slight *increase* in code.

In addition, reusability is based on again taking advantage of the effort made in previous software components. Although there are some approaches where the reused parts can be modified (adapted) from project to project [12], the ideal option is to reuse it exactly as it was, benefiting from all the acquired validation, something that is guaranteed by encapsulation, restricting that the module could be modified at the moment of reusability.

3.3 Modifiability

Whatever the software system is, predictiveness cannot be complete and, unavoidably, prediction errors will sometimes occur. In that case a question we must ask ourselves is whether making predictive software, i.e., reducing modification frequency, entails an increase in the cost of modification, thus eventually compromising overall maintenance. To answer this, we would need to know what kind of software is most maintainable in the following way:

- it *predicts* specification changes in order to reduce the number of future changes to software.
- once a failure in prediction occurs, the *modification* can be made smoothly.

The question is how are these two properties compatible and to what extent.

It is well known that redundancy also compromises modifiability, but, at the same time, every software developer knows that excessive compression (cryptic models, code or documentation) also hinders modifiability. Wolff's new concept of software [42] is based on compression, based on the fact that short software is more manageable and that the reduction of redundancy eases modifiability and extensibility. In the end, despite its predictive shortcomings, the MDL principle (as a preference for compressed models) is not valid for software development because it has been experimentally proved that extremely compressed models are not appropriate for reusability, as for other software quality factors, such as comprehensibility, testability and modifiability itself.

Is there then any good compromise between compression and avoidance of redundancy? The answer is again to realise that avoidance of redundancy can be achieved without excessive compression. In other words, there are an infinite number of irreduceable models (without redundancy), such as intensional models, which are not the most compressed models.

The explanatory paradigm of ML and philosophy of science is the most appropriate one to ensure functionality, reusability, modifiability and maintenance. Some other factors such as traceability, modularity, cohesion, comprehensibility and intelligibility can also be partially redefined under the paradigm of machine learning or philosophy of science (especially the explanatory view). For instance, performance can be seen in terms of lazy vs. eager learning methods [29]. Eager learning works with a model, whereas lazy learning predicts each new instance by comparing it with old cases. In the case of software, eager learning obviously requires more effort at development time and revision is more complicated, but performance and reusability are not compromised.

Nevertheless, from the ML experimental and theoretical results on the complexity of lazy methods, a medium or large size predictive system must necessarily be based on eager learning methods, and, in the following, we will take for granted that this is the case.

4   Predictive Software Life-Cycle

In section 2, the five main common stages between science and software were presented just as they are, without explicit influence between them. The analogy is now exploited to re-design the software life-cycle with the goal of making it predictive, and introducing model revision as one of the most important (and reiterative) stages.

4.1 A New Life Cycle

Figure 2 represents a mixture between an automated software construction cycle and scientific theory evolution. The terminology is used indistinctly, by either borrowing a term from philosophy of science (or ML) or by using a term from software engineering.

The process begins by gathering the data and partial requirements of the problem and *inducing* a first model from these examples usually with the help of background knowledge which consists of reusable software components of previous projects and some other information about the domain of the reality from which the problem originates. The next stages are quite similar to the classical or automated life-cycles, depending on the degree of formalisation of the model and the automation of the transformation stage. The first result of the process is a program which can be contrasted / validated with more use examples or with real operation. This comparison may trigger a partial or whole revision of the model, which is followed by a rederivation of the program.

Obviously, this cycle could be more detailed depending on the automated or non-automated character of each stage. For instance, in a non-automated developing schema, an analysis stage could be introduced between an induced partial specification and the model, without using previous software. The design would convert this initial model into a refined model by using the repositories.

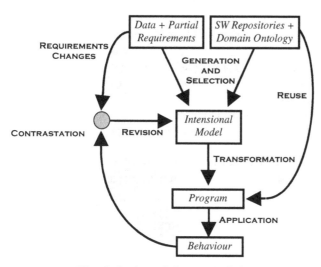

Fig. 2. *Predictive Software Life-Cycle*

4.2   Towards the Automation of the Predictive Life-Cycle

As the analogy suggests, at present, the goal would be to (partially) automate the process by using techniques from ML. However, automated inductive methods are not yet ready for most of the complex software problems we face. Nonetheless, specifications are getting increasingly more complex and more data-based, and ML techniques are becoming more powerful to justify the inductive software paradigm practically and economically. Partridge [33] presents some successful cases of automated construction of software from sample data.

There are two generic approaches for research towards this difficult goal: 1) to evolve simple, fully-automated software systems into more complex systems; and 2) to develop semi-automated systems. Both approaches highlight a revival of declarative paradigms, because declarative languages are more mature for automating the stages of the previous life-cycle, and more intelligible.

For the first *via*, logic programming is clearly the most appropriate paradigm at present. Inductive Logic Programming (ILP) [32] represents the automation of the stage of generation and selection from examples and background knowledge. The automation of the transformation stage is ensured by many years of research in transformation techniques (see e.g. [35]). The automation of the revision of the model can be found in works usually originated in non-monotonic approaches inside AI, by using logical theories [9] or more software specific approaches [1]. Finally, the application stage is performed directly through SLD-resolution or after a specialisation stage (see e.g. [2]) for improving performance.

The problems of scalability appear at all the stages, but more critically in the first stage. From the first recovery of specifications by using ILP [10], and after the application for inducing simple algorithms shown in part III of [7], the prospect of ILP for program synthesis has sometimes been discredited and biased. Nowadays, ILP is addressing more complex problems, so the predictive declarative programming paradigm can address medium-complexity problems, such as web-agents, controllers in changing environments, software assistants, and the like. Nonetheless, we must recognise the main problems of ILP for software engineering: background knowledge usage bottleneck and knowledge mobilisation [18].

For the second *via*, the most important issue is the intelligibility of software, i.e., if some part of the model (or the code) is automatically generated from the user's requirements, it must be intelligible to humans, in order to ensure good coordination with manually generated software and allowing for manual maintenance and revisions. In this case, the use of declarative languages is even more justified.

5. Conclusions and Future Work

This paper has focused on the view of programs as scientific theories or, more precisely, software development as learning. This analogy forces a reconsideration of the quality factors of software and the software construction life-cycle. New software characteristics are distinguished, mainly that software must be predictive, in order to minimise future modifications, and other software factors are redefined. Induction will be more important than deduction in the future, when automation is possible for complex systems.

Software systems must receive feedback from the user about the quality of its task: adequacy to user's needs, efficiency, robustness, etc., and they must update to the user's demands dynamically. In other words, software systems must learn from the environment and user's needs, in an interactive way quite similar to query or interactive learning [3].

The recent aim for automation of induction has driven us to highlight and encourage the productive translations of ML techniques to software engineering. Although full automation is not possible at the moment, the analogy, the revision of factors and the new life-cycle are useful for traditionally developed software. This is the keypoint of the paper, to highlight that a change in attitude (or paradigm) in software construction can be useful in practice even without any automation at all.

In a broader context, many historical traits of the short life of software engineering (in contrast to the long life of philosophy of science) can also be better understood. For instance, many techniques and paradigms of software engineering in the last decades can be seen as tools and mechanisms to ease compression while preserving intensionality (avoidance of exceptions), such as structured programming, object-oriented programming, encapsulation, polymorphism, etc.

Moreover, the emphasis placed on the inductive phase of modelling to make software more predictive matches the increasing relevance that requirement elicitation has been acquiring in software engineering theory and practices in the last decade.

At present, the authors are developing inductive algorithms and systems for other more powerful declarative languages, for which transformation and specialisation techniques are also developed [35], [2]. In particular, the induction of functional logic programs has been attempted [20][21] in order to allow the acceptance of more expressive and complex requirement cases as examples, which is usual in software applications. The system FLIP [16] is specially designed to induce recursive programs and it also supports the use of background knowledge, with the long-term goal of automating [22] more and more parts of the whole process.

As future work, from a much more practical point of view, software is a very appropriate place to experiment new techniques from AI and ML (see e.g. [40]). Moreover, AI and ML can expand their commercial applications in this area. Many ML paradigms and techniques [31] can be used in different processes and stages of software construction: evaluation criteria like cross-validation, query learning [3], reinforcement learning applied to constructive languages [23], explanation-based learning, [14], data mining for knowledge-based software, analogical reasoning, case-based reasoning, genetic computation, etc.

In summary, our analogy also shows that until machine intelligence (and ML) approaches human ability more closely, fully automated programming will remain a fallacy. In the meantime, in accordance with the analogy presented here and in an effort to reach the Utopia of "intelligent software" [30], a more prosperous methodology for software construction could be devised from the nascent "predictive software".

Acknowledgements

First of all, the authors would like to thank Jesús Alcolea for the introduction to Fetzer's work. Other people have helped to develop these ideas: Jaume Agustí, Vicent Pelechano and Enrique Hernández. Finally, this work also benefited from a short discussion held with John Lloyd, Steve Muggleton and Luc de Raedt about the possibilities of the use of ILP for software practice at the the "*JICSLP'98 CompulogNet Area Meeting on Computational Logic and Machine Learning*" [20].

References

1. Alferes, J.J.; Leite, J.A.; Pereira, L.M.; Przymusinska, H.: Przymusinski, T.C. "Dynamic Logic Programming", in Freire et al. (eds) Proc. Joint Conf. of Declarative Prog., pp. 393-408, 1998.
2. Alpuente, M.; Falaschi, M.; Vidal, G. "Partial Evaluation of Functional Logic Programs" *ACM Trans. on Programming Languages and Systems*, 20(4):768-844, 1998.
3. Angluin, D. "Queries and concept learning" *Machine Learning* 2, No. 4, 319-342, 1988.
4. Banerji, R.B. "Some insights into automatic prog. using a pattern recognition viewpoint" in Biermann et al. (eds.): *Automatic program construction techniques*, Macmillan, 1984.
5. Barron, A.; Rissanen, J.; Yu, B. "The Minimum Description Length Principle in Coding and Modeling" *IEEE Transactions on Information Theory*, Vol. 44, No. 6, 2743-2760, 1998.

6. Basili, V.R. "The Experimental Paradigm in Software Engineering" in Rombach et al. (eds.) *Experimental Software Engineering Issues*, LNCS no. 706, Springer-Verlag, 1993.

7. Bergadano, F.; Gunetti, D. *Inductive Logic Programming*, The MIT Press, 1996

8. Berry, D.M.; Lawrence, B. "Requirements Engineering" *IEEE Software*, 26-29, Mar. 1998.

9. Botilier, C.; Becher, V. "Abduction as belief revision" *Art. Intelligence* 77, 43-94, 1995.

10. Cohen, W. "Recovering Software Specifications with Inductive Logic Programming" in K. Ford, (ed.), *Proc. of the AAAI Conference*, pages 142-148, Seattle, WA, 1994.

11. Colburn, T.R. "Program Verification, Defeasible Reasoning, and Two Views of Computer Science" in *Minds and Machines* 1, 97-116, 1991.

12. Davis, M. J. "Adaptable, Reusable Code" Symp. on Sw Reusability, Seattle, apr. 1995, ACM.

13. De Millo, R.; Lipton, R.J, Perlis, A.J. "Social Processes and Proofs of Theorems and Programs" *Communications of the ACM* 22 (5), 271-280, 1979.

14. Dietterich, T.G.; Flann, N.S. "Explanation-Based Learning and Reinforcement Learning: A Unified View" *Machine Learning*, 28, 169-210, 1997.

15. Dijkstra, E.W. "Notes on Structured Programming" in O.Dahl *et al.* (eds.) *Structured Programming*, New York, Academic Press 1972.

16. Ferri, C.; Hernández-Orallo, J.; Ramírez-Quintana, M.J. "The FLIP System. From Theory to Implementation", submitted to Machine Learning, Special Issue on ILP'99.

17. Fetzer, J.H. "Philosophical Aspects of Program Verification" *Minds & Machines* 1, 197-216, 1991.

18. Flener, P. and Yilmaz, S. "Inductive synthesis of recursive logic programs: achievements and prospects", *The Journal of Logic Programming*, 41, 141-195, 1999.

19. Hernández-Orallo, J.; García-Varea, I. "Explanatory and Creative Alternatives to the MDL Principle", *Foundations of Science*, Kluwer, to appear.

20. Hernández-Orallo, J.; Ramirez-Quintana, M.J. "Induction of Functional Logic Programs", Lloyd (ed.) JICSLP'98 CompulogNet Meeting on Computational Logic and ML, 49-55, 1998.

21. Hernández-Orallo, J.; Ramírez-Quintana, M.J. "A Strong Complete Schema for Inductive Functional Logic Programming", in Flach, P.; Dzeroski, S. (eds.) *Inductive Logic Programming'99* (ILP'99), in LNAI 1634, pp. 116-127, Springer-Verlag 1999.

22. Hernández-Orallo, J.; Ramírez-Quintana, M.J. "Predictive Software", submitted to Automated Software Engineering Journal, Special Issue on Inductive Programming.

23. Hernández-Orallo, J. "Constructive Reinforcement Learning", *International Journal of Intelligent Systems*, Wiley, to appear.

24. Hoare, C.A.R. "An Axiomatic Basis for Computer Programming" *Communications of the ACM* 12, 576-580, 583, 1969.

25. IEEE Std. 982.1-1988 "IEEE Standard Dictionary of Measures to Produce Reliable Software" *The IEEE*, June, 1988.

26. IEEE/ANSI Std. 610.12 "IEEE Standard Glossary of Software Engineering Terminology" *The IEEE*, February, 1991.

27. ISO/IEC 9126, "Information technology. Software Product Evaluation. Quality characteristics and guidelines for their use" *Intl. Org. for Standardization and Intl. Electrotechnical Commission*, 1991.

28. Lieberherr, K.J. *Adaptive Object-Oriented Software: The Demeter Method with Propagation Patterns*, PWS Publishing Company, Boston, 1996.

29. López de Mántaras, R.; Armengol, E. "Machine Learning from examples: Inductive and Lazy Methods" *Data & Knowledge Engineering* 25, 99-123, 1998.

30. Maes, P. "Intelligent Software" *Scientific American* 273 (3), September, 1995.

31. Mitchell, Tom M., *Machine Learning*, McGraw-Hill International Editions, 1997.

32. Muggleton, S.; De Raedt L. "Inductive Logic Programming — theory and methods" *Journal of Logic Programming*, 19-20:629-679, 1994.

33. Partridge, D. "The Case for Inductive Programming" *IEEE Computer*, pp. 36-41, Jan 1997.
34. Pettorossi, A.; Proietti, M., "Rules and Strategies for Transforming Functional and Logic Programs" *ACM Computing Surveys,* Vol. 28, no. 2, June 1996.
35. Pettorossi, A.; Proietti, M., "Developing Correct and Efficient Logic Programs by Transformation" *Knowledge Engineering Review*, Vol. 11, No. 4, December 1996.
36. Popper, K.R., *Conjectures and Refutations: The Growth of Scientific Knowledge* Basic Books, New York 1962, Harper, New York, 1965, 1968.
37. Rumbaugh, J.; Blaha, M.; Premerlani, W.; Eddy, F.; Lorensen, W., *Object-Oriented Modeling and Design*, Prentice Hall 1991.
38. Scherlis, W.L.; Scott, D.S. "First Steps Towards Inferential Programming" in R.E.A. Mason (ed.) *Information Processing* 83, pp- 199-212, 1983.
39. Shrager, J.; Langley, P., *Computational Models of Scientific Discovery and Theory Formation*, Morgan Kaufmman, 1990.
40. Srinivasan, K.; Fisher, D. "Machine Learning Approaches to Estimating Software Development Effort" *IEEE Transactions on Software Engineering*, Vol. 21, No. 2, Feb. 1995.
41. Thagard, P. "Explanatory coherence", *Behavioural & Brain Sciences*, 12 (3), 435-502, 1989.
42. Wolff, J.G. "Towards a new concept of software", *Software Engineering J.*, IEE, Jan. 1994.

What Is '*Mathematicalness*' in Software Engineering?
— Towards Precision Software Engineering —

Hidetaka Kondoh

Systems Development Laboratory, Hitachi, Ltd.
1099 Ohzenji, Asao, Kawasaki 215-0013, Japan
kondoh@memeber.ams.org

1 Introduction

What kind of human activities do theories (*theoretical computer science*) and practices (*industrial software development*) on software most resemble? Hoare and He (1998) adopted the following viewpoint; the relationship between theoretical computer science and real-world software development corresponds to that of physical sciences and classical fields of engineering, *e.g.* mechanical engineering or aero-dynamical engineering. From this viewpoint, they successfully showed an approach towards a unified theory intended for industrial programming.

Here, we take a distinct viewpoint because of the difference between *underlying logics* of each scientific field, *i.e.* physical sciences and theoretical computer science. The underlying logic of physical sciences is *inductive* in principle, and this inductive nature of physical theories is inevitable since the physical world is given to us independent of ourselves. In this case, we must formulate properties of the physical world and then develop physical theories via comparisons between theoretical predictions and experimental results.

On the other hand, a computer program is just an implementation of some computable function which is defined in a *deductive* formal system. Such *deductive* underlying logic governing software is quite an important character of this field, hence it must be taken into account when developing software. We therefore take an approach different from that of Hoare and He.

Our approach is this: the relationship between theories and practices on software corresponds to that of mathematical logic and *living* mathematics (which we call '*ordinary mathematics*') done by *working* mathematicians (in the sense of the title of Mac Lane (1971)) as their daily work. We therefore claim that software engineers should develop their products just like working mathematicians develop mathematics; *i.e.*, software should be developed *really mathematically*.

Now most formal methods claim to be 'mathematical'; but *are they really mathematical?* Are they truly desirable approach to mathematical software development? Such a question, whether one thing is 'mathematical' or not, may seem very subjective and a matter of taste. We, however, claim that this question

T. Maibaum (Ed.): FASE 2000, LNCS 1783, pp. 163–177, 2000.

can be answered objectively as far as from the viewpoint of 'mathematicalness' as stated above, *i.e.* to define 'to be mathematical' as *cultural properties commonly kept by working mathematicians*. At this point, we only point out that such working mathematicians' culture has been successfully stable for sufficiently long time (at least from Hilbert's proposal of the axiomatism in the early of this century) and, hence, that our definition of mathematicalness is not arbitrary.

According to the above definition of mathematicalness, we reconsider the basic question, whether formal methods are mathematical or not, and will answer "NO", and explain why formal methods are not actually mathematical from the viewpoint of working mathematicians.

To answer this question, we will analyze activities of working mathematicians and will reveal several 'ideas' (actually some kind of *misconceptions* we think), which unfortunately prevent formal methods from becoming widely accepted in the field of industrial software even though such ideas are commonly considered to be useful or even strong points of formal methods. In Section 2, we will discuss the differences between 'to be mathematical' from the viewpoint of working mathematicians and 'to be logical' in the sense of mathematical logic on which formal methods are based. In Section 3, we will analyze the differences between mathematicians' proofs and formal proofs of formal methods.

After discussing those misconceptions, in Section 4, we will show the similarity between software and mathematics; *i.e.*, the correspondence between macro structures found in software development (*e.g.*, architectural patterns, design patterns, *etc.*) and macro structures found in mathematical arguments. Then we propose a novel concept of *mathematical* software engineering, which we call '*Precision Software Engineering*', on the basis of this correspondence between software and mathematics. Finally, we will point out remaining themes necessary for realizing this concept as an industrially applicable discipline so that future software engineering will become truly mathematical and produce reliable software.

2   Is '*Logicalness*' $\iff$ '*Mathematicalness*'?

In this section, we analyze the difference in the viewpoints of working mathematicians and mathematical logicians, and we evaluate whether formal methods are actually mathematical or not.

Each formal method is based on some formal system such as axiomatic set theory, a system of modal or temporal logics, *etc.* These formal systems are originated from mathematical logic or theoretical computer science, which is applied mathematical logic. Hence, formal methods are *(mathematico-) logical*. It seems to us that, on the basis of this fact, most formal methods claim to be 'mathematical'.

It is, however, not necessarily true that a thing is mathematical if and only if it is logical. One direction (mathematicalness implies logicalness) is clearly true. This is because mathematics is a deductive language; *i.e.*, all the notions and the statements in mathematics are formalizable in a logical system, say axiomatic set theory.

The other direction (mathematico-logicalness implies mathematicalness) is, however, much more problematic. This implication would have been trivially true if we had taken the mathematical logicians' viewpoint of mathematics. But as we stated in §1, we adopted the working mathematicians' viewpoint as the definition of 'to be mathematical'. Hence, we must carefully analyze what 'mathematical' means in the working mathematicians' community.

There are many criticisms against mathematical logic. These are given by working mathematicians (*e.g.*, Jean Dieudonné (1982)). These criticisms are mainly due to working mathematicians' misunderstandings about and prejudices against mathematical logic. Mathematical logic is clearly an important part of our culture just like mathematics is.

We, however, think that these criticisms must be reconsidered more seriously so that we can learn some lessons from them by carefully analyzing why working mathematicians display such hostility against mathematical logic. Such criticisms show the following facts: (1) most working mathematicians do not regard mathematical logic as *the logic for ordinary mathematics*; (2) mathematics analyzed from the mathematico-logical viewpoint is *irrelevant* to ordinary mathematics which working mathematicians love and develop.

Why does such an unfortunate gap between mathematical logicians and working mathematicians occur? This gap is due to the nature of mathematical logic; *i.e.*, its complete *reductionistic* nature. For example, consider the following set of formulae:

$$\forall x.\, x^{-1} \cdot x = e,$$
$$\forall x.\, e \cdot x = x,$$
$$\forall x, y, z.\, x \cdot (y \cdot z) = (x \cdot y) \cdot z.$$

These are very familiar axioms of groups and most working mathematicians consider this mathematical structure very important.

From the mathematico-logical viewpoint, however, these formulae are no more than sentences of first-order equational logic with one constant symbol and two function symbols (one is unary, the other binary). That is, mathematical logic cannot explain nor even pay any attention to the importance of these axioms in ordinary mathematics.

Just like this example of the group structure, mathematical logic reduces any mathematical structures to formulae in a formal system and also reduces proof techniques based on such structures to combinations of primitive inference rules of this formal system by discarding their *pragmatic* significance for working mathematicians. This is because the main purpose of mathematical logic is to analyze logical but *not* mathematical structures of mathematical arguments.

On the other hand, working mathematicians consider mathematical structures very useful and important, and also regard that proof techniques based on such structures indispensable in developing ordinary mathematics as their daily work (*cf. e.g.*, Mac Lane (1986)). *E.g.*, in most books on mathematics, the group structure is frequently used in developing mathematical theories.

In other words, mathematical logic, especially proof theory, reduces all the mathematical contents into *meaningless* syntax in a formal system and then analyzes such syntactic objects to obtain some information, say logical complexities of mathematical notions. We call such a nature of mathematical logic *reductionistic*. From such a viewpoint, all intuition (or *semantics* in a very vague sense) on mathematical objects held by working mathematicians are completely abandoned. Every mathematical theory is reduced to a collection of purely syntactic phrases and the liveness of such a theory on the working mathematicians' *Platonic world* is completely lost.

Criticisms to mathematical logic raised by working mathematicians can be summarized like this: *"mathematical logic neither helps our imagination in the living mathematical world nor gives any hints for proving theorems about our mathematical world; the logical structure shown by mathematical logic has hardly any relation to our 'logic' of living ordinary mathematics."*

Moreover, mathematical logicians do their daily work (*i.e.*, research on mathematical logic) not mathematico-logically but mathematically. That is, they live in their own world of imaginations.

Hence, *mathematical logicians themselves are actually working mathematicians!* They are working mathematicians in fields different from those of ordinary mathematics. But there is an essential difference between mathematical logicians and ordinary working mathematicians. Their viewpoints on ordinary mathematics are quite different. Mathematical logicians observe ordinary mathematics from the meta-level (in the sense of metamathematics) so view it *syntactically*, while working mathematicians live in the world of this ordinary mathematics: *i.e.*, ordinary mathematics is at the object-level for them; hence, they view it *semantically*.

Software formalists (we hereafter denote 'researchers on formal verification' by this term) often claim that one of strong points of formal methods is to allow software engineers to reason the correctness of software purely syntactically. Such a claim clearly shows that software formalists view software development from the meta-level. This viewpoint is quite similar to the mathematical logicians' one on ordinary mathematics but is *never* the working mathematicians' one on it nor the logicians' one on logic itself.

From these observations, we answer "NO" to the basic question whether formal methods are mathematical. Formal methods force their users to work in a very strictly defined formal syntax just like mathematical logic analyzes ordinary mathematics. Working mathematicians, on the other hand, think semantically and do their daily work in a natural language in a very rigorous manner with minimal use of formal syntax (*i.e.*, mathematical formulae) only when using such formalism is more compact and clearer to express their mathematical ideas than expressing such ideas in a natural language.

Any formal syntax has a strong tendency to force its users to work syntactically rather than semantically, even though syntactical manipulations are much
more inefficient than working with semantical imaginations. In the next section,
we will observe the fact that mathematicians' productivity is unbelievablly high
when we compare it to that of software engineers. One of keys of their high
productivity is that they are thinking semantically rather than syntactically
about mathematical objects. In the next section, we will reveal the secret how
mathematicians attain such high productivity.

3   Are Formal Proofs Imperative?

NOTICE: Hereafter, the term 'mathematics' will be used in a broader sense
than in §2; *i.e.*, as the generic name for all the deductive sciences including
mathematical logic and theoretical computer science as well as (ordinary) mathematics. The term '(working) mathematicians' therefore denotes researchers in
all such fields. When we use these terms in the narrower sense as in §2, we affix
an adjective 'ordinary'.

Many formal methods are supported by (semi-)automatic provers or proof-
checkers. Users of such methods can verify the consistency of their specifications
and the correctness of programs with respect to specifications completely formally supported by such provers/proof-checkers running on a computer. Hence,
those formal methods claim that such possibility of formal verifications is one
of strong points of themselves. Is this possibility really a strong point? Are such
formal verifications compatible with reasonable productivity of software?

Now we estimate working mathematicians' productivity and compare it with
the productivity of software engineers. It is very difficult to estimate the amount
of *semantical contents* in a mathematical paper and almost impossible to compare such an amount with the amount of a program. It is, however, possible to
estimate the amount of *syntactical objects* denoting such semantical contents. In
estimating such syntactical amount, the next example will give some insights.
Let X be a set, $\sqsubseteq$ and $\leq$ be partial orders on X, and $\equiv$ and $\simeq$ be equivalence
relations induced by these partial orders, respectively. Suppose $x \sqsubseteq y \Rightarrow x \leq y$
for all $x, y \in X$. Then, it is trivial that $x \equiv y \Rightarrow x \simeq y$ for all $x, y \in X$. But if
we want to prove this trivial theorem formally (in, say Gentzen's NK) we need
more than 10 steps. It is well known from constructive programming that every
formal proof step exactly corresponds to a step of a program.

We can therefore roughly estimate the amount of a program-like formal object
denoting the contents in a mathematical paper by multiplying its number of lines
by 10 or more (if proofs of that paper contain large 'gaps' which novices cannot
fill in, then 1,000 or even more would be appropriate) to obtain the corresponding
LOC (lines of code) as software. This means a 20-page paper (it is not so long as
a mathematical paper) with 30 lines per page corresponds to at least 6,000 LOC
as a program. In fact, this estimation may be too small since most mathematical
papers are very technical and contain many 'gaps' which only professionals can

fill in, so we should estimate the amount of contents of such a paper as at least 60,000 LOC (here, still a rather small scaling factor 100 is used). Even if a mathematician produces only one paper per year, his productivity about the mathematical contents corresponds to 5,000 LOC per month!

This would be surprising productivity if he were a software engineer. At first sight, this comparison may seem to be unfair, but it is not so unfair. Suppose there were a *formal mathematician* who do mathematics completely formally (perhaps using some formal-proof development tools). Note that his aim is not to record existing mathematical theories formally but to develop his own novel mathematical theory just like usual mathematicians do. Then, such a formal mathematician had to have his productivity as high as the above LOC value in order that he could write a paper (per year) containing equivalent mathematical contents to the above (*non-formal but rigorous*) mathematician's one. We should aware that activities of such formal mathematicians are almost the same as those of software engineers. In fact, they can be said '*programmers in mathematics*'.

The fact that the above comparison seems unfair shows an important point. That is, *software engineers have been handicapped already compared with mathematicians*. Software engineers' handicap is that their final products must be completely formal, computer programs. Most of software engineers do not think formally at the current state-of-art, but their productivity has been significantly reduced already in order to produce formal objects. In the case of mathematics, if there were formal mathematicians, they would be handicapped, too. Therefore, the productivity 5,000 LOC per month required for such formal mathematicians sounds unrealistic, and such unreality is solely due to their way of working, *i.e.* syntactical manipulation instead of semantical imagination, because mathematical (*i.e.*, semantical) contents of formal mathematicians' products are completely the same as those of ordinary mathematicians' ones.

To understand such formal mathematicians' handicaps, we should remind that in mathematical papers there are many 'gaps' which only very trained people can fill in. In fact, mathematicians attain their surprisingly high productivity mainly because they do not prove their theorems formally. They leave some 'gaps' in proofs unfilled, and such 'gaps' are actually not true gaps (*i.e.*, flaws of proofs). They are *trivial* for intended readers of such papers. Mathematicians do not want to spend their time filling in such 'trivial gaps' completely.

Formal proofs (say, of the correctness of software) do not allow the smallest 'gaps', even if such 'gaps' are actually trivial for software engineers. Proving formally decreases productivity of software engineers from that with semantical thinking to the level of syntactical thinking; *i.e.*, programming. The secret of mathematicians' surprising productivity is thus: they limit use of formal languages in describing and proving mathematical properties as little as possible and then keep their productive semantical imagination as much as possible.

Note that *no mathematical logicians, theoretical computer scientists, nor software formalists have ever written a paper in which their theorems are proved formally*. That is, any researchers on formal systems do their daily work mathematically (in the sense of §2) but NEVER formally.

If software engineers are requested to prove the correctness of their programs complete formally, then they will be doubly handicapped. They must not only produce completely formal products (programs) but also work with such products completely formally. Then software engineers' performance in provings will surely be decreased from the level of mathematicians' performance in provings to that of formal mathematicians' one.

Software engineers' mission is to produce software with reasonable reliability and performance within a given budget. For software engineers, activities such as designing software and proving its correctness are their daily work; these activities just correspond to stating theorems about mathematical objects and proving them for working mathematicians, or stating metatheorems about properties of formal systems and proving such metatheorems for software formalists. *It is quite unfair to request that only software engineers must prove the correctness of their products formally.* Though it is true that the main part of a software engineer's product is a formal object (*i.e.*, a computer program), such a formal artefact is produced in the very final step of their daily work. A correctness proof of a program is only a way to guarantee the quality of their product. For software engineers, a correctness proof is not their ends but a mean of quality assurance.

The following fact is empirically well known among working mathematicians: in a seminar, if a theorem is stated and a sketch of its proof is shown and also if most of the participants in that seminar think that it is correct, then *the statement of the theorem itself is true in most cases* even if the original proof sketch may contain serious flaws when a proof is written in detail. In verifying the correctness of software, 'a theorem' above corresponds to the correctness. For software engineers, the correctness of software is very important but achieving absolutely correct correctness proofs lies outside their principal aim.

Most formal verifications are methods that directly guarantee *the correctness of correctness proofs* and then inform us of the correctness of software. As mentioned above, this approach is outside software engineers' principal aim. To remedy this problem, the notion of 'verification' in the Cleanroom Method, Linger et al. (1979), gives a good hint. In this method, 'correctness proofs' are planned to be done rigorously (but never formally) as verification-reviews by a small design team consisting of several engineers. This approach to correctness proofs is quite similar to checking proof sketches by participants in a seminar of working mathematicians. Hence, the notion of and the approach to verification in the Cleanroom Method, in its spirit, quite resemble the daily activities of working mathematicians. This method has been successfully applied to real projects. Overall productivity is reported to be the same or improved compared with that in conventional (without any correctness proofs) developments even though correctness are proved in this method, *cf.* Gibson (1997).

The Cleanroom Method verification is limited to the scale of individual procedure and cannot be applied to larger scales. In the next section, keeping the spirit of this method (*i.e.*, focusing the correctness of software but never that of correctness proofs), we will show an approach to mathematical software development by comparing *macro structures* in software and mathematics.

4   The Software-Mathematics Structural Correspondence

In this section, we analyze the structural resemblance between software and mathematics by focusing their macro structures.

Constructive Programming is an approach to systematically derive programs from their specifications written in some version of intuitionistic (*i.e.*, constructive) logics, say a higher-order intuitionistic type theory, instead of the usual classical (*i.e.*, two-valued) logic. This approach is based on the following de Bruijn-Curry-Howard correspondence between programming and logic; *cf.* Nordström et al. (1990), Luo (1994), and Hindley (1997):

Table 1. The de Bruijn-Curry-Howard Correspondence

Programming	Logic
Specification	Proposition
Program	Proof

The problem of the constructive programming approach is its too *microscopic* and *reductionistic* viewpoint. There are many textbook on the same mathematical theme, but we say that some are well-written and some are poor even if later ones had no gaps in proofs and no typos. If these books are considered formally then they are equivalent, since each book gives the same main theorem and shows its proof. The difference between such well-written books and poor ones lies in the style of their presentation.

Well-written books show intuitively clear and natural definitions capturing essential notions adequately, provide many useful lemmata, and prove the main theorem in a very beautiful and reusable way. Just like this, a program at the programming-in-larges level, which is so large that it needs software engineering, is expected to have a beautiful internal structure consisting of understandable and stable-against-modification components in order to decrease efforts in its maintenance.

The constructive programming approach has another problem, the difficulty of formal proofs as we discussed in §3. Therefore, we must admit that this approach is quite difficult to be applied to industrial software development.

We, however, think that this constructive programming approach has its own interests; *i.e.*, this approach gives hints to consider an analogy between programming and mathematics/logic. In the constructive programming approach, this analogy is quite formal but stays at the *programming-in-smalls* level. If we relax this analogy to be informal and extend it to a more macro scale, the *programming-in-larges* level, then we can find a correspondence between structures found in software development and those used in mathematical activities at various levels of granularity. This correspondence is shown in Table 2. We now analyze this *Software-Mathematics Structural Correspondence* more carefully. Note that the base of our analysis is the correspondence shown in Table 1.

Table 2. The Structural Correspondence between Software and Mathematics

Software Development	Mathematical Activity
Basic Control Structure (Repetitive Loop, Conditional, ... etc.)	Elementary Proof Step (Mathematical Induction, Case Analysis, ... etc.)
Idiom (Useful Combination of Control Structures)	Proof Technique (Conventional Technique for Fragmental Proof)
Abstract Data Type (Collection of Operations on Common Data)	Theory on a Mathematical Notion (Collection of Lemmata on a Mathematical Notion)
Design Pattern (Specific Combination of (Possible) Classes and Specific use of their Interdependencies)	Proof Tactics (Specific Combination of Subgoals (Lemmata) and Specific use of their Interdependencies)
Architectural Pattern (Specific Combination of Specification of Components)	Theory Strategy (Collection of Basic Definitions and the Main Theorem)
Software System	Mathematical Theory (Structure formed by Definitions, Theorems & Proofs)
Domain	Mathematical Field (Basic Framework for Mathematical Thinking with Common Vocabulary)

- **Basic Constrol Structure *vs.* Elementary Proof Step**

    The lowest level of the correspondence, between a *basic control structure* and an *elementary proof step*, is essentially formal in the sense of the constructive programming approach. *E.g.*, a sequential composition corresponds to the cut rule in logic, a conditional corresponds to the disjunction elimination in logic, and a terminating repetition corresponds to an induction on a well-founded ordering.

- **Idiom *vs.* Proof Technique**

    An *idiom* in programming is a specific pattern of combination of basic control structures. As stated above, control structures correspond to elementary proof steps. Hence, an idiom corresponds to a specific pattern of combination of elementary proof steps in mathematics. Such a pattern is a *proof technique*; *e.g.*, Fermat's method of 'infinite descent', Reid (1988), (often used in elementary number theory) is a specific combination of a *reductio ad absurdum* and a mathematical induction.

- **Abstract Data Type *vs.* Theory on a Mathematical Notion**

    An *abstract data type* (or a *class* in the object-oriented paradigm) is a collection of operations acting on a common data to be encapsulated. As we have seen in Table 1, a specification of an operation corresponds to a proposition. Hence, a specification of an abstract data type (or a class) corresponds to a (usually miniature) *theory on a specific mathematical notion* and an implementation of an abstract data type (or a class) is in correspondence with a proof of such a theory. Most typical example of such a theory on a mathematical notion is group theory (though it is not miniature). This correspondence is well-known and is a basis for the algebraic approach to abstract data types, Ehrig and Mahr (1985).

- **Design Pattern *vs.* Proof Tactics**

    A *design pattern* is a specific combination of classes and specific dependencies (inheritance relations) among them. As shown above, classes correspond to theories of mathematical notions. In mathematics, a *proof tactics* is a collection of conventional knowledge on matters such as what lemmata should be stated in order to prove the desired theorem and how to use dependencies between theorems. In many cases in mathematical theories, those lemmata form a miniature theory on an auxiliary mathematical notion which is used to develop the proof of an upper-level proposition. Hence, a design pattern corresponds to a proof tactics in mathematics.

- **Software System *vs.* Mathematical Theory**
  Before considering the relationship between architectural patterns and theory strategies, we analyze the next pair (*i.e.*, software systems and mathematical theories) since each of the former pair is a skeleton of corresponding one in the latter pair; hence, the discussion on the second pair is expected to be more intuitive than that on the first one.

A *software system* is developed according to its specification, has some interface with its environment, and is implemented as a collection of various components interacting one another; each component has its own specification and interfaces to other components. At the side of mathematics, by a *mathematical theory*, we mean the contents of a mathematical book or a paper. It consists of a collection of definitions and theorems (some of them are *main theorems*, for which the book or the paper is written) and their proofs. Of course, in order to show main theorems, many auxiliary definitions, lemmata and their proofs are necessary. Such organic collection of these mathematical items form a mathematical theory. This just corresponds to a non-trivial programming-in-larges software system as follows:

- the (functional) specification of a whole software system corresponds to statements of main theorems as a whole (by taking their conjunction);
- the specification of a component corresponds to the statement of a lemma which is used to prove main theorems;
- the implementation of this component corresponds to the proof of this lemma;
- a component, which is provided as a *library* and is outside of the development project of the system, corresponds to an 'external' lemma whose statement is borrowed from some reference and is used without a proof;
- (definitions of) mathematical notions for describing the statement of main theorems corresponds to (definitions of) abstract data types used to give the functional specification of the software system;
- (definitions of) auxiliary notions used to describe statements of lemmata are in correspondence with (definitions of) abstract data types for interfaces among components.

Note that a mathematical monograph contains quite a lot of materials; *e.g.*, Barendregt's "*The Lambda Calculus*" (1981) has the contents as much as *ca.* 400,000 LOC (> 600 pages × 30 lines/page × 20 (as a scaling factor); in this case, the author estimates the scaling factor to be a very small value 20, since that book hardly contains any 'gaps' in proofs), which is large enough as non-trivial programming-in-larges software.

- **Architectural Pattern *vs.* Theory Strategy**

An *architectural pattern* is a specific pattern of a collection of specifications of components, interfaces among these components and an interface with an external environment for the system which is expected to build with this architectural pattern. Each component is given a *partial* specification; *i.e.*, this specification is so weak that it cannot uniquely define the external function of the component. An architectural pattern therefore is a template for constructing software systems.

Now consider the mathematical side. A *strategy for developing a mathematical theory* is characterized as its starting point (basic definitions), its pattern of the goal (*i.e.*, the pattern of main theorem(s)), and patterns of several important auxiliary lemmata. For example, in λ-calculus or rewriting systems alike, if we want to show the Church-Rosser Theorem (*i.e.*, the congruence of reductions), then we have several choices. One of them is to show it via the Hindley-Rosen Diamond Lemma. Another is to use parallel reduction. Each of them gives a strategy for developing the reduction theory of such a calculus. In this example, the goal, the concrete statement of the Church-Rosser Theorem, depends on each reduction system; hence, the Church-Rosser Theorem is the name of a family of *similar* statements. Just like this, each of the Hindley-Rosen Lemma and the notion of parallel reduction is a family of similar statements and that of similar notions, respectively. As we have seen in this example, a theory strategy is a template to build many concrete mathematical theories; in this case, each strategy (*i.e.*, via the Hindley-Rosen Lemma or via parallel reduction) is a template to construct a concrete rewriting theory of various rewriting systems. As we have shown the correspondence between software systems and mathematical theories, we can conclude that architectural patterns and theory strategies corresponds to each other.

- **Domain *vs.* Mathematical Field**

A *domain* has its own basic vocabulary to describe problems and each term in such vocabulary carries its own specific meaning and restrictions for its use. Similarly, a *mathematical field* defines a basic framework and a common vocabulary for mathematical thinking. For example, it is often said by working mathematicians that algebraists think with the equality, $=$, while analysts use the inequality, $\leq$. This means that $=$ is a basic notion in algebra, but it is not the case in analysis. In analysis, $=$ is a compound notion shown by a pair of two $\leq$'s ($x = y$ from $x \leq y$ and $y \leq x$) by taking limits of appropriate sequences. To show another example, let's see what the field of λ-calculus is. When we read Barendregt's encyclopedic monograph (1981), it tells us that we should investigate such a calculus on four aspects: *i.e.*, conversion relations, reduction relations, equational theories, and models. These are the most basic vocabulary in λ-calculus and give the most basic thinking-framework in developing similar various calculi.

Differences between Software Engineers and Working Mathematicians

We have seen that macro structures known in software engineering well correspond to macro structures in mathematics. *There is, however, an essential dif-*

ference between software engineering and mathematics in handling such macro structures. Mathematicians are very rigorous in using their mathematical macro structures. They very carefully analyze limitations of usage of these structures: *e.g.*, under what condition a lemma can be used, what additional conditions are needed for a mathematical construction to preserve a desirable property, *etc.* Software engineers treat their macro structures such as architectural patterns, Buschmann et al. (1996), and design patterns, Gamma et al. (1995), in very intuitive and empirical manners. They have found such reusable structures but have never analyzed their rigorous properties.

A design pattern can be said a structure with several holes, each of which is expected to be filled by a class or an object. Current works on design patterns, however, do not analyze necessary properties for such holes: *e.g.*, what a class invariant is necessary for a class to fill a specific hole of the pattern; what preconditions/postconditions are expected for a specific method supported by a hole-filling class. In the case of an architectural pattern, it is a macro structure with holes for large components and interactions among them. We should therefore know rigorously about necessary properties of each component to fill each hole. We also need to know about under what conditions additional properties of these components are preserved all over the architecture. For example, what additional conditions are necessary to extend the deadlock-freeness of each component to this architecture as a whole. Without knowledge about properties of these macro structures, software engineers either cannot safely reuse them in building reliable software systems or must prove the correctness of the software from scratch every time they use macro structures.

There are several works on formal descriptions of such software macro structures. *Most of them, however, are at the level of description.* They are not at the level of analysis of their properties. Careful analysis and accumulating such rigorous properties are essential and far more important than describing structures formally, because if we knew their properties rigorously, we could correctly use those macro structures in constructing software systems with high reliability and could prove its correctness efficiently on the basis of such rigorous properties.

5   Towards Precision Software Engineering

So far, we have discussed how we can make software engineering truly mathematical. The key idea is the use of macro structures such as architectural patterns and design patters with their own rigorous theories.

In other words, software engineering must not only describe the structure itself (with, say, UML or some kind of architecture description languages) but also develop a rigorous miniature theory (*mini-theory* for short) for each software macro structure, which has holes to be filled (instantiated) by some components. Each such mini-theory must clarify rigorous properties of each structure: *e.g.*, invariants of the structure, relationships among invariants of components to fill holes of that structure, properties preserved by that structure and additional condition (if necessary) for this preservation. Such properties on a macro structure form an *ad hoc* (in the sense of mathematical logic) but useful mini-theory ('theory' exactly in the sense of mathematical theories) on this structure. These mini-theories can be used in proving correctness of software systems built up with those structures. Then software engineers can *safely* use such macro structures in building reliable software and rigorously proving its correctness *efficiently*. This situation is completely parallel to the situation in mathematics: *i.e.*, working mathematicians first empirically found useful mathematical structures such as groups, rings, and topological spaces; then, for such structures, mathematicians developed *ad hoc* but rich theories such as group theory, general topology, *etc.*; and now, they can effectively use such theories on mathematical structures in developing their own mathematical theories by proving their own theorems efficiently on the basis of such theories in order to output their *products*; namely, mathematical papers and books.

We call such an truly mathematical discipline of software engineering as *Precision Software Engineering*. This discipline must consists of *ad hoc* mini-theories on *empirically useful* software macro structures just like mathematics consists of theories on mathematical structures like groups, rings, *etc.* which are *ad hoc* from the mathematico-logical viewpoint. There are much materials, namely generic meta-theories such as many variations of programming logics and calculi for concurrency, provided by theoretical computer science (including researches on formal methods), which are applicable to build up such mini-theories for Precision Software Engineering.

The most important difference between Precision Software Engineering and formal methods is the difference in viewpoints and not that of meta-theories on which they are based. Most formal methods aim to formally *describe* software with a language (as a concretization of some generic meta-theories) and to prove the correctness of software formally. On the other hand, Precision Software Engineering stresses to rigorously *analyze* software macro structures and to construct their own *logically ad hoc* (but *logically consistent*, of course) and *practically useful* mini-theories on reusable such structures on the basis of generic meta-theories. This approach to software engineering gives a good interface between software engineering and theoretical computer science. That is, the latter provides *generic* meta-theories on the nature of computation, while the former develops *ad hoc* mini-theories on software macro structures and methodologies to work with such mini-theories founded on generic meta-theories.

Precision Software Engineering is not already-established discipline, but there are several interesting works which share the spirit of Precision Software Engineering. The most significant and already practical one is the Cleanroom Method, which captured the essential spirit of mathematical proof and applied it correctness proofs of programs, *cf.* Linger et al. (1979). Bertrand Meyer's Design by Contract is also a practical approach to program correctness on the basis of an interesting analogy that the precondition and the postcondition of a procedure can be seen as the contract of the provider and users of the procedure, and this approach covers the object-oriented paradigm, *cf.* Meyer (1997).

Another very ambitious and quite interesting works on more macro-scale structures is Dines Bjørner's Domain Theory (1997 and 1998), where Bjørner tries to develop theories on various application domains of software by describing each application domain by a formal specification language RSL to standardize the vocabulary of the domain, then analyzing properties of each domain very rigorously (in fact, formally) and finally obtaining its properties (invariants of the application domain and many useful lemmata) in the form of formal sentences in RSL.

Yet another interesting rigourous approach on macro-scale structures is Bjørner et al. (1997), which characterizes Michael Jackson's (originally not so rigourous) Problem Frames (1995) in software development; and the notion of the Problem Frame, in turn, was inspired from G. Polya's classical work(1957) on the classification of mathematical problems for solving them.

Also interesting works are on formal definitions of practically useful design/modeling languages like UML, so-called Precise Semantics of Software Modeling Techniques: *e.g.*, Broy et al. (1998). If UML have such formal foundations and properties and limitations of various design transformations on that languages are analyzed rigorously, then working software engineers can effectively work with UML in a very rigorous and safe manner.

There have been many proposals to make programming mathematical. Among others, Hoare (1986) clearly showed the correspondence between programming and mathematics. Those proposals are, however, at the programming level; *i.e.*, within the programming-in-smalls scope and actually from the mathematico-logical viewpoint in stead of working mathematicians' one. The novelty of our proposal is its scope. Our approach offers a way for more upper design processes in software development to become mathematical on the basis of the Software-Mathematics Correspondence shown in Table 2, which we have found.

As a (mainly academic) research field, Precision Software Engineering may also be called *Abstract Software Engineering* just in the sense of *abstract* algebra. In fact, the principal aim of Precision Software Engineering is to establish *abstract (mini-)theories* of empirically useful software macro structures independent from how those structures are concretely implemented (in C, Java, *etc.*). This is quite analogous how abstract algebra was born. For example, groups were originally found by Galois as very concrete objects; *i.e.*, substitutions of solutions of algebraic equations. Later, Noether and other mathematicians abstracted and purified the notion of groups and established modern abstract group theory. Other branches of abstract algebra were also emerged by abstracting originally very concrete mathematical objects (*i.e.*, various number systems like $\mathbb{Z}$, $\mathbb{Q}$, and $\mathbb{C}$). Like this, what are necessary in current complicated software development is abstract theories of useful design patterns, software architectures and so on. Therefore, when both of Abstract Software Engineering as a research field and Precision Software Engineering as an engineering discipline are established, working software engineers can efficiently develop highly reliable software, and then, *software engineering can become a truly* modern *engineering field like other conventional ones, e.g. aircraft engineering.*

Acknowledgements

The author wishes to express his deepest thanks to Professor Roger Hindley, who told the author much about logicians' viewpoint and also about historical conflicts between working mathematicians and logicians. Discussions with him form the basis of Section 2. The author also much thanks to Professor Henk Barendregt, whose enthusiasm to make programs more beautiful strongly motivated the author to think about a more rational way of software development and to initiate this work. The author wishes to express his sincere gratitudes for Professor Dines Bjørner, who kindly gave the author's group a lecture on his Domain Theory, and he also gave the author several comments on a draft of this paper, which inspired and encouraged the author very much. The author also owes some of inspiration appeared in this work to Professor Tony Hoare (as well as his book) whose interests and comments on a draft of this work also encouraged the author so much. Constructive criticisms given by Mr. Hirokazu Yatsu, Professor Tetso Tamai, Professor Motoshi Saeki and Dr. Kazuhito Ohmaki much helped the author in clarifying the notion of Precision Software Engineering. Last but not least, the author wishes to thank Professor Kenroku Nogi, Mr. Shigeru Otsuki, and Mr. Hirokazu Tanabe for their encouragements and warm advices which were very helpful for the author to improve the current work.

References

Barendregt, H. P. (1981): *The Lambda Calculus*, North-Holland.

Bjørner, D. (1997): *UNU/IIST's Software Technology R&D in Africa, Asia, Eastern Europe, and Latin America: 'Five' Years — a Personal View*, UNU/IIST Report No. 90.

Bjørner, D. (1998): *Domains & Requirements, Software Architecture & Program Organization*, Full Day Seminar in IFIP '98, Budapest.

Bjørner, D., et al. (1997): Michael Jackson's Problem Frames: Towards Methodological Principles of Selecting and Applying Formal Software Development Techniques and Tools, in *Proceedings of 1st ICFEM*, 263–270.

Broy, M., et al. (1998): *PSMT — Workshop on Precise Semantics of Software Modeling Techniques*, Tech. Report of TUM I9803.

Buschmann, F., et al. (1996): *A System of Patterns*, John Wiley & Sons.

Dieudonné, J. (1982): in *Penser les mathématiques*, Editions du Seuil.

Ehrig, H. and B. Mahr (1985): *Fundamentals of Algebraic Specification 1*, Springer-Verlag.

Gamma, E., et al. (1995): *Design Patterns*, Addison-Wesley.

Gibson, R. (1997): *Cleanroom Software Engineering Practice* (by S. A. Baker et al.), 116–134, Idea Group Publishing.

Hoare, C. A. R. (1986): *The Mathematics of Programming*, Clarendon Press, Oxford.

Hoare, C. A. R., and He, J. (1998): *Unifying Theories of Programming*, Prentice Hall.

Jackson, M. (1995): *Software Requirements & Specification*, Addison-Wesley.

Linger, R. C., et al. (1979): *Structured Programming*, Addison-Wesley.

Luo, Z. (1994): *Computation and Reasoning*, Clarendon Press, Oxford.

Mac Lane, S. (1971): *Categories for the Working Mathematician*, Springer-Verlag.

Mac Lane, S. (1986): *Mathematics: Form and Function*, Springer-Verlag.

Meyer, B. (1997): *Object-Oriented Software Construction*, 2nd ed., Prentice Hall.

Nordström, B., et al. (1990): *Programming in Martin-Löf's Type Theory*, Clarendon Press, Oxford.

Polya, G. (1957): *How to Solve It*, 2nd ed, Princeton Univ. Press.

Reid, M. (1988): *Undergraduate Algebraic Geometry*, Cambridge Univ. Press.

Shaw, M. and Garlan, D. (1996): *Software Architecture*, Prentice Hall.

A Formal Approach to Heterogeneous Software Modeling

Alexander Egyed and Nenad Medvidovic

University of Southern California
Computer Science Department
Los Angeles, CA 90089-0781, USA
{aegyed,neno}@sunset.usc.edu

Abstract. The problem of consistently engineering large, complex software systems of today is often addressed by introducing new, "improved" models. Examples of such models are architectural, design, structural, behavioral, and so forth. Each software model is intended to highlight a *particular view* of a desired system. A combination of multiple models is needed to represent and understand the *entire system*. Ensuring that the various models used in development are consistent relative to each other thus becomes a critical concern. This paper presents an approach that integrates and ensures the consistency across an architectural and a number of design models. The goal of this work is to combine the respective strengths of a powerful, specialized (architecture-based) modeling approach with a widely used, general (design-based) approach. We have formally addressed the various details of our approach, which has allowed us to construct a large set of supporting tools to automate the related development activities. We use an example application throughout the paper to illustrate the concepts.

1 Introduction

The software community places great hopes on software modeling notations and techniques to ease a variety of development challenges. The intellectual toolset available to software developers has been steadily enriched with more powerful and more comprehensive models. At the same time, the growing number of heterogeneous models has resulted in an observable split within this community: one part of the community is working on and with special-purpose development models; another part focuses on general-purpose models. Special-purpose models tend to focus on individual software development issues and are typically accompanied by powerful analytical evaluation tools. General-purpose models, on the other hand, address a wider range of issues that arise during development, typically resulting in a family of models that span and relate those issues.

This split has impacted the two communities' visions of how software development challenges are best addressed. A special-purpose approach is typically centered around a single design notation with a narrow modeling and analysis focus (e.g., an architecture description language, or ADL [14]). A general-purpose approach embraces a *family* of design notations with a much broader, system-wide focus (e.g., the Unified Modeling Language, or UML [1]). Thus, for instance, UML emphasizes

T. Maibaum (Ed.): FASE 2000, LNCS 1783, pp. 178-192, 2000.

modeling practicality and breadth, while ADLs tend to emphasize rigor and depth. Both these perspectives are needed to address the broad spectrum of rapidly changing situations that arise in software development. Our previous work has demonstrated that the two perspectives can indeed play complementary roles in *modeling and analyzing software architectures* [10,12,16]. We have recently begun using combinations of the general- and special-purpose approaches to aid us in the task of *sound software refinement*: refining high-level software models (i.e., architectures) into lower-level models (i.e., designs and implementations) in a manner that preserves the desired system properties and relationships [7].

This paper discusses the issues we have encountered in attempting to bridge the two perspectives and the solutions we have developed to address those issues. In particular, we have augmented our ADL-based approach to modeling, analysis, simulation, and evolution of architecturally relevant aspects of a system (e.g., system-level structure and interactions, performance, reliability), with the strengths of UML: supporting a broad range of both high- and low-level development concerns with a widely adopted, standard notation.

Integrating an ADL-based approach with UML is a non-trivial task. One difficulty arises from the difference in the modeling foci, language constructs, and assumptions between an ADL and UML. Therefore, the first critical challenge is to ensure that the model, as specified in the ADL, is transferred into UML as faithfully as possible, and vice versa. Another difficulty is a by-product of the numerous modeling notations within UML (component, class, object, state chart, use case, activity, etc. diagrams): one view of a system model, as depicted in one notation (e.g., class diagram), may be inconsistent with another view, as depicted in another notation (e.g., activity diagram). Thus, the second critical challenge is to ensure that changes made in one view are reflected as faithfully as possible in another.

We have developed and exploited two techniques to deal with these two challenges. They are illustrated in Figure 1. The figure depicts the relationship between the UML modeling constructs ("Core UML") and the constructs of an ADL, such as Rapide [6] or C2 [18]. As indicated in the figure, only a certain, small number of ADL constructs can be represented in "Core UML". This should come as no surprise since, as discussed above, ADLs are special-purpose notations that tend to favor rigor and formalism - concepts that are less present in UML due to its practitioner-oriented,

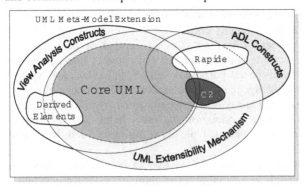

general-purpose nature. However, UML provides a mechanism that allows "Core UML" to be extended to address new modeling needs (depicted by the "UML Extensibility Mechanism" ellipse in Figure 1). We exploit this feature of UML to address the first challenge: supporting the transformation of an ADL model into a UML model and vice

Fig. 1. Extending and Augmenting UML; challenges to represent ADL and analysis Constructs in UML.

versa.[1] The second challenge deals with ensuring the consistency across UML's modeling notations. Since this area has not been addressed by the designers of UML, the strategy we pursue is to augment UML with constructs that maintain the relationships among the modeling elements *across* different notations (depicted by the "View Analysis Constructs" ellipse in Figure 1). In tandem, the two techniques allow us to specify, refine, and integrate the heterogeneous models supported by an ADL and by the different UML notations, alleviating the shortcomings of both languages in the process.

The remainder of the paper is organized as follows. Section 2 presents our approach to software architecture modeling, analysis, and simulation. Section 3 outlines our technique for transferring architectural decisions into UML. Section 4 focuses on ensuring the consistency among UML models, both across different UML notations and across levels of abstraction (e.g., high-level vs. low-level design). Our conclusions round out the paper.

2   Our Approach to Architecture-Based Development

The concepts discussed in this paper are independent of the application domain, the specifics of the chosen architectural style, and the modeling language(s). For illustration purposes, we have selected the C2 architectural style [18]. C2 serves solely as a vehicle for exploring our ideas. It allows us to discuss the development issues relevant at the architectural level and motivates the discussion of transforming an architectural model into UML. This section also highlights certain approaches to software modeling and analysis that are not available in UML.

An architecture in the C2 style consists of components, connectors (buses), and their configurations. Each component has two connection points, a "top" and a "bottom." Components communicate solely by exchanging messages. The top (bottom) of a component can only be attached to the bottom (top) of one bus. It is not possible for components to be attached directly to each other: buses always have to act as intermediaries between them. However, two buses can be attached together.

We illustrate the above concepts with an example. The architecture we use is a logistics system for routing incoming cargo to a set of warehouses, shown in Figure 2. The *DelPort, Vehicle,* and *Warehouse* components are objects that keep track of the states of a delivery port, a transportation vehicle, and a warehouse, respectively. Each may be instantiated multiple times in a system. The *DelPortArt, VehicleArt,* and *WarehouseArt* components are responsible for graphically depicting the states of their respective objects to the end-user. The *CargoRouter* organizes the display based on the actual number of port, vehicle, and warehouse instances in the system. The *Clock* provides consistent time measurement to interested components, while the *NextShipment* component determines when cargo arrives at a port, keeps track of available transport vehicles at each port, and tracks the cargo during its delivery to a warehouse. The *GraphicsBinding* component renders the drawing requests sent from the *CargoRouter* using a graphics toolkit, such as Java's AWT. The five connectors

---

[1] Note that a portion of Rapide falls outside this "extended UML" in Figure 1. This is a reflection of the fact that UML is not always able to support all features of a given ADL [12].

receive, filter, and route the messages sent by components to their appropriate recepients.

2.1 Architectural Analysis

To support architecture modeling, analysis, implementation, and evolution, we have developed a formal *type system* for software architectures [8,11,13]. We treat every component specification at the architectural level as an *architectural type*. We distinguish architectural types from *basic types* (e.g., integer, boolean, string, array, record, etc.). A component has a name, a set of internal state variables, a set of interface elements, an associated behavior, and (possibly) an implementation.

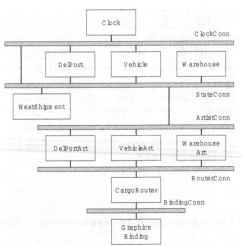

Fig. 2. Architecture of the cargo routing system

Each interface element has a direction indicator (*prov*ided or *req*uired), a name, a set of parameters, and (possibly) a result. Component behavior consists of an invariant and a set of operations. The invariant is used to specify properties that must be true of all component states. Each operation has preconditions, postconditions, and (possibly) a result. Like interface elements, operations can be *prov*ided or *req*uired. The preconditions and postconditions of required operations express the *expected* semantics for those operations. We separate the interface from the behavior, defining a mapping function from interface elements to operations. This function is a total surjection: each interface element is mapped to exactly one operation, while each operation implements at least one interface. An interface element can be mapped to an operation only if the types of its parameters are subtypes of the corresponding variable types in the operation, while the type of its result is a supertype of operation's result type. This property directly enables a single operation to export multiple interfaces.

This set of definitions allows us to formally treat two distinct development activities: evolution of individual components via subtyping [8] and analysis of an architecture for conformance among interacting components. In this paper we focus on the latter. The left side of Figure 3 shows the relevant definitions of interface parameter conformance and operation conformance.[2] The right side of Figure 3 is a reflection of our experience that components need not always be able to fully interoperate in an architecture, but that mismatches should be allowed under certain situations (e.g., COTS reuse). The two extreme points on the spectrum of type conformance are: *minimal type conformance*, where at least one service (interface and

---

[2] The definitions are specified in Z, a language for modeling mathematical objects based on first order logic and set theory [17]. Z uses standard logical connectives ($\land$, $\lor$, $\Rightarrow$, etc.) and set-theoretic operations($\in$, $\cup$, $\subseteq$, etc.). The complete formal defintion of the type system is given in [11].

```
┌─ Param_Conformance ──────────────┐   ┌─ Minimal_Type_Conformance ──────────┐
  Basic_Type_Conformance              Interface_Conformance
  Param_Name_Conformance              Behavior_Conformance
  Prm_Conf : Int_Element ⇸ Int_Element  Architecture
├──────────────────────────────────┤   ├─────────────────────────────────────┤
  ∀ ie1, ie2 : Int_Element •          ∀ c1 : Component | c1 ∈ components •
    (ie1, ie2) ∈ Prm_Conf             ∃ c2 : Component | c2 ∈ components ∧ (c1, c2) ∈ Comm_Link •
    ⇔                                   (∃ ie1, ie2 : Int_Element |
    (ie1, ie2) ∈ Prm_Nam_Conf ∧         ie1 ∈ c1.interface ∧ ie2 ∈ c2.interface •
    (∀ p1, p2 : Variable |              ie1.name = ie2.name ∧
    p1 ∈ ie1.params ∧ p2 ∈ ie2.params ∧ p1.name = p2.name •   ie1.dir = REQ ∧ ie2.dir = PROV ∧
    (p2.type, p1.type) ∈ Basic_Conf)    (ie1, ie2) ∈ Prm_Conf ∧
                                        (c1.int_op_map(ie1),
                                        c2.int_op_map(ie2)) ∈ Oper_Conf)
```

```
┌─ Oper_Conformance ───────────────┐
  Basic_Type_Conformance
  Logical_Implication
  Oper_Conf : Operation ⇸ Operation       ┌─ Full_Type_Conformance ──────────────┐
├──────────────────────────────────┤        Interface_Conformance
  ∀ o1, o2 : Operation •                     Behavior_Conformance
    (o1, o2) ∈ Oper_Conf                     Architecture
    ⇔                                      ├──────────────────────────────────────┤
    (∀ v1 : Variable | v1 ∈ o1.vars •        ∀ c1 : Component; ie1 : Int_Element |
    ∃ v2 : Variable | v2 ∈ o2.vars •           c1 ∈ components ∧ ie1 ∈ c1.interface ∧ ie1.dir = REQ •
    (v1.type, v2.type) ∈ Basic_Conf ∨        ∃ c2 : Component; ie2 : Int_Element |
    (v2.type, v1.type) ∈ Basic_Conf) ∧         c2 ∈ components ∧ (c1, c2) ∈ Comm_Link ∧
    (o1.precond, o2.precond) ∈ Logic_Impl ∧    ie2 ∈ c2.interface ∧ ie2.dir = PROV •
    (o2.postcond, o1.postcond) ∈ Logic_Impl ∧  ie1.name = ie2.name ∧
    (o1.result, o2.result) ∈ Basic_Conf        (ie1, ie2) ∈ Prm_Conf ∧
                                               (c1.int_op_map(ie1), c2.int_op_map(ie2)) ∈ Oper_Conf
```

Fig. 3. Formal specification of architectural type conformance predicates

corresponding operation) required by each component is provided by some other component along its communication links; and *full type conformance*, where every service required by every component is provided by some component along its communication links.

2.2   Example of Architectural Analysis

We illustrate architectural type conformance with a simple example drawn from the cargo routing application (recall Figure 2). Figure 4 shows partial models of the *DelPort* and *DelPortArt* components, specified in the C2SADEL ADL [13]. The two components are *intended* to interact in the cargo routing system (i.e., there is a communication path between them in the architecture via *StateConn* and *ArtistConn*). In the example from Figure 4, *DelPortArt* requires one service: *unloadShipment*, which is mapped to its operation *or1*. *DelPort* provides an operation, *op1*, with a matching interface (as required by the interface parameter conformance predicate in Figure 3). Thus, to establish type conformance, we must make sure that the pre- and postconditions of the two operations are properly related as specified in the operation conformance and minimal type conformance predicates in Figure 3. To do so, we must establish that the following relationships hold:

- *DelPortArt or1 pre* ⇒ *DelPort op1 pre*
  `(s ∉ contents) ⇒ true`
  Since *DelPort*'s *op1* does not have any preconditions, the right-hand side (RHS) of the implication becomes `true`. Therefore the entire implication evaluates to true regardless of the truth value of its left-hand side (LHS).
- *DelPort op1 post* ⇒ *DelPortArt or1 post*
  `((~cap = cap + ShpSize(s)) ∧ (s ∈ ~cargo)) ⇒ (s ∈ ~contents)`

```
component DelPortComponent is {            component DelPortArtComponent is {
state { cap : Int; max_cap : Int;          state { selects : \set Int;
        cargo : \set Shipment;                     UniqueID : Int \x Int -> Int; }
        ShpSize : Shipment -> Int }         invariant { #selects \eqgreater 0; }
invariant { cap \eqgreater 0 \and          interface {
            cap \eqless max_cap; }           prov ip1: selectShipment(port : Int;
interface {                                                            shp : Int);
  prov ip1: unloadShipment(s : Shipment);    req ir1: unloadShipment(s : Shipment); }
  req ir1: Tick(); }                        operations {
operations {                                 prov op1: {
  prov op1: {                                  let pid : Int; sid : Int;
    let s : Shipment;                          post (#~selects = #selects + 1) \and
    post (~cap = cap + ShpSize(s))                  (UniqueID(pid,sid) \in selects); }
         \and (s \in ~cargo); }             req or1: {
  req or1: {                                   let s : Shipment;
    let time : STATE_VARIABLE;                    contents : STATE_VARIABLE;
    post ~time = 1 + time; } }                 pre (s \not_in contents);
map {                                          post (s \in ~contents); } }
  ip1 -> op1 (s -> s);                      map {
  ir1 -> or1 (); }                            ip1 -> op1 (port -> pid, shp -> sid);
}                                             ir1 -> or1 (s -> s); }
                                           }
```

Fig. 4. Partial specification of the DelPort and DelPortArt components. # denotes set cardinality; ~ denotes the value of a variable after the operation executes; STATE_VARIABLE is a placeholder for any basic type

The two matching interface elements (*unloadShipment*) of the *DelPort* and *DelPortArt* components have matching parameters (s), which are mapped to the respective components' operation variables (also s). *DelPortArt*'s variable contents is of type STATE_VARIABLE, which is intended to generically describe the internal state of another component in a required operation.[3] contents can be unified with the *DelPort* internal state variable cargo, so that the implication becomes

$$((\sim\text{cap} = \text{cap} + \text{ShpSize(s)}) \land (\text{s} \in \sim\text{cargo})) \Rightarrow (\text{s} \in \sim\text{cargo})$$

This implication is of the form $(A \land B) \Rightarrow B$ and is also true: an implication can be false only if its RHS (B) evaluates to false; however, in this case that would result in the LHS $(A \land B)$ also evaluating to false, making the implication true.

We have thus established that, at the least, minimal type conformance holds in the architectural interaction between *DelPort* and *DelPortArt*.

2.3   Architectural Simulation

The example above demonstrate how an architecture can be analyzed statically for desired properties. Another way in which we have been able to analyze C2-style architectures has been through early simulations of applications, built based on the applications' architectural models. To this end, we have exploited C2's event-based nature: one can rapidly construct a partial implementation of an architecture that mainly focuses on the components' external (asynchronous message) interfaces. For example, a prototype of the cargo routing application discussed above was initially implemented and later augmented to include a foreign-language user interface by a single developer in a matter of hours [2]. Our support tools also allow insertion of event monitors and filters to explicitly observe message traffic and assess dynamic properties of the architecture. Any inconsistencies in the architecture not detected by

---

[3]   For a more formal and in-depth treatment of STATE_VARIABLE types, see [11]

type conformance checking, such as inconsistencies in component interaction protocols, are likely to manifest themselves during simulations.

2.4 Tool Support

The activities described in this section (architecture modeling, analysis, simulation, implementation, and evolution) are supported by DRADEL, a component-based development environment [13], and a light-weigt simulation and implementation infrastructure [9]. Three of DRADEL's components are particularly relevant to this discussion (a fourth component will be discussed in Section 3):

- The *TopologicalConstraintChecker* component analyzes an architecture for adherence to design heuristics and architectural style rules. Currently, this component ensures the rules of the C2 style, but can be easily replaced with components enforcing other kinds of design rules.
- The *TypeChecker* component implements the rules of our architectural type system, briefly discussed in Section 2.1. The *TypeChecker* automatically performs the conformance checks such as those shown in Section 2.2.
- The *CodeGenerator* component automatically generates architecture implementation skeletons discussed in Section 2.3. The skeletons are generated based on a component's architectural model specified in C2SADEL: all message generation, marshalling, and unmarshalling code is produced, as is a stub for the component's internal (application-specific) behavior. Component stubs are then completed manually. The amount of effort needed to complete a stub depends on the desired faithfulness of the prototype implementation to the final system and it can range from a few to several hundred lines of code.

3   Refining an Architectural Model into a UML Model

Once an architectural model is constructured and its analysis and simulation demonstrate the presence (or absence) of properties of interest, the model can be used as a basis for system design and implementation. This requires the transfer of information from the architectural model to a (high-level) design and subsequent refinement of that design. One way to effectively accomplish this task is by transferring the application model from an ADL to a notation better suited for addressing lower-level design issues. We employ UML [1] to that end.

UML is a semi-formally defined design language with a large, extensible set of modeling features that span a number of modeling diagrams (see Section 1). Our previous work has studied in depth the relationsip between ADLs and UML [10,12,16]. One outcome of this research has been a set of well-defined strategies one could employ to meaningfully transfer an ADL model into UML. Based on this work, we have recently augmented the DRADEL environment discussed in Section 2.4 to include *UMLGenerator*, a component that transforms a C2SADEL specification into a UML model. *UMLGenerator* uses a set of formally defined rules that specify how each C2SADEL construct is transformed into a corresponding (set of) UML construct(s). The rules make use of predefined UML constructs, as well as *stereotypes*, UML's built-in extensibility mechanisms. Stereotypes allow the addition of attributes to existing modeling elements (via *tagged values*) and the restriction of modeling element semantics (via *constraints*). The constraint portion of a stereotype is formally specified in UML's Object Constraint Language (OCL) [19]. For example, the compositional rules of the C2 architectural style, discussed in Section 2, can be specified using a UML stereotype as follows.

Stereotype C2Architecture for instances of meta class Model

[1] A C2 architecture is made up of only C2 model elements.

```
SELF.OCLTYPE.MODELELEMENT->FORALL(ME|ME.STEREOTYPE= C2COMPONENT OR
ME.STEREOTYPE = C2CONNECTOR OR ME.STEREOTYPE = C2ATTACHOVERCOMP OR
ME.STEREOTYPE = C2ATTACHUNDERCOMP OR ME.STEREOTYPE = C2ATTACHCONNCONN)
```

[2] Each C2Component has at most one C2AttachConnAbove.

```
LET COMPS=SELF.OCLTYPE.MODELELEMENT->SELECT(ME|ME.STEREOTYPE=C2COMPONENT),
COMPS->FORALL(C | C.ASSOCEND.ASSOCIATION->SELECT(A |
            A.STEREOTYPE = C2ATTACHCONNABOVE)->SIZE <= 1)
```

[3] Each C2Component has at most one C2AttachConnBelow.
Similar to the constraint above.

[4] Each C2Component must be attached to some connector.

```
LET COMPS=SELF.OCLTYPE.MODELELEMENT->SELECT(ME|ME.STEREOTYPE=C2COMPONENT),
COMPS->FORALL(C | C.ASSOCEND.ASSOCIATION->SIZE > 0)
```

[5] Each C2Connector must be attached to some connector or component.

```
LET CONNS=SELF.OCLTYPE.ELEMENTS->SELECT(E|E.STEREOTYPE=C2CONNECTOR),
CONNS->FORALL(C | C.ASSOCEND.ASSOCIATION->SIZE > 0)
```

The above stereotype describes only one portion of C2 and is accompanied by other stereotypes defining C2 components and connectors, their interactions, and the internal makeup of individual components and connectors as specified in C2SADEL [13]. This complete specification of C2 concepts in terms of UML stereotypes was used as the basis for implementing the *UMLGenerator* component. Figure 5 shows a partial and somewhat simplified set of C2SADEL-to-UML transformation rules as encoded in the *UMLGenerator*.

```
Internal Component Object → Class
State Variable → Class Private Attribute
Component Invariant → Tagged Value + Class Documentation
Provided Operation → Class Operation
Required Operation → Class Documentation
    Operation Pre/Post Condition → Pre/Post Condition on Class Operation
    Message Return Type → Return Type on Class Operation
    Message Parameter → Parameter (Name + Type) on Class Operation
Architecture Configuration (explicit invocation) → (Object) Collaboration Diagram
    Component Instance → Internal Component Object Class Instance
    Connector Instance → «Interface» Class Instance
    Component/Connector Binding → Object Link (instance of an association)
Component → «C2-Component» Class
    Internal Component Object → «C2-Component» Class Attribute
    Component Top Interface → «Interface» Class
    Component Bottom Interface → «Interface» Class
    Outgoing Message → «Interface» Class «out» Operation
Incoming Message → «Interface» Class «in» Operation
```

Fig. 5. Excerpt from the rule set for transforming C2SADEL into UML. «» denotes stereotypes

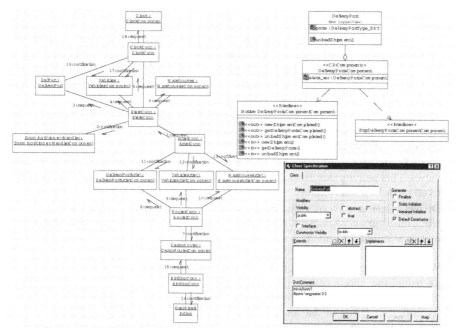

Fig. 6. Partial UML model of CargoRouter architecture (using Rational Rose™)

The UML specification resulting from this transformation is stored as a Rational Rose™ model [15]. A portion of the Rose model for the cargo router architecture from Figure 2 is shown in Figure 6: it depicts the entire architecture as a UML collaboration diagram (left) and the attributes of and class diagram corresponding to the *DeliveryPort* component (right). This automatically generated Rose model is consistent with the architectural model and is used as the basis for further, possibly manual refinement of the architecture as discussed below.

4   Design Refinement and Analysis

Architectural refinement enables us to transform our C2 architecture into a (high-level) UML design. Since that design will likely be further refined into lower-level designs (and an implementation), those subsequent refinements may become inconsistent with the original architecture. This is particularly likely if the refinements are done manually. This section will discuss how a refinement can be automated by employing a technique that augments UML (recall Figure 1).

4.1   View Integration Framework

To enable automated design analysis we have devised and applied a view integration framework, accompanied with a set of activities and techniques for identifying mismatches in an automatable fashion [3]. This approach exploits redundancy between views: for instance, if view A contains information about view B, this information can be seen as a constraint on B. The view integration framework is used to enforce such constraints and, thereby, the consistency across the views. In addition to constraints and consistency rules, our framework also defines *what* information can be exchanged and *how* it can be exchanged. This is critical for automating the process of identifying and resolving inconsistencies since direct comparison between views is usually infeasible. Our framework has three major activities:

- **Mapping** identifies related pieces of information and thereby describes what information is overlapping. Mapping is often done manually, e.g., via naming dictionaries and traceability matrices.
- **Transformation** simplifies (i.e., abstracted) detailed views or generalizes specific views. This activity describes how information can be exchanged and results in derived modeling information.
- **Differentiation** traverses the model to identify mismatches. *Mapping* indicates what information should be compared; *Transformation* indicates how that information should be compared.

We will illustrate these concepts using the cargo router example. Figure 7 depicts an excerpt of its design in UML in the form of a class diagram. This design varies considerably from the high-level design we generated in Section 3. As the design is further modified, it will become increasingly difficult to see whether the changes are consistent with the original architecture, depicted in Figure 2. Again, note that the architectural and design views show distinct but overlapping

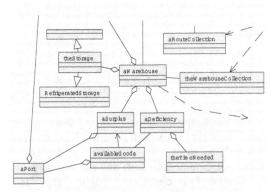

Fig. 7. Design Refinement of CargoRouter

information; this redundancy between the views is used in the form of constraints in helping to verify consistency. It has been our observation that the major challenge of view integration is not the actual comparison of views (*Differentiation*) but instead the *Transformation* and *Mapping* of modeling information [3]. Since *Mapping* tends to be predominantly manual, *Transformation* becomes the key enabling technology for automated view integration. We, therefore, discuss it on more detail.

4.2 Transformation

Figure 8 captures the three major dimensions of view transformation [3]. Software modeling views can be seen as abstract or concrete on the one hand, and generic or specific on the other. The abstract-concrete dimension was foreshadowed in Section 3 where the C2 architecture was the abstract view and the generated UML model was the concrete view. Note that a view's level of abstraction is relative. Thus, for in-

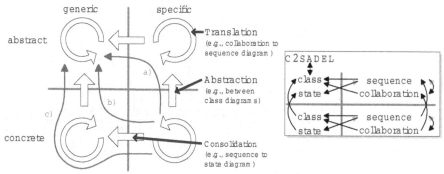

Fig. 8. Two dimensions of views with three dimensions of view transformations. Paths a-d denote possible transformation paths from concrete-specific to abstract.

stance, the derived UML model depicted in Figure 6 is concrete relative to the C2 view but abstract relative to the class diagram in Figure 7.[4]

The generic-specific dimension denotes the generality of modeling information. For instance, a class diagram naturally describes a general relationship between classes, whereas a sequence diagram describes a specific scenario. Another way of saying this is that constructs in general views must capture the union of all specific views, and that a specific view must fit within the boundaries of its respective generic one. The level of generality/specificity is, again, in the eye of the beholder (e.g., a view is more generic than some views and more specific than others).

Having two dimensions of views implies three types of transformation axes: *Abstraction* to capture vertical transformation, *Consolidation* to capture horizontal transformation, and *Translation* to capture transformation within a single quadrant (both input and output views are of the same category). We have also observed that often only uni-dimensions transformations can be fully automated (e.g., [4,5]) - usually going from concrete to abstract or from specific to generic.

The framework depicted in Figure 8 allows us to combine simple transformation techniques to enable more complex transformations in support of the integration of C2SADEL and UML. Figure 8 depicts one such complex transformation going from the lower right quadrant (e.g., a concrete sequence diagram) to the upper left quadrant (e.g., an abstract class diagram). The three paths ("a" to "c") indicate the three alternative transformation scenarios on how to get there. Path "a" first abstracts the sequence diagram and then consolidates it to yield a class diagram view. Path "b" first consolidates and then abstracts. Path "c" consolidates, translates, and abstracts. There are of course other variations using additional translations. The translation step may seem redundant since it does not seem to put us any closer to the target quadrant. Nevertheless, translation can help us in circumventing a non-existing transformation by translating to another view that can be abstracted/consolidated or by switching to a more reliable abstraction/consolidation method not available within the current view.

---

[4] Note that the implementation is the most concrete view of a system.

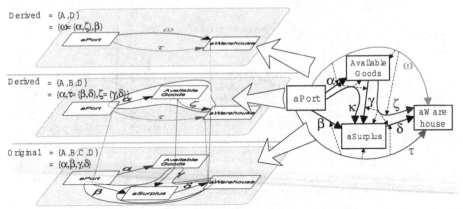

Fig. 9. Representation of Abstraction Transformation (multiple views and their storage)

The right hand-side of Figure 8 depicts existing transformations our approach currently supports (e.g., concrete class to abstract class, sequence to state, etc.). Note that a few arrows are double-headed, with the second head drawn in a light gray shade. These cases denote examples where the reverse transformation is semi-automated.

4.3   Implication of Transformation for Consistency Checking

Complex transformations are not just a serial execution of individual transformations. To enable complex transformations we also need to address the issue of how to capture and maintain modeling information – in particular, how to handle derived modeling information [3]. Thus, transformation methods need to be integrated in order to avoid the two fundamental problems that may arise:

1. Transformation Redundancy: a modeling element should be transformed at most once using the same transformation method, thus avoiding transformation redundancy.
2. Multiple Derived Results: multiple transformations of a modeling element using different transformation methods may result in multiple results. The model must therefore support multiple interpretations.

Figure 9 demonstrates both issues using *relation abstraction* (a method that collapses relations among multiple modeling elements into simpler relations). The bottom-most layer on the left hand-side shows an excerpt of the class diagram from Figure 7 with four classifiers (boxes) and a number of relations (links) between them. The middle layer is more abstract in that the classifier *aSurplus* has been eliminated and a more abstract relation (τ) has been created to replace it. The top-most layer further eliminates the classifier *availableGoods*. We now have three views. If we were to store the views separately, we might eventually introduce inconsistencies between them. For instance, any changes to the bottom view would require updates to all its higher-level abstractions. This would likely become unmanageable in a large-scale system with a large number of user-created views plus all their transformations. Furthermore, if we again take the bottom view and abstract *aSurplus* away, we are duplicating both effort and storage since we are not aware of the previous abstraction. The right hand-side of Figure 9 depicts a possible solution for these two problems. It suggests using an n-ary relationship among modeling elements. The figures on the left are now simply projections of the model on the right. The underlying model on the right minimizes information duplication. Note that UML does not support n-ary relationships among many of its modeling elements, partially motivating our decision to augment it. Revisiting Figure 1, the problem of how to deal with derived modeling elements can only be solved by augmenting the model.

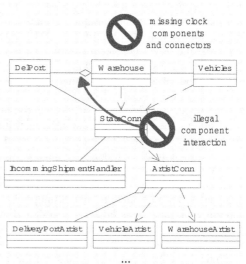

Fig. 10. Except of Abstracted Class Diagram

4.4 Consistency Checking

The issues discussed in sections 4.1 and 4.2 form the foundation that allows us to check the relative consistency of two or more UML models. Thus, in order to ensure the consistency of the UML model in Figure 7 with respect to the original C2 architecture in Figure 2 (or Figure 6) we can automatically derive the transformation paths, perform the actual transformations (the refinement of the C2 model and the abstraction of the class diagram), and then compare their respective results (two class diagrams at similar levels of abstraction). Figure 10 shows an excerpt of the abstraction from Figure 7 using a set of abstraction rules discussed in Section 4.2 and completely specified in [4]. We can now observe that the architecture differs from the design in several ways: the design does not include the *Clock* component or its related connector and depicts some component interactions (e.g., *DelPort* to *Warehouse*) that are not defined in the architecture.

Although it is possible that both these cases are results of deliberate design decisions, transformation has enabled us to easily compare the two views and quickly highlight their inconsistencies. The human designer can then either address the inconsistencies or ignore them. To date, we have automated a part of our view integration framework in a tool called UML/Analyzer [3]. The abstracted view depicted in Figure 10 can be derived automatically using our tool.

5   Conclusion

This paper addressed architectural modeling using a specialized approach, C2, and showed how it can be used to complement a general-purpose modeling language, UML. We discussed the benefits of C2 and UML as well as the need for integrating their respective strengths. The integration of C2 and UML is not a trivial undertaking and we introduced two techniques to enable it: *constraining UML* and *augmenting it*. We showed how to represent C2 in UML (Section 3) in order to illustrate *constraining UML* and how to perform complex transformations and view integration (Section 4) in order to illustrate *augmenting UML*.

This paper also presented formal approaches to software development to support a variety of development activities (specification, analysis, and modeling). Formalism plays a major role during all of those activities. Formalism is also the foundation of automation. The benefits of automation were illustrated throughout this paper. In Section 2, we discussed the analytic powers of special-purpose models like C2. Using C2 we were able to automatically analyze static and dynamic properties of our system. Automation then helped us in further refining our special-purpose C2 model into a general-purpose UML model (Section 3). This automated refinement capability removed a major obstacle to model integration since no manual labor was required in making tools and models work together. Finally, automation supported us during model validation. We illustrated automated consistency checking between views and demonstrated this using a C2 architecture and its corresponding UML design (Sec. 4).

To date, we have automated many of the concepts discussed in this paper and created two tool suites: SAAGE (Dradel+Rose) to enable architectural modeling and refinement; and UML/Analyzer (also integrated with Rose) to enable automated transformations and consistency checking. It is our long-term vision to further extend the automation support to other aspects of the software life cycle.

6 Acknowledgements

This research is sponsored by DARPA through Rome Laboratory under contract F30602-94-C-0195 and by the Affiliates of the USC Center for Software Engineering: http://sunset.usc.edu/CSE/Affiliates.html.

7 References

1. Booch, G., Jacobson, I., Rumbaugh, J.: The Unified Modeling Language User Guide, Addison-Wesley, 1998
2. DARPA. Evolutionary Design of Complex Software (EDCS): Demonstration Days 1999. http://www.if.afrl.af.mil/programs/edcs/demo-days-99/
3. Egyed, A.: "Integrating Architectural Views in UML," Qualifying Report, Technical Report, Center for Software Engineering, University of Southern California, USC-CSE-99-514, http://sunset.usc.edu/TechRpts/Papers/usccse99-514/usccse99-514.pdf, 1999
4. Egyed, A. and Kruchten, P.: Rose/Architect: a tool to visualize software architecture. *Proceedings of the 32nd Annual Hawaii Conference on Systems Sciences* (1999)
5. Koskimies, K., Systä, T., Tuomi, J., and Männistö, T. (1998) "Automated Support for Modelling OO Software," IEEE Software, January, pp. 87-94.

6. Luckham, D.C. and Vera, J.: "An Event-Based Architecture Definition Language." IEEE Transactions on Software Engineering, vol. 21, no. 9, pages 717-734, September 1995.
7. Medvidovic, N., Egyed, A., and Rosenblum, D.S.: Round-Trip Software Engineering Using UML: From Architecture to Design and Back. In Proceedings of the Second International Workshop on Object-Oriented Reengineering (WOOR'99), Toulouse, France, September 6, 1999.
8. Medvidovic, N., Oreizy, P., Robbins, J.E., and Taylor, R.N.: Using Object-Oriented Typing to Support Architectural Design in the C2 Style. In Proceedings of the Fourth ACM SIGSOFT Symposium on the Foundations of Software Engineering (FSE4), pp. 24-32, San Francisco, CA, October 16-18, 1996.
9. Medvidovic, N., Oreizy, P., and Taylor, R.N.: Reuse of Off-the-Shelf Components in C2-Style Architectures. In Proceedings of the 1997 Symposium on Software Reusability (SSR'97), pp. 190-198, Boston, MA, May 17-19, 1997. Also in Proceedings of the 1997 International Conference on Software Engineering (ICSE'97), pp. 692-700, Boston, MA, May 17-23, 1997.
10. Medvidovic, N. and Rosenblum, D.S.: Assessing the Suitability of a Standard Design Method for Modeling Software Architectures. In Proceedings of the First Working IFIP Conference on Software Architecture (WICSA1), pp. 161-182, San Antonio, TX, February 22-24, 1999.
11. Medvidovic, N., Rosenblum, D.S., and Taylor, R.N.: A Type Theory for Software Architectures. Technical Report, UCI-ICS-98-14, Department of Information and Computer Science, University of California, Irvine, April 1998.
12. Medvidovic, N., Rosenblum, D.S., Robbins, J.E., Redmiles, D.F.: Modeling Software Architectures in the Unified Modeling Language. In submission.
13. Medvidovic, N., Rosenblum, D.S., and Taylor, R.N.: A Language and Environment for Architecture-Based Software Development and Evolution. In Proceedings of the 21st International Conference on Software Engineering (ICSE'99), pp. 44-53, Los Angeles, CA, May 16-22, 1999.
14. Medvidovic, N., and Taylor, R.N.: A Classification and Comparison Framework for Software Architecture Description Languages. IEEE Transactions on Software Engineering, to appear, 2000.
15. Rational Software Corporation, Rational Rose 98: Using Rational Rose
16. Robbins, J.E., Medvidovic, N., Redmiles, D.F., and Rosenblum, D.S.: Integrating Architecture Description Languages with a Standard Design Method. In Proceedings of the 20th International Conference on Software Engineering (ICSE'98), pp. 209-218, Kyoto, Japan, April 19-25, 1998.
17. Spivey, J.M.: The Z notation: a reference manual. Prentice Hall, New York, 1989.
18. Taylor, R.N., Medvidovic, N., Anderson, K.N., Whitehead, E.J., Jr., Robbins, J.E., Nies, K.A., Oreizy, P., and Dubrow, D.L.: A Component- and Message-Based Architectural Style for GUI Software. IEEE Transactions on Software Engineering, vol. 22, no. 6, pp. 390-406, 1996.
19. Warmer, J.B., Kleppe, A.G.: The Object Constraint Language: Precise Modeling With UML, Addison-Wesley, 1999

Formal Specification of Object-Oriented Meta-modelling

Gunnar Övergaard

Royal Institute of Technology, Stockholm, Sweden

Abstract. Modelling languages such as the Unified Modeling Language are used during the early phases of system development to capture requirements and to express high-level designs. Many such languages have no universally fixed interpretations since different development projects often use key concepts, like Class, Generalization and Association, in slightly different ways. Therefore *meta-modelling*, i.e. the precise specification of the concepts used in a model, is of importance in order to avoid misunderstandings.

The BOOM framework, presented in this paper, is intended for this kind of meta-modelling. The framework consists of a collection of modelling constructs specified with a small object-oriented language. The framework is simple enough for an engineer to adjust the modelling concepts to project specific needs. It includes all necessary aspects of language specification, among them definition of abstract syntax, well-formedness rules, and dynamic semantics. To demonstrate its use, this paper includes a specification of some of the constructs defined in the Unified Modeling Language.

1   Introduction

There are many object-oriented system development methods used by industry today [5, 15, 17, 6, 1, 16]. Since these languages are used in the early phases of system development, expressiveness is more important than precision. Therefore, the languages typically have a rich and well-specified graphical syntax but no rigorous semantics. Some of these languages even include constructs for modifying the semantics of the language: the Unified Modeling Language [10] includes the Stereotype construct which enables the developer to modify the semantics of a construct as well as its notation. Only very few of the development methods have a formal specification, and these methods are usually developed for a specific organisation or a specific type of application, like SDL [4]. Methods that have received wider acceptance are usually informally specified.

However, informally and incompletely defined languages have several drawbacks. The system specifications in such languages will not have unique interpretations. A model can unintentionally be interpreted differently by different people, both within the project and outside the project. It is also hard to envisage effective computer tools that support the system development process, if the tool cannot access the intended meaning of the models.

T. Maibaum (Ed.): FASE 2000, LNCS 1783, pp. 193–207, 2000.

To avoid these problems, a modelling language needs a kind of formal semantics which is easy to understand and which can be easily modified. The definition must admit changes in the structure of the language constructs, in the meaning of these constructs, and in the combination of the constructs. The definition must be presented in an accessible way, so that system developers can understand and adjust it at need – it has to be a flexible language. At the same time, the specification must be rigorous enough to avoid unnecessary ambiguities.

Several different formal specification methods exist today (see e.g. the *Formal Methods* home page at *http://www.comlab.ox.ac.uk/archive/formal-methods. html*). These methods are based upon different kinds of formalisms. During the last decade, object-orientation has influenced the formal community resulting in formal object-oriented methods [2, 18]. In these methods, precision is combined with the advantages of object-orientation, such as encapsulation and inheritance.

A major reason for choosing an object-oriented formal specification language instead of a traditional one is that the intended user is acquainted with the object-oriented paradigm. In this way, there is no conceptual shift between the object-oriented *modelling language* and the object-oriented *specification method*. Moreover, just as an object-oriented technique, including factoring out commonalities, encapsulation and localization of information, is preferable for system development, it is also appropriate for language specification. Traditionally, the abstract syntax of a construct is separated from the definition of the rule that state when the construct is well-formed. Moreover, the specification of the dynamic semantics of the language is often separated from the rest of the specification. Understanding or adjusting the definition of a construct given in a traditional specification will therefore be much more difficult than in a specification using an object-oriented technique, since in the traditional specification the complete definition of the construct is spread out over several places.

Another advantage with an object-oriented specification technique is that it may include a library of predefined components in a language specification. Since different object-oriented modelling languages use similar constructs, each new specification does not have to start from scratch. Deviations from the predefined definition can be expressed in subclasses of the components.

Together the components form a so-called meta-model, i.e. they constitute a model of an object-oriented modelling language. The different kinds of constructs in the language are expressed with classes in the meta-model, and the associations between these classes state the relationships between the constructs. The methods that are defined in the classes in the meta-model specify both the well-formedness rules and the dynamic semantics of the language.

In this paper we present a meta-model for specification of modelling languages. The purpose of the meta-model is to provide a framework for defining the different constructs in such a language. The idea of this kind of framework arose from our participation in the team developing and enhancing the Unified Modeling Language. This paper is organized as follows: The next section presents a framework for specification of modelling languages, while Section 3 demonstrates its usage by expressing some of the constructs defined in the Unified Modeling Language in the framework. This paper ends with some concluding remarks.

2   BOOM – A Framework for Formal Specification

In this section we present BOOM, a framework for specification of object-oriented modelling languages. It includes all necessary aspects of language specification, among them definition of abstract syntax, well-formedness rules, and dynamic semantics. The framework consists of a meta-model of such languages and a formal specification language called ODAL which is used for defining the classes in the meta-model. ODAL is a simple, strongly typed object-oriented language with a familiar syntax. Its semantics is specified using the π-calculus [8]. In this it follows the principles from e.g. Walker [19] and Jones [7] where it is shown how the π-calculus is used to define object-oriented programming languages. The complete semantics of ODAL is approximately 50 pages and is out of the scope of this paper.

In BOOM we adopt a *localization principle* that implies a specification technique in which the semantics of the different kinds of relationships are separated from other kinds of constructs. For example, the specification of an object construct states that, among other things, an object has a set of relationships, but the specification of the construct does not include any of the semantics of these relationships. The meaning of a particular kind of relationship is defined separately. Hence, when a new kind of object construct is defined in the modelling language, features like atomic transactions, persistence etc. are included in the definition, but not features based on a relationship of a specific kind. Similarly, the definition of a class construct is made without any assumptions about e.g. the existence of a generalization construct.

BOOM includes all meta levels in one model, i.e. different meta levels are not separated into different models. This enables BOOM to express languages that support meta-modelling, like languages that include a meta-class construct or that allow explicit relationships to cross meta levels.

It should be noted that BOOM is not a model of a CASE-tool. The purpose of BOOM is to specify the semantics of modelling languages, i.e. its purpose is not to provide a model of how such a language should be implemented. There are several aspects which are not considered during the development of BOOM but which must be included in the design of a tool, like efficiency, storage etc.

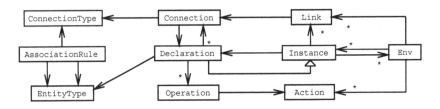

Fig. 1. A subset of BOOM in UML notation.

The core of BOOM contains approximately 30 classes for defining class-like constructs, binary relationships, instances and links, i.e. each class defines the abstract syntax as well as the static and the dynamic semantics of a construct. These classes are accompanied by a set of classes for specification of operations and actions. Moreover, BOOM contains classes for stating rules how different constructs may be connected to each other. Together, these classes form a framework for specification of modelling languages.

If BOOM does not contain a class which specifies the desired semantics exactly, a new class can be added. This new class usually becomes a subclass of an already existing class in BOOM, modifying selected parts of the existing class by overriding or extending some of its definitions.

Below we describe parts of BOOM. In Section 3, we use BOOM for specification of some of the constructs in the Unified Modeling Language [10].

2.1   Class-like Constructs

In BOOM class-like constructs in a modelling language, such as a Class construct or a Data Type construct, are expressed with the class Declaration. It specifies a construct which declares a set of features, and may create instances that offer these features. There may both be structural features, like attributes and associations to other class-like constructs, as well as be behavioural features, like operations and methods. In BOOM structural features are basically expressed with the Connection class, which specifies binary, directed relationships between Declarations, while the Operation class in BOOM is used for specifications of behavioural features. Hence, a Declaration includes a set of Connections and a set of Operations. In accordance with the localization principle a Declaration depends only on the existence of its Connections and Operation, not on their specific kinds. The semantics of the different kinds of features are specified within (subclasses of) the Connection class and the Operation class.

The different kinds of instance constructs in a model, like Object and Data Value, are expressed as instances of the BOOM class Instance. In an object-oriented model, an instance is created by, and therefore follows the declaration in, a class-like construct. This implies that an Instance is associated with a Declaration (its creator, or origin), and that the Instance has a set of Links corresponding to the set of Connections declared in its Declaration, as well as that it can perform the behaviour declared in the Operations of its Declaration.

Since BOOM defines all meta levels within one model, a Declaration must be an instance of another Declaration. The class Declaration is therefore a subclass of Instance. This implies that relationships between class-like constructs, like generalization between classes, are expressed with Links between Declarations.

The detailed specifications of Declaration, Instance and their subclasses are made in ODAL, a formal object-oriented language. Due to the scope of this paper we have excluded most of these details. However, some examples are to be found in the following. Although ODAL has not been presented in this paper, we believe that a reader who is familiar with object-oriented languages will have no problem of understanding these examples.

CLASS Instance
VARIABLES
   origin : Declaration,
   links : Link*
INVARIANT
   origin ≠ NULL
METHODS
initialize (o : Declaration,
        c : Connections) : Instance
   origin := o;
   FOREACH con IN c DO
     links ADD con createLink ()
entityType () : EntityType
   origin instanceKind ()
evaluateAction (a : Action) : Boolean
   . . .
        ⋮

CLASS Declaration SUPERCLASS Instance
VARIABLES
   operation : Operation*,
   connection : Connection*,
   instanceType : EntityType,
   name : Name
INVARIANT
   name ≠ NULL AND instanceType ≠ NULL
METHODS
addConnection (c : Connection) : Boolean
   IF SELF lookupConnection (c name ()) = NULL AND
     ruleset allowedConnection (
      SELF instanceKind (),
      c target () instanceKind (),
      c connectionType ()) THEN
     connection ADD c; TRUE
   ELSE FALSE
lookupConnection (n : Name) : Connection
   COLLECT c IN connection SUCHTHAT c name () = n
instanceKind () : EntityType
   instanceType
createInstance () : Instance
   instanceType source () NEW (SELF, connection)
        ⋮

For example, the meaning of adding a new Connection to a Declaration is defined in the *addConnection* operation in the Declaration class. It states that two conditions must be fulfilled: there must not be another Connection within the Declaration with the same name as the new one, and this kind of Connection must be allowed between the kinds of instances represented by the Declaration and by the target of the Connection. (The *ruleset* referenced in the operation specifies the allowed combinations. See Section 2.3.) If these conditions are fulfilled the Connection is added and the operation results in *true*.

2.2 Relationships

BOOM defines binary directed relationships, called Connections, between Declarations, and corresponding binary directed relationships, called Links, between Instances. A Link can only exist between two Instances if a corresponding Connection is declared between their Declarations (cf. the declaration of a variable and the variable slot). Hence, such relationship constructs, like Pointers, are easily specified using (a subclass of) the Connection class.

CLASS Connection
VARIABLES
   name : Name,
   target : Declaration,
   instanceType : ConnectionType
INVARIANT
   target ≠ NULL AND name ≠ NULL AND
   instanceType ≠ NULL
METHODS
target () : Declaration
   target
connectionType () : ConnectionType
   instanceType
createLink () : Link
   Link NEW (SELF)
      ⋮

CLASS Link
VARIABLES
   origin : Connection
   value : Instance*
INVARIANT
   origin ≠ NULL
METHODS
connectionType () : ConnectionType
   origin connectionType ()
      ⋮

If the modelling language contains more complex relationship constructs, like N-ary relationships or bi-directional relationships, a more complex mapping onto BOOM is required. Since the semantics of an N-ary relationship is in many ways similar to a class (each of its links is connected to a collection of instances), and a bi-directional relationship can be seen as a special case of an N-ary relationship, it is therefore not surprising that they are expressed in the same way as a class. For example, the different end-points of the relationship must have unique names which correspond to the requirement that the attributes of a class must have unique names. Hence, such a relationship is specified by mapping the relationship itself onto a Declaration, and the relationship's end-points onto Connections included in the Declaration (see the example in Section 3.2.)

2.3   Mapping Language Entities onto BOOM Classes

BOOM uses an explicit mapping between the names of the class-like and object-like constructs in a modelling language and the BOOM classes that specify the constructs. There are a few reasons for doing this. First, BOOM contains a set of predefined classes that have already been given names. When there is a mismatch between the name used in the modelling language and the name used in BOOM, a mapping resolves the conflict. Second, several constructs may be specified with the same BOOM class, e.g. a N-ary relationship may have the same semantics as an ordinary class. Instead of duplicating the BOOM class, both Class and N-ary Relationship may be mapped onto the same BOOM class. Third, to be able to compare constructs in different languages the names of the BOOM classes should not interfere. Finally, once the mapping of the language constructs onto BOOM classes has been established, the names used in the modelling language can be used. If, for example, the semantics of a construct is later modified, only the mapping has to be changed (possibly after adding a new class to BOOM which includes the changes.)

The mapping is done using three classes called EntityType, ConnectionType and LinkType. Each of them pairs a modelling construct name and a BOOM class; EntityType pairs the name with (a subclass of) the class Instance, while ConnectionType pairs the name and (a subclass of) the class Connection, and LinkType pairs the name with (a subclass of) the class Link. To express that a new entity is being defined in the modelling language, the class that the modelling constructs maps onto, is instantiated.

For example, assume that the Class construct has the semantics as defined by the Declaration class in BOOM, and that the semantics of the Object construct is specified by the Instance class. Moreover, assume that each object can have a set of pointers to other objects, i.e. the language includes a Pointer construct and therefore also a PointerDeclaration construct; the semantics of the Pointer construct is assumed to be defined by the Link class while the PointerDeclaration construct is specified with the Connection class. The mapping of these modelling constructs onto BOOM is defined by the following statements:

```
mapping ADD (EntityType NEW (CLASS, Declaration));
mapping ADD (EntityType NEW (OBJECT, Instance));
mapping ADD (ConnectionType NEW (POINTERDECLARATION, Connection));
mapping ADD (LinkType NEW (POINTER, Link));
```

When a new object is to be created, the BOOM class which the name OBJECT maps onto, i.e. Instance, is instantiated.

BOOM also requires that all allowed combinations of kinds of connections and kinds of declarations are explicitly enumerated. In this way it is stated what kinds of connections are meaningful between different kinds of constructs; no other combinations are allowed. For this purpose BOOM uses an explicit set of association rules. Each rule is expressed with a tuple of entity and connection names: ⟨*kind of source, kind of target, kind of connection*⟩.

In our small example, classes can declare pointers to classes. We therefore state that a class can be connected to a class with a pointer declaration. This is done with the following expression:

```
ruleset ADD (AssociationRule NEW (CLASS, CLASS, POINTERDECLARATION));
```

If a declaration of a connection is added to the model which does not conform to any of the association rules, the model is not well-formed, i.e. its semantics is not defined.

After defining how the different language constructs are mapped onto the BOOM classes that specify their semantics, and after stating what connections may be used between the different constructs, we can now define how the constructs in the language are connected to each other. We are using a graphical notation to do this. Figure 2 shows the different language constructs we have defined in our small example.

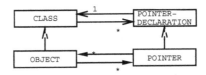

Fig. 2. A fragment of a meta-model of our example language.

A box denotes the language construct with the name equal to the string inside the box. An arrow from one box to another implies that an occurrence of the construct denoted by the source box contains a set of references to occurrences of the construct denoted by the target box. A declaration of a relationship is denoted by an open arrow head, while a closed arrow head denotes the connection itself. The multiplicity of the contained set is defined by the number or the interval at the arrow head ('*' denotes unlimited, i.e. any number of instances is allowed). A dashed arrow denotes an *instance-of* relationship.

The multiplicities stated on in these diagrams are included in the definition of the corresponding BOOM classes. The multiplicity on an arrow:

- from a Declaration to a Connection is included in the invariant of the Declaration
- from a Connection to a Declaration is always '1' (cf. there is only one type in a variable declaration)
- from an Instance to a Link is always '*', since the actual number of Links is always determined by the multiplicity on the arrow between the corresponding Declaration and Connection (see also the specification of the Instance class in Section 2.1).
- from a Link to an Instance is included in the invariant of the Link

Hence, in our small meta-model we have stated that an object may have a set of pointers, and that each pointer may reference a set of objects. Furthermore, an object is an instance of, i.e. it originates from, a class. A class may declare a set of pointers, and each of these references a class.

3   Formal Specification of UML Using BOOM

In this section we exemplify how BOOM is used for specification of modelling languages by presenting how some of the constructs in the Unified Modeling Language (UML) [10] can be expressed in BOOM. We will not present all the details regarding the BOOM classes but concentrate on the usage of BOOM. More detailed descriptions of the semantics can be found in e.g. [12, 11, 13]. In this paper we will focus our presentation on a few constructs in UML: Class, Association and Package.

3.1   Class Construct

In UML a class is a description of a set of objects that share the same structure and behaviour. More specifically, a class declares a set of attributes, and a set of operations, and may be attached to a collection of associations. (Due to the scope of this paper we ignore the other constructs for specification of behaviour, such as Methods and State Machines.) In BOOM the Declaration class specifies precisely this: it has a name, contains a set of Operations and a set of Connections. Hence, we use Declaration for specification of the Class construct.

Each attribute of the class declares a name and a reference to a data type. In BOOM the Connection class specifies a named connection to a (subclass of) Declaration. However, an attribute has a multiplicity stating how many data values an instance of the class should hold, which is absent in Connection. (We ignore some other properties of the Attribute construct, but these can be added similarly.) Therefore, a new class is defined in BOOM, called MultiplicityConnection. This class is a subclass of Connection; it adds an extra attribute, *multiplicity*, and a set of corresponding methods. Furthermore, the class also defines the extra semantics implied by the multiplicity property.

The operations of a UML class are defined similarly to attributes using (subclasses of) the class Operation in BOOM.

The specification of the Data Type construct can also be done with the Declaration class, because the construct supports the same features as the Class construct. However, instances of these two constructs have different semantics. They are therefore specified using two different BOOM classes: Object is an ordinary kind of instance, while a Data Value cannot modify its own state. Therefore, the Object construct is specified using the Instance class, while Data Value is specified using the TokenInstance subclass of Instance.

In UML the connection between an object and a data value is called an Attribute Link. It corresponds to an attribute in the object's class, and it holds the actual attribute values. However, the number of data values referenced by the attribute link must fulfil the requirement stated by the multiplicity declared by the attribute. This is specified in the NumberedLink class in BOOM.

Hence, we state how these constructs are mapped onto BOOM and how they may be connected with the following ODAL expressions:

```
mapping ADD (EntityType NEW (CLASS, Declaration));
mapping ADD (EntityType NEW (DATATYPE, Declaration));
mapping ADD (EntityType NEW (OBJECT, Instance));
mapping ADD (EntityType NEW (DATAVALUE, TokenInstance));
mapping ADD (ConnectionType NEW (ATTRIBUTE, MultiplicityConnection));
mapping ADD (LinkType NEW (ATTRIBUTELINK, NumberedLink));
ruleset ADD (AssociationRule NEW (CLASS, DATATYPE, ATTRIBUTE));
```

The meta-model defining these constructs and how they are related to each other is found in Figure 3.

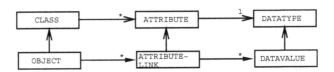

Fig. 3. A fragment of a meta-model presenting the Class and Attribute constructs of UML.

Note that this kind of diagram only present the constructs and how they are related. The detailed formal semantics of each construct is specified with the ODAL language, and is found in the BOOM classes that each construct maps onto.

3.2   Association Construct

The Association construct of UML is a relationship with at least two end-points. These end-points are similar to the attributes of a class; they have a name and a multiplicity. (Once again we ignore some of its properties, but these can be specified using the same technique as in the case of *multiplicity*.) We therefore define the Association End construct to be specified by the MultiplicityConnection class. This class has an extra attribute representing the multiplicity, as well as some methods using this attribute. The Association construct itself can be specified with the Declaration construct, since in UML an Association can create instances, called Links, and it has a name and includes operations for reading and modifying the end-points of these Links. There is, however, an extra requirement that must be fulfilled by an Association which is absent in a Class: it must have at least two association end-points (see Figure 4). Therefore, a new class is defined in BOOM, called AssociationDeclaration. It is a subclass of Declaration; the difference is that the subclass has an extended invariant stating the extra requirement. (In fact, there are also other differences between the N-ary Association construct and the Class construct, and all these differences are captured by the AssociationDeclaration class in BOOM.)

To specify the UML Association construct the following ODAL expression establish the mapping between the constructs:

```
mapping ADD (EntityType NEW (ASSOCIATION, AssociationDeclaration));
mapping ADD (ConnectionType NEW (ASSOCIATIONEND, MultiplicityConnection));
ruleset ADD (AssociationRule NEW (ASSOCIATION, CLASS, ASSOCIATIONEND));
```

Similarly, the Link and Link End constructs of UML correspond to the Object and Attribute Link constructs. However, Link End has an additional requirement: it must be connected to exactly one instance, and not to a set of instances. Hence, a new BOOM class is defined: SingleLink.
These two constucts are mapped onto BOOM with the following expressions:

```
mapping ADD (EntityType NEW (LINK, Instance));
mapping ADD (LinkType NEW (LINKEND, SingleLink));
```

The meta-model specifying these constructs and how they are related to each other is presented in Figure 4.

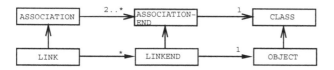

Fig. 4. A fragment of a meta-model presenting the Association and Link constructs of UML.

Once again, the details of the specifications are to be found in the BOOM classes. The diagram only presents the constructs and their relationships. A formal specification in ODAL of some of the relationship constructs in UML is found in [11].

3.3   Package Construct

In UML Packages are used for grouping elements, such as Classes and Packages, into units that act as name spaces for their contained elements, i.e. each contained element must have a unique name within the package. Furthermore, a package is not instantiable, which implies that it does not exist at the object level; its sole purpose from a semantic point of view is to define a name space. We will use the Package construct of UML to exemplify how relationships at the model level are expressed in BOOM by specifying that packages can contain classes.

In BOOM the specific connection between two instances is expressed with a Link, while the declaration of that connection is expressed with a (subclass of) Connection. This implies that the relationship between a specific package and its contents is expressed with a Link. Hence, the declaration of this Link is expressed between the creator of the package and the creator of the contents. We therefore introduce the MetaClass and the MetaPackage constructs. When these constructs are instantiated, Classes and Packages are created. Hence, the Contents relationship, stating that a package may contain classes, is declared from MetaPackage to MetaClass. In this way each package has a link expressing the connection between the package and its contained classes.

To specify the MetaClass construct we use the MetaDeclaration class of BOOM, which is a subclass of Declaration, but which creates Declarations instead of Instances. The MetaPackage construct might also have been specified with the MetaDeclaration class, but the construct has an additional constraint: it must have a containment relationship (see Figure 5). Therefore, the MetaPackage construct is mapped onto the NamespaceDeclaration, which is a subclass of MetaDeclaration.

```
mapping ADD (EntityType NEW (METAPACKAGE, NamespaceDeclaration));
mapping ADD (EntityType NEW (METACLASS, MetaDeclaration));
```

The Contents construct is specified with a subclass of Connection, because its semantics affects the uniqueness of the contained classes' names as well as the semantics of the element-lookup operation. The actual connection between a package and its contained classes is defined with a Link.

```
mapping ADD (ConnectionType NEW (CONTENTSDECLARATION, ContentsConnection));
mapping ADD (LinkType NEW (CONTENTS, Link));
ruleset ADD (AssociationRule NEW (METAPACKAGE, METACLASS, CONTENTSDECLARATION));
```

As packages are not instantiable, the Package construct is mapped onto the NonInstantiableDeclaration, which is a subclass of Declaration. The difference between the two is that the subclass cannot create instances.

```
mapping ADD (EntityType NEW (PACKAGE, NonInstantiableDeclaration));
```

The meta-model specifying the contents relationship between the Package construct and the Class construct is presented in Figure 5.

3.4   Class and Association Constructs Revisited

In this section we give two examples showing why the BOOM framework supports adjustments of the modelling language. In UML, not only packages but also classes may contain other classes. This implies that the container class acts as the

Fig. 5. A fragment of a meta-model presenting the Package and Contents constructs of UML.

name space of the contained classes. Since we already have specified the meaning of the containment relationship, and thanks to the localization principle, it is very simple to add this extension to the current specification. We only need to do two modifications of the specification: i) the set of association rules is extended with the possibility for a class to have a containment relationship to other classes, and ii) the mapping of the MetaClass construct onto the BOOM class which specifies its semantics is changed. Instead of mapping it onto MetaDeclaration it is mapped onto NamespaceDeclaration, which has the same semantics as a MetaDeclaration, but with the additional invariant constraint of always including a containment relationship. No other modification is needed in the specification. The meta-model is updated accordingly (see Figure 6).

```
mapping REPLACE (EntityType NEW (METACLASS, NamespaceDeclaration));
ruleset ADD (AssociationRule NEW (METACLASS, METACLASS, CONTENTSDECLARATION));
```

The second example is the Association Class construct. In UML, an association may have attributes attached to it. These attributes model information that belongs to the relationship itself and not to any of the associated classes. This kind of association is called an Association Class for it acts both as an association and as a class. To specify the Association Class construct in BOOM, we use the same BOOM classes as for Association and Link, but we add to the specification rules that makes it possible for the construct to contain links and attribute links.

```
mapping ADD (EntityType NEW (ASSOCIATIONCLASS, AssociationDeclaration));
mapping ADD (EntityType NEW (LINKOBJECT, Instance));
ruleset ADD (AssociationRule NEW (ASSOCIATIONCLASS, DATATYPE, ATTRIBUTE));
ruleset ADD (AssociationRule NEW (ASSOCIATIONCLASS, CLASS, ASSOCIATIONEND));
```

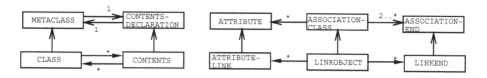

Fig. 6. A fragment of a meta-model presenting the additions made to the model: Class containment and Association Class.

This example shows how simple it is to add a new construct to the language if the necessary BOOM classes are available. Note that already existing classes can be reused when defining new classes.

3.5   Other Meta-modelling Approaches

A few other approaches to meta-modelling of modelling languages have been presented:

MOF The *Meta Object Facility* (MOF) [9] is a meta-meta model, i.e. a model for modelling meta-models. The MOF has been accepted as a standard by the Object Management Group (OMG), and it is, for example, used as the foundation for defining UML. The main purpose of the MOF is "to provide a set of CORBA [Common Object Request Broker Architecture [14]] interfaces that can be used to define and manipulate a set of interoperable metamodels" [9, 1-1]. This implies that the MOF can be used for defining repository services for storing computer representations of models, for information management as well as for data warehouse management. Hence, the MOF is a model for meta-data management and meta-data interoperability. The focus is on tool vendors and tool interoperability. However, the MOF is not intended for specification of the semantics of a meta-model. The meaning of the different constructs in a meta-model has to be expressed by other means.

CDIF The *CASE Data Interchange Format* [3] is a standard for interchange formats between CASE tools. It is not specific for object-oriented models, and can be used for several different kinds of models, like process models and data-flow models. The models in CDIF are defined using *Entity-Relationship-Attribute* models. These models are defined at three levels of models: model, meta-model and meta-meta model. No run-time semantics or modelling semantics is given as the focus is on interchange of information between CASE tools.

4   Concluding Remarks

In this paper we have presented BOOM, a framework for formal specification of modelling languages. The framework consists of a formal specification language and a meta-model of object-oriented modelling languages. The meta-model offers a set of predefined components to be used when specifying such a modelling language. Hence, the specification work does not have to start from scratch each time, but can be based an already existing specification. Differences between the actual semantics and the semantics offered by the components are specified in user-defined subclasses of the components.

The framework offers different levels of abstractions for the specification of a language: what constructs exist, how the constructs are interconnected, a mapping from the constructs to BOOM classes, and the detailed semantics defined in the BOOM classes. In this way, all the details need not be covered for understanding the specification of a language. This paper focuses on the first three layers; a description of the last layer can be found in e.g. [13, 11].

The practical usage of the framework is demonstrated by the specification of the Unified Modeling Language, and this paper presents how some of the constructs in UML have been specified. This paper also demonstrates that many typical modifications of a modelling language, like adding variations to existing constructs, or modifying the detailed semantics of a construct, can be easily performed in the framework. In our work we have also used BOOM for specifying other parts of UML, e.g. specification of the abstract syntax, the static and the dynamic semantics of the Collaboration, the Use Case and the Subsystem constructs.

There are three major areas that will benefit from the BOOM framework, all of them requiring formal and adjustable specification techniques. Use of the BOOM framework will facilitate tailoring of the modelling language in a development process: the BOOM classes define the abstract syntax and semantics of language constructs, such as Class, Association, and Object. The definitions of the constructs used in a project must capture the desired semantics to ensure that the constructs are used consistently within the project. Moreover, the framework facilitates the development of tools for performing intelligent operations on models, such as checking for internal consistency or conformance between parts of the model. The BOOM classes can be used to define precisely what such operations mean. Finally, we claim that BOOM is of particular use for the UML development community, where the absence of a proper and flexible semantics makes it difficult to relate the many different approaches and extensions.

References

[1] G. Booch. *Object-Oriented Design with Applications*. Redwood City, 1991.
[2] E.H. Dürr and J. van Katwijk. VDM++ - A Formal Specification Language for Object-oriented Designs. In *Computer Systems and Software Engineering. Proceedings of CompEuro'92*, pages 214–219. IEEE Computer Society Press, 1992.
[3] Electronic Industries Association, 2500 Wilson Blvd. Arlington, VA 22201. *EIA/IS-107: CDIF / Framework for Modeling and Extensibility*, 1997. http://www.eia.org/eig/cdif/how-to-obtain-standards.html.
[4] International Telecommunication Union (ITU), Place des Nations, CH-1211 Geneva 20, Switzerland. *Recommendation Z.100 (03/93) - CCITT specification and description language (SDL)*, 1993. http://www.itu.int/itudoc/itu-t/rec/z.html.
[5] I. Jacobson, G. Booch, and J. Rumbaugh. *The Unified Software Development Process*. Addison-Wesley, 1999.
[6] I. Jacobson, M. Christerson, P. Jonsson, and G. Övergaard. *Object-Oriented Software Engineering: A Use Case Driven Approach*. Addison-Wesley, 1993.
[7] C. B. Jones. A pi-calculus Semantics for an Object-Based Design Notation. In E. Best, editor, *CONCUR'93: 4th International Conference on Concurrency Theory Lecture Notes in Computer Science 715*. Springer-Verlag, 1993.

[8] R. Milner, J. Parrow, and D. Walker. A Calculus of Mobile Processes, I. *Information and Computation*, 100:1–40, 1992.

[9] *Meta Object Facility (MOF) Specification*, September 1997. On-line documentation: http://www.omg.org/pub/docs/ad/97-08-{14,15}.pdf.

[10] Object Management Group, Framingham Corporate Center, 492 Old Connecticut Path, Framingham MA 01701-4568. *OMG Unified Modeling Language Specification, version 1.3*, June 1999. http://www.omg.org/cgi-bin/doc?ad/99-06-08.

[11] G. Övergaard. A Formal Approach to Relationships in the Unified Modeling Language. In M. Broy, D. Coleman, T. S. E. Maibaum, and B. Rumpe, editors, *Proceedings PSMT'98 Workshop on Precise Semantics for Software Modeling Techniques*, pages 91–108. Technische Universität, München, Germany, TUM-I9803, April 1998.

[12] G. Övergaard. A Formal Approach to Collaborations in the Unified Modeling Language. In R. France and B. Rumpe, editors, *Proceedings of UML'99 – The Unified Modeling Language: Beyond the Standard, Lecture Notes in Computer Science 1723*, pages 99–115. Springer-Verlag, 1999.

[13] G. Övergaard and K. Palmkvist. A Formal Approach to Use cases and Their Relationships. In P.-A. Muller and J. Bézivin, editors, *Proceedings of the Unified Modeling Language: UML'98: Beyond the Notation, Lecture Notes in Computer Science 1618*. Springer-Verlag, 1999.

[14] A. Pope. *The Corba Reference Guide : Understanding the Common Object Request Broker Architecture*. Addison-Wesley, 1998.

[15] T. Reenskaug, P. Wold, and O. A. Lehne. *Working with Objects: The OOram Software Engineering Method*. Manning Publications, 1996.

[16] J. Rumbaugh, M. Blaha, W. Premerlani, F. Eddy, and W. Lorensen. *Object-Oriented Modeling and Design*. Prentice-Hall, Englewood Cliffs, 1991.

[17] B. Selic, G. Gullekson, and P. Ward. *Real-Time Object-Oriented Modeling*. John Wiley and Sons, 1994.

[18] S. Stepney, R. Barden, and D. Cooper. *Object Orientation in Z*. Springer-Verlag, 1992.

[19] D. Walker. Objects in the π-Calculus. *Information and Computation*, 116:253–271, 1995.

Verification of Object Oriented Programs Using Class Invariants

Kees Huizing, Ruurd Kuiper, and SOOP*

Eindhoven University of Technology, PO Box 513, 5600 MB Eindhoven,
The Netherlands,
keesh@win.tue.nl, wsinruur@win.tue.nl

Abstract. A proof system is presented for the verification and derivation of object oriented programs with as main features strong typing, dynamic binding, and inheritance. The proof system is inspired on Meyer's
system of class invariants [12] and remedies its unsoundness, which is already recognized by Meyer. Dynamic binding is treated in a flexible way:
when throughout the class hierarchy overriding methods respect the pre-
and postconditions of the overridden methods, very simple proof rules
for method calls suffice; more powerful proof rules are supplied for cases
where one cannot or does not want to follow this restriction.
The proof system is complete relative to proofs for properties of pointers
and the data domain.

1 Introduction

Although formal verification is not very common in the discipline of object oriented programming, the importance of formal specification is generally acknowledged ([12]). With the increased interest in component based development, it
becomes even more important that components are specified in an unambiguous manner, since users or buyers of components often have no other knowledge
about a component than its specification and at the same time rely heavily on its
correct functioning in their framework. The specification of a class, sometimes
called *contract*, usually contains at least pre- and postconditions for the public
mehtods and a class invariant.

A class invariant expresses which states of the objects of the class are consistent, or "legal". An object that doesn't satisfy the class invariant has an
uninterpretable state that should only occur during an update of the object.
Therefore, whenever an object is handed over from one piece of the code to the
other (and therefore possibly from one developer to another), one should be able
to assume the class invariant to hold for the object. Of course, this is what the
term "invariant" conveys. Nevertheless, the usual practice in verification is too

---

* Research group Systematic Object Oriented Programming, at the time of conception
  of this paper consisting of Lex Bijlsma, Rik van Geldrop, Louis van Gool, Kees
  Hemerik, Kees Huizing, Ruurd Kuiper, Onno van Roosmalen, Jaap van der Woude,
  and Gerard Zwaan

T. Maibaum (Ed.): FASE 2000, LNCS 1783, pp. 208–221, 2000.

weak to guarantee this invariance. According to this practice, one proves that every (public) method that starts in a state satisfying the invariant will also terminate in a state satisfying the invariant. As Meyer already remarks, this does not in general guarantee invariance [12] and hence, leads to unsoundness. When the call chain of methods can visit a certain object twice, the second call may find the object in an inconsistent state, i.e., not satisfying the invariant. This situation of *reentrance*, sometimes called *call-back*, occurs in many object oriented designs. Another problem may occur when a class invariant depends on the state of more than one object. In this case, changing the state of one object may break the invariant of another [15]. In this paper, this problem is called *vulnerability*.

To overcome these problems, we formulate a proof system that does guarantee true invariance of the class invariants. This leads to more proof obligations than just "assuming that the invariant holds before, prove that it holds after", but it makes problems with call-backs and fragile base classes [15] visible as early as possible in the development.

Proof theoretic approaches comparable to ours but not dealing specifically with the questions addressed in the present paper, i.e., call-backs and vulnerability, can be found in, e.g., [9,14,13,8,10]. A somewhat more different proof theoretic approach appears in [1]. A semantically oriented approach, aiming for automated object-oriented verification, is proposed in [6].

2   Framework

2.1   Programming Language

The proof system works in principle for any object oriented, strongly typed programming language. For our notation, we stay closely to Java [3]. With strongly typed, we mean that every expression has a static type and that type incompatibilities render a program illegal.

Furthermore, we expect our language to have dynamic binding, so we assume that values of expressions have a *dynamic type* that can be different from the static type of the expression. We assume that there is a subtype relation of types, which is a partial order. We assume that the language is *type safe*, i.e., the dynamic type of an expression is always a subtype of the static type. In practice, a language is seldom type safe in the sense that every legal, or compilable, program is type safe. Of course, one could design proof rules to prove that a program is indeed type safe. We will not go into this further. Inheritance follows subtyping. When C is a subclass of D, C is also a subtype of D.

2.2   Object References

An object reference is an expression that refers to an object or equals the special constant null. The value null does not refer to an object, hence it cannot be dereferenced, i.e., no method call or other member access can be applied to null.

We thus assume that object references are never undefined (such as pointing to garbage). This assumption can be achieved by having no explicit object deletion in the language but relying on automatic garbage collection instead. Non-**null** object references are equal if and only if they refer to the same object. Object references may occur in statements as well as in assertions.

The special variable **this** always refers to the currently active object, i.e., the object to which the currently executing method belongs. We assume that the only object that can be changed at any moment during execution is the currently active object. This can be achieved by not allowing assignments to fields of other objects, or more severely, only allowing access to objects via method calls. This latter restriction is advised in many object oriented design methodologies.

We assume that the static type of object references is always known. The proof system can derive equality and inequality of reference and type expressions. About the type system we assume:

1. the subtype relation $<:$ is transitive and reflexive;
2. we do not have subsumption, i.e., $A <: B$ does not imply that any expression of type A is of type B;
3. if $o.x$ is a type correct expression, it refers to a member that is declared in (a supertype of) the dynamic type of o; this member is uniquely determined, though not statically. If o is **null**, the value of the expression is undefined.

A new object of class C is created by the expression **new** $C()$. After creation, the *constructor* associated to class C, if it exists, is executed. In this paper, we allow at most one constructor per class. For the purpose of the proof system, we consider the expression **new** as a method call. The result value is a reference to the newly created object.

2.3   Assertion Language

The assertion language is first order predicate logic with local program variables as free variables. Concerning instance variables (also known as attributes), there is a slight complication, since their value depends on the object they belong to. Therefore, instance variables should always be prefixed with a reference to the object they belong to. In many cases, this reference is **this**, and this reference is silently assumed when we omit it, but it may be any other expression that yields an object reference.

Every assertion in the proof system is associated to a class. For the pre- or post-condition of a method, it is the class that the method belongs to; for class invariants it is that class, obviously; for annotations in the code it is the class the code is associated to. This class is called the type of the assertion. When an assertion is prefixed with an object reference, it is to be evaluated in the context of that object. We define this syntactically, as follows:

Definition: Let P be an assertion of type C and o an object reference of type C or a subtype thereof. Then we define $o.P \equiv P[\text{this}/o])$.

An unprefixed assertion is silently assumed to have **this** as a prefix.

If $o = \text{null}$, the value $o.P$ is undefined. Note that **this** never has value **null**.

2.4   Proof System

In an object-oriented program, the notion of a main program has more or less disappeared, leaving a set of classes for the "user" (programmer, developer) to work with. Therefore, the purpose of a proof system for object-orientation is not to prove a certain program correct, but to prove a system of classes correct. To achieve this, to every class we associate a class invariant and a pair of pre/postconditions to every method in the class. This specification can be used to infer properties about his own program. The proof system provides a method to prove that the class indeed satisfies its specification. Before we go into class invariants, we first give a sketch how pre- and postconditions are used in the proof system.

The idea is to put at certain places in the program text assertions that should be true whenever program execution arrives at that point. This is proved by fulfilling proof obligations, which are either implications in predicate logic, or Hoare-triples[7]. All methods are annotated with assertions. A legal annotation has assertions in at least the following places:

- before and after the body of the method;
- before and after every method call (including **new** statements).

Assume that an annotated method m in class C looks as follows (because the Java-style braces that surround blocks of code clash with Hoare-triple braces, we use **begin** and **end** for program blocks):

```
{pre}
void m(void) begin
    {Q₁}
    ... // code without method calls
    {R₁}
    o₁.method₁();
    {Q₂}
    .
    .
    .
    {R_{n-1}}
    o_{n-1}.method_{n-1}();
    {Q_n}
    ... // code without method calls
    {R_n}
end
{post}
```

So every method call $o_i.\text{method}_i$ is surrounded by a pair (R_i, Q_{i+1}), and the other pieces of code (so-called *local code segments*) by pairs (Q_i, R_i). To get consistent subscripting, it may be necessary to insert an empty statement between Q_1 and R_1 or Q_n and R_n, in case the method begins or ends with a method call.

Then we have the following proof three obligations. How to fulfill the last two, we will address later.

1. prove:

$$\text{this}.pre \Rightarrow Q_1$$

$$R_n \Rightarrow \text{this}.post$$

2. for every two assertions Q_i and R_i that are separated by local code P_i, prove the Hoare triple:

$$\{Q_i\}P_i\{R_i\}$$

3. for every two assertions R_i and Q_{i+1}, surrounding method call $o.\text{method}_i()$, prove:

$$\{R_i\}o.\text{method}_i()\{Q_{i+1}\}$$

We have simplified matters somewhat. We assumed that the method has no parameters, and we assume that the method body can indeed be written as a sequence of local code segments and method calls. It is relatively straigthforward to remove these simplifications; we will not go into this.

The second type of proof obligations, we call *local proof obligations*. How these proofs are established is not the concern of this paper. One can substitute one's favourite proof system, applied to one's favourite programming language, using one's favourite assertion language.

Regarding the third proof obligation, we recall the proof obligation for ordinary procedure calls. In that case, we would have to prove

$$R_i \Rightarrow pre_{\text{method}_i} \text{ and } post_{\text{method}_i} \Rightarrow Q_{i+1}$$

where pre_m and $post_m$ are the pre- and postcondition of the procedure, [4].

For method calls, the situation is somewhat more complicated and how to formulate the proof obligation in that case is the subject of the next section.

2.5   Proving Pre- and Postconditions for Methods

Before we discuss what has to be done for methods, we introduce some notation.

Notation

- $\mathcal{T}_d(o), \mathcal{T}_s(o)$ denote dynamic resp. static type of o
- $o.m$ denotes method m of the dynamic type of o (cf. Java method call)
- $o{:}m$ denotes method m of the *static* type of o
- m_C denotes method m in class C, so $o{:}m = m_{\mathcal{T}_s(o)}$
- $D <: C$ denotes that D is a subtype of C; note that the subtype relation is reflexive, so $D = C$ implies $D <: C$.

Methods are specified by pre- and postconditions, just like procedures in ordinary sequential programming languages. Apart from a funny syntax to specify the first parameter, the important difference with procedures is that methods have *dynamic binding*. From the syntax of a method call like $o.m()$, we can not deduce which method will be executed, and, consequently, we do not know which pre/postcondition pair should be used. We propose two different solutions, which do not necessary exclude each other.

1. During class design, make sure that an overriding method (a method of a subclass that redefines a method of a superclass), can really substitute the method it overrides. I.e., the precondition of the overriding method should be weaker than the precondition of the method it overrides, and the postcondition should be stronger[1]. This leads to the proof obligations: For any two types $D <: C$ that both define method m, prove:

    - $pre_{m_C} \Rightarrow pre_{m_D}$
    - $post_{m_D} \Rightarrow post_{m_C}$

    Now we may use the following axiom in our proofs:

    $$\{o.pre_{am}\}o.m()\{o.post_{am}\}$$

2. Keep information about the dynamic type of an object in the assertions; then use the following axiom:

    $$\{T_d(o) = C \wedge o.pre_{m_C}\}o.m()\{o.post_{m_C}\}$$

    At object creation, dynamic type information is inserted into the assertions, for instance by the following axiom:

    $$\{true\}o = \mathbf{new}\ C()\{T_d(o) = C\}$$

    Likewise for assignment:

    $$\{T_d(o') = C\}o = o'\{T_d(o) = C\}$$

    These axioms take care of the type information, but of course don't capture all of the behaviour of object creation and assignment; we assume that the rest of the proof system takes care of that.

    These two solutions do not exclude each other. Nevertheless, if 1 is used for a certain class C, then the associated proof obligations must be proved for C and all its subtypes. An advantage of approach 2 is that no such additional proof obligations are incurred. However, an advantage of approach 1 over approach 2 is that no dynamic type information needs to be recorded in the assertions.

---

[1] This is basically the methodology as elaborated in more detail in [10]

3   Class Invariants

The proof system described above can be unwieldy. One of the key issues of object oriented design is that objects represent something, possibly an object in the real world, or a more abstract entity, which is more than just the data that it contains. This means that, whenever one uses an object in a correctness proof, one may assume that it satisfies certain semantic properties. These properties are commonly shared among all objects of the same type and since object types are represented by classes in object oriented languages, they are called *class invariants* [12]. This is essentially an extension of the notion of *representation invariant*. Representation invariants are a well-known and powerful concept in the verification of data structures. In addition to representation invariants, a class invariant may talk about properties of linked objects too. Class invariants simplify the specification of methods by factoring out common properties. Furthermore, class invariants help simplifying correctness proofs: at a method call, there is in general only a proof obligation for the precondition of the method, not for the invariant of the called object, as we will see later.

We associate a class invariant with every class (when omitted, we assume the invariant to be *true*), and we write I_C for the invariant associated to class C. We use the notation $o.I$ for the class invariant of the actual class of o evaluated in the context of the object referred to by o. Note that this depends on the dynamic type of o, and without information about this dynamic type, we cannot deduce anything from $o.I$. This is different from the expression $o.P$ where P is a known predicate. The expression $o.I$, however, is merely an expression and is not an abbreviation for a predicate. Similar to the pre/postconditions for methods, we give two approaches.

1. Make sure that the invariant of a subtype is a strengthening of the invariant of the supertype. Formally,

   Proof obligation: Whenever $D <: C$, then prove $I_D \Rightarrow I_C$, $pre_{M_C} \Rightarrow pre_{M_D}$, and $post_{M_D} \Rightarrow post_{M_C}$.
   Then we can use the following

   Axioms:

   $$o.I \Rightarrow o{:}I \quad o{:}pre_m \Rightarrow o.pre_m \quad o.post_m \Rightarrow o{:}post_m$$

   This approach captures an important principle of object-oriented design: a subclass should be a specialization of its superclass, hence properties that hold for objects of a certain type C (here modelled by the class invariant I_C) should also hold for objects of subtypes of C.

2. Collect dynamic type information in assertions and use the following rules:

   $$\frac{\mathcal{T}_d(o) = C}{o.I \Leftrightarrow o.I_C} \quad \frac{\mathcal{T}_d(o) = C}{o.pre_m \Leftrightarrow o.pre_{m_C}} \quad \frac{\mathcal{T}_d(o) = C}{o.post_m \Leftrightarrow o.post_{m_C}}$$

Soundness of these rules follows from [10], where, in a different setting, the same proof obligations appear. In fact, the proof obligation of $pre_{M_C} \Rightarrow pre_{M_D}$ compromises completeness when D has more variables (attributes) than C. In that case, approach 2 can be used, or approach 1 should be refined along the lines of [10].

3.1   Where Do Class Invariants Hold?

Until now, we have not defined what it means for a class to satisfy its specification. We will do that now.

For pre/postcondition pairs, we would want that a method that is called in a state where the precondition holds should terminate in a state where the postcondition holds.

For class invariants, it is less evident what should be required. It is unrealistic to have class invariants hold all the time. When the data in an object changes, it is often not possible to keep the invariant valid during the whole process. However, when an object is handed over, or when a method is invoked on an object, this object should be in a consistent state. Otherwise, the receiver of the object can hardly do anything useful with it. Since it is the purpose of class invariants to describe that an object is in a consistent state, we would want our class invariants to hold in these states.

Definition 1. *A class invariant I_C is valid if it holds for all existing objects of type C during the following points of program execution:*

- *at the beginning of any method execution, except for a new object at the beginning of the execution of its constructor*
- *at the end of any method execution.*

3.2   Proof Obligations for Class Invariants

We want to design a proof system that allows us to derive validity for class invariants. For this purpose, we have to extend the system of section 2 with additional proof obligations.

3.3   Simple Case

In the simplest case it suffices to prove that the invariant of an object holds at exit of any method that changes the object, including any constructor of that object:

1. For any constructor $c()$ of class C prove $\{true\}body_c\{I_C\}$
2. for any plain method $m()$, prove $\{pre_m \wedge I\}body_m\{post_m \wedge I_C\}$

This proof system may be unsound, however, when there is *re-entrance*. Re-entrance occurs when a chain of method calls returns to an object earlier in the chain. For example, consider an object α that executes a method m. Halfway, m calls a method on object β and this methods calls back on α by method n. When n starts, m is not finished, so the proof obligation above does not guarantee that α's invariant holds. Re-entrance is in particular possible in situations where call-back mechanisms are exploited.

To accommodate this, we have to require that the invariant holds just before any method call in the body of a method. This leads to the following structure.

- **assumption** At the beginning of the method body and after every method call, *assume* that the invariant holds.
- **obligation** At the end of the method body and before every method call, *prove* that the invariant holds.

Note that we can strengthen the assumption with invariants of any other object, for instance, objects that are handed to a method via parameters can be assumed consistent.

This is not enough, however. Suppose object o refers to object p in its invariant. Then, changing p may invalidate the invariant of o. This suggests the following definition. This is the so-called *forward-backward* problem, described by Meyer. In this example, two objects keep references to one another. When this is expressed in the invariant of one of these objects, this invariant could be violated by changing the other object. This notion is captured in the following definition.

Definition 2. *When object reference o of type D occurs in invariant I_C, we say that objects of class C are* vulnerable to *(objects of) class D. o is called the* vulnerability reference.

Given an execution state, an object α is semantically vulnerable to *an object β if a change to β can invalidate the invariant of α.*

The idea now is to strengthen the proof obligation above with obligations to prove the invariants of all objects that are vulnerable to the current class. For this purpose, we need a reference to the vulnerable object. The next section deals with this problem.

3.4   Referencing Vulnerable Objects

Suppose we have a linked list of objects of class C. Every object has a field n that references the next object in the list (possibly `null`), and an integer field x. If we want to express that the list is strictly decreasing, we need as invariant

$I_C : x \neq \texttt{null} \rightarrow x > n.x$

Then, each object in the list is vulnerable to the next one. For instance, a method m that increases x would maintain the invariant of the current object, but would invalidate the invariant of the previous object in the list. So we need a proof obligation that can talk about the previous object in the list, although in general objects don't have such a reference, as this example shows. This problem is not restricted to this example. In many cases, there are one-way references and when such a reference occurs in the invariant, the referenced object cannot talk about the object that is vulnerable to its changes.

For this purpose, we introduce *logical variables* (sometimes called freeze variables or specification variables, [4]) in the method body that refer to the vulnerable objects. For every method in class B and expression o of type B occurring in the invariant of class A, the assertion at the start of the method body may be strengthened by expressions of the form

$$X.o = \texttt{this} \vee X = \texttt{null}$$

where X is of type A.

3.5 Proof System

Gathering these ideas together, we come to the following scheme of proof obligations.

Let M be a method of class C, annotated as in section 2.4, let $r_1 \ldots r_k$ be the vulnerability references of C, then do the following[2] for every $1 \leq i \leq n$.

1. (pre-condition) choose object references $p_1, \ldots, p_m$, and prove
   $pre \wedge p_1.I \wedge \ldots \wedge p_m.I \wedge (X_1.r_1 = \texttt{this} \vee X_1 = \texttt{null}) \wedge \ldots \wedge (X_k.r_k = \texttt{this} \vee X_k = \texttt{null}) \Rightarrow Q_1$
   when M is a constructor, none of the p_i may equal $\texttt{this}$;
2. (local code segment P_i) prove $\{Q_i\} P_i \{R_i\}$;
3. (pre condition method call $o_i.M_i$) prove $R_i \Rightarrow o_i.pre_{M_i}$;
4. (local invariant) $R_i \Rightarrow I$;
5. (vulnerable invariants) for every vulnerability reference r_j prove $X_j \neq \texttt{null} \wedge R_i \Rightarrow X_j : I$;
6. (post-condition method call) choose object references $q_1, \ldots, q_m$ and prove
   $o_i.post_{M_i} \wedge q_1.I \wedge \ldots \wedge q_m.I \Rightarrow Q_i$;
7. (post-condition) $R_n \Rightarrow post$.

Remarks

ad 1 These invariants are free to choose. Any object reference that is in scope can be used, referring via member fields of the current object or via parameters of M. Object references that are not in scope are not forbidden, but are useless in proofs.

ad 2 For this, we rely on the underlying proof system. Note that P_i does not contain any method calls.

---

2 When method M is inherited from a superclass B, these proof obligations have to be redone in case the invariant of C is stronger than the invariant of B.

ad 3 Again, two approaches can be followed here. When it has been proved that $pre_{M_C^i} \Rightarrow pre_{M_D^i}$ for every class $D <: C$, it suffices to prove $o_i : pre_{M^i}$. Otherwise, some type information about o_i must be used.

ad 6 Analogous to 3, when it has been proved that $post_{M_D^i} \Rightarrow post_{M_C^i}$, then the proof obligation reduces to $o_i : post_{M_i} \wedge$ etc. Otherwise, type information about o_i must be used.

4   Example

This example shows how to deal with vulnerability. Consider two classes A and B, where objects in A hold a reference to those in B, but not the other way round. Changing the value of an object in class B may invalidate the invariant of an object in class A. Hence, objetcs in class A are vulnerable to B.

```
{IA: x>ref.y}
class A begin
    B ref;
    int x;
end

{IB: true}
class B begin
    int y;

    void dec() begin
        {Q1}
        y:=y-1;
        {R1}
    end;

    void inc() begin
        {Q2}
        y:=y+1;
        {R2}
    end
end
```

Obviously, $dec()$ leaves I_A intact, whereas $inc()$ doesnot necessarily. To prove the correctness of $dec()$, we choose

$$Q_1 : (X.ref = this \vee X = \texttt{null}) \wedge y = N \wedge X.x > X.ref.y$$

(the last conjunct is the invariant for X).

$$R_1 : X.x > N \wedge y = N - 1$$

$X.x > N$ follows from the fact that $X.x$ is immutable to this segment and $X.ref.y = \texttt{this}.y = N$. From R_1 the required $X.x > X.ref.y$ can easily be deduced.

The proof obligation that R_2 implies $X.I$ cannot be satisfied, which is of course what we want.

5   Soundness and Completeness

This section briefly sketches the proofs of soundness and completeness.

To define these notions, we assume that there is always a main program that starts out with no objects allocated. As far as verification is concerned, we consider this main program as a method body with pre- and postconditions equivalent to *true*.

Following [11], we define an execution of the program as a maximal, in our case also terminating, sequence of transitions between program states.

Definition 3. *An execution e of program P is a terminating transition sequence* $\sigma_0 \xrightarrow{l_1} \ldots \xrightarrow{l_n} \sigma_n$ *where the σ_i denote program states and each label l_i either denotes*

1. *a local tranisition, i.e., a sequence of local steps, corresponding to a local code segment, not involving method calls or object creation; which local transitions are allowed is defined by the semantics of the programming language that is used and is not of interest here;*
2. *or a method call $o.m()$;*
3. *or a return transition, corresponding to the termination of a method; which method is terminated is determined by the balance of calls and returns in the previous part of the execution sequence.*

Since we are only studying partial correctness, we can restrict ourselves to terminating executions. This means in particular that dereferencing of null-referencing will never occur, since this would lead to abortion.

We assume that the proof system is sound for local transitions, i.e., whenever $\{Q\}P\{R\}$ has been proven for a local code segment P, it is true, i.e., every terminating execution of P starting in a state satisfying Q will end in a state satisfying R.

In the following, the phrase "all class invariants hold" (in a state σ or during an execution e), means that the invariants of all allocated objects (in σ or in the states of e) evaluate to true.

Theorem 1 (Soundness). *Let a program be given with all proof obligations satisfied and an execution sequence with all class invariants holding in σ_0. Then all class invariants hold for all objects at all states σ_i in the transition sequence.*

Proof Let a program and an execution sequence $e = \sigma_0 \xrightarrow{l_1} \ldots \xrightarrow{l_n} \sigma_n$ be given as in the theorem. Note that all states σ_i correspond to points in the code that are annotated in the correctness proof. By induction to i, we prove that all class invariants hold during e and furthermore that the assertions from the correctness proof hold in the corresponding states. For $i = 0$ it holds by assumption. For $i > 0$, there are three cases.

1. l_i denotes a local transition in class C for code segment P_j. By induction, $[\![Q_j]\!]\sigma_{i-1}$ and by soundness of the proof system for local transitions and p.o. (proof obligation) 2, $[\![R_j]\!]\sigma_i$. Now consider an object α of class D. If D is not vulnerable to C, it is obvious that $[\![\alpha.I_D]\!]\sigma_{i-1} \Leftrightarrow [\![\alpha.I_D]\!]\sigma_i$. If $[\![\alpha]\!]\sigma_{i-1} = [\![\mathtt{this}]\!]\sigma_{i-1}$, and hence $[\![\alpha]\!]\sigma_i = [\![\mathtt{this}]\!]\sigma_i$, then $[\![\alpha.I_C]\!]\sigma_i$ follows from $[\![R_j]\!]\sigma_i$ and p.o. 4. If D is vulnerable to C via r, we know by p.o. 5 that $R \Rightarrow (X \neq \mathtt{null} \Rightarrow X : I)$. Since X is a free variable here and we have soundness for local transitions, this must hold for any valuation of X, in particular for $X = \alpha$. Since α refers to an actual object, it can't be $\mathtt{null}$ and, knowing that $[\![R_j]\!]\sigma_i$, $[\![\alpha.I]\!]\sigma_i$ must be true.

2. l_i denotes a method call $o_j.M_j$. When this is not a constructor, no object has changed state between σ_{i-1} and σ_i and hence all invariants are maintained. When the method call is a constructor call, a new object has been created in σ_i. For this object, however, the invariant is not required at σ_i. Furthermore, by induction $[\![R_j]\!]\sigma_{i-1}$ and then by p.o. 3, $[\![o_i.pre_{M_j}]\!]\sigma_{i-1}$. By the semantics of the method call, we then know that $[\![pre]\!]\sigma_i$ and because all invariants are maintained, $[\![p_k.I]\!]$ holds for arbitrary p_k. When we choose a valuation for the X_k that satisfies $X_k.r_k = \mathtt{this} \vee X_k = \mathtt{null}$ (which is always possible), we know that $[\![Q_1]\!]\sigma_i$ because of p.o. 1.

3. l_i denotes a return transition. Then no objects have changed their state and hence all invariants are maintained. The proof that $[\![Q_j]\!]\sigma_i$ is analogous to the previous point, now using p.o. 6 and p.o. 7.

end of proof

In the following definition, an annotation of the program refers to the annotation in section 3.5, in which postconditions may be strengthened. Why this is, is explained below.

Theorem 2 (Completeness). *Let a program be given of which all executions satisfy at method calls the corresponding preconditions and at both calls and returns all class invariants. Then there exists an annotation of the program and the classes such that all proof obligations are fulfilled.*

We have to allow that postconditions are strengthened, because otherwise it may be impossible to fulfill proof obligation 6.

Now we can prove completeness if we have a complete proof system without class invariants. Then we can strengthen the postconditions in such a way that they imply the necessary class invariants.This must be possible, since the class invariants are holding in the corresponding states, by assumption.

This proof depends on the existence of a complete proof system for the chosen object oriented programming language. In the literature various proof systems can be found ([2,5]), although they differ somewhat from our approach.

6   Conclusion

The above approach extends the practical applicability of Object Oriented verification using pre and post conditions and invariants; its soundness and completeness is argued. One could perhaps view the notion of completeness as not fully satisfactory - we are studying other notions that do not depend on changing contracts, viz. strengthening postconditions, taking into account the extension with subclasses.

Future work considers furthering the practical use of the approach through establishing simplifying (preferably syntactical) restrictions. Correctness of the resulting method could then be argued on the basis of the framework presented here.

References

1. M. Abadi and K.R.M. Leino, *A Logic of Object-Oriented Programs*, in TAPSOFT '97, LNCS 1214, Springer, 1997.

2. P.H.M. America and J.J.M.M. Rutten, *A Parallel Object-Oriented Language: Design and semantic foundations*, PhD thesis, Free University of Amsterdam, 1989.

3. K. Arnold and J. Gosling, *The Java programming language, 2nd ed.*, Addison-Wesley, 1997.

4. K.R. Apt and E.-R. Olderog, *Verification of sequential and concurrent programs*, Springer-Verlag, 1991.

5. F.S. de Boer, *Reasoning about dynamically evolving process structures: A proof theory for the parallel object-oriented language POOL*, PhD thesis, Free University of Amsterdam, 1991.

6. U. Hensel, M. Huisman, B. Jacobs, and H. Tews, *Reasoning about Classes in Object-Oriented Languages: Logical Models Tools*, in ESOP at ETAPS 1998, Springer-Verlag, 1998.

7. C.A.R. Hoare, *An axiomatic basis for computer programming*, Communications of the ACM, 12, pp. 576–583, 1969.

8. H.B.M. Jonkers, *Upgrading the pre- and postcondition technique*. In VDM '91: Formal Software Development Methods, LNCS 551, Springer-Verlag, 1991.

9. K. Rustan M. Leino, *Toward Reliable Modular Programs*, Phd. Thesis, California Institute of Technology, Pasadena, 1995.

10. B. Liskov and J. Wing, *A behavioral notion of subtyping*, ACM TOPLAS , 16:6, pp. 1811-1841, 1994.

11. Z. Manna and A. Pnueli, *The Temporal Logic of Reactive and Concurrent Systems*. Springer-Verlag, 1992.

12. B. Meyer, *Object-Oriented Software Construction*, Prentice Hall, 1988.

13. A. Poetzsch-Heffter and P. Müller, *Logical foundations for typed object-oriented languages*, in D. Gries and W.P. de Roever, editors, Programming Concepts and Methods (PROCOMET), 1998.

14. A. Poetzsch-Heffter, *Specification and verification of object-oriented programs*, Habilitation, TU Muenchen, 1997.

15. C. Szyperski, *Component software : Beyond object-oriented programming*, Addison-Wesley, 1998.

16. J.Warmer, A. Kleppe, *The Object Constraint Language*, Addison-Wesley, 1999.

Verification of Object-Z Specifications by Using Transition Systems: Application to the Radiomobile Network Design Problem

Pablo Gruer, Vincent Hilaire, and Abder Koukam

Université de Technologie de Belfort Montbéliard
4 rue du château
90010 Belfort Cedex, FRANCE
Pablo.Gruer@utbm.fr

Abstract. This paper presents a technique for verifying specifications which uses the object-oriented state-based language Object-Z. The technique is based upon translation of Object-Z specifications into transition systems. The translation of Object-Z into a transition system allows one to use established techniques and tools in order to verify the specifications. We present the basis of our translation approach and then illustrate it by a case study. The case study consists in proving properties of our antennae parameter setting problem specification.

1 Introduction

Formal specification must fulfill two roles. The first is to provide the underlying rationale for the system under development. The second is to guide subsequent design and implementation phases. For example, the model checking approach may be very useful in order to verify a formula related to the specification. Furthermore this verification can be carried out automatically using model checking tools. While most specification formalisms are suited for the first role, few enable automatic verification of systems properties.

Among specification formalisms, Z [7] has received considerable attention. Furthermore, there exist object oriented extensions of this formalism, such as Object-Z [1], which allow for class structured specifications. These formalisms are well suited for concise and comprehensible description of software but automatic analysis tools are very rare, and often restrict to syntactic checking.

Our approach consists in translating an Object specification towards a transition system. Transition systems are behavioral models of software systems which can provide an operational semantic to specifications. Moreover, with transition systems, one can use established techniques [5] and tools, such as STeP [4], in order to prove some properties of Object-Z specifications. Nevertheless, defining an operational semantics for Object-Z is a difficult task. The richness of the specification language, that benefits from the first order predicate notation, is one of the reasons of the difficulty. For instance, operations described by quantified predicates often produce a set of transitions rather than a single transition.

T. Maibaum (Ed.): FASE 2000, LNCS 1783, pp. 222–236, 2000.

Yet, the set of transitions represents an atomic operation and, in order for the semantic to be correct, this atomicity must be preserved in some fashion.

This paper presents a verification technique based on translation rules of Object-Z specifications into transition systems. Rather than an exhaustive presentation of the transformation rules, we address some difficulties that originate in the richness of the specification language. We do not present a formal treatment of this question in this paper, but illustrate it with the case study. Consequently, this work should be considered as the result of an experience on verification of Object-Z specifications by means of transition systems, with STeP as the verification tool. The general organization of this paper is as follows. Section 2 introduces Object-Z and transition systems. Section 3 presents the main idea of the verification technique, i.e., transforming an Object-Z class into a transition system. Section 4 presents the antenna parameter setting problem, its specification and its verification with the STeP environment. Eventually section 5 concludes with an outline of future research.

2   Basic Concepts

2.1   Object-Z

Object-Z [1] is a formal specification language which extends Z [7] by introducing object-orientation. Both are based upon set theory and first order predicate logic. Specification written in those languages include two parts: the system state and operations on states. Operations are constrained by pre and post conditions. Specification of an operation is enclosed in a definition scope called schema. Object-Z allows to group portions of the state and related operations in a class schema. It allows modularity, composition and inheritance. We propose an example of an Object-Z class based upon the *"heap of matches"* game. Two players, identified as player 0 and player 1, alternate in taking matches from a heap. The player whose turn has arrived decides whether he takes one, two or three matches. The player who takes the last match is the game's looser. The Object-Z description of the game class is the following:

Move
$\Delta(heap, turn)$
$take? : [1..3]$

$heap \geq take?$
$heap' = heap - take?$
$turn' = 1 - turn$

$\Box((turn = 0) \Rightarrow \bigcirc(turn = 1))$
$\Box((turn = 1) \Rightarrow \bigcirc(turn = 0))$

Variables _heap_ and _turn_ specify respectively the number of matches in the heap and the current player identity. States are seen as bindings of model variables to values: the state of an object of the _Game_ class is determined by the value bound to variables _heap_ and _turn_. All _Object − Z_ classes include a schema named _INIT_ to specify the set of initial states of the class. The _Move_ schema specifies the class operation, a game move, and illustrates some notational conventions of _Object − Z_. The Δ statement indicates the portion of the state that is modified by the operation. Schemas that define operations are splitted in two zones by a short horizontal line. The upper zone specifies the portion of state involved in the operation and the operation parameters. The lower zone is occupied by predicates that express operation conditions. Another notational convention refers to the so-called _before/after_ predicates. Primed variable names denote the value to which the variable is bound after the operation, unprimed variable names denote the value to which the variable was bound before the operation. Consequently, predicates without primed variables can be seen as operation preconditions and predicates with mixed primed and unprimed variables describe the effect of the operation on the state (i.e., the variable binding). Finally, a variable name followed by the question mark (?) distinguishes an operation's input parameter and a variable name followed by the exclamation mark (!) distinguishes an operation's output parameter. As for operation schemata, the class schema can be separated in two zones by a short horizontal line. The lower zone, if present, includes one or more temporal logic formulas, the history invariants. As we will examine in the sequel, history invariants allow to express liveness and safety constraints on the computations an object of the class can undergo, see [6] for a discussion on _Object − Z_ classes and history invariants. In our example, the given invariants state that game players should alternate in executing game moves. From the given specification of _Move_ operation, this constraint is satisfied by all the possible computations of any instance of the game and the history invariants could be omitted.

2.2   Transition Systems

We intend to use transition systems to provide a semantics to classes of _Object − Z_. The intended meaning or "type" of an Object-Z class is the set of computations that objects of the class can undergo. A transition system is a compact representation of a set of computations and therefore appears as an adequate representation for the semantics of an Object-Z class. Furthermore, a number of verification techniques have been defined to check transition system models against temporal logic formulas.

A transition system $S = <\mathcal{V}, \Sigma, \mathcal{T}_e, \mathcal{T}_c, \Theta>$ includes a set $\mathcal{V}$ of typed variables, a set Σ of states, a set $\mathcal{T}_e$ of elementary transitions, a set $\mathcal{T}_c$ of compound transitions and an initial conditions Θ. Variables $\mathcal{V} = \mathcal{V}_i \cup \mathcal{V}_o \cup \mathcal{V}_p$ group in three classes: input ($\mathcal{V}_i$), output ($\mathcal{V}_o$) and private ($\mathcal{V}_p$). We assume that all common types and most of the classical type constructors are available, as it is the case for STeP. A state $s \in \Sigma$ is a valuation of the private variables. As for Z specifications, the state is determined by the value to which each variable is bound. If $v \in \mathcal{V}_p$ is a variable, we will note $s[v]$ the value bound to v in state s. Naturally, state s considered as a valuation function can be inductively extended to expressions of any kind. Particularly the initial condition Θ is a predicate such that, s_0 is an initial state if and only if $s_0[\Theta] = true$. We say that s_0 satisfies Θ, which is noted $s_0 \vDash \Theta$.

The sets $\mathcal{T}_e$ and $\mathcal{T}_c$ contain respectively the elementary and the compound transitions. Both represent state changes, i.e., functions of the kind: $\Sigma \to \mathbb{P}\,\Sigma$.

Generally, an elementary transition $\tau \in \mathcal{T}_e$ is described by its transition relation ρ_τ, i.e., a conjunction of predicates. As for the Z notation, we adopt the *before/after* convention to write those predicates. Among many possible general forms for a transition relation, we adopt the following:

$$\rho_\tau = Pre(\tau) \wedge (v_1' = Exp_1) \wedge \cdots \wedge (v_n' = Exp_n)$$

where $Pre(\tau)$, a predicate with only unprimed variables, is the transition's precondition: s is a source state for τ if and only if $s \vDash Pre(\tau)$. For each conjoint $(v_i' = Exp_i)$, $v_i \in \mathcal{V}_p \cup \mathcal{V}_o$ and Exp_i is an expression without primed variables. The set $\{v_1, \cdots, v_n\} \subseteq \mathcal{V}_p \cup \mathcal{V}_o$ is the subset of variables which change value as a consequence of the transition triggering. Finally, in the case of elementary transitions, unless otherwise stated, we assume that for each $v \notin \{v_1, \cdots, v_n\}$, there is an unwritten conjoint $(v' = v)$, meaning that variables that do not appear in $\rho(\tau)$ are supposed to be left unchanged by the transition.

Compound transitions are subsets of elementary transitions noted $[\tau_1; \cdots; \tau_n]$. Compound transitions should be considered as atomic: components of compound transitions do not interleave with other transitions of S. We introduce compound transitions to account for the atomicity of Object-Z class operations, as will be seen in section 3.1. We note $\mathcal{V}'(\rho_\tau)$ the set of primed variables of transition relation ρ_τ. A compound transition $[\tau_1; \cdots; \tau_n]$ is coherent if and only if:

$$\forall \tau_i, \tau_j \in [\tau_1, \cdots, \tau_n] \bullet i \neq j \Rightarrow \mathcal{V}'(\rho_{\tau_i}) \cap \mathcal{V}'(\rho_{\tau_j}) = \varnothing$$

A computation of transition system $S = <\mathcal{V}, \Sigma, \mathcal{T}_e, \mathcal{T}_c, \Theta>$ is a sequence

$$\sigma : s_0, s_1, \cdots, s_j, \cdots$$

of states such that $s_0 \vDash \Theta$ and for every $s_i, i \geq 0$, at least one of the following possibilities is verified:

- There is a $\tau \in \mathcal{T}_e$ such that $s_i \vDash Pre(\tau)$ and $s_{i+1} \in \tau(s_i)$.
- There is a coherent compound transition $[\tau_1; \cdots; \tau_n] \in \mathcal{T}_c$ that verifies what follows. Let $\mathcal{E} = \{\tau_1^e, \cdots, \tau_m^e\}$ be the set of components of τ_c enabled in s_i (i.e., for all j, $s_i \vDash Pre(\tau_j^e)$), then $\mathcal{E} \neq \varnothing$ and $s_{i+1} \in \tau_1^e(s_i) \cap \cdots \cap \tau_m^e(s_i)$.

We note $\mathcal{C}(S)$ the set of all computations of transition system S.

3   Verification Technique

3.1   From Object-Z Classes to Transition Systems

A class specification written in Object-Z can bee seen as the description of an abstract machine. Objects of the class are instances capable of producing computations of the machine, as sequences of state changes caused by operations. The aim of the proposed transformation is to obtain, from the definition of the class, written in Object-Z, a compact representation of the set of computations an object of the class can produce. This representation is intended to take the form of a transition system. The intended result of the transformation is a triple $(S, \mathcal{A}, \mathcal{H})$ where $S =< \mathcal{V}, \Sigma, \mathcal{T}_e, \mathcal{T}_c, \Theta >$ is a transition system as defined in section 2.2, $\mathcal{A}$ and $\mathcal{H}$ are sets of linear temporal logic (LTL) formulas called respectively axioms and history invariants. A simple Object-Z class definition has the following elements:

ClassName _____
   type definitions
   constant definitions
   state schema
   initial state schema
   operations
   _____
   history invariants

An Object-Z class named cl is characterized by the following sets. $Attr(cl)$ is a set of class attributes, declared in the _state schema_, $Param(cl)$ is a set of operation parameters. Both are subsets of a set of identifiers such that $Attr(cl) \cap Param(cl) = \varnothing$.

$State(cl) \subseteq Attr(cl) \nrightarrow Val$ is the set of class states, a subset of the finite partial functions from attributes to values. The set Val contains all possible values of attributes of any type. Finally, $Op(cl)$ is the set of class operations. We introduce the auxiliary functions $\pi_i : Op(cl) \rightarrow \mathbb{P}\, Param(cl)$ and $\pi_o : Op(cl) \rightarrow \mathbb{P}\, Param(cl)$ that give respectively the set of input and output parameters of an operation.

We explain now the translation of a simple Object-Z class named cl towards a model $(S^{cl}, \mathcal{A}^{cl}, \mathcal{H}^{cl})$, with $S^{cl} =< \mathcal{V}^{cl}, \Sigma^{cl}, \mathcal{T}_e^{cl}, \mathcal{T}_c^{cl}, \Theta^{cl} >$ and illustrate it with the _heap of matches_ game. We state that:

$$\mathcal{V}_p^{cl} = Attr(cl), \quad \mathcal{V}_i^{cl} = \bigcup_{o \in Op(cl)} \pi_i(o), \quad \mathcal{V}_o^{cl} = \bigcup_{o \in Op(cl)} \pi_o(o)$$

so that, for the *Game* class we have $\mathcal{V}_p^{Game} = \{heap, turn\}$, $\mathcal{V}_i^{Game} = \{take?\}$ and $\mathcal{V}_o^{Game} = \varnothing$.

State schema of the form $[declaration\ part \mid Ax_1; \cdots; Ax_n]$ declares attributes and, optionally, states a list of axioms relative to declared attributes. Axioms $Ax_1, \cdots, Ax_n$ are first order predicates on the attributes defined in the declaration part. We state that:

$$\mathcal{A}^{cl} = \{Ax_1, \cdots, Ax_n\}$$

The general form of the initial state schema is $INIT \mathrel{\widehat{=}} [Pr_1; \cdots; Pr_m]$ where the $Pr_i(i \in [1..m])$ are first order predicates on the class attributes. We state that:

$$\Theta^{cl} = Pr_1 \wedge \cdots \wedge Pr_m$$

so that, for the *Game* class we have $\Theta^{Game} = (heap = 46) \wedge (turn = 0)$.

The class operations $OperationName \mathrel{\widehat{=}} [declaration\ part \mid predicate\ list]$ are the portion of the specification which is translated towards the transitions of S^{cl}. In many cases, an operation gives rise to a set of elementary transitions. Let $\mathcal{T}^o = \{\tau_1, \cdots, \tau_i\}$ be the set of elementary transitions resulting from operation $o \in Op(cl)$. We distinguish the following cases:

- if $\mathcal{T}^o$ is a singleton (i.e., $\mathcal{T}^o = \{\tau\}$), then $\tau \in \mathcal{T}_e^{cl}$.
- if $\mathcal{T}^o = \{\tau_1, \cdots, \tau_n\}$, with $n > 1$ then let $\tau_c = [\tau_1; \cdots; \tau_n] \in \mathcal{T}_c^{cl}$, provided that τ_c is coherent.

Given the richness of the Object-Z language, a detailed definition of all the translation rules from operations into transitions is a difficult task. We will illustrate some aspects of the translation principles through the *Game* example and also through the case study. Operation *Move* of the *Game* class gives rise to transition τ^{Move} as follows. The predicate with unprimed attributes determines the precondition: $Pre(\tau^{Move}) = (heap \geq take?)$. The predicates with mixed unprimed and primed attributes determine the rest of the transition relation. In the case of the *Game* example, the transition relation is straightforward:

$$\rho_{\tau^{Move}} = (heap \geq take?) \wedge (heap' = heap - take?) \wedge (turn' = 1 - turn)$$

and we have: $\mathcal{T}^{Game} = \mathcal{T}^{Move} = \{\tau^{Move}\}$.

Finally, the *history invariants* part of the class specification contains a list of LTL formulas $H_1, \cdots, H_p$. We state that:

$$\mathcal{H}^{cl} = \{H_1, \cdots, H_p\}$$

So that we have $\mathcal{H}^{Game} = \{\Box((turn = 0) \Rightarrow \bigcirc(turn = 1)), \Box((turn = 1) \Rightarrow \bigcirc(turn = 0))\}$. Operations that translate to compound transitions are typically those which are specified by quantified formulas. In the case study we present rules to obtain compound transitions from operation specifications in which variables bound by quantifiers have finite types, such as intervals of natural integers.

3.2   Validity, Satisfiability, and Consistency

We present now the meaning of sets $\mathcal{A}$ and $\mathcal{H}$ that have been introduced in section 3.1. We use the fact that computations of transition systems can be models of LTL formulas. Mathematical logic gives a precise meaning to the word *model*, by defining the satisfaction relation between *"universe of discourse"* entities (models) and logic formulas. Let us begin by a quick remind of LTL formulas and their satisfaction relation.

LTL extends predicate calculus with new logical operators such as $\bigcirc$, $\mathcal{U}$, $\square$, $\Diamond$, called the temporal operators. If F_1 and F_2 are well-formed formulas so are $\bigcirc F_1$, $F_1 \mathcal{U} F_2$, $\square F_1$ and $\Diamond F_1$. State formulas are formulas without temporal operators. State-quantified formulas are formulas such that temporal operators do not appear in the scope of quantifiers.

The natural model for LTL formulas on a set $V = \{v_1, \cdots, v_n\}$ of variables are the so called Chains, i.e., sequences of valuations of V noted:

$$\sigma : s_0, \cdots, s_j, \cdots$$

with, for all j, $s_j : V \rightarrow Dom(V)$, where $Dom(V)$ denotes the domain where all variables of V take their values. We note $s[v]$ the value of variable $v \in V$ in state s. The satisfaction relation ($\vDash$) is defined as follows. If F is a state formula, then $(\sigma, j) \vDash F$, i.e σ satisfies F at position j, if and only if $s_j \vDash F$ (i.e., $s_j[F]$ = true). If F_1 and F_2 are temporal formulas, the relation $\vDash$ is defined inductively: $(\sigma, j) \vDash \bigcirc F_1$ if and only if $(\sigma, j + 1) \vDash F_1$; $(\sigma, j) \vDash F_1 \mathcal{U} F_2$ if and only if there exists $k \geq j$ such that $(\sigma, k) \vDash F_2$ and for all i such that $j \leq i < k$, $(\sigma, i) \vDash F_1$; $(\sigma, j) \vDash \Diamond F_1$ if and only if $(\sigma, j) \vDash \text{true} \mathcal{U} F_1$; $(\sigma, j) \vDash \square F_1$ if and only if $(\sigma, j) \vDash \neg \Diamond \neg F_1$. The set of chains that satisfy an LTL formula F is noted $Sat(F)$.

Given an *Object-Z* class cl and its associated semantic entity $(S^{cl}, \mathcal{A}^{cl}, \mathcal{H}^{cl})$, the set $\mathcal{A}^{cl} = \{A_1, \cdots, A_m\}$ of axioms defines the state space of cl as the set:

$$\{s \in \Sigma^{cl} \mid s \vDash A_1 \wedge \cdots \wedge A_m\}$$

In other words, the axioms restrict the set Σ^{cl} of states of the transition system in order to ensure that $\mathcal{A}^{cl}$ is valid.

To define the meaning of the history invariant set, let us remind section 2.2, where we defined the set $\mathcal{C}(S)$ of computations of a transition system. We state that S^{cl} is consistent, with the set $\mathcal{H}^{cl} = \{H_1, \cdots H_n\}$ of history invariants if $Sat(H_1 \wedge \cdots \wedge H_n) \cap \mathcal{C}(S^{cl}) \neq \varnothing$. In other words, $\mathcal{H}^{cl}$ is expected to be satisfiable relatively to S^{cl}.

4   Case Study

4.1   The Radio-Mobile Network Example

In order to illustrate the specification and verification approach, we choose an example from the Radio-Mobile Network (RMN) design problem. Radio-mobile

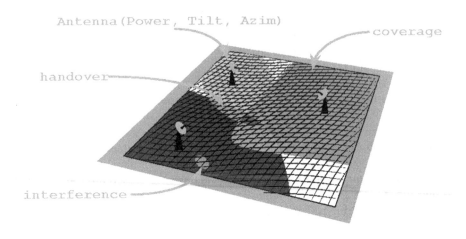

Fig. 1. Antenna parameter setting problem

communication relies on a network of antennae to cover a given area of territory, in order to ensure communication services such as mobile phones. The design of a RMN includes three main stages: antennae positioning, parameter setting and frequency allocation.

We are concerned here with the parameter setting stage: once the antennae locations have been determined in the positioning stage, the parameter setting problem deals with the issue of Quality of Service (QoS) optimization. The antenna parameter problem has yet been presented. Indeed, [3] gives an implemented solution to the problem, and in [2] we specify the problem and we simulate the specification.

For each antenna, three parameters need generally to be adjusted: emission power, tilt and azimuth. On the other hand, QoS includes several aspects, such as coverage, traffic, interference and handover. To optimize QoS, a trade-off must be found. For instance, coverage and handover ask for higher emission power while interference avoidance asks for lesser radio energy.

In order to solve the parameter setting problem, the area to cover is partitioned into a set of meshes whose size vary from 25 to 100 square meters, depending on the type of land, as illustrated by figure 1, which resumes the parameters setting problem.

For the sake of clarity, we restrict our example to the of emission power setting problem, of which we present now a formal description. Given a set $A = \{a_1, \cdots, a_n\}$ of antennae and a set $M = \{m_1, \cdots, m_k\}$ of meshes, the following functions define the radio-propagation upon the considered area. Function $Fade : M \times A \to \mathbb{R}$ allows to calculate the mesh-local variation of the field emitted by each antenna. Function $Power : A \to \mathbb{R}$ gives the radio-electric emission power of each antenna. Function $F : M \times A \to \mathbb{R}$ allows to calculate the field intensity in any mesh, due to each antenna emission. As a matter of fact, for mesh m_i and antenna a_j, the field intensity can be calculated as $F(m_i, a_j) = f(Fade(m_i, a_j), Power(a_j))$, for a given function f. In this example we assume that f is simply the product between emission power and attenuation:

$$F(m_i, a_j) = Fade(m_i, a_j) * Power(a_j)$$

4.2 Specification

The specification of the antennae parameter setting problem is structured in three classes. The first specifies the terrain upon which antennae are situated, the second specifies an antennae and the latter specifies the system as a whole. We suppose that antennae and meshes numbers are fixed and known. They are specified by the following schema.

Types $MESHID$ and $ANTENNAID$ allow to identify each mesh and each antenna. Constant function Fade gives, for each antenna, the field attenuation in any mesh and thereby allows to calculate field intensity in any mesh, due to any antenna. We adopt the view of identifying discrete emission power levels, as defined by type $POWERLEVEL$. The only state variable is $Field$ which, for any mesh, gives a field intensity vector indexed by the set of antennae identifiers, the contribution of each antenna to the mesh's field. Operation $ChangeField$ allow to calculate the contribution of an antenna to the field after a change in antenna's emission power. Operation $MeasureField$ returns, for a given antenna, the field it contributes to any mesh. Operation $DetectInterference$ returns, for a given antenna, the indication of whether it interferes another antenna in any mesh.

__ $Terrain$ _____

$n : \mathbb{N}$ [number of antennae]
$k : \mathbb{N}$ [number of meshes]
_____
$n < k$

$MESHID == [1..k]$
$ANTENNAID == [1..n]$
$POWERLEVEL == [0..100]$

$Fade : MESHID \times ANTENNAID \rightarrow \mathbb{R}$

$\forall i : MESHID, j : ANTENNAID \bullet 0 \le Fade(i,j) < 1$

$Field : MESHID \rightarrow (ANTENNAID \rightarrow \mathbb{R})$

__ $INIT$ _____
$\forall m : MESHID; \; a : ANTENNAID \bullet Field(m)(a) = 0$

$\ulcorner$ _ChangeField_ $\underline{\hspace{6cm}}$
$\Delta Field$
$EmitedPower?: POWERLEVEL$
$AntId?: ANTENNAID$

$\forall\, m: MESHID\, \bullet$
$Field'(m) = Field(m) \oplus \{AntId? \mapsto Fade(m, AntId?) * EmitedPower?\}$

$\ulcorner$ _MeasureField_ $\underline{\hspace{5cm}}$
$AntId?: ANTENNAID$
$FieldMeasure!: MESHID \rightarrow \mathbb{R}$

$\forall\, m: MESHID\, \bullet\, FieldMeasure!(m) = Field(m)(AntId?)$

$\ulcorner$ _DetectInterference_ $\underline{\hspace{5cm}}$
$AntId?: ANTENNAID$
$Interfered!: MESHID \rightarrow \mathbb{B}$

$\forall\, m: MESHID\, \bullet\, Interfered!(m) =$
$\exists\, a: ANTENNAID\, \bullet\, a \neq AntId? \wedge Field(m, a) \geq gate_Q \wedge$
$\quad Field(m, AntId?) \geq gate_S$

An antenna is specified by its identity, emission power and coverage attributes and operations. Operation _SetCoverage_ determines, from field intensity, the meshes covered by the antenna. Operation _SetPower_ bases on interference to determine whether the antenna increases or decreases its emission power. Operation _Emit_ outputs the antenna's emission power.

$\ulcorner$ _Antenna_ $\underline{\hspace{8cm}}$

$n: \mathbb{N}$	[number of antentennae]
$k: \mathbb{N}$	[number of meshes]

$n < k$

$MESHID == [1..k]$
$ANTENNAID == [1..n]$
$POWERLEVEL == [0..100]$

$AntId: ANTENNAID$
$EmissionPower: POWERLEVEL$
$Covered: MESHID \rightarrow \mathbb{B}$
$Coverage: \mathbb{N}$

$$\begin{array}{|l}
\hline
\quad INIT \rule{3cm}{0.4pt} \\
\; EmissionPower = 0 \\
\; Coverage = 0 \\
\hline
\end{array}$$

$$\begin{array}{|l}
\hline
\quad SetCoverage \rule{2cm}{0.4pt} \\
\; \Delta(Covered, Coverage) \\
\; Identity! : ANTENNAID \\
\; FieldMeasure? : MESHID \rightarrow \mathbb{R} \\
\hline
\; Identity! = AntId \\
\; \forall\, m : MESHID \bullet Covered'(m) = (FieldMeasure?(m) > gate_Q) \\
\; Coverage' = \#(Covered' \rhd true) \\
\hline
\end{array}$$

$$\begin{array}{|l}
\hline
\quad SetPower \rule{3cm}{0.4pt} \\
\; \Delta(EmissionPower) \\
\; Identity! : ANTENNAID \\
\; Interfered? : MESHID \rightarrow \mathbb{B} \\
\hline
\; Identity! = AntId \\
\; \#(Interfered? \rhd true) < I_{max} \;\wedge \\
\quad EmissionPower' = EmissionPower + \Delta_1 Power \\
\; \#(Interfered? \rhd true) \geq I_{max} \;\wedge \\
\quad EmissionPower' = EmissionPower - \Delta_2 Power \\
\hline
\end{array}$$

$$\begin{array}{|l}
\hline
\quad Emit \rule{3cm}{0.4pt} \\
\; Identity! : ANTENNAID \\
\; Power! : POWERLEVEL \\
\hline
\; Identity! = AntId \\
\; Power! = EmissionPower \\
\hline
\end{array}$$

The system composed of antennae and meshes is specified by *CommunicationSystem* class. It includes an instance of the *Terrain* class and a set of instances of the *Antenna* class, indexed by the set of antenna identifiers.

$$\begin{array}{|l}
\hline
\quad CommunicationSystem \rule{2cm}{0.4pt} \\
\; terrain : Terrain \\
\; antenna : ANTENNAID \rightarrow Antenna \\
\hline
\; \forall\, a : ANTENNAID \bullet antenna(a).AntId = a \\
\hline
\quad INIT \rule{3cm}{0.4pt} \\
\; terrain.INIT \\
\; \forall\, a : ANTENNAID \bullet antenna(a).INIT \\
\hline
\end{array}$$

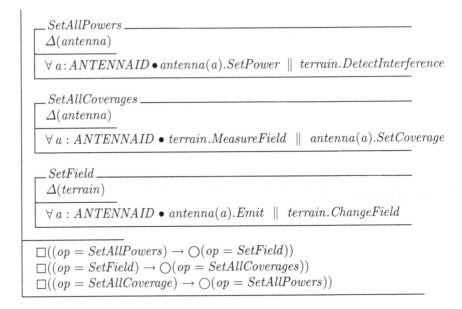

4.3   Verifying the Object-Z Specification

Obtaining the Transitions System   We discuss now some components of
the transition system that results from the Object-Z specification of the case
study. We do not express formally in this work the rules that guide such a transformation. Rather, we give an informal presentation to justify the transitions
resulting from some constructs frequently used in the case study. An important
issue concerns the evaluation of compound transitions by evaluating sequentially
their elementary component transitions. This can be made under some conditions that we present below.

Many assertions that specify the operations of our model are universally quantified formulas, with bound variables ranging in sets $MESHID$ and $ANTENNAID$.
The general idea to translate such assertions into transitions is as follows. With
formula:

$$\forall\, i : [1..k] \bullet Pre_i \wedge (var_i' = Exp_i)$$

where Pre_i is a precondition, var_i is a variable name and Exp_i is an expression,
we associate the compound transition $[\tau_1; \cdots ; \tau_k]$ such that for all $i \in [1..k]$,
the transition relation is:

$$\rho(\tau_i) = Pre_i \wedge (var_i' = Exp_i)$$

If for all $i, j \in [1..k]$ we have $i \neq j \Rightarrow var_i \neq var_j$ then we have a coherent
transition. Moreover, this compound transition can be evaluated sequentially if
neither Pre_i nor Exp_i contain any variable other than var_i.

Another Z construct frequently used in our specification is the range restriction
operator ($\rhd$). We used it when, given a predicate on $Mesh$, we had to count

the domain elements that mapped to true. A general rule to translate such a construct towards a set of transitions, is the following. Given a predicate $Pred : [1..k] \rightarrow \mathbb{B}$, with formula:

$$count' = \#(Pred(i) \triangleright true)$$

we associate the compound transition $[(count' = 0); \tau_1; \cdots ; \tau_k]$ such that for all $i \in [1..k]$, the transition relation is:

$$\rho(\tau_i) = Pred(i) \wedge (count' = count + 1)$$

Indeed, this is not a coherent compound transition but we can obtain the expected result by evaluating sequentially each one of the component elementary transitions.

We dealt with some other aspects of the Object-Z specification, such as aggregation, before translation towards transition systems. As a matter of fact, we inspired from the approach to class aggregation presented in [6]. As an example, the *CommunicationSystem* class results from the aggregation of classes *Terrain* and *Antenna*. Operations of the aggregate class were defined by applying operator $\|$ to operations of component classes. To obtain the translation of those operations towards transitions of the transition system, we first applied schema transformations due to the $\|$ operator of [6]. As an example, consider the *SetField* operation, which refers to operation $antenna(a).Emit \ \| \ terrain.ChangeField$. We have:

$$\begin{array}{|l}
\hline
\_antenna(a).Emit \ \| \ terrain.ChangeField \_\rule{4cm}{0.4pt} \\
\Delta(terrain) \\
\hline
ChangeField.AntId? = Emit.Identity! \\
Terrain.EmitedPower? = Emit.Power! \\
terrain \ \underline{Terrain :: ChangeField} \ terrain' \\
\hline
\end{array}$$

where, according to operation $antenna(a).Emit$, we have:

$$Identity! = antenna(a).AntId$$

and

$$Power! = antenna(a).EmissionPower$$

On the other hand, remind that relation $terrain \ \underline{Terrain :: ChangeField} \ terrain'$ states that *terrain* and *terrain'* are related by the aggregated operation exactly as they are related by operation *ChangeField* of class *Terrain*. If we apply the equalities and the definition of the $terrain \ \underline{Terrain :: ChangeField} \ terrain'$ relation, we obtain:

$$\begin{array}{|l}
\hline
\_antenna(a).Emit \parallel terrain.ChangeField _____ \\
\Delta(terrain) \\
\hline
\forall\, m : MESHID \bullet Field'(m) = Field(m) \oplus \{\, antenna(a).AntId \mapsto \\
Fade(m, antenna(a).AntId) * antenna(a).EmissionPower\,\} \\
\hline
\end{array}$$

which is the predicate to be translated towards transitions.

Verifying with STeP: Some Implementation Details The use of STeP
as a verification tool requires the expression of the resulting transition system
according to the STeP transitions syntax. As the later do not include the notion
of compound transitions defined in section 2.2, we defined an implementations
of compound transitions based on the sequential evaluation of elementary transitions components. To ensure atomicity of compound transitions we used lock
variables. We factorized sets of transitions by implementing loop constructs. Finally, Functions on domain $MESHID$ (respectively $ANTENNAID$) were implemented as arrays indexed by $[1..k]$ (respectively $[1..n]$) and functions on domain
$MESHID \times ANTENNAID$ were implemented as arrays indexed by $[1..k] \times [1..n]$.
As an example consider operation $SetCoverage$ of class $Antenna$, which produced
the following transition relations:

$$\rho_1 = (lock = FREE) \wedge (index' = 1) \wedge (Coverage' = 0) \wedge (lock' = TAKEN)$$
$$\rho_2 = (index \geq 1) \wedge (index \leq k) \wedge (FieldMeasure?[index] \geq gate_Q) \wedge$$
$$(Covered'[index] = \text{true}) \wedge (Coverage' = Coverage + 1) \wedge (index' = index + 1)$$
$$\rho_3 = (index \geq 1) \wedge (index \leq k) \wedge (FieldMeasure?[index] < gate_Q) \wedge$$
$$(Covered'[index] = \text{false}) \wedge (index' = index + 1)$$
$$\rho_4 = (index > k) \wedge (index' = 0) \wedge (lock' = FREE)$$

We used the STeP model-checker to verify the satisfiability of the history
invariants of class $CommunicationSystem$, on a simple communication system
composed of two antennae and ten meshes. The STeP model-checker proves
or refutes validity of LTL formulas relatively to a transition system. to establish the satisfiability of history invariant H one must actually establish that
$\neg\,H$ is not valid. Concerning our case study, we checked separately each one
of the three temporal formulas of class $CommunicationSystem$. For instance,
the satisfiability of the first formula was checked by establishing that formula
$\neg \diamondsuit\neg\,((op = SetAllPowers) \rightarrow \bigcirc(op = SetField))$ was not valid.
We first verified some properties of separated classes. For the $Antenna$ class, we
verified the satisfiability of formula $F_1 = \diamondsuit(Coverage \geq Cov_{min})$ with Cov_{min}
being a minimal number of covered meshes. This property represents the possibility of an important result to be obtained, i.e., an antenna covering at least
a minimal number of meshes. As already mentioned, the STeP model-checker
proves or refutes validity of LTL formulas relatively to a transition system. Consequently, STeP was asked to verify formula $\square(Coverage < Cov_{min})$. A counterexample was rapidly established by STeP. The number of states visited by the

model-checker was 48. Next we verified a safety property, expressed by formula $F_2 = \Box((Coverage \leq k) \Rightarrow (EmmissionPower < 100))$, to mean that even when all meshes are covered by an antenna, the maximal power level is not exceded. This property was refuted by STeP with a counterexample, thereby motivating a change in the *Antenna* specification. The modified version satisfied F_2, but verifying this formula took considerable amounts of time, visiting more than 200000 states.

5   Conclusion

Formalisms like Z and Object-Z include in a unique specification language two important conceptual domains. On one side, by adopting the first order predicate notation, they belong to the *specify with logic* realm. On the other side, as they describe system state and operations on states, Object-Z also relates to more operational styles of specification. In this work on verification of Object-Z specifications we propose some rules to transform an Object-Z class into a transition system, in order to use verification tools such as the STeP environment. Rather than general rules, we present the approach by applying it to a case-study. The proposed informal rules transform operations of the class in sets of simple transitions grouped in indivisible compound transitions to represent operations of the class. Future research should concentrate on a better understanding of problems related to the transformations from Object-Z operations towards compound transitions, that preserve! the properties of operations expressed with first order predicates. Formal presentation of a set of well defined transformation rules is also necessary to consolidate the approach.

References

1. Roger Duke, Paul King, Gordon Rose, and Graeme Smith. The Object-Z specification language. Technical report, Software Verification Research Center, Department of Computer Science, University of Queensland, AUSTRALIA, 1991.
2. V. Hilaire, T. Lissajoux, and A. Koukam. AGENTCHARTS: AN OPERATIONAL MODEL FOR MULTI-AGENT SYSTEMS. In *International Conference on Advanced Computer Systems ACS'98*, 1998.
3. T. Lissajoux, V. Hilaire, A. Koukam, and A. Caminada. Genetic algorithms as prototyping tools for multi-agent systems: Application to the antenna parameter setting problem. In Springer Verlag, editor, *Lecture Note in Artificial Intelligence*, number 1437 in LNAI, 1998.
4. Z. Manna, N. Bjoerner, A. Browne, and E. Chang. STeP: The Stanford Temporal Prover. *Lecture Notes in Computer Science*, 915:793–??, 1995.
5. Zohar Manna and Amir Pnueli. *Temporal Verification of Reactive Systems: Safety*. Springer, 1995.
6. Graeme Paul Smith. *An Object-Oriented Approach To Formal Specification*. PhD thesis, University of Queensland, 1992.
7. J. M. Spivey. *The Z Notation: A Reference Manual*. Prentice Hall, 1992.

A Model for Describing Object-Oriented Systems from Multiple Perspectives

Torsten Nelson, Donald Cowan, and Paulo Alencar

Computer Systems Group, University of Waterloo
{torsten,dcowan,alencar}@csg.uwaterloo.ca

Abstract. We present work on a formal model for the composition of object-oriented modules, or *hyperslices*, which represent different perspectives on the system being built. With the model, we should be able to study existing approaches such as subject-oriented programming, as well as extend other object-oriented languages, such as the UML, to accommodate the use of hyperslices. We show here a sample of the specification language that accompanies the formal model, and a small example of its use.

1 Introduction

The idea of dividing a system description into various perspectives, each of which portrays some aspect of the system, has been the topic of recent intensive research. Techniques such as subject-oriented programming [9] and aspect-oriented programming [14] explore the possibilities of having multiple representations of the same entity from the problem domain. The need arises for a formal model that brings together what is common about the various multiple-perspective methods, particularly within the object-oriented paradigm. Such a model would allow for strengthening of existing techniques with the possibility for formal proofs and consistency checks, and serve as the basis for extending popular design and implementation languages with multiple-perspective capabilities. This work attempts to fill this gap.

In section 2 we discuss the need for multiple-perspective decomposition and present its different categories. We then discuss issues related to multiple-perspective decomposition restricted to the object-oriented paradigm in section 3. Section 4 shows the proposed model, followed by a small example of its use in section 5.

2 Multiple-Perspective Decomposition

One of the most widely accepted tenets of software development is the fact that complex problems must be divided into smaller parts that are easier to understand and work with. Traditional approaches to modeling such as structured analysis and object orientation take a top-down approach, where a system is decomposed into several parts, each of which is again decomposed until each part is simple and cohesive. The parts are then implemented independently and composed to form the desired software system. The exact nature of the entities that form each part varies between approaches, but typically

T. Maibaum (Ed.): FASE 2000, LNCS 1783, pp. 237–248, 2000.

each unit of the decomposition is encapsulated in a procedure (*functional* decomposition), module, or class (*object* decomposition). It is common to think of each of these units as pieces in a larger puzzle, all of which fit together to form the solution.

Recently, new approaches to problem decomposition have been the subject of research. It is often useful to view the entire problem from a single perspective, discarding all the problem elements that are not relevant to the perspective, and thereby reducing problem complexity. The problem then becomes easier to understand and manage than when viewed in its entirety. In contrast to the top-down approach for functional decomposition mentioned in the previous paragraph, each perspective can be thought of as a glass sheet with some aspect of a painting: one sheet may have a black outline of the painting; another, its colors; others may have shadings, textures, and so on. Superimposing all glass sheets forms the complete painting.

What distinguishes this "multiple-perspective" decomposition from other forms of divide-and-conquer is the fact that the decomposed parts are not disjoint. In other approaches to decomposition, any entity from the problem domain appears in only one of the pieces after decomposition - no entity appears in more than one piece. By contrast, an entity may appear in any number of perspectives, and its definition can be different in each perspective.

We frame our concept of perspective in software engineering rather broadly using the following two definitions.

- A description of a software system has *multiple perspectives* if it is explicitly divided into two or more partial descriptions, and there are entities from the problem domain that appear in more than one partial description.
- A *method* uses multiple perspectives if it enforces the description of software with multiple perspectives and provides rules governing how perspectives are related to one another.

These definitions allow a wide variety of methods to be thought of as using multiple perspectives. We divide them into three categories according to the kind of partial description used: architectural, domain-specific, and user-defined perspectives. Our research focuses on methods that allow user-defined perspectives. In order to clarify the relationships among the proposed models, we discuss the three categories of multiple-perspective methods.

2.1 Architectural Perspectives

Structured analysis methods such as the one proposed by Gane and Sarson [8] use two different diagrams to describe a system: a module hierarchy chart describing the division of the system into modules, and a data flow diagram describing how data was transferred between the modules. Each diagram represents a partial description of the system, and contains representations of the same entities from the problem domain, and therefore fit our definition of a perspective. Modern object-oriented analysis and design methods such as the Object Modeling Technique (OMT) [18], Coad and Yourdon [5], UML [3], and others, all use different perspectives to describe a software system.

However, in all of the above, the perspectives are defined by the method and reflect different modeling or descriptive capabilities. For instance, a model may define structural relationships between entities, such as containment or association, while another may define behavioral aspects of each entity. Each perspective is usually described using a different language. This kind of description is often called an *architectural* perspective since each represents a certain aspect of the system's architecture. An important characteristic of architectural perspective decomposition is that it is independent of the problem domain. Dividing a problem into structural and behavioral views tells you nothing about the problem itself [13].

2.2 Domain-Specific Perspectives

There are other methods that allow the use of predefined perspectives, but instead of reflecting architectural aspects, the perspectives represent aspects of a specific problem domain. An example of this kind of method is the ISO standard for Open Distributed Processing (ODP) [11], which is geared towards the description of distributed systems. In ODP, systems may be described from any of five viewpoints. The five were chosen because they represent different and important perspectives relevant to the domain of distributed systems. These are *domain-specific* perspectives.

2.3 User-Defined Perspectives (Hyperslices)

Other methods allow for the decomposition of a problem into *user-defined* perspectives. These depend on the domain of concern, and therefore may be different from problem to problem. Also, the number of perspectives is not limited or predefined by the method. Methods supporting this type of decomposition were first developed for use in requirements elicitation, where it is common to have different stakeholders who have different ideas about the problem at hand, all of which must be captured. All perspectives are usually, but not always, described using the same language.

Various approaches have been proposed that allow user-defined perspectives. The approaches work at various levels of abstraction, and give different names to the units of decomposition. Table 1 lists some of these approaches.

Approach	Unit name	Level of abstraction
ViewPoints [7]	viewpoint	requirements analysis
Role models [15]	role	design
Contracts [10]	contract	design
Aspect-oriented programming [14]	aspect	implementation
Subject-oriented programming [9]	subject	implementation

Table 1. Approaches to decomposition with multiple user-defined perspectives

As can be seen from the table, the field is quite overloaded with different terminology for similar concepts. In recent work, Tarr et al. have coined the terms *Multi-Dimensional Separation of Concerns (MDSC)* to designate the discipline of multiple-perspective decomposition, and *hyperslice* to designate a unit of decomposition that follows this discipline, at any level of abstraction [20].

The most appropriate definition of hyperslice for our purposes is Daniel Jackson's concept of *view*:

"A view is a partial specification of the whole program, in contrast to a module, which is a specification - often complete - of only part of the program" [12].

A hyperslice, like a "view", specifies some aspect of the entire program.

The form of decomposition afforded by hyperslices is useful in many levels of software design. During requirements elicitation, for instance, the engineer often has to deal with many different people who are stakeholders in the system to be developed. Each of these stakeholders may have different perceptions about the problem at hand and of the desired behavior of the system. Hyperslices are a natural way of representing each stakeholder's perspective on the system so that later a coherent picture can be formed. The same advantages found at the requirements analysis phase carry over into later phases. Having design and implementation modules that correspond to user requirements provides easy requirements tracing. In the next section we discuss the use of hyperslices with object-oriented systems.

While the ideas behind MDSC are useful, there are issues that must be tackled when applying it, One of the most pressing of which is is *consistency*. When we allow more than one representation of an entity, we must somehow ensure that the representations do not contradict each other. Being able to detect inconsistencies and deal with them is one of the challenges of MDSC, and formal models that allow reasoning are an indispensable aid towards achieving this goal. Easterbrook et al. have studied mechanisms for dealing with inconsistencies when using requirements-level hyperslices [6].

There are also conflicts that do not manifest themselves as logical inconsistencies, but as a form of interference between hyperslices; the goals of the viewpoints may be mutually interdependent and actions taken by one may cause undesired behavior in the other. This is analogous to the problem of feature interaction in telephone systems [4]. A formal model should aid in the detection of such interactions.

There is yet no formal model to allow a comparative study of the properties of the various existing approaches to hyperslices; our work intends to fill that gap. However, mention should be made of *Ku* [19], a formal object-oriented language for hyperslices currently under development at Imperial College. Once our model and Ku are both complete, it will be interesting to compare analytical results derived from the two independent studies.

3   Object-Oriented Hyperslices

While the concepts behind MDSC (Multi-Dimensional Separation of Concerns) are widely applicable, much of the work in the field involves its use together with the object-oriented paradigm. Many of the shortcomings of object-orientation are addressed by MDSC. Among these are rigid classification hierarchies, scattering of requirements across classes, and tangling of aspects related to various requirements in a single class or module. For a detailed treatment and motivation for the use of multiple perspectives in object-orientation, we refer the reader to Tarr et al. [20].

We are interested in the subset of MDSC that deals with object-oriented systems. We consider a hyperslice to be a module that conforms to some accepted model of object-orientation, made up of classes and class relationships such as containment and inheritance. For an object-oriented system to fit into the category of MDSC, however, there must be entities from the problem domain that appear in more than one module. That is, there must be classes in different modules that represent separate aspects of the same entity. Since a hyperslice is meant to be a complete encapsulation of some relevant aspect of the system, the classes in a hyperslice should not have any links to classes of other hyperslices. Each hyperslice should be a well formed unit that can be understood in isolation.

As an example, one of the hyperslices in a system may be concerned with displaying information about the various objects that concern the system. The classes in this hyperslice should have methods to output information, and whatever attributes that are relevant to these methods. Other attributes or methods, such as those concerned with synchronization, or with some form of computation over the data, should not appear in this hyperslice. However, the hyperslice should contain all classes that have an output aspect to them.

Splitting an object-oriented description into various hyperslices gives a level of separation of concerns that offers significant advantages over traditional approaches. Among these advantages are the following:

Requirements-based modularization since entities are allowed to appear in more than one unit of decomposition, and to be only partially specified in any one unit, it is possible to have units that encapsulate a single requirement from the problem domain. For instance, if some of the data is to be stored and retrieved from a network server, a hyperslice would be defined containing all classes that have data belonging in the server. Each class would have only enough detail defined to allow the relevant storage operations to be performed. The same classes might appear in other hyperslices, but no mention of server storage would be found in them.

Decentralized development since classes can be represented differently in different hyperslices, classes need no longer be owned by developers who are responsible for all details regarding that class, but each developer can be responsible for a part of the shared class.

Unanticipated composition designs for separate programs can be thought of as hyperslices of an integrated application; a hyperslice-enabled method would allow the developer to describe how the programs are to be joined together.

Software evolution along the same lines, features can be added to existing systems as separate hyperslices; this would allow changes to be made without requiring modifications to existing designs. An example of hyperslices applied to evolution can be found in [2].

3.1 Composing Hyperslices

Since each hyperslice is a plain object-oriented module, it can in theory be described using any object-oriented language, at any level of abstraction. Having defined the hyperslices, they must now be composed to form a complete system. This is where the

MDSC paradigm differs from other approaches to decomposition. Some approaches, such as that advocated by module interconnection languages, define interfaces for modules, with provided and required functionality, and match provided functions with required ones across modules. Others, such as frameworks, use inheritance as the basic composition mechanism. In MDSC, each hyperslice is well formed and independent, and does not require other hyperslices. There are classes, however, that exist in various hyperslices. In order to form the desired system, we must establish the *correspondence* between these classes.

Correspondence is the specification of what elements match between hyperslices, and the semantics of each match. There are many ways in which matching can affect the overall behavior of the system. Matched classes may have complementing behavior, or one's behavior may override the other, or they may interact in more complex ways.

The granularity of correspondence is an issue. Using classes as the unit of correspondence (also called *join point* [14]) seems to be too coarse. There are many different ways in which we may wish to specify that entire classes are matched, and the model would require a large variety of different correspondence operators. On the other hand, using single program statements is too fine-grained. Specifying correspondence would require understanding implementation details, and would be very complex. In our model, we choose the middle road and use methods as the smallest elements that can be matched. Ossher and Tarr argue in favor of this approach [16]. We define correspondence operators that allow methods to be matched with various different semantics. The semantics describe what method bodies are executed in response to a method call.

Another issue with regard to correspondence is *object binding*. This is the specification of how objects of classes with corresponding methods are bound to each other at runtime. The description of correspondence is class-based, meaning that a method from a class is said to correspond to a method in another class. However, the semantics of correspondence are observed during method invocation on particular runtime objects. If a method invocation results in the execution of a method in an object of a different class, we must be able to determine exactly what the target object is. The binding specification describes how to determine correspondence between runtime objects.

4   The Hyperslice Model

We are interested in studying object-oriented hyperslices with operation-level correspondence. A language to allow hyperslice composition is under development. This is a class-based language that uses methods as the smallest indivisible unit. It is not meant to be an executable object-oriented language, but a means to specify formally compositions that can be done in any object-oriented design or implementation language. The language has two parts, one for class definition and one for composition.

The model allows us to study properties of techniques that use operation-level correspondence such as subject-oriented programming [9], and serves as a semantic basis for the extension of other object-oriented languages with the required mechanism for multi-dimensional separation of concerns. Since subject-oriented programming already represents an embodiment of MDSC at the implementation level, one of our interests is in extending design-level languages such as UML.

4.1 Class Language

The class language defines the classes present in the system, as well as the call graph between the methods of these classes. The semantics of correspondence are specified in terms of transformations in the call graph structure.

Each class is defined as a set of methods. A method has a name and a list of other methods that it calls. The internal state of a method is irrelevant. Each method call in this list is decorated with the modal symbols □ (*always*) and ◇ (*possibly*). At this stage, the language is untyped, and does not support parameters to methods, or return values.

Data attributes are not modeled. Instead, they may be represented as methods, the data being the internal state of the method. In fact, any method that does not call any other methods can be thought of as an attribute. This approach is related to the one used by Abadi and Cardelli in their object calculus [1]. Figure 1 shows the syntax of the class language, while figure 2 shows a sample class definition.

hyperslice ::= *class*{*class*}
class ::= **class** *name* "{" *method*{, *method*} "}"
method ::= *name*["(" { *called-method* } ")"]
called-method ::= □*name*|◇*name*
name ::= an identifier containing letters, hyphens, or a period. The period separates class
        names from method names.

Fig. 1. Class definition language syntax

```
class Tree {nodes, find( □ nodes, ◇ travel-left, ◇ travel-right ),
           travel-left (□ nodes), travel-right (□ nodes) }
```

Fig. 2. Sample class definition

Note that the names inside the parenthesis are not arguments, but the list of methods that the method calls. In the example above, the class named *Tree* has four methods. The methods *find, travel-left,* and *travel-right* will always call method *nodes*. The method *find* may, in addition, call methods *travel-left* and *travel-right*. The method call list may contain methods from other classes, specified by stating the class and method names separated by a period (as in `Tree.find`).

4.2 Composition Language

A composition is specified using *calling contexts*. At the highest level is the program calling context. By default, in any context, calling a method results in that method being executed. Method correspondence expressions can be used to change the effects of method calls. An expression is formed by two method names connected by a correspondence operator. Each expression can also introduce new calling contexts that have scope limited to the execution of the method that precedes the context.

Operator	Call	Execution
Unidirectional		
a followed-by b	a	$a; b$
a preceded-by b	a	$b; a$
a replaced-by b	a	b
Bidirectional		
a merge b	a	$a; b$
= a followed-by $b \wedge b$ followed-by a	b	$b; a$
a swap b	a	b
= a replaced-by $b \wedge b$ replaced-by a	b	a

Table 2. Method correspondence operators

Table 2 shows the correspondence operators and their meaning in terms of method calls and executions. The semicolon is used to denote sequence: $a; b$ means that method a will be executed and immediately followed by the execution of method b.

The bidirectional operators merely combine unidirectional ones and exist to add brevity to specifications. Many others are possible besides the two shown previously. Figure 3 shows the syntax of the composition language.

context ::= "{" {*expression*} "}"
expression ::= *name*[*context*] | *name*[*context*] *operator name*[*context*]
operator ::= followed-by | preceded-by | replaced-by | merge | swap

Fig. 3. Composition language syntax

Composition expression examples:

$a\{b$ **followed-by** $c\}$ Calls to a will result in the execution of a. During the execution of a, calls to b will result in the execution of b, followed by the execution of c.

$x\{p$ **followed-by** $q\}$ **preceded-by** $y\{r$ **swap** $q\}$ A call to x will result in the execution of y followed by the execution of x. In the execution of y, calls to r are replaced with the execution of q, and calls to q are replaced with the execution of r. In the execution of x, calls to p will result in the execution of p followed by the execution of q.

4.3   Object Binding

The composition operators are described at the class level. However, their effects are at the object level. A correspondence operator defines what happens when a call is made to a specific object. That call may result in the execution of methods in a different object. We need a way to determine the object referred to in the execution. Once that is determined, objects are bound to each other throughout their lifetime.

If there is a correspondence expression that matches a method call in a class a to a method execution in a different class b, there must be a binding expression detailing how objects of class a are to be bound to objects of class b. A binding expression has the form *a operator b*, where a is the class that has the method called, b is the class that has the method executed in response to the call, and *operator* is a binding operator. There can only be one binding expression involving any given pair of classes.

Currently, our language supports only three binding operators: *binds-to-unique*, *binds-to-any*, and *binds-to-all*. The expression *a binds-to-unique b* means that an object of class a is bound to any object of class b, as long as b has not yet been bound to any other object of class a. If such an object does not exist, one must be created. Another kind of binding is *binds-to-any*. The expression *a binds-to-any b* means that an object of class a can be bound to any existing object of class b. Finally, *binds-to-all* means that an object of class a will be bound to all existing objects of class b.

The effect of *binds-to-unique* is to create a one-to-one correspondence between objects. If *a binds-to-unique b*, then for each object of class a there will be an object of class b. The effect of *binds-to-any* is to create a many-to-one correspondence. If *a binds-to-any b*, a single object of class b is sufficient; all objects of class a can bind to that object. Finally, *binds-to-all* creates a many-to-many correspondence. In this case, when a method is called on an object of class a, the corresponding method of class b will be executed for all objects of class b.

5   Example: Concurrent File System

In this example we will take two independent modules, a simple file system and a concurrency control unit, and consider them as two hyperslices, or separate aspects, of an integrated system. The system is to give support for concurrency to the file system.

Hyperslice 1: file system A simple file system hyperslice contains two classes: `File` and `Directory`. Both allow *read* and *write* operations.

Hyperslice 2: shared buffer The shared buffer hyperslice contains a single class, *Mutex*, which encapsulates a shared buffer for use in a concurrent environment by multiple threads. The shared buffer contains three methods: *read, write*, and *cs*. Many readers can access the buffer at the same time, but writers require exclusive access. The *cs* method implements the critical section, which is where the buffer is actually manipulated.

Our intention is to combine the two hyperslices to produce a file system that supports execution in a concurrent environment, i.e., that allows many simultaneous users to read from a file or directory, but requires exclusive access to write in either of them. Figure 4 shows the class definitions for the two hyperslices.

```
class File { read( ), write( ) }
class Directory { read( ), write( ) }
class Mutex { read( □ cs ), write( □ cs ), cs( ) }
```

Fig. 4. Class definitions

The *Mutex* class provides synchronization for the desired system. Our intent is for users to still be able to use the File and Directory classes normally. However, before the file system operations can be used, the synchronization process must happen. This means that the appropriate Mutex method must be executed before the file system method. We use a correspondence expression to make sure that this happens, and that the appropriate file system method is executed when the Mutex object enters the critical section. The four required correspondence expressions are shown in figure 5.

```
File.read replaced-by Mutex.read { cs replaced-by File.read }
File.write replaced-by Mutex.write { cs replaced-by File.write }
Directory.read replaced-by Mutex.read
            { cs replaced-by Directory.read }
Directory.write replaced-by Mutex.write
            { cs replaced-by Directory.write }
```

Fig. 5. Correspondence expressions

The four expressions have similar structures. Let's examine the first line. When the user calls the read method of a File object, the read method of a Mutex object will be executed instead. The method will go through the read access protocol for the shared buffer. When it becomes possible to read the shared buffer, the cs method will be called. However, the context specified that File.read be executed instead. The file is then read. When File.read returns, the rest of the Mutex.read method is executed, releasing any locks that may be necessary. Figure 6 shows the flow of control between the hyperslices.

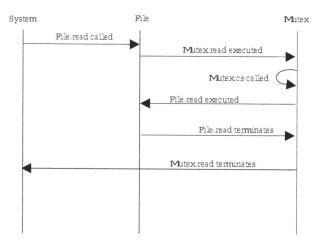

Fig. 6. Flow of control after correspondence

```
File binds-to-unique Mutex
Directory binds-to-unique Mutex
```

Fig. 7. Object binding expressions

The effect of the binding expressions, shown in figure 7 is to ensure that each *File* or *Directory* object will have its own *Mutex* object. This will allow each file to have its own concurrency access; while a file is being read, a different file can be written. Had we used *binds-to-any*, instead, we would have all files sharing a single Mutex object, which would have the effect of only allowing the file system to write to a single file at a time. This illustrates how the behavior of the system can be modified by changing the binding expressions.

6   Work in Progress

Many issues still need to be tackled before the model can be used as a basis for the extension of object-oriented approaches. The language is still untyped, and methods support neither arguments nor return values. Dealing with these will require work on the semantics of the correspondence operators, since the parameters or return types of a called method may differ from those of the executed method. The language also needs support for inheritance and more complex types of object binding.

We use transformations to achieve the desired semantics mandated by the correspondence operations. Since conventional object-oriented languages offer no primitives that are equivalent to these operators, the model becomes more useful if the systems described can be converted into systems in the conventional object-oriented model. This can be accomplished by a set of semantics-preserving transformations that would modify the existing classes to apply the functionality dictated by the correspondence operators.

The formal model underlying the language is under development using the PVS language and theorem prover [17].

7   Conclusion

We are providing the formal infrastructure for reasoning about multiple-perspective object-oriented systems. Our model is based on method-level correspondence, and is simple yet capable of describing the complex relationships that are necessary for this form of separation of concerns. We use call graphs to define the structure of individual hyperslices. Correspondence operations are used to specify changes in the call graph structure, and binding operators specify how runtime objects are matched. The example shown in this work is small, but illustrates the potential for using the model languages in hyperslice composition.

Once the model has been further expanded to include more object-oriented mechanisms such as inheritance, we intend to use it for formal reasoning about systems defined in many of the existing approaches such as subject-oriented programming. In particular, we are interested in consistency checking, a constant problem when using this form of decomposition. We also wish to use our semantic infrastructure as the basis for extending other object-oriented languages with multiple-perspective capabilities.

References

[1] Martin Abadi and Luca Cardelli. *A Theory of Objects*. Springer-Verlag, 1996.

[2] Paulo Alencar, Donald Cowan, Carlos Lucena, and Torsten Nelson. Viewpoints as an evolutionary approach to software system maintenance. In *Proceedings of IEEE International Conference on Software Maintenance*, October 1997.

[3] Grady Booch, James Rumbaugh, and Ivar Jacobson. *Unified Modeling Language User Guide*. Addison-Wesley, 1998.

[4] E. J. Cameron, N. Griffeth, Y.-J. Lin, M. Nilson, and W. Schnure. A feature interaction benchmark for IN and Beyond. In W. Bouma and H. Velthuijsen, editors, *Feature Interactions in Telecommunications Systems*, pages 1–23. IOS Press, 1994.

[5] P. Coad and E. Yourdon. *Object-Oriented Analysis*. Prentice Hall, 1989.

[6] Steve Easterbrook and Bashar Nuseibeh. Using ViewPoints for inconsistency management. *Software Engineering Journal*, 11(1):31–43, January 1996.

[7] A. Finkelstein, J. Kramer, B. Nuseibeh, L. Finkelstein, and M. Goedicke. Viewpoints: a framework for integrating multiple perspectives in system development. *International Journal of Software Engineering and Knowledge Engineering*, 2(1):31–57, 1992.

[8] C. Gane and T. Sarson. *Structured Systems Analysis: Tools and Techniques*. Prentice Hall, 1979.

[9] William Harrison and Harold Ossher. Subject-oriented programming (a critique of pure objects). In *Proceedings of OOPSLA '93*, pages 411–428. ACM, 1993.

[10] I. M. Holland. Specifying reusable components using contracts. In *Proceedings of ECOOP '92*, 1992. Lecture Notes in Computer Science no. 615.

[11] ISO. *ITU Recommendation X.901-904 – ISO/IEC 10746 1-4: Open Distributed Processing – Reference Model – Parts 1-4*. ISO, 1995.

[12] Daniel Jackson. Structuring Z specifications with views. *ACM Transactions on Software Engineering and Methodology*, 4(4):365–389, October 1995.

[13] Michael Jackson. *Software Requirements and Specifications: a lexicon of principles, practices and prejudices*. Addison-Wesley, 1995.

[14] Gregor Kiczales, J. Lamping, A. Mendhekar, C. Lopes, J. Loingtier, and J. Irwin. Aspect-oriented programming. In *Proceedings of ECOOP '97*, 1997.

[15] Bent Bruun Kristensen. Roles: Conceptual abstraction theory and practical language issues. *Special Issue of Theory and Practice of Object Systems (TAPOS) on Subjectivity on Object-Oriented Systems*, 1996.

[16] Harold Ossher and Peri Tarr. Operation-level composition: a case in (join) point. In *Proceedings of the 1998 ECOOP Workshop on Aspect-Oriented Programming*, 1998.

[17] S. Owre, J. M. Rushby, and N. Shankar. PVS: A prototype verification system. In Deepak Kapur, editor, *11th International Conference on Automated Deduction (CADE)*, volume 607 of *Lecture Notes in Artificial Intelligence*, pages 748–752, Saratoga, NY, June 1992. Springer-Verlag.

[18] James Rumbaugh, Michael Blaha, William Premerlani, Frederick Eddy, and William Lorensen. *Object-Oriented Modeling and Design*. Prentice Hall, 1991.

[19] Mark Skipper and Sophia Drossopoulou. Formalising composition-oriented programming. In *Proceedings of the 1999 ECOOP Workshop on Aspect-Oriented Programming*, 1999.

[20] Peri Tarr, Harold Ossher, William Harrison, and S. Sutton. N degrees of separation: Multi-dimensional separation of concerns. In *Proceedings of the 21st International Conference on Software Engineering*, pages 107–119, 1999.

Stepwise Introduction and Preservation of Safety Properties in Algebraic High-Level Net Systems

J. Padberg, K. Hoffmann, and M. Gajewsky

Technical University Berlin
Institute for Communication and Software Technology
{padberg, hoffmann, gajewsky}@cs.tu-berlin.de

Abstract. Our approach of rule-based refinement[1] provides a formal description for the stepwise system development based on Petri nets. Rules with a left-hand and a right-hand side allow replacing subnets in a given algebraic high-level net system. The extension of these rules supports the preservation of system properties. In this paper we extend the preservation of safety properties significantly. We define rules, that introduce new safety properties. In our new approach we propose first the verification of properties at the moment they can be expressed and then their preservation further on. Hence, properties can be checked as long as the system is still small. Moreover, introducing properties allows checking these for the relevant subpart only. Changes that are required later on can be treated the same way and hence preserve the system properties. Hence, we have made a step towards a formal technique for the stepwise system development during analysis and design.

Keywords: algebraic high-level net systems, rule-based refinement, temporal logic, safety properties, safety preserving morphisms, safety introducing rules, safety preserving rules

1 Introduction

The need to ensure quality of software systems yields a demand for formal techniques for the assertion of system properties. The verification of a (sub)system usually takes place, after the system has been modeled. This is on the one hand costly, since it is a large and complex system. On the other hand subsequent changes require the repeated verification of the whole system once more. The approach we are suggesting solves this problem. We propose to introduce safety properties already during the stepwise development of the system model. Our approach is based on the rule-based refinement of Petri nets.

Petri nets have a long and successful story. The integration with data type descriptions has led in the 80's to powerful specification techniques (a summary can be found in [JR91]). These techniques together with an adequate

---

[1] This paper continues our research on rule-based refinement of algebraic high-level nets, we have first introduced at FASE 98 [PGE98].

T. Maibaum (Ed.): FASE 2000, LNCS 1783, pp. 249–265, 2000.

tool support, e.g. [JCHH91, Jen92, Gru91, DG98, OSS94] are widely applied in practical system development. Here, we use algebraic high-level net systems [Vau87, PER95, GPH00], an integration of place/transition nets (as in [Rei85] or algebraically in [MM90]) with algebraic specifications in the sense of [EM85]. Rule-based refinement of nets is obtained by the instantiation of high-level replacement systems [EHKP91] by algebraic high-level net systems. Rules are given as a span of morphisms, mapping the interface to the left-hand as well as to the right-hand side. The application of a rule to a net system is a transformation and yields again a net system. This target net system is roughly the original one, where one subnet is replaced by another. Refinement rules, moreover have an additional morphism from the left-hand side to the right-hand side. This morphism then ensures the preservation of system properties in the sense of [MP92].

In this paper safety properties are expressed in terms of certain temporal formulas over the markings of the net system. We introduce several morphisms of algebraic high-level net systems. Namely place preserving and transition gluing morphisms preserve safety properties. That is, if the safety properties hold in the domain of a morphisms then it holds in the codomain as well. We then present safety preserving rules yielding safety preserving transformations. Moreover, we present safety introducing rules. These add a new subnet together with a safety property over this subnet. Hence, new safety properties are introduced into the model and then preserved. The main result of this paper is that the introduced morphisms give rise to safety preserving rules and transformations in Theorems 1 and 2. Furthermore, rules for the introduction of new safety properties preserve the old safety properties and add new ones (see Theorem 3). Our approach allows the explicit introduction of safety properties as soon as they are expressible in the model. So once the corresponding system part is modeled the relevant safety properties can be expressed and verified. Hence, the verification takes place as soon as possible and more important as long as the model is fairly small. Moreover, we have the possibility to verify the safety properties for the relevant part only. Subsequently they are preserved throughout the remaining development process. In Concept 11 we describe this impact of our technical results.

The first step to a rule-based refinement preserving safety properties has been presented for algebraic high-level net systems at FASE 98 [PGE98]. We here give the new class of transition gluing morphisms. We show that these morphisms preserve safety properties and allow safety preserving rules (see Theorem 2). Moreover, our approach now comprises nets with an initial marking, i.e. net systems. Hence, we expand the notion of place preserving morphisms and ensure the desired properties (see Theorem 1). And we extend our approach to allow rules that explicitly introduce new safety properties. Details concerning the proofs and the lemmas in the appendix can be found in [GPH00].

This paper is organized as follows: First in Section 2 we illustrate our notions by an example. Then (Section 3) we give the formal definitions and state our results. At last we summarize our results and discuss future work.

2   Example: Medical Information System

In this section we motivate the notions and results of this paper in terms of a small example inspired by a case study [Erm96] of the medical information system called Heterogeneous Distributed Information Management System (HDMS). On the one hand the aim of this section is to introduce the basic notions of the model (algebraic high-level net system), temporal logic formulas, and rule-based refinement on an intuitive level. On the other hand we demonstrate how safety properties are preserved using place preserving and transition gluing morphisms. These safety properties have to be proven only once for the rule introducing them. Our notions concerning safety introducing and preserving rules capture the intuitive understanding of such development steps, that cannot violate given safety properties. In Section 3 these notions are given formally.

An algebraic high-level net system consists — roughly speaking — of a Petri net with inscriptions of an algebraic specification defining the data type part of

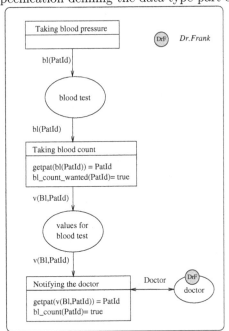

the net system and an initial marking. The tokens are data elements of a *Spec*-Algebra [EM85]. Figure 1 shows a sample net system, the subsystem blood count BC. The net system is inscribed with terms over the specification **BC-Spec** sketched below. The idea of the net system BC is to model the following situation at the hospital: The blood test of a patient arrives at the laboratory, denoted by the transition *Taking blood pressure*. Then the blood count is carried out, if demanded. Finally, the doctor is notified about the measured values. All these activities are represented as transitions in the net system BC. Furthermore we give the initial marking of BC.

Figure 1: Start Net System BC

We merely state the sorts and operations of **BC-Spec** used explicitly in the subsequent initial markings.

  sorts: Name, Patient, PatId, Pat Record, Blood Test, ...
  opns : patient: Name, Sex, Adress, PatId → Patient
      getpat: Patient → PatId
      mk_patrecord: Patient, Presc → PatRecord
      bl: PatId → Blood Test

We here consider the A-quotient term algebra (see [EM85]), the algebra generated according to the specification over carrier sets for names, doctors, resources etc. Assuming the carrier sets $A_{Name} = \{Smith, Miller, \ldots\}$ and $A_{Doctor} = \{Dr.\ Frank, Dr.\ Brown \ldots\}$ we have the following initial marking M_{BC} given by $(Dr.\ Frank, \textbf{doctor})$. Dr. Frank is at the ward, which is represented by the token on the place **doctor**.

We are now going to enhance the model with the blood value measurement of a patient at the ward. We achieve this by first adding patients and their ward documents and the taking of blood pressure and blood test to the start net system BC, i.e. the application of the rule r_{int}, depicted in Figure 2.

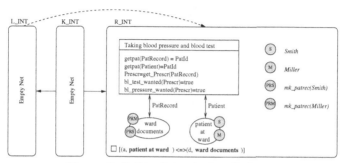

Figure 2: Safety Introducing Rule r_{int}

In general, rules are split into a deleting part L, an adding part R and an interface K which is preserved. The rule r is then given by $r = (L \xleftarrow{u} K \xrightarrow{v} R)$ where u and v are specific morphisms. The application of a rule to an algebraic high-level net system informally means replacing a subnet specified by the left-hand side of the rule with a net system specified by the right-hand side. More precisely, the rule r is applied to a net system G via an occurrence morphism $g : L \rightarrow G$. Then the deletion step and the construction step is defined using two pushouts (for formal definition see Appendix A). In our example the application of the rule r_{int} to the net system BC yields the net system BVM1[2], which consists of the right-hand side of the rule r_{int} and the start net system BC. The initial marking of the net system on the right-hand side of r_{int} is given by patients and their patient records, that is we have

$$(Smith, \textbf{patient at ward}) \oplus (mk\_patrec(Smith, \ldots), \textbf{ward documents}) \oplus$$
$$(Miller, \textbf{patient at ward}) \oplus (mk\_patrec(Miller, \ldots)\textbf{ward documents})$$

The net system R_INT on the right-hand side of the rule r_{int} in Figure 2 is provided with an additional safety property. Such rules can be shown to be safety introducing (see Definition 9 and Theorem 3). Safety introducing rules are provided with additional safety properties for the right-hand side net system. This safety property is introduced to the resulting net system for each application of the rule. For the correct treatment of a patient we have to ensure the following: "whenever some patient is at the ward the corresponding patient record is within

---

[2] Due to space limitation we do not give the intermediate net systems BVM1, BVM2, or BVM3 explicitly here.

the ward documents". This safety property is not relevant before application of r_{int} and even not expressible. After application of r_{int} however it becomes crucial. First of all it has to be true on the level of rules, that is we have to verify it for the net system R_INT. The safety property obviously holds in R_INT. As this kind of rule preserves safety properties (see Theorem 3), it also holds in the net system BVM1 resulting of the application of r_{int} to BC. In Definition 6 we define temporal logic formula over nets systems and their validity with respect to markings. Intuitively, a temporal logic formula states facts about markings and is given in terms of data elements of tokens on places. That is, the static formula $(a, \textbf{patient at ward}) \iff (d, \textbf{ward documents})$ is true for a marking M where a patient a is at the ward if and only if the corresponding patient record d is at the ward. This is given formally by $getpat(a) = getpat(d)$ for $a \in A_{Patient}$ and $d \in A_{PatRecord}$. The always operator in the safety property $\Box[(a, \textbf{patient at ward}) \iff (d, \textbf{ward documents})]$ states that this is true for all reachable markings.

In Figure 3 we give the rule r_{tg-tbp} that identifies the transitions *Taking blood pressure* and *Taking blood pressure and blood test*. Applying r_{tg-tbp} to the net system BVM1 yields the net system BVM2, that contains no longer isolated elements. As the morphism from L_TG-TBP to R_TG-TBP is transition gluing the safety property is preserved. Moreover the safety property holds in BVM2 as tg-rules preserve safety properties (see Theorem 2).

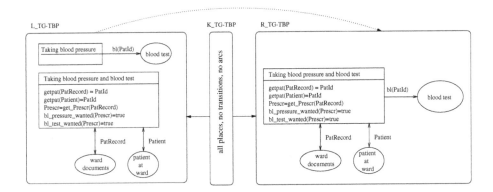

Figure 3: Transition Gluing Rule r_{tg-tbp}

In order to introduce the planning of the next measurement we apply rule r_{pp} depicted in Figure 4 to the net system BVM2. This yields the net system BVM3, which consists of the net system BVM2 extended by the net system for planning of the next measurement. Rule r_{pp} describes the insertion of the place **values for hypertension test** and the subsequent transition and the place **schedule**. This describes that the values of the hypertension test influence the schedule of the next measurement. As the rule r_{pp} does not change the environment of places, it is called *place preserving* (see Definition 4). Applying this rule we again preserve the safety property. Especially, the introduced safety property is propagated to the resulting net system. The preservation of safety properties by place preserving rules is stated in Theorem 1.

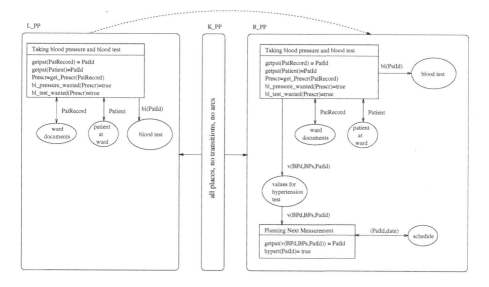

Figure 4: Place Preserving Rule r_{pp}

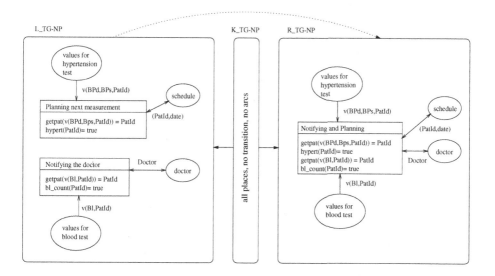

Figure 5: Transition Gluing Rule r_{tg-np}

Finally we model that notifying the doctor and planning of the next measurement are done synchronously. Both values for hypertension test and for blood test have to be available. This is achieved by the rule r_{tg-np} in Figure 5 that glues the corresponding transitions. Since it is transition gluing it is compatible with the safety property (as stated in Theorem 2). This means, that in the derived net system BVM in Figure 6 still the safety property $\square[(a, \textbf{patient at ward}) \Longleftrightarrow (d, \textbf{ward documents})]$ holds.

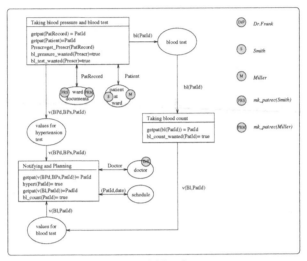

Figure 6: Final Net System BVM

The main result of this paper is that we can introduce new safety properties, which have to be proven for the right-hand side of the safety introducing rules only. They are preserved by place preserving and transition gluing rules. In this way we can extend our example net system BVM by adding further safety properties. The given rules satisfy sufficient conditions to ensure the propagation of safety properties. This is a great advantage for software development as safety properties can be proven in a subsystem of the whole model.

3   Safety Introducing and Preserving Rules

In this section we present our important conceptual result concerning a method for handling safety properties during software development. This result is supported by our main technical results stating the introduction and preservation of safety properties by special kinds of rules (For a review of rules and transformations see Appendix A). We formally define algebraic high-level (AHL) net systems given on an intuitive level in Section 2. For AHL net systems we introduce different notions of morphisms needed for safety preservation and their integration with rules. Based on the notion of safety property we also define safety preserving morphisms and rules. In our main theorems we show that the previously defined rules are in fact safety preserving.

A detailed version of our notions, results and proofs can be found in [GPH00], but would definitely exceed the scope of the paper.

Definition 1 (Algebraic High-Level Net System). *An algebraic high-level (AHL) net system is given by*

$$N = (SPEC, A, P, T, pre, post, cond, \widehat{m})$$

with

- $SPEC \in |\mathbf{SPEC}|$: *an algebraic specification with $SPEC = (\Sigma, E)$ (see [EM85]),*
- $A \in |\mathbf{Alg(SPEC)}|$ *a SPEC algebra,*
- P : *the set of places,*
- T : *the set of transitions,*
- $pre, post : T \to (T_{OP}(X) \times P)^{\oplus}$
  the pre- and postcondition functions of T, defining for each transition with adjacent arcs the arc inscriptions and the weight, (see Def. 15 for $\oplus$-operator)
- $cond : T \to \mathcal{P}_{fin}(EQNS(\Sigma))$
  the function that maps each transition to a finite set of conditions over the signature with variables representing the firing conditions, and
- $\widehat{m} \in (A \times P)^{\oplus}$ *the initial marking (see Def. 15).*

In contrast to [PGE98] AHL net systems comprise an initial marking. Examples of AHL net systems are depicted in the figures in Section 2. AHL net systems are provided with distinguishable tokens. These are denoted by tuples (a, p), where $a \in A$ is a data element and $p \in P$ is the place it resides on. Tokens are moved over the set of places by firing of transitions. This firing behaviour is given by adding and subtracting of tokens to and from a marking. This is achieved using the corresponding monoid operations (see Def. 16 in Appendix B), the tokens and a consistent assignment of variables.

Subsequently, we introduce various notions of morphisms for AHL net systems. These notions are based on the restriction of the initial marking, given in Definition 18 in Appendix B, and the pre- and post set, see Definition 17. All morphisms are specializations of so called loose morphisms. These give rise to the category **QAHLSys** which is of fundamental importance in the proofs of our main theorems.

Definition 2 (AHL Net System Morphisms and Categories). *Given two AHL net systems $N_i = (SPEC_i, A_i, P_i, T_i, pre_i, post_i, cond_i, \widehat{m_i})$ for $i = 1, 2$ then an algebraic high-level (AHL) net system morphisms $f : N_1 \to N_2$ given by $f = (f_\Sigma, f_A, f_P, f_T)$ with*

- $f_\Sigma : SPEC_1 \to SPEC_2$ *is a specification morphism,*
- $f_A : A_1 \to V_{f_\Sigma}(A_2)$ *is a homomorphism in $\mathbf{Alg(SPEC_1)}$,*
- $f_P : P_1 \to P_2$ *maps places to places in $\mathbf{Set}$, and*
- $f_T : T_1 \to T_2$ *maps transitions to transitions in $\mathbf{Set}$,*

and the following abbreviations

- $f_{insc} := (f_\Sigma \times f_P)^{\oplus} : (T_{OP1}(X) \times P_1)^{\oplus} \to (T_{OP2}(X) \times P_2)^{\oplus}$
- $f_M := ((f_\Sigma, f_A) \times f_P)^{\oplus} : (A_1 \times P_1)^{\oplus} \to (A_2 \times P_2)^{\oplus}$
- $f_C := \mathcal{P}_{fin}(f_\Sigma^{\#})$

for the induced mappings of arc inscriptions, markings, respectively conditions, are called

loose

- for any $t \in T_1$ we have $f_{insc}(pre_1(t)) \leq pre_2(f_T(t))$
  $f_{insc}(post_1(t)) \leq post_2(f_T(t))$ no "old" arcs are lost
- $f_C \circ cond_1 \subseteq cond_2 \circ f_T$ possibly adding transition guards
- $f_M(\widehat{m_{1|p}}) \leq \widehat{m_{2|f_P(p)}}$ placewise lesser initial marking of N_1
- $A_1 \cong V_{f_\Sigma}(A_2)$ compatibility of models as f_A is an isomorphism

This class of morphisms gives rise to the category **QAHLSys**.

transition preserving

if they are loose and

- $f_{insc} \circ pre_1 = pre_2 \circ f_T$
  $f_{insc} \circ post_1 = post_2 \circ f_T$
       no "new" arcs adjacent to "old" transitions are allowed
- $f_C \circ cond_1 = cond_2 \circ f_T$ compatibility of transition guards

This class of morphisms gives rise to the category **AHLSys**.

place preserving

if it is a loose morphism and the following place preserving conditions hold:

- $f_\Sigma : SPEC_1 \rightarrow SPEC_2$ is persistent, that is for the corresponding free functor $F_{f_\Sigma} : \mathbf{Alg(SPEC_1)} \rightarrow \mathbf{Alg(SPEC_2)}$ we have $V_{f_\Sigma} \circ F_{f_\Sigma} \cong ID$ (see [EM85]).
- $\bullet(f_P(p)) = (f_\Sigma \times f_T)^\oplus(\bullet p)$
  and $(f_P(p))\bullet = (f_\Sigma \times f_T)^\oplus(p\bullet)$ for all $p \in P_1$
  (see Def. 17 for pre and post sets)
       no "new" arcs adjacent to "old" places are allowed
- f_T, f_P, and f_Σ are injective
- $\widehat{m_{2|f_P}} = f_M(\widehat{m_1})$ no "new" tokens on "old" places are allowed
- $f_C \circ cond_1 = cond_2 \circ f_T$ compatibility of transition guards

transition gluing

if it is a loose morphism and the following holds:

- f_P and f_Σ are isomorphisms
- $f_M(\widehat{m_1}) = \widehat{m_2}$ no "new" tokens
- f_T is surjective s. t. for $t_2 \in T_2$
  $pre_2(t_2) = \sum_{t \in f_T^{-1}(t_2)} f_{insc}(pre_1(t))$, and analogously for post,
       summing up all arcs from the source transitions
- $cond_2(t_2) = \bigcup_{t \in f_T^{-1}(t_2)} f_C \circ cond_1(t)$ for $t_2 \in T_2$
       summing up all conditions from the source transitions

Note, that these notions are novel and especially designed for safety preservation. In fact, place preserving and transition gluing morphisms preserve safety properties, because basically the environments of places are preserved. Moreover, the treatment of the initial marking, namely placewise comparison, yields cocompleteness.

Example 1 (Morphisms in Example). Transition preserving morphisms are depicted in Figures 2,3, 4, and 5 by $\rightarrow$ as there are no transitions in the interfaces of the rules. The morphisms in Figure 2 and 4 denoted by $\rightarrow\!\!\!\rightarrow$ are place preserving, because new arcs are adjacent only to new places. Figures 3 and 5 depict transition gluing morphisms by $\cdots\!\!\!\triangleright$.

For the integration of place preserving and transition gluing morphisms with rules in Definition 4 and 5 we use strict morphisms yielding an HLR system, see [EHKP91, EGP99].

Definition 3 (Strict Morphisms). *Given a transition preserving AHL net system morphism $f : N_1 \to N_2$ with $f = (f_\Sigma, f_A, f_P, f_T)$ and $N_i = (SPEC_i, A_i, P_i, T_i, pre_i, post_i, cond_i, \widehat{m_i})$ for $i = 1, 2$. f is called*

1. *marking strict*
   if $f_M(\widehat{m_1}|_p) = \widehat{m_2}|_{f_P(p)}$ the initial marking of the source net is placewise equal to the target net.
2. *strict*
   if it is marking strict, and moreover f_P, f_T, and f_Σ are injective, and f_Σ is strict in **SPEC**.

Definition 4 (PP-Rules). *A pair (r, f) is called pp-rule, if $r = (L \xleftarrow{u} K \xrightarrow{v} R)$ is a rule with strict transition preserving morphisms u, v and a place preserving morphism $f : L \to R$ with $f \circ u = v$.*

Definition 5 (TG-Rules). *A pair (r, f) is called tg-rule, if $r = (L \xleftarrow{u} K \xrightarrow{v} R)$ is a rule with strict transition preserving morphisms u, v and a transition gluing morphism $f : L \to R$ with $f \circ u = v$.*

Example 2 (Rules in Example). According to Example 1, the rules in Figure 2 and 4 are pp-rules. Figures 3 and 5 denote tg-rules.

The next definition concerns safety properties based on formulas, see also [PGE98], and their translation via (arbitrary) morphisms. Subsequently, Definition 7 specifies safety preserving morphisms.

Definition 6 (Safety Property, Formulas, Translations).

1. *The set of static formulas $\mathcal{F}$ is given inductively: For $\lambda(a, p) \in (A \times P)^\oplus$ we have the atoms $\lambda(a, p) \in \mathcal{F}$. Furthermore $(\varphi_1 \in \mathcal{F} \Longrightarrow \neg\varphi_1 \in \mathcal{F})$, and $(\varphi_1 \in \mathcal{F}, \varphi_2 \in \mathcal{F} \Longrightarrow \varphi_1 \wedge \varphi_2 \in \mathcal{F})$.*
   The validity of formulas is given w.r.t. the marking of a net. Let $m \in (A \times P)^\oplus$ be a marking of N then: $m \models_N \lambda(a, p)$ iff $\lambda(a, p) \leq m$, and $m \models_N \neg\varphi_1$ iff $\neg(m \models_N \varphi_1)$, and $m \models_N \varphi_1 \wedge \varphi_2$ iff $(m \models_N \varphi_1) \wedge (m \models_N \varphi_2)$.
2. *Let φ be a static formula over N. Then $\Box\varphi$ is a **safety property**. The safety property $\Box\varphi$ holds in N under m iff φ holds in all states reachable from m:*
$$m \models_N \Box\varphi \Longleftrightarrow \forall m' \in [m\rangle : m' \models_N \varphi$$
   For the initial marking $\widehat{m}$ we also write $N \models \Box\varphi$ instead of $\widehat{m} \models_N \Box\varphi$.
3. *The **translation** $\mathcal{T}_f$ of formulas over N_1 along a morphism $f = (f_\Sigma, f_A, f_P, f_T) : N_1 \to N_2$ to formulas over N_2 is given for atoms by*
$$\mathcal{T}_f(\lambda(a, p)) = \lambda(f_A(a), f_P(p))$$
   The translation of formulas is given recursively by $\mathcal{T}_f(\neg\varphi) = \neg\mathcal{T}_f(\varphi)$, $\mathcal{T}_f(\varphi_1 \wedge \varphi_2) = \mathcal{T}_f(\varphi_1) \wedge \mathcal{T}_f(\varphi_2)$ and $\mathcal{T}_f(\Box\varphi) = \Box\mathcal{T}_f(\varphi)$.

Definition 7 (Safety Preserving Morphism). *A morphism* $f : N_1 \to N_2$ *is called safety preserving, iff for all safety properties* $\Box\varphi$ *we have* $N_1 \models \Box\varphi \Longrightarrow N_2 \models T_f(\Box\varphi)$.

Definition 8 captures the notion of safety preserving rules. There must be a safety preserving morphism both on the level of the rule as well as on the level of its application, i.e. the transformation.

Definition 8 (Safety Preserving Rule and Transformation). *Given a rule* $r = (L \leftarrow K \to R)$ *in an HLR system and an arbitrary morphism* $f : L \to R$. *The pair* (r, f) *is a safety preserving rule, iff*

1. f *is a safety preserving morphism*
2. *given a net* N_1, *and an occurrence* $g_1 : L \to N_1$, *the direct transformation* $N_1 \overset{r}{\Longrightarrow} N_2$ *yields a safety preserving morphism* $\overline{f} : N_1 \to N_2$.

We denote the direct transformation by $N_1 \overset{(r,f)}{\Longrightarrow} N_2$ *and call it safety preserving transformation, short sp-transformation.*

Generally, it is difficult to determine in advance whether the application of a rule yields a special kind of morphism. However, the theory of Q-transformation introduced in [Pad96, Pad99] and reviewed in Appendix A yields sufficient criteria. These are employed in the proofs of the subsequent theorems. Proofs can can be sketched here only due to space limitation, for details see [GPH00].

Theorem 1 (PP-Rules are Safety Preserving [PGE98]).

Proof. (Sketch) For condition 1 of Definition 8 the corresponding proof of Theorem 3.5 (Place Preserving Morphisms Preserve Safety Properties) in [PGE98] is lifted to AHL net systems which involves a detailed treatment of the initial marking. Analogously, for condition 2 the proof of Theorem 4.2 (Rule-Based Refinement Preserves Safety Properties) in [PGE98] has to be extended.

Theorem 2 (TG-Rules are Safety Preserving).

Proof. (Sketch) Condition 1 of Definition 8 is due to the fact that transition gluing morphism reflect firing. Condition 2 can be shown by showing the Q-conditions of Definition 14 in Appendix A. For pushouts in **QAHLSys** it can be proven by contradiction that their components are pushouts in the underlying categories. Furthermore, the initial marking and the set of transition conditions of the pushout object is given by the supremum of the (translated) markings and conditions of the source net systems. These facts are basically used for the proof of preservation of pushouts and inheritance of transition gluing morphisms. Analogously, inheritance of transition gluing morphisms under coproducts uses the componentwise construction and corresponding facts about the initial marking and transition conditions.

Our last main theorem concerns rules that introduce new safety properties. In fact, these are safety preserving as well. The introduction of safety properties by rules is given by safety properties satiesfied by the AHL net system R and preserved by the occurence of R in the AHL net system N_2. Hence then N_2 also satisfied this property. In this sense it is introduced.

Definition 9 (Safety Introducing). *Given a rule $r = (L \leftarrow K \rightarrow R)$ and a safety property $\Box\varphi$ over R s.t. $R \models \Box\varphi$. If $o : R \rightarrow N_2$ is safety preseving for all transformations $N_1 \stackrel{r}{\Longrightarrow} N_2$, r is called safety introducing rule.*

Definition 10 (SI-Rule). *A rule of the form $r = (\emptyset \leftarrow \emptyset \rightarrow R)$ is called si-rule.*

Example 3 (SI-Rule in Example). Figure 2 depicts an si-rule. The safety property $\Box[(a, \textbf{patient at ward}) \Longleftrightarrow (d, \textbf{ward documents})]$ is introduced.

Theorem 3 (SI-Rules are Safety Introducing and Preserving).

Proof. (Sketch) The application of an si-rule to a net N yields the coproduct $N + R$ and an occurence $o : R \rightarrow N + R$ which is a coproduct injection and therefore place preserving. These morphisms preserve safety properties. Furthermore, the unique morphism $\emptyset : \emptyset \rightarrow R$ (from the left-hand side to the right-hand side) is place preserving. Thus si-rules are a special case of pp-rules and Theorem 1 yields the stated proposition.

Main Conceptual Result 11 (Stepwise Development of Safe Models). *The concept of introducing safety properties (see Definition 10) enables development of an AHL net system hand-in-hand with its safety properties. The safety property has to be proven only once for the right-hand side of the rule. Subsequent refinement by si-rules, pp-rules, or tg-rules does not only preserve the explicitly introduced, but also all implicit safety properties (see Theorems 1, 2, and 3). Hence, employing these kinds of rules in the development of a system supports the development of safe models.*

4   Conclusion

In this paper we have presented our approach of rule-based refinement based on the introduction and preservation of safety properties. The technical results concern algebraic high-level net systems. For those we present safety preserving morphisms, rules and transformations. Place preserving morphisms preserve safety properties, since the adjacency of the places is not changed. Transition gluing morphisms preserve safety properties since the glued transitions has the union of the pre and post domains of the mapped transitions. Both classes of morphisms satisfy the $\mathcal{Q}$ conditions (see Apendix A). Thus, we obtain safety preserving rules and transformations. Safety introducing rules add a new isolated subnet, that satisfies some new safety property. Moreover, these rules preserve safety properties as the corresponding morphism is place preserving.

Conceptually, we have extended our approach of rule-based refinement. Rule-based refinement is a formal description of stepwise development of system model. This technique is especially useful in early phases of the software development process. Each step is given by an application of rules. These rules introduce new safety properties or preserve those that already hold in the system. These steps can even be taken in parallel provided some independence conditions are satisfied (for these results see [Pad96, Pad99]). Moreover, the compatibility with horizontal structuring techniques (as given in [Pad99]) requires detailed knowledge of the transformation as well as the structuring technique. This can be expressed in independence conditions as they are given in our approach. The applicability fo safety introducing as well as preserving rules is the same as for usual rules in net transformation systems. The structure of the rules may prohibit the application of a rule to a given net. This is the case if its application could violate either the net or the safety property.

Future work concerns further system properties. Rule-based refinement has to be extended to comprise further system properties. Our approach is designed to include any system property provided it can be expressed using morphisms. Hence, we are going to investigate various morphism classes for certain properties. Liveness is one of those properties that are most interesting for this line of research.

References

[DG98]   W. Deiters and V. Gruhn. Process Management in Practice - Applying the FUNSOFT Net Approach to Large-Scale Processes. *Automated Software Engineering*, 5:7–25, 1998.

[EGP99]   H. Ehrig, M. Gajewsky, and F. Parisi-Presicce. *High-Level Replacement Systems with Applications to Algebraic Specifications and Petri Nets*, volume 3: Concurrency, Parallelism, and Distribution, chapter 6, pages 341–400. World Scientific, Handbook of Graph Grammars and Computing by Graph Transformations edition, 1999.

[EHKP91]   H. Ehrig, A. Habel, H.-J. Kreowski, and F. Parisi-Presicce. Parallelism and concurrency in High Level Replacement Systems. *Math. Struc. in Comp. Science*, 1:361–404, 1991.

[EM85]   H. Ehrig and B. Mahr. *Fundamentals of Algebraic Specification 1: Equations and Initial Semantics*, volume 6 of *EATCS Monographs on Theoretical Computer Science*. Berlin, 1985.

[Erm96]   C. Ermel. Anforderungsanalyse eines medizinischen Informationssystems mit Algebraischen High-Level-Netzen. Technical Report 96-15, TU Berlin, 1996.

[GPH00]   Maike Gajewsky, Julia Padberg, and Kathrin Hoffmann. Safety Introducing and Preserving Rules for Algebraic High-Level Net Systems. Technical report, Technical University Berlin, 2000. to appear.

[Gru91]   V. Gruhn. *Validation and Verification of Software Process Models*. PhD thesis, Universität Dortmund, Abteilung Informatik, 1991.

[JCHH91] K. Jensen, S. Christensen, P. Huber, and M. Holla. *Design/CPN. A Reference Manual.* Meta Software Cooperation, 125 Cambridge Park Drive, Cambridge Ma 02140, USA, 1991.

[Jen92]   K. Jensen. *Coloured Petri Nets. Basic Concepts, Analysis Methods and Practical Use*, volume 1: Basic Concepts. Springer Verlag, EATCS Monographs in Theoretical Computer Science edition, 1992.

[JR91]   K. Jensen and G. Rozenberg, editors. *High-Level Petri-Nets: Theory and Application.* 1991.

[MM90]   J. Meseguer and U. Montanari. Petri Nets are Monoids. *Information and Computation*, 88(2):105–155, 1990.

[MP92]   Zohar Manna and Amir Pnueli. *The Temporal Logic of Reactive and Concurrent Systems, Specification.* 1992.

[OSS94]   A. Oberweis, G. Scherrer, and W. Stucky. INCOME/STAR: Methodology and Tools for the Development of Distributed Information Systems. *Information Systems*, 19(8):643–660, 1994.

[Pad96]   J. Padberg. *Abstract Petri Nets: A Uniform Approach and Rule-Based Refinement.* PhD thesis, Technical University Berlin, 1996. Shaker Verlag.

[Pad99]   Julia Padberg. Categorical Approach to Horizontal Structuring and Refinement of High-Level Replacement Systems. *Applied Categorical Structures*, 7(4):371–403, December 1999.

[PER95]   J. Padberg, H. Ehrig, and L. Ribeiro. Algebraic high-level net transformation systems. *Mathematical Structures in Computer Science*, 5:217–256, 1995.

[PGE98]   J. Padberg, M. Gajewsky, and C. Ermel. Rule-Based Refinement of High-Level Nets Preserving Safety Properties. In E. Astesiano, editor, *Fundamental approaches to Software Engineering*, pages 221–238, 1998. Lecture Notes in Computer Science 1382.

[Rei85]   W. Reisig. *Petri Nets*, volume 4 of *EATCS Monographs on Theoretical Computer Science.* 1985.

[Vau87]   J. Vautherin. Parallel System Specification with Coloured Petri Nets. In G. Rozenberg, editor, *Advances in Petri Nets 87*, pages 293–308, 1987. 266.

A   Review of High-Level Replacement Systems

Here we briefly review the concepts of high-level replacement (HLR) systems in the sense of [EHKP91], a categorical generalization of graph grammars. High-level replacement systems are formulated for an arbitrary category $\mathbf{C}$ with a distinguished class $\mathcal{M}$ of morphisms.

Definition 12 (Rules and Transformations). *A rule $r = (L \xleftarrow{u} K \xrightarrow{v} R)$ in $\mathbf{C}$ consists of the objects L, K and R, called left-hand side, interface (or gluing object) and right-hand side respectively, and two*

morphisms $K \xrightarrow{u} L$ and $K \xrightarrow{v} R$ with both morphisms $u, v \in \mathcal{M}$, a distinguished class of morphisms in $\mathbf{C}$. Given a rule $r = (L \xleftarrow{u} K \xrightarrow{v} R)$ a direct transformation $G \xLongrightarrow{r} H$, from an object G to an object H is given by two pushout diagrams

$$
\begin{array}{ccccc}
L & \xleftarrow{u} & K & \xrightarrow{v} & R \\
{\scriptstyle g_1}\downarrow & {\scriptstyle (1)}\ {\scriptstyle g_2} & \downarrow & {\scriptstyle (2)} & \downarrow{\scriptstyle g_3} \\
G & \xleftarrow{c_1} & C & \xrightarrow{c_2} & H
\end{array}
$$

(1) *and* **(2)** *in the category $\mathbf{C}$. The morphisms $L \xrightarrow{g_1} G$ and $R \xrightarrow{g_3} H$ are called occurrences of L in G and R in H, respectively. By an occurrence of rule $r = (L \xleftarrow{u} K \xrightarrow{v} R)$ in a structure G we mean an occurrence of the left-hand side L in G.*

A transformation sequence $G \overset{*}{\Longrightarrow} H$, *short transformation, between objects G and H means G is isomorphic to H or there is a sequence of $n \geq 1$ direct transformations:*
$$G = G0 \overset{r_1}{\Longrightarrow} G1 \overset{r_2}{\Longrightarrow} \ldots \overset{r_n}{\Longrightarrow} Gn = H.$$

Definition 13 (High-Level Replacement System). *Given a category $\mathbf{C}$ together with a distinguished class of morphisms $\mathcal{M}$ then $(\mathbf{C}, \mathcal{M})$ is called a HLR-category if $(\mathbf{C}, \mathcal{M})$ satisfies the HLR-Conditions (see [EGP99]).*

The main idea in the following definition is to enlarge the given HLR-category in order to include morphisms, that are adequate for refinement. The $\mathcal{Q}$-conditions [Pad99] state additional requirements, that an HLR-category has to satisfy for the extension to refinement morphisms.

Definition 14 ($\mathcal{Q}$: Refinement Morphism [Pad99]). *Let $\mathbf{QCat}$ be a category, so that $\mathbf{C}$ is a subcategory $\mathbf{C} \subseteq \mathbf{QCat}$ and $\mathcal{Q}$ a class of morphisms in $\mathbf{QCat}$.*

1. *The morphisms in $\mathcal{Q}$ are called $\mathcal{Q}$-morphisms, or refinement morphisms.*
2. *Then we have the following $\mathcal{Q}$-conditions:*
   Closedness: *$\mathcal{Q}$ has to be closed under composition.*
   Preservation of Pushouts: *The inclusion functor $I : \mathbf{C} \to \mathbf{QCat}$ preserves pushouts, that is, given $C \overset{f'}{\longrightarrow} D \overset{g'}{\longleftarrow} B$ a pushout of $B \overset{f}{\longleftarrow} A \overset{g}{\longrightarrow} C$ in $\mathbf{C}$, then $I(C) \overset{I(f')}{\longrightarrow} I(D) \overset{I(g')}{\longleftarrow} I(B)$ is a pushout of $I(B) \overset{I(f)}{\longleftarrow} I(A) \overset{I(g)}{\longrightarrow} I(C)$ in $\mathbf{QCat}$.*
   Inheritance of $\mathcal{Q}$-morphisms under Pushouts: *The class $\mathcal{Q}$ in $\mathbf{QCat}$ is closed under the construction of pushouts in $\mathbf{QCat}$, that is, given $C \overset{f'}{\longrightarrow} D \overset{g'}{\longleftarrow} B$ a pushout of $B \overset{f}{\longleftarrow} A \overset{g}{\longrightarrow} C$ in $\mathbf{QCat}$, then $f \in \mathcal{Q} \Longrightarrow f' \in \mathcal{Q}$.*
   Inheritance of $\mathcal{Q}$-morphisms under Coproducts: *The class $\mathcal{Q}$ in $\mathbf{QCat}$ is closed under the construction of coproducts in $\mathbf{QCat}$, that is, for $A \overset{f}{\longrightarrow} B$ and $A' \overset{f'}{\longrightarrow} B'$ we have $f, f' \in \mathcal{Q} \Longrightarrow f + f' \in \mathcal{Q}$ provided the coproduct $A + A' \overset{f+f'}{\longrightarrow} B + B'$ of f and f' exists in $\mathbf{QCat}$.*
3. *A $\mathcal{Q}$-rule (r, q) is given by a rule $r = L \overset{u}{\longleftarrow} K \overset{v}{\longrightarrow} R$ in $\mathbf{C}$ and a $\mathcal{Q}$-morphism $q : L \to R$, so that $K \overset{u}{\longrightarrow} L \overset{q}{\longrightarrow} R = K \overset{v}{\longrightarrow} R$ in $\mathbf{QCat}$.*

The next fact states the class $\mathcal{Q}$ is also preserved under transformations.

Lemma 1 ($\mathcal{Q}$-Transformations [Pad99]). *Let $\mathbf{C}, \mathbf{QCat}, \mathcal{Q}$, and $I : \mathbf{C} \to \mathbf{QCat}$ satisfy the $\mathcal{Q}$-conditions. Given a $\mathcal{Q}$-rule (r, q) and a transformation $G \overset{r}{\Longrightarrow} H$ in $\mathbf{C}$*

defined by the pushouts **(1)** *and* **(2)***, then there is a unique $q' \in \mathcal{Q}$, such that $q' \circ c_1 = c_2$ and $q' \circ g_1 = g_3 \circ q$ in $\mathbf{QCat}$. The transformation $(G \overset{}{\Longrightarrow} H, q' : G \to H)$, or short $G \overset{(r,q')}{\Longrightarrow} H$, is called $\mathcal{Q}$-transformation. $R \overset{g_3}{\longrightarrow} H \overset{q'}{\longleftarrow} G$ is pushout of $G \overset{g_1}{\longleftarrow} L \overset{q}{\longrightarrow} R$ in $\mathbf{QCat}$.*

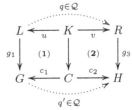

B   Algebraic High-Level Net Sytems

Definition 15 (Category CMON of Free Commutative Monoids). *Let P be a set. Then $(P^{\oplus}, \lambda, \oplus)$ is called the free commutative monoid generated by P, s.t. for all $u, v, w \in P^{\oplus}$ the following equations hold:*

- $\lambda \in P^{\oplus}$
- $v \oplus \lambda = \lambda \oplus v = v,$
- $u \oplus (v \oplus w) = (u \oplus v) \oplus w$
- $v \oplus w = w \oplus v$

  Elements w of the free commutative monoid $P^{\oplus}$ are called linear sums. They can be represented as $w = \sum_{p \in P} \lambda_p \cdot p$ with coefficients $\lambda_p \in \mathbb{N}$ and $p \in P$. They can be considered as multisets.
  Free commutative Monoids together with set-based monoid homomorphism define the category **CMON**.

Definition 16 (Operations of Free Commutative Monoids). *Free commutative monoids imply the operations $\oplus, \ominus, \leq$ and $\geq$ on linear sums. These are the obvious addition, subtraction and comparison of coefficients on linear sums.*
Let $M_1, M_2 \in P^{\oplus}$ with $M_1 = \sum_{p \in P} \lambda_p \cdot p$ and $M_2 = \sum_{p \in P} \lambda'_p \cdot p$, then

$$M_1 \leq M_2 \quad , \text{ if } \forall p \in P : \lambda_p \leq \lambda'_p$$
$$M_1 \geq M_2 \quad , \text{ if } \forall p \in P : \lambda_p \geq \lambda'_p$$
$$M_1 \oplus M_2 = \sum_{p \in P} (\lambda_p + \lambda'_p) \cdot p$$
$$M_1 \ominus M_2 = \sum_{p \in P} (\lambda_p - \lambda'_p) \cdot p, \text{ if } M_1 \leq M_2$$

Lemma 2 (Induced Functions of Place Vector). *Let $m \in (A \times P)^{\oplus}$ Then we have $m : P \to A^{\oplus}$. Similarily, let $m \in (T_{OP}(X) \times P)^{\oplus}$. Then we have $m : P \to T_{OP}^{\oplus}(X)$.*

Definition 17 (Pre- and Post Set). *Given an AHL net system $N = (SPEC, A, P, T, pre, post, cond, \widehat{m})$ then we define*

$$\bullet p = \sum_{t \in T} post(t)(p) \cdot t \in (T_{OP}(X) \times T)^{\oplus}$$

and

$$p \bullet = \sum_{t \in T} pre(t)(p) \cdot t \in (T_{OP}(X) \times T)^{\oplus}$$

Definition 18 (Restrictions of Place Vector). *Given $m \in (A \times P)^{\oplus}$ and let $P' \subseteq P$, then there is $m_1 \in (A \times P')^{\oplus}$ and $m_2 \in (A \times (P \setminus P'))^{\oplus}$ such that $m = m_1 \oplus m_2$.*
  We define $m_{|P'} = m_1$.
  Moreover there are two important special cases:

1. $P' = \{p\}$ *denoted with $m_{|p}$*
2. $P' = f_P(P_0)$ *for some function $f_P : P_0 \to P$, denoted with $m_{|f_P}$*

Lemma 3 (Restrictions are Compatible with Monoid-Operations). *Let $P' \subseteq P$ and $m \in (A \times P)^{\oplus}$ and $p \in P_1$. Then we have*

$$
\begin{array}{rll}
(1) & (m \oplus m')_{|P'} &= m_{|P'} \oplus m'_{|P'} \\
(2) & (m \ominus m')_{|P'} &= m_{|P'} \ominus m'_{|P'} \\
(3) & m \leq m' \Longrightarrow m_{|P'} \leq m'_{|P'} \\
(4) & f_M(m)_{|f_P} &= f_M(m) \\
(5) & f_M(m_{1|f_P}) &= m_{2|f_P(p)} \Longleftrightarrow m_1(p) = m_2(f_P(p))
\end{array}
$$

Ready-Simulation Is Not Ready to Express a Modular Refinement Relation

Françoise Bellegarde, Jacques Julliand, and Olga Kouchnarenko

LIFC, Univ. Franche-Comté, 16, route de Gray, 25030 Besançon Cedex France
{bellegar,julliand,kouchna}@lifc.univ-fcomte.fr,
http://lifc.univ-fcomte.fr

Abstract. The B method has been successfully used to specify many industrial applications by refinement. Previously, we proposed enriching the B event systems by formulating its dynamic properties in LTL. This enables us to combine model-checking with theorem-proving verification technologies. The model-checking of LTL formulae necessitates that the B event system semantics is a transition system. In this paper, we express the refinement relation by a relationship between transition systems. A result of our study shows that this relation is a special kind of simulation allowing us to exploit the partition of the reachable state space for a modular verification of LTL formulae. The results of the paper allow us to build a bridge between the above view of the refinement and the notions of observability characterized as simulation relations by Milner, van Glabbeek, Bloom and others. The refinement relation we define in the paper is a ready-simulation generalization which is similar to the refusal simulation of Ulidowsky. The way the relation is defined allows us to obtain a compositionality result w.r.t. parallel composition operation.

For complex systems, it is important in practice to associate a design by refinement with a design by a parallel composition of their components. This refinement relation has two main applications:
- it allows the splitting of the refined transition system into modules;
- it allows the construction of complex systems by a parallel composition of components.

It makes sense to qualify the refinement relation as being modular.

1 Introduction

In this paper, we express the refinement semantics as a relation between transition systems because we want to associate the verification of LTL formulae in the framework of a refinement design of reactive systems.

The B refinement method has been successfully used to specify many reactive systems: case studies such as an elevator [2], an industrial automatism [3], a steam-boiler case study [4], as well as industrial applications such as *MÉTÉOR* [7] by *Matra Transport International*, and the *SPECTRUM* project [23] by *GEC-Marconi Avionics Limited*.

T. Maibaum (Ed.): FASE 2000, LNCS 1783, pp. 266–283, 2000.
© Springer-Verlag Berlin Heidelberg 2000

The B refinement method [1, 6] is used to specify reactive systems by event systems. In [12, 14], we propose to enrich this specification wiht dynamic properties formulated in the Linear Temporal Logic (LTL). We can then combine model-checking with theorem proving techniques. For that the verification has to take place both at the syntactic level for theorem proving and at the operational level for the verification of LTL formulae by model-checking. At the operational level, the specification is expressed with a transition system. At this level, the refinement relates transition systems between themselves. In [14, 18], we show that the refinement splits the refined transition system into modules. This allows us to verify some LTL properties separately on each module and to let what remains to be proved. For that, the refinement needs to be defined between transition systems. Therefore, the refinement verification takes place also at the operational level.

The results of the paper allow us to build a bridge between the above view of the refinement and the notions of observability characterized as simulation relations by Milner, van Glabbeek, Bloom and others.

We define the refinement relation as a simulation which allows us to exploit a partition of the refined reachable state space. With such a partition we are able to avoid the model-checking blow-up by verifying LTL formulae in a modular way [14]. Moreover, we want this refinement relation to be compositional w.r.t. parallel composition through refinement. That is why we call "modular" our refinement relation.

This paper is organized as follows. After giving preliminary notions in Section 2, Section 3 defines the behavior semantics of the transition systems derived from the B refinement design. Then, we define the transition system modular refinement relation in Section 4. Its expressiveness is studied in Sections 5 and 6. In Section 7, we illustrate the use of our framework on the example of the robot carrying parts from an arrival device towards two exit devices. Then, Section 8 explains how the refinement relation is used in the context of a verification tool set which combines automatic-proof and model-checking technologies. We end by some related works and some perspectives.

2   Preliminaries

In this paper we are concerned with a relationship between *transitions systems* which is a binary relation on their sets of states. In this framework, a predicate transformer is a function transforming sets of states into sets of states.

A **transition systems** is a pair $\langle S, \rightarrow \rangle$, where S is a set of states and $\rightarrow$ is a transition relation on S ($\rightarrow \subseteq S \times S$).

Definition 1. (*$pre[\psi]$ and $post[\psi]$ **predicate transformers**) *Given a relation* ψ *between two set of states* S_1 *and* S_2 *(*$\psi : S_1 \times S_2$*), we define* $pre[\psi] : 2^{S_2} \times 2^{S_1}$ *and* $post[\psi] : 2^{S_1} \times 2^{S_2}$ *by*

- $pre[\psi] \stackrel{def}{=} \lambda X.\{q_1 \in S_1 \ s.t. \ (\exists q_2 \in X \ s.t. \ q_1 \psi q_2)\}$
- $post[\psi] \stackrel{def}{=} \lambda X.\{q_2 \in S_2 \ s.t. \ (\exists q_1 \in X \ s.t. \ q_1 \psi q_2)\}$

So, for $S_2' \subseteq S_2$, $pre[\psi](S_2')$ represents the set of predecessors of the states of S_2' via the relation ψ, and, for $S_1' \subseteq S_1$, $post[\psi](S_1')$ represents the set of successors of the states of S_1' via ψ. Some useful results concerning the pre and $post$ predicate transformers can be found in [22] as, for example, the two following propositions.

Proposition 1. *For any relation ψ from a set S_1 to a set S_2 ($\psi \subseteq S_1 \times S_2$), we have:*

- *For any X_1, X_2 subsets of S_2, $pre[\psi](X_1 \cup X_2) = pre[\psi](X_1) \cup pre[\psi](X_2)$.*
- *For any X_1, X_2 subsets of S_1, $post[\psi](X_1 \cup X_2) = post[\psi](X_1) \cup post[\psi](X_2)$.*

We adopt the following notations:

- We denote by Id_S the *identity* function on 2^S.
- We denote by $\tilde{\alpha}$ the dual of a function $\alpha \ : \ 2^{S_1} \rightarrow 2^{S_2}$ that is $\tilde{\alpha} \stackrel{def}{=} \lambda X.\overline{\alpha(\overline{X})}$.
- We denote the composition of two relations $\psi \subseteq S_1 \times S_2$ and $\phi \subseteq S_2 \times S_3$ by their juxtaposition $\psi \ \phi$.
- We denote the composition of two predicate transformers $\alpha \ : \ X \rightarrow Y$ and $\beta \ : Y \rightarrow Z$ by $\beta \circ \alpha \ : X \rightarrow Z$.

Proposition 2. *Let be $\rightarrow \subseteq S \times S$. Then $pre[\rightarrow^2] = pre[\rightarrow] \circ pre[\rightarrow]$.*

We give hereafter the definition of Galois connections and some results about them. More information can, e.g., be found in [19, 21].

Definition 2. (Galois connections) *Let S_1 and S_2 be two sets of states. A connection from 2^{S_1} to 2^{S_2} is a pair of monotonic functions (α, γ), where $\alpha \ : \ 2^{S_1} \rightarrow 2^{S_2}$ and $\gamma \ : \ 2^{S_2} \rightarrow 2^{S_1}$, such that $Id_{S_1} \subseteq \gamma \circ \alpha$ and $\alpha \circ \gamma \subseteq Id_{S_2}$.*

It is well-known that α and γ determine each other in a unique manner. These characterizations allow obtaining in [16] a proposition showing the links between the binary relation ψ from S_2 to S_1 and the connections from 2^{S_2} to 2^{S_1} in term of predicate transformers pre and $post$.

Proposition 3. (Connections generated by a binary relation on states) *If $\psi \subseteq S_1 \times S_2$, then the pair $(post[\psi], \widetilde{pre}[\psi])$ is a connection from 2^{S_1} to 2^{S_2}, and $(pre[\psi], \widetilde{post}[\psi])$ is a connection from 2^{S_2} to 2^{S_1}.*

3   Behavioral Semantics of Systems Derived from the B Design

In this paper we look at the B refinement at the operational semantic level since it splits the refined transition system into modules. This allows a modular verification of some LTL properties.

We define an operational semantics of a B specification under the form of a labeled transition system. We denote by S a set of states. We introduce a finite set of *variables* $V \stackrel{\text{def}}{=} \{x_1, \dots, x_n\}$. Let l be an injective function which allows us to give values to the states as a conjunction of variable/value equalities. Let q be a state, and $v_1, \dots, v_n$ be values, then $l(q)$ ($l(q)$ holds in q) is defined by $x_1 = v_1 \wedge \cdots \wedge x_n = v_n$. Usually, to describe LTL formulae semantics, the set of all the propositions holding in a state q is considered to be a label of q. We consider one of them $l(q)$ since, then, we know that a proposition P holds in q by $l(q) \Rightarrow P$ holds.

We call *invariant* a predicate I which holds on each state, and, as such, formulates a safety property of the system. A specification in B always requires such an invariant. A predicate I is an invariant of an interpreted transition system iff $\forall q \in S, l(q) \Rightarrow I$.

Let $Act \stackrel{\text{def}}{=} \{a, b, \dots\}$ be a nonempty alphabet of interpreted *actions*. The actions affect state variables. A labeled transition relation $\rightarrow$ ($\subseteq S \times Act \times S$) is defined as a set of triples (q, a, q') (written "$q \stackrel{a}{\rightarrow} q'$"). The interpreted transition system $TS = \langle S, Act, \rightarrow, l \rangle$ has the state space $S \stackrel{\text{def}}{=} \{q, q', q_1, \dots\}$, labeled transition relation $\rightarrow \subseteq S \times Act \times S$, and the state interpretation function l.

The transition relation $\rightarrow$ can be extended on a sequence of transitions in the standard way: q' is reachable from q, written $q' \in (\rightarrow)^*(q)$, (or there is a *path* σ from q to q') if there exist states $q_1, \dots, q_n$ and transitions $t_1, \dots, t_{n-1}$ respectively labeled by $a_1, \dots, a_{n-1}$ such that

$$(q =) \, q_1 \stackrel{a_1}{\rightarrow} q_2 \dots \stackrel{a_{n-1}}{\rightarrow} q_n \, (= q').$$

We note $\Upsilon_{TS}(q)$ the set of the paths of the transition system TS beginning in q. Given the path $\sigma = q \stackrel{a}{\rightarrow} q' \stackrel{b}{\rightarrow} q'' \stackrel{c}{\rightarrow} \dots$ in $\Upsilon_{TS}(q)$, we define its trace, note $tr(\sigma)$ by $tr(\sigma) \stackrel{\text{def}}{=} abc \dots$.

Moreover, given a state q, any proposition P such that $l(q) \Rightarrow P$ can be used to verify a LTL formula along a path which contains q in its trace.

As usual, the inverse relation $(\rightarrow)^{-1}$ denotes the predecessor relation on states, and we can say that q' is reachable from q, $q \, (\rightarrow)^* \, q'$, iff $q' \, ((\rightarrow)^*)^{-1} \, q'$.

4   Modular Refinement Relation

In this section we consider two interpreted transition systems $TS_1 = \langle S_1, Act_1, \rightarrow_1, l_1 \rangle$ and $TS_2 = \langle S_2, Act_2, \rightarrow_2, l_2 \rangle$ giving the operational semantics of two systems at two levels of refinement. We say that TS_2 is a *refinement* of TS_1.

The syntactical requirements of the B refinement are expressed as follows:

1. The refinement introduces *new* actions, so $Act_1 \subseteq Act_2$.
2. The invariant I_2, commonly called the *gluing* invariant (for instance, cf. [6]), expresses how the variables from the two interpreted transition systems are linked. More precisely, the invariant of the refined system is $I_2 \wedge I_1$.

4.1   Modular Refinement as State Space Partition

We exploit the B refinement so that we can build a partition of the state space.

First, we define a binary relation $\mu \subseteq S_2 \times S_1$ allowing us to express the relation between values of two consecutive interpreted transition systems.

Definition 3. (Glued states) *The state $q_2 \in S_2$ is glued to $q_1 \in S_1$, written as $q_2 \; \mu \; q_1$, iff $l(q_2) \wedge I_2 \Rightarrow l(q_1)$.*

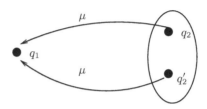

Fig. 1. State space partition idea

The glue relation μ allows us to define an equivalence relation $\sim_\mu$ between states of the second level transition system. Formally, two states q_2 and q_2' of the TS_2 are equivalent iff there exists a state q_1 of TS_1 s.t. $q_2 \; \mu \; q_1$ and $q_2' \; \mu \; q_1$ (see Figure 1). Indeed, we get an equivalence since giving two distinct states q_2 and q_2' we cannot have two distinct states q_1 and q_1' satisfying the above implication. When there are states of TS_2 glued to the state q_1 of TS_1, the state q_1 gives its name q_1 to an element of the partition.

Definition 4. (Equivalence class name) *Let X be an equivalence class of $S_2/\sim_\mu$. The state $q_1 \in S_1$ is the name of X iff, for a state $q_2 \in X$, we have $q_2 \; \mu \; q_1$.*

4.2   Modular Refinement as a Relation

In this section we consider the refinement of an interpreted transition system as a simulation and we motivate it as a path set inclusion. Our purpose is to define a refinement relation to be a simulation allowing us to exploit the partition of the reachable state space for a modular verification of LTL formulae. For that, we restrict μ into a relation ρ which relates a refined transition system to one of its abstraction, and, we restrict ρ^{-1} into a relation ξ which relates a transition system to one of its refinement. These relations are useful to distinguish some elements of the partition of the state space.

This partition is used first, to prove an invariant of a module, and second, to verify propositional components of a LTL formula which is verified on a module.

From a Refined Transition System to One of Its Abstraction Let us call ρ a relation included into μ between the states of TS_2 and TS_1 which satisfies the following requirements:

1. In order to describe the refinement, we keep the transitions of TS_2 labeled over Act_1 but the *new* ones (from $Act_2 \setminus Act_1$) introduced by the refinement are considered as *non observable* τ moves. These τ moves hide the transitions of the modules viewed as interpreted transition systems. Indeed, the transitions of a module with state space S are the τ moves between the states of S (cf. Figure 2).

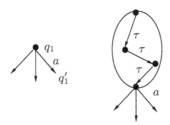

Fig. 2. Silent moves

2. In the above modules, it is certainly not desirable that τ moves take control forever. So, we want no deadlock and no infinite path of τ moves.

Let $Act_{1\tau} \stackrel{\text{def}}{=} Act_1 \cup \{\tau\}$. For each $a \in Act_{1\tau}$, we note $q \stackrel{a}{\Longrightarrow} q'$ when there is $n \geq 0$ such that $q \stackrel{\tau^n a}{\longrightarrow} q'$. Intuitively, a transition $\stackrel{a}{\Longrightarrow}$ allows us to absorb a finite number of τ before the action a. Notice that Milner in [17] uses $\stackrel{a}{\Longrightarrow}$ for $\stackrel{\tau^n a \tau^m}{\longrightarrow}$ with $n, m \geq 0$ but we force m to be equal to 0. The reason is that the occurrence of an action a determines the end of a path of a module. Notice that all the paths of a module are finite ones.

Definition 5. *Let $TS_1 = \langle S_1, Act_1, \rightarrow_1, l_1 \rangle$ and $TS_2 = \langle S_2, Act_{1\tau}, \rightarrow_2, l_2 \rangle$ be respectively a transition system and its refinement. Let a be in Act_1. The relation $\rho \subseteq S_2 \times S_1$ is defined as the greatest binary relation included into μ and satisfying the following clauses:*

1. *(strict transition refinement)* $(q_2 \, \rho \, q_1 \wedge q_2 \stackrel{a}{\rightarrow}_2 q'_2) \Rightarrow (\exists q'_1 \; s.t. \; q_1 \stackrel{a}{\rightarrow}_1 q'_1 \wedge q'_2 \, \rho \, q'_1)$
2. *(stuttering transition refinement)*
   $(q_2 \, \rho \, q_1 \wedge q_2 \stackrel{\tau}{\rightarrow}_2 q'_2 \stackrel{a}{\Longrightarrow}_2 q''_2) \Rightarrow (\exists q'_1 \; s.t. \; q_1 \stackrel{a}{\rightarrow}_1 q'_1 \wedge q'_2 \, \rho \, q_1 \wedge q''_2 \, \rho \, q'_1)$

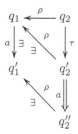

3. **(lack of new deadlock)** $(q_2 \; \rho \; q_1 \wedge q_2 \nrightarrow_2) \Rightarrow (q_1 \nrightarrow_1)$

4. **(non τ-divergence)** $q_2 \; \rho \; q_1 \Rightarrow \neg \, (q_2 \xrightarrow{\tau} q_2' \xrightarrow{\tau} q_2'' \xrightarrow{\tau} \cdots \xrightarrow{\tau} \cdots)$

Notice that the presence of Clause 4 guarantees the monotonicity of an iterative construction of the relation ρ and, this way, the existence of this relation.

The relation ρ implements the modular refinement viewed as a path set inclusion. Given Υ_{TS_1} and Υ_{TS_2}, sets of paths of TS_1 and TS_2, we can see that

1. Clauses 1 and 2 of ρ-definition mean that every path of Υ_{TS_2} refines some path in Υ_{TS_1} (see Figure 3).

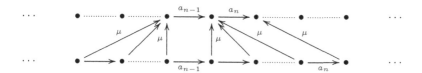

Fig. 3. Path refinement.

2. Clause 4 means that the refinement does not authorize infinite *new* paths composed only with new transitions in TS_2. In terms of graph, such infinite paths are cycles, so, there always must be a way out of these cycles, if any, by a strongly fair transition since such a transition, which is always eventually taken, forbids the infinite loop.

3. Clause 3 implies that any deadlock in Υ_{TS_2} corresponds to a deadlock in Υ_{TS_1} which means that new deadlocks are forbidden.

From an Abstract Transition System to One of Its Refinement

Definition 6. *Let $TS_1 = \langle S_1, Act_1, \rightarrow_1, l_1 \rangle$ and $TS_2 = \langle S_2, Act_{1\tau}, \rightarrow_2, l_2 \rangle$ be respectively a transition system and its refinement. Let a be in Act_1. The relation $\xi \subseteq S_1 \times S_2$ is the greatest binary relation included into ρ^{-1} and satisfying the following clause:*

(non-determinism) $(q_1 \overset{a}{\rightarrow}_1 q_1' \wedge q_1 \xi q_2)) \Rightarrow (\exists q_2', q_2'' \ s.t. \ q_1 \xi q_2' \wedge q_2' \overset{a}{\Longrightarrow}_2$

$q_2'' \wedge q_1' \xi q_2'')$

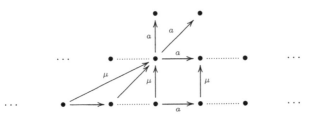

The construction stays monotonic.

Again, we explain the ξ relation in terms of the path set inclusion. If there is an *internal* non-deterministic choice among the transitions of Υ_{TS_1} which begins at the same state q_1 (see Definition 6), then there exists (at least) one of these transitions which is refined by some path $\sigma_2 \in \Upsilon_{TS_2}$ (see Figure 4).

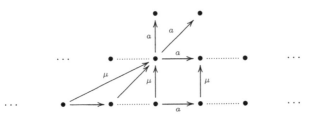

Fig. 4. Internal non-deterministic choice refinement.

Intuitively, the above notions of refinement mean that we observe the system more often taking into account additional details about its behavior. In terms of traces, the trace of the path σ_1 is embedded into the trace of the transitions in σ_2, or, in other words, we find the path σ_1 by removing the transitions labeled by *new* (from $Act_2 \setminus Act_1$) actions from the path σ_2 but this holds only if the transition systems are deterministic. In the presence of a non-deterministic choice, it is possible that some traces disappear among a non-deterministic set of transitions, but at least one trace remains.

The relation ξ allows us to define some elements of a partition of the refined state space $S_2/\sim_\mu$ as modules, i.e., $X \in S_2/\sim_\mu$ of name $q_1 \in S_1$ (i.e. the equivalence class name, see Definition 4) is also a module (named q_1) if and only if, for all the states q_2 in X, we have $q_1 \xi q_2$. So, from a designer point of view, "ξ holds" means that TS_1 is refined by TS_2.

As a consequence of the definition of ξ, there can be no deadlock and no livelock inside a module. Moreover, each path $\tau^* a$ refines a a-transition beginning in q_1. Finally, the set of the labels of all the transitions beginning in q_1 is equal to the set of the labels a of all the paths $\tau^* a$. This last consequence will be shown in Section 5.2.

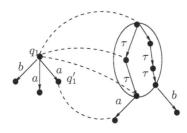

Fig. 5. Module

5   Modular Refinement as a Simulation

In this section, we consider the modular refinement relation $\eta \stackrel{\text{def}}{=} \xi^{-1}$. So, from a designer point of view, η holds means that TS_2 refines TS_1. We show that the modular refinement relation can be viewed as a special kind of τ-*simulation* which is derived from the observational equivalence of Milner [17] between a refined transition system and its abstraction. Finally, it is a generalization of the *ready* simulation of [10].

5.1   Modular Refinement as a τ-Simulation

In this section, we are interested in a view of the modular refinement as a τ-simulation from TS_2 to TS_1.

From the relation η, Proposition 3 allows us to generate a Galois connection $(post[\eta], \widetilde{pre}[\eta])$. The construction is inspired by [16]. Notice that the above authors are looking for building an abstraction when we are interested in a modular refinement. We choose this approach to show a τ-simulation because we see better the role of the modules by the way of the predicate transformers $post[\eta]$ and $\widetilde{pre}[\eta]$. Notice that the Milner's approach observes each time two related states, so it does not allow to consider a whole module (a set of states) which is related to one abstract state.

Let X be a subset of the refined state space S_2 ($X \subseteq S_2$). Then $post[\eta](X)$ is the set of the module names, i.e.,

$$post[\eta] \stackrel{\text{def}}{=} \lambda X.\{q_1 \in S_1 s.t. \ (\exists q_2 \in X \ s.t. \ q_2 \ \eta \ q_1)\}$$

Let X be a subset of the abstract state space S_1 ($X \subseteq S_1$). Then $\widetilde{pre}[\eta](X)$ is the union of the state space of the modules named in X, i.e.,

$$\widetilde{pre}[\eta] \stackrel{\text{def}}{=} \lambda X.\bigcup_{i \in I} X_i \ s.t.$$
$$(\forall i. \ i \in I \Rightarrow X_i \in S_2/{\sim_\mu}) \wedge (\forall q_2.q_2 \in X_i \Rightarrow (\exists q_1 \in X \ s.t. \ q_2 \eta q_1))$$

By using this Galois connection we show that the modular refinement is a kind of τ-simulation which is derived from the observational equivalence of Milner [17]. Now we give the definition of a η-simulation.

Definition 7. ($\sqsubseteq_\eta$) *Let* $TS_2 = \langle S_2, Act_{1\tau}, \rightarrow_2 \rangle$ *and* $TS_1 = \langle S_1, Act_1, \rightarrow_1 \rangle$ *be two transition systems and* η *be a relation from* S_2 *to* S_1 ($\eta \subseteq S_2 \times S_1$). *Define* $S_2 \sqsubseteq_\eta S_1$ *if and only if* $((\xrightarrow{\tau}_2)^*)^{-1}(\xrightarrow{a}_2)^{-1} \eta \subseteq \eta (\xrightarrow{a}_1)^{-1}$ *for all* $a \in Act_1$.

If $S_2 \sqsubseteq_\eta S_1$, we say that S_2 η-simulates S_1. This η-simulation is closely related to the τ-simulation in the sense of Milner. The difference is that in the *tau-simulation* the action a can be the empty action, and that τ-transitions can follow a.

In Theorem 1, we show that, by modular refinement, S_2 η-simulates S_1. For that, we need another predicate transformer in the refined transition system. Recall that a refined transition system TS_2 has silent moves whereas an abstract transition system TS_1 has no silent moves. For TS_2, the predicate transformer $pre[\rightarrow_2]$ is extended to $pre^{\tau^*a}[\rightarrow_2]$ to take into account the silent moves.

Definition 8. ($pre^{\tau^*a}[\rightarrow_2]$ **predicate transformer**) *Given the relation* $\rightarrow_2$: $S_2 \times S_2$, *we define* $pre^{\tau^*a}[\rightarrow_2]$: $S_2 \times S_2$ *by*
$$pre^{\tau^*a}[\rightarrow_2] \overset{def}{=} \lambda X_2.\{q_2 \in S_2 \text{ s.t. } (\exists q_2' \in X_2 \text{ s.t. } q_2' \overset{a}{\Longrightarrow} q_2)\}.$$

The definition of pre^{τ^*a} is not a problem because there is no infinite τ-path (see Clause 4 of Definition 5). Notice that Proposition 1 applies to $pre^{\tau^*a}[\rightarrow_2]$ by finite composition of $pre[\rightarrow_2]$ because of Proposition 2.

We need the following lemma to prove that S_2 η-simulates S_1.

Lemma 1. *Let* η *be the relation between the two transition systems* $TS_2 = \langle S_2, Act_{1\tau}, \rightarrow_2, l_2 \rangle$ *and* $TS_1 = \langle S_1, Act_1, \rightarrow_1, l_1 \rangle$. *Let* (α, γ) *be the Galois connection* $(post[\eta], \widetilde{pre}[\eta])$. *Then, we have*

$$\alpha \circ pre^{\tau^*a}[\rightarrow_2] \circ \gamma \subseteq pre[\rightarrow_1].$$

Proof. Let q_i be the name of a module Y_i (see Definition 4). Then

$$\alpha \circ pre^{\tau^*a}[\rightarrow_2](Y_i)$$

gives the modules names of the set $P = pre^{\tau^*a}[\rightarrow_2](Y_i)$ by Definition of α. All the elements of the set P are related to a predecessor of q_i by Clauses 1 and 2 of Definition 5. Therefore, this is included into the set $pre[\rightarrow_1](\{q_i\})$.

Let X be a subset of the abstract state space S_1 ($X \subseteq S_1$). Then, $\gamma(X) = \bigcup_{i \in I} Y_i$ where the Y_i's are the modules in S_2 the names of which are elements $\{q_1, q_2, \ldots, q_i, \ldots\}$ of X. Therefore,

$$\alpha \circ pre^{\tau^*a}[\rightarrow_2] \circ \gamma(X) = \alpha \circ pre^{\tau^*a}[\rightarrow_2] \left(\bigcup_{i \in I} Y_i \right)$$

which is equal to $\bigcup_{i \in I} (\alpha \circ pre^{\tau^*a}[\rightarrow_2] (Y_i))$ by Propositions 1 and 2.

Since $\alpha \circ pre^{\tau^*a}[\rightarrow_2] (Y_i)$ is included into $pre[\rightarrow_1](\{q_i\})$ for all $i \in I$, we obtain that $\bigcup_{i \in I} (\alpha \circ pre^{\tau^*a}[\rightarrow_2] (Y_i))$ is included into $\bigcup_{i \in I} pre[\rightarrow_1](\{q_i\})$. The latter is included into $pre[\rightarrow_1](X)$.

Theorem 1. *Let η be the relation between the two transition systems $TS_2 = \langle S_2, Act_{1\tau}, \rightarrow_2, l_2 \rangle$ and $TS_1 = \langle S_1, Act_1, \rightarrow_1, l_1 \rangle$. Then $S_2 \sqsubseteq_\eta S_1$.*

We slightly adapt the proof from [16] to our case by using Lemma 1, Definition 2 and Definition 7.

So, the modular refinement relation is an η-simulation. However, this result uses only Definition 5 of ρ. In the next section, we will point up the role played by the non-determinism.

5.2   Modular Refinement as a Generalization of the Ready-Simulation

In this section, we see the modular refinement relation η as a generalization of the ready-simulation of [10].

For that we will keep the ready-set definition (see [9, 10]) for the abstract system as $readies(q_1) = \{a \in Act_1 \text{ s.t. } q_1 \xrightarrow{a}_1\}$, and, we will simply replace $\rightarrow_2$ by $\Longrightarrow_2$ for the refined system, i.e., $readies(q_2) = \{a \in Act_{1\tau} \text{ s.t. } q_2 \stackrel{a}{\Longrightarrow}_2\}$. Moreover, we take into account the non-divergence of τ.

Theorem 2. *Let $TS_1 = \langle S_1, Act_1, \rightarrow_1, l_1 \rangle$ and $TS_2 = \langle S_2, Act_{1\tau}, \rightarrow_2, l_2 \rangle$ be two transition systems. If $(q_2 \ \eta \ q_1)$ then $readies(q_1) = \bigcup\limits_{q_2 \ s.t. \ q_2 \eta q_1} readies(q_2)$.*

Proof. $\subseteq$) It is immediate by Definition 6.
$\supseteq$) It is immediate by Clauses 1 and 2 of Definition 5.

Therefore, η implies the equality of the *readies* as it is the case for the ready simulation of [10]. This result points up that the set of a module exiting actions is equal to the set of this module name (see Definition 4) exiting actions.

Furthermore, the equality of the *readies* allows us to define ξ as follows:

Definition 9. *Let $TS_1 = \langle S_1, Act_1, \rightarrow_1, l_1 \rangle$ and $TS_2 = \langle S_2, Act_{1\tau}, \rightarrow_2, l_2 \rangle$ be respectively a transition system and its refinement. Let a be in Act_1. The relation $\xi \subseteq S_1 \times S_2$ is the greatest binary relation included into ρ^{-1} and satisfying the following clause:*
(readies) $(q_1 \xrightarrow{a}_1 q_1' \wedge q_1 \ \xi \ q_2)) \Rightarrow (readies(q_1) = \bigcup\limits_{q_2 \ s.t. \ q_1 \xi q_2} readies(q_2))$

Theorem 3. *Definition 6 and Definition 9 are equivalent.*

Proof. $\Rightarrow$) It is immediate by Theorem 2.
$\Leftarrow$) It is immediate because Clause readies of Definition 9 implies Clause non-determinism of Definition 6.

Notice that Definition 9 is easily implementable since it is enough to verify the equality of the *readies* when verifying that Definition 5 holds.

6   Compositionality of the Modular Refinement

We give a result concerning the compositionality of the modular refinement relation η w.r.t. a parallel composition operation which is important for the application of the modular refinement in practice since it allows to build complex systems by a parallel composition of components.

Definition 10. (Parallel composition) *Let* $TS_i = \langle S_i, Act_i, \rightarrow_i, l_i \rangle$ *and* $TS_j = \langle S_j, Act_j, \rightarrow_j, l_j \rangle$ *be two transition systems. The parallel composition of* TS_i *and* TS_j *is* $TS_i \| TS_j \stackrel{def}{=} \langle S, Act_\tau, \rightarrow, l \rangle$ *where* S *is the set of the* $q\|q''$ *(* $q \in S_i$ *and* $q'' \in S_j$*),* Act *is the union of* Act_i *and* Act_j*,* l *is the product of* l_i *and* l_j*. Let* $\alpha \in Act_\tau$*, for* $k \in \{i, j\}$*, the transition relation* $\rightarrow$ *is defined by combining individual actions in parallel as follows.*

$$[PAR1]\ \frac{q \xrightarrow{\alpha}_k q'}{q\|q'' \xrightarrow{\alpha} q'\|q''} \qquad [PAR2]\ \frac{q \xrightarrow{\alpha}_k q'}{q''\|q \xrightarrow{\alpha} q''\|q'}$$

This definition means that all moves of parallel composition are moves of either TS_1 or of TS_2.

In the following theorem, η denotes the modular refinement relation linking transition systems as well as their parallel compositions.

Theorem 4. *Let* $q_2\ \eta\ q_1$ *and* $q_4\ \eta\ q_3$*. We have:*

1. $q_2\|q_4\ \eta\ q_1\|q_3$
2. $q_4\|q_2\ \eta\ q_3\|q_1$

Proof. We prove the result for 1, the second proof being similar.

For the result 1, we show that $\mathcal{S}$ verifies clauses of Definitions 5 and 6, where

$$\mathcal{S} \stackrel{def}{=} \{(q_1\|q_3, q_2\|q_4)\ s.t.\ q_2\ \eta\ q_1\ \&\ q_4\ \eta\ q_3\}$$

for $q_1, q_2, q_3, q_4 \in S$. Now, suppose $(q_1\|q_3, q_2\|q_4) \in \mathcal{S}$.

1. First, we consider Definition 5. Let $q_2\|q_4 \xrightarrow{\alpha} \tilde{q}$ with $\alpha \in Act_\tau$. There are four cases:

   (a) $q_2 \xrightarrow{a}_2 q_2'$, and $\tilde{q} = q_2'\|q_4$. Then, because $q_2\ \eta\ q_1$, we have $q_1 \xrightarrow{a}_1 q_1'$ with $q_2'\ \eta\ q_1'$ by Clause 1 of Definition 5; hence also $q_1\|q_3 \xrightarrow{a} q_1'\|q_3$ by $[PAR1]$ rule of Definition 10, and $(q_1'\|q_3, q_2'\|q_4) \in \mathcal{S}$.

   (b) $q_4 \xrightarrow{a}_4 q_4'$, and $\tilde{q} = q_2\|q_4'$. We get the result in the same way than the case above by using $[PAR2]$ rule of Definition 10.

   (c) $\alpha = \tau$, and $q_2 \xrightarrow{\tau}_2 q_2'$. Moreover, we derive $q_2' \Longrightarrow_2 q_2''$ and $q_2\|q_4 \xrightarrow{\tau} q_2'\|q_4 \Longrightarrow q_2''\|q_4\ (= \tilde{q})$. Then, because $q_2\ \eta\ q_1$, we have $q_1 \xrightarrow{a}_1 q_1'$ with $q_2'\ \eta\ q_1$ and $q_2''\ \eta\ q_1'$ by Clause 2 of Definition 5; hence, we also get $q_1\|q_3 \xrightarrow{a} q_1'\|q_3$ by $[PAR1]$ rule of Definition 10, and $(q_1\|q_3, q_2'\|q_4)$ and $(q_1'\|q_3, q_2''\|q_4)$ are in $\mathcal{S}$.

(d) $\alpha = \tau$, and $q_4 \xrightarrow{\tau}_4 q_4'$. We have the result by the same argument than the case above.

2. Second, we consider Definition 6. Let $q_1 \| q_3 \xrightarrow{\alpha} \tilde{q}$ with $\alpha \in Act$. There are two cases:

(a) $q_1 \xrightarrow{a}_1 q_1'$, and $\tilde{q} = q_1' \| q_3$. Then, because $q_2 \, \eta \, q_1$, we have $q_1 \, \xi \, q_2$. By Definition 6, there exists q_2', q_2'' s.t. $q_1 \, \xi \, q_2' \wedge q_2' \xRightarrow{a}_2 q_2'' \wedge q_1' \, \xi \, q_2''$. By [$PAR1$] rule of Definition 10, we have $q_2' \| q_4, q_2'' \| q_4$ s.t. $q_1 \| q_3 \, \xi \, q_2' \| q_4 \wedge q_2' \| q_4 \xRightarrow{a} q_2'' \| q_4 \wedge q_1' \| q_3 \, \xi \, q_2'' \| q_4)$, and $(q_1 \| q_3, q_2' \| q_4)$ and $(q_1' \| q_3, q_2'' \| q_4)$ are in $\mathcal{S}$.

(b) We have the same proof for the case $q_3 \xrightarrow{a}_3 q_3'$ and $\tilde{q} = q_1 \| q_3'$.

This compositionality result permits the modular design of the system into separate components. So, the attribute "modular" of the refinement relation η expresses the modular design ability as well as the partition of the refined system state space into modules.

7   Example

The definition of the modular refinement relation is motivated by the conditions expressed in terms of path set refinement as we saw in Section 4. We illustrate the refinement design with a simple example of a robot carrying parts inspired from [3]. It shows how the modules appear in the refined reachability graph, and how the non-determinism decreases during the refinement process. This last point justifies the clause non-determinism of Definition 6. The robot's example is voluntarily simple. We have studied the modular refinement relation about less trivial applications such as the protocol $T = 1$ [13], a BRP protocol [5] and so on.

We suppose the carrier device (CD) carries one part at a time from an arrival device AD located to its left towards two exit devices located respectively to the left (EDL) and the right (EDR) of the carrier device (see Figure 7).

The two refinement levels of transition systems (presented in Figure 8 and Figure 6 by their reachability graphs) model the transportation of parts by the carriage device on the exit devices. The first level ignores the movement of the carriage device and how parts arrive in it. The second level introduces the rotation movement of the carrier device.

At the first level of abstraction (see Figure 8), we are not concerned which of the exit devices is receiving the part. This introduces what we call an internal non-determinism in the abstract transition system. The variables are CD, EDL, EDR. Here, the invariant is well-typing: $CD, EDL, EDR \in \{free, busy\}$. Initially, all the devices are $free$. The actions that can be observed are the loading of a part (label L), the deposit of a part (label U), the exit of a part from the left exit device (label ExL) and the exit of a part from the right exit device (label ExR). The interpretation of the eight different states appears graphically. For example, $l(q_5)$ is $CD = busy \wedge EDL = free \wedge EDR = busy$. One can notice two transitions labeled by U originating from q_1 (internal non-determinism).

The second level of refinement (see Figure 6) introduces the observation of the two rotations, from the left to the right (RoR) and from the right to the left (RoL) that the carrier device must do in order to deposit a part either to the left or to the right. The glue invariant is $I_2 \stackrel{\text{def}}{=} (CD' = CD \wedge EDL' = EDL \wedge EDR' = EDR \wedge Pos \in \{l, r\})$.

A plausible behavior may remove the internal non-determinism by forcing the carrier device to unload on the left exit device if it is turned toward the left; respectively, to unload on the right exit device if it is turned toward the right (in position). Moreover, the rotation towards the left becomes a priority in the other situations since the arrival device is located to the left. This imposed behavior is supposed to minimize the number of rotations towards the right.

We verify that S_2 is a modular refinement of S_1 by substituting τ transitions by transitions labeled by RoL, RoR and verifying Definitions 5 and 6. Moreover, one can notice how the refinement introduces a partition of the refined transition system into modules. Notice in the example that the two transitions labeled by U exiting from the module of name q_1 are the reflection of the two transitions labeled by U exiting from q_1 at the abstract level. So, the traces containing U and beginning with q_1 remain. So, we have $readies(q_1) = readies(q'_{11}) \cup readies(q'_{12})$ where q'_{11} and q'_{12} are the two states in the module of name q_1.

Another plausible behavior may remove the internal non-determinism by simply forcing the carrier device to unload on the left (left first) when both devices are free. This imposed behavior is, as above, supposed to optimize the number of rotations since the arrival device is located to the left.

Notice that there is only one transition labeled by U exiting from the module q_1 which is the reflection of the two transitions labeled by U exiting from q_1 at the abstract level. So, some traces containing U and beginning by q_1 disappear between the abstract and the refined level but at least one trace containing U remains. We can use other strategies such as, for example, forcing the carrier device to unload on the exit device which has been freed the first (first free, first busy).

8 Application

As safety and liveness properties are essential for reactive systems, the verification uses different methods which are based either on the model or on the system description. The model-based verification methods use the labeled transition systems techniques equipped with logics or behavior equivalences. The methods which are working on the system description via its denotational semantics, prove theorems about the system behavior by using an appropriate logic. The theorem provers or the proof assistants are semi-automatic in contrast with the model-checkers, but they can handle infinite systems.

To get the advantages of both methods in verifying that the B event system satisfies its dynamic properties (expressed by LTL formulae), it is very interesting to be able to combine model-checking with theorem proving in the same verification tool set [8]. In [12, 14, 18], we propose an original combination of the above techniques. Proof is used when fully automatic (for example, tautology checker in propositional calculus). At the abstract level of the refinement, model-checking is used for dynamic property verification. The proposed refinement relation allows us to cross both techniques at the best of their advantages and possibilities. This is made possible because the proposed refinement relation determines modules in the refined reachability graph (for that, see [8]).

For finite state transition systems, the refinement verification and the module construction are implementable by an on-the-fly traversal of the refined transition system reachability graph. This is implemented as a component of a verification tool set [8].

9   Conclusion and Related Works

We are following an approach using both automatic-proof and model-checking technologies. This cooperation is permitted because of the refinement methodology [12, 14] which has been proposed to specify reactive systems and to verify their dynamic properties expressed in the LTL.

We have defined a formal framework for this methodology: the modular refinement relation between an abstract and a refined transition systems derived from the B design.

Since we apply the modular relation η to finitely branching transition systems, and since η does not accept the τ-divergence, it is closely related to the *refusal simulation* as defined by Ulidowsky in [24]. The refusal simulation is also a generalization of the ready simulation of Bloom et al. [10]. The main difference between the modular refinement relation η and the refusal simulation is in the non-determinism clause of Definition 6. This clause requires that q_1 relates to q_2, i.e., that the module of name q_1 exists but the refusal simulation does not. This constraint is the key to obtain the equality of the readies (see Theorem 2). Therefore, the modular refinement relation, which is also a generalization of the ready simulation, seems to be strictly included in the refusal simulation.

We can also relate the clauses of Definition 5 to the clauses $(a), (\epsilon), (O), (\Delta)$, (S) of van Glabbeek in [11] by taking into account of the fact that there is no silent moves in the abstract transition system. Therefore, we could situate the modular refinement relation as a *divergence sensitive stability respecting completed simulation* in the van Glabbeek' spectrum.

Another contribution of this work is that it gives a good semantics which authorizes us to compare the modular refinement relation with other refinement definitions [20, 15]. We anticipate that without the non-determinism, it is also equivalent to Lamport's TLA refinement.

One of the consequences of Theorem 4 is that the modular refinement relation is preserved w.r.t. the parallel composition. This allows us to keep the same refinement notion for both modular design and modular verification of reactive systems.

The partition of the refined system state space into modules is the second reason to call modular our refinement relation. It facilitates the verification by taking into account the system modularity introduced by the refinement. Accordingly we are currently building the verification tool set [8].

References

[1] J. R. Abrial. *The B Book*. Cambridge University Press - ISBN 0521-496195, 1996.

[2] J. R. Abrial. Extending B without changing it (for developing distributed systems). In *1st Conference on the B method*, pages 169–190, Nantes, France, November 1996.

[3] J. R. Abrial. Constructions d'automatismes industriels avec B. In *Congrès AFADL*, ONERA-CERT - Toulouse, France, May 1997. Invited lecture.

[4] J. R. Abrial, E. Börger, and H. Langmoeck. *Specifying and Programming the Steam Boiler Control*. LNCS 1165. Springer Verlag, 1996.

[5] J. R. Abrial and L. Mussat. Specification and design of a transmission protocol by successive refinements using B. LNCS, 1997.

[6] J. R. Abrial and L. Mussat. Introducing dynamic constraints in B. In *Second Conference on the B method*, LNCS 1393, pages 83–128, Montpellier, France, April 1998. Springer Verlag.

[7] P. Behm, P. Desforges, and J.M. Meynadier. MÉTÉOR: An industrial success in formal development. In *Second conference on the B method*, LNCS 1393, Montpellier, France, April 1998. Springer Verlag. Invited lecture.

[8] F. Bellegarde, J. Julliand, and H. Mountassir. Model-based verification through refinement of finite B event systems. In *Formal Method'99 B User Group Meeting*, CD-ROM publication, 1999.

[9] B. Bloom. *Ready Simulation, Bisimulation, and the Semantics of CCS-Like Languages*. PhD thesis, MIT, August 1989.

[10] B. Bloom, S. Istrail, and A. R. Meyer. Bisimulation can't be traced. *Journal of the ACM*, 42(1):232–268, January 1995.

[11] R. J. van Glabbeek. The linear time - branching time spectrum II: The semantics of sequential systems with silent moves. In *Proc. CONCUR'93, Hildesheim, Germany, LNCS 715*, pages 66–81. Springer-Verlag, August 1993.

[12] J. Julliand, F. Bellegarde, and B. Parreaux. De l'expression des besoins à l'expression formelle des propriétés dynamiques. *Technique et Science Informatiques*, 18(7), 1999.

[13] J. Julliand, B. Legeard, T. Machicoane, B. Parreaux, and B. Tatibouet. Specification of an integrated circuits card protocol application using B and linear temporal logic. In *Second conference on the B method*, LNCS 1393, pages 273–292, Montpellier, France, April 1998. Springer Verlag.

[14] J. Julliand, P.A. Masson, and H. Mountassir. Modular verification of dynamic properties for reactive systems. In *International Workshop on Integrated Formal Methods (IFM'99)*, York, Great Britain, 1999.

[15] L. Lamport. A temporal logic of actions. 16:872–923, May 1994.

[16] C. Loiseaux, S. Graf, J. Sifakis, A. Bouajjani, and S. Bensalem. Property preserving abstractions for the verification of concurrent systems. *Formal Methods in System Design*, 6:1–35, January 1995.

[17] R. Milner. *Communication and Concurrency*. Prentice Hall Int., 1989.

[18] H. Mountassir, F. Bellegarde, J. Julliand, and P.A. Masson. Coopération entre preuve et model-checking pour vérifier des propriétés LTL. In *submission AFADL'2000*, 2000.

[19] O. Ore. Galois connections. *Trans. Amer. Math. Soc.*, (55):493–513, February 1944.

[20] A. Pnueli. System specification and refinement in temporal logic. In *Proc. 12th Conf. Found. of Software Technology and Theor. Comp. Sci., New Delhi, India, LNCS 652*, pages 1–38. Springer-Verlag, December 1992.

[21] L. E. Sanchis. Data types as lattices : retractions, closures and projections. *RAIRO Informatique Théorique et Applications*, 11(4):329–344, 1977.

[22] J. Sifakis. Property preserving homomorphisms of transition systems. In *Proc. Logics of Programs Workshop, Pittsburgh, LNCS 164*, pages 458–473. Springer-Verlag, June 1983.

[23] H. Treharne, J. Draper, and S. Schneider. Test case preparation using a prototype. In *Second conference on the B method*, LNCS 1393, pages 293–312, Montpellier, France, April 1998. Springer Verlag.

[24] I. Ulidowski. Equivalences on observable processes. In *Proceedings of the 7th Annual IEEE Symposium on Logic in Computer Sciences IEEE, New-York, IEEE Computer Society Press*, pages 148–161, 1992.

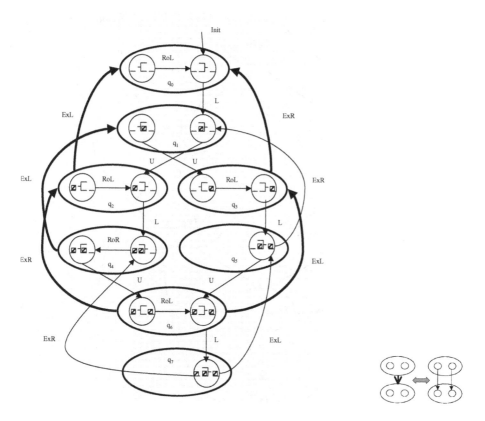

Fig. 6. A refined transition system (in position).

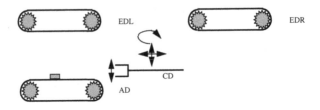

Fig. 7. The physical system.

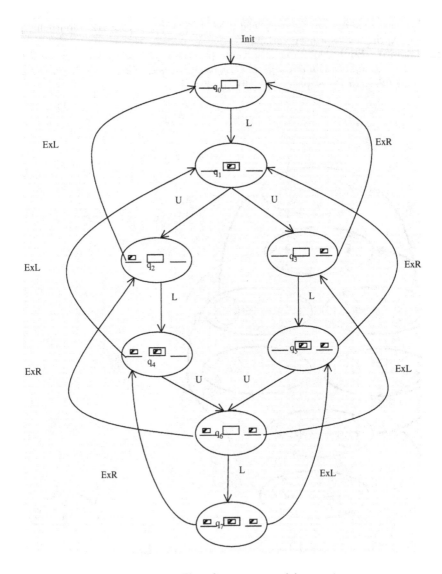

Fig. 8. The abstract transition system.

Java Program Verification
via a Hoare Logic with Abrupt Termination

Marieke Huisman and Bart Jacobs

Computing Science Institute, University of Nijmegen
Toernooiveld 1, 6525 ED Nijmegen, The Netherlands
{marieke,bart}@cs.kun.nl

Abstract. This paper formalises a semantics for statements and expressions (in sequential imperative languages) which includes non-termination, normal termination and abrupt termination (*e.g.* because of an exception, break, return or continue). This extends the traditional semantics underlying *e.g.* Hoare logic, which only distinguishes termination and non-termination. An extension of Hoare logic is elaborated that includes means for reasoning about abrupt termination (and side-effects). It prominently involves rules for reasoning about while loops, which may contain exceptions, breaks, continues and returns. This extension applies in particular to Java. As an example, a standard pattern search algorithm in Java (involving a while loop with returns) is proven correct using the proof-tool PVS.

1 Introduction

Java is quickly becoming one of the most widely used programming languages. Being able to establish the correctness of Java programs is thus of evident importance. In [19] a tool is presented which translates Java classes into logical theories (of the proof tools Isabelle [26] or PVS [23, 24]). The translation involves a particular semantics for statements and expressions, which forms a basis for proving correctness formulas. But "[...] reasoning about correctness formulas in terms of semantics is not very convenient. A much more promising approach is to reason directly on the level of correctness formulas." (quote from [3, p. 57]). Hoare logic is a formalism for doing precisely this.

The first contribution of this paper is a precise description of the semantics of statements and expressions underlying [19]. It involves abrupt termination as a prominent feature. The present description is more detailed than the one in [19] and more abstract in two aspects. First, and most importantly, it is not formulated in the language of PVS or Isabelle, but in a general type theoretical language involving records and variants. This means that the reader need not be familiar with particulars of (the language of) PVS or Isabelle. Secondly, the semantics described here is not especially focused on Java, and may apply to other languages with similar forms of abrupt termination.

The second contribution consists of a concrete and detailed elaboration and adaptation of existing approaches to programming logics with exceptions, notably from [9, 22, 21] (which are mostly in weakest precondition form). This

T. Maibaum (Ed.): FASE 2000, LNCS 1783, pp. 284–303, 2000.

elaboration and adaptation will be done for a real-world programming language like Java. Although the basic ideas used here are the same as in [9, 22, 21], the elaboration is different. For example, we have many forms of abrupt termination, and not just one sole exception, and we have a semantics of statements and expressions as particular functions (actually coalgebras, or maps in a Kleisli category, see [18]), and not a semantics of traces.

The logic presented here did not arise as a purely theoretical exercise, but was developed during actual verification of Java programs. For example, the ability to handle abnormalities was crucially needed for the vector class verification from [17], especially when dealing with **for** loops with **return** statements in their bodies.

Regarding the semantics that we shall be using, we recall that in classical program semantics and Hoare logic the assumption is that statements will either terminate normally, resulting in a successor state, or will not terminate at all, see *e.g.* [6, Chapter 3] or [28, Section 2.2]. In the latter case one also says that the statement hangs, typically because of a non-terminating loop. Hence, statements may be understood as partial functions from states to states. Writing Self for the state space, we can see statements as "state transformer" functions

$$ \mathsf{Self} \longrightarrow \mathsf{lift}[\mathsf{Self}] \quad (= 1 + \mathsf{Self}) $$

where 1 is a one-element set and $+$ is disjoint union. This classical view of statements turns out to be inadequate for reasoning about Java programs. Java statements may hang, or terminate normally (like above), but they may additionally "terminate abruptly" (see *e.g.* [13, 4]). Abrupt termination may be caused by an exception (typically a division by 0), a return, a break or a continue (inside a loop). Abrupt (or abnormal) termination is fundamentally different from non-termination: abnormalities may be temporary because they may be caught at some later stage, whereas recovery from non-termination is impossible.

Abrupt termination requires a modification of the standard semantics of statements and expressions, resulting in a failure semantics, as for example in [28, Section 5.1]. Here, statements will be modeled as more general state transformer functions

$$ \mathsf{Self} \xrightarrow{\;\;\mathsf{stat}\;\;} 1 + \mathsf{Self} + \mathsf{StatAbn} $$

where StatAbn forms a new option, which itself can be subdivided into four parts:

$$ \mathsf{StatAbn} = \mathsf{Exception} + \mathsf{Return} + \mathsf{Break} + \mathsf{Continue} $$

These four constituents of StatAbn will typically consist of a state in Self together with some extra information (*e.g.* the kind of exception, or the label of a break). This structure of the codomain of our Java state transformer functions will be captured formally in a type StatResult, see Section 4.

In classical Hoare logic, expressions are viewed as functions

$$ \mathsf{Self} \longrightarrow \mathsf{Out} $$

where Out is the type of the result. Also this view is not quite adequate for our purposes, because it does not involve non-termination, abrupt termination or side-effects. In contrast, an expression in Java may hang, terminate normally or terminate abruptly. If it terminates normally it produces an output result (of the type of the expression) together with a state (since it may have a side-effect). If it terminates abruptly, this can only be because of an exception (and not because of a break, continue or return). Hence an expression of type Out will be (in our view) a function of the form:

$$\text{Self} \xrightarrow{\quad\text{expr}\quad} 1 + (\text{Self} \times \text{Out}) + \text{ExprAbn}$$

The first option 1 captures the situation where an expression hangs. The second option Self × Out occurs when an expression terminates normally, resulting in a successor state together with an output result. The final option ExprAbn describes abrupt termination—because of an exception—for expressions. Again, this will be captured by a suitable type ExprResult in Section 4.

This abstract representation of statements and expressions as "one entry / multiexit" functions (terminology of [9]) forms the basis for the current work. It will be used to give meaning to basic programming constructs like composition, if-then-else, and while.

Hoare logic for a particular programming language consists of a series of deduction rules for special sentences, involving constructs from the programming language, like assignment, if-then-else and composition, see Section 3. In particular, while loops have received much attention in Hoare logic, because they involve a judicious and often non-trivial choice of a loop invariant. For more information, see *e.g.* [6, 14, 2, 11, 3]. There is what we would like to call a "classical" body of Hoare logic, which applies to standard constructs from an idealised imperative programming language. This forms a well-developed part of the theory of Hoare logic. It is couched in general terms, and not aimed at a particular programming language. This generality is an advantage, but also a disadvantage, in particular when one wishes to reason about a specific programming language. In this paper, an extension of standard Hoare logic is presented in which the different output options of statements and expressions will result in different kinds of sentences (for e.g. Break or Return), see Section 5 below.

We should emphasise that the extension of Hoare logic that is introduced here applies to only a small (sequential, non-object-oriented) part of Java. Hoare logics for reasoning about concurrent programs may be found in [3], and for reasoning about object-oriented programs in [8, 1]. There is also more remotely related work on "Hoare logic with jumps", see [10, 5] (or also Chapter 10 by De Bruin in [6]), but in those logics it is not always possible to reason about intermediate, "abnormal" states. And in [27] a programming logic for Java is described, which, in its current state, does not cover forms of abrupt termination—the focus point of this work.

This paper is organised as follows. Section 2 sketches the type theory and logic in which we shall be working. Section 3 briefly discusses the basics of Hoare logic. Section 4 discusses the formalisation of the semantics of Java statements and expressions in type theory. It also describes Hoare logic of normal termination. Section 5 discusses our extension of Hoare logic of abrupt termination. Proof rules for abruptly terminating while loops are discussed in Section 6. Section 7 gives an example of the use of Hoare logic of abrupt termination. Finally, we end with conclusions and future work in Section 8.

2 Basic Type Theory and Logic

In this section we shall present the simple type theory and (classical) higher-order logic in which we will be working. It can be seen as a common abstraction from the type theories and logics of both PVS and Isabelle/HOL[1]. Using this general type theory and logic means that we can stay away from the particulars of the languages of PVS and Isabelle and make this work more accessible to readers unfamiliar with these languages. Due to space restrictions, the explanation will have to be rather sketchy.

Our type theory is a simple type theory with types built up from:[2] type variables $\alpha, \beta, \ldots$, type constants nat, bool, string (and some more), exponent types $\sigma \to \tau$, labeled product (or record) types $[\mathsf{lab}_1 : \sigma_1, \ldots, \mathsf{lab}_n : \sigma_n]$ and labeled coproduct (or variant) types $\{\mathsf{lab}_1 : \sigma_1 \mid \ldots \mid \mathsf{lab}_n : \sigma_n\}$, for given types $\sigma, \tau, \sigma_1, \ldots, \sigma_n$. New types can be introduced via definitions, as in:

$$\mathsf{lift}[\alpha] : \mathsf{TYPE} \stackrel{\text{def}}{=} \{\mathsf{bot}: \mathsf{unit} \mid \mathsf{up}: \alpha\}$$

where unit is the empty product type $[\,]$. This lift type constructor adds a bottom element to an arbitrary type, given as type variable α. It is frequently used.

For exponent types we shall use the standard lambda abstraction $\lambda x : \sigma . M$ and application NL notation. For terms $M_i : \sigma_i$, we have a labeled tuple $(\mathsf{lab}_1 = M_1, \ldots, \mathsf{lab}_n = M_n)$ inhabiting the labeled product type $[\mathsf{lab}_1 : \sigma_1, \ldots, \mathsf{lab}_n : \sigma_n]$. For a term $N : [\mathsf{lab}_1 : \sigma_1, \ldots, \mathsf{lab}_n : \sigma_n]$ in this product, we write $N.\mathsf{lab}_i$ for the selection term of type σ_i. Similarly, for a term $M : \sigma_i$ there is a labeled or tagged term $\mathsf{lab}_i M$ in the labeled coproduct type $\{\mathsf{lab}_1 : \sigma_1 \mid \ldots \mid \mathsf{lab}_n : \sigma_n\}$. And for a term $N : \{\mathsf{lab}_1 : \sigma_1 \mid \ldots \mid \mathsf{lab}_n : \sigma_n\}$ in this coproduct type, together with n terms $L_i(x_i) : \tau$ containing a free variable $x_i : \sigma_i$ there is a case term $\mathsf{CASES}\ N\ \mathsf{OF}\ \{\mathsf{lab}_1\ x_1 \mapsto L_1(x_1) \mid \ldots \mid \mathsf{lab}_n\ x_n \mapsto L_n(x_n)\}$ of type τ. These introduction and elimination terms for labeled products and coproducts are required to satisfy standard (β)- and (η)-conversions.

Formulas in higher-order logic are terms of type bool. We shall use the connectives $\wedge$ (conjunction), $\vee$ (disjunction), $\supset$ (implication), $\neg$ (negation, used with

---

[1] Certain aspects of PVS and Isabelle/HOL are incompatible, like the type parameters in PVS versus type polymorphism in Isabelle/HOL, so that the type theory and logic that we use is not really in the intersection. But with some good will it should be clear how to translate the constructions that we present into the particular languages of these proof tools. See [15] for a detailed comparison.

[2] In this paper we only use non-recursive types, but in the translation of Java constructs like `catch` and `switch` we also use the (recursive) list type constructor.

rules of classical logic) and constants true and false, together with the (typed) quantifiers $\forall x\colon \sigma.\varphi$ and $\exists x\colon \sigma.\varphi$, for a formula φ. There is a conditional term IF φ THEN M ELSE N, for terms M, N of the same type, and a choice operator $\varepsilon x\colon \sigma.\varphi(x)$, yielding a term of type σ. We shall use inductive definitions (over the type nat of natural numbers), and also reason with the standard induction principle. All this is present in both PVS and Isabelle/HOL.

3   Basics of Hoare Logic

Traditionally, Hoare logic allows one to reason about simple imperative programs, containing assignments, conditional statements, while and for loops, and block statements with local variables. It provides proof rules to derive the correctness of a complete program from the correctness of parts of the program. Sentences (also called asserted programs) in this logic have the form $\{P\}\, S\, \{Q\}$, for partial correctness, or $[P]\, S\, [Q]$, for total correctness. They involve assertions P and Q in some logic (usually predicate logic), and statements S from the programming language that one wishes to reason about. The partial correctness sentence $\{P\}\, S\, \{Q\}$ expresses that if the assertion P holds in some state x and *if* the statement S, when evaluated in state x, terminates normally, resulting in a state x', then the assertion Q holds in x'. Total correctness $[P]\, S\, [Q]$ expresses something stronger, namely: if P holds in x, *then* S in x terminates normally, resulting in a state x' where Q holds. Some well-known proof rules are:

$$\frac{\{P\}\, S\, \{Q\} \qquad \{Q\}\, T\, \{R\}}{\{P\}\, S;T\, \{R\}}\,[\text{comp}] \qquad \frac{\{P \wedge C\}\, S\, \{Q\} \qquad \{P \wedge \neg C\}\, T\, \{Q\}}{\{P\}\, \text{if } C \text{ then } S \text{ else } T\, \{Q\}}\,[\text{if}]$$

$$\frac{\{P \wedge C\}\, S\, \{P\}}{\{P\}\, \text{while } C \text{ do } S\, \{P \wedge \neg C\}}\,[\text{while}]$$

The predicate P in the while rule is often called the loop invariant.

Most classical partial correctness proof rules immediately carry over to total correctness. A well-known exception is the rule for the while statement, which needs an extra condition to prove termination. Consider for example the program (fragment) while true do skip. For every predicate P, it is easy to prove $[P]\, \text{skip}\, [P]$. But the whole statement never terminates, so we should not be able to conclude $[P]\, \text{while true do skip}\, [P \wedge \text{false}]$. An extra condition, which guarantees termination, should be added to the rule. The standard approach is to define a mapping from the underlying state space to some well-founded set and to require that every time the body is executed, the result of this mapping decreases. As this can happen only finitely often, the loop has to terminate. Often this mapping is called the variant (in contrast to the loop invariant). This gives the following proof rule for total correctness of while statements.

$$\frac{[P \wedge C \wedge \text{variant} = n]\, S\, [P \wedge \text{variant} < n]}{[P]\, \text{while } C \text{ do } S\, [P \wedge \neg C]}$$

3.1   Some Limitations of Hoare Logic

Hoare logic has had much influence on the way of thinking about (imperative) programming, but unfortunately it also has some shortcomings. First of all, it is not really feasible to verify non-trivial programs by hand. Most computer science students—at some stage during their training—have to verify some well-known algorithm, such as quicksort. At that moment they often decide never to do this again. One would like to have a tool, which does most of the proving automatically, so that the user only has to interfere at crucial steps in the proof. Secondly, classical Hoare logic enables reasoning about an ideal programming language, without side-effects, exceptions, abrupt termination of statements, *etc.* However, most widely-used (imperative) programming languages do have side-effects, exceptions and the like.

In our project [16, 19] we aim at reasoning about real, widely-used programming languages. Thus far we concentrated on Java. The first step of our project is to provide a formal semantics to Java statements and expressions, in the higher-order logic and type theory from the previous section. Reasoning about a particular Java program can only be done after it is translated into type theory, for which we use our translation tool. In the logic, the user can write down required properties about the program—using partial and total correctness sentences—and try to prove these. Via appropriate rewrite rules—used as "interpreter"—many properties for non-looping, non-recursive programs can be proven without user interaction. This translation (to PVS) and reasoning are described in more detail elsewhere [19], while this paper presents more details of the formal semantics of Java. The underlying memory model is explained in [7].

As mentioned in the introduction, reasoning that is directly based on the semantics of the programming language is often not appropriate for looping or recursive programs. These kinds of programs require the use of a special purpose logic, such as Hoare logic. Gordon [12] describes how the rules of Hoare logic are mechanically derived from the semantics of a simple imperative language. This enables both semantic and axiomatic reasoning about programs in this language. What we describe next may be seen as a deeper elaboration of this approach, building on ideas from [9, 22, 21].

4   Semantics of Java Statements and Expressions

This section describes in more detail how the semantics of Java statements and expressions is formalised in type theory. Statements and expressions are regarded as state transformer functions, possibly producing a new state with a tag telling whether the state is normal or abnormal. This will be explained first. The last part of this section (Subsection 4.4) describes our first extension of classical Hoare logic, namely Hoare logic of normal termination for Java-like languages, which incorporates side-effects. Section 5 describes the more substantial extension of Hoare logic with abrupt termination.

4.1   Statements and Expressions as State Transformers

In this section we will describe state transformers for statements and expressions in type theory. As explained in the introduction, an extra possibility has to be added (besides non-termination and normal termination) to capture abrupt termination of statements and expressions: statements and expressions are modeled as functions with types $\mathsf{Self} \to 1 + \mathsf{Self} + \mathsf{StatAbn}$ and $\mathsf{Self} \to 1 + (\mathsf{Self} \times \mathsf{Out}) + \mathsf{ExprAbn}$, respectively. For convenience, the output types are represented in two steps, via the variant types $\mathsf{PreStatResult}$ and $\mathsf{PreExprResult}$.

$$\mathsf{PreStatResult}[\mathsf{Self}, A] : \mathsf{TYPE} \stackrel{\mathrm{def}}{=} \qquad \mathsf{PreExprResult}[\mathsf{Self}, \mathsf{Out}, A] : \mathsf{TYPE} \stackrel{\mathrm{def}}{=}$$

$$\{\, \mathsf{hang} : \mathsf{unit}, \qquad\qquad\qquad \{\, \mathsf{hang} : \mathsf{unit},$$
$$\mid \mathsf{norm} : \mathsf{Self}, \qquad\qquad\qquad \mid \mathsf{norm} : [\,\mathsf{ns} : \mathsf{Self}, \mathsf{res} : \mathsf{Out}\,],$$
$$\mid \mathsf{abnorm} : A \,\} \qquad\qquad\qquad \mid \mathsf{abnorm} : A \,\}$$

These definitions involve type variables $\mathsf{Self}, \mathsf{Out}$ and A. Further, we have two different types for abnormalities. Expressions only terminate abruptly, because of an exception, while statements can also terminate abruptly because of a **break**, **continue** or **return** [13]. Below, in Section 4.2, the meaning of these statements will be described in more detail.

$$\mathsf{StatAbn}[\mathsf{Self}] : \mathsf{TYPE} \stackrel{\mathrm{def}}{=}$$

$$\{\, \mathsf{excp} : [\,\mathsf{es} : \mathsf{Self}, \mathsf{ex} : \mathsf{RefType}\,] \qquad \mathsf{ExprAbn}[\mathsf{Self}] : \mathsf{TYPE} \stackrel{\mathrm{def}}{=}$$
$$\mid \mathsf{rtrn} : \mathsf{Self}$$
$$\mid \mathsf{break} : [\,\mathsf{bs} : \mathsf{Self}, \mathsf{blab} : \mathsf{lift}[\mathsf{string}]\,] \qquad [\,\mathsf{es} : \mathsf{Self}, \mathsf{ex} : \mathsf{RefType}\,]$$
$$\mid \mathsf{cont} : [\,\mathsf{cs} : \mathsf{Self}, \mathsf{clab} : \mathsf{lift}[\mathsf{string}]\,]\,\}$$

An (expression or statement) exception abnormality consists of a state together with a reference to an exception object. The reference is represented as an element of a special type $\mathsf{RefType}$ (see [7]), which does not play a rôle in the sequel. A return abnormality only consists of a (tagged) state, and break and continue abnormalities consist of a state, possibly with a label (given as string).

Finally, we define abbreviations $\mathsf{StatResult}$ and $\mathsf{ExprResult}$ by substitution as:

$$\mathsf{StatResult}[\mathsf{Self}] \stackrel{\mathrm{def}}{=} \mathsf{PreStatResult}[\mathsf{Self}, \mathsf{StatAbn}[\mathsf{Self}]]$$
$$\mathsf{ExprResult}[\mathsf{Self}, \mathsf{Out}] \stackrel{\mathrm{def}}{=} \mathsf{PreExprResult}[\mathsf{Self}, \mathsf{Out}, \mathsf{ExprAbn}[\mathsf{Self}]]$$

To summarise, in our formalisation, statements are modeled as functions from Self to $\mathsf{StatResult}[\mathsf{Self}]$, and expressions as functions from Self to $\mathsf{ExprResult}[\mathsf{Self}, \mathsf{Out}]$, for the appropriate result type Out.

There is one technicality that deserves some attention. Sometimes an expression has to be transformed into a statement, which is only a matter of forgetting the result of the expression. However, in our formalisation we have to do this transformation explicitly, using a function E2S.

e: Self $\rightarrow$ ExprResult[Self, Out] $\vdash$

$$E2S(e) : \text{ Self} \rightarrow \text{StatResult[Self]} \overset{\text{def}}{=}$$

$$\lambda x: \text{Self. CASES } e\,x \text{ OF } \{$$
$$| \text{ hang} \mapsto \text{hang}$$
$$| \text{ norm } y \mapsto \text{norm}(y.\text{ns})$$
$$| \text{ abnorm } a \mapsto \text{abnorm}(\text{excp}(\text{es} = a.\text{es}, \text{ex} = a.\text{ex}))\,\}$$

In the last line an expression abnormality (an exception) is transformed into a statement abnormality.

4.2   Throwing and Catching Abnormalities

Based on the types representing statements and expressions various program constructs can be formalised. This will be done here, and in the next subsection. We start with statements dealing with abrupt termination. We shall use the notation $[\![S]\!]$ to denote the interpretation (translation) of the Java statement or expression S in type theory.

Abnormalities can both be thrown and be caught, basically via re-arranging coproduct options. We shall describe constructs for both throwing and catching in type theory. Abrupt termination affects the flow of control: once it arises, all subsequent statements are ignored, until the abnormality is caught, see the definition of composition ";" in the next subsection. From that moment on, the program executes normally again. We shall discuss breaks and returns in some detail, and only sketch continues and exceptions.

Break A break statement can be used to exit from any block. If a break statement is labeled, it exits the block with the same label. Typically, a break statement with label lab must occur inside a (nested) block with the same label lab, so that it can not be used as an arbitrary goto. Unlabeled break statements exit the innermost switch, for, while or do statement. A Java break statement is translated as

$$[\![\text{break}]\!] \overset{\text{def}}{=} \text{BREAK}$$
$$[\![\text{break label}]\!] \overset{\text{def}}{=} \text{BREAK-LABEL}(\text{"label"})$$

where BREAK and BREAK-LABEL(s), for s: string, are defined as functions Self $\rightarrow$ StatResult[Self]:

$$\text{BREAK} \overset{\text{def}}{=} \lambda x: \text{Self. abnorm}(\text{break}(\text{bs} = x, \text{blab} = \text{bot}))$$
$$\text{BREAK-LABEL}(s) \overset{\text{def}}{=} \lambda x: \text{Self. abnorm}(\text{break}(\text{bs} = x, \text{blab} = \text{up } s))$$

There is an associated function CATCH-BREAK which turns abnormal states, because of breaks with the appropriate label, back into normal states.

ll : lift[string], s : Self $\rightarrow$ StatResult[Self] $\vdash$

    CATCH-BREAK$(ll)(s)$: Self $\rightarrow$ StatResult[Self] $\overset{\text{def}}{=}$

        λx : Self. CASES $s\,x$ OF {
            | hang $\mapsto$ hang
            | norm y $\mapsto$ norm y
            | abnorm a $\mapsto$ CASES a OF {
                    | excp e $\mapsto$ abnorm(excp e)
                    | rtrn z $\mapsto$ abnorm(rtrn z)
                    | break b $\mapsto$ IF b.blab $= ll$
                            THEN norm(b.bs)
                            ELSE abnorm(break b)
                    | cont c $\mapsto$ abnorm(cont c) } }

In the Java translation [19] every labeled block is enclosed with CATCH-BREAK applied to the appropriate label:

$$[\![\texttt{label:body}]\!] \overset{\text{def}}{=} \text{CATCH-BREAK}(\text{up}(\text{``label''}))([\![\text{body}]\!])$$

Similarly, every switch, while, for and do statement is enclosed with CATCH-BREAK applied to bot.

Return When a return statement is executed, the program immediately exits from the current method. A return statement may have an expression argument; if so, this expression is evaluated and returned as the result of the method. The translation of the Java return statement (without argument) is $[\![\texttt{return}]\!] =$ RETURN where RETURN is defined in type theory as:

$$\text{RETURN} : \text{Self} \rightarrow \text{StatResult[Self]} \overset{\text{def}}{=} \lambda x : \text{Self. abnorm(rtrn } x)$$

This statement produces an abnormal state. Such a return abnormality can be undone, via appropriate catch-return functions. In our translation of Java programs, such a function CATCH-STAT-RETURN is wrapped around every method body that returns void. First the method body is executed. This may result in an abnormal state, because of a return. In that case the function CATCH-STAT-RETURN turns the state back to normal again. Otherwise, it leaves the state unchanged.

$s \colon \mathsf{Self} \to \mathsf{StatResult}[\mathsf{Self}] \; \vdash$

$\mathsf{CATCH\text{-}STAT\text{-}RETURN}(s) \colon \mathsf{Self} \to \mathsf{StatResult}[\mathsf{Self}] \; \overset{\mathrm{def}}{=}$

$\lambda x \colon \mathsf{Self}. \; \mathsf{CASES} \; s \, x \; \mathsf{OF} \; \{$

$\quad | \; \mathsf{hang} \mapsto \mathsf{hang}$

$\quad | \; \mathsf{norm} \, y \mapsto \mathsf{norm} \, y$

$\quad | \; \mathsf{abnorm} \, a \mapsto \mathsf{CASES} \; a \; \mathsf{OF} \; \{$

$\qquad\qquad | \; \mathsf{excp} \, e \mapsto \mathsf{abnorm}(\mathsf{excp} \, e)$

$\qquad\qquad | \; \mathsf{rtrn} \, z \mapsto \mathsf{norm} \, z$

$\qquad\qquad | \; \mathsf{break} \, b \mapsto \mathsf{abnorm}(\mathsf{break} \, b)$

$\qquad\qquad | \; \mathsf{cont} \, c \mapsto \mathsf{abnorm}(\mathsf{cont} \, c) \, \} \, \}$

The translation of a **return** statement with argument is similar, but more subtle. First the value of the expression is stored in a special local variable, and then the state becomes abnormal, via the above RETURN. Instead of CATCH-STAT-RETURN a function CATCH-EXPR-RETURN is used, which eventually turns the state back to normal and, in that case, returns the output that is held by the special variable.

Continue Within loop statements (`while`, `do` and `for`) a `continue` statement can occur. The effect is that control skips the rest of the loop's body and starts re-evaluating the (update statement, in a `for` loop, and) Boolean expression which controls the loop. A `continue` statement can be labeled, so that the `continue` is applied to the correspondingly labeled loop, and not to the innermost one.

Within the translation of loop statements, the function CATCH-CONTINUE is used, which catches abnormal states, because of continues with the appropriate label. The definitions of CONTINUE and CATCH-CONTINUE are similar to those of BREAK and CATCH-BREAK, respectively.

Exceptions An exception can occur for two reasons: it can either be thrown explicitly, or implicitly by a run-time error. Java provides a statement `try ... catch ... finally` to catch exceptions. Our formalisation contains statements THROW, TRY-CATCH and TRY-CATCH-FINALLY which realise throwing and catching of exceptions. They do not play a rôle in the rest of this paper.

4.3   The Formalisation of Composite Statements and Expressions

The semantics of program constructs is described compositionally. For example, $[\![S; T]\!]$ is defined as $[\![S]\!] \, ; [\![T]\!]$, where "$;$" is the translation of the statement composition operator $;$. It is defined on $s, t \colon \mathsf{Self} \to \mathsf{StatResult}[\mathsf{Self}]$ as:

$s \, ; t \; \colon \; \mathsf{Self} \to \mathsf{StatResult}[\mathsf{Self}] \; \overset{\mathrm{def}}{=} \; \lambda x \colon \mathsf{Self}. \; \mathsf{CASES} \; s \, x \; \mathsf{OF} \; \{$

$\qquad\qquad\qquad\qquad\qquad\qquad\qquad | \; \mathsf{hang} \mapsto \mathsf{hang}$

$\qquad\qquad\qquad\qquad\qquad\qquad\qquad | \; \mathsf{norm} \, y \mapsto t \, y$

$\qquad\qquad\qquad\qquad\qquad\qquad\qquad | \; \mathsf{abnorm} \, a \mapsto \mathsf{abnorm} \, a \, \}$

$$
\begin{array}{l}
c\colon \mathsf{Self} \to \mathsf{ExprResult}[\mathsf{Self}, \mathsf{bool}],\, s\colon \mathsf{Self} \to \mathsf{StatResult}[\mathsf{Self}],\, x\colon \mathsf{Self} \vdash \\
\quad \mathsf{NoStops}(c, s, x) \;:\; \mathsf{nat} \to [\mathsf{result}\colon \mathsf{bool}, \mathsf{state}\colon \mathsf{Self}] \stackrel{\mathrm{def}}{=} \\
\quad\quad \lambda n\colon \mathsf{nat}.\ \mathsf{IF}\ \forall m\colon \mathsf{nat}.\, m < n \supset \\
\qquad\qquad\qquad \mathsf{CASES}\ \mathsf{iterate}(\mathsf{E2S}(c)\,;s, m)\, x\ \mathsf{OF}\ \{ \\
\qquad\qquad\qquad\quad \mid \mathsf{hang} \mapsto \mathsf{false} \\
\qquad\qquad\qquad\quad \mid \mathsf{norm}\, y \mapsto \mathsf{CASES}\ c\, y\ \mathsf{OF}\ \{ \\
\qquad\qquad\qquad\qquad\qquad \mid \mathsf{hang} \mapsto \mathsf{false} \\
\qquad\qquad\qquad\qquad\qquad \mid \mathsf{norm}\, z \mapsto z.\mathsf{res} \\
\qquad\qquad\qquad\qquad\qquad \mid \mathsf{abnorm}\, b \mapsto \mathsf{false}\, \} \\
\qquad\qquad\qquad\quad \mid \mathsf{abnorm}\, a \mapsto \mathsf{false}\, \} \\
\qquad\qquad \mathsf{THEN}\ \ \mathsf{CASES}\ \mathsf{iterate}(\mathsf{E2S}(c)\,;s, n)\, x\ \mathsf{OF}\ \{ \\
\qquad\qquad\qquad\quad \mid \mathsf{hang} \mapsto (\mathsf{result} = \mathsf{false}, \mathsf{state} = x) \\
\qquad\qquad\qquad\quad \mid \mathsf{norm}\, y \mapsto (\mathsf{result} = \mathsf{true}, \mathsf{state} = y) \\
\qquad\qquad\qquad\quad \mid \mathsf{abnorm}\, a \mapsto (\mathsf{result} = \mathsf{false}, \mathsf{state} = x)\, \} \\
\qquad\qquad \mathsf{ELSE}\ (\mathsf{result} = \mathsf{false}, \mathsf{state} = x)
\end{array}
$$

$$
\begin{array}{l}
c\colon \mathsf{Self} \to \mathsf{ExprResult}[\mathsf{Self}, \mathsf{bool}],\, s\colon \mathsf{Self} \to \mathsf{StatResult}[\mathsf{Self}],\, x\colon \mathsf{Self} \vdash \\
\quad \mathsf{NormalStopNumber?}(c, s, x) \;:\; \mathsf{nat} \to \mathsf{bool} \stackrel{\mathrm{def}}{=} \\
\quad\quad \lambda n\colon \mathsf{nat}.\ (\mathsf{NoStops}(c, s, x)\, n).\mathsf{result} \wedge \\
\qquad\qquad\qquad \mathsf{CASES}\ c\, \big((\mathsf{NoStops}(c, s, x)\, n).\mathsf{state}\big)\ \mathsf{OF}\ \{ \\
\qquad\qquad\qquad\quad \mid \mathsf{hang} \mapsto \mathsf{false} \\
\qquad\qquad\qquad\quad \mid \mathsf{norm}\, y \mapsto \neg(y.\mathsf{res}) \\
\qquad\qquad\qquad\quad \mid \mathsf{abnorm}\, a \mapsto \mathsf{false} \}
\end{array}
$$

$$
\begin{array}{l}
c\colon \mathsf{Self} \to \mathsf{ExprResult}[\mathsf{Self}, \mathsf{bool}],\, s\colon \mathsf{Self} \to \mathsf{StatResult}[\mathsf{Self}],\, x\colon \mathsf{Self} \vdash \\
\quad \mathsf{AbnormalStopNumber?}(c, s, x) \;:\; \mathsf{nat} \to \mathsf{bool} \stackrel{\mathrm{def}}{=} \\
\quad\quad \lambda n\colon \mathsf{nat}.\ (\mathsf{NoStops}(c, s, x)\, n).\mathsf{result} \wedge \\
\qquad\qquad\qquad \mathsf{CASES}\ (\mathsf{E2S}(c)\,; s)\, \big((\mathsf{NoStops}(c, s, x)\, n).\mathsf{state}\big)\ \mathsf{OF}\ \{ \\
\qquad\qquad\qquad\quad \mid \mathsf{hang} \mapsto \mathsf{false} \\
\qquad\qquad\qquad\quad \mid \mathsf{norm}\, y \mapsto \mathsf{false} \\
\qquad\qquad\qquad\quad \mid \mathsf{abnorm}\, a \mapsto \mathsf{true} \}
\end{array}
$$

Fig. 1. Auxiliary functions NoStops, NormalStopNumber? and AbnormalStopNumber? for the definition of WHILE in type theory

ll: lift[string], c: Self $\rightarrow$ ExprResult[Self, bool], s: Self $\rightarrow$ StatResult[Self] $\vdash$

$\quad$ WHILE$(ll)(c)(s)$: Self $\rightarrow$ StatResult[Self] $\stackrel{\text{def}}{=}$

$\quad\quad \lambda x$: Self. LET $iter_body = $ E2S(c); CATCH-CONTINUE$(ll)(s)$,
$\quad\quad\quad\quad\quad\quad NormalStopSet =$
$\quad\quad\quad\quad\quad\quad\quad\quad$ NormalStopNumber?$(c,$ CATCH-CONTINUE$(ll)(s), x)$
$\quad\quad\quad\quad\quad\quad AbnormalStopSet =$
$\quad\quad\quad\quad\quad\quad\quad\quad$ AbnormalStopNumber?$(c,$ CATCH-CONTINUE$(ll)(s), x)$ IN
$\quad\quad\quad$ IF $\exists n$: nat. $NormalStopSet\, n$
$\quad\quad\quad$ THEN $\big($iterate$(iter\_body, \varepsilon n$: nat. $NormalStopSet\, n)$; E2S$(c)\big)\, x$
$\quad\quad\quad$ ELSIF $\exists n$: nat. $AbnormalStopSet\, n$
$\quad\quad\quad$ THEN $\big($iterate$(iter\_body, \varepsilon n$: nat. $AbnormalStopSet\, n)$; $iter\_body\big)\, x$
$\quad\quad\quad$ ELSE hang

Fig. 2. WHILE in type theory, using definitions from Figure 1

Thus if statement s terminates normally in state x, resulting in a next state y, then $(s;t)\, x$ is $t\, y$. And if s hangs or terminates abruptly in state x, then $(s;t)\, x$ is $s\, x$ and t is not executed. This binary operation ; forms a monoid with the following skip statement as unit.

$$\text{skip} : \text{Self} \rightarrow \text{StatResult[Self]} \stackrel{\text{def}}{=} \lambda x\text{: Self. norm}\, x$$

Skip and composition are used in the following iterate function.

$$\text{iterate}(s, n) : \text{Self} \rightarrow \text{StatResult[Self]} \stackrel{\text{def}}{=} \lambda x\text{: Self. IF } n = 0$$
$$\text{THEN skip}$$
$$\text{ELSE iterate}(s, n - 1)\,;\, s$$

It will be used in the definition of the WHILE function, see Figures 1 and 2. All Java language constructs are formalised in a similar way, following closely the Java language specification [13].

The translation of the Java while statement depends on the occurrence of a label (immediately before the while):

$$[\![\text{while(cond)}\{\text{body}\}]\!] \stackrel{\text{def}}{=} \text{CATCH-BREAK(bot)(}$$
$$\text{WHILE(bot)}([\![\text{cond}]\!])([\![\text{body}]\!]))$$
$$[\![\text{lab:while(cond)}\{\text{body}\}]\!] \stackrel{\text{def}}{=} \text{CATCH-BREAK(bot)(}$$
$$\text{WHILE(up("lab"))}([\![\text{cond}]\!])([\![\text{body}]\!]))$$

The outer CATCH-BREAK(bot) makes sure that the while loop terminates normally if an unlabeled break occurs in its body. Figure 2 shows the definition of WHILE in type theory, making use of the auxiliary functions from Figure 1. The earlier given function iterate is applied to the composite statement

$$\text{E2S(cond)}\,;\, \text{CATCH-CONTINUE(lift\_label)(body)}$$

where lift_label is either bot or up("lab"). Below, this statement will be referred to as the iteration body. It first evaluates the condition (for its side-effect, discarding its result), and then evaluates the statement, making sure that occurrences of a continue (with appropriate label) in this statement are caught. The sets NormalStopNumber? and AbnormalStopNumber? in Figure 1 characterise the point where the loop will terminate in the next iteration, either because the condition becomes false, resulting in normal termination of the loop, or because an abnormality occurs in the iteration body, resulting in abnormal termination of the loop. From the definitions it follows that if NormalStopNumber? or AbnormalStop-Number? is non-empty, then it is a singleton. And if both are non-empty, then the number in NormalStopNumber? is smaller or equal than the number in Abnormal-StopNumber?. Therefore, the WHILE function first checks if NormalStopNumber? is non-empty, and subsequently if AbnormalStopNumber? is non-empty. In both cases, the iteration body is executed the appropriate number of times, so that the loop will terminate in the next iteration. In the case of normal termination this is followed by an additional execution of the condition (for its side-effect), and in the case of abnormal termination this is followed by an execution of it-eration body, resulting in abrupt termination. If both sets NormalStopNumber? and AbnormalStopNumber? are empty, the loop will never terminate (normally or abruptly), thus hang is returned. Basically, this definition makes WHILE a least fixed point, see [18] for details.

4.4   Hoare Logic with Normal Termination for Java-like Languages

Having described some ingredients of the semantics of statements and expres-sions of Java-like languages, we can formalise the notions of partial and to-tal correctness in this context. For the moment we only consider normal ter-mination. The predicates PartialNormal? and TotalNormal? formalise the no-tions of partial and total correctness, using variables pre, post: Self $\to$ bool and stat: Self $\to$ StatResult[Self].

$$\text{PartialNormal?(pre, stat, post)} : \text{bool} \stackrel{\text{def}}{=} \forall x\colon \text{Self. pre}\, x \supset \text{CASES stat}\, x \text{ OF } \{$$
$$\mid \text{hang} \mapsto \text{true}$$
$$\mid \text{norm}\, y \mapsto \text{post}\, y$$
$$\mid \text{abnorm}\, a \mapsto \text{true} \}$$

$$\text{TotalNormal?(pre, stat, post)} : \text{bool} \stackrel{\text{def}}{=} \forall x\colon \text{Self. pre}\, x \supset \text{CASES stat}\, x \text{ OF } \{$$
$$\mid \text{hang} \mapsto \text{false}$$
$$\mid \text{norm}\, y \mapsto \text{post}\, y$$
$$\mid \text{abnorm}\, a \mapsto \text{false} \}$$

It is easy to prove the validity of all the well-known Hoare logic proof rules, using definitions like $\{P\}\,[S]\,\{Q\} = \text{PartialNormal?}(P, [S], Q)$. Even more, it is also easy to incorporate side-effects into these rules.

We also can formulate (and prove) extra proof rules, capturing the correctness of abruptly terminating statements. For instance, the next rule states that if we have a labeled block, containing some statement S, followed by an appropriately labeled **break** statement, then it suffices to look at the correctness of S.

$$\frac{[P]\,S\,[Q]}{[P]\,\mathsf{CATCH\text{-}BREAK}(l)(S\,;\mathsf{BREAK\text{-}LABEL}(l))\,[Q]}$$

It is immediately clear how to formulate similar rules for other abnormalities.

5   Hoare Logic with Abrupt Termination

Unfortunately, the proof rules for normal termination do not give enough power to reason about arbitrary Java-like programs. To achieve this, it is necessary to have a "correctness notion" for being in an abnormal state, *e.g.* if execution of S starts in a state satisfying P, then execution of S terminates abruptly, because of a **return**, in a state satisfying Q. To this end, we introduce the notions of abnormal correctness. They will appear in four forms, corresponding to the four possible kinds of abnormalities. Rules will be formulated to derive the (abnormal) correctness of a program compositionally. These rules will allow the user to move back and forth between the various correctness notions.

The first notion we introduce is partial break correctness (with notation: $\{P\}\,S\,\{\mathsf{break}(Q,l)\}$), meaning that if execution of S starts in some state satisfying P, and execution of S terminates in an abnormal state, because of a **break**, then the resulting abnormal state satisfies Q. If the **break** is labeled with **lab**, then $l = \mathsf{up}(\text{"lab"})$, otherwise $l = \mathsf{bot}$.

Naturally, we also have total break correctness ($[P]\,S\,[\mathsf{break}(Q,l)]$), meaning that if execution of S starts in some state satisfying P, then execution of S will terminate in an abnormal state, satisfying Q, because of a **break**. If this **break** is labeled with a label **lab**, then $l = \mathsf{up}(\text{"lab"})$, otherwise $l = \mathsf{bot}$. Continuing in this manner leads to the following eight notions of abnormal correctness.

partial break correctness	$\{P\}\,S\,\{\mathsf{break}(Q,l)\}$
partial continue correctness	$\{P\}\,S\,\{\mathsf{continue}(Q,l)\}$
partial return correctness	$\{P\}\,S\,\{\mathsf{return}(Q)\}$
partial exception correctness	$\{P\}\,S\,\{\mathsf{exception}(Q,e)\}$
total break correctness	$[P]\,S\,[\mathsf{break}(Q,l)]$
total continue correctness	$[P]\,S\,[\mathsf{continue}(Q,l)]$
total return correctness	$[P]\,S\,[\mathsf{return}(Q)]$
total exception correctness	$[P]\,S\,[\mathsf{exception}(Q,e)]$

It is tempting to change the standard notation $\{P\}\,S\,\{Q\}$ and $[P]\,S\,[Q]$ into $\{P\}\,S\,\{\mathsf{norm}(Q)\}$ and $[P]\,S\,[\mathsf{norm}(Q)]$ to bring it in line with the new notation, but we will stick to the standard notation for normal termination.

The formalisation of these correctness notions in type theory is straightforward. As an example, we consider the predicate PartialReturn? of partial return correctness. It is used to give meaning to the notation $\{P\}\,[\![S]\!]\,\{\mathsf{return}(Q)\}$ = PartialReturn?$(P,[\![S]\!],Q)$.

$$\mathsf{pre},\mathsf{post}\colon \mathsf{Self}\to \mathsf{bool},\mathsf{stat}\colon \mathsf{Self}\to \mathsf{StatResult}[\mathsf{Self}]\ \vdash$$

$$\mathsf{PartialReturn?}(\mathsf{pre},\mathsf{stat},\mathsf{post})\ :\ \mathsf{bool}\ \stackrel{\mathrm{def}}{=}$$

$$\forall x\colon \mathsf{Self.}\,\mathsf{pre}\,x \supset \mathsf{CASES}\ \mathsf{stat}\,x\ \mathsf{OF}\ \{$$
$$\mid \mathsf{hang}\mapsto \mathsf{true}$$
$$\mid \mathsf{norm}\,y\mapsto \mathsf{true}$$
$$\mid \mathsf{abnorm}\,a\mapsto \mathsf{CASES}\ a\ \mathsf{OF}\ \{$$
$$\mid \mathsf{excp}\,e\mapsto \mathsf{true}$$
$$\mid \mathsf{rtrn}\,z\mapsto \mathsf{post}\,z$$
$$\mid \mathsf{break}\,b\mapsto \mathsf{true}$$
$$\mid \mathsf{cont}\,c\mapsto \mathsf{true}\,\}\,\}$$

Many straightforward proof rules can be formulated and proven, for these correctness notions, like

$$\{P\}\,\mathsf{RETURN}\,\{\mathsf{return}(P)\} \qquad\qquad \frac{[P]\,S\,[\mathsf{return}(Q)]}{[P]\,S\,;T\,[\mathsf{return}(Q)]}$$

And finally there are rules to move between two correctness notions, from normal to abnormal and vice versa. Here are some examples for the return statement.

$$\frac{\{P\}\,S\,\{\mathsf{return}(Q)\}}{\{P\}\,\mathsf{CATCH\text{-}STAT\text{-}RETURN}(S)\,\{Q\}} \qquad \frac{\{P\}\,S\,\{Q\}}{} \qquad \frac{[P]\,S\,[\mathsf{return}(Q)]}{[P]\,\mathsf{CATCH\text{-}STAT\text{-}RETURN}(S)\,[Q]}$$

Most of these proof rules are easy and straightforward to formulate, and they provide a good framework to reason about programs in Java-like languages. But while loops are more interesting.

6   Hoare Logic of While Loops with Abnormalities

In classical Hoare logic, reasoning about while loops involves the following ingredients. (1) An invariant, *i.e.* a predicate over the state space which remains true as long as the while loop is executed; (2) a condition, which is false after normal termination of the while loop; (3) a body, whose execution is iterated a number of times; (4) (when dealing with total correctness) a variant, *i.e.* a mapping from the state space to some well-founded set, which strictly decreases every time the body is executed. To extend this to abnormal correctness, we first look at a silly example of an abruptly terminating while loop.

```
while (true) { if (i < 10) { i++; } else { break; } }
```

This loop will always terminate, and we can find some variant to show this, but after termination we can not conclude that the condition has become false. We need special proof rules, from which, in this case, we can conclude that after termination of this while loop $i < 10$ does not hold (anymore). This desire leads us to the development of special rules for partial and total abnormal correctness of while loops. Below, we will describe the partial and total break correctness rules in full detail, the rules for the other abnormalities are basically the same.

6.1 Partial Break While Rule

Suppose that we have a while loop $\mathsf{WHILE}(l_1)(C)(S)$, which is executed in a state satisfying P. We wish to prove that if the while loop terminates abruptly, because of a break, then the result state satisfies Q—where P is the loop invariant and Q is the predicate that holds upon abrupt termination (in the example above: $i \geq 10$). A natural condition for the proof rule is thus that if the body terminates abruptly, because of a break, then Q should hold. Furthermore, we have to show that P is an invariant if the body terminates normally.

$$\frac{\{P\}\,\mathsf{E2S}(C)\,;\mathsf{CATCH\text{-}CONTINUE}(l_1)(S)\,\{P\} \quad \{P\}\,\mathsf{E2S}(C)\,;\mathsf{CATCH\text{-}CONTINUE}(l_1)(S)\,\{\mathsf{break}(Q,l_2)\}}{\{P\}\,\mathsf{WHILE}(l_1)(C)(S)\,\{\mathsf{break}(Q,l_2)\}}\ \ [\text{partial-break}]$$

Thus, assume: (1) if the iteration body $\mathsf{E2S}(C)\,;\mathsf{CATCH\text{-}CONTINUE}(l_1)(S)$ is executed in a state satisfying P and terminates normally, then P still holds, and (2) if the iteration body is executed in a state satisfying P and ends in an abnormal state, because of a break, then this state satisfies some property Q. Then, if the while statement is executed in a state satisfying P and it terminates abruptly, because of a break, then its final state satisfies Q.

Soundness of this rule is easy to see (and to prove): suppose we have a state satisfying P, in which $\mathsf{WHILE}(l_1)(C)(S)$ terminates abruptly, because of a break. This means that the iterated statement $\mathsf{E2S}(C)\,;\mathsf{CATCH\text{-}CONTINUE}(l_1)(S)$ terminates normally a number of times. All these times, P remains true. However, at some stage the iterated statement must terminate abruptly, because of a break, labeled l_2, and then the resulting state satisfies Q. As this is also the final state of the whole loop, we get $\{P\}\,\mathsf{WHILE}(l_1)(C)(S)\,\{\mathsf{break}(Q,l_2)\}$.

6.2 Total Break While Rule

Next we formulate a proof rule for the total break correctness of the while statement. Suppose that we have a state satisfying $P \wedge C$ and we wish to prove that execution of $\mathsf{WHILE}(l_1)(C)(S)$ in this state terminates abruptly, because of a break, resulting in a state satisfying Q. We have to show that (1) the iteration body terminates normally only a finite number of times (using a variant), and (2) if the iteration body does not terminate normally, it must be because of a break, resulting in an abnormal state, satisfying Q. This gives:

$$[P \wedge C] \text{ E2S}(C) \text{; CATCH-BREAK}(l_2)(\text{CATCH-CONTINUE}(l_1)(S)) \text{ [true]}$$
$$\{P \wedge C \wedge \text{variant} = n\} \text{ E2S}(C) \text{; CATCH-CONTINUE}(l_1)(S) \{P \wedge C \wedge \text{variant} < n\}$$
$$\dfrac{\{P \wedge C\} \text{ E2S}(C) \text{; CATCH-CONTINUE}(l_1)(S) \{\text{break}(Q, l_2)\}}{[P \wedge C] \text{ WHILE}(l_1)(C)(S) [\text{break}(Q, l_2)]} \qquad \text{[total-break]}$$

The first condition states that execution of the iteration body followed by a CATCH-BREAK, in a state satisfying $P \wedge C$, always terminates normally, thus the iteration body itself must terminate either normally, or abruptly because of a break. The second condition expresses that if the iteration body terminates normally, the invariant and condition remain true and some variant decreases. Thus, the iteration body can only terminate normally a finite number of times. Finally, the last condition of this rule requires that when the iteration body terminates abruptly (because of a break), the resulting state satisfies Q. Soundness of this rule is easy to prove.

In [9] a comparable rule "(R9)" is presented, which is slightly more restrictive: it requires that the abnormality occurs when the variant becomes 0. In our case we require that it should occur at some unspecified stage.

7   An Example Verification of a Java Program in PVS

To demonstrate the use of Hoare logic with abrupt termination, we consider the following pattern match algorithm in Java.

```
class Pattern {
  int [] base;
  int [] pattern;
  int find_pos () {
    int p = 0, s = 0;
    while (true)
      if (p == pattern.length) return s;
      else if (s + p == base.length) return -1;
          else if (base[s + p] == pattern[p]) p++;
              else { s++; p = 0; } } }
```

This algorithm is based on a pattern match algorithm described in [25]. The it-ti construction proposed there is programmed in Java as a while loop, with a condition which always evaluates to true. The loop is exited using one of two return statements. Explicit continues, as used in [25], are not necessary, because the loop body only consists of one if statement. In [21, Chapter 5] a comparable algorithm is presented which searches the position of an element in a 2-dimensional array via two (nested) while loops. If the element is found, an exception is thrown, which is caught later. This has the same effect as a return. The algorithm is derived from a specification, via rules for exceptions.

This find_pos algorithm in itself is not particularly spectacular, but it is a typical example of a program with a while loop, in which a key property holds upon abrupt termination (caused by a return). The task of the algorithm is, given two arrays base and pattern, to determine whether pattern occurs in base, and if so, to return the starting position of the first occurrence of pattern. The algorithm checks—in a single while loop—for each position in the array base whether it is the starting point of the pattern—until the pattern is found. If the pattern is found, the while loop terminates abruptly, because of a return.

In the verification of this algorithm, we assume that both pattern and base are non-null references. In the proof our Hoare logic rules are applied, until substatements do not contain loops anymore. Then in principle everything can be rewritten automatically, and no user-interaction is required. We shall briefly discuss the invariant, variant and exit condition.

Some basic ingredients of the invariant for this while loop are:

- the value of the local variable p ranges between 0 and pattern.length;
- the value of s + p ranges between 0 and base.length, so that the local variable s is always between 0 and base.length − p;
- for every value of p, the sub-pattern pattern[0],... ,pattern[p-1] is a sub-array of base;
- for all i smaller than s, i is not a starting point for an occurence of pattern (*i.e.* pattern has not been found yet).

To prove termination of the while loop, a variant with codomain nat × nat is used, namely (base.length − s, pattern.length − p). If the loop body terminates normally, the value of this expression strictly decreases, with respect to the lexical order on nat × nat. Either s is increased by one, so that the value of base.length − s decreases by one, or s remains unchanged and p is increased by one, in which case the value of the first component remains unchanged and the value of the second component decreases.

The exit condition states that if the pattern occurs, then p = pattern.length and the value s, which is the starting point of the first occurence of pattern, will be returned, else, if the pattern does not occur, s = base.length and −1 will be returned. Being able to handle such exit conditions is a crucial feature of the Hoare logic described in this paper.

The correctness of this algorithm is shown in PVS 2.2 in two lemmas. The first lemma states that if the pattern occurs in base, its starting position will be returned, the other lemma states that if pattern does not occur, −1 will be returned. Each proof consists of approximately 250 proof commands. The crucial step in the proof is the application of the total return while rule with appropriate invariant. Rerunning the proofs takes approximately 5000 seconds on a Pentium II, 300 MHz.

8   Conclusions and Future Work

We have presented the essentials of a semantics of (Java) statements and expressions with abrupt termination and of an associated Hoare logic. This forms part of a wider project for reasoning about Java programs. The logic presented here is heavily used in a verification case study [17] focussing on a class from

Java's standard library. Future work includes extending the semantics and proof rules to the "Annotated Java" language JML [20], consisting of standard Java with correctness assertions added as comments. Ultimately, our tool [19] should translate these assertions into appropriate verification conditions.

Acknowledgements Thanks are due to Rustan Leino for his sharp comments on an earlier version of this paper and to Joachim van den Berg for helpful discussions. Hans Meijer suggested to use the algorithm used in Section 7 as example verification.

References

[1] M. Abadi and K.R.M. Leino. A logic of object-oriented programs. In M. Bidoit and M. Dauchet, editors, *TAPSOFT'97: Theory and Practice of Software Development*, volume 1214 of *LNCS*, pages 682–696. Springer-Verlag, 1997.

[2] K.R. Apt. Ten years of Hoare's logic: A survey—part I. *ACM Trans. on Progr. Lang. and Systems*, 3(4):431–483, 1981.

[3] K.R. Apt and E.-R. Olderog. *Verification of Sequential and Concurrent Programs*. Springer, 2nd rev. edition, 1997.

[4] K. Arnold and J. Gosling. *The Java Programming Language*. Addison-Wesley, 2nd edition, 1997.

[5] E.A. Ashcroft, M. Clint, and C.A.R. Hoare. Remarks on "Program proving: jumps and functions by M. Clint and C.A.R. Hoare". *Acta Informatica*, 6:317–318, 1976.

[6] J.W. de Bakker. *Mathematical Theory of Program Correctness*. Prentice Hall, 1980.

[7] J. van den Berg, M. Huisman, B. Jacobs, and E. Poll. A type-theoretic memory model for verification of sequential Java programs. Techn. Rep. CSI-R9924, Comput. Sci. Inst., Univ. of Nijmegen, 1999.

[8] F.S. de Boer. A WP-calculus for OO. In W. Thomas, editor, *Foundations of Software Science and Computation Structures*, number 1578 in LNCS, pages 135–149. Springer, Berlin, 1999.

[9] F. Christian. Correct and robust programs. *IEEE Trans. on Software Eng.*, 10(2):163–174, 1984.

[10] M. Clint and C.A.R. Hoare. Program proving: jumps and functions. *Acta Informatica*, 1:214–224, 1972.

[11] M.J.C. Gordon. *Programming Language Theory and its Implementation*. Prentice Hall, 1988.

[12] M.J.C. Gordon. Mechanizing programming logics in higher order logic. In *Current Trends in Hardware Verification and Automated Theorem Proving*. Springer-Verlag, 1989.

[13] J. Gosling, B. Joy, and G. Steele. *The Java Language Specification*. Addison-Wesley, 1996.

[14] D. Gries. *The Science of Programming*. Springer, 1981.

[15] W.O.D. Griffioen and M. Huisman. A comparison of PVS and Isabelle/HOL. In J. Grundy and M. Newey, editors, *Proceedings of the 12 International Workshop on Theorem Proving in Higher Order Logics (TPHOLs '98)*, volume 1479 of *LNCS*, September 1998.

[16] U. Hensel, M. Huisman, B. Jacobs, and H. Tews. Reasoning about classes in object-oriented languages: Logical models and tools. In *Proceedings of European Symposium on Programming (ESOP)*, volume 1381 of *LNCS*, pages 105–121. Springer-Verlag, March 1998.

[17] M. Huisman, B. Jacobs, and J. van den Berg. A case study in class library verification: Java's Vector class (abstract). In B. Jacobs, G.T. Leavens, P. Müller, and A. Poetzsch-Heffter, editors, *Formal Techniques for Java Programs*, volume 251 - 5/1999 of *Informatik berichte FernUniversität Hagen*, 1999.

[18] B. Jacobs and E. Poll. A monad for basic Java semantics. Techn. Rep. CSI-R9926, Comput. Sci. Inst., Univ. of Nijmegen, 1999.

[19] B. Jacobs, J. van den Berg, M. Huisman, M. van Berkum, U. Hensel, and H. Tews. Reasoning about classes in Java (preliminary report). In *Object-Oriented Programming, Systems, Languages and Applications (OOPSLA)*, pages 329–340. ACM Press, 1998.

[20] G.T. Leavens, A.L. Baker, and C. Ruby. Preliminary design of JML: A behavioral interface specification language for Java. Technical Report 98-06c, Iowa State University, Department of Computer Science, January 1999.

[21] K.R.M. Leino. *Toward Reliable Modular Programs*. PhD thesis, California Inst. of Techn., 1995.

[22] R. Leino and J. van de Snepscheut. Semantics of exceptions. In E.-R. Olderog, editor, *Programming Concepts, Methods and Calculi*, pages 447–466. North-Holland, 1994.

[23] S. Owre, S. Rajan, J.M. Rushby, N. Shankar, and M.K. Srivas. PVS: Combining specification, proof checking, and model checking. In R. Alur and T.A. Henzinger, editors, *Computer-Aided Verification (CAV '96)*, volume 1102 of *LNCS*, pages 411–414, New Brunswick, NJ, July/August 1996. Springer-Verlag.

[24] S. Owre, J. Rushby, N. Shankar, and F. von Henke. Formal verification for fault-tolerant architectures: Prolegomena to the design of PVS. *IEEE Transactions on Software Engineering*, 21(2):107–125, February 1995.

[25] D. Parnas. A generalized control structure and its formal definition. *Communications of the ACM*, 26(8):572–581, 1983.

[26] L.C. Paulson. *Isabelle - a generic theorem prover*, volume 828 of *LNCS*. Springer-Verlag, 1994. With contributions by Tobias Nipkow.

[27] A. Poetzsch-Heffter and P. Müller. A programming logic for sequential Java. In S.D. Swierstra, editor, *Programming Languages and Systems*, LNCS, pages 162–176. Springer, Berlin, 1999.

[28] J.C. Reynolds. *Theories of Programming Languages*. Cambridge University Press, 1998.

Foundations for Software Configuration Management Policies Using Graph Transformations*

Francesco Parisi-Presicce[1] and Alexander L. Wolf[2]

[1] Dip. Scienze dell'Informazione, Universitá degli Studi di Roma *La Sapienza*
Via Salaria 113, 00198 Roma, Italy,
`parisi@dsi.uniroma1.it`
[2] Department of Computer Science, University of Colorado at Boulder
Boulder, Colorado, USA,
`alw@cs.colorado.edu`

Abstract. Existing software configuration management systems embody a wide variety of policies for how artifacts can evolve. New policies continue to be introduced. Without a clean separation of configuration management policies from configuration management mechanisms, it is difficult to understand the policies as well as difficult to reason about how they relate. We introduce a formal foundation for specifying configuration management policies by viewing the policies in terms of graph transformation systems. Not only are we able to precisely capture the semantics of individual policies, we can, for the first time, describe formal properties of the relationship between policies.

1 Introduction

Managing the evolution of interrelated software artifacts is a central activity in software engineering. This activity is often referred to as *version control* or, more generally, as *configuration management* (CM) [13]. Among the many relationships that exist among software artifacts, three are the principal concern of CM.

- *Revision:* a relationship reflecting the history of modifications made to an artifact over time. A revision of an artifact is considered to be a *replacement* for a previous revision of that artifact.

---

* This work was performed while A.L. Wolf was a visitor at the Dip. di Scienze dell'Informazione, supported in part by the Universitá degli Studi di Roma *La Sapienza* and by the Air Force Materiel Command, Rome Laboratory, and the Defense Advanced Research Projects Agency under Contract Numbers F30602-94-C-0253 and F30602-98-2-0163. The work of F. Parisi-Presicce was partially supported by the EC under TMR Network GETGRATS (GEneral Theory of GRAph Transformation Systems) and Esprit Working Group APPLIGRAPH.

T. Maibaum (Ed.): FASE 2000, LNCS 1783, pp. 304–318, 2000.

- *Variant:* a relationship reflecting the variation in the realizations of an artifact to fit within different contexts. A variant of an artifact is considered to be an *alternative* to other variants of that artifact, where an alternative is chosen based on an environmental concern such as target operating system.
- *Configuration:* a set of artifacts considered to be complete and compatible with respect to some model of a system. A configuration is made up of one revision of one variant (i.e., a *version*) of each distinct artifact that is a component of the system.

Tools supporting the CM activity are responsible for recording the relationships among versions of artifacts in a *repository*, as well as for enforcing the *policies* by which developers are permitted to manipulate artifacts to create versions and their relationships. In effect, version relationships induce a graph, called the *version graph*, and policies determine a set of legal version graphs.

Looking at the landscape of CM tools, we can see a large number and wide variety of policies [3]. For example, SCCS [11] directly supports only revisions and not variants. Access to artifacts is controlled through a mechanism called *check-out/check-in* in which a developer must first lock an artifact before it can be modified, and then must release that lock before the changes become visible, and available, to other developers. New revisions are added successively to form a linear chain of versions for each artifact in the repository (Figure 1a). RCS [14] extends SCCS by supporting a version tree for each artifact, where variants are indicated by branches in the tree and revisions are indicated by successive versions forming a trunk or limb of the tree (Figure 1b). CVS [1] is a variant of RCS that does not support locking. Instead, CVS allows developers to concurrently make changes to private copies and then later merge them. In effect, CVS turns the RCS version tree into a more general directed acyclic graph (Figure 1c). DVS [2] is a variant of SCCS that follows the locking paradigm and supports revisions, but adds a grouping mechanism based on arbitrary sets of artifacts. The groups, called *collections*, are themselves artifacts and, therefore, are subject to locking and exhibit a recorded revision history (Figure 1d).

SCCS, RCS, CVS, and DVS represent just a small sampling of the many policies that have been invented. New ones appear regularly, some of which are quite involved. An example is a policy that embodies a "deep" semantics for the versioning of collections (e.g., the policy introduced by Lin and Reiss in their programming environment POEM [8]). A deep semantics requires that whenever a new version of an artifact is created, then new versions of any containing collections must also be created. Clearly, this is a recursive definition when collections are themselves treated as artifacts that can be contained in other collections. A simple illustration appears in Figure 2. In 2a is an empty collection. A second version of the collection contains two artifacts, an empty collection and an atomic artifact, as shown in 2b. When an artifact is added to the empty collection, this results in the creation of a new version of that collection, which in turn results in a new version of the top-level collection, as shown in 2c. Notice that the third version of the top-level collection shares the same version of the atomic artifact with the second version of the top-level collection.

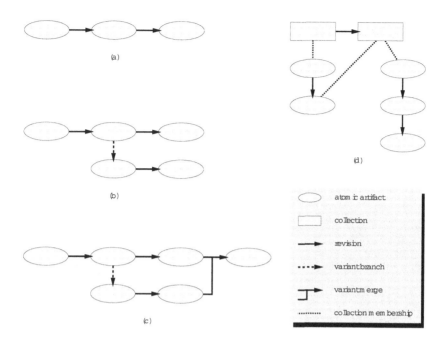

Fig. 1. Example Version Graphs.

Typically, CM policies are embedded deeply within the implementations of CM tools. As a way to make the tools more flexible, van der Hoek et al. [15] have logically separated CM policies from CM mechanisms. Their approach is to define a generic abstraction of a CM repository and to provide a programmatic interface to that repository. Specific CM policies are then realized by programming against this interface. While the approach has been successfully employed in the implementation of a wide variety of CM policies, it suffers from the fact that those policies are being captured at the low level of implementation code written in a procedural programming language. Significant leverage could be achieved if the policies could instead be defined declaratively and at a higher level of abstraction. In particular, a declarative and higher-level specification could lead to a better understanding of the policies, as well as a more appropriate basis upon which to reason about various properties of the policies.

We have begun to develop an improved method for specifying CM policies. The foundation for this method is the theory of *graph transformation systems*. Graph transformation provides an ideal perspective from which to view the problem, since the evolution of artifacts in a CM repository can be seen as a deliberate and regulated transformation of version graphs. We can use this perspective to flexibly define a CM policy in terms of either or both the allowed and the disallowed version graphs, such that the operations applied to an artifact repository are suitably constrained to follow the policy. Perhaps more importantly, we can

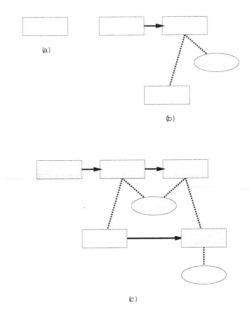

Fig. 2. An Example of "Deep" Collection Versioning.

begin to perform meaningful analyses of the relationships among the policies themselves. For instance, if we wish to institute a new policy, is the existing repository compatible with that policy? If we wish to combine the work of two development teams, each of which uses a different CM tool incorporating a different CM policy, will they conflict? If we wish to integrate two policies to form a third, what are the possible ways to do this and what are the properties of the possible policies that arise? The ability to answer these and other such questions has not previously been possible and represents a significant contribution to the field of software configuration management.

This paper introduces our approach to specifying CM policies using graph transformation systems. In the next section we briefly review the basics of graph transformation systems. Section 3 details our use of graph transformation to specify CM policies. Our ability to reason about the relationship between different CM policies is illustrated in Section 4. We conclude in Section 5 with a look at related and future work.

2   Background on Graph Transformation Systems

In this section we recall the basic definitions and properties of typed graphs and typed graph transformation systems. A *graph* $G = (N, E, src, tar)$ is given by a set N of nodes, a set E of edges and functions $src, tar : E \rightarrow N$ that assign source and target nodes to edges. A *graph morphism* $f = (f_N, f_E) : G \rightarrow G'$ is given by functions $f_N : N \rightarrow N'$ and $f_E : E \rightarrow E'$ such that $src' \circ f_E = f_N \circ src$ and $tar' \circ f_E = f_N \circ tar$. With identities and composition being defined componentwise, this defines the category **Graph**. To structure graphs [4, 5, 6], let $TG \in$ **Graph** be a fixed graph, called *typed graph*. A *TG-typed graph* (G, t_G) is given by a graph G and a graph morphism $t_G : G \rightarrow TG$. A *(type-preserving) morphism of TG-typed graphs* $f : (G, t_G) \rightarrow (G', t_{G'})$ is a graph morphism $f : G \rightarrow G'$ that satisfies $t_{G'} \circ f = t_G$. With composition and identities this yields the category **Graph**$_{TG}$. Note that **Graph**$_{TG}$ is the comma category **Graph** over TG, thus it is complete and cocomplete.

While the type graph TG can be used to classify the components of a graph, *labels* are needed to distinguish elements of the same type. If $C = (C_N, C_E)$ is a pair of disjoint, possibly infinite, sets, a *C-labelled graph* is a graph G as above along with two labelling functions $c_N : N \rightarrow C_N$ and $c_E : E \rightarrow C_E$. For simplicity, the adjective "labelled" will be omitted in the rest of the paper.

Definition 1 (Retyping Functors). *Any graph morphism $f : TG \rightarrow TG'$ induces a* backward retyping functor $f^< :$ **Graph**$_{TG'} \rightarrow$ **Graph**$_{TG}$, *defined by $f^<((G', t_{G'})) = (G^*, t_{G^*})$ and $f^<(k' : (G', t_{G'}) \rightarrow (H', t_{H'})) = k^* : (G^*, t_{G^*}) \rightarrow (H^*, t_{H^*})$ by pullbacks and mediating morphisms as in the following diagram,*

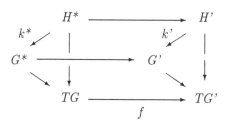

and a forward retyping functor $f^> :$ **Graph**$_{TG} \rightarrow$ **Graph**$_{TG'}$, *given by $f^>((G, t_G)) = (G, f \circ t_G)$ and $f^>(k : (G, t_G) \rightarrow (H, t_H)) = k$ by composition.*

As shown in [5], backward and forward retyping functors are left and right adjoints.

In general, the algebraic approaches to graph transformations (see [12] for a complete treatment) are based on the concept of gluing of graphs, modeled by pushouts in suitable categories: in the Double Pushout (DPO) approach a derivation step is based on a two pushout construction in the category **Graph**$_{TG}$ of (labeled, typed) graphs and graph morphisms while, in the SPO approach, it is defined by a single pushout in the category **Graph**$^P_{TG}$ of (labeled) graphs and partial morphisms. Our approach is based on double pushouts, although the specific example investigated use particular kinds of rules that do not erase and thus can be thought of as rules in either approach.

A *TG-typed graph rule* is a span $((L, t_L) \xleftarrow{l} (K, t_K) \xrightarrow{r} (R, t_R))$ where (L, t_L), (K, t_K), (R, t_R) are typed over the same type graph TG and l, r are TG-typed graph morphisms. The left graph (L, t_L) is matched to the actual graph when the rule is applied and the right graph (R, t_R) is substituted to the occurrence of (L, t_L). The span expresses which items of (L, t_L) are related to which items of (R, t_R), and the interface graph (K, t_K) contains the items preserved by the rule application.

TG-typed rules and TG-typed rule morphisms (as triples $f = (f_L, f_K, f_R)$ of TG-typed graph morphisms compatible with the spans) define, with the componentwise identities and composition, the category $\mathbf{Rule}_{TG}$ as the comma category $\mathbf{Rule}$ over TG. Since $\mathbf{Rule}$ is complete and cocomplete, so is $\mathbf{Rule}_{TG}$.

Definition 2 (Typed Graph Transformation System Specification).
A typed graph transformation system specification (tgts-specification) $\mathbf{G} = (TG, P, \pi)$ *consists of a type graph* TG, *a set of rule names* P *and a mapping* $\pi : P \to | \mathbf{Rule}_{TG} |$, *associating with each rule name a TG-typed rule.*

Definition 3 (Morphisms of Typed Graph Transformation Systems).
A morphism of tgts-specifications (tgts-morphism), $f = (f_{TG}, f_P) : \mathbf{G} \to \mathbf{G}'$ *from* $\mathbf{G} = (TG, P, \pi)$ *to* $\mathbf{G}' = (TG', P', \pi')$ *is given by an injective type graph morphism* $f_{TG} : TG \to TG'$ *and a mapping* $f_P : P \to P'$ *between the sets of rule names, such that* $f_{TG}^{>}(\pi(p)) = \pi'(f_P(p))$ *for all* $p \in P$.

As shown in [5], tgts-specifications and morphisms form a category, called **TGTS** closed under colimits.

Notation If G and G' have the same type, $G \cap G'$ denotes the tgts G'' where the range of π'' is $\pi(P) \cap \pi'(P')$ regardless of the set P'' of names chosen (G'' is well defined up to isomorphism)

Given a tgts-specification $\mathbf{G} = (TG, P, \pi)$, a *direct derivation* $p/m :$ $(G, t_G) \Rightarrow (H, t_H)$ over $\mathbf{G}$ from a graph (G, t_G) via a rule p and a matching morphism $m : (L, t_L) \to (G, t_G)$ is given by the following double pushout diagram

$$
\begin{array}{ccccc}
(L, t_L) & \xleftarrow{\ l\ } & (K, t_K) & \xrightarrow{\ r\ } & (R, t_R) \\
\downarrow{\scriptstyle m} & & \downarrow{\scriptstyle k} & & \downarrow{\scriptstyle h} \\
(G, t_G) & \xleftarrow{\ l'\ } & (D, t_D) & \xrightarrow{\ r'\ } & (H, t_H)
\end{array}
$$

in $\mathbf{Graph}_{TG}$, where $\pi(p) = ((L, t_L) \xleftarrow{l} (K, t_K) \xrightarrow{r} (R, t_R))$. (G, t_G) is called the *input*, and (H, t_H) the *output* of $p/m : (G, t_G) \Rightarrow (H, t_H)$. A *derivation* $p_1/m_1, \dots, p_n/m_n : (G, t_G) \Rightarrow (H, t_H)$ over $\mathbf{G}$ from a graph (G, t_G) via rules $p_1, \dots, p_n$ and matching morphisms $m_1, \dots, m_n$ is a sequence of direct derivations over $\mathbf{G}$, such that the output of the i'th direct derivation is the input of the $(i + 1)$'st direct derivation. The set of all derivations over $\mathbf{G}$ is denoted $Der(\mathbf{G})$ and, considering $Der(\mathbf{G})$ as the behavior of $\mathbf{G}$, the following property [5] holds:

Proposition 1 (Preservation of Behavior). *Let* $f = (f_{TG}, f_P) :$ $\mathbf{G} \to \mathbf{G}'$ *be a tgts-morphism. For each derivation* $d : (G, t_G) \Rightarrow$

(H, t_H) with $d = (p_1/m_1; \ldots; p_n/m_n)$ in $Der(\mathbf{G})$ there is a derivation $f(d) : f_{TG}^>(G, t_G) \Rightarrow f_{TG}^>(H, t_H)$ in $Der(\mathbf{G'})$, where $f(d) = (f_P(p_1)/f_{TG}^>(m_1); \ldots; f_P(p_n)/f_{TG}^>(m_n))$. Moreover, $f_{TG}^<(f(d) : f_{TG}^>(G, t_G) \Rightarrow f_{TG}^>(H, t_H)) = (d : (G, t_G) \Rightarrow (H, t_H))$.

In other words, any graph generated in $\mathbf{G}$ can be generated in $\mathbf{G'}$ after appropriate translation via the type morphism.

The formalism presented so far is not sufficient to model the rules in the example of Fig. 2 in the preceding section. What is needed is to add to the rules some *context* conditions which prevent the application of a rule even in the presence of a match m.

Definition 4 (Application Conditions).

- *An* application condition *for a match* $m : L \to G$ *is a total graph morphism* $c_i : L \to L_i$.
- *A* positive *application condition* c_i *is satisfied by* m *if there exists a (total) graph morphism* $n : L_i \to G$ *such that* $n \circ c_i = m$.
- *A* negative *application condition* c_i *is satisfied by* m *if there is* **no** *(total) graph morphism* $n : L_i \to G$ *such that* $n \circ c_i = m$.
- *A conditional rule is a rule* p *with a set of application conditions Cond and a derivation* $p/m : (G, t_G) \Rightarrow (H, t_H)$ *takes place only if the match* m *satisfies every condition in Cond.*

Notation In the remainder of the paper, the pushout object of two morphisms $a \to b$ and $a \to c$ in a cocomplete category is denoted by $b +_a c$. Similarly, in a complete category, the pullback object of the morphisms $b \to d$ and $c \to d$ is denoted by $b \times_d c$.

3   Formalization of CM Policies

Informally a policy for a software configuration manager describes (among other things) how and when an artifact can be *checked out* for a possible modification; how and who can *check in* an artifact after a possible modifications; how to introduce new versions.

Furthermore, a policy specifies which kinds of structures are forbidden and should never be constructed (an example is a cycle of version dependencies) when introducing new versions. Finally, a policy should keep track of the *current* environment and be able to specify which developers can access which parts of the systems, each with the allowed set of rules to modify the repository model.

We are not addressing here the problem of describing and integrating different environments, which will be tackled in a subsequent paper. The objective is to give a formal framework to describe wanted and unwanted structures.

Definition 5 (Policy). *A policy* A *is a triple* (T, Pos, Neg) *where*

- $T = (C, TG)$ *is the type of the policy consisting of a set* C *of labels and a type graph* TG

– *Pos is a (C, TG)-graph transformation system*
– *Neg is a set of (C, TG)-graphs and (C, TG)-graph morphisms*

The three components are denoted by $T(A)$, $Pos(A)$ and $Neg(A)$, respectively and $GPos(A)$ denotes the set of graphs generated by $Pos(A)$ (starting from the empty graph).

Interpretation The first component describes the "type" of the policy, with the type graph TG indicating what kind of entitiess it deals with (for example, artifacts can only be subject to revisions or the 'receiving' end of a membership relation can only be a collection) and the labels in C denoting, for example, the numbering to be used for revisions or for variants. The second component $Pos(A)$ describes intentionally the graphs that the policy intends to generate by giving the rules to do so. The third component describes the unwanted structures in an extensional way. Any graph $H \in Neg(A)$ indicates that no graph containing H (via a morphism) can be accepted. Any morphism $N \to E$ contained in $Neg(A)$ indicates that no graph containing N can be accepted unless it contains also E. Formally, a graph G is acceptable by H if there is no morphism $H \to G$ and a graph G is acceptable by $N \to E$ if any injective morphism $N \to G$ can be extended to a morphism $E \to G$ such that $N \to E \to G = N \to G$. In general, a set of graphs $\mathbf{G}$ is acceptable by $Neg(A)$ if any $G \in \mathbf{G}$ is acceptable by every $N \to E \in Neg(A)$.

Example 1. The definitions are illustrated with a formalization of the policy *REV* that allows the explicit revision of artifacts. Since the policy does not delete any item, the rules have $L = K$ and thus only $K \to R$ is shown. The policy is over the type graph T_R

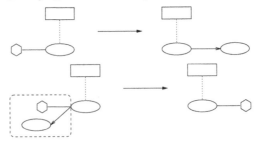

where the rectangle represents a collection that contains the connected artifact, the hexagon is a tag indicating that the connected artifact is checked-out and the loop on the ellipsis that the artifact can have a revision. $Pos(REV)$ contains one rule that allows a checked-out artifact to be checked-in and declared a revision of the previously checked-out artifact, and one rule that allows the checking-out of an artifact provided that it has not been checked-out already and does not have a revision (for the rule to be applicable, the matching morphism cannot be extendable to the part [negative condition] enclosed in the dashed rectangle).

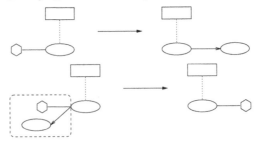

Pos(REV) also contains the three rules needed to implement the "deep" collection versioning (not included for lack of space), a rule to add a new artifact to an existing collection and a rule with empty left hand side to introduce one node representing a new collection.

(The user determines which of the two rules is "current".)

Neg(REV) contains only two graphs: one stating that no artifact can be a revision of itself and the other that an artifact can have only one revision.

Definition 6. *A policy A is* coherent *if GPos(A) satisfies Neg(A), i.e., if its rules cannot generate a graph containing an unwanted graph.*

A coherent policy A is closed *if any graph not in GPos(A) is rejected by Neg(A), i.e., if the positive and negative parts of A describe all the graphs over* $T(A) = (C, TG)$

Example 2. (cont.)

It is not difficult to check that the policy *REV* given above is a coherent policy since the second rule controls (at check-out time) that an artifact is not already revisioned and can be checked-out, while the only way to introduce a revision is by the first rule and only for checked-out artifacts.

In order to compare policies, it is helpful to view any $H \in Neg(A)$ as the identity morphism $H \rightarrow H$ (**NOT** to be interpreted as a morphism $N \rightarrow E$ in *Neg(A)* !) . This allows us to treat *Neg(A)* as a tgts with rules $(H \leftarrow H \rightarrow H)$ and $(N \leftarrow N \rightarrow E)$ and thus to use tgts-morphisms. Policies can be compared by comparing their two significant components *Pos* and *Neg*. Consider for example a pessimistic policy *PES* which prescribes that only the last version of an artifact can be further versioned and an optimistic policy *OPT* which allows any version, and not only the last one, to be versioned again. The pessimistic policy generates only graphs that are acceptable by the optimistic policy, while the converse need not be true, i.e., $GPos(PES) \subseteq GPos(OPT)$. Furthermore, any graph rejected by *OPT* is also rejected by *PES* which deals with a particular version (the last one) among those dealt with by *OPT*. This situation can be formalized by the notion of subsumption

Definition 7 (Subsumption). *A policy A* subsumes *a policy B of the same type* (C, TG) *if* $GPos(B) \subseteq GPos(A)$ *and* $Neg(A) \subseteq Neg(B)$.

The idea can be generalized by a morphism between policies

Definition 8 (Policy Morphism). *A policy morphism* $f : A \rightarrow B$ *between policies A and B is a triple* (f_T, f_P, f_N) *where*

- $f_T = (f_C, f_{TG}) : (C_A, TG_A) \rightarrow (C_B, TG_B)$ *is a pair consisting of a total function and a total (untyped) graph morphism*

- $f_P : Pos(A) \rightarrow Pos(B)$ and $f_N : Neg(B) \rightarrow Neg(A)$ are tgts-morphisms as in Def.3 with respect to the type morphism f_T.

Remark 1. A tgts-morphism f_N indicates that policy A rejects at least all the graphs that policy B rejects (up to retyping) and possibly more. A tgts-morphism f_P indicates that, up to the retyping induced by f_T, policy B has all the rules of policy A and thus can generate all the graphs generated by A (Prop.1). Hence if the types of A and B are the same and there is at least one policy morphism $A \rightarrow B$, then B subsumes A. The converse is in general not true because f_P relates the **rules** of the two policies: there may not be any tgts-morphism $f_P :$ $Pos(A) \rightarrow Pos(B)$ and yet $GPos(A) \subseteq GPos(B)$.

Policy morphisms can easily be composed componentwise: each component is the composition of functions (f_C), of graph morphisms (f_{TG}) or of tgts-morphisms $(f_P$ and $f_N)$ which is associative with the usual identities. Working componentwise, we can prove the following result

Theorem 1. *The category POLICY of policies and policy morphisms is closed under finite colimits*

Intuitively, the pushout of two policy morphisms $A_0 \rightarrow A_1$ and $A_0 \rightarrow A_2$ constructs a new policy $A_1 +_{A_0} A_2$ by taking the pushout of the positive rules and the pullback of the negative graphs and morphisms. The policy so constructed need not be coherent even if the policies A_i are coherent. We address this problem at the end of the next section with Theorem3.

4   Relationships Between Policies

In this section we investigate ways of combining policies to obtain other policies. Unless otherwise specified, we consider policies of the same type $T = (C, TG)$. This assumption is harmless and simplifies the treatment (any graph of type $T_0 = (C_0, TG_0)$ can be considered of type $T_1 = (C_1, TG_1)$ provided that there exists a morphism $f_T : (C_0, TG_0) \rightarrow (C_1, TG_1)$) by allowing "set-theoretic" manipulations of policies.

There are (at least) three different ways of combining the negative parts $Neg(A)$ and $Neg(B)$ to obtain the negative part of their combination. The resulting policy rejects a graph G if it contains

- a subgraph forbidden by either A or B
- a subgraph forbidden by A and one forbidden by B
- a subgraph forbidden by both A and B

More formally

Definition 9 (Negative Strategies). *For sets of morphisms $Neg(A)$ and $Neg(B)$, define*

- $CA(Neg(A), Neg(B)) = Neg(A) \cup Neg(B)$
- $CD(Neg(A), Neg(B)) = \{N_A + N_B \rightarrow E_A + E_B : N_A \rightarrow E_A \in Neg(A), N_B \rightarrow E_B \in Neg(B)\} \cup \{H_A + H_B : H_A \in Neg(A), H_B \in Neg(B)\}$
- $DA(Neg(A), Neg(B)) = Neg(A) \cap Neg(B)$

Interpretation A graph is rejected by $CA(Neg(A), Neg(B))$ if it is rejected by policy A or by policy B or by both: it is a CAutious strategy rejecting a graph even if one of the policies could accept it. A graph is rejected by $DA(Neg(A), Neg(B))$ if it is rejected by both policies for the same reason: it is a DAring strategy rejecting a graph only if there is no choice. A graph is rejected by $CD(Neg(A), Neg(B))$ if it is rejected by both policies for possibly different reasons.

Analogous to the negative part, there are (at least) three different ways of combining the generative parts $Pos(A)$ and $Pos(B)$ to obtain the positive part of the combination of the policies A and B.

Definition 10 (Positive Strategies). *Given graph transformation systems* $Pos(A)$ *and* $Pos(B)$, *define*

- $CA(Pos(A), Pos(B)) = Pos(A) \cap Pos(B)$
- $CD(Pos(A), Pos(B)) = \{p_A + p_B : p_A \in Pos(A), p_B \in Pos(B)\}$
- $DA(Pos(A), Pos(B)) = Pos(A) \cup Pos(B)$

Interpretation The graphs generated by $CA(Pos(A), Pos(B))$ are (some of) the graphs generated by both $Pos(A)$ and $Pos(B)$: a CAutious strategy. The graphs generated by $DA(Pos(A), Pos(B))$ includes all the graphs in $GPos(A) \cup GPos(B)$ along with the graphs obtained by the "interaction" of the rules of the two sets: a DAring strategy. The graphs generated by $CD(Pos(A), Pos(B))$ are those obtained by taking the disjoint union of one graph generated by $Pos(A)$ and one by $Pos(B)$.

Policies can be combined by selecting one strategy for the generative part and one for the rejecting part.

Definition 11. *Given policies* A *and* B, *the combination of* A *and* B *with strategies* X *and* Y *is denoted by* $[X, Y](A, B)$ *and is the policy* C *where*
$Pos(C) = X(Pos(A), Pos(B))$ *and*
$Neg(C) = Y(Neg(A), Neg(B))$
for $X, Y \in \{DA, CD, CA\}$

The first result on combining policies is a straightforward application of the definitions

Proposition 2. *If* A *and* B *are policies such that there exists a policy morphism from* A *to* B, *then*

1. $[DA, DA](A, B) = B$
2. $[CA, CA](A, B) = A$

The main problem in combining policies is to predict the behavior of the resulting policy. In particular, the two policies to be combined could "interfere" with each other where one of the two generates a graph which is rejected by the other policy. Which of the different ways of combining two coherent policies generates again a coherent policy ? The remaining part of this section is devoted to giving partial answers to this question. One special case is already treated in the previous Proposition. The two **extreme** ways of combining policies use DAring strategies for both components generating more graphs than the two policies generate individually and rejecting only when both policies agree, and CAutious strategies for both components generating a "small" set of graphs and rejecting a graph when just one of the policies rejects it.

Proposition 3.   1. If A and B are coherent, then $C = [CA, CA](A, B)$ is coherent
   2. There exist coherent policies A and B such that $D = [DA, DA](A, B)$ is not coherent.

Proof. (Sketch)(1) Since $GPos(C) \subseteq GPos(A) \cap GPos(B)$ and $Neg(C) = Neg(A) \cup Neg(B)$, if $G \in Neg(C)$ is a subgraph of $H \in GPos(C)$, then it is a graph generated by both A and B contradicting the coherence of A if $G \in Neg(A)$ or the coherence of B if $G \in Neg(B)$.
(2) Consider in fact a type graph for both policies consisting of 2 isolated nodes (call them **a** and **b**). Policy A (resp. B) has only one rule generating from the empty graph one with a single node of type **a** (resp. **b**). Both policies reject all the graphs that contain a node of type **b** and a node of type **a**. The two policies are obviously coherent but $Pos(D)$ contains a graph with one node of type **a** and one node of type **b** and thus rejected by definition of $Neg(D)$.

The next few results try to narrow the gap between these two extremes.

Proposition 4. If A and B are coherent, then $[CA, X](A, B)$ is coherent for any $X \in \{CA, CD, DA\}$

Proposition 5. (a) For any $X \in \{CA, CD, DA\}$, if $[X, CA](A, B)$ is coherent, then so are $[X, CD](A, B)$ and $[X, DA](A, B)$
(b) There exist coherent policies A, B, P, and Q such that $[CD, DA](P, Q)$ and $[CD, CD](A, B)$ are not coherent.

The crucial case is when the largest number of graphs is generated while allowing either policy to reject a graph.

Theorem 2. If $[DA, CA](A, B)$ is coherent, then $[X, Y](A, B)$ is coherent for any $X, Y \in \{CA, CD, DA\}$

Example 3. (cont.)
   Consider the policy VAR over the same type graph $T_V = T_R$ used for the policy REV but where the loop on the artifact node indicates a variant of an

artifact. $Pos(VAR)$ contains one rule that allows a checked-out artifact to be checked-in and declared a variant of the previously checked-out artifact, and one rule that allows the checking-out of an artifact provided that it has not been checked-out already.

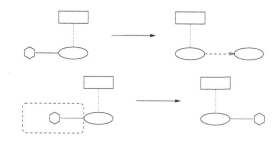

(Again the user selects the "current" rule)

$Pos(VAR)$ also contains rules to add a new collection and to add a new artifact within an existing collection.

$Neg(VAR)$ contains only two graphs: one stating that no artifact can be a variant of itself, and the other one that no more than two variants can be merged at a time.

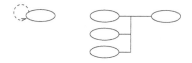

Again it is easy to check that VAR is a coherent policy.

The two policies REV and VAR can be thought of the same type, namely T_R with **two** distinct loops, one denoting revision and one denoting variant.

CLAIM The policy $M = [DA, CA](REV, VAR)$ is coherent.

In fact, the interaction of the rules of REV and VAR cannot generate the forbidden graphs since, for example, REV is coherent and the rules in $Pos(VAR)$ cannot generate "variant" arcs. In other words, there are **no** forbidden graphs over the "common" type consisting of the graph T_R without the loop.

The idea behind this example can be generalized. To determine whether the most "dangerous" combination $[DA, CA]$ of coherent policies is coherent, it is sufficient to check only the forbidden graphs of either policy which are of the common type.

Theorem 3. *Let A and B be coherent policies over types T_A and T_B, respectively, and $f_A : T \to T_A$, $f_B : T \to T_B$ type morphisms with $f : T \to T_A +_T T_B$. Denote by $A*$ and $B*$ the policies A and B, respectively, viewed over the type $T_A +_T T_B$. The policy $[DA, CA](A*, B*)$ is coherent if and only if the policy $(DA(A*, B*), NEG)$ is coherent, where*
$NEG = \{n \in Neg(A*) \cup Neg(B*) : f^>(f^<(n)) = n\}.$

Notice that $[DA, CA](A*, B*)$ corresponds to the pushout object (in POL-ICY) with respect to the empty set of shared policy rules (cf. Theorem 1).

We close this section with a simple result involving closed policies.

Definition 12. *Policies A and B over the same type are equivalent if* $GPos(A) = GPos(B)$ *and* $Neg(A) = Neg(B)$.

Proposition 6. *Policies A and B are equivalent if and only if A subsumes B and B subsumes A.*

Theorem 4. *Given closed policies A and B, $[DA, CA](A, B)$ is coherent if and only if A and B are equivalent*

5   Conclusion

The use of graph transformation systems to model various aspects of software engineering is well established. In the particular area of configuration management, three efforts stand out as representative of related work.

- Heimbigner and Krane [7] use graph transformation systems to model the software build process, which is an orthogonal activity to versioning within the general area of configuration management. The build process describes how tools (e.g., compilers and linkers) should be applied to artifacts (e.g., source files) to derive other artifacts (e.g., object and executable files).
- Westfechtel [16] has developed a graph transformation framework for describing the structure of documents and a particular policy for how document structures should evolve.
- Mens [9] uses labelled typed graphs to represent reusable software components and conditional graph rewriting for describing a particular policy by which those components should evolve.

Our work contrasts with these and related efforts in that it is more generally applied to multiple policies, and to understanding the relationships among those policies.

The choices of DA, CA and CD to construct new policies are just "policies" themselves on policy building : under investigation are more general ways of putting policies together. Also under study are the possible ways of converting a non-coherent policy into a coherent one by modifying either Neg (easy) or Pos (not as easy) or both. Such modifications could be modelled within the rule–base framework itself ([10]).

Our future work is aimed at modeling the full spectrum of existing CM policies and finding further critical properties that relate them to each other. Going further, we plan to design and build a tool to take as input policies specified as graph transformation systems and produce as output policy enforcement code in a procedural programming language. As a first target, we will generate policies implemented as calls to the library functions of the NUCM configuration management repository [15].

References

[1] B. Berliner. CVS II: Parallelizing Software Development. In *Proceedings of 1990 Winter USENIX Conference*, pages 341–352. USENIX Association, January 1990.

[2] A. Carzaniga. *Distributed Versioning System Manual, Version 1.2*. Department of Computer Science, University of Colorado, Boulder, Colorado, June 1998.

[3] R. Conradi and B. Westfechtel. Version Models for Software Configuration Management. *ACM Computing Surveys*, 30(2):232–282, June 1998.

[4] A. Corradini and R. Heckel. A compositional approach to structuring and refinement of typed graph grammars. In *Proc. SEGRAGRA'95 (Graph Rewriting and Computation)*, volume 2 of *ENTCS*, pages 167–176. Elsevier, 1995.

[5] M. Große–Rhode, F. Parisi Presicce, and M. Simeoni. Spatial and temporal refinement of typed graph transformation systems. In *Proc. MFCS'98 (Mathematical Foundations of computer Science)*, volume 1450 of *Lecture Notes in Computer Science*, pages 553–561, 1998.

[6] M. Große–Rhode, F. Parisi Presicce, and M. Simeoni. Refinements of graph transformation systems via rule expressions. In *Proc. Sixth Intl. Workshop on Theory and Application of Graph Transformations (TAGT'98)*, Lecture Notes in Computer Science, 1999. To appear.

[7] D. Heimbigner and S. Krane. A Graph Transformation Model for Configuration Management Environments. In *SIGSOFT '88: Proceedings of the Third Symposium on Software Development Environments*, pages 216–225. ACM SIGSOFT, November 1988.

[8] Y.-J. Lin and S.P. Reiss. Configuration Management with Logical Structures. In *Proceedings of the 18th International Conference on Software Engineering*, pages 298–307. Association for Computer Machinery, March 1996.

[9] T. Mens. Conditional Graph Rewriting as an Underlying Formalism for Software Evolution. In *Proceedings of the International Symposium on Applications of Graph Transformation with Industrial Relevance*, Lecture Notes in Computer Science. Springer-Verlag, 1999. To appear.

[10] F. Parisi Presicce. Transformations of graph grammars. In *Proc. 5th Int. Workshop on Graph Grammars*, volume 1073 of *Lecture Notes in Computer Science*, pages 426–442, 1996.

[11] M.J. Rochkind. The Source Code Control System. *IEEE Transactions on Software Engineering*, SE–1(4):364–370, December 1975.

[12] G. Rozenberg, editor. *Handbook of Graph Grammars and Computing by Graph Transformation*, volume 1. World Scientific, New Jersey, 1997.

[13] W. Tichy. Tools for Configuration Management. In *Proceedings of the International Workshop on Software Versioning and Configuration Control*, pages 1–20, January 1988.

[14] W.F. Tichy. RCS, A System for Version Control. *Software—Practice and Experience*, 15(7):637–654, July 1985.

[15] A. van der Hoek, A. Carzaniga, D.M. Heimbigner, and A.L. Wolf. A Reusable, Distributed Repository for Configuration Management Policy Programming. Technical Report CU–CS–849–98, Department of Computer Science, University of Colorado, Boulder, Colorado, September 1998.

[16] B. Westfechtel. A Graph-Based System for Managing Configurations of Engineering Design Documents. *International Journal of Software Engineering and Knowledge Engineering*, 6(4):549–583, December 1996.

Analyzing Non-functional Properties of Mobile Agents

Pascal Fradet, Valérie Issarny, and Siegfried Rouvrais

IRISA/INRIA, Campus Universitaire de Beaulieu, 35042 Rennes, France
{fradet,issarny,rouvrais}@irisa.fr

Abstract. The mobile agent technology is emerging as a useful new way of building large distributed systems. The advantages of mobile agents over the traditional client-server model are mainly non-functional. We believe that one of the reasons preventing the wide-spread use of mobile agents is that non-functional properties are not easily grasped by system designers. Selecting the right interactions to implement complex services is therefore a tricky task. In this paper, we tackle this problem by considering efficiency and security criteria. We propose a language-based framework for the specification and implementation of complex services built from interactions with primitive services. Mobile agents, RPC, remote evaluation, or any combination of these forms of interaction can be expressed in this framework. We show how to analyze (i.e. assess and compare) complex service implementations with respect to efficiency and security properties. This analysis provides guidelines to service designers, enabling them to systematically select and combine different types of protocols for the effective realization of interactions with primitive services.

1 Introduction

Code mobility is gaining more acceptance as a useful and hopefully future technology [1]. In particular, the mobile agent technology is emerging as a new way of building large distributed systems. Here, we consider a mobile agent as an entity in which code, data and execution state can explicitly migrate from host to host in heterogeneous networks [3]. Other types of interaction exist; let us cite remote evaluation or the classical RPC-based client-server[1] (i.e. remote procedure calls). Functionally, all that can be implemented using mobile agents can also be achieved by using RPC communication protocols. The advantages/drawbacks of mobile agents compared to RPC are mainly non-functional [9]. The motto being to move the computation to the data rather than the data to the computation, mobile agents can improve performances by reducing the bandwidth usage. On the other hand, they pose new security problems, namely how to protect agents against malicious hosts (or *vice versa*).

---

[1] In our context, we consider them both as degenerate forms of mobile agents. Remote evaluations execute remotely the code on a single server. A RPC amounts to sending a request (not a code) to a primitive service.

T. Maibaum (Ed.): FASE 2000, LNCS 1783, pp. 319–333, 2000.

In this paper, we are specifically concerned with the use of mobile agents for the construction of complex services. By complex services we mean client requests built from primitive services available over networks composed of various devices ranging from powerful workstations to PDAs. Clearly, there is not a single best interaction protocol to combine such a variety of primitive services. The goal of this paper is to guide the choice of the adequate protocols (mobile agent, remote evaluation, RPC or a mixture) depending on the efficiency and security properties that the complex service requires. There have been experiments comparing performance of those different forms of interaction, but to the best of our knowledge, the formal assessment of non-functional properties of mobile computation has not been addressed so far. Yet, the need for formalization is obvious when dealing with security properties. On the other hand, mobility complicates seriously the specification and analysis of non-functional properties. Thus, we decided to restrict ourselves to a simple language of services but to tackle the analysis and comparisons of interaction protocols using a formal approach.

We specify complex services as simple expressions where primitive services and treatments are represented as basic functions. These expressions are mainly used to specify dependencies. The specification also includes information about the place (host), and non-functional properties of basic services. The abstract expressions are refined into concrete expressions, which make implementation choices (number of agents and their route) syntactically explicit. Mobile agents, RPC, remote evaluation or any combination of these forms of interactions can be represented, analyzed, and compared with respect to performance and security properties. The notion of performance considered in this paper is the total size of data exchanged in the interactions, whilst the notion of security focused on is confidentiality. The proposed framework enables designers to analyze (i.e assess and compare) various implementations of a complex service and to select the one that suits best their overall design goals. In addition, our framework can conveniently be integrated in a design environment supporting the abstract description of service software architectures, which further eases the actual implementation of services.

This paper is structured as follows. Section 2 introduces the basic setting of our abstract model of interactions using two simple functional languages. It further shows how to automatically refine expressions from one language (the specification) to the other (the implementation). Section 3 addresses the analysis of the implementations of complex services with respect to efficiency and security. Section 4 briefly discusses the practical application of our model through its combination with the architectural description of service architectures. Section 5 reviews related work and concludes.

2   Functional Models of Interactions

We describe complex services (i.e. client requests) as functional expressions where primitive functions represent services (i.e. basic services offered by providers) or treatments (i.e. basic actions defined by clients). Such complex services can be specified at two levels of abstraction. At the *abstract level*, a client request is a simple (abstraction-less, recursive-less) functional expression. This expression specifies the functional semantics of the request and makes the dependencies between basic services clear. At the *concrete level*, expressions can be seen as a collection of remote evaluation, mobile agent or RPC interactions. Compared to abstract expressions, implementations choices such as the number, the type, the path (or route) and the composition of interactions are now explicit. The benefit of concrete expressions is that they can be easily analyzed with respect to non-functional properties such as efficiency or security. A way to assess implementation choices is to compile the abstract client request into concrete expressions which can be analyzed and compared.

In this section, we present in turn the abstract language, the concrete language, and their relationship.

2.1 Abstract Language

The abstract language used to specify complex services is given in Figure 1. A service is either a tuple of independent expressions, a primitive function applied to an expression, or a data. *Service* and *Treatment* denote respectively the set of primitive services and the set of client actions. *Data* denotes the data provided by clients with their requests; it could be seen as the 0-ary treatment functions. The semantics of such expressions is straightforward and relative to an environment (e) associating a meaning to each primitive functions and data identifiers (see Figure 2).

$$E \ ::= \ (E, ..., E) \ \big| \ fE \ \big| \ d$$

where $f \in Primitive = Service \cup Treatment$ and $d \in Data$

Fig. 1. Abstract language

$$
\begin{aligned}
\mathcal{E}_a \ &: \ Exp_a \ \rightarrow \ Env \ \rightarrow \ Value \\
\mathcal{E}_a[\![(E_1, \ldots, E_n)]\!] \ e \ &= \ (\mathcal{E}_a[\![E_1]\!] \ e, \ldots, \mathcal{E}_a[\![E_n]\!] \ e) \\
\mathcal{E}_a[\![f \ E]\!] \ e \ &= \ (e \ f) \ (\mathcal{E}_a[\![E]\!] \ e) \\
\mathcal{E}_a[\![d]\!] \ e \ &= \ e \ d
\end{aligned}
$$

Fig. 2. Semantics of abstract expressions

Examples. Let us take two examples of abstract expressions that will be considered throughout the paper. One of the simplest example is requesting a basic service s on a data d, and applying a treatment t on the result. This is specified as:

$$t(s\ d) \tag{1}$$

An instance of this kind of service is taken in [8] to illustrate the benefit of mobile agents compared to RPC interactions. In their weather forecast example, the services are requests to a picture database. The data d specifies a picture, the service s (actually the database) returns the picture matching the specification d, and t is an image processing treatment (e.g. a filter). If t decreases drastically the size of the image then it is clearly more bandwidth efficient to implement the service as a mobile agent. The treatment t is then executed on the server and only the much smaller image is sent back to the client.

As a more complex example, consider the following expression:

$$t(s_1(d_1, s_2\ d_2), t_3(s_3\ d_3)) \tag{2}$$

Such an expression may represent a service to book plane and train tickets depending on various criteria: for example, the sub-expression $t_3(s_3\ d_3)$ is a request (d_3) to a train company service (s_3) returning schedules that are then filtered (by t_3) to retain only daily trains going to the airport; independently, the service s_2 returns a list of possible destinations according to the criteria d_2 (e.g. hotel descriptions); the service s_1 takes a list of possible dates (d_1) and a list of destinations $(s_2\ d_2)$ and returns a list of flights; then, the final treatment t matches selected flights and trains.

□

Abstract expressions specify the functionality of complex services as well as dependencies between base services and treatments. For the latter example, the base service s_2 must be accessed before s_1, whereas s_3 can be accessed independently. Even if abstract expressions are particularly simple, they are sufficient to model many realistic complex services and to pose interesting challenges.

2.2   Concrete Language

The concrete language makes implementation choices explicit. Its syntax is described in Figure 3. A concrete expression is a collection of let-expressions, each one representing an interaction (i.e. a mobile agent, a remote evaluation or remote procedure call). We use a uniform representation for the interactions, in the sense that RPC and remote evaluation protocols are seen as particular agents in our concrete language. An interaction is a continuation expression A applied to a data argument D. Continuation-passing-style (CPS) [13] is the standard technique to encode a specific evaluation order in functional expressions. We use it here to express the sequencing of basic services and treatments. A function f now takes an additional argument, a continuation A, and applies it to the result of its evaluation. The CPS version of a function f such that $f d = d'$ is a function $\overline{f}$ which takes an additional argument A (a continuation), and applies it to the result of its evaluation, that is $\overline{f}\ A\ d = A\ d'$. The continuation represents the sequence of primitive services or treatments that remain to be executed. The functions $go_{i,j}$ denote migrations from a place i to a place j^2. Functionally, the go functions are just the identity. Once combined with continuation expressions, they suffice to express the agent's route precisely. The special continuation end terminates the evaluation of an interaction. The semantics of the concrete language is described in Figure 4.

$$
\begin{aligned}
E &::= \textbf{let}\ (r_1, ..., r_n) = A\ D\ \textbf{in}\ E\ \Big|\ D \\
A &::= f\ A\ \Big|\ go_{id_1, id_2}\ A\ \Big|\ end \\
D &::= (D_1, ..., D_n)\ \Big|\ d\ \Big|\ r
\end{aligned}
$$

where $f\ \in\ \overline{Primitive}$, $id_i\ \in\ Place$, and $d\ \in\ Data$

Fig. 3. Syntax of concrete language

$$
\begin{aligned}
\mathcal{E}_c\ &:\ Exp_c\ \rightarrow\ Env\ \rightarrow\ Value \\
\mathcal{E}_c[\![\textbf{let}\ (r_1, ..., r_n) = A\ D\ \textbf{in}\ E]\!]\ e\ &=\ (\lambda(r_1, ..., r_n).\mathcal{E}_c[\![E]\!]\ e)(\mathcal{A}_c[\![A]\!]\ e\ (\mathcal{D}_c[\![D]\!]\ e)) \\
\mathcal{E}_c[\![D]\!]\ e\ &=\ \mathcal{D}_c[\![D]\!]\ e \\[6pt]
\mathcal{A}_c[\![f\ A]\!]\ e\ &=\ e\ f\ (\mathcal{A}_c[\![A]\!]\ e) \\
\mathcal{A}_c[\![go_{id_1, id_2}\ A]\!]\ e\ &=\ \mathcal{A}_c[\![A]\!]\ e \\
\mathcal{A}_c[\![end]\!]\ e\ &=\ \lambda d.d \\[6pt]
\mathcal{D}_c[\![(D_1, ..., D_n)]\!]\ e\ &=\ (\mathcal{D}_c[\![D_1]\!]\ e, ..., \mathcal{D}_c[\![D_n]\!]\ e) \\
\mathcal{D}_c[\![d]\!]\ e\ &=\ e\ d
\end{aligned}
$$

Fig. 4. Semantics of concrete expressions

Examples. The expression $t(s\ d)$ can be implemented in two different ways: either by RPC (i.e. processing the treatment at the client place) or by using a mobile agent (i.e. executing the treatment at the service place). Two concrete

---

^{2} Actually, even if some migrations could be deduced from the locations of base services, the go functions are needed to specify where treatments are to be executed.

expressions correspond to these two options. Let us write $\bar{s}$ and $\bar{t}$ for the CPS versions of s and t, and write c and 1 to denote the client place and service place respectively. The first, RPC-based, implementation is represented by the following expression:

$$\textbf{let } r_1 = go_{c,1}(\bar{s}(go_{1,c} \; end)) \; d \; \textbf{ in}$$
$$\textbf{let } r_2 = \bar{t} \; end \; r_1 \qquad\qquad \textbf{ in}$$
$$r_2$$

The data d is transmitted to place 1 $(go_{c,1})$, the remote service s is called and its result is returned to the client $(go_{1,c})$. Then, the treatment is performed locally by the client. The second, agent-based, implementation is represented by the expression:

$$\textbf{let } r_1 = go_{c,1}(\bar{s}(\bar{t}(go_{1,c} \; end))) \; d \; \textbf{ in}$$
$$r_1$$

The treatment is transmitted and executed at the service place (i.e. 1).

Let us describe now two possible implementations of the abstract complex service (2) presented earlier. We assume that the three base services s_1, s_2, and s_3 are located at different places, respectively 1, 2 and 3. The implementation based on two RPC protocols to interact with s_1 and s_2 and a mobile agent for s_3 with a remote treatment t_3 can be represented by the following concrete expression:

$$\textbf{let } r_1 = go_{c,3}(\bar{s_3}(\bar{t_3}(go_{3,c} \; end))) \; d_3 \quad \textbf{ in}$$
$$\textbf{let } r_2 = go_{c,2}(\bar{s_2}(go_{2,c} \; end)) \; d_2 \qquad \textbf{ in}$$
$$\textbf{let } r_3 = go_{c,1}(\bar{s_1}(go_{1,c} \; end)) \; (d_1, r_2) \textbf{ in}$$
$$\textbf{let } r_4 = \bar{t} \; end \; (r_3, r_1) \qquad\qquad\qquad \textbf{ in}$$
$$r_4$$

Figure 5-a gives the graphical representation of the interactions, where boxes represent the client and the service places, and arrows represent the data-flow between the components. Dashed-arrows indicate the place where the treatments are executed. The implementation based on a mobile agent protocol to interact with both s_1 and s_2 and on a RPC protocol to interact with s_3 can be represented by:

$$\textbf{let } r_1 = go_{c,3}(\bar{s_3}(go_{3,c} \; end)) \; d_3 \qquad\qquad \textbf{ in}$$
$$\textbf{let } r_2 = \bar{t_3} \; end \; r_1 \qquad\qquad\qquad\qquad \textbf{ in}$$
$$\textbf{let } r_3 = go_{c,2}(\bar{\bar{s_2}}(go_{2,1}(\bar{s_1}(go_{1,c} \; end)))) \; (d_1, d_2) \quad \textbf{ in}$$
$$\textbf{let } r_4 = \bar{t} \; end \; (r_3, r_2) \qquad\qquad\qquad\qquad \textbf{ in}$$
$$r_4$$

The graphical representation of this complex-service is given in Figure 5-b.

$\square$

Of course, different implementations of the same abstract expression are functionally equivalent. As we see in the next section, a concrete expression is functionally equivalent to the abstract expression it implements.

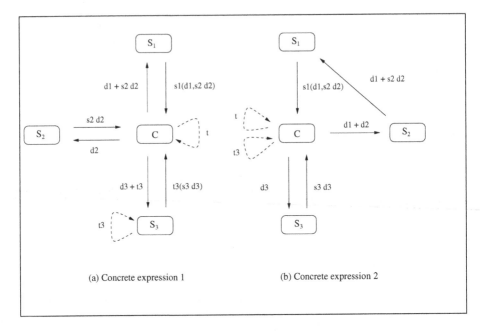

(a) Concrete expression 1   (b) Concrete expression 2

Fig. 5. Graphical representations of two implementations

2.3 From Abstract to Concrete Expressions

We outline here how to compile an abstract expression into a concrete one. The compilation process depends on three choices: the number and constituents of agents, their route, and the place for the execution of each treatment. The third choice is represented by an environment (p) mapping any primitive function to its location (i.e. the server providing the service or the execution environment). The two first choices are represented as a list of lists of primitive functions. The outer list represents the agents whereas inner lists describe the route of each agent. For example, the choices corresponding to the concrete expression depicted in Figure 5-a are summarized in the following list of agents:

$$[[t_3; s_3]; [s_2]; [s_1]; [t]]$$

That is, there are four interactions; for example, the first one (i.e. sublist $[t_3; s_3]$) is a mobile agent that calls s_3 and then applies t_3. Of course, not all agent lists are valid. A valid list of lists must include all the different treatments and services of the abstract expression and must respect the dependencies of the abstract term.

Given a valid list of agents and an environment (p) mapping primitive functions to places, it is easy to translate an abstract expression into a concrete one. This compilation is described by the function *Abs2Conc* given in Figure 6. *Abs2Conc* takes a list of agents ll and produces a let-expression for each of them. It supposes that all functions have been renamed so that a function in the list denotes unambiguously a call in the expression. For each sub-list l (i.e. an agent),

$Abs2Conc$ extracts (using the function $SubExp$) the sub-expressions $(E_1, \ldots, E_n)$ of the global expression E involving the primitives in l. For example:

$$SubExp \; [t_3; s_3] \; (t(s_1(d_1, s_2 \; d_2), t_3(s_3 \; d_3))) = t_3(s_3 \; d_3)$$

and

$$SubExp \; [t_3; s_3; s_2] \; (t(s_1(d_1, s_2 \; d_2), t_3(s_3 \; d_3))) = (s_2 \; d_2, t_3(s_3 \; d_3))$$

$Abs2Conc \; : \; Exp_a \; \rightarrow \; List(List(Primitive)) \; \rightarrow \; (Exp_c, Env)$

$Abs2Conc \; E \; nil \; e \; = \; (E, e)$
$Abs2Conc \; E \; (l.ll) \; e \; =$
    $\underline{let} \; (E_1, ..., E_n) = \; SubExp(l, E) \; \underline{in}$
    $\underline{let} \; (X_1, e_1) = \; Agent[\![(E_1, \ldots, E_n)]\!] \; l \; client \; end \; e \; \underline{in}$
    $\underline{let} \; (X_2, e_2) = \; Abs2Conc \; E[r_i/E_i] \; ll \; e_1 \; \underline{in}$
    $(\mathbf{let} \; (r_1, \ldots, r_n) = X_1 \; \mathbf{in} \; X_2 \; , \; e_2)$

$Agent \; : \; Exp_a \; \rightarrow \; List(Primitive) \; \rightarrow \; Place \; \rightarrow \; Cont \rightarrow \; Env \; \rightarrow \; (Exp, Env)$

$Agent[\![E]\!] \; nil \; i \; k \; e \; = \; (go_{client,i} \; k \; E \; , \; e)$
$Agent[\![(E_1, \ldots, f E_i, \ldots, E_n)]\!] \; (f.l) \; i \; k \; e \; =$
    $Agent[\![(E_1, \ldots, E_i, \ldots, E_n)]\!] \; l \; (p \; f) \; (\overline{f}(go_{(p \; f),i}k))$
                             $e[\overline{f} \; \leftarrow \; \lambda c.\lambda(x_1, \ldots, x_n). \; c \; (x_1, \ldots, e \; f \; x_i, \ldots, x_n)]$

Fig. 6. Translation algorithm

Each collection of sub-expressions is translated into an agent using the function $Agent$. The function $Agent$ takes the sub-expressions to compile, the ordered list which indicates the sequentialization of services and treatments, the current place (initially the client place), the current continuation (initially the final continuation end) and the primitive function environment. Calls to services and treatments are sequentialized using CPS and $go_{i,j}$ are inserted according to the environment p. The environment e is updated to reflect the fact that new CPS versions of primitive functions are introduced. The correctness of the translation is expressed by the following property:

PROPERTY: $(E_c, e_c) = Abs2Conc \; E_a \; ll \; e_a \; \Rightarrow \; \mathcal{E}_a[\![E_a]\!] \; e_a = \mathcal{E}_c[\![E_c]\!] \; e_c$

In theory, the function $Abs2Conc$ could be used to produce automatically all possible implementations of an abstract term, enabling their analysis and their comparison. It suffices to consider all possible valid agent lists, that is to say,

all possible arrangements of primitive functions respecting the abstract dependencies, and for each of them, every admissible permutations. The algorithm to
verify that an agent list is valid is a simple check of the order of functions appearing in the list $w.r.t$ the dependencies of the abstract term. In practice, this
use of $Abs2Conc$ might be considered only for small abstract expressions. In fact,
there are up to 2^{n-1} agent arrangements (where n is the number of primitive
functions), and up to $p!$ possible routes for an agent with p primitives.

We see in Section 4 more practical ways to use the compilation function
$Abs2Conc$.

3   Analyzing Performance and Security Properties

Concrete expressions make the analysis of performance and security properties
easy. The number and paths of agents of our concrete expressions are explicit in
the syntax. The only additional information needed is basic properties associated
with primitive objects (data, functions, codes, places, ...). We consider that this
information is given via environments mapping primitive objects to performance
or security properties. The definitions of analyses are expressed similarly as the
semantic functions of Figure 4; actually our analyses can be seen as abstract
semantics/interpretations of concrete expressions. For performance properties,
the measure we consider is the amount of traffic generated on the network. For
security properties, we focus on confidentiality properties, without considering
integrity for space reasons.

3.1   Performance

To estimate the cost (in terms of bandwidth) of the implementation of a complex-
service, we consider two environments e_s and e_f. The environment e_s associates
primitive functions to the size of their source code. For primitive services, this
size is zero: services are tied to servers and do not travel on the network. The
environment e_f associates each data to a size and each primitive function f to an
abstract function s_f yielding the size of the result of f depending of the size of its
argument (i.e. $s_f(size\ x) = size(f\ x)$). Sizes can be represented numerically or
symbolically [3]. Of course, it is not always possible to know precisely in advance
the sizes of results (e.g. number of hits for a query to an arbitrary database). In
such cases, approximations such as the average or maximum sizes should be
considered.

Using the two environments e_s and e_f, the amount of traffic involved by an
implementation is evaluated by the function $Cost_E$ (see Figure 7). Compared to
the semantics of Figure 4, the environment (e_f) now associates data and primitive functions to performance properties and the $raison\ d'etre$ of $go_{i,j}$ functions
becomes clear now. Note that the environment e_s is only read and used as a

---

[3] Numerical values are easy to normalize and compare whereas symbolic values are
more generic and represent more faithfully the reality. Both fit in our framework and
we do not dwell on this issue any further in this paper.

global constant. The cost of a let-expression is the cost of its sub-expressions. The cost of the body (E) is evaluated with its variables (r_i) associated with their size (d_i). The function $Cost_A$ evaluates the cost of an agent and takes as parameters the environment e_f, the size of the agent $(Source[\![A]\!]$, where α_{go} is the size of an instruction go), and the size of its data (d). The cost of an expression $go_{i,j}A$ is the cost of the continuation A plus the cost of transmitting the data and the agent source code ($i = j$ implies that there is no migration and therefore no transmission induced). More precisely, the transmission cost involved with a migration is:

$$\alpha_{i,j}(s + Sum\ d)$$

where $Sum\ d$ represents the total size of data (i.e. the summation of all the basic sizes in d), s denotes the size of the agent source code, and the coefficient $\alpha_{i,j}$ permits to take into account the bandwidth between places i and j (i.e. the quality of the connection).

$$
\begin{aligned}
&Cost_E\ :\ Exp_c\ \rightarrow\ Env\ \rightarrow\ Size\\
&Cost_E[\![\mathbf{let}\ (r_1,\ldots,r_n) = A\ D\ \mathbf{in}\ E]\!]\ e_f = \underline{let}\ (d_1,\ldots,d_n) = \mathcal{A}_c[\![A]\!]\ e_f\ (\mathcal{D}_c[\![D]\!]\ e_f)\ \underline{in}\\
&\qquad\qquad\qquad\qquad\qquad\qquad\qquad\qquad\quad Cost_E[\![E]\!]\ (e_f[r_i\ \leftarrow\ d_i])\\
&\qquad\qquad\qquad\qquad\qquad\qquad\qquad\qquad\ + Cost_A[\![A]\!]\ e_f\ (Source[\![A]\!])\ (\mathcal{D}_c[\![D]\!]\ e_f)\\
&Cost_E[\![D]\!]e_f \qquad\qquad\qquad\qquad\qquad = 0\\
\\
&Cost_A[\![f\ A]\!]\ e_f\ s\ d \qquad\qquad\qquad\ \ = e_f\ f\ (Cost_A[\![A]\!]\ e_f\ s)\ d\\
&Cost_A[\![go_{i,j}\ A]\!]\ e_f\ s\ d \qquad\qquad\ = Cost_A[\![A]\!]\ e_f\ s\ d\ +\\
&\qquad\qquad\qquad\qquad\qquad\qquad\qquad\quad\ \underline{if}\ i = j\ \underline{then}\ 0\ \underline{else}\ \alpha_{i,j}(s\ +\ Sum\ d)\\
&Cost_A[\![end]\!]\ e_f\ s\ d \qquad\qquad\qquad = 0\\
\\
&Source[\![f\ A]\!] \qquad\qquad\qquad\qquad\quad = e_s\ f\ +\ Source[\![A]\!]\\
&Source[\![go_{i,j}\ A]\!] \qquad\qquad\qquad\quad = \alpha_{go} + Source[\![A]\!]\\
&Source[\![end]\!] \qquad\qquad\qquad\qquad\quad = 0
\end{aligned}
$$

Fig. 7. Cost evaluation

Example. Let us consider the simple expression $t(s\ d)$ again and suppose that the abstract environments are:

$$e_f = [d\ \leftarrow\ 10^4; s\ \leftarrow\ \lambda x.10^7; t\ \leftarrow\ \lambda x.x div 10]$$
$$e_s = [s\ \leftarrow\ 0; t\ \leftarrow\ 10^5]$$

That is to say, the request is of $10Kb$, the database s returns $10Mb$ images, the treatment t divides image size by 10, the size of the source of t is $100Kb$, whereas, by convention, the size of the service s is null. The performance of an implementation choice ll for this expression is represented by:

$$\underline{let}\ (E, e_f') = Abs2Conc\ [\![t(s\ d)]\!]\ ll\ e_f\ \underline{in}\ Cost_E\ [\![E\ ]\!]\ e_f'$$

Assuming that the cost of a *go* (α_{go}) is null and that $\alpha_{i,j} = 1$ for all places i and j, the cost of the associated RPC implementation (see Section 2.2) is $1.001 \ 10^7$ (the data and the complete picture travel on the network, i.e. $10Kb + 10Mb$) and the cost of the mobile agent implementation (see Section 2.2) is $1.11 \ 10^6$ (the data, the reduced size picture, and the code of the treatment travel on the network i.e. $10Kb + 1Mb + 100Kb$).

□

We have focused on the volume of transmission implied by an implementation. Other criteria, such as time efficiency could be considered as well. Some additional information such as the service response times or communication delays should be introduced in environments but the analysis would remain similar.

3.2 Security

Security is regarded by many designers as the most critical issue to address before promoting the use of mobile agents in large service-provisioning systems. There are now good and accepted techniques to protect hosts from malicious mobile agents. However, protecting mobile agent from malicious hosts is a much more difficult task [11]. The analysis of security properties can be of a great help to the system designer. In particular, this kind of information should permit to rule out implementations that make sensitive data or treatments travel through untrusted hosts.

In our framework, each object (data, code, place) is associated with a value taken from a lattice of security levels. As before, we consider two environments. The environment e_s associates server places to the security level they insure[4] and treatments to the security level their source requires to roam safely. The environment e_f associates each primitive function f to an abstract function s_f returning the security level of the result of f depending of the security level of its argument. The environment e_f also contains the security level associated to data. In the following, we consider confidentiality (non-divulgation) properties. Integrity (i.e. non-modification) properties are dual and can be analyzed likewise.

The analysis in Figure 8 checks if confidentiality requirements are met by a given concrete expression. The function $Conf_E$ is defined as a recursive scan of the expression and returns a boolean. The symbols $\sqsubseteq, \perp, \sqcup$ denote respectively the partial order relation, the smallest element, and the join of the lattice of security levels. The expression $\bigsqcup d$ denotes the least upper bound of all the confidentiality levels in d. The auxiliary function Lub evaluates the confidentiality level required by the source code of an agent; this is the least upper bound of the levels of all its treatments. Note that the environment e_s is only read and is used as a global constant. The function $Conf_A$ takes as parameters the expression to check, the environment e_f, the current place (initially *client*), the confidentiality level of the source code ($Lub[\![A]\!]$) and the confidentiality level of the data.

---

[4] When there is no knowledge on the security of a place, the lowest security level should be taken.

Checking an agent amounts to verifying at each step that the level required by the current data ($\bigsqcup d$) and by the source code (c) is less or equal than the one insured by the current place (e_s p). Furthermore, for each migration $go_{i,j}$, the confidentiality level required by the data and the code must be less or equal than the confidentiality level insured by the network connection from place i to j ($\alpha_{i,j}$).

$Conf_E$: Exp_c $\rightarrow$ Env $\rightarrow$ $Bool$

$Conf_E[\![\textbf{let } (r_1,\ldots,r_n) = A\ D\ \textbf{in } E]\!]\ e_f = \underline{let}\ (d_1,\ldots,d_n) = \mathcal{E}_c[\![A]\!]\ e_f\ (\mathcal{D}_c[\![D]\!]\ e_f)\ \underline{in}$
$\qquad\qquad\qquad\qquad\qquad\qquad\qquad\qquad\qquad\qquad Conf_E[\![E]\!]\ (e_f[r_i \leftarrow d_i])\ \wedge$
$\qquad\qquad\qquad\qquad\qquad\qquad\qquad\qquad\qquad\qquad Conf_A[\![A]\!]\ e_f\ client\ (Lub\ [\![A]\!])\ (\mathcal{D}_c[\![D]\!]\ e_f)$
$Conf_E[\![D]\!]\ e_f \qquad\qquad\qquad\qquad\qquad\qquad = true$

$Conf_A[\![X]\!]\ e_f\ p\ c\ d \qquad\qquad\qquad\quad = (\bigsqcup d \sqcup c)\ \sqsubseteq\ e_s\ p\ \wedge$
$\qquad\qquad\qquad\qquad\qquad\qquad\qquad\qquad \underline{Case}\ X\ \underline{in}$
$\qquad\qquad\qquad\qquad\qquad\qquad\qquad\qquad\quad f\ A\ \ \ : e_f\ f\ (Conf_A[\![A]\!]\ e_f\ p\ c)\ d$
$\qquad\qquad\qquad\qquad\qquad\qquad\qquad\qquad\quad go_{i,j}\ A\ :\ (\bigsqcup d \sqcup c)\ \sqsubseteq\ \alpha_{i,j}\ \wedge$
$\qquad\qquad\qquad\qquad\qquad\qquad\qquad\qquad\qquad\qquad\qquad Conf_A[\![A]\!]\ e_f\ j\ c\ d$
$\qquad\qquad\qquad\qquad\qquad\qquad\qquad\qquad\quad end\ \ \ \ : true$

$Lub\ [\![t\ A]\!] \qquad\qquad\qquad\qquad\qquad = (e_s\ t) \sqcup Lub\ [\![A]\!]$
$Lub\ [\![s\ A]\!] \qquad\qquad\qquad\qquad\qquad = Lub\ [\![A]\!]$
$Lub\ [\![go_{i,j}\ A]\!] \qquad\qquad\qquad\quad = Lub\ [\![A]\!]$
$Lub\ [\![end]\!] \qquad\qquad\qquad\qquad\quad = \bot$

Fig. 8. Confidentiality checking

In the context of mobile agents, integrity properties, that is to say the non-modification of data and treatments, is as important as confidentiality. Checking integrity requirements can be specified in much the same way as confidentiality. One difference is that once a treatment is executed on a host, it is not necessary to check its integrity until the end of the agent's route (whereas the confidentiality of treatment has to be checked for the complete journey).

4   Practical Uses of the Model

For our model to be of practical interest, it should be integrated within a design environment. At the implementation level, the environment should be based on a platform offering both RPC and mobile agent interactions (such as the Grasshopper platform [5] based on CORBA middleware). At an abstract level, an environment based on architecture description language is an ideal ground for our approach [10]. Software architecture lies at the heart of successful large design [4]. The main contribution of this promising research area is to abstract away from the implementation details (macroscopic view of the system) and to mostly concentrate on the organization of the system to be specified, built and/or analyzed. This structural model is composed of components interconnected by connectors. The components are usually seen as processing units described by their behaviors and interfaces whereas the connectors are an abstract way of specifying the interaction protocols between those components.

In order to apply our approach, primitive services will be represented by components, interactions by connectors, and the location of base services (i.e. physical place) together with their associated attributes must be provided by the architecture description (i.e. functionality, efficiency and security levels). Several uses of such a framework can be considered:

- *Refinement of component.* Suppose that a component is specified as a complex service in our abstract language. The goal of the designer might be to refine this component into an architecture built from basic services. This refinement can be represented as a concrete expression. In other words, our approach can be used to choose the connectors. The naive generation of all the possible implementations is rapidly untractable if the complex service is not trivial. There are however admissible heuristics that permits to reduce this complexity. For example, if a treatment always increases the size of its inputs, then a simple mobile agent interaction will generate more bandwidth consumption than a RPC. Also asking for certain security properties permits to filter out many unsafe implementations.
- *Verification.* Given an architecture, the designer may want to verify that the protocols used are valid with respect to non-functional properties such as security. The architecture can be represented as a concrete expression and the analysis of Section 3.2 used to check the property.
- *Adaptation.* Given an architecture, the designer may want to change some parameters (such as service locations, bandwidth of connections, etc.) in order to meet non-functional requirements. The use of analyses in this context is much less problematic than in the context of refinement. Most parameters are already fixed and the best choice for the remaining ones can be found without combinatory explosion. For example, one may focus on optimal routes for fixed mobile agent in order to minimize bandwidth usage. Similarly, the security analysis may guide the designer in the use of securized connections, encrypted programs [14], or tamper-proof hardware, in order to ensure a security property.

5   Conclusion

Little work has been done towards evaluating non-functional properties of mobile agents. Some comparisons of RPC based *vs* mobile agent based applications on a given network have been done (e.g. see [6]). These approaches to performance evaluation are purely experimental. Furthermore, they do not consider hybrid interactions mixing mobile agents, remote evaluations, and remote procedure calls. To the best of our knowledge, Carzaniga, Picco, and Vigna [2] were the first to provide some basic hints (relative to bandwidth consumption) to select the adequate interactions. Their simple performance model was extended for network load and execution time by Straßer and Schwehm [16] for a sequence of mixed interactions of RPCs and agent migrations. In our framework, these approaches boil down to analyzing a concrete expression where the size of all requests and replies is fixed.

Several formalisms have been proposed to model mobility. Variants of the π-calculus (e.g. the Ambiant-calculus [1]) are very powerful models of computation. They contain an explicit notion of space composed of components (code or physical device) that move through locations. They describe precisely the distribution, mobility, or inter-communication of a group of agents and can provide some security checks to control the channels of communication. Their final goal is to propose a language for modeling Internet applications. The calculus of Sekiguchi and Yonezawa [15] is an extension of the lambda-calculus closer to our proposal. Their goal was to describe and compare different mobile agents movement mechanisms (like Obliq, Telescript, etc.).

The goal of our work is to analyze non-functional properties in order to guide designers in building large distributed systems. As a first step, we found it more reasonable to consider a simple language. On the other hand, our approach is formal and takes into account any kind of hybrid interactions. There are many avenues for further research. One is to investigate the integration of other service interaction protocols in our model. In [12], Picco identifies three paradigms that can be used to design distributed applications exploiting code mobility (i.e. remote evaluation, mobile agent, and code on demand). In code on demand interactions the client sends a request and gets a function to be processed locally. Modeling these applet-like interactions implies a higher-order version of our language (i.e. services may return treatments). Other important language extensions are non deterministic choice and iteration. In addition, more complex inter-service dependencies could be specified by adding variables and the let construction in the abstract language. Another plan for future work is to consider other non-functional properties like fault tolerance and to complete the integration of our model within a software architecture design environment. We are currently looking at the ASTER environment [7] associated with a platform providing both mobile agent and RPC interactions. Although some extensions should be considered, we believe however that our approach paves the way towards the systematic selection of interactions in service architectures.

Acknowledgments

This work has been partially supported by grants from the C3DS project[5].

---

[5] Control and Coordination of Complex Distributed Services. ESPRIT Long Term Research Project Number 24962 - www.newcastle.research.ec.org/c3ds

References

[1] L. Cardelli. Abstractions for mobile computations. In Jan Vitek and Christian D. Jensen, editors, *Secure Internet Programming, Security Issues for Mobile and Distributed Objects*, volume 1603 of *LNCS*, pages 51–94. Springer, 1999.

[2] Antonio Carzaniga, Gian Pietro Picco, and Giovanni Vigna. Designing distributed applications with mobile code paradigms. In R. Taylor, editor, *Proceedings of the 19th International Conference on Software Engineering (ICSE'97)*, pages 22–32. ACM Press, may 1997.

[3] David M. Chess, Colin G. Harrison, and Aaron Kershebaum. Mobile agents: Are they a good idea? Research report RC 19887, IBM Research Division, T. J. Watson Research Center, Yorktown Heights, NY 10598, february 1994.

[4] David Garlan and Mary Shaw. An introduction to software architecture. In V. Ambriola and G. Tortora, editors, *Series on Software Engineering and Knowledge Engineering, Vol 2*, Worlds Scientific Publishing Company, pages 1–39. 1993.

[5] IKV++ GmbH. Grasshopper - www.ikv.de/products/grasshopper/index.html.

[6] L. Ismail and D. Hagimont. A performance evaluation of the mobile agent paradigm. In *Proceedings of the Conference on Object-Oriented Programming, Systems, Languages, and Applications*, pages 306–313, 1999.

[7] Valérie Issarny and Titos Saridakis. Defining open software architectures for customized remote execution of web agents. *Autonomous Agents and Multi-Agent Systems Journal. Special Issue on Coordination Mechanisms and Patterns for Web Agents*, 2(3):237–249, september 1999.

[8] Dag Johansen. Mobile agent applicability. In *2nd International Workshop on Mobile Agents, MA'98, Stuttgart, Germany*, volume 1477 of *Lecture Notes in Computer Science*, pages 80–98. Springer, september 1998.

[9] Danny B. Lange and Mitsuru Oshima. Seven good reasons for mobile agents. *Communications of the ACM, Multiagent Systems on the Net and Agents in E-commerce*, 42(3):88–89, march 1999.

[10] Nenad Medvidovic and Richard N. Taylor. A framework for classifying and comparing architecture description languages. *SIGSOFT Software Engineering Notes*, 22(6):60–76, november 1997.

[11] Jonathan T. Moore. Mobile Code Security Techniques. Technical Report MS-CIS-98-28, University of Pennsylvania, Department of Computer and Information Science, may 1998.

[12] Gian Pietro Picco. *Understanding, Evaluating, Formalizing, and Exploiting Code Mobility*. Ph.d. thesis, Politecnico di Torino, Italy, february 1998.

[13] John C. Reynolds. The discoveries of continuations. *Lisp and Symbolic Computation*, 6(3/4):233–248, november 1993.

[14] T. Sander and C. Tschudin. Towards mobile cryptography. In *Proceedings of the IEEE Symposium on Research in Security and Privacy*, Research in Security and Privacy, Oakland, CA, may 1998. IEEE Computer Society Press.

[15] T. Sekiguchi and A. Yonezawa. A calculus with code mobility. In Chapman and Hall, editors, *Proc. 2nd IFIP Workshop on Formal Methods for Open Object-Based Distributed Systems (FMOODS)*, pages 21–36, London, 1997.

[16] Markus Straßer and Markus Schwehm. A Performance Model for Mobile Agent Systems. In H. R. Arabnia, editor, *Proceedings of the International Conference on Parallel and Distributed Processing Techniques and Applications PDPTA'97*, pages 1132–1140, Las Vegas, 1997.

Specification of an Automatic Manufacturing System: A Case Study in Using Integrated Formal Methods*

Heike Wehrheim

Universität Oldenburg
Fachbereich Informatik
Postfach 2503, D–26111 Oldenburg, Germany
wehrheim@informatik.uni-oldenburg.de

Abstract. An automatic manufacturing system serves as a case study for the applicability of an *integrated formal method* to the specification of software systems. The formal method chosen is *CSP-OZ*, an integration of the state-oriented formalism Object-Z with the process algebra CSP. The practicability as well as limitations of CSP-OZ are studied. We furthermore employ a graphical notation (class diagrams) from the Unified Modelling Language to describe the *architectural view* of the system. The correctness of the obtained specification is checked by a translation into the input language of the CSP model checker FDR and a following property check.

1   Introduction

Recently, there is an emerging interest in formal methods which combine specification techniques for different views on systems. In particular, methods integrating static aspects (data) and dynamic aspects (behaviour) are investigated (see for example [Obj99, Que96, GP93, TA97, GS97, Smi97, MD98]). The advantage of these methods is that different views on a system can be conveniently modelled. Integrated methods are in particular important for the specification of *software* for reactive systems, which have to cope with a number of different aspects of systems: large data descriptions, dynamic behaviour, timing constraints and analog components. In this paper, we investigate the usefulness and applicability of an integrated formal method to the specification of software for manufacturing systems. The formalism chosen is CSP-OZ [Fis97], a combination of the process algebra CSP [Hoa85] and an object-oriented extension of Z, Object-Z [DRS95]. CSP-OZ integrates a state-oriented with a behaviour-oriented view and thus allows to specify different aspects of a system within a single formalism. A semantics for the combined formalism has been given in [Fis97].

---

* This work was partially funded by the Leibniz Programme of the German Research Council (DFG) under grant Ol 98/1-1.

T. Maibaum (Ed.): FASE 2000, LNCS 1783, pp. 334–348, 2000.

Our case study is the specification of a *holonic manufacturing system*. This case study is part of the german research program "Integration of Software Specification Techniques"[1]. The term "holon" has its origin in the greek word "holos" (whole) and describes an autonomous, flexible agent. The term "holonic manufacturing systems" refers to systems where the transportation of material within the plant are managed by holonic transportation systems, i.e. transportation systems without drivers and without central scheduling device [WHS94]. The purpose of the manufacturing system is the processing of workpieces by different machine tools. Two stores in the plant serve as containers for workpieces. The holonic transportation agents are responsible for transportation of workpieces between machine tools and stores. The throughput of workpieces in the plant should be as high as possible. An elaborate communication protocol between machine tools, stores and transportation agents ensures that the agent with the smallest cost for transportation is used for a particular transportation job.

The CSP-OZ specification models an abstract view of the system, considering the *activities* of machine tools and agents as a modelling entity, i.e. we do not specify the manufacturing system on machine level describing movements of roboter arms etc., but rather have concentrated on the software used in the different components. A particular focus was laid on the specification of the communication scheme between components and the influence of the data part thereon. The specification clearly showed the strength of CSP-OZ as a specification formalism for software systems but also revealled some weaknesses, for instance the lack of specifying timing constraints.

An additional aim of the work presented here was to investigate the possibility of integrating more informal graphical notations, used in industry, with a formal method. As a first approach, we have chosen to use the class diagrams of UML for the specification of the communication structure of the system. This turned out to fit well to the object-oriented method CSP-OZ; thedifference to an ordinary use of class diagrams lies in the interpretation of associations in the context of distributed communicating systems: since objects may be (and in our case are) physically distributed, all interactions among active objects have to be interpreted as *communications* (in the sense of message exchanges via channels).

An advantage of using formal methods in the specification of software is their precise formal semantics. This advantage can best be exploited when some property checking on the specification can also be performed. Using a technique proposed in [FW99] – translating CSP-OZ specifications into the input language of the CSP model checker FDR [FDR97] – we carry out some correctness checks on the specification, most notably a check for *deadlock-freedom*. Given the complex communication protocol among machine tools and transportation agents, deadlock-freedom is not trivial to achieve.

In Section 2 we start with a brief introduction of our specification formalism CSP-OZ. Section 3 presents (part of) the specification of the manufacturing system, and Section 4 describes the property check on the specification.

---

[1] http://tfs.cs.tu-berlin.de/projekte/indspec/SPP/index.html.

2   CSP-OZ

CSP-OZ is an *object-oriented formal method* combining Object-Z [DRS95] (an object-oriented extension of Z) with the process algebra CSP. The general idea is to augment the state-oriented Object-Z specification with the specification of behaviour in the style of CSP. A CSP-OZ specification describes a system as a collection of interacting objects, each of which has a prescribed structure and behaviour. Communication takes place via *channels* in the style of CSP. CSP-OZ has a formal semantics on the basis of CSPs failure-divergence model [Fis97].

In general, a CSP-OZ specification consists of a number of paragraphs, introducing classes, global variables, functions and types. Instances of the classes can be combined via CSP composition operators. Here, we will briefly describe the form of class specifications and illustrate them by a small example of a one-place buffer. A CSP-OZ class has the following basic structure:

$Name(formal\ parameters)$	
inherit *superclass*	[inherited superclasses]
chan *channelname*	[channel definitions]
main = ...	[CSP-Part]
type and constant definitions	[Z-Part]
state schema, initial state schema	
operation schemas	

The state schema gives the *attributes* of a class, the operation schemas their *methods*. The initial state schema fixes the initial values of attributes. For every method which can be called on an instance of the class, a corresponding channel has to be defined. In the operation schemas methods are defined by *enable* and *effect predicates*, which give the enabling conditions for an application of an method and its effect on the attributes and communicated values. The parameters of a method can be of type *input* (denoted x?), *output* (x!) or *simple* (solely x). A simple parameter is one on which both communication partners agree, there is no direction in the flow of communication value. Simple parameters can for instance be used for *object references*: in a distributed setting, a method call m to a particular object O (usually written as $O.m$, where O is a reference to the object) can now be expressed, using communication via channels, as $m.O$, where m is the name of a channel and O an instantiation of a simple parameter.

Every class may *inherit* attributes and methods from one or more other classes. A class may have a number of formal parameters, which have to be replaced by actual parameters when the class is instantiated. In the CSP-Part of the specification the behaviour of a class is defined, i.e. the order of execution of methods is fixed (sometimes also called the *synchronisation constraint* of the class). The CSP-Part describes the *data-independent* part of behaviour, it may not refer to attributes of the class (therefore all parameters of channel names occur as input parameters, $chan$?x). The data-dependent aspects are encoded in the enabling conditions of the methods. Thereby a clean separation of data and behaviour aspects is obtained.

Below a CSP-OZ specification of a class *Buffer* is given. The basic type of elements in the buffer is *Element*.

[*Element*]

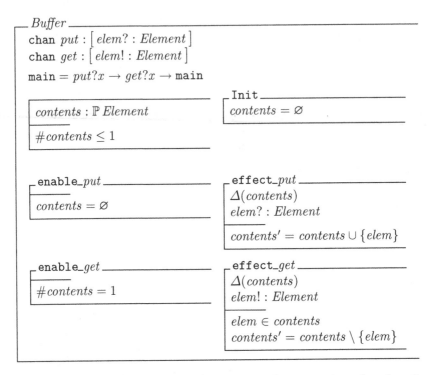

The class has one attribute *contents* (specified in the state schema) and methods *put* and *get*. A primed attribute name stands for the value of the attribute after the execution of the method. The Δ-declaration declares the attributes which may be changed by the method. The CSP-Part specifies that *put* and *get* methods may only be used alternately. This is also guaranteed by the enabling conditions of the methods, i.e. we could as well either leave out the CSP-Part or set the enabling conditions of methods to true without changing the behaviour of class *Buffer*.

2.1   CSP Operators

In this example, we have used just one CSP operator, the prefix operator $\rightarrow$. In the specification of the manifacturing system, a number of other operators will be used, which are now briefly explained.

- ;   denotes sequential composition of processes;
- ||| denotes parallel composition with no synchronisation, $\|_A$ is parallel composition with synchronisation on all events in the set A, i.e. the components of a parallel composition have to jointly execute events in A;

- $\backslash A$ is hiding of events in the set A;
- $\square$ is an external choice; external means that the choice can be influenced by an environment requesting certain events;
- $[name1 \leftarrow name2]$ is a renaming of $name1$ into $name2$.

Furthermore, most operators may be used in a replicated version, e.g. $||| \ a : A \bullet P(a)$ is a parallel composition of all processes $P(a)$, where a is in A.

A last operator is to be explained, which will be used quite often: the CSP *timeout* operator. The intention of this operator is to abstractly model a timeout in the absense of a notion of time in CSP. The process $P \rhd Q$ has the following behaviour: with any visible action of P, the choice between P and Q is decided, if no action from P happens, the process times out and behaves like Q.

A more thorough introduction to CSP can be found in [Hoa85, Ros97], an introduction to Z in [Spi92], to Object-Z in [Smi00].

3   Specification

Next, we present the specification of the automatic manufacturing system. This case study is part of the german DFG priority program "Integration of specification techniques with applications in engineering". The automatic manufacturing system consists of the following parts: two stores (In and Out), one for workpieces to be processed (the in-store), one for the finished workpieces (the out-store), a number of holonic transportation systems (hts) ($T1, T2, \dots$) and three machine tools (short: wzm for german "<u>W</u>erk<u>z</u>eug<u>m</u>aschinen") A, B and C for processing the workpieces. Every workpiece has to be processed by all three machine tools in a fixed order ($In \rightarrow A \rightarrow B \rightarrow C \rightarrow Out$). The hts' are responsible for transportation of workpieces between machine tools and stores. The hts' work as autonomous agents, free to decide which machine tool to serve (within some chosen strategy). Initially the in-store is full and the out-store as well as all wzm are empty. When a wzm is empty or contains an already processed workpiece it broadcasts a request to the hts in order to receive a new workpiece or to deliver one. The hts' (when listening) send some offer to the wzm, telling them their cost for satisfying the request. Upon receipt of offers the wzm decides for the best offer and give this hts the order, which then executes it. This way, all workpieces should be processed by all three tools and transported from the in- to the out-store.

The specification language we employ is an *object-oriented* formal method. The specification thus consists of a number of classes, somehow related to one another. To facilitate the understanding of the overall structure of the specification, we describe it by means of a *class diagram* (in the style of the Unified Modelling Language, UML). Class diagrams are (so far) not part of the formal method CSP-OZ, we just use them as a graphical means for showing the structure of specifications. Class diagrams show the static structure of the model, in particular, the things that exist, their internal structure and their relationships to other things. In particular, we find: boxes, denoting *classes*; arrows, describing *generalisation* (inheritance); simple arcs, standing for *associations* and arcs

with filled diamonds at the end, denoting *compositions*. An association shows a
possible interaction between two classes. A composition is a strong form of an
association: it describes a relationship between a "whole" and its parts, where
the existence of the parts depends on the whole. Class diagrams are traditionally
used for data modelling. In this paper we take a different view on class diagrams.
All classes in the diagram are assumed to be *active*. When using class diagrams
in the description of distributed communicating systems, active objects most
often reside on different locations, hence any interaction has to take the form of
a *communication*. Thus associations and compositions stand for some particular
form of composition (now in the process algebra sense) of the classes, using communication via channels for interaction. Associations are parallel compositions
with communication via the channels which are the *names* of the association.
Composition is stronger: the class and its components are combined in parallel
but now all channels between the class and its components are hidden to the
outside.

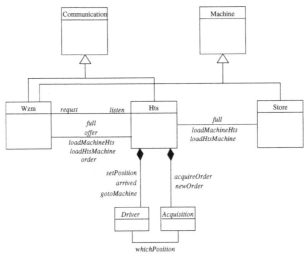

Fig. 1. Class diagram for manufacturing system

In Figure 1 the class diagram for the manufacturing system is given. The main
classes of our specification are *Wzm*, *Hts* and *Store*. The class diagram furthermore contains two superclasses from which these classes are derived: a superclass *Machine* specifying the basic behaviour of stores and machine tools (with
attributes like contents and methods like loading), and a superclass *Communication* defining a protocol for broadcast communication. The class *Hts* embodies
two other classes: one for managing the driving in the plant hall (*Driver*) and a
class for acquisition of new orders (*Acquisition*). The use of composition and not
association here implies that every *Hts* inevitably has components *Driver* and
Acquisition.

Class specifications. The classes themselves are now specified with CSP-OZ.
At the end we will see how they can be combined by CSP operators in order

to achieve the above depicted structure. We start with the definition of a basic type and some abbreviations: *Workpiece* is the basic type for workpieces, *Wzm* specifies the set of all machine tools, *Hts* the holonic transportation systems, and *Store* the stores.

$$[Workpiece] \qquad\qquad Wzm == \{A, B, C\}$$
$$Hts == \{T_1, T_2\} \qquad\qquad Store == \{In, Out\}$$
$$Machines == Stores \cup Wzm$$

The type *Coord* is used to describe the position of machines and agents in the hall. *Status* describes the status of workpieces in machines (processed or not yet processed): $Coord == \mathbb{N} \times \mathbb{N}$, $Status == \{finished, notFinished\}$.

We start with the specification of the superclass *Machine*. It should capture the basic common properties of machine tools and stores: they may contain a number of workpieces (limited by some capacity), they may load and deload workpieces, and tell others whether they are empty or full.

Machine(*id* : *Machines*)

chan $full : [h : Hts; m : \{id\}; b! : \mathbb{B}]$
chan $loadHtsMachine : [h : Hts; m : \{id\}; w? : Workpiece]$
chan $loadMachineHts : [m : \{id\}; h : Hts, w! : Workpiece]$

	Init
$contents : \mathbb{P}\ Workpiece$	$contents = \varnothing$
$capacity : \mathbb{N}_1$	
$\#contents \le capacity$	

effect_*full*

$b! : \mathbb{B}$

$b = (\#contents = capacity)$

enable_*loadMachineHts*	**effect_***loadMachineHts*
$contents \ne \varnothing$	$\Delta(contents)$
	$h : Hts, w! : Workpiece$
	$w \in contents$

enable_*loadHtsMachine*	**effect_***loadHtsMachine*
$\#contents < capacity$	$\Delta(contents)$
	$h : Hts, w? : Workpiece$
	$contents' = contents \cup \{w\}$

The first part of the specification describes the basic interface between machines and hts. Afterwards the attributes of the class are defined and the initial state values are given. The last part gives the enabling conditions and effects for the execution of operations (e.g. only load workpieces from a machine to an hts when the machine is not empty). Since we just define the basic ingredients of machines here, we have no CSP behaviour descriptions.

The superclass *Communication* provides two protocols for broadcast communication between agents and machine tools. Here is one point where we reach the limits of CSP-OZ: CSP with its *synchronous* communication paradigm cannot exactly describe the radio communication between tools and agents. Radio communication is somehow a mixture of synchronous and asynchronous communication: the sender may always send its message (asynchronously), the receiver can only receive the message when it listens at exactly the time the message is sent (synchronously). Since we have no notion of time in our specification language, we model this type of communication with the CSP timeout operator: the sender tries a synchronous communication with every receiver; when this fails it may timeout. Similarly the receiver can timeout when no communication is possible. This behaviour is modelled by the processes *BROADCAST* and *LISTEN*, which have the set of receivers (*to*), senders (*from*) respectively, and the communication channel (*comm*) as parameters.

Communication
$BROADCAST(to, comm) =$
   $||| \ rec : to \bullet ((comm?x.rec?y \rightarrow SKIP) \rhd SKIP)$
$LISTEN(from, comm) =$
   $||| \ sender : from \bullet ((comm!from?x?y \rightarrow SKIP) \rhd SKIP$

The class *Wzm* specifying machine tools is a subclass of both *Machine* and *Communication* (i.e. we have multiple inheritance here). Inheritance is semantically the *conjunction* of the Z part of the superclass with the Z part of the subclass, and *parallel composition* of the CSP parts with synchronisation on all events that occur in both CSP specifications. The process equations of the superclass are inherited by the subclass and may be used by them (code re-use). This is for instance the case for the protocols of superclass *Communication*: inheritance makes the two process names accessible within the subclass *Wzm*. The basic behaviour of a wzm is as follows: it has to find an hts fetching some workpiece for it, load a workpiece, process it, find another hts to take it over, deload it and start again from the beginning. Additionally it always has to be able to tell others wether it is full or empty. This behaviour is specified by the CSP process of class *Wzm*. The search for an hts proceeds as follows: the wzm broadcasts a request to all hts (telling them whether it is full or empty), the hts that have listened may send a reply offering some cost for the transport. The wzm then chooses the offer with the smallest cost and tries to order this hts. If the ordering does not succeed (the hts may have decided for another job), they choose another offer until either the order succeeds or no further offers are available upon which the wzm makes its request again.

$\underline{\quad Wzm\quad}$

inherit *Machine, Communication*

chan *process, choose, noOffers*

chan $request : \big[\, h : Hts;\ m : \{id\};\ b! : \mathbb{B} \,\big]$

chan $offer : \big[\, h : Hts;\ m : \{id\};\ cost? : \mathbb{N} \,\big]$

chan $order : \big[\, h : Hts;\ m : \{id\} \,\big]$

$
\begin{aligned}
\textbf{main} \quad &= FULL \,\|\|\, WORK \\
FULL \quad &= full?x \rightarrow FULL \\
WORK \quad &= FINDHTS;\ loadHtsMachine?x \rightarrow process \rightarrow \\
&\qquad FINDHTS;\ loadMachineHts?x \rightarrow WORK \\
FINDHTS &= BROADCAST(Hts, request); \\
&\qquad LISTEN(Hts, offer);\ CHOOSE \\
CHOOSE \quad &= choose \rightarrow ((order?x \rightarrow SKIP) \rhd CHOOSE)) \\
&\qquad \square\ noOffers \rightarrow FINDHTS
\end{aligned}
$

$status : Status$
$offers : \text{seq}(Hts \times \mathbb{N})$
$orderTo : Hts$

$\underline{\quad \textbf{Init}\quad}$
$offers = \langle\,\rangle$
$status = finished$

$\underline{\quad \textbf{enable\_}request\quad}$
$status = finished$

$\underline{\quad \textbf{effect\_}request\quad}$
$h : Hts, b! : \mathbb{B}$

$b = (contents \neq \varnothing)$

$\underline{\quad \textbf{effect\_}offer\quad}$
$\Delta(offers)$
$h : Hts, cost? : \mathbb{N}$

$offers' = offers \frown \langle (h, cost) \rangle$

$\underline{\quad \textbf{enable\_}choose\quad}$
$offers \neq \langle\,\rangle$

$\underline{\quad \textbf{effect\_}choose\quad}$
$\Delta(offers, orderTo)$

$\exists\, n \in \mathbb{N} : (orderTo', n)\ \text{in}\ offers \wedge \forall (h, m)\ \text{in}\ offers : n \leq m$
$offers' = offers \upharpoonright ((Hts \times \mathbb{N}) \setminus \{(orderTo', n)\})$

$\underline{\quad \textbf{effect\_}order\quad}$
$h : Hts$

$h = orderTo$

$\underline{\quad \textbf{enable\_}noOffers\quad}$
$offers = \langle\,\rangle$

The basic behaviour of wzms is specified by the CSP process **main**, all data
dependent aspects are specified within the CSP part (for instance the choice
for the offer with the smallest cost is encoded in the effect schema of operation
choose). This allows for a clear separation of static and dynamic aspects, and

also allows for an easy change (for instance when other criteria should be used for choosing an offer).

The class *Hts* describes the principle behaviour of a holonic transportation agent. The driving and order acquisition specific aspects are specified within the components *Driver* and *Acquisition*. Since the most interesting part of an hts (negotiation with wzms) is specified within the component *Acquisition* we refrain from giving the specification of classes *Hts* and *Driver* here and instead concentrate on *Acquisition*. The main task of class *Acquisition* is the negotiation of new orders. Initially it waits for a call from class *Hts* to acquire a new order. It asks for its current position and listens to the requests made by the wzm. All received requests have to be checked whether they can be satisfied, for instance, if the requesting wzm is full, it has to be checked whether the wzm, next to the requesting one, is empty (in order to asure that a workpiece can also be delivered). This check is encoded in the effect of operation *full*: all wzm are asked whether they are full (*ASK*) and the set of current requests is modified according to the answer. From all satisfiable requests the one with the least cost (distance from current position to wzm) is chosen and an offer is made to the requesting wzm. If this offer succeeds and an order is accomplished, class *Acquisition* informs the *Hts* about this. If the offer does not succeed, the set of current requests is emptied and finding a new order starts again.

$\underline{\quad Acquisition(master : Hts)\quad}$

```
inherit  Broadcast
```

chan $newOrder : \left[\, ord! : Wzm \times \mathbb{B} \,\right]$
chan $whichPosition : \left[\, pos? : Coord \,\right]$
chan $listen : \left[\, h : \{master\};\; wzm : Wzm;\; b? : \mathbb{B} \,\right]$
chan $offer : \left[\, h : \{master\};\; wzm : Wzm;\; cost! : \mathbb{N} \,\right]$
chan $order : \left[\, h : \{master\};\; wzm : Wzm \,\right]$
chan $requestsThere, noRequests, emptyRequests, acquireOrder$

main $= acquireOrder \rightarrow whichPosition?x \rightarrow FINDORDER$
$FINDORDER = LISTEN(Wzm, listen);$
$\quad (requestsThere \rightarrow ASK;$
$\qquad ((offer?x \rightarrow ((order?x \rightarrow newOrder?x \rightarrow \mathbf{main})$
$\qquad\qquad \vartriangleright emptyRequests \rightarrow FINDORDER))$
$\qquad\qquad \vartriangleright emptyRequests \rightarrow FINDORDER)$
$\qquad \square\ (noRequests \rightarrow FINDORDER))$
$\quad \square\ (noRequests \rightarrow FINDORDER)$
$ASK = |||\ ma : Machines \bullet (full?x!ma?y \rightarrow SKIP)$

	$\underline{\quad Init\quad}$
$currRequests : \mathbb{P}(Wzm \times \mathbb{B})$	$currRequests = \varnothing$
$orderFrom : Wzm$	
$position : Coord$	

___effect_*newOrder*_____

$\Delta(currOffers)$
$ord! : Wzm \times \mathbb{B}$

$first(ord) = orderFrom, ord \in currRequests$
$currOffers' = \varnothing$

___effect_*whichPosition*_____   ___effect_*emptyRequests*_____

$\Delta()$ $\Delta(currRequests)$
$pos? : Coord$
                                        $currRequests' = \varnothing$
$pos = position$

___enable_*noRequests*_____   ___enable_*requestsThere*_____

$currRequests = \varnothing$ $currRequests \neq \varnothing$

___effect_*listen*_____

$\Delta(currRequests)$
$wzm : Wzm, b? : \mathbb{B}$

$currRequests' = currRequests \cup \{(wzm, b)\}$

___enable_*offer*_____   ___effect_*order*_____

$currRequests \neq \varnothing$ $\Delta(orderFrom)$
                                        $wzm : Wzm$

                                        $orderFrom' = wzm$

___effect_*offer*_____

$\Delta()$
$wzm : Wzm, cost! : \mathbb{N}$

$\exists b \in \mathbb{B} : (wzm, b) \in currRequests \land$
$\forall (m, q) \in currRequests \bullet$
$\qquad dist(position, target(wzm, b)) \leq dist(position, target(m, q))$
[function target determines the position of the target of the request]
$cost = dist(position, place(wzm))$

___effect_*full*_____

$\Delta(currRequests)$
$wzm : Wzm, b? : \mathbb{B}$

$currRequests' =$
$\quad currRequests \setminus \{(w, f) \bullet (if\ f\ then\ next(w) = wzm \land b)\ \lor$
$\qquad\qquad\qquad\qquad (if\ \neg f\ then\ prev(w) = wzm \land \neg b)\}$

This completes the part of the class specifications. Due to lack of space we leave out the specifications of the other classes.

System specification. The classes now have to be instantiated and the created objects have to be combined to give the automatic manufacturing system. First we define a process *compoHts* describing the composition of *Hts* with *Driver* and *Acquisition*. Composition in class diagrams is translated into a parallel composition of components, where in contrast to ordinary association, the synchronised events are hidden afterwards. The synchronisation set is derived from the inscriptions of the association arcs in the class diagram: *Driver* and *Acquisition* synchronise on the set $A = \{whichPosition\}$, *Hts* with *Driver* and *Acquisition* on $B = \{setPosition, setId, arrived, gotoMachine, newOrder, acquireOrder\}$. We also carry out the renaming here which is induced by the association between *Hts* and *Wzm* in which the participants of the association have different roles (channel names *request* and *offer* at the ends of the association). However, we could also have chosen to use a linked parallel composition between *Hts* and *Wzm*.

$$compoHTS(id) =$$
$$(Hts(id) \parallel_B (Driver(id) \parallel_A Acquisition(id))) \setminus (A \cup B)[listen \leftarrow request])$$

The automatic manufacturing system is then obtained as a parallel composition of an appropriate number of class instances. In the choice of synchronisation sets we have to be a little more careful now: some channel names (e.g. *loadHtsMachine*) occur on more than one association; since the associations are however not ternary, this is not ment to be a synchronisation of three or more objects. In this case synchronisation now has to be distinguished by parameters and not by channel names alone. All parameters used for this purpose should be *simple* and stand for the identities of the involved objects. As an example: $Store(In)$ and all hts synchronise on $loadMachineHts.In$, whereas $Wzm(A)$ and the hts synchronise on $loadMachineHts.A$.

$$
\begin{array}{c}
Store(In) \\
\parallel_C \\
(\parallel\!\parallel\!\parallel hts : Hts \bullet compoHTS(hts)) \\
AutoManuSystem = \quad\quad \parallel_D \\
(\parallel\!\parallel\!\parallel wzm : Wzm \bullet Wzm(wzm)) \\
\parallel_E \\
Store(Out)
\end{array}
$$

where we have the following synchronisation sets:

$C = \{loadMachineHts.In, full.T1.In, full.T2.In\},$

$D = \{loadMachineHts.A, loadMachineHts.B, loadMachineHts.C,$

$\quad loadHtsMachine.T1.A, loadHtsMachine.T1.B, loadHtsMachine.T1.C,$

$\quad loadHtsMachine.T2.A, loadHtsMachine.T2.B, loadHtsMachine.T2.C,$

$full.T1.A, full.T1.B, full.T1.C, \quad full.T2.A, full.T2.B, full.T2.C,$

$request, offer, order\},$

$E = \{loadHtsMachine.T1.Out, loadHtsMachine.T2.Out,$

$full.T1.Out, full.T2.Out\}.$

This completes the specification of the automatic manufacturing system. So far, this models the manufacturing system on a rather abstract level; we have for instance not modelled how the loading and deloading of workpieces is handled on the actual machine level. Nevertheless, the specification contains all activities performed by the system and describes the communication scheme for interaction. The communication scheme of a system is the major source for errors leading to deadlocks of the system. In the next section, we describe how we can prove deadlock freedom of our specification.

4   Verification

The verification of the manufacturing system follows ideas proposed in [FW99] (building on ideas of [MS98]): the CSP-OZ specification is translated into the CSP dialect of the model-checker FDR [FDR97], which can then be used to verify properties on the specification. The formal basis for this translation is the failure-divergence semantics of CSP-OZ classes. The CSP dialect of FDR is a combination of CSP with a functional language. The functional part of FDR-CSP can be used for modelling the Z-part of the specification. The translation cannot handle CSP-OZ completely, but a rather large portion of it. The translation for instance requires instantiation of basic types and restriction of variables to finite domains; however we do not have to eliminate nondeterminism from the specification, which usually has to be done when "executing" a formal specification.

For the manufacturing system, we thus have to choose some concrete set of values for the basic type *Workpiece* and we have to restrict *Coord* to a finite space (say $1\ldots10\times1\ldots10$). The most severe restriction, necessary for model-checking, concerns the initial values of the stores. We have not given the specification of the stores here, but of course the in-store has to be filled with a certain number of workpieces. Ideally, the model-checker should be able to verify deadlock-freedom of the specification for *any* number of workpieces in the in-store. However, this is beyond the range of model checkers like FDR. We thus have to perform the model-checking for a fixed number of workpieces in the store.

Having chosen these concrete values, the specification can be translated into FDR-CSP[2]. Two properties have been checked on the translated specification:

1. Deadlock-freedom and
2. adherence to the correct ordering of processing.

---

[2] At the moment the translation has to be done manually, but an implementation is under development.

By the second point, we mean that every workpiece has to be processed by the machine tools in the correct order. The second property was verified by *hiding* all events besides the event *process* and only observing the ordering of processing workpieces. This shows that every workpiece of the in-store is correctly carried to the wzm and processed in the right order. As an example for the performance of FDR on the case study: the labelled transition system for an instantiation with two hts and three wzm has 4213677 states and the second property can be checked in 1008 seconds cpu time on a SPARC Ultra.

The verification detected three errors in the first specification: an incorrect setting of initial values of one class, a wrong order of events in the CSP-part of a class and a wrong synchronisation set in the parallel composition of classes. So, although we cannot claim to have verified correctness of the specification for all possible instantiations of the system, we have been able to use a model-checker to find general errors.

5   Conclusion

In this paper we investigated the applicability of an integrated formal method to the specification of an industrial-scale software system. The case study clearly showed the advantages of using CSP-OZ, in particular the need for a formalism combining behaviour and data specification, but also revealed some drawbacks, for instance the inability of expressing timing requirements. The later aspect would especially be important when evaluating the performance (throughput in time) of the manufacturing system.

Besides designing a specification, we were also able to prove correctness properties of the design by means of a translation into the input language of the model checker FDR. The model checking process however always relies on fixing a particular instantiation of the system.

The case study also demonstrated the usefulness of employing graphical modelling languages in the design of the specification. We intend to further extend the possibilities of using object-oriented design methods together with CSP-OZ, especially the UML profile UML-RT [SR98], which seems to be well suited for the description of distributed communicating systems.

References

[DRS95]   R. Duke, G. Rose, and G. Smith. Object-Z: A specification language advocated for the description of standards. *Computer Standards and Interfaces*, 17:511–533, 1995.

[FDR97]   Formal Systems (Europe) Ltd. *Failures-Divergence Refinement: FDR2 User Manual*, Oct 1997.

[Fis97]   C. Fischer. CSP-OZ: A combination of Object-Z and CSP. In H. Bowman and J. Derrick, editors, *Formal Methods for Open Object-Based Distributed Systems (FMOODS '97)*, volume 2, pages 423–438. Chapman & Hall, 1997.

[FW99]   C. Fischer and H. Wehrheim. Model-checking CSP-OZ specifications with FDR. In K. Araki, A. Galloway, and K. Taguchi, editors, *Proceedings of the 1st International Conference on Integrated Formal Methods (IFM)*, pages 315–334. Springer, 1999.

[GP93]   J.F. Groote and A. Ponse. Proof theory for μ-CRL: A language for processes with data. In *Semantics of specification languages*, Workshops in Computing. Springer, 1993.

[GS97]   A. J. Galloway and W. Stoddart. An operational semantics for ZCCS. In M. Hinchey and Shaoying Liu, editors, *Int. Conf. of Formal Engineering Methods (ICFEM)*. IEEE, 1997.

[Hoa85]   C. A. R. Hoare. *Communicating Sequential Processes*. Prentice-Hall, 1985.

[MD98]   B. P. Mahony and J.S. Dong. Blending Object-Z and Timed CSP: An introduction to TCOZ. In *The 20th International Conference on Software Engineering (ICSE'98)*, pages 95–104. IEEE Computer Society Press, April 1998.

[MS98]   A. Mota and A. Sampaio. Model-checking CSP-Z. In *Proceedings of the European Joint Conference on Theory and Practice of Software*, volume 1382 of *LNCS*, pages 205–220, 1998.

[Obj99]   Object Management Group. *OMG Unified Modeling Language Specification*, June 1999. version 1.3.

[Que96]   J. Quemada, editor. *Revised working draft on enhancements to LOTOS (V4)*. ISO, 1996.

[Ros97]   A. W. Roscoe. *The Theory and Practice of Concurrency*. Prentice-Hall, 1997.

[Smi97]   G. Smith. A semantic integration of Object-Z and CSP for the specification of concurrent systems. In J. Fitzgerald, C. B. Jones, and P. Lucas, editors, *Proceedings of FME 1997*, volume 1313 of *LNCS*, pages 62–81. Springer, 1997.

[Smi00]   G. Smith. *The Object-Z Specification Language*. Kluwer Academic Publisher, 2000.

[Spi92]   J. M. Spivey. *The Z Notation: A Reference Manual*. Prentice-Hall International Series in Computer Science, 2nd edition, 1992.

[SR98]   B. Selic and J. Rumbaugh. Using UML for modeling complex real-time systems. Technical report, ObjecTime, 1998.

[TA97]   K. Taguchi and K. Araki. Specifying concurrent systems by Z + CCS. In *International Symposium on Future Software Technology (ISFST)*, pages 101–108, 1997.

[WHS94]   E. Westkämper, M. Höpf, and C. Schaeffer. Holonic manufacturing systems. In Lake Tahoe HMS Consortium, editor, *Holonic manufacturing systems*, 1994.

A Case Study on Using Automata in Control Synthesis

Thomas Hune and Anders Sandholm

BRICS*, Department of Computer Science
University of Aarhus, Denmark
{baris,sandholm}@brics.dk

Abstract. We study a method for synthesizing control programs. The method merges an existing control program with a control automaton. We have used monadic second order logic over strings to specify the control automata. Specifications are translated into automata by the Mona tool. This yields a new control program restricting the behavior of the old control program such that the specifications are satisfied. The method is presented through a concrete example.

1 Introduction

In the following we will describe some practical experience on synthesizing programs for the LEGO® RCX™ system. The synthesis is based partly on an existing simple program and partly on an automaton generated by the tool Mona [7].

Writing control programs can often be an error prone task, especially if a number of special cases must be taken into account. Time is often spent on handling special case or failure situations rather than solving the actual problem at hand. A number of different methods and tools have been developed to ease this task. One well known method is based on a control automaton running in parallel with the actual program [12, 13]. The automaton controls the input and output events of the program. This is a way of restricting the sequences of I/O actions occurring.

The automata controlling the I/O actions can be specified in different ways, e.g. by specifying it directly in some suitable notation, or by a logical formula. We have chosen the latter approach. There are various logics which could be used as specification language. We have chosen to use monadic second order logic over strings (M2L) [2] for a number of reasons. First of all M2L has a number of nice properties such as being expressive and succinct. For instance, having second order quantification M2L is more expressive than LTL. Furthermore, there are succinct M2L-formulae of size n which have minimal corresponding automata of non-elementary size. Secondly, the tool Mona [7] implements a translation from M2L formulae to minimal deterministic automata (MDFA) accepting the language specified by the formula. The automata generated do not contain any

---

* Basic Research in Computer Science,
  Center of the Danish National Research Foundation.

T. Maibaum (Ed.): FASE 2000, LNCS 1783, pp. 349–362, 2000.

acceptance condition for infinite executions so we will only be considering safety properties.

The method we study here is a variation of classical synthesis as described in e.g. [10, 12], in that the method is partly based on an existing control program. The aim of the synthesis described here is to restrict the behavior of an existing (hopefully very simple) control program such that it satisfies certain given properties. The executions of the existing control program are restricted by the control automaton having I/O events as alphabet. These events define the interface between the existing control program and the specification.

For studying the method we will look at a control program for a moving crane. We have implemented the method for this example in the LEGO® RCX™ system [9]. Using the LEGO® RCX™ system is interesting for at least two reasons. First of all the environment of the RCX™ system and especially the programming language is quite restricted, so it is not obvious that implementing the method is feasible at all. Secondly, using the LEGO® RCX™ system one can build actual physical systems for testing the control programs. We have built the crane and used it with different control programs.

The language running on the LEGO® RCX™ brick (RCX™ language) is an assembly-like language with a few high level features, like a notion of task or process. Programs are written on a PC and downloaded to the RCX™ brick where they are interpreted.

1.1 Related Work

The use of finite state automata for controlling systems is not novel. Ramadge and Wonham [12] give a survey of classic results.

The method used in this paper has been used successfully in <bigwig> [13], a tool for specifying and generating interactive Web services. Our method for control synthesis is used as an integral part of <bigwig> to define safety constraints. In fact, via use of a powerful macro mechanism [1] the method has been used to extend the Web programming language in <bigwig> with concepts and primitives for concurrency control, such as, semaphores and monitors.

1.2 Outline of the Paper

In the following section we will outline the method. A short presentation of the LEGO® system is given in Section 3. In Section 4 the crane example is presented. The logic-based specification language is presented in Section 5, and the merge of automata with the RCX™ code in Section 6. Finally, Section 7 rounds off with conclusions, and suggestions for future work.

2 Outline of the Method

The two main components of the synthesis is a basic control program and an automaton. From these two components we generate a control program which is ready for use. We do not have any special requirements to what a control program is, like no side effects, since in our case the control program is the only program running on the RCX™ brick. The interface between the two components is a predefined set of I/O actions. This will typically be all commands in the program for reading sensors or manipulating actuators.

Given a basic control program and an implementation of the automaton we merge these. Each instruction in the basic control program using one of the I/O actions is transformed to a sequence of instructions first calling the automaton and based on the response from the automaton performing the action or not. Section 6.3 will discuss different approaches to what should happen, when a given action is not allowed by the automaton.

Since the automaton is invoked only when the basic control program is about to make an I/O action, it can only restrict the possible I/O behaviors of the control program, not add new I/O actions. Only looking at sequences of I/O actions the basic control program must therefore be able to generate all sequences present in the solution. Since the automaton will prune away unwanted sequences, the basic control program might also generate unwanted sequences. The basic control program should not implement any kind of priority scheme, unless one is sure that combining this with the safety specification will not lead to deadlocks.

The hope is that writing such basic control programs should be a simple task. In general the basic control program could be one always being able to read any sensor and give any command to the actuators. This amounts to generating the star operation of the input alphabet. However, there will often be a correspondence between input and output which it would be natural to have in a basic the control program. This is the case in the example shown later.

One could see the basic control program as implementing the method for controlling the sequences of I/O actions and the automaton defining the allowed policy for these. This suggests that with one implementation of a basic control program it is possible to test different specifications or strategies (policies) only by changing the control automaton. Therefore, a fast (automatic) way of getting an implementation of an automaton from a specification and merging this with the control program allows for testing different specifications fast.

3   The LEGO® System

The studies we have conducted are based on the LEGO® RCX™ system and the associated RCX™ language. The language is an assembly like language with some high level concepts like concurrent tasks. The language is restricted in a number of ways, e.g. it is possible to address only 32 integer variables and allows only ten tasks in a program. Furthermore, one cannot use symbolic names in programs. However, we have not encountered problems with the mentioned restrictions during our experiments.

A small operating system is running on the RCX™ with processes for handling I/O and one process running an interpreter for the RCX™ language. The RCX™

brick has three output ports (for motors and lights) and three input ports. Four kinds of sensors for the input ports are supplied by LEGO®: touch, temperature, rotation, and light.

3.1   The RCX™ Language

A program consists of a collection of at most ten tasks. There is no special way to communicate between tasks but all variables are shared, providing a way of communication. A task can start another task with the command StartTask(i) and stop it with the command StopTask(i). Starting a task means restarting it from the beginning. That is, there is no command for resuming the execution of a task nor spawning an extra "instance" of a task.

The language has some commands for controlling the actuators, the main ones being On(li) and Off(li) where li is a list of ports. The commands SetFwd(li) and SetRwd(li) sets the direction of the ports in li to forward and reverse respectively. There are also a number of instructions for manipulating variables. All of these take three integer arguments. The first argument specifies the target variable, the second the type of the source, and the third the source. The most important types of sources are: variables (the third argument is then the number of the variable), constants (the third argument is then the value), and sensor readings (the third argument is then the number of the sensor). These types of sources can be used in the instruction SetVar(i,j,k) for assigning a value to a variable. In the instructions for calculating like SumVar(i,j,k), SubVar(i,j,k), and MulVar(i,j,k) sensor readings are not allowed.

Loops can be defined in two ways, either by the Loop(j,k) instruction or by the While(j,k,l,m,n) instruction. The arguments of the Loop indicates how many times the body should be iterated in the same way as the source of the instructions for calculating. The While loop is iterated as long as the condition specified by the arguments is satisfied. The first two and last two arguments specify the sources of a comparison as in an assignment and l specifies a relation from the set $\{=, <, >, \neq\}$.

There is also a conditional, If(j,k,l,m,n), with the condition specified as in the While construct and an Else branch can be specified as well.

One can block a task for a given time using the Wait(j,k) statement. When the specified time has passed, execution of the task is resumed.

During execution a task is either enabled or blocked. A task can be blocked by a StopTask(i) instruction, by a Wait(j,k) instruction, or by finishing its execution (reaching the end of the code). Initially only task zero is enabled. The enabled tasks are executed in a round robin fashion, where each task executes one instruction and then leaves control for the next task.

The statements presented above constitute the part of the RCX™ language which we have used for implementing control automata.

4   Example

As an example we will look at a crane which we will program in the RCX™ language. We have built the crane and tested it with different control programs. The crane is run by three motors connected to the RCX™. One motor is driving the wheels, one is turning the turret around, and one is moving the hook up and down. The input for the three motors are three touch sensors, which is all the RCX™ brick has room for. This means we can only turn motors on and off. Therefore the crane alternates between moving forward and backward each time the motor is turned on. The direction of turret and the hook is controlled in a similar way.

A very basic control program for the crane could consist of four tasks. One task for setting up the sensors and motors, and starting the other tasks. For each of the three inputs, one task for monitoring input and controlling the motor correspondingly. Task 1 for monitoring sensor 0 would then be

```
BeginOfTask 1
Loop 2, 0                    'An infinite loop
  SetFwd "0"                 'Set direction of motor 0 to forward
  SetVar 1, SENSOR, 0        'Var1 := Sensor0
  While VAR, 1, 3, CONST, 1  'While Var1 != 1
    SetVar 1, SENSOR, 0
  EndWhile
  On "0"                     'Start motor 0
  Wait CONST, 100            'Wait
  SetVar 1, SENSOR, 0        'Var1 := Sensor0
  While VAR, 1, 3, CONST, 1  'While Var1 != 1
    SetVar 1, SENSOR, 0
  EndWhile
  Off "0"                    'Stop motor 0
  Wait CONST, 100                'Wait
  ... repeat the code replacing SetFwd "0" with SetRwd "0" ...
EndLoop
EndOfTask
```

The Wait statements ensures that one touch of the sensor is not read as two touches. We could of course have tested for this but for our example this will do. The two other tasks for controlling the remaining two motors look similar, only the numbers of variables, sensors and motors are different.

For the purpose of illustrating the presented method we choose to place the following constraints on the behavior of the crane. First of all we only want one thing happening at a time, so we will not allow for two motors to be turned on at the same time. Pressing the touch sensor could now be seen as a request which the control program may grant (and start the motor) when all the motors are stopped. Moreover, we want that moving the hook has higher priority than the wheels and the turret. Requests from the other two are handled in order of arrival. The first constraint on the behavior is basically mutual exclusion which is nontrivial to implement in the RCX™ language (this is an integrated part of the implementation of the automata-based approach described in Section 6). On top of this we have a mixed priority and queue scheme.

5   Logic-Based Specifications

Basically we could keep the initial simple control program if we had a way of pruning out some unwanted executions. To be able to implement the constraints we have to change the initial control program slightly. This is done by considering touching a sensor as a request. The motor can be turned on when the request is accepted. Even with these changes the program is still a simple to write. Execution of the program gives rise to a sequence of events. In our case we will consider input (requests), and two kinds of output (start and stop motor) as events. We then implement the automaton accepting the language over these events satisfying the introduced constraints. With this approach we can thus keep the control program simple.

Traditionally, control languages are described by automata which are in some cases a good formalism to work with. However, having experience in using logic for specifying properties, we will take that approach here. In this section we describe the use of a logic formalism from which we can automatically generate automata.

5.1   Terminology

An *automaton* is a structure $A = (Q, q^{in}, \Sigma, \rightarrow, F)$, where Q is a set of states with initial state $q^{in} \in Q$, Σ is a finite set of events, $\rightarrow \subseteq Q \times \Sigma \times Q$ is the transition relation, and $F \subseteq Q$ the set of acceptance states. We shall use $q_1 \xrightarrow{\sigma} q_2$ to denote $(q_1, \sigma, q_2) \in \rightarrow$. A sequence $w = \sigma_0 \sigma_1 \ldots \sigma_{n-1} \in \Sigma^*$ is said to be *accepted* by the automaton A if there exists a run of A which reads the sequence w and ends up in an accepting state q. So we have $q_1, \ldots, q_{n-1} \in Q$ and $q \in F$, such that $q^{in} \xrightarrow{\sigma_0} q_1 \xrightarrow{\sigma_1} \ldots \xrightarrow{\sigma_{n-2}} q_{n-1} \xrightarrow{\sigma_{n-1}} q$. We shall denote by $L(A)$ the *language* recognized by an automaton, that is, $L(A) = \{ w \in \Sigma^* \mid A \text{ accepts } w \}$.

In order to be able to define the notion of a legal control language, one partitions the event set Σ into *uncontrollable* and *controllable* events: $\Sigma = \Sigma_u \cup \Sigma_c$. The controllable events can be disabled by the control automaton at any time, whereas the uncontrollable ones are performed autonomously by the system without any possible interference by the control automaton, which merely has to accept the fact that the particular uncontrollable event has occurred. Thus a control language must in some sense, which is defined precisely below, respect the uncontrollableness of certain events. Furthermore, since our method only allows restrictions concerning safety properties, it does not make sense to have non-prefix-closed languages as control languages. That is, we define the notion of control language as follows.

Let $pre(L)$ denote the prefix closure of a language L, and let $unc(L)$ denote closure of L under concatenation of uncontrollable events. That is, let

$$pre(L) = \{\, v \in \Sigma^* \mid \exists w \in \Sigma^* : vw \in L \,\} \text{ and}$$
$$unc(L) = \{\, vw \in \Sigma^* \mid v \in L \wedge w \in \Sigma_u^* \,\}.$$

A language, L over $\Sigma = \Sigma_u \cup \Sigma_c$ is called a *control language* if it satisfies the two properties $pre(L) = L$ and $unc(L) = L$.

When using deterministic finite state automata to specify sets of sequences, checking for prefix closedness is easy. One just has to make sure that all transitions from non-accepting states go to non-accepting states. Similarly, checking closure under concatenation of uncontrollable events is straightforward for deterministic automata.

What is new here, in comparison to the use of our method in [13], apart from the new domain of LEGO® RCX™ robots, is the partition into controllable and uncontrollable events and the resulting additional restrictions and computations.

5.2   Specification Logic

It would be nice if instead of converting the informal requirement in Section 4 into an automaton, one could write it formally in a specification formalism closer to natural language. That is, we would like to be able to write something like the following.

- Only one motor can be turned on at a time;
- If the wheels get turned on, then the hook must not be requesting and the wheels must have been the first to make a request; and
- If the turret gets turned on, then the hook must not be requesting and the wheels must have been the first to make a request.

We therefore turn to a formalism that is as expressive as finite state automata and yet still allows for separation of the declaratively specified requirements (previously our control automaton) and the operational part of the control program (the existing RCX™ program).

Experience has shown that logic is a suitable specification formalism for control languages. For the purpose of defining controllers for LEGO® RCX™ robots, we have chosen to use M2L. One might argue in favor of other specification formalisms such as high-level Petri Nets [6] or Message Sequence Charts [11]. Being a logic formalism, however, M2L has the advantage that specifications can be developed iteratively, that is, one can easily add, delete, and modify parts of a specification. It also has a readable textual format. Moreover, the formalism in use should be simple enough that a runtime checker, such as an automaton, can actually be calculated and downloaded to the RCX™ brick. Thus, M2L is powerful and yet just simple enough to actually subject it to automated computation.

Experience in using M2L as a language for defining control requirements has shown that only the first-order fraction of the logic is used in practice [1,

13]. We shall thus consider only first order quantifications, though second-order quantifications could be added at no extra cost.

The abstract syntax of the logic is given by the following grammar:

$$\phi ::= \exists p : \phi' \mid \forall p : \phi' \mid \neg \phi' \mid \phi' \wedge \phi'' \mid \phi' \vee \phi'' \mid \phi' \Rightarrow \phi'' \mid \sigma(t) \mid t < t'$$
$$t ::= p \mid t + 1$$

That is, M2L has the constructs: universal and existential quantifications over first order variables (ranging over positions in the sequence of events), standard boolean connectives such as negation, conjunction, disjunction, and implication, and basic formulae, $\sigma(t)$, to test whether an event σ can be found at position t, and $t < t'$, to test whether position t is before position t'. It also has operations on terms, such as, given a position t one can point out its successor $(t+1)$, and simple term variables (p).

A formula ϕ in M2L over the event set Σ will – when interpreted over a finite sequence of events w – either evaluate to true or to false and we shall write this as $w \models \phi$ or $w \not\models \phi$, respectively. The *language* associated with ϕ is $L(\phi) = \{ w \in \Sigma^* \mid w \models \phi \}$. The language associated with an M2L formula is guaranteed to be regular. In fact, it has been known since the sixties that M2L characterizes regularity [2, 4].

The Mona tool implements the constructive proof of the fact that for each M2L formula there is a minimal deterministic finite state automaton accepting the language of the formula. That is, Mona translates a particular M2L formulae, ϕ, into its corresponding minimal deterministic finite state automata (MDFA), A, such that $L(\phi) = L(A)$.

Example 1. Let $\Sigma = \{a, b, c\}$. The M2L formula to left

$$\forall p, p'' : (p < p'' \wedge a(p) \wedge a(p''))$$
$$\implies \exists p' : p < p' < p'' \wedge b(p')$$

is true for sequences in which any two occurrences of a will have an occurrence of b in between. Using Mona, one can compute the automaton corresponding to the formula above. The resulting automaton appears to the right.

Example 2. With this logic-based specification language in place, we can write a specification of the requirements given in the example. The logic-based specification looks quite complex at first. However, because of it's modular structure we find it easier to handle than the automaton. The basic formulae for the elements of the alphabet are req1(t), req2(t), req3(t), turnon1(t), turnon2(t), turnon3(t), turnoff1(t), turnoff2(t), and turnoff1(t). The first three are uncontrollable events of the alphabet and the rest are controllable events of the alphabet. A predicate is true if the event at position t is the mentioned event. Using these basic predicates we can define some basic predicates like all motors are stopped by:

$$\text{off1}(t) = (\forall t' : t' < t \Rightarrow \neg\text{turnon1}(t')) \lor$$
$$(\forall t' : (t' < t \land \text{turnon1}(t')) \Rightarrow$$
$$\exists t'' : t' < t'' \land t'' < t \land \text{turnoff1}(t''))$$

Similarly, we define predicates `off2(t)` and `off3(t)` and using these we can define a predicate, `alloff(t)`, specifying that all the motors are turned off.

$$\text{alloff}(t) = \text{off1}(t) \land \text{off2}(t) \land \text{off3}(t)$$

We can specify that motor 1 has been requested to be turned but has not yet been turned on by the following predicate:

$$\text{request1}(t) = \exists t' : t' < t \land \text{req1}(t') \land (\forall t'' : (t' < t'' \land t'' < t) \Rightarrow \neg\text{turnon1}(t''))$$

Predicates `request2(t)` and `request3(t)` are specified similarly. Using this we can define a predicate specifying that the first request which has not been acknowledged is one.

$$\text{req1first}(t) = \text{req1}(t) \land \forall t' : (t' < t \land \text{request1}(t') \land$$
$$\forall t'' : (t' < t'' \land t'' < t) \Rightarrow \neg\text{request1}(t'')) \Rightarrow$$
$$((\text{req2}(t') \Rightarrow \exists t'' : t' < t'' \land t'' < t \land \neg\text{req2}(t'')) \land$$
$$(\text{req3}(t') \Rightarrow \exists t'' : t' < t'' \land t'' < t \land \neg\text{req3}(t'')))$$

Again, predicates `req2first(t)` and `req3first(t)` are specified similarly. With these basic predicates as building blocks we can give a specification closely related to the informal requirements of the example.

$$\forall t : (\text{turnon1}(t) \lor \text{turnon2}(t) \lor \text{turnon3}(t)) \Rightarrow \text{alloff}(t) \land$$
$$\forall t : \text{turnon2}(t) \Rightarrow (\neg\text{req1}(t) \land \text{req2first}(t)) \land$$
$$\forall t : \text{turnon3}(t) \Rightarrow (\neg\text{req1}(t) \land \text{req3first}(t)),$$

An informal specification for the control of the crane containing three properties was given in Section 5.2. Each of these properties corresponds to one of the lines in the predicate above. For instance the first line of the predicate specifies that if a motor is turned on then all the motors are turned off. This corresponds to the first property that only one motor can be turned on at a time. Similar for the remaining two lines and properties.

Since our basic control program specifies the order of the events in the individual tasks (first `req`, then `turnon`, and then `turnoff`), this specification will define the wanted behavior.

From this specification Mona generates the minimal deterministic automaton which has 46 states and 276 transitions (six from each state).

Should we want to change the control language of our example in such a way that all three tasks have equal priority, the overall structure of the control automaton would change. As the following example will show, modifying the logical formula is indeed quite comprehensible in the case of the LEGO® crane requirements.

Example 3. Say that we would like to change the requirements such that all motors are given equal priority, that is, they will be turned on in a first come first served manner. Using the logic-based specification, all we have to do is to change the last two lines of our specification slightly resulting in the following fifo requirement.

$$\forall t : (\mathtt{turnon1}(t) \vee \mathtt{turnon2}(t) \vee \mathtt{turnon3}(t)) \Rightarrow \mathrm{alloff}(t) \wedge$$
$$\forall t : \mathtt{turnon1}(t) \Rightarrow \mathrm{req1first}(t) \wedge$$
$$\forall t : \mathtt{turnon2}(t) \Rightarrow \mathrm{req2first}(t) \wedge$$
$$\forall t : \mathtt{turnon3}(t) \Rightarrow \mathrm{req3first}(t).$$

Note that the sub-formulae, such as, `alloff()` and `req2first()` are reused from the previous specification. As we can see it is relatively easy to change the specification using the previously defined primitives.

From this specification Mona generates an automaton with 79 states and 474 transitions.

6   Merging Automata and RCX™ Code

Given a control automaton and the basic control program, one can synthesize the complete control program. In this section we describe how to translate an automaton into RCX™ code and how this is merged with the existing RCX™ control program. For our example we have done this by hand. It should be clear from this section that only standard techniques are used and these can easily be carried out automatically.

6.1   Wrapping the RCX™ Code

The execution of the basic control program is restricted to sequences allowed by a control automaton as follows. Firstly, RCX™ code is generated for the control automaton and then this code is merged with the existing RCX™ code. Merging RCX™ code with an automaton can in some sense be considered a program transformation. Each statement involving a request or writing to an output port is replaced by a block of code that tests whether the operation is legal according to the control automaton. For our example an action should be delayed if the control automaton does not allow it. Transforming the code for turning motor 0 on, will lead to the following piece of code.

```
While VAR, 4, 3, CONST, 1 'While automaton has not accepted the command
  SetVar 31, CONST, 1      'Arg := on0, the argument for the automaton
  GoSub 0                  'Run the automaton
  SetVar 4, VAR, 22        'Local success:= global success
EndWhile
On "0"                     'Execution of the actual command
```

We have chosen to implement the automaton as a subroutine. Since arguments for subroutines are not allowed in the language, passing an argument to the automaton has to be done via a global variable. Similarly, since a subroutine cannot return a value, return values are also placed in global variables for the process to read. The while loop delays the action until the automaton accepts execution of it.

6.2   Implementing Mutual Exclusion and Automata

However, the idea described above is not sufficient since we will not allow more tasks to use the automaton simultaneously. In the RCX™ language the problem is obvious since we are using shared variables for passing arguments and results. In general, we also need exclusive access to the automaton since the outcome of the automaton depends on its state when execution begins. If a process accesses the automaton while it is used by another process, the state variable might be corrupted. Therefore we must have exclusive access to the automaton.

In our implementation we have used Dijkstra's algorithm to implement mutual exclusion between several processes [3]. But any correct mutual exclusion algorithm would of course do. The algorithm uses some shared variables but this is no problem in the RCX™ language since all variables are shared. There are no gotos in the RCX™ language. Therefore, we have used an extra while loop and a success variable for each task. Except from these details, the algorithm is followed directly.

An automaton is implemented in the standard way by representing the transition relation as nested conditionals of depth two branching on the current state and the input symbol respectively. The current state and the input symbol is represented by one variable each. This gives us a way to combine the run of an automaton with the execution of standard RCX™ code with wrapped input/output statements.

6.3   Variations of the Method

In the example an action is delayed if the control automaton does not grant permission at once. Depending on the problem to be solved the action taken when permission is not granted can vary. That is, there are various ways of handling this temporary lack of controller acknowledgment:

 - as in the above example where the task is *busy wait* asking the controller over and over whether its label had been enabled; but
 - one could also simply *cancel* or ignore the statement requesting permission and continue execution. This could be done by replacing the busy waiting while loop by an if statement.

The former would often be the preferred approach in cases where the internal state of the code is important, such as, in our example, or in a train gate controller. The latter would be a good choice in cases where the code is written in a reactive style, constantly changing output action based on newly read input, e.g. in autonomous robots.

The property implemented by the automaton in the example was specific to the problem. One could also imagine using the method for general properties e.g. for protecting hardware against malicious sequences of actions. This leaves at least two options of where to put the automaton:

- as in the example above where the automaton was put *alongside the wrapped RCX™ code*. Placing the code implementing the automaton at this level seems a natural choice when dealing with properties about the behavior of a specific RCX™ program solving a particular problem.
- If the property is of a more general kind, one should rather place the automaton *at the level of the operating system*.

So far we have only considered untimed properties. One could easily imagine using automata with discrete time as control automata. This would open for a whole new range of properties to be specified, e.g. a minimum delay between two actions. In the example it would be possible to specify properties like that a minimum time of 5 seconds should pass between stopping the crane and starting to move the hook.

On the RCX™ this could be realized by having a variable representing the discrete time. This variable could be updated by a task consisting of an infinite loop waiting for one time unit and then updating the variable. Assuming variable number zero represents the time, it could be updated by:

```
SetVar 0, CONST, 0       'Initialize the timer
Loop CONST, 0            'An infinite loop
  Wait CONST, 10         'Wait for 1 sec.
  SumVar 0, CONST, 1     'Update the timer
EndLoop
```

7   Conclusion

We have used control automata in conjunction with basic control programs for synthesizing complete control programs. Using this method one can add to a basic control program a control automaton which will ensure certain safety properties are satisfied. We have used M2L to specify the control automata and the Mona tool to translate formulae into automata.

The approach has been implemented in the setting of the LEGO® RCX™ system. This has allowed for the possibility of testing the implementations on real physical systems.

Based on our experiments we find the method well suited for synthesis of programs ensuring safety properties like the ones we have used. We find the main advantage of the method is the ease of testing different specifications. The separation of the active control program and the restricting automaton also allows for ensuring (new) safety specifications to existing control programs. In critical systems one might consider the automaton only for monitoring actions, not restricting these, to avoid deadlocks.

The main disadvantage of the method is the restriction to safety properties. Since the all concurrent tasks must access the automaton there is a danger of this becoming bottleneck.

Future work There is an overhead connected with gaining exclusive access to the automaton and running it. How much time is spent on gaining access to the automaton of course depends on the arrival of input events. It would be interesting to calculate some specific times for this given some input sequences. A tool for translating RCX™ programs to timed models supported by Uppaal [8] exists [5]. Using Uppaal one can "measure" the time spent by a program from an input is read until the response arrives.

The example presented in this paper only has one component (one crane) and the control restrictions are consequently imposed on that particular component only. One could easily imagine having several components in a distributed environment working to achieve a common goal. By use of modular synthesis and distributed control [12] via independence analysis [13] one can statically infer information about which constraints to put locally on the components and which to put on the (most often necessary) central controller.

References

[1] Claus Brabrand. Synthesizing safety controllers for interactive Web services. Master's thesis, Department of Computer Science, University of Aarhus, December 1998. Available from `http://www.brics.dk/~brabrand/thesis/`.

[2] J.R. Büchi. Weak second-order arithmetic and finite automata. *Z. Math. Logik Grundl. Math.*, 6:66–92, 1960.

[3] E.W. Dijkstra. Solution of a problem in concurrent programming control. *Communications of the ACM*, 8(9):569, September 1965.

[4] C.C. Elgot. Decision problems of finite automata design and related arithmetics. *Transactions of the American Mathematical Society*, 98:21–52, 1961.

[5] T. Hune. Modelling a real-time language. In *Proceedings of Fourth International Workshop on Formal Methods for Industrial Critical Systems*, 1999.

[6] K. Jensen and G. Rozenberg, editors. *High-level Petri Nets – Theory and Application*. Springer-Verlag, 1991.

[7] N. Klarlund and A. Møller. *MONA Version 1.3 User Manual*. BRICS Notes Series NS-98-3 (2.revision), Department of Computer Science, University of Aarhus, October 1998.

[8] K. G. Larsen, P. Pettersson, and W. Yi. UPPAAL in a nutshell. *In Springer International Journal of Software Tools for Technology Transfer*, 1(1+2), 1997.

[9] LEGO.   *Software   developers   kit*,   November   1998.   See `http://www.legomindstorms.com/`.

[10] Z. Manna and A. Pnueli. Synthesis of communicating processes from temporal logic specifications. *ACM Transactions on Programming Languages and Systems*, 6(1):68–93, January 1984.

[11] S. Mauw and M. A. Reniers. An algebraic semantics of Basic Message Sequence Charts. *The Computer Journal*, 37(4):269–277, 1994.

[12] Peter J. G. Ramadge and W. Murray Wonham. The control of discrete event systems. *Proceedings of the IEEE*, 77(1):81–98, January 1989.

[13] Anders Sandholm and Michael I. Schwartzbach. Distributed safety controllers for Web services. In Egidio Astesiano, editor, *Fundamental Approaches to Software Engineering, FASE'98*, Lecture Notes in Computer Science, LNCS 1382, pages 270–284. Springer-Verlag, March/April 1998. Also available as BRICS Technical Report RS-97-47.

Formal System Development with KIV

Michael Balser, Wolfgang Reif, Gerhard Schellhorn, Kurt Stenzel, and
Andreas Thums

Abt. Programmiermethodik
Universität Ulm, 89069 Ulm, Germany
{balser,reif,schellhorn,stenzel,thums}@informatik.uni-ulm.de

1   Overview

KIV is a tool for formal systems development. It can be employed, e.g.,

- for the development of safety critical systems from formal requirements specifications to executable code, including the verification of safety requirements
  and the correctness of implementations,
- for semantical foundations of programming languages from a specification of
  the semantics to a verified compiler,
- for building security models and architectural models as they are needed for
  high level ITSEC [7] or CC [1] evaluations.

Special care was (and is) taken to provide strong proof support for all validation
and verification tasks. KIV can handle large scale formal models by efficient
proof techniques, multi-user support, and an ergonomical user interface. It has
been used in a number of industrial pilot applications, but is also useful as an
educational tool for formal methods courses. Details on KIV can be found in [9]
[10] [11] and under http://www.informatik.uni-ulm.de/pm/kiv/.

2   Specification Language

KIV supports both the functional and the state-based approach to describe
hierarchically structured systems.

The functional approach uses higher-order algebraic specifications. The first-
order part is a subset of CASL [2]. Specifications are built up from elementary
specifications with the operations enrichment, union, renaming, parameteriza-
tion and actualization. Specifications have a loose semantics and may include
generation principles to define inductive data types. Specification components
can be implemented by stepwise refinement using modules with imperative programs. The designer is subject to a strict decompositional design discipline leading to modular systems with compositional correctness. As a consequence, the
verification effort for a modular system becomes linear in the number of its
modules.

For the state-based approach KIV uses abstract state machines (ASMs, [5])
over algebraically specified data types. The semantics of an ASM is the set of

T. Maibaum (Ed.): FASE 2000, LNCS 1783, pp. 363–366, 2000.

traces generated by the transition relation defined by the rules of the ASM. ASMs are implemented using a compositional refinement notion. Correctness of a refinement requires the commutativity of diagrams for corresponding traces. An important instance of ASM refinement is compiler correctness, e.g. for Prolog [13]. A modularization theorem allows to decompose the correctness proof for each refinement into subproofs for arbitrary subdiagrams [4]. Correctness proofs use Dynamic Logic, a program logic for imperative programs.

In KIV, formal specifications of software and system designs are represented explicitly as directed acyclic graphs called *development graphs*. Each node corresponds to a specification component, an ASM, a module or an ASM refinement. Each node has a *theorem base* attached. Theorem bases initially contain axioms, ASM rules and automatically generated proof obligations for refinements. The theorem base also stores theorems added by the user (proved and yet unproved ones), and manages proofs and their dependencies.

3   Proof Support

In KIV, proofs for specification validation, design verification, and program verification are supported by an advanced interactive deduction component based on *proof tactics*. It combines a high degree of automation with an elaborate interactive proof engineering environment. Deduction is based on a sequent calculus with proof tactics like simplification, lemma application, and induction for first-order reasoning and a proof strategy based on symbolic execution and induction for the verification of implementations with imperative programs using Dynamic Logic [6].

To automate proofs, KIV offers a number of *heuristics* [10]. Among others, heuristics for induction, unfolding of procedure calls, and quantifier instantiation are provided. Heuristics can be chosen freely, and changed any time during the proof. Additionally, a 'problem specific' heuristic exists which is easily adaptable to specific applications. Usually, the heuristics manage to find 80 – 100 % of the required proof steps automatically.

The conditional rewriter in KIV (called *simplifier*) handles thousands of rules very efficiently, using the compilation technique of [8] with some extensions like AC-rewriting and forward reasoning. As the structure of a formula helps to understand its meaning, the KIV simplifier preserves this structure. The user explicitly chooses the rewrite and simplification rules. Different sets of simplification rules can be chosen for different tasks.

Frequently, the problem in engineering high assurance systems is not to verify proof obligations affirmatively, but rather to interpret failed proof attempts that may indicate errors in specifications, programs, lemmas etc. Therefore, KIV offers a number of *proof engineering* facilities to support the iterative process of (failed) proof attempts, error detection, error correction and re-proof. Dead ends in proof trees can be cut off, proof decisions may be withdrawn both chronologically and non-chronologically. Unprovable subgoals can be detected by automatically generating counter examples. This counter example can be traced backwards through the proof to the earliest point of failure. Thereby the user is assisted in the decision whether the goal to prove is not correct, proof decisions were incorrect, or there is a flaw in the specification. After a correction the goal must be re-proved. Here another interesting feature of KIV, the strategy for proof reuse, can be used. Both successful and failed proof attempts are reused automatically to guide the verification after corrections [12]. This goes far beyond proof replay or proof scripts. We found that typically 90% of a failed proof attempt can be recycled for the verification after correction.

The *correctness management* in KIV ensures that changes to or deletions of specifications, modules, and theorems do not lead to inconsistencies, and that the user can do proofs in any order (not only bottom up). It guarantees that only the minimal number of proofs are invalidated after modifications, that there are no cycles in the proof hierarchy and that finally all used lemmas and proof obligations are proved (in some sub-specification).

4   User Interface

KIV offers a powerful graphical user interface which has been constantly improved over the years. The intuitive user interface allows easy access to KIV for first time users, and is an important prerequisite for managing large applications. The interface is object oriented, and is implemented in Java to guarantee platform independency.

The top-level object of a development, the development graph, is displayed using daVinci [3], a graph visualization tool which automatically arranges large graphs conveniently. The theorem base, which is attached to each development node, is arranged in tables, and context sensitive popup menus are provided for manipulation. While proving a theorem, the user is able to restrict the set of applicable tactics by selecting a context, i.e. a formula or term in the goal, with the mouse. This is extremely helpful for applying rewrite rules, as the set of hundreds of rewrite rules is reduced to a small number of applicable rules for the selected context. Proofs are presented as trees, where the user can click on nodes to inspect single proof steps.

In large applications, the plentitude of information may be confusing. Therefore, important information is summarized, and more details are displayed on request. Different colors are used to classify the given information. Additionally a special font allows the use of a large number of mathematical symbols.

KIV automatically produces LaTeX documentation for a development on different levels of detail. Specifications, implementations, theorem bases, proof protocols, and various kinds of statistics are pretty printed. The user is encouraged to add comments to specifications, which are also used to automatically produce a data dictionary. As several users may work simultaneously on a large project, the documentation facilities of KIV are very important. The automatically extracted information can also be included into reports.

References

1. CCIB-98-026. *Common Criteria for Information Technology Security Evaluation, Version 2.0.* ISO/IEC JTC 1, May 1998. available at http://csrc.nist.gov/cc.
2. CoFI: The Common Framework Initiative. Casl – the CoFI algebraic specification language tentative design: Language summary, 1997. Available at http://www.brics.dk/Projects/CoFI.
3. M. Fröhlich and M. Werner. Demonstration of the interactive graph visualization system *daVinci*. In R. Tamassia and I. Tollis, editors, *DIMACS Workshop on Graph Drawing '94. Proceedings*, LNCS 894, Berlin, 1994. Princeton (USA), Springer. http://www.informatik.uni-bremen.de/~davinci/.
4. G. Schellhorn. *Verifikation abstrakter Zustandsmaschinen.* PhD thesis, Universität Ulm, Fakultät für Informatik, 1999. (to appear, in German).
5. Y. Gurevich and J. Huggins. The semantics of the c programming language. In E. Börger, H. Kleine Büning, G. Jäger, S. Martini, and M.M. Richter, editors, *Computer Science Logic.* Springer LNCS 702, 1993.
6. D. Harel. *First Order Dynamic Logic.* LNCS 68. Springer, Berlin, 1979.
7. ITSEC. *Information Technology Security Evaluation Criteria, Version 1.2.* Office for Official Publications of the European Communities, June 1991.
8. S. Kaplan. A compiler for conditional term rewriting systems. In *2nd Conf. on Rewriting Techniques and Applications. Proceedings.* Bordeaux, France, Springer LNCS 256, 1987.
9. W. Reif. The KIV-approach to Software Verification. In M. Broy and S. Jähnichen, editors, *KORSO: Methods, Languages, and Tools for the Construction of Correct Software – Final Report*, LNCS 1009. Springer, Berlin, 1995.
10. W. Reif, G. Schellhorn, and K. Stenzel. Interactive Correctness Proofs for Software Modules Using KIV. In *COMPASS'95 – Tenth Annual Conference on Computer Assurance*, Gaithersburg (MD), USA, 1995. IEEE press.
11. W. Reif, G. Schellhorn, K. Stenzel, and M. Balser. Structured specifications and interactive proofs with KIV. In W. Bibel and P. Schmitt, editors, *Automated Deduction – A Basis for Applications.* Kluwer Academic Publishers, Dordrecht, 1998.
12. W. Reif and K. Stenzel. Reuse of Proofs in Software Verification. In R. Shyamasundar, editor, *Foundation of Software Technology and Theoretical Computer Science. Proceedings*, LNCS 761, pages 284–293, Berlin, 1993. Bombay, India, Springer.
13. G. Schellhorn and W. Ahrendt. Reasoning about Abstract State Machines: The WAM Case Study. *Journal of Universal Computer Science (J.UCS)*, 3(4):377–413, 1997. Available at http://hyperg.iicm.tu-graz.ac.at/jucs/.

More About TAS and IsaWin — Tools for Formal Program Development

Christoph Lüth[1] and Burkhart Wolff[2]

[1] Bremen Institute of Safe Systems (BISS), FB 3, Universität Bremen
cxl@informatik.uni-bremen.de
[2] Institut für Informatik, Albert-Ludwigs-Universität Freiburg
wolff@informatik.uni-freiburg.de

Abstract. We present a family of tools for program development and verification, comprising the transformation system TAS and the theorem proving interface IsaWin. Both are based on the theorem prover Isabelle [8], which is used as a generic logical framework here. A graphical user interface, based on the principle of direct manipulation, allows the user to interact with the tool without having to concern himself with the details of the representation within the theorem prover, leaving him to concentrate on the main design decisions of program development or theorem proving.

Introduction

Interactive theorem proving and program development may be more of a challenge than fully automatic techniques, but at the same time it is more powerful. The tools presented here have been designed to make this task as straightforward as possible. They are based on the Isabelle system, which provides a flexible logical framework and combines interactive proof with powerful automatic proof techniques. Isabelle is complemented with a graphical user interface, which is easy to learn and does not burden the user with unnecessary command language syntax and other technicalities. Moreover, the tools and methods can be used for a wide variety of logics or formal methods.

The tools form an integrated system for formal program development, in which TAS is used for transformational program development, and IsaWin for discharging the incurred proof obligations. However, both tools can be used separately as well.

In this extended abstract, we will give a brief overview over TAS and IsaWin. Since TAS and IsaWin have been presented on previous ETAPS conferences [3, 5], the presentation will concentrate on recent improvements.

The Transformation Application System TAS

TAS is a system for formal transformational program development. In a nutshell, formal program development with TAS proceeds as follows. The user begins by

T. Maibaum (Ed.): FASE 2000, LNCS 1783, pp. 367–370, 2000.

stating an initial specification with respect to a particular signature. The signature, corresponding to an Isabelle theory, is edited in an external file, and contains definitions of operations, data types, axioms, etc. The initial specification is transformed by applying correctness-preserving transformation rules, either generated automatically from existing theorems or taken from a library of predefined transformations. A particular feature of TAS is that transformation rules are based on theorems, which means that we can prove their correctness in a precise logical sense.

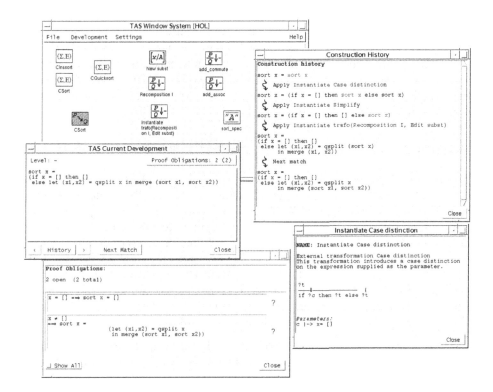

Fig. 1. Screenshot of TAS. Windows, clockwise from top left: the notepad, the construction history, a transformation, the proof obligations and the construction area.

Figure 1 shows a screenshot of TAS. The principle of direct manipulation means that the user should not have to remember the names of transformation rules, theorems, or other objects, but should instead be able to work with meaningful gestures as often as possible. Hence, transformation rules, substitutions and other intermediate results are placed on the *notepad*, where they are represented by icons and can be manipulated by drag&drop. Transformational development takes place in the *construction area*, where the current specification can be manipulated by *pointing* — we can mark a particular subterm and apply a transformation to it, or ask for all applicable transformations.

TAS is generic over the formal method employed, as long as it supports a notion of *correctness-preserving refinement*. Instantiations of TAS include higher-order logic, where the refinement is based on logical equivalence, and the process calculus CSP, where the refinement is based on the usual refinement of processes.

IsaWin

IsaWin is a graphical user interface for the theorem prover Isabelle. It can be used together with TAS to discharge the proof obligations arising from transformational developments, or as a stand-alone interface to Isabelle. It allows access to all of Isabelle's basic functionality, such as forward and backward resolution, simplification and classical reasoning. An instantiation of IsaWin with the embedding of the algebraic specification language CASL into Isabelle will be presented at the TACAS conference [7].

What's New?

The new developments build on the strengths of TAS and IsaWin: the graphical user interface and its principle of direct manipulation. The basic idea is that we can not relieve users of design decisions during the development or proving process, but we can support them as much as possible. To this end, we attempt to provide only as much information as needed, eliding unnecessary details but preserving the essentials. Details should remain available, but only per user request. The interface should be *quiet* [2]. Of course, users need to be knowledgeable in the particular logic or formal method used, but they should not have to remember names or syntactic representations of transformations, theorems or operations.

The recent improvements can be grouped as follows:

- *Search functions* look for applicable transformations or theorems in a particular situation. The user can mark a subterm, and have the system list all applicable transformations or theorems in a chooser.
- The *transformation library* allows transformations to be grouped into different folders (to distinguish e.g. complex design transformations from simple logical transformations). Further, the system supports the interactive, fully automatic *generation* of transformations from theorems.
- Pervasive use of *interactive hypertext*. E.g. by clicking on the name of an applied transformation rule in the history, the rule itself is displayed; a principle which is used whenever a name is displayed.
- With the *filer*, we can import signatures and specifications from the file system.
- TAS supports the *reuse of developments* by allowing the generation and abstraction of transformation rules from transformational developments.
- A new instantiation of TAS to support a variation of Back and Wright's *refinement calculus* [1] is currently being developed.

More Information

For details of the system architecture underlying TAS and IsaWin, and in particular the generic graphical user interface, we refer to [6]. The wider context of TAS and IsaWin, the UniForM project, is described in [4]. Further information and the tools themselves are available from our web page:

http://www.informatik.uni-bremen.de/~agbkb/

System Requirements

To compile TAS and IsaWin, a full Standard ML compiler (such as Standard ML of New Jersey) which furthermore implements the Posix modules from the SML Basis Library is needed. To run TAS and IsaWin, the Tcl/Tk shell (wish, version 8.0 or newer) is needed as well.

Binary distributions are available for Solaris and Linux (SuSE distribution), but the wish needs to be available locally. On these systems, TAS and IsaWin need at least 32 MB to run, and 64 MB to run comfortably.

References

[1] R.-J. Back and J. von Wright. *Refinement Calculus*. Springer Verlag, 1998.
[2] R. Bornat and B. Sufrin. Jape's quiet interface. In N. Merriam, editor, *User Interfaces for Theorem Provers UITP '96*, Technical Report, pages 25–34. University of York. Electronic proceedings available at http://www.cs.york.ac.uk/~nam/uitp96/proceedings.html, 1996.
[3] Kolyang, C. Lüth, T. Meier, and B. Wolff. TAS and IsaWin: Generic interfaces for transformational program development and theorem proving. In M. Bidoit and M. Dauchet, editors, *TAPSOFT 97': Theory and Practice of Software Development*, number 1214 in LNCS, pages 855–859. Springer Verlag, 1997.
[4] B. Krieg-Brückner, J. Peleska, E.-R. Olderog, and A. Baer. The UniForM workbench, a universal development environment for formal methods. In J. M. Wing, J. Woodcock, and J. Davies, editors, *FM'99 — Formal Methods. Proceedings, Vol. II*, number 1709 in LNCS, pages 1186–1205. Springer Verlag, 1999.
[5] C. Lüth, H. Tej, Kolyang, and B. Krieg-Brückner. TAS and IsaWin: Tools for transformational program development and theorem proving. In J.-P. Finance, editor, *Fundamental Approaches to Software Engineering FASE'99. Joint European Conferences on Theory and Practice of Software ETAPS'99*, number 1577 in LNCS, pages 239–243. Springer Verlag, 1999.
[6] C. Lüth and B. Wolff. Functional design and implementation of graphical user interfaces for theorem provers. *Journal of Functional Programming*, 9(2):167–189, March 1999.
[7] T. Mossakowski. CASL — from semantics to tools. In *TACAS 2000 — Tools and Algorithms for the Construction and Analysis of Systems*. Springer Verlag, 2000. To appear in LNCS.
[8] L. C. Paulson. *Isabelle - A Generic Theorem Prover*. Number 828 in LNCS. Springer Verlag, 1994.

Using Maude*

Manuel Clavel[1], Fransisco Durán[2], Steven Eker[2], Patrick Lincoln[2],
Narciso Martí-Oliet[3], Jose Meseguer[2], and Jose F. Quesada[4]

[1] Department of Philosophy, University of Navarre, Spain
[2] SRI International, Menlo Park, CA 94025, USA
[3] Facultad de Ciencias Matemáticas, Universidad Complutense, Madrid, Spain
[4] CICA (Centro de Informática Científica de Andalucía), Seville, Spain

Maude is a wide-spectrum reflective logical language based on rewriting logic [7] that can be used to specify, prototype, and formally analyze concurrent software systems, specification languages, logics, and theorem provers. Because of its efficient implementation, it can also be used as a programming language and as a meta-tool to generate other tools. This paper gives a brief introduction to the language and illustrates with examples some of the features of the current version, available free of charge together with examples, documentation, and papers from SRI: see `http://maude.csl.sri.com`. The key characteristics of Maude can be summarized as follows:

- *Based on rewriting logic.* This makes it particularly well suited to express concurrent and state-changing aspects of systems declaratively.
- *Wide-spectrum.* Rewriting logic is a logical and semantic framework for both specification and efficient execution.
- *Multiparadigm.* Since rewriting logic conservatively extends equational logic, an equational style of functional programming is naturally supported in a sublanguage. A declarative style of concurrent object-oriented programming is also supported with a simple logical semantics.
- *Reflective.* Rewriting logic is reflective [4, 1]. The design of Maude capitalizes on this fact to support a novel style of *metaprogramming* with very powerful module-combining and module-transforming operations that surpass those of traditional parameterized programming.
- *Internal Strategies.* The strategies controlling the rewriting process can be defined by rewrite rules and can be reasoned about inside the logic [4, 5, 1].

Maude's implementation has been designed with the explicit goals of supporting executable specification and formal methods applications, of being easily extensible, and of supporting reflective computations. Although it is an interpreter, its advanced semicompilation techniques support flexibility and traceability without sacrificing the performance of up to 1.665 million rewrites per second in the free theory and between 131 thousand, and 1 million rewrites per second if associativity and commutativity axioms are used, on a 500MHz Alpha.

* Supported through Rome Laboratories contract F30602-97-C-0312, by DARPA and NASA through Contract NAS2-98073, by Office of Naval Research Contract N00014-96-C-0114, and N00014-99-C-0198.

T. Maibaum (Ed.): FASE 2000, LNCS 1783, pp. 371–374, 2000.
© Springer-Verlag Berlin Heidelberg 2000

A Decision Procedure for Bands

Bands are idempotent semigroups. Deciding the word problem for bands is a subtle problem, since the naive approach of using the idempotency equation as a string rewriting rule yields a nonconfluent system. The Maude module below specifies the confluent and terminating equational system proposed by Siekmann and Szabo [8]. The subtle part is that, even though the rules are string rewriting rules applied *modulo* associativity, the added conditional rule has to compare *sets* of elements in appropriate substrings. Thus, in addition to a sort List with an associative concatenation operator, we also need an auxiliary sort Set with an associative and commutative union operation and an idempotency equation. This illustrates Maude's support for rewriting *modulo* equational axioms. All combinations of associativity, commutativity, and left and right identity are supported.

```
fmod ASSOC-IDP is protecting QID .
  sorts List Set .   subsorts Qid < List Set .
  op __ : List List -> List [assoc] .        *** list concatenation
  op _,_ : Set Set -> Set [assoc comm] .     *** set union
  op {_} : List -> Set .                     *** set of a list
  var I : Qid .   var S : Set .   vars L P Q : List .
  eq S,S = S .   eq L L = L .                *** set and list idempotence
  ceq L P Q = L Q if {L} == {Q} and {L P} == {L} .
  eq {I} = I .   eq {I L} = I,{L} .
endfm
```

We can then decide the equality of two given words by equality, e.g.,

```
reduce 'a 'b 'c == 'a 'b 'c 'b 'a 'b 'c
```

It is not difficult to see that both words are reductions, using the idempotency equation as a rule, from the common ancestor 'a 'b 'a 'b 'c 'b 'a 'b 'c.

Reflection and the META-LEVEL

Rewriting logic is reflective [4, 1] in the precise sense that there is a finitely presented rewrite theory U such that for any finitely presented rewrite theory T (including U itself) we have the following equivalence

$$T \vdash t \longrightarrow t' \iff U \vdash \langle \overline{T}, \overline{t} \rangle \longrightarrow \langle \overline{T}, \overline{t'} \rangle$$

where $\overline{T}$ and $\overline{t}$ are terms representing T and t as data elements of U. In Maude reflection is efficiently supported through its predefined META-LEVEL module, which provides key functionality for the universal theory U. In particular, META-LEVEL has sorts Term and Module, whose respective terms are metarepresentations $\overline{t}$ and $\overline{T}$, for t term and T a module (that is, a rewrite theory). For example, a term $t = f(a,g(b))$, in a module FOO, with a, b constants of sort Foo is metarepresented as $\overline{t} = {}'f[\{'a\}Foo,'g[\{'b\}Foo]]$. META-LEVEL has a number of functions for performing metalevel computations in the universal theory [2]. In particular, the meta-apply function applies at the metalevel a rule in a module to a term. Its operator declaration is

```
op meta-apply : Module Term Qid Substitution MachineInt -> ResultPair .
```

The first and second arguments are metarepresentations $\overline{T}$, and $\overline{t}$ for a module T and a term t; the third argument is the label of the rule, the fourth is a substitution instantiating some variables in the rule, and the fifth is a number indicating the match instance with which we want to rewrite. Since matching may be performed *modulo* axioms such as associativity, commutativity and/or identity, in general a rule may match a subject term in several different ways. The result of applying the function is a pair, consisting of the (metarepresentation of) the rewritten term and the matching substitution in case of success, or an error constant and the empty substitution in case of failure.

A Reflective Example

The following example demonstrates the use of the Maude metalevel. The example consists of defining a metalevel function `findAllRewrites` that, given a term t in a module T, will find (the representation of) all one-step rewrites from t. Note that `meta-apply` only applies a rule at the top of the subject term, whereas here we want all one-step rewrites at all term positions.

```
fmod META is protecting META-LEVEL .
  sort TermSet .  subsort Term < TermSet .
  var T : Term .  var S : Substitution . var L : Qid .
  vars TL Before After : TermList .  vars OP SORT : Qid .
  var N : MachineInt .  op first : ResultPair -> Term .
  op ~ : -> TermList .  eq ~, TL = TL .  eq TL, ~ = TL .  op {} : -> TermSet .
  op _|_ : TermSet TermSet -> TermSet [assoc comm id: {}] .
  op meta-apply1 : Term Qid MachineInt -> Term .
  op findAllRewrites : Term Qid -> TermSet .
  op findTopRewrites : Term Qid MachineInt -> TermSet .
  op findLowerRewrites : Term Qid -> TermSet .
  op rewriteArguments : Qid TermList TermList Qid -> TermSet .
  op rebuild : Qid TermList TermSet TermList -> TermSet .
  eq meta-apply1(T, L, N) = first(meta-apply(['FOO], T, L, none, N)) .
  eq T | T = T .  eq first({T, S}) = T .
  eq findAllRewrites(T, L) = findTopRewrites(T, L, 0) | findLowerRewrites(T, L) .
  eq findTopRewrites(T, L, N) = if meta-apply1(T, L, N) == error* then {}
       else meta-apply1(T, L, N) | findTopRewrites(T, L, N + 1) fi .
  eq findLowerRewrites({OP}SORT, L) = {} .
  eq findLowerRewrites(OP[TL], L) = rewriteArguments(OP, ~, TL, L) .
  eq rewriteArguments(OP, Before, T, L) = rebuild(OP, Before, findAllRewrites(T, L), ~) .
  eq rewriteArguments(OP, Before, (T, After), L) =
       rebuild(OP, Before, findAllRewrites(T, L), After) |
         rewriteArguments(OP, (Before, T), After, L) .
  eq rebuild(OP, Before, {}, After) = {} .
  eq rebuild(OP, Before, T, After) = OP[Before, T, After] .
  eq rebuild(OP, Before, (T | TS), After) = (OP[Before, T, After]) |
       rebuild(OP, Before, TS, After) .
endfm
```

Given a module FOO with only one rule labeled `'one`, the following finds all one step rewrites from `f(a, g(b))`.

```
reduce findAllRewrites('f[{'a}Foo,'g[{'b}Foo]], 'one).
```

Applications

Maude is a wide-spectrum language and an attractive formal meta-tool for building many advanced applications and formal tools. Substantial applications include: a module system for Maude implemented in Maude [6], an inductive theorem prover; a Church-Rosser checker (both part of a formal environment for Maude and for the CafeOBJ language [3]); an HOL to Nuprl translator; a proof assistant for the Open Calculus of Constructions (OCC); and a translator from J. Millen's CAPSL specification language to the CIL intermediate language. In addition, several language interpreters and strategy languages, several object-oriented specifications—including cryptographic protocols and network applications—and a variety of executable translations mapping logics, architectural description languages and models of computation into the rewriting logic reflective framework have been developed by different authors.

We thank everyone on the Maude team for their contributions to the system and this paper. We thank our colleagues working on similar systems such as CafeOBJ and ELAN for interesting discussions and helpful comments.

References

[1] Manuel Clavel. Reflection in general logics and in rewriting logic, with applications to the Maude language. Ph.D. Thesis, University of Navarre, 1998.

[2] Manuel Clavel, Francisco Durán, Steven Eker, Patrick Lincoln, Narciso Martí-Oliet, José Meseguer, and José Quesada. Maude: specification and programming in rewriting logic. SRI International, January 1999, http://maude.csl.sri.com.

[3] Manuel Clavel, Francisco Durán, Steven Eker, and José Meseguer.   Building equational proving tools by reflection in rewriting logic.   In *Proc. of the CafeOBJ Symposium '98, Numazu, Japan.* CafeOBJ Project, April 1998. http://maude.csl.sri.com.

[4] Manuel Clavel and José Meseguer. Reflection and strategies in rewriting logic. In J. Meseguer, editor, *Proc. First Intl. Workshop on Rewriting Logic and its Applications*, volume 4 of *Electronic Notes in Theoretical Computer Science*. Elsevier, 1996. http://www.elsevier.nl/cas/tree/store/tcs/free/noncas/pc/volume4.htm.

[5] Manuel Clavel and José Meseguer.   Internal strategies in a reflective logic.   In B. Gramlich and H. Kirchner, editors, *Proceedings of the CADE-14 Workshop on Strategies in Automated Deduction (Townsville, Australia, July 1997)*, pages 1–12, 1997.

[6] Francisco Durán.   A reflective module algebra with applications to the Maude language. Ph.D. Thesis, University of Malaga, 1999.

[7] José Meseguer.   Conditional rewriting logic as a unified model of concurrency. *Theoretical Computer Science*, 96(1):73–155, 1992.

[8] J. Siekmann and P. Szabo. A noetherian and confluent rewrite system for idempotent semigroups. *Semigroup Forum*, 25:83–110, 1982.

Author Index